DOING
Comparative
POLITICS

THIRD EDITION

DOING
Comparative
POLITICS

AN INTRODUCTION TO
APPROACHES & ISSUES

Timothy C. Lim

LYNNE
RIENNER
PUBLISHERS

BOULDER
LONDON

Published in the United States of America in 2016 by
Lynne Rienner Publishers, Inc.
1800 30th Street, Boulder, Colorado 80301
www.rienner.com

and in the United Kingdom by
Lynne Rienner Publishers, Inc.
3 Henrietta Street, Covent Garden, London WC2E 8LU

Library of Congress Cataloging-in-Publication Data
Names: Lim, Timothy C., 1960– author.
Title: Doing comparative politics : an introduction to approaches and issues
  / by Timothy C. Lim.
Description: Third edition. | Boulder, Colorado : Lynne Rienner, [2016] |
  Includes bibliographical references and index.
Identifiers: LCCN 2016028546 | ISBN 9781626374508 (paperback : alk. paper)
Subjects: LCSH: Comparative government.
Classification: LCC JF51 .L56 2016 | DDC 320.3—dc23
LC record available at https://lccn.loc.gov/2016028546

British Cataloguing in Publication Data
A Cataloguing in Publication record for this book
is available from the British Library.

Printed and bound in the United States of America

The paper used in this publication meets the requirements
of the American National Standard for Permanence of
Paper for Printed Library Materials Z39.48-1992.

5 4 3 2 1

Contents

List of Figures   ix
Acknowledgments   xi

1   Getting Into Comparative Politics   1

What Is Comparative Politics? 3
What Is Politics? 9
What Does It Mean to Compare? 13
Why Compare? 15
What Is Comparable? 17
What Are the Advantages of the Comparative Method? 20
The Importance of Method and Theory 22

Part 1 Doing Comparative Politics

2   Comparing to Learn, Learning to Compare   27

Comparing and Open-Mindedness 28
Comparing and Critical Thinking 28
Strategies of Comparing 29
The Logic of Comparative Analysis 30
Concrete Models of Comparative Analysis 43
Conclusion 58

3   Thinking Theoretically in Comparative Politics   61

Why Study Theory? 61
Theory in Comparative Politics 67
Theoretical Divisions: Rationality, Structure, and Culture 71
Rationality: A Nontechnical Introduction 72
The Structural Tradition 78

The Cultural Tradition 86
A Hybrid Tradition: Institutionalism 93
Separation or Synthesis? 96
Bringing Everything Together 97

Part 2 The Questions

4   Why Are Poor Countries Poor?
    Explaining Economic Underdevelopment   103

Defining Poverty 105
To Be Poor or Not to Be Poor? A Rational Choice Perspective
    on Poverty 108
Cultural Explanations of Poverty: The Bad and the Good 119
Keeping the Poor Down? Structural Explanations of Poverty 126
Conclusion 136

5   Why Has East Asia Prospered?
    Explaining Economic Growth in
    Japan, South Korea, Taiwan, and China   139

Rationality, the Strong State, and Rapid Economic Growth in
    East Asia 143
Culture and Capitalist Development in East Asia 156
Global Capitalism and the Rise of East Asia 168
Explaining China's Economic Rise 179
Conclusion 186

6   What Makes a Democracy?
    Explaining the Breakdown of Authoritarian Rule   189

Defining Democracy: A Never-Ending Debate? 190
Economic Development and Democracy:
    A Necessary Relationship? 195
Agents of Democratization: Rational Choice and Democratic
    Transition 204
Structure and Rationality: Competition or Synthesis? 216
A Missing Link? Culture and Democracy 218
Taking the Next Step 228

7   Why Do People Kill?
    Explaining Genocide and Terrorism   233

Definitions: Genocide and Terrorism 236
Strategic Killers? Rational Choice Explanations of Genocide
    and Terrorism 245
The Culture of Killing: Cultural Approaches to Explaining Collective
    Political Violence 257
The Power of Culture: Making Genocide and Terrorism Possible 261
Choice or Fate? A Structural View of Genocide and Terrorism 271
Conclusion 277

8   Why Collective Action?
    Explaining the Rise of Social Movements   279
    What Is a Social Movement? 281
    Social Movements and Rationality 285
    Structural Accounts of Social Movements 295
    Culture and Social Movements 302
    The Three Perspectives and the Arab Spring 310
    Conclusion 317

Part 3 The Future of Comparative Politics

9   Globalization and the Study of Comparative Politics   321
    What Is Globalization? 323
    Implications of Globalization in Comparative Politics 326
    Globalization and the Three Research Traditions 328
    Conclusion 340

Glossary   341
Selected Bibliography   361
Index   383
About the Book   409

Figures

1.1	Some Key Concepts in Comparative Politics: State, Nation, Nation-State, Government, and Country	5
1.2	A Few Definitions of Comparative Politics	6
1.3	Wal-Mart vs. the World, 2015 Estimates	13
1.4	The Importance of History	15
1.5	Three Purposes of Comparing: A Summary	18
1.6	The Black Box of Explanation	22
2.1	Independent and Dependent Variables	31
2.2	Firearm-Related Homicide Rates in the United States and Canada, 2012	32
2.3	Estimates of Civilian Firearms Ownership and Homicide Rates in Selected Countries	34
2.4	Twins, Aging, and the Logic of the MSS Design	37
2.5	Suicide Rates in Selected Countries	38
2.6	Ethnic Conflict or Ecological Violence in Darfur?	47
2.7	Example of a Within-Case Comparison: Russian Economic Development	54
2.8	Summary of Skocpol's Comparative Research Design	57
3.1	Correlation and Causation	65
3.2	Agency and Structure	70
3.3	A Sampling of Theories in Comparative Politics	72
3.4	Rational Choice Analysis: Key Questions	79
3.5	Comparing Chess and the Structural Approach in Comparative Politics	81
3.6	The Structural Approach: Key Questions	85
3.7	Definition of Culture: Core Features	89

3.8   Gendercide and Women   92
3.9   Three Legs of Comparative Analysis: Theory, Method, and
        Evidence   98
4.1   Countries with the Highest Fertility Rates, per Capita GDP,
        and GDP per Capita Rankings, 2014   111
4.2   Corruption in Equatorial Guinea   119
4.3   Max Weber, the Protestant Ethic, and the Rise of Capitalism   120
4.4   Why Professional Athletes Go Broke: A Cultural Explanation?   124
4.5   What Is Dependence?   128
4.6   Net Transfer of Financial Resources from Poor Countries to
        Rich Countries, Selected Years   131
4.7   Lending Interest Rates in Selected Countries, 2010–2014   132
4.8   The International Monetary Fund and Its Critics   133
5.1   How "Rich" Is East Asia?   140
5.2   Map of East Asia with Japan, South Korea, Taiwan, and China   141
5.3   Tri-Modal Structure of the Capitalist World-System   170
5.4   Flying Geese Model   172
5.5   China's Average Annual Real GDP Growth Rate, 1960–2014   180
5.6   The Contradictions of Chinese Development? Strong Public
        Investment and Runaway Corruption   182
6.1   Major Prodemocracy Protests: From China to MENA   207
6.2   Authoritarian Regime Types and Democratic Transition   214
6.3   Freedom House's Democracy Score for Postcommunist
        Countries, 2014   229
7.1   Definition of Genocide from the Convention on the
        Prevention and Punishment of the Crime of Genocide   238
7.2   Some Definitions of Terrorism   244
7.3   The UN Peacekeeping Operation in Rwanda   249
7.4   The Suicide Terrorist Attack Against US Forces in Lebanon   252
7.5   Defining Ideology   264
8.1   The Distinction Between Mass Mobilization and
        Social Movements   280
8.2   Selected Definitions of a Social Movement
        (and Mass Mobilization)   283
8.3   Measuring Social Movement Outcomes: Success or Failure?   286
8.4   New Social Movements   289
9.1   Benjamin Barber's "McWorld"   322

Acknowledgments

I am grateful to all those who adopted the first two editions of this book and for the positive and constructive responses that I have received, which inspired many of the myriad revisions in this new edition. I am also grateful to Lynne Rienner herself, not only for giving me an opportunity to publish a third edition of *Doing Comparative Politics,* but also for offering valuable editorial advice.

I also wish to thank the hundreds of students at Cal State Los Angeles (CSLA) who have taken my course Foundations of Comparative Politics, many of whom have variously offered praise or critical feedback; in either case, I appreciate the comments. Among those CSLA students, I must specifically thank Francisco Mendez and Jacqueline Vargas for volunteering to help copyedit and provide a student's view of my manuscript.

Not least, I am grateful to my wife, Dr. Atsuko Sato, and my daughter, Ailani Sato-Lim, for their continuing support.

—*Timothy C. Lim*

1

Getting Into Comparative Politics

Scholars who study comparative politics, and all scholars for that matter, are generally concerned with answering questions, or with providing explanations for the myriad processes, issues, and events that shape the world in which we live. Of course, answering questions first requires that we *ask* questions. In the field of comparative politics, these questions have generally revolved around large-scale political, social, and economic changes that occur primarily at the domestic or national level. Examples of such large-scale change include social revolutions (e.g., the French Revolution of 1789, the Russian Revolution of 1917, or the Chinese Revolution of 1949), nation-building, economic transformation and development (e.g., the shift from a rural economy to a capitalist-industrial economy), political development (especially democratization), among others. The foregoing list of issues leads to fairly obvious, albeit broad, questions: Why do social revolutions occur, and why are some successful, while others are not? Why did some countries industrialize long ago, while many other countries only began to industrialize fairly recently? Why have some countries democratized, while others remain decidedly nondemocratic? Part of "getting into comparative politics" means asking the sorts of questions around which the field revolves.

Given the importance of questions, it would be useful to introduce a few more, some big and some not so big; some very clearly part of the domain of comparative politics, and some perhaps much less so:

- Why does the United States lead the rest of the industrialized world— by a very wide margin—in the number of gun homicides?
- Why are there still so many desperately poor peoples and desperately poor countries in the world? Conversely, how have some peoples and countries been able to become rich and prosperous in only a generation or so?

1

- Why do some mass protests against violent and repressive governments work while others fail miserably?
- Why do high school students in the United States—in the richest country on the planet—do relatively poorly on international tests of math and science?

The foregoing list is purposely bookended by two questions not normally asked in the field of comparative politics, in that they are both centered on the United States and are both about "smaller" (albeit far from unimportant) issues. I do this for one simple reason: to highlight the fact that the field of comparative politics, in principle, can cover a very diverse range of issues and is not limited to the study of foreign countries. I will discuss both these points later in the chapter. First, however, I want to say something about the issue of "answers," for finding answers is also a part— a very big part—of getting into comparative politics. For all the questions just posed, there are many possible answers. Some answers may seem very persuasive, and others may seem completely unconvincing. On the question about gun homicides, for example, controversial director Michael Moore argued in his Oscar-winning 2002 film *Bowling for Columbine* that the high level of gun violence in the United States is largely due to a "culture of fear." This culture of fear, he posited, is constantly reproduced through policies and practices that exacerbate insecurity throughout US society; more important, it pushes Americans to resolve problems and interpersonal conflict through violence, a reaction that in turn creates a self-confirming cycle: fear begets violence, which begets more fear, which begets even more violence, and so on. A culture of fear may not explain everything we need to know about gun violence in the United States, but according to Moore, it is almost certainly a major element—perhaps *the* major element—of any explanation that purports to tell us why Americans are so prone to shooting each other. Is Moore right? Or is his argument completely baseless? *How do we know?* More broadly, how do we know if *any* argument—especially one that deals with complex social, political, or economic phenomena—is valid or even plausible? This book is designed, in part, to help you answer these sorts of questions. Learning how to evaluate specific arguments, however, is secondary to the overarching goal of this book, which is to enable you to better understand and explain social, political, or economic processes, events, and outcomes *on your own*.

So what does any of this have to do with comparative politics? The answer is this: comparative politics provides us with a ready array of conceptual and analytical tools that we can use to address and answer a wide range of questions about the social world, including the question "Why are there so many gun homicides in the United States?" Put another way, comparative politics provides a systematic, coherent, and practical way to understand and make better sense of the things that happen in the world around us, from our own neighborhoods to the world at large. In a broader sense, moreover, comparative politics is relevant to almost anyone, even and especially to those who assume that the field is only about studying foreign countries. This is because, as a general procedure or approach, comparative politics can be applied to a huge variety of problems, from the mundane to the sublime, in a wide variety of areas. Explaining gun violence is just one example, but there are many others. Consider the following potpourri of questions and issues: Can a single-payer national healthcare system work in the United States? Are fundamentalist religious beliefs and democracy always and forever incompatible? Is vast economic inequality a necessary byproduct of a capitalist system? Will the legalization of all drugs, including the decriminalization of marijuana, significantly reduce crime and make drug use safer?

To repeat: a comparative politics approach is well suited for addressing all the foregoing questions and many others. At this point, of course, the reasons may not be clear, but they will become much clearer as we proceed. It is also important to say, at this early juncture, that comparative politics is not the only, nor is it always the best, approach one can use. Nonetheless, virtually any student or concerned citizen (not to mention scholar or policymaker) will benefit tremendously from cultivating and developing a comparative politics approach or, to put it more colloquially, from simply getting into comparative politics. With all this in mind, the next important step we need to take is to clarify what the term *comparative politics* means and what it implies. As we will see, this is easier said than done.

What Is Comparative Politics?

Many textbooks on comparative politics provide a clear, seemingly simple answer to the question "What is comparative politics?" Perhaps the simplest is one introduced earlier: "Comparative politics is the study of politics *in foreign* countries" (Zahariadis 1997, p. 2, emphasis added). Few texts, though, stop there. Most also emphasize that comparative politics, in slightly more formal terms, involves both a *method* of study and a *subject* of study. As a method of study, comparative politics is—not surprisingly—premised on comparison or comparative analysis. As a subject of study, comparative politics focuses on **understanding** and explaining political phenomena that take place *within* a **state**, **society**, **country**, or **political system**. (See Figure 1.1 for a discussion of these various terms.)[1] This slightly more detailed definition of the field gives us a better sense of what comparative politics is and how it may differ from other fields of inquiry, although, as will be discussed later, it is a definition that can raise more questions than it answers. Still, defining comparative politics as a method of study based on comparison and a subject of study based on an examination of political phenomena in various countries highlights several important points. First, it immediately tells us that the field is ostensibly concerned with *internal* or domestic dynamics, which helps to distinguish comparative politics from **international relations** (IR)—a field of study largely, though not exclusively, concerned with the external relations or foreign policies of states. Second, it tells us that comparative politics is, appropriately enough, concerned with political phenomena. Third, and perhaps most important, it tells us that the field is not only characterized but also *defined* by a comparative method of analysis. I might also point out that this second definition does not automatically exclude the United States (as the first does) from the field of comparative politics: the United States is a state or country in exactly the same sense that France, Japan, India, Mexico, South Korea, Zimbabwe, or Russia is.[2]

As already noted, though, the second definition of comparative politics raises a number of other questions and issues. Can comparative politics, for example, focus only on what happens *inside* countries? In other words, is it possible to understand the politics of a place without understanding and accounting for the impact of external or transnational/international forces? This is a very important question, but there are several others: What is meant by *political* phenomena—or by politics more generally? Are economic, social, and cultural phenomena also political, or do they fall into a completely different category? Regarding the question of method, we might also ask: What does it mean to compare? Is comparison in comparative politics different from, say, comparison in sociology, history, chemistry, or any other field of study? Even more basically, *why* do we compare? That is, what's the point of making comparisons in the first place? And last, *how* do we compare?

The Importance of Definitions

In posing so many questions, I realize that I also might have raised a question in *your* mind, namely, why make things so complicated? Isn't it possible to just be satisfied with a very short and easy-to-understand definition? The simple answer is no. One reason is clear: *definitions are important.* Very important. This is partly because they tell us what is included in the field of study and what is left out. Consider the definition suggested earlier: "Comparative politics is the study of politics in foreign countries." This definition, at least implicitly, leaves out the United States (or really any other country, depending on the nationality of the reader). But it is not clear why the United States should receive such special consideration. Is it because the United States is different from all other countries—literally incomparable? Or is there some other, less obvious reason? We are left to wonder. Consider, too, the point made in the foregoing paragraph on the notion of politics: Does a study of *politics* in foreign countries mean that we

Figure 1.1 Some Key Concepts in Comparative Politics: State, Nation, Nation-State, Government, and Country

The terms *state, nation, nation-state, government,* and *country* are often used interchangeably, especially in the popular press and media in general. Although this practice is not entirely unwarranted, it is important to recognize that the terms are not synonymous. A state, for example, is a legal concept that is premised on a number of conditions: a permanent population, a defined territory, and a *national* government capable of maintaining effective control over its territory. In addition, many scholars (following **Max Weber**) argue that a state must have a monopoly on the *legitimate* use of physical force or violence within a given territory. Notice that the definition of state includes a reference to government, which can be defined as the agency or apparatus through which a body exercises authority and performs its functions. In this definition, governments need not be part of a state; moreover, multiple governments may exist within a single state. We can find governments in all sorts of places—in a university or school (that is, the student government) or in **sovereign** "nations" (for example, a Native American tribal council)—and at many levels. Cities, counties, provinces, and whole regions (for example, the European Union) can also have their own separate governments.

The example of Native Americans is a useful way to differentiate a nation from a state. A nation, in the simplest terms, can be defined as a group of people who recognize each other as sharing a common identity. This common identity can be based on language, religion, culture, or a number of other *self-defined* criteria. This makes the concept of the nation inherently subjective or **intersubjective**. Nations do not require states or governments to exist, nor must nations exist within a single defined territory. One can speak, for example, of nations that transcend borders, such as the Nation of Islam. Combining the definitions of state and nation creates the concept of the nation-state. Technically speaking, a nation-state would only exist if nearly all the members of a single nation were organized in a single state, without any other distinct communities being present (Willets 1997, p. 289). From this perspective, despite its prevalent usage, many scholars argue that there are no true nation-states and that the concept should be entirely abandoned. But there are what we might call *national states*—states in which a common identity is forged around the concept of nationalism itself (for more on this issue, see Eley and Suny 1996). For example, people living in the United States may be divided by a wide range of religious, cultural, ethnic, linguistic, and other differences. Yet they all may share a common sense of "being American." Practically speaking, the term *national state* is often used as a synonym for *nation-state*. The notion of a national state, moreover, comes close to the more concrete concept of country, which may be defined as a distinct political system of people sharing common values and occupying a relatively fixed geographic space (Eley and Suny 1996). *Country* is the most generic of the terms referred to here.

do *not* study economic, social, or cultural issues and concerns in those same foreign countries? Does it mean we only examine those things that governments or states do? If the answer to the last two questions is yes, it would necessarily mean that a lot of potentially important issues and concerns would be left out in the study of comparative politics. Yet this would clearly be a mistake.

Given the complexities of defining the field, there continue to be a variety of definitions of comparative politics. Admittedly, at least in a broad or generic sense,[3] most definitions of comparative politics are now on the same basic page. At the same time, there are still subtle and usually unstated differences. (For a sampling of various definitions of comparative politics, see Figure 1.2.) Thus, despite some basic consensus, it is nonetheless worthwhile to explore, in greater depth, the various aspects of how to define the field of comparative politics. For without greater exploration, a number of important, even fundamental, issues may go unquestioned. My intention, however, is not to provide *the* definition of comparative politics.

Figure 1.2 A Few Definitions of Comparative Politics

"Comparative politics involves the systematic study and comparison of the world's political systems. It seeks to explain differences between as well as similarities among countries. In contrast to journalistic reporting on a single country, comparative politics is particularly interested in exploring patterns, processes, and regularities among political systems" (Wiarda 2000, p. 7).

Comparative politics is "the study and comparison of domestic politics across countries" (O'Neil 2015, p. 5).

"What is comparative politics? It is two things, first a world, second a discipline. As a 'world,' comparative politics encompasses political behavior and institutions in all parts of the earth. . . . The 'discipline' of comparative politics is a field of study that desperately tries to keep up with, to encompass, to understand, to explain, and perhaps to influence the fascinating and often riotous world of comparative politics" (Lane 1997, p. 2).

"Comparative politics . . . involves no more and no less than a comparative study of politics—a search for similarities and differences between and among political phenomena, including political institutions (such as legislatures, political parties, or political interest groups), political behavior (such as voting, demonstrating, or reading political pamphlets), or political ideas (such as liberalism, conservatism, or Marxism). Everything that politics studies, comparative politics studies; the latter just undertakes the study with an explicit comparative methodology in mind" (Mahler 2000, p. 3).

Instead, my goal is to help you understand the complexities and subtleties of defining the field. One of the best ways to accomplish this is by asking the type of questions posed earlier. Next, of course, I need to try to *answer* these questions, which is what I will endeavor to do in the remainder of this chapter.

In thinking about the definition of comparative politics, it is useful to recognize that comparative politics is not the only field in political science that focuses on countries or states as the primary **units of analysis**. Scholars in international relations, as suggested earlier, are also intimately concerned with countries or, more accurately, states. But IR scholarship is typically more interested in examining relations between and among states—that is, with their *interactions* in an international system. Even though this has not precluded IR scholars from looking at what happens inside states or countries, a good deal of research in the field has tended to treat states as undifferentiated wholes, which is to say that IR scholars (especially those associated with, until fairly recently, the dominant research school in IR, **realism** or **neorealism**) assume that states are *functionally alike* when interacting with other states. This is a critical assumption, largely because it suggests that it is possible to explain the behavior of states or countries *without* a careful examination of their internal working and makeup (internal workings and makeup include such things as a country's political and economic systems, its cultural **norms** and traditions, and its specific historical experiences and **institutions**). The reasoning behind this assumption stems from the belief that the international system is **anarchic**, such that each and every state is forced to behave in similar ways regardless of its internal makeup or its domestic politics. The logic here is both simple and compelling: in an anarchic (as opposed to **hierarchic**) system, states must compete with other states for security, power, and influence. They must do so precisely because there is no ultimate rule-maker and rule-enforcer for the system as a whole. Lacking an ultimate authority, individual states (or actors) are forced onto the same basic path when dealing with other states. Each state must, in other words, do those things that ensure its own long-term survival. This generally means, among other things, building a strong army, developing a network of mutually beneficial military-strategic alliances, maintaining a diplomatic corps, gathering intelligence, and engaging in military conflict when necessary.

In this view, the internal makeup of a country is *relatively* unimportant in terms of explaining or predicting its external behavior. Thus, for example, a liberal democracy with a strong **presidential system** (such as the United States) would behave—with regard to its foreign policy decisions—in the same way that a single-party, **communist**-led dictatorship would.[4] In a similar vein, we would expect a state governed by an **Islamic** fundamentalist regime, say Iran, to act in essentially the same manner as any other state. A more salient consideration would be the size and military capacity of a country. That is, a large, militarily powerful country would behave differently from a small, militarily weak country. The foregoing discussion, I should stress, is highly simplified and stylized; in addition, it fails to account for wide and significant divergences within IR scholarship.[5] Nonetheless, it is a useful way to grasp what has long been a basic distinction between IR and comparative politics. This is necessary if only because so many people, including some political scientists (at least those outside of IR and comparative politics), are largely oblivious to the differences between the two fields. Yet for the most part, the two fields have developed along very different lines, both theoretically and methodologically, and have only occasionally intersected in a significant and meaningful manner. This is reason enough to spend a lot of time defining comparative politics, for if we cannot even distinguish it from related fields, how can we reasonably talk about a comparative politics approach?

The strong tendency, in IR, to gloss over the domestic or internal characteristics of states or countries left a huge gap to be filled. Comparative politics has, almost by default, filled this gap, a fact reflected in earlier definitions of the field. In this respect, we might say that, whereas IR is generally based on an outside-in approach, comparative politics has generally been based on an inside-out approach. The different emphases of the two fields have in turn produced (at least in the past) a very clear-cut division of (intellectual) labor. Thus, as Nikolaos Zahariadis pointed out:

> Comparative research tends to be geographic in orientation; that is comparativists generally describe themselves either as country specialists or as Europeanists, Africanists, Asianists, and so on. [Ironically, this has led many "comparativists," in practice, to eschew engaging in comparative research; instead, many have become narrowly, even exclusively, focused on their country of expertise.] In contrast, divisions in international relations are more thematic and involve issues such as international conflict or international political economy that transcend geographic boundaries. (1997, p. 4)

Zahariadis is correct, but his observations do not go far enough. The division of labor between comparative politics and IR has resulted not only in different orientations and research interests but also in a belief, particularly among IR scholars in the **realist** school, that there is a very high, even impenetrable, wall between domestic and international politics.

Can the Internal Politics of a Place and the Impact of External Forces Be Understood Separately?

All this brings us back to an integrally related issue, one raised earlier in the chapter—whether is it possible to understand the internal politics of a place without understanding the impact of external forces. *My* answer to this question is a simple and unequivocal no. This impossibility, I think, has been true for a very long time (at least since the beginnings of **colonialism** in the fifteenth century) but is particularly true today. Processes such as **globalization** in all its various dimensions (a topic covered at length in Chapter 9), in particular, have made it nearly impossible to understand the internal dynamics of a country without looking at what happens on the "outside." In practice, virtually all comparativists recognize this, although there is still a great deal of disagreement over the relative importance of internal versus external factors. Some scholars argue that external and, particularly, system-level factors—such as the **structure** of the world economy or particular relationships of **dependence** between poor and rich countries—are extremely and sometimes overwhelmingly important. Others argue that although such things matter, what matters most are the individual attributes of societies and their states. These individual attributes may derive from particular historical experiences, from culture, from specific types of institutional arrangements, and so on. The debate between these two sides is related to the main theoretical approaches in comparative politics, which we will cover in much more depth in subsequent chapters. For now, suffice it to say that although almost all comparativists now recognize the peril of defining the field strictly in terms of what happens inside a country, state, or society, there is no consensus on exactly what this means.

Another Definition of Comparative Politics

Admitting that comparative politics cannot be limited to looking at what happens inside a country or other large social unit, I should stress, does not mean that we need to completely abandon any distinctions among fields of study, and especially between comparative politics and IR. We do need, however, to amend our definition of comparative politics. Thus, rather than defining comparative politics as a subject of study based on an examination of political phenomena *within* or *in* countries, we can say that comparative politics examines the interplay of domestic and external forces on the politics of a given country, state, or society. This amended definition, unfortunately, still does not tell us if it is legitimate to separate the study of politics from economics, society, culture, and so on. It is to this question that we turn next.

What Is Politics?

Traditionally (that is, prior to the 1950s), comparative politics mainly involved *describing* the basic features of political systems. Most research in comparative politics, moreover, operated on the premise that politics referred exclusively to the *formal* political system—that is, to the concrete institutions of government (such as the parliament, the congress, and the bureaucracy) and to the constitutional and judicial rules that helped governments function.

Accordingly, early studies tended to be little more than factual and generally superficial accounts of how particular institutions of government operated and were organized or how certain laws were written and then passed. Such accounts may be useful and even necessary, but they can tell only a small part of what we need to know about politics. Even those political processes and actors closely associated with the formal political system—such as political parties, elections, foreign and domestic decisionmaking—were left out of these early studies. Politics, in short, was conceived of in very narrow terms.

A Process-Oriented Definition of Politics

This narrowness began to change in the 1950s, when scholars laid a new foundation for the field of comparative politics and for political science more generally. There are several complex reasons for this, most of which are not necessary to discuss for present purposes. Suffice it to say, then, that the traditional concern with the formal and legalistic conceptualization of politics was challenged and ultimately cast aside in favor of a broader view. An influential article by Roy Macridis and Richard Cox (1953) symbolized this change. The two authors argued that the preoccupation with formal political institutions and judicial rules was too close to the study of law and not close enough to the study of politics, which, in contrast to the study of law, "observed that relations between society and authority were governed by judicial but also by informal rules and sometimes by brute force" (cited in Zahariadis 1997, p. 7). Although Macridis and Cox (along with several other prominent scholars) succeeded in breaking the hold of **formalism/ legalism** in comparative politics, they did so only to a limited extent. This was true for two basic reasons. First, although the move away from formalism/ legalism opened the door to comparative study of a broader range of political institutions and processes, politics was still defined primarily if not solely in relation to activities that involved the state or the government. Second, the discipline of political science generally and comparative politics specifically remained tied to the idea that politics—as a subject of study—could be separated from economics, sociology, history, geography, anthropology, or any other field in the social sciences and humanities.

The limitations of this latter view become particularly clear, noted Adrian Leftwich, "when one considers concrete problems in modern societies, such as unemployment in the industrial societies on the one hand, and rural poverty in the Third World on the other. The harder you think about these issues, the more difficult it is to identify them as strictly economic, social, or political in their causes or consequences" (1983, p. 4). I agree, which is why in this book we will begin with a concept of politics that is broader than what is offered in many traditional textbooks. This alternative definition, what we might call a *process-oriented* or *processual* definition

(Stoker and Marsh 2002), sees politics as part-and-parcel of a larger *social process*. In this view, politics "is about the uneven distribution of power in society [or between societies], how the struggle over power is conducted, and its impact on the creation and distribution of resources, life chances and well-being" (p. 9). This process-oriented definition, as should be clear, makes it difficult if not impossible to maintain firm boundaries between disciplines. To see this, consider, for example, how uneven distributions of power in societies come about in the first place. Are these uneven power distributions the product of history? Or do contemporary economic forces play the determinative role? What about the effects of culture, religion, custom, or even geography? Is it possible to say that one type of factor always predominates, or is there an inextricable interaction among these different forces—be they economic, social, political, cultural, geographic, and so on? The answer to all these questions is, I believe, fairly clear, and it boils down to the conclusion that politics is integrally and necessarily tied to history, culture, economics, geography, and a variety of other forces. In practice, I think, most comparativists agree with this view of politics, which is why comparative political analysis today tends to be wide-ranging and inclusive.

In addition to transcending disciplinary boundaries, a process-oriented definition of politics has at least two other implications. First, it clearly takes politics out of the governmental arena and puts it into almost all domains of life. These other domains include virtually all social and civil institutions and actors, such as churches, factories, corporations, trade unions, political parties, think tanks, ethnic groups and organizations, women's groups, organized crime, and so on. Second, a process-oriented definition of politics reinforces our amended definition of comparative politics stated earlier (namely, "as a field that looks at the interplay of domestic and external forces on the politics of a given country, state, or society"). For it is clear that politics—as a struggle for power over the creation and distribution of resources, life chances, and well-being—is not something that can be easily compartmentalized into the domestic and international. This is because the activities that determine the distribution and use of resources (at least for the past few hundred years) are rarely confined to a single, clearly defined political territory; thus, as all politics is local (according to one popular saying), all politics is also potentially international and global.

Losing Focus?

There are, I should note, many political scientists who would disagree with this broad conception of politics. We are already familiar with the basic argument, which essentially reverses the problem of narrow definitions. To wit: while narrow definitions exclude a lot of potentially important "stuff," overly broad definitions may include too much. That is, because there are no neat boundaries telling us what is and what is not included in the scope of the definition, we are studying both everything and nothing. Zahariadis, for example, would like us to differentiate politics from "corporate decisions"; the latter, he asserted, "affect only a specific corporation" (1997, p. 2). Yet just a little reflection tells us this is not always the case. Certainly there are myriad decisions made within a corporation (or within a family, factory, church, or other social institution) with very limited or no public or societal impact. At the same time, it is also true that a vast number of "private" corporate decisions have a clear and sometimes profound public dimension. By their very nature, in fact, many corporate decisions have a deep influence on how resources are obtained, used, produced, and distributed. Moreover, in an era of mega-corporations—where the largest firms are bigger, and often immensely bigger, than many countries in terms of command over economic resources—the suggestion that corporate decisions do not have a far-reaching public impact is difficult to maintain. Consider, in this regard, Wal-Mart. In the 2015 fiscal year, Wal-Mart's total revenue (domestic plus international) amounted to $486 billion (*Wal-Mart 2015 Annual Report*), which was more than the estimated **gross domestic product** (GDP) of all but thirty-eight countries that same year. More specifically, in 2015, Wal-Mart's revenues put it between Belgium, with a GDP (based on a **purchasing power party** [PPP] valuation) of $492 billion, and Switzerland, with a GDP of $481 billion. Needless to say, Wal-Mart's revenues vastly exceeded the GDP of most of the world's smaller countries. Haiti's GDP, to cite just one example, was a paltry $18 billion in 2015, or about 4 percent of Wal-Mart's total sales. (All GDP figures cited in KNOEMA 2015; see Figure 1.3 for additional details.) It is not hard to see that Wal-Mart's corporate decisions, in general, can and often do have a much greater political impact than decisions made in Haiti. Where, then, do we draw the line between public and private decisions? Is it even possible to do so? I would argue that the line, in some respects, has simply become too blurred to be of major significance today.

Admittedly, though, it would be a mistake for politics to be defined as "everything including the kitchen sink." Indeed, as I discuss in subsequent chapters (and as suggested earlier), it is often necessary to provide clear-cut, precise definitions. This is especially true when trying to develop an argument or when trying to support a specific **hypothesis** or claim. After all, if one cannot precisely or adequately define what it is being studied—say democracy or terrorism—how can one possibly claim to say anything meaningful about that subject? In defining an entire field of study, however, precision is less important, but not irrelevant. The trick, then, is to develop a definition that is neither too narrow nor too unfocused. One solution, albeit a pragmatic one, is to acknowledge that the politics about which comparativists (and other political scientists) are most concerned, according to Gerry Stoker and David Marsh, is primarily *collective* as opposed to interpersonal,

---

Figure 1.3　Wal-Mart vs. the World, 2015 Estimates

The table below shows where Wal-Mart would rank, based on total revenue compared to GDP, if it were a country. The comparison, of course, is overly and perhaps fatally simplistic, but nonetheless gives a rough indication of the economic size and power of the company relative to a range of countries.

Rank	Country	Purchasing Power–Adjusted GDP ($ billions)
1	United States	18,125
10	France	2,634
20	Taiwan	1,125
30	South Africa	725
—	**Wal-Mart**	**486**[a]
40	Singapore	471
50	Qatar	346
60	Ireland	238
70	New Zealand	165
80	Libya	103
90	Côte d'Ivoire	77
100	Democratic Republic of Congo	62

Sources: Figure for Wal-Mart based on the 2015 fiscal year, and includes total revenues for Wal-Mart US, Wal-Mart International, and Sam's Club (*Wal-Mart 2015 Annual Report*, http://stock.walmart.com/files/doc_financials/2015/annual/2015-annual-report.pdf). GDP figures cited in KNOEMA 2015.
Note: a. Total sales.

---

and it involves interaction both *within* the public arena—that is, in the government or state—and also *between* the public arena and social actors or institutions (2002, p. 10). No doubt, this qualification will still be unsatisfactory to many political scientists, but it is also one upon which a large number of comparativists have chosen to base their research and analysis.

　　With all this in mind, let us now turn to the other major aspect of comparative politics—comparing—by posing a simple question.

What Does It Mean to Compare?

In thinking about what it means to compare, let us first consider what Charles Ragin, a prominent social scientist, has to say: "Thinking without comparison is unthinkable. And, in the absence of comparison, so is all scientific thought and scientific research" (Ragin 1987, p. 1, citing Swanson 1971, p. 141). Although Ragin was citing another scholar, his own position is clear: in *all* the sciences—social and natural—researchers, scholars, and students are invariably engaged in making some sort of comparison. If this is so (and it is fair to say that it is), then there is very little that sets comparative politics apart (on the surface, at least) from other fields of study. This is to say that the comparative strategies used by comparativists are not in principle different from the comparative strategies used by other political scientists or by sociologists, economists, psychologists, historians, and so on. But it does not mean that absolutely no differences exist: (very) arguably, one practice that sets comparative politics apart from other fields is the explicit and direct focus on the comparative method—as opposed to simply or informally "comparing."[6]

The comparative method, as I will discuss in detail in the following chapter, is a distinctive mode of comparative analysis. According to Ragin (1987), it entails two main predispositions. First, it involves a bias toward (although certainly not an exclusive focus on) **qualitative analysis**, which means that comparativists tend to look at cases *as wholes* and to compare whole cases with each other. Thus the tendency for comparativists is to talk of comparing Germany to Japan, or the United States to Canada. This may not seem to be an important point, but it has significant implications, one of which is that comparativists tend to eschew—or at least put less priority on—**quantitative analysis**, also known as **statistical** or **variable**-centered **analysis** (Ragin 1987, pp. 2–3). In the social sciences, especially over the past few years, this orientation away from quantitative and toward qualitative analysis definitely sets comparativists apart from other social scientists. Even within comparative politics, however, this is beginning to change. The second predisposition among comparativists is to value *interpretation* and *context* (pp. 2–3). This means, in part, that comparativists (of all theoretical orientations, I might add) begin with the assumption that "history matters." Saying that history matters, I should caution, is much more than pointing out a few significant historical events or figures in an analysis; instead, it involves showing exactly how historical processes and practices, as well as long-established institutional arrangements, impact and shape the contemporary environment in which decisions are made, events unfold, and struggles for power occur. It means, in other words, demonstrating a meaningful continuity between the past and the present. This is not easy to do, but for a comparativist using history, it is often an essential task. (See Figure 1.4.)

Although understanding the predisposition of comparativists is important, this still doesn't tell us what it means to compare—a question that may seem easy to answer, but in fact is not. Just pointing out or describing differences and similarities between any two countries, for example, is not by any account the be-all and end-all of comparative analysis. Indeed, staying strictly at the level of superficial description—for example, China has a **Confucian** heritage, whereas the United States does not; both France and Russia experienced **social revolutions**—one will never genuinely engage in

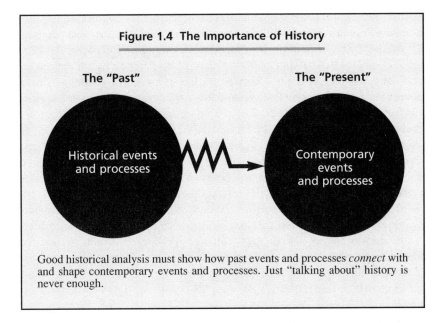

Figure 1.4 The Importance of History

The "Past"

The "Present"

Historical events and processes

Contemporary events and processes

Good historical analysis must show how past events and processes *connect* with and shape contemporary events and processes. Just "talking about" history is never enough.

comparative *analysis,* no matter how accurate the observations. And revealing anything meaningful or insightful about political phenomena is even less likely. Comparing, then, involves much more than pointing out similarities or differences between two or more entities. Just what else is involved in comparative analysis is the topic of our next chapter, so I will reserve the remainder of this discussion on the topic until then. In the meantime, we need to address another basic and essential question.

Why Compare?

To be good comparativists, we need to know *why* we compare. In other words, what is the purpose of comparing? On this question, Giovanni Sartori (1994) offered us a very simple answer: we compare to **control**. By control, Sartori meant to say—albeit in a very loose way—that we use comparisons as a way to check (verify or falsify) whether our claims or assertions about certain phenomena are valid by controlling for, or holding constant, certain variables. Take the statements "poverty causes corruption" or, conversely, "corruption causes poverty"; "**authoritarianism** is more conducive to high levels of economic growth than democracy"; and "social revolutions are caused by relative deprivation." How do we know, Sartori asked, whether any of these statements is true, false, or something else? "We know," Sartori answered, "by looking around, that is, by *comparative checking*" (p. 16, emphasis added). It is important to understand that, in most comparative analyses, actual **control variables** are not used. This issue may not be very clear right now and, for our purposes, is not critical. The main point is this: different types of comparisons allow a researcher to treat a wide variety of similarities *or* differences (depending on the particular comparative principle used) as if they are control variables. In so doing, the researcher can safely eliminate a whole range of potentially significant factors and instead concentrate on those variables deemed most important. This is what Michael Moore implicitly did in his film when, to show that his argument was right, he compared the United States and Canada. More specifically, he asserted that because the two countries shared a number of common features, for example, a high rate of gun ownership, ethnic diversity, and exposure to violence in entertainment, none of the commonalities could explain why the United States was a such violent society. In other words, in that comparison, he was treating all the similarities between the two countries as control variables in order to assess how lower or higher levels of fear impact the gun homicide rate in the two countries.

Unfortunately, comparative checking usually cannot (indeed, can almost never) provide definitive answers. This is true, in part, because comparative checking is an imperfect mode of analysis, at least when comparing many complex real-world cases. It is also true, in more substantive terms, because comparison is not the best method of control in scientific analysis. There are much better methods of control, such as the **experimental method** and statistical control. "But," as Sartori also noted, "the experimental method has limited applicability in the social sciences, and the statistical one requires many cases" (1994, p. 16), something that research in comparative politics generally lacks (this is referred to as the **small-N** problem). Like it or not, therefore, comparison often represents only a second-best method of control in the social sciences and comparative politics.

Despite its second-best status, comparing to control is an undeniably important purpose of comparative analysis. Yet many comparativists, especially those with a strong predisposition toward qualitative and historical analysis, are not always, or even mostly, involved in (formally and rigorously) testing hypotheses through their comparisons (Ragin 1987, p. 11). Instead, as Ragin noted, many comparativists "*apply* **theory** to cases in order to interpret them" (p. 11, emphasis in original). We will see examples of this in subsequent chapters, but what Ragin meant, in part, is that comparativists recognize that countries or other types of **macrosocial** units all, in important ways, have a unique story to tell. Ragin suggested, therefore, that some researchers are often most interested in using comparative analysis to get a better grasp of these *individual* "stories," rather than primarily using them as a way to verify or falsify specific arguments or hypotheses. In other words, for these researchers, in-depth understanding is the goal of comparative analysis. Comparing to understand, to put it in slightly different terms, means that researchers use comparison to see what other cases can tell them about the specific case or country in which they have the most interest.

In a similar vein, some comparativists assume that the sheer complexity of real-world cases makes control a worthwhile but difficult, if not impossible, goal to achieve. Instead, they advocate a more pragmatic approach that attempts to build theoretical generalization—or **explanation**—through an accumulation of case-based knowledge (this is sometimes referred to as **analytical induction**). In this view, it is understood that no case, by itself, or no comparison of a small number of cases is sufficient to test a theory or general claim. This is largely because the overwhelming complexity of any given case makes any test problematic and highly contingent. Instead, each case or each small-N comparison provides comparativists another piece (albeit often a very complicated piece in and of itself) to work into a much larger puzzle. I will come back to this issue—and specifically the issue of **complex causality**—later.

Even though the foregoing discussion may be a little confusing, the key point is simply that, although researchers use comparisons for different reasons, doing comparative politics requires that you be aware of *your* reason and rationale for making a comparison. Figure 1.5 provides a summary of the three general purposes of comparing.

What Is Comparable?

Another important question about comparing involves the issue of exactly what one can compare. What, to put it simply, is comparable? Again, the answer may seem obvious at first blush, especially in the context of comparative politics. For instance, it certainly seems reasonable to assert that countries (governments, societies, or similar entities) are comparable. Yet why should this be the case? One basic answer is that all countries share at least some common attributes—for example, they all occupy a territory defined by political boundaries, they all represent the interests of a political community, they are all recognized (albeit not always officially as in the case of Taiwan or Palestine) by other countries or states, and so on. Implicitly, this is why most everyone assumes, to paraphrase a common saying, that oranges can be compared to other oranges, and apples can be compared to other apples (while, of course, apples and oranges cannot be compared to each other). At the same time, countries each differ in some meaningful ways. Indeed, it is fair to say that differences are crucially important in any type of comparative analysis. After all, if all countries were exactly alike, there would be no reason to compare them. Think about this last point for just a moment. Why, to repeat the basic question, is there nothing to be learned from comparing two completely identical units of analysis? Methodologically speaking, the answer is clear: comparing completely

Figure 1.5 Three Purposes of Comparing: A Summary

	Comparing to *Control*	Comparing to *Understand*	Comparing to *Explain*
Basic strategy or purpose	Comparative checking	Interpretation	Analytical induction
Logic or approach to comparative analysis	Researcher uses a range of cases as a way to test (verify or falsify) a specific claim, hypothesis, or theory.	Researcher is primarily interested in a single case and uses different cases or general theories as a way to learn more about the case being studied.	Researcher uses cases as a way to build a stronger theoretical explanation. Cases are used in a step-by-step manner, with each case contributing to the development of a general theory.
Simple example	(1) *Begin with a claim:* A high level of gun ownership will lead to a high level of gun-related homicide.	(1) *Begin with case (and issue):* The high level of homicides in South Africa.	(1) *Begin with general theory:* Structural theory of democratization.
	(2) *Test the claim:* Researcher examines a range of countries in order to control for gun ownership; if countries with the highest rates of gun ownership have low rates of gun-related homicides (and vice versa), the claim is falsified and must be rejected.	(2) *Use existing theories and other cases to better understand case:* Researcher uses a range of theories on gun violence to better understand why South Africa is the most violent country in the world. Researcher also uses other cases to see what those cases can tell him about South Africa.	(2) *Use various cases to strengthen the theory:* Researcher begins by looking at the democratization process in Mexico. This examination may lead researcher to revise elements of theory; the researcher then looks at Taiwan, Poland, and Ukraine. Each case is used as a steppingstone in developing or strengthening original theory.

identical units does not allow us to assess the significance of any particular variable. In this respect, we might say that comparing apples to oranges generally makes more sense than comparing oranges to oranges or apples to apples.

Thus, to determine what we can compare, we can begin by saying that we can compare "entities whose attributes are in part shared (similar) and in part non-shared" (Sartori 1994, p. 17). Accordingly, we can say that countries are comparable to each other—as are provinces or states (such as California and Texas), cities, and neighborhoods—because all countries share certain attributes, but also differ from each other in a variety of ways. Saying all this, however, still doesn't tell us all we need to know. Is it appropriate, for instance, to compare the United States to Côte d'Ivoire, Japan, Indonesia, Guinea-Bissau, or New Zealand? Similarly, is it appropriate to compare California to Rhode Island or New York state, or Los Angeles to Philadelphia (or Seoul, London, or Paris)? It depends on what the researcher is hoping to accomplish; it depends on what the focus of analysis is; it depends on the particular research design the researcher plans to use; and it depends on the range of similarities and differences between or among the units of comparison. This is an obvious point; still, it is one worth making because, when phrased as a question—"On what does our comparison depend?"—it forces the researcher to think more carefully about how to design their study. It forces the researcher, as well, to *justify* the comparisons ultimately made.

What we can compare, I should stress, is definitely not limited to countries or other geographic entities (more on this in Chapter 2). Nor is it necessarily limited to comparable data from two or more countries. Such a restriction, for example, would automatically exclude comparatively oriented but single-country (or single-unit) **case studies**, including such classic comparative studies as Alexis de Tocqueville's *Democracy in America* ([1835] 1988) and Emile Durkheim's *The Elementary Forms of the Religious Life* ([1915] 1961) (both cited in Ragin 1987, p. 4). As Ragin explained it, "Many area specialists [i.e., researchers who concentrate on a single country] are thoroughly comparative because they implicitly compare their chosen case to their own country or to an imaginary or theoretically decisive ideal-typic case" (p. 4). Other scholars, including Sartori, would disagree, or at least would be quite skeptical of the claim that single-country case studies can be genuinely comparative. Sartori wrote, for example, "It is often held that comparisons can be 'implicit.' . . . I certainly grant that a scholar *can be* implicitly comparative without comparing, that is, provided that his one-country or one-unit study *is* embedded in a comparative context and that his concepts, his analytic tools, are *comparable*. But how often is this really the case?" (1994, p. 15, emphasis in original).[7] Sartori made a good point, but so too did Ragin. My own view is that single case studies can be comparative if the researcher is clear about the "comparative context." But this is far less difficult than Sartori implies. (I will return to a discussion of this point in the following chapter.) There is, I might also note, a special type of case study, which is referred to as a **within-case comparison**. A within-case comparison examines an ostensibly single case over time, during which there is a significant change in the variable or variables under investigation.[8] As I discuss further in Chapter 2, this is actually a type of binary comparison, and one that is unequivocally comparative.

We are not going to resolve the debate here. Suffice it to say, then, that doing comparative analysis requires far more than just looking at a foreign country or just randomly or arbitrarily picking two or more countries to study in the context of a single paper or study. It is, instead, based on a general *logic* and on particular strategies that guide (but do not necessarily) determine the comparative choices we make. Understanding the logic of comparative analysis, in fact, is essential to doing comparative politics. Needless to say, this will also be an important topic of discussion in Chapter 2. But to conclude for now our general discussion of comparing, it would be useful to consider some of the advantages of the comparative method (a topic also addressed in the following chapter).

What Are the Advantages of the Comparative Method?

Earlier I noted that comparativists tend to look at *cases as wholes* and to compare whole cases with each other. There are important advantages to this practice, the first and most important of which, perhaps, is that it enables researchers to deal with complex causality (or causal complexity). At one level, complex causality is an easy-to-grasp concept. After all, there is little doubt that much of what happens in the "real world" is an amalgam of economic, cultural, institutional, political, social, and even psychological processes and forces. Not only do all these processes and forces exist independently (at least to some extent), but they also *interact* in complicated, difficult-to-discern, and sometimes unpredictable (or contingent) ways. Thus, in studying a particular phenomenon—say, political violence—it is likely that several or even dozens of factors are at play. Some factors may be primarily economic, such as poverty, unemployment, and unequal income distribution. Other factors may be cultural (for example, specific religious values and practices, community norms), political (for example, lack of democracy or a skewed distribution of political power, which itself could be based on religious or ethnic differences), socioeconomic (for example, strong **class**-based divisions), and so on. An adequate understanding of political violence may have to take all these factors into account and will likely have to specify their interrelationship and interaction within certain contexts. Ragin provided a very useful, three-point summary of complex causality:

> First, rarely does an outcome of interest to social scientists have a single cause. The conditions conducive for strikes, for example, are many; there is no single condition that is universally capable of causing a strike. Second, *causes rarely operate in isolation.* Usually, it is *the combined effect* of various conditions, *their intersection in time and space,* that produces a certain outcome. *Thus, social causation is often both multiple and conjectural, involving*

different combinations of causal conditions. Third, a specific cause may have opposite effects *depending on context.* For example, changes in living conditions may increase or decrease the probability of strikes, depending on other social and political conditions. . . . The fact that some conditions have contradictory effects depending on context further complicates the identification of empirical regularities because it may appear that a condition is irrelevant when in fact it is an essential part of several causal combinations in both its presence and absence state. (1987, p. 27, emphasis added)

The point to remember is that other methods of inquiry (such as the experimental method and statistical analysis) cannot, in general, adequately deal with complex causality. Comparative (case-oriented) analysis, by contrast, is especially—perhaps uniquely—suited for dealing with the peculiar complexity of social phenomena (Rueschemeyer 1991). Why? Quite simply because comparative analysis, to repeat a point made earlier, can and often does deal with cases as a whole—meaning that a full range of factors can be considered at once within particular historical contexts (which themselves vary over time). This is especially apparent with regard to deviant or anomalous cases. Comparative analysis can help explain why, for example, some relatively poor countries—such as India, Mauritania, and Costa Rica—are democratic, when statistically based studies would predict just the opposite.[9] To account for such anomalous cases (as many comparativists might argue), we need to look very closely at the particular configuration of social, cultural, socioeconomic, and political forces in these individual countries, and understand how, from a historical perspective, these configurations emerged and developed. We also need to understand how external forces and relationships interacted with the domestic environment to produce the specific results that they did. None of this is likely to be achieved, to repeat, without considering the whole context of each individual case.

A second, strongly related advantage is that comparative analysis (especially when carried out in a qualitative as opposed to quantitative manner) allows the researcher to better understand or explain the relationship between and among factors. Quantitative or statistical research, by contrast, does a very good job in showing that relationships *exist* (for example, that capitalist development is related to democratization) but does not generally do a good job at telling us what the nature or underlying dynamic of this relationship is. To use a metaphor from aviation, we might say that quantitative analysis shows a strong **correlation** between engine failure and plane crashes, but it typically does not tell us the exact reasons (or the chain of causal events leading to the crash—since not all engine problems, even very similar ones, lead to the same outcome, and vice versa). To find out the reasons planes crash, therefore, investigators almost always have to look inside the "black box" or flight data recorder (see Figure 1.6).[10] They have to analyze the myriad factors—some of which will undoubtedly be

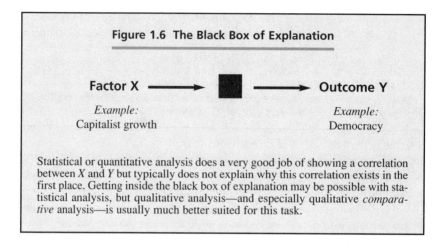

Figure 1.6 The Black Box of Explanation

Factor X ⟶ ■ ⟶ Outcome Y

Example:
Capitalist growth

Example:
Democracy

Statistical or quantitative analysis does a very good job of showing a correlation between X and Y but typically does not explain why this correlation exists in the first place. Getting inside the black box of explanation may be possible with statistical analysis, but qualitative analysis—and especially qualitative *comparative* analysis—is usually much better suited for this task.

unique to individual flights—to determine the cause of any particular crash. Even this may not be enough: quite frequently, investigators have to literally reassemble the fragments of the destroyed plane to determine the chain of causal events. To be sure, the cause is sometimes obvious and does not require intensive investigation, but more often than not, the *incident as a whole* needs to be examined in order to develop a complete explanation.

The Importance of Method and Theory

The metaphor of the black box is instructive, but we should be careful not to take it too far, for comparative analysis is more than just opening up the black box and analyzing its contents. It also involves—as might already be apparent from my discussion of the two types of comparative research strategies—a process of a priori conceptualization. At the most basic level, this simply means that the selection of cases to investigate should not be purely random or arbitrary but should be guided by certain criteria, some of which derive from the particular research design we choose. Yet before we even get to the research design, important choices have to be made regarding the factors (or variables) we consider significant in the first place. These choices are guided by theory. In Chapter 3, I talk much more about theory. For now, then, let me highlight one general point: theory has a bad reputation among students. Part of the blame, I think, falls on professors who do not help students understand why theory is not only important but is something none of us can do without (whether in an academic discipline or in everyday life). As I will make clear, we all theorize about the world, all the time. Yet just because we all theorize does not mean we all do it equally well—this is especially true for those of you who operate on the assumption that theories have nothing to do with the "real world," or that one can explain or understand anything simply by appealing to the "facts" (a view reflected in the oft-heard statement "Let the facts speak for them-selves"). One way to rectify this problem is to simply become more self-conscious and explicit about theory/theorizing; this has the added benefit, I might add, of helping oneself become a more disciplined, critical, and ana-lytic thinker. Thinking theoretically about comparative politics, in this re-gard, has value well beyond the confines of this particular subfield. The same can be said about thinking comparatively, which is the topic of our next chapter.

To sum up, *doing comparative politics* requires, minimally, a clear-eyed understanding of what comparative politics is, of what it means to compare, and of the importance and necessity of theory. There is, of course, more to doing comparative politics than just these three requirements, but they con-stitute an essential foundation upon which everything else will stand.

Notes

1. Terms that appear in boldface type are defined in the book's glossary.

2. This seems an obvious point about which most scholars would agree. Yet the distinction between US politics and comparative politics still exists in the United States. There are, of course, plenty of reasons for this, one of which is that it is nat-ural for people to see their own country or society as separate and distinct from other places. Nonetheless, there is no solid justification for the distinction. As Lee Sigelman and G. H. Gadbois nicely put it, "the traditional distinction between American and comparative politics is . . . intellectually indefensible. . . . Compari-son presupposes multiple objects of analysis . . . one compares something to or with something else" (1983, cited in Sartori 1994, p. 14).

3. Most researchers in the field, as noted, can probably agree on a basic, but very general, definition of comparative politics (such as the ones listed in Figure 1.2). There is far less agreement, however, on how the field should be constituted in terms of a particular theoretical or even methodological approach. In a wide-ranging discussion on the role of theory in comparative politics, for example, some of the leading names in comparative politics and comparative analysis fail to achieve a con-sensus on what is or should be the theoretical core of the field (see Kohli et al. 1995).

4. I should note, however, that there has never been unanimous agreement on this point. Indeed, one of the main areas of controversy in international relations theory today revolves around the "democratic peace thesis" (Doyle 1995). The crux of this argument is that liberal (or democratic) states do not go to war with other lib-eral states. In essence, advocates of the democratic peace thesis argue that there is something unique about the *internal* constitution of liberal states that changes their behavior in relation to other liberal states.

5. For obvious reasons, I cannot provide a detailed and nuanced discussion of international relations theory here. Fortunately, there are a number of very good in-troductory texts that do just this. One good book to start with is *The Globalization of World Politics: An Introduction to International Relations* (2014), edited by John Baylis, Steve Smith, and Patricia Owens (and now in its sixth edition).

6. Despite the fact that the field is defined in terms of particular method—that is, comparison—there are many scholars in the field of comparative politics who, ac-cording to Giovanni Sartori, "have no interest, no notion, no training, in comparing"

(1994, p. 15). The reason, I might note, may have more to do with the ethnocentric way the field has been defined than with the scholars themselves. To understand this point, consider the fact that comparative politics (in the United States) has been defined, most simplistically, as "studying other countries." Thus, as Sartori put it, "a scholar who studies only American presidents is an Americanist, whereas a scholar who studies only French presidents is not" (p. 14). The US-based scholar who decides to study only France, in other words, is only classified as a "comparativist" by dint of his or her interest in a country other than the United States.

7. Later, Sartori stated his case more strongly. "I must insist," he contended, "that as a 'one-case' investigation the case study cannot be subsumed under the comparative *method* (though it may have comparative merit)" (1994, p. 23, emphasis in original).

8. One prominent comparativist, Dietrich Rueschemeyer, seemed to agree with me on this point. As he put it, "Even in single-case studies comparative awareness and especially a longer time span of investigation can—logically analogous to cross-country comparisons—make the structural conditions of different event sequences more visible" (1991, p. 29).

9. Costa Rican democracy, especially, has been an issue of special interest to comparativists, since it constitutes, according to Dietrich Rueschemeyer, Evelyne Stephens, and John Stephens, "the real exception to the pattern [of authoritarianism] prevailing in Central America" (1992, p. 234).

10. Rueschemeyer, Stephens, and Stephens made a very strong argument on this point. They noted that, although cross-national statistical work has shown an undeniable and very strong link (correlation) between capitalist development and democracy, this correlation, by itself (and no matter how many times it is replicated), "does not carry its own explanation." "It does not," they continued, "identify the causal sequences accounting for the persistent relation, not to mention the reason why many cases are at odds with it. Nor can it account for how the same end can be reached by different historical routes. The repeated statistical finding has a peculiar 'black box' character that can be overcome only by theoretically well grounded empirical analysis" (1992, p. 4).

Part 1
Doing Comparative Politics

2

Comparing to Learn, Learning to Compare

With a few exceptions, most introductory textbooks on comparative politics spend very little time discussing the question of how to compare.[1] It is not entirely clear why this is, but as I noted in the preceding chapter, comparative politics is the only field in political science that is explicitly defined in terms of a particular method. For this reason alone it makes sense to devote serious attention to the issue of comparison. But there is another good reason: learning how to compare is an extremely useful and valuable skill—and not just in the context of comparative politics. Indeed, as one pair of comparativists put it, "Comparison is the engine of knowledge" (Dogan and Pelassy 1990, p. 8). Comparative analysis, in other words, is indispensable to learning more about the world in which we live. Significantly, this learning can sometimes take place almost by accident. French historian Fernand Braudel explained it this way: "Live in London for a year," he wrote, "and you will not get to know much about England. But through comparison, in the light of your surprise, you will suddenly come to understand some of the more profound and individual characteristics of France, which you did not previously understand because you knew them too well" (Braudel 1972, p. 24, cited in Dogan and Pelassy 1990, p. 8). For students living in the United States, the lesson is equally true: live in Tokyo (Berlin, Mexico City, Johannesburg, etc.) for a year, and you will learn much more about the United States than any of those places, because your experiences in a new environment will compel you to notice more, and think more deeply, about life in the United States. Comparing, in short, can help open your eyes to the world—including or especially your *own* world—in a manner that simply would not be possible otherwise. Of course, a newfound vision does not come automatically. Many people can look at the world around them and see absolutely nothing new. Worse still, they may look around the world merely to confirm already closely held, but incorrect or distorted, beliefs.

Comparing and Open-Mindedness

Learning to compare, therefore, entails more than just a capacity to look at (or live in) a foreign place. It also requires a willingness to *understand* and *evaluate* differences, as well as similarities, in an *open-minded* manner. Unfortunately, none of this is easily taught inside a classroom (in the same way, say, that a professor can teach a simple math equation or the definition of a basic concept). This especially applies to open-mindedness, for open-mindedness is an attribute that comes as much from the inside as it does from the outside. As a student and as a human being, in other words, you must make a commitment to this general principle, or else it is likely that you will not learn a great deal from this or any book. At the same time, just reminding yourself to be open-minded is not enough. Many of our most ingrained biases are those of which we are completely unaware—those that we do not consider biases at all, but simply natural or self-evident truths. Unfortunately, this tendency is not limited to students. In particular, the development of comparative politics as a field of study has been clearly influenced by the belief, on the part of US academics—especially in the early to middle twentieth century—that the economic and political systems of the United States were the standards by which all other countries were to be judged. In fact, many US social scientists of that era were very firm in their beliefs that the United States occupied a special place in the world. "The reasons," as Howard Wiarda nicely put it,

> go to the heart of the American experience, to the deeply held belief that the United States is different [from] and *superior* to European and all other nations, the widespread conviction at the popular level that the United States had little to learn from the rest of the world, the near-universal belief of Americans in the superiority of their institutions and their attitudes that the rest of the world must learn from the United States and never the other way around. (1991, p. 12, emphasis added)

In retrospect, it is easy to blame US scholars for their **ethnocentrism**; yet it is important to note, as Mattei Dogan and Dominque Pelassy did, that one of the best ways to first recognize and then avoid the trap of ethnocentrism is through comparison. "Indeed," as they put it, "the very concept of ethnocentrism simply cannot exist without the comparative exercise. Only with exposure to other cultures does one become conscious of possible intellectual occlusion" (1990, p. 9).

Comparing and Critical Thinking

An important and clearly related aspect of open-mindedness is critical thinking. By critical, I do not mean quick to judge (as in, "My mom was really critical of my nose ring"). I mean just the opposite. That is, to be critical means to engage in a process of careful, well-considered, and reflective evaluation. If you make comparisons in a superficial, haphazard, or unreflective manner, you might as well not bother. For you are not only unlikely to develop any meaningful insights, but you also run the risk of constructing a dangerously distorted or entirely erroneous analysis. Unfortunately, as with open-mindedness, thinking critically is not easy to teach. Professors can talk all day about the importance of and necessity for thinking critically, but you must first be willing to make the effort to discipline your mind to do so. This said, it would still be useful to offer a few more words about critical thinking.

One nice perspective on critical thinking is provided by Daniel J. Kurland, who wrote in 1994 in *I Know What It Says . . . What Does It Mean:* "Broadly speaking, critical thinking is concerned with reason, intellectual honesty, and open-mindedness, as opposed to emotionalism, intellectual laziness, and closed-mindedness" (cited in Fowler n.d.). This, in turn, involves a number of concrete practices, the most important of which are "following evidence where it leads; considering all possibilities; relying on reason rather than emotion; being precise; considering a variety of possible viewpoints and explanations; weighing the effects of motives and biases . . . not rejecting unpopular views out of hand; being aware of [and self-reflective about] one's own prejudices and biases; and not allowing them to sway one's judgment" (cited in Fowler n.d.). Anyone who follows these guidelines will almost certainly become a better, stronger student of comparative politics and of life more generally. As I have already said, none of this is easy to teach, much less learn. Fortunately, comparative analysis provides a useful path toward good critical thinking, since it encourages—and, if done right, forces—you to put into practice many of the points raised here. Even more, I believe that comparative analysis is *the* ideal framework for critical thinking in the social sciences. So how does one "do it right"? It is to this issue we turn next.

Strategies of Comparing

There is no one way—or even a best way—to do comparative analysis. In fact, as we'll see in the following sections, there are numerous principles and models one can use to carry out comparative analysis, all of which are equally valid. "Equally valid," though, does not mean that each type of comparison is equally suited for different tasks, purposes, or questions. This is a key point. For it is, on one level, the questions you ask and the goal you wish to achieve that should determine the comparative framework you use, and not the other way around. Comparisons are also determined, I need to emphasize, by the characteristics and availability of the things (i.e., units of analysis) that need to be compared. As might be evident, the discussion that follows will address some fairly abstract points; yet this chapter is meant to be mostly practical in nature. More specifically, I will address a number of basic questions: What are the specific ways of comparing? How does one go about choosing the cases used in comparative analysis? Once you have selected your case or cases for comparison, how many should be compared—one, two, three, a dozen, or perhaps the whole universe of countries (or other units of analysis) that currently make up the world? What are the specific advantages and disadvantages of the different comparative principles and models? I will address all of these questions in this chapter. It is necessary to start, however, with a discussion of the general principles or logic of comparing.

The Logic of Comparative Analysis

The first point to remember—one already mentioned—is this: doing comparative analysis correctly *requires* a basic understanding of the logic or general principles of comparative research design. This point cannot be overstated. To do comparative analysis properly, one must absolutely, positively have a firm grasp of the logic of comparing. Without this understanding, many if not most comparisons will be useless, since they can easily lead researchers and others to distorted or just plain wrong conclusions. Fortunately, the essential principles—or the basic logic—of comparative analysis are not necessarily hard to grasp. For the purposes of this book, the focus will be on three of the most general and least-complicated comparative principles: the **most similar systems** (MSS), the **most different systems** (MDS), and the **method of agreement** (MoA). To be sure, these are not the only principles for comparative analysis. Many comparativists, for example, draw from John Stuart Mill's seminal book *A System of Logic: Ratiocinative and Inductive* ([1843] 1967). In his book, Mill introduced a range of other comparative principles, including the **method of difference** and **indirect method of difference**. The MSS, MDS, and MoA, however, are arguably the most commonly used, easiest to learn, and simplest to apply. More important, they underlie most other comparative designs and specific comparative models; they also offer a scientific way toward knowing when our arguments are right, wrong, or something else.

The Most Similar Systems Design

As the name implies, the most similar systems strategy is based on finding two or more very similar social systems, typically countries. More specifically, it is based on matching up and then comparing two or more systems that share a whole range of similarities (political, social, demographic, economic, cultural, and so on) but also differ in at least a couple of important respects. Adam Przeworski and Henry Teune—whose book *The Logic of Comparative Social Inquiry* (1970) is considered by many to be the bible on contemporary comparative analysis in the social sciences—gave as an example the Scandinavian countries (Sweden, Norway, Finland) or the two-party systems of the Anglo-Saxon countries (that is, the United States and Britain), which are viewed as archetypical most similar systems "because these countries share many economic, cultural, and political characteristics" (p. 32). In methodological terms, the important point is that the characteristics the systems share can, in principle, be held constant and can therefore be considered irrelevant in explaining a particular social or political phenomenon (the **dependent variable**) that *varies* between or among the systems. Having "controlled for" a range of variables, the comparativist can focus on finding a significant *dissimilarity* between the two systems, which can then be put forward as *the* causal factor or key **independent variable**. To put it in slightly different terms, the independent variable, as with the dependent variable, also varies between the two units of analysis. (See Figure 2.1 for further discussion of independent and dependent variables.)

Figure 2.1 Independent and Dependent Variables

In an *experimental* setting, the independent variable is the variable controlled or (intentionally) manipulated by the researcher in order to observe its effect. The dependent variable is the phenomenon that is in some way affected by the independent variable. In comparative politics and other social scientific research, however, experimental designs, as we have learned, are generally not possible. This means that the independent variable cannot be manipulated but must instead be analyzed retrospectively or indirectly. For instance, a researcher studying presidential elections may make the following claim: "When the unemployment rate exceeds 7.0 percent, incumbent presidents are not reelected." In this example, the dependent variable is the reelection of incumbent presidents. The independent variable is the overall unemployment rate. To assess the relationship between the independent and dependent variables, a researcher could collect (historical) data on unemployment rates from several countries. If the researcher found that in every instance the unemployment rate was greater than 7 percent at the time of a presidential election that the incumbent lost, the initial hypothesis would be strengthened. In this case, to reiterate the main point, the independent variable is not manipulated by the researcher but is instead evaluated indirectly or retrospectively through the use of historical data. (This example is from "Writing Political Science," http://www.unc.edu/depts/wcweb/handouts/polisci.htm.)

To some researchers, it is, strictly speaking, erroneous to talk about independent and dependent variables in the type of analysis illustrated here. For our purposes, therefore, we need to be clear that the terms *independent variable* and *dependent variable* are used in a less formal but still clear-cut manner by most comparativists. To repeat: the independent variable is the one that you think of as causal, and the dependent variable is the one that you think of as being affected by the independent variable.

The MSS Design in Practice:
Comparing the United States and Canada

To help make this discussion even more concrete, consider the example from Chapter 1: a comparison of the United States and Canada, two most similar systems. If we use these two countries or systems to try to answer a by now familiar research question—"Why is the gun homicide rate higher in the United States than in any other advanced, industrialized country?"— we can immediately control for or hold constant a wide range of potentially significant variables. Again, this is what Michael Moore did, at least in a very casual and implicit manner, in *Bowling for Columbine*. Specifically, because the United States and Canada share so many attributes—such as high per capita gross domestic product, moderate levels of poverty and unemployment, a relatively high level of ethnic and racial diversity, exposure to violent movies and video games, a Christian-based heritage, similar levels of immigration, and so on—we can assume that no one of these similarities is responsible for the appreciably higher gun homicide rate in the United States. Conversely, we can also deduce that none is responsible for the relatively low rate of gun-related homicides in Canada. (See Figure 2.2 for details on gun-related homicide rates; statistics on major assaults involving firearms in the two countries are also included.) Accordingly, we are able to turn our attention to identifying a significant difference or differences between the systems or units of analysis that can account for the variance in gun-related homicides between the two countries. It is this difference (or differences) that is key.

So what is *the* key difference (or differences) between the two countries that might account for the higher level of gun-related homicide in the United States? Before saying anything more, I must stress that definitively

---

Figure 2.2 Firearm-Related Homicide Rates in the United States and Canada, 2012

	United States	Canada
Intentional homicides (per 100,000 population)	3.5	0.5
Total number of intentional homicides	8,813	172
Major assaults involving firearms (per 100,000 population)	52.8	5.5
Total number of major assaults involving firearms	143,119	1,459

Source: Government of Canada 2014.

answering this question is both beyond the scope of this chapter and also a task that I expressly want to avoid. Instead, my intention is to highlight how a researcher can use comparative principles to address the question in a scientific manner. Keeping the last point in mind, some observers have pointed to the extraordinarily high level of gun ownership in the United States, as well as the legal-institutional and historical factors that make the high levels of gun ownership possible. Michael Moore did not consider gun ownership to be a key factor in his argument (although he did try to "test" for it), but given its salience, it is worth subjecting this factor to a bit more comparative scrutiny. According to one of the most meticulous estimates available, in 2007 there were about twenty-seven times more (civilian) firearms in the United States (roughly 270 million, but perhaps much more) than in Canada (10 million), although on a **per capita** basis, the difference is not as dramatic: in the United States there were between 83 and 97 firearms for every 100 people, whereas in Canada there were between 25 and 38 guns for every 100 people, a difference of roughly three to one (but as much as four to one) (*Small Arms Survey* 2007, p. 47). In this view, one can make a plausible (or at least prima facie) argument that the level of gun ownership must be part of the explanation for the high gun-related homicide rate in the United States. Common sense tells us, too, that there must be some relationship between the easy availability of guns and the number of gun-related homicides in a society, although common sense is not always right.

Indeed, a little more comparative checking will tell us that the issue is not so clear-cut. Among industrialized democracies, Finland and Switzerland have the second and third highest rates of gun ownership (behind the United States), at 69 and 61 per 100 people, respectively (based on the "high estimate" given in the 2007 *Small Arms Survey*). Yet their respective levels of gun-related homicides are much lower than that in the United States, and, in the case of Finland, even lower than Canada's (see Figure 2.3). Conversely, a few countries with relatively low gun ownership rates— compared to the United States, Finland, Switzerland, and Canada—have extremely high gun homicides rates. Brazil, the Philippines, and Colombia are prime examples (see Figure 2.3). None of this is to say that we must reject the claim that gun ownership is an important variable, but we know that, *by itself,* it cannot explain the relatively high number of gun-related murders in the United States (remember our discussion of complex causality). There must, in short, be another factor (or set of factors) that sets the United States apart. One possibility, discussed in Chapter 1, is Michael Moore's thesis, which revolves around the idea that gun violence in the United States is driven by a "culture of fear." It would not be hard, in fact, to put the two variables together in the context of a single argument: a heightened sense of fear in the United States leads not only to higher rates of gun ownership, but also to a much greater propensity to actually use

Figure 2.3 Estimates of Civilian Firearms Ownership and Homicide Rates in Selected Countries

	Number of Civilian Firearms (average of high and low estimates) (2006)[a]	Low Estimate of Number of Firearms per 100 People (2006)[a]	High Estimate of Number of Firearms per 100 People (2006)[a]	Homicide Rate per 100,000 Population[b] (2012)	Firearm Homicide Rate per 100,000 Population (2000)[a]
United States	270,000,000	83.0	97.0	4.7	2.97
Germany	30,000,000	24.0	36.0	0.8 (2011)	0.47
France	19,000,000	30.0	34.0	1.2	—
Mexico	15,500,000	15.0	15.0	21.5	3.70
Brazil	15,300,000	8.8	8.8	25.2	—
Yemen	11,500,000	32.0	90.0	4.8 (2010)	—
Canada	9,950,000	25.0	38.0	1.6	0.54
Italy	7,000,000	6.9	17.3	0.9	—
Philippines	3,900,000	3.4	6.1	8.7	—
England	3,400,000	3.3	7.8	1.6	0.12
Switzerland	3,400,000	31.0	61.0	0.6 (2011)	0.56
Colombia	3,100,000	5.4	9.1	30.8	51.80
Australia	3,050,000	15.0	16.0	1.1	0.31
Finland	2,900,000	41.0	69.0	2.1	0.43
Sweden	2,800,000	23.0	40.0	0.9	—

Sources: Firearm ownership data from *Small Arms Survey 2007;* homicide rate data from United Nations Office on Drugs and Crime (UNODC) n.d., "Homicide Counts and Rates"; firearm homicide data from UNODC n.d., *Seventh United Nations Survey.*

Notes: a. Dates are not consistent due to unavailability of data.

b. Average is of high and low estimates from various sources, including Interpol, the World Health Organization (WHO), the UNODC, and national sources.

firearms against others. There are likely—indeed, almost certainly—other significant factors and arguments as well. And, it is up to the comparativist to find these factors, which is a task that is made much more manageable through a well-designed comparative framework.

Limitations of the MSS design. It is important to understand that *no* comparison of the United States and Canada (or of any pair of countries) by itself will *prove* that gun ownership or a "culture of fear" or some other factor is the cause of the high rate of gun-related homicides in the United States. There are two basic reasons for this. First, and most obvious, a comparison of only two cases does not and cannot provide a strong enough empirical basis for making hard conclusions or big claims. (On this last point,

I should note that MSS comparisons can involve more than two cases, but, when comparing large-scale social units, it is exceedingly difficult to incorporate more than a handful of comparative cases into a single comparison.) A moment's reflection should help us understand why a comparison of only two or a handful of cases is problematic. Specifically, with only a limited number of cases, there is no way to be sure that your findings are any more than coincidental or happenstance. Think about the example used earlier on the relationship between gun ownership and firearm-related deaths. If a researcher compared, say, only England and the United States (as two most similar cases), he might easily conclude that there is a hard-and-fast **causal relationship** between the two variables. But jumping to that conclusion is dangerous, since another comparison (whether based on the MSS principle or something else) might show no relationship at all, or might point to a different factor. To put it very simply, if only a single comparison is done, the researcher cannot know what's missing.

Second, and far less obvious, it is important to understand that, even though the United States and Canada (or the United States and England) may be very similar systems, they are not as alike as they might appear to be at first glance. Indeed, the closer we look, the more differences we are likely to find, to the point, some might argue, that the two countries no longer seem very similar at all, let alone "most similar." This is a serious and real limitation. After all, if the United States and Canada (or any other set of countries or cases) have too many differences, the logic of the MSS design falls apart, since it becomes increasingly difficult to know which differences are important and which are irrelevant. The main methodological point, to repeat, is this: if there are too many differences between the United States and Canada, we cannot simply assume that the one difference we identify (for example, a high level of private gun ownership in the United States versus a lower level of private gun ownership in Canada, or a "culture of fear" versus a "culture of security") is the only difference that matters. The MSS design, in this sense, suffers from an unavoidable and significant flaw when applied to complex, real-world social systems. Simply put, no matter how similar two (or more) large-scale social systems may seem, there are bound to be so many differences, big and small, that it would be impossible, in strict methodological terms, to establish exactly which differences have causal significance and which do not (Hopkin 2002, p. 254).

At the same time, there still may be good reason for classifying large social systems, such as the United States and Canada, as most similar systems. The key point is this: when using the MSS principle, it is possible to set aside a (large) range of differences between two or more MSS units of analysis. This is possible, in small part, because many differences can be considered trivial—often this can be determined through basic comparative checking. More important, though, it is possible because most research does not begin with a blank slate. Instead, through previous studies (typically carried out by other researchers and analysts), it will be fairly clear that a wide range of factors are immaterial to an explanation of gun-related homicides or other phenomena. Thus, if (albeit, a very important "if") the many differences between two or more systems have already been eliminated as potential causes, they can be safely disregarded. For example, the population of the United States is about nine times larger than Canada's population (the US population is about 313 million compared to Canada's population of just under 34 million). This is, to be sure, a big difference. Yet previous research, as well as comparative checking, shows that there is no clear-cut correlation, still less a causal relationship, between population size and gun-related homicide rates. Accordingly, this difference (and others subject to the same scrutiny) can be safely ignored.

The importance of differences in the MSS design: A recap. When using the MSS design it is important to remember the key point: the differences between most similar systems are more important than the similarities. Differences are *crucial* to the logic of the MSS comparison. To put it in slightly different terms, in a vast sea of similarities, there should be at least two meaningful differences between the systems. One of these differences will be among the many potential explanatory or independent variables. The other difference must be in the dependent variable. With regard to this latter point, in particular, comparativists like to say that the MSS design requires variance in the dependent variable. Figure 2.4 provides another way to think about the importance of differences in the MSS design using the example of identical twins.

The Most Different Systems Design

Not surprisingly, the logic of the most different systems design is largely the reverse of that of the MSS design. This is most evident in the general approach of the MDS design, which (in ideal terms) is to find two systems that are different in almost every respect, except for the variable or variables under investigation.[2] The basic idea, to borrow from the discussion of the MSS design, is to find, in a vast sea of differences, key similarities between very dissimilar systems. The logic of the MDS design, I should note, is counterintuitive: many novice comparativists automatically assume that very dissimilar systems can and should not be compared (recall the earlier discussion of the oft-heard phrase "You can't compare apples to oranges"). But as made clear in the first chapter, this is not at all the case.

Here is a second point that needs to be highlighted: in contrast to the MSS design, variance on the dependent variable is neither required nor desired. In fact, the existence or strength of the dependent variable must be

Figure 2.4 Twins, Aging, and the Logic of the MSS Design

One useful way to easily and clearly grasp the logic upon which an MSS comparison is based is to consider differences between identical twins. Obviously, twins (which we can consider to be separate units of analyses or systems) share the widest range of similarities that two human beings can: in this regard, they are almost perfect examples of two most similar systems. Yet twins do not develop exactly alike: over time, differences invariably arise. A difference—such as facial aging—can be identified as a dependent variable: an outcome or phenomenon that is the product of some other factor or set of factors. With this in mind, consider a study by Bahman Guyuron and colleagues (2009) titled "Factors Contributing to the Facial Aging of Identical Twins." The authors were intrigued by the perceived differences in facial aging between twins. To the researchers, that one difference meant that some other difference had to have caused one twin to appear older than the other. Thus, the task of the researchers was to find out what other differences may have caused or resulted in one twin appearing older than the other. These other differences are the independent variables. The task, in other words, was to find key differences in a sea of similarities. In their study, the following factors (plus a few others) were identified as key: smoking, increased sun exposure, alcohol consumption, and marital status (divorcees looked older, widows and widowers looked younger). Remember, though: if a pair of identical twins was truly identical—if there were no differences at all between them—then a comparison of the two would make no (scientific) sense.

generally the same in all cases, for, in an MDS design, the researcher is attempting to show that the relationship between the presumed independent variable or variables and a dependent variable holds across a wide variety of vastly divergent settings. This means, in practical terms, that the comparativist will often select cases in terms of the dependent variable. If a researcher wants to identify the causes of religious or ethnic conflict, for example, they may only look for cases in which such conflict was/is present. It is important to note, however, that not everyone agrees on the merit of this practice. As B. Guy Peters pointed out, "there are disputes over the appropriateness of selecting cases on the dependent variable, with qualitative researchers arguing that this is essential, and quantitative researchers arguing that it invalidates most findings" (1998, p. 67). I cannot resolve the debate here, except to say that comparativists, in general, put greater emphasis on qualitative analysis. One reason for this, moreover, is clear: most comparativists simply have too few cases from which to select.

To make this discussion more understandable, let's consider one hypothetical example to illustrate the central logic of the MDS design. This example borrows from Adam Przeworski and Teune (1970), whose work was mentioned earlier. In their discussion of the MDS design, Przeworski and Teune began with a focus on suicide rates (the dependent variable). In looking around the world, it was immediately apparent that some societies had (or have) very high rates of suicide, some very low rates, and some right in between. The overall variance, though, was and continues to be quite significant (see Figure 2.5). This raised an obvious question, namely, what factor or factors explain why some societies have high rates of suicide while others have very low or moderate rates? Methodologically, there are several ways we can examine this question, but an MDS design is a good choice in light of the available data. (At the outset, it is important to emphasize that a real-world analysis on the causes of suicide would be far, far more complex than what is presented here. Still, an MDS design provides a useful way of approaching this very complex issue.)

Consider the following set of countries: Guyana, Japan, and Estonia. Each has a nearly identical rate of male suicide. Yet, at least at a general level, they might properly be regarded as three most different systems: Guyana is a small, relatively poor, ethnically and culturally diverse country located in South America; Japan is a large, generally homogeneous, and economically wealthy country in East Asia; and Estonia, a former Soviet republic, is a middle-income, partly heterogeneous society located along the Baltic Sea (between Latvia, Russia, and Finland). There are a host of other political, social, and cultural differences as well, so the primary objective is to find a *common factor* in all three countries that could help explain their

Figure 2.5 Suicide Rates in Selected Countries (per 100,000; most recent year available)

	Year	Male Suicide Rate	Female Suicide Rate
Lithuania[a]	2005	68.1	12.9
Guyana	2005	33.8	11.6
Japan	2006	34.8	13.2
Estonia	2005	35.5	7.3
Kuwait	2002	2.5	1.5
Tajikistan	2001	2.9	2.3
Guatemala	2003	3.4	0.9
Haiti[b]	2003	0.0	0.0

Source: World Health Organization 2008.
Notes: a. Lithuania has the highest suicide rate in the world.
   b. Haiti, along with Antigua and Barbuda, Honduras, Saint Kitts and Nevis, São Tomé and Príncipe, Egypt, Syria, Iran, Jamaica, and Peru, have the lowest rates of suicide (data for these countries, however, are between ten and thirty years old).

relatively high rates of (male) suicide. We could follow the same procedure, it is worth pointing out, with three other most different systems (say, Kuwait, Tajikistan, and Guatemala), but all with very *low rates* of male suicide. The logic here is exactly the same, but now we are looking for the common factor or factors that help explain why suicide is a relatively rare occurrence among those three countries.

In both sets of comparative cases, I must emphasize, we run into the same type of limitation previously addressed with regard to the MSS design, albeit in reverse. Specifically, the closer we look at Guyana, Japan, and Estonia (or Kuwait, Tajikistan, and Guatemala), the more similarities we are likely to find. How do we know, then, which similarities are or are not causally significant? On one level, the answer is that we cannot know for sure, but on another level, we can use the same process of elimination as with the MSS design. Similarities shared by *all* countries, for example, can be discounted; while other potentially important similarities can be tested for separately through parallel comparative or other types of analysis.

Before concluding this discussion, it would be useful to refer to one additional and more pertinent example of—at least for students of comparative politics—an MDS comparison. This example is provided by Theda Skocpol, a prominent sociologist and comparativist. In her influential book *States and Social Revolutions* (1979), Skocpol compared late-eighteenth-century France, early-twentieth-century Russia, and mid-twentieth-century China in an effort to explain the causes of successful social revolutions. It is useful to note that Skocpol did not explicitly base her analysis on a most different systems design (instead, she referred to Mill's methods of agreement and difference), but it is fairly clear that she applied the basic, and very simple, principles of the MDS strategy. Consider her explanation for why she chose to focus on France, Russia, and China. To wit, she recognized that the three countries, in three distinct periods of time, were very different in many ways (that is, they were clearly most different systems). Yet they "exhibited important similarities in their Old Regimes and revolutionary processes and outcomes—similarities more than sufficient to warrant their treatment together as one pattern calling for a coherent causal explanation" (p. 41). In other words, the key reasons for comparing late-eighteen-century France, early-twentieth-century Russia, and mid-twentieth-century China, according to Skocpol, derived first from the profound similarities each shared with regard to the dependent variable, which she defined as a social revolution characterized by the creation of a "centralized, bureaucratic, and mass-incorporating nation-state with enhanced great-power potential in the international arena" (p. 41). Second, and just as important, Skocpol argued that the cause (or primary reason) of social revolutions in all three countries (that is, the independent variables) was essentially the same. In short, her stated research design, at least the main part of her design, followed the logic of the MDS approach very closely. It is useful to point out, too, that Skocpol's choice of cases spanned almost two centuries; this tells us that cases do not have to come from the same time period in order to be compared.

* * *

The basic logic of the most different systems design is really quite simple. Just remember that it is not merely a matter of finding very different systems, but of finding different systems in which there is little variance on the dependent variable. Once this is done, the researcher is set up to look for a key similarly with regard to independent variable. Like the MSS design, however, the MDS design is far from perfect. There is no guarantee, for example, that the findings from an MDS design will unequivocally, or even confidently, identify causal relationships, which are generally what social scientists are most interested in determining. To see this, let us reconsider the example of suicide among most different systems. Assuming we found a common characteristic among our three examples from earlier (Guyana, Japan, and Estonia)—say, a high level of alcoholism or social alienation—how do we know that either of these is the root cause? Indeed, it may be the case (and likely is) that alcoholism or alienation is the product of a third, still unidentified factor. (In this sense, alcoholism or alienation may be symptomatic rather than causal.) And it may be, moreover, that this third factor is different in all three societies. This raises a second, perhaps more serious problem with the MDS system design, namely that it cannot adequately deal with **multiple causation** (Ragin 1987). In other words, there is no reason to presume that a certain phenomenon (such as social revolution or suicide) is necessarily the product of one and only one cause. Very different causes may produce the same or similar results. Similarly, different combinations of causes may produce the same result. If a comparativist uses an MDS design without considering these possibilities, they may end up with distorted or completely unfounded conclusions. As I will discuss later, this limitation is not a deal breaker. With a carefully designed *mixed* comparative strategy (i.e., a single comparative framework that incorporates multiple principles and models), it is possible to ameliorate the limitations of any single principle or model. This brings us to the third comparative principle, the method of agreement.

The Method of Agreement

The method of agreement is perhaps the most intuitive of the three comparative principles under discussion. Accordingly, the basic logic is quite simple, and probably can be best understood through an example. Suppose a researcher is interested in explaining instances of large-scale, popular uprising in nondemocratic regimes, the type of uprising that occurred throughout the Middle East and North Africa at the end of 2010 and into 2011, which is most commonly referred to as the Arab Spring. Now consider the following list of possible causes (note that the list of factors will likely be based on existing studies of popular uprisings, as well as the comparativist's own research-based hypotheses):

a. Long-standing economic malaise with attendant problems (e.g., high unemployment and underemployment, low incomes, pervasive poverty).
b. Persistent and rising levels of socioeconomic inequality.
c. Emergence of strong class-based identities in the working and middle classes.
d. Increasing levels of urbanization, education, and social activism.
e. Aging dictator.
f. Better and more general access to social media and related sites (e.g., Facebook, Twitter, Instagram, and YouTube).
g. A galvanizing or dramatic incident directed against or perpetrated by the regime.
h. A deterioration of regime cohesion (e.g., the military elite begin to function independently of the political leadership).

The next step is to see which, if any, of these factors are present (or absent) among the cases in our examination. In this scenario, it is useful to have as many comparative cases as possible. Fortunately, this is a much easier task using the MoA than the MSS or MDS designs, since one does not have to worry about finding appropriate sets of cases that fulfill the requirements of the most similar or most different systems principles. Instead, using the MoA, the researcher can simply examine all those cases in which the dependent variable is present (or absent), without having to worry if the cases are "most similar" or "most different." Using the MSS principle, in contrast, it may be very difficult to find more than two or three cases that are *both* most similar systems, *and* have clear variance on a particular dependent variable. But back to the basic point: in a study of the Arab Spring, the researcher can include *all* those countries in which a large-scale, popular uprising took place—such as Tunisia, Egypt, Libya, Yemen, Syria, Bahrain, Algeria, Oman, among others. (Note: for the purposes of this example, it does not matter if the uprising successfully overthrew the existing regime.) Once this is done, the researcher's main task is to see if there are commonalities across all of the cases. If there are, the researcher could tentatively conclude that those common factors (or a single common factor) help to explain the emergence of large-scale popular uprisings. Conversely, the researcher examines all those cases in which there was no popular uprising. (The Arab Spring is discussed in more detail in Chapter 8.) In a number of real-world studies, I might note, researchers have implicitly or explicitly used the MoA in trying to explain the origins of the Arab Spring. One particularly salient factor is the role of social media (see, for example, Howard et al. 2011). These studies, it is important to add, do not generally assert that the existence of social media was the only causal variable; instead, they argue that it was a necessary ingredient, as it enabled citizens to coalesce and then organize in a manner that had been hitherto impossible under the repressive circumstances that characterize authoritarian regimes.

As with MSS and MDS comparisons, however, the researcher needs to be very careful in drawing hard-and-fast causal conclusions using only the MoA. There are several easily discernable reasons for this, but I will highlight just the most important one. Namely, demonstrating that a factor (or small set of factors) is present in a range of cases does not and cannot establish **causation**. The factor identified could be largely irrelevant, or it could be secondary, or it could be an effect rather than a cause. Keep in mind, on this point, that the design of the MoA does not allow the researcher to eliminate a range of other variables. Similarities via the MSS principle, or difference via the MDS principle, in other words, are not controlled for in the method of agreement. In the example of the Arab Spring, in fact, some researchers have strongly criticized the conclusion that social media played a primary or even secondary causal role. In one study, for instance, Gadi Wolfsfeld, Elad Segev, and Tamir Sheafer (2013) argued that the use of social media *followed* rather than preceded protest activity. In this view, social media, at best, played a complementary role. This is an important debate, about which there is intense disagreement. Important as the debate is, it is well beyond the scope of this chapter to settle. Suffice it to say that, despite its limitations, the MoA is an important, albeit far from perfect, methodological tool.

The upshot? While the MoA is useful and appropriate in comparative analysis, it should not be relied upon as a standalone method of analysis. Instead, the method of agreement might be best employed in conjunction with other methods, and as a starting point of analysis.

The Three Cs

In stressing the limitations of the MoA, the MDS, and MSS designs, my intention, again, is not to confuse or frustrate you, still less dissuade you from using them in your own analysis. Rather, my intention is to emphasize the need for *caution, care,* and *constraint*—the three Cs. Too often students (and policymakers, journalists, pundits, and even professional researchers, including professors) tend to jump to hard conclusions or to make big generalizations based on both good (i.e., properly designed and logical) and bad comparisons. This is not a good idea, to say the least, and it is not intellectually or methodologically justifiable. At the same time, comparative analysis is an indispensable tool for researchers of all stripes, and for anyone trying to make better sense of the world. Indeed, sometimes it is the only viable methodological tool available. The main lessons, therefore, are simply to understand, first, how to make good comparisons, and second, how to avoid making bad comparisons. The third lesson is to recognize the advantages *and* limitations of the basic principles of comparative analysis.

Concrete Models of Comparative Analysis

As we've just seen, the MSS, MDS, and MoA are the basic principles for organizing comparative analysis. As Dogan and Pelassy pointed out, however, they do not provide a sufficient sense of "the different possibilities offered to the researcher [and student] who has to delineate the area of analysis and choose the countries to be included in the comparison" (1990, p. 111). Fortunately, Dogan and Pelassy (as well as a number of other scholars) helped to fill this gap. Specifically, the authors listed several specific *models* open to comparativists. These include, but are not limited to: (1) the case study in comparative perspective; (2) **binary analysis** or a comparison of two units; (3) a multiunit comparison involving three or more units; and (4) a **mixed design**. With respect to the case study, I would also add two very closely related models (mentioned earlier): *analytical induction* and *within-case comparison*. In the remainder of this chapter, I will spend time discussing each of these models, albeit in general terms. There are a couple of reasons why I do not provide in-depth, highly detailed discussions. First, it would probably do little good to overwhelm you with methodological minutiae, much of which will not be fully understandable until you have a good chance to actually *do* some real comparative analysis on your own. Second, once the basic *principles* of comparative analysis are understood, the various models can be grasped with relative ease. Thus, an extended discussion is, for the most part, not necessary. With these points firmly in mind, let us begin with a look at the first model of comparative analysis, the case study in comparative perspective. (One quick note: I used the term *model* to differentiate the upcoming discussion with the just-completed discussion of the *logic* or *principles* of comparative analysis. As just suggested, too, the models discussed in this chapter are typically premised on a specific comparative principle or logic. In other words, comparative models are built upon a specific comparative principle; the two go hand-in-hand, but are nonetheless distinct concepts.)

The Case Study in Comparative Perspective

In comparative politics, a case study is typically associated with an *in-depth* examination of a specific country or political system, as in the Mexican case, the Japanese case, or the French case. In this regard, it would be natural to assume that the "case" in a case study is always a country, and that a case is just a synonym for the term *unit of analysis*. However, both assumptions would be wrong. Perhaps it would best, then, to begin this section by answering the question "What is a case?" Unfortunately, as with the question of what comparative politics is, the answer is not as clear-cut as one might think or hope. Is a case, as Charles Ragin and Howard Becker (1992) asked, a generic category, such as a country, a society, a family, a community, an organization/institution, or even an individual? Is it a historically or theoretically constituted category: for example, an "authoritarian personality"? Or is a case a specific event, such as an anticolonial revolution? The simple response is that all these various examples represent—or can represent—cases. I emphasize "can" because, as Ragin and Becker pointed out, a "case is not inherently one thing or another, but a way station in the process of producing social science" (p. 225). More simply, Ragin and Becker were suggesting that cases are not self-evident. Indeed, researchers often only determine what their case is, or what the parameters of their case are, in the course of their research.

Admittedly, this is an abstract and perhaps distracting way of trying to describe a case. For our purposes, then, I will rely on a highly simplified and very practical definition. It is also one that seems to underlie many, if not most, case studies. Specifically, this definition recognizes that researchers typically base their cases on three basic characteristics. First, a case usually centers on a specific issue or concern (e.g., terrorism, industrialization, revolution, a **social movement**). Second, a case is often, although not always, based on a delimited geographic space, such as Germany, Texas, Tokyo, or the Kurdish community (the Kurdish community generally lives in the contiguous areas of Turkey, Iraq, Iran, Armenia, and Syria; this illustrates the fact that a "delimited geographic space" can be transnational, and not just national or subnational). Third, a case generally covers a specific period of time. Using these three characteristics, it becomes easy to identify and create a case. For example, "far-left terrorism in early post-war Italy" would be a case, as would "Tea Party conservatism in US politics since 2008" (this latter example is based on 2013 research by Williamson and Skocpol). Again, this is a purposely simplified definition, one about which many scholars might disagree. (For an extended discussion of how to conceptualize a case, see Ragin and Becker's *What Is a Case?* [1992], which is an entire 242-page book devoted to the question.) At the same time, the foregoing delineation of a case provides novice comparativists a not unreasonable starting point.

Can a Single Case Study Be Comparative?

While providing a basic definition of a case is necessary, another, perhaps more basic question looms in the background. To wit, can a single case study even be *comparative*? It is important to not gloss over this question, for, if a single case study *cannot* be comparative, then I really have no business discussing it here. As I already pointed out, some scholars, such as Giovanni Sartori, are highly skeptical of the idea that a single case study can be genuinely comparative. Sartori raised a legitimate concern. After all, there are many scholars (especially **area studies** specialists) who treat their cases as unique or literally incomparable and, therefore, *noncomparable*. There is some rationale for this, as the case study approach assumes that the particular historical, political, cultural, and social *context* surrounding an issue or concern always creates a distinctive or original sequence of events. At the same time, when the researcher is even partly concerned with understanding or explaining more general political, social, or economic phenomena (such as far left terrorism, rapid capitalist industrialization, or social revolution), comparative analysis is extremely difficult to avoid, even if one wants to do so. Consider the issue of *rapid* capitalist industrialization: How can we judge what is rapid or what is slow without comparing cases? Although this is an admittedly trite example, it is not difficult to raise more substantive, deeper questions. For instance, how can we even speak of capitalist development in one place and time without recognizing that capitalism is a general process that profoundly impacts all cases, albeit with differential results (thus setting the stage for more meaningful comparative analysis)? The answer to both questions is easy: we cannot. That is, in trying to explain or understand broader political, social, or economic phenomena in a single place (or case), we are compelled to think in a comparative manner.

This is what I meant when, in Chapter 1, I discussed the need for the researcher to be clear about the "comparative context" when doing a case study. The comparative context refers, in part, to the existing research and knowledge on a particular process or event. The effort to position your case study within the body of this knowledge necessitates a comparative approach. You need to determine, for example, whether your case fits a pattern or is, in some meaningful way, unique. Even if "unique," you are required to compare your case to others to know what exactly sets it apart. Doing this makes a single case study comparative. It is certainly true that not all researchers do this, especially student researchers: blissful or even willful ignorance of other cases is not uncommon. However, when attention is paid to the comparative context, when an effort is made to position your case within a larger body of knowledge, then it becomes possible for a case study to be comparative.

How to Do a Case Study in Comparative Perspective: Basic Guidelines
Unfortunately, recognizing that case studies can and sometimes must be comparative does not tell us *how to use* a case in comparative analysis. Even more unfortunate, at least for beginning comparativists, is that there is no single, step-by-step procedure for doing so. The discussion that follows,

then, is meant to be a loose (and extremely simple) guide, rather than a strict set of instructions, on how to do a case study in comparative perspective.

The first general rule of doing a case study in comparative perspective is one suggested earlier: to see your case *in relation* to others. This requires you to be familiar with both similar and dissimilar cases, even if you do not explicitly or systematically incorporate these other cases into your analysis. If you were doing a case study of "ethnic conflict" in Darfur (Sudan), for example, you would be well advised to read about ethnic conflict in Sri Lanka, Chechnya, Indonesia, the former Yugoslavia, and other relevant places. In a study of Darfur, moreover, it would be particularly useful to know about other conflicts (ethnic and otherwise) in Africa. These might include past and ongoing conflicts in Angola, Burundi, Congo, Eritrea/Ethiopia, Nigeria, Rwanda, Sierra Leone, and Zimbabwe. Knowing about these other conflicts enables you to see more clearly how distinctive the Darfur case really is or how representative it is of the broader problem of (ethnic) conflict. Indeed, as should already be clear, you *cannot* make a conclusion about the distinctive or representative nature of the conflict in Darfur (or anywhere else) without knowing something about comparable cases.

Examining your case in relation to others also provides you a cursory but still important method of control for any claims you make about your case. Indeed, many a case study has been ruined by the analyst's blithe ignorance of other relevant cases. After examining the Darfur case in depth, for example, an observer might find evidence that it is not an ethnic conflict at all, but instead is fundamentally a product of an ecological crisis and, more specifically, of desertification caused by global warming—UN Secretary-General Ban Ki-moon made just this argument in 2007. As Ban wrote, "It is no accident that the violence in Darfur erupted during [a] drought." Ban, to his credit, also engaged in some comparative checking by noting, "violence in Somalia grows from a similarly volatile mix of food and water insecurity [caused by drought]. So do the troubles in Ivory Coast and Burkina Faso" (p. A15). But a good comparativist will also look at other cases in the region (and elsewhere) to see if the relationship between desertification and social conflict (née ethnic conflict) holds up. If this "comparative checking" shows that there are many other places experiencing desertification that are *not* embroiled in widespread social conflict, it immediately tells the comparativist that other factors *must* be considered, and perhaps that there is a particular intersection of political, social, ethnic, and ecological forces at play. It could even be that the relationship between desertification and social conflict is specious or highly contingent. (Discovering this could be the product of comparative analysis or a more in-depth examination of a particular case, or both—see Figure 2.6 for more discussion.) The main point, again, is this: "seeing your case in relation to others" allows the researcher

---

Figure 2.6 Ethnic Conflict or Ecological Violence in Darfur?

Ban Ki-moon's focus on desertification and global warming as key factors behind the conflict in Darfur has sparked a vigorous debate. One of the leading supporters of this view—and one of Ban's close advisers—is Jeffrey Sachs. Sachs (2007) did not argue that desertification is the only factor behind the violence in Darfur, but he suggested that it is a very important one. Ban's opinion, I should note, was also shaped by Stephan Faris, who wrote a short article in *Atlantic Monthly* titled "The Real Roots of Darfur" (2007). Others, however, have argued that among the many contributing factors to the conflict in Darfur, desertification is, at best, of minor significance. Nick Hutchinson, for example, wrote: "A case can be made that the tragic drought and widespread famine of 1984–85 lead to localised conflicts pitting pastoralists against farmers. . . . But the real Darfur tragedy escalated in 2003, when government forces were firmly aligned against a rebellion of pastoralists" (2008, p. 10). Most significant, this escalation took place against a backdrop of increasing "greening" of the Sahel outside Darfur, which had begun as early as 1987. Researchers at the Tyndall Center for Climate Change, Hutchinson noted, speculated that the region had shifted to a wetter climate regime. In other words, the relationship between conflict and ecological change was exactly opposite what Ban and others had claimed. Why did Ban miss this (if he did)? According to Hutchinson, the reason was clear: "Close attention to detail is invaluable in geography. When debating 'climate wars' and Darfur, research rather than rhetoric is paramount" (p. 10).

The lesson is the same for students of comparative politics doing a case study: pay close attention to detail and do your research. And, of course, it also helps immensely to see your case in relation to others. Keeping these points in mind will be invaluable in determining not only who is right about the primary causes of the long-standing, disastrous, and deadly conflict in Darfur, but also what the best solutions might be.

---

to easily and efficiently assess, albeit at a general level, the plausibility of her argument.

Dogan and Pelassy gave us a second, strongly related rule for doing a case study in comparative perspective. As they put it, a case study in comparative perspective is one that "aims at generalization" (1990, p. 122). This takes us a step further than just examining a case in relation to others. For what Dogan and Pelassy were telling us is that we need to self-consciously fit our case into the bigger (theoretical) picture. They explained it this way:

> To view Morocco in the perspective of the Arab world, to consider the Nazi experience within the framework of the **totalitarian** model, or to study recent Turkish history in the light of problems raised by development means including the monograph in a series of comparative studies. Sometimes the general

perspective is clearly stated [that is, is explicit], and sometimes it is implicit. But it must be present for the monograph to become a real [comparatively oriented] *case study.* (p. 122, emphasis added)

Let's consider Dogan and Pelassy's rule in light of the preceding example of ethnic conflict in Darfur. Aiming at generalization with this case means, among other things, consciously attempting to discern where the Darfur case fits in with regard to existing theories of ethnic or social conflict. Is the Darfur case representative of a general pattern or model of ethnic (social) conflict? If so, which one and why? Or is Darfur a truly unique case, theoretically and empirically speaking? Even, or especially, if the researcher decides that Darfur is a unique case, it is important to understand that this, too, has broader implications for theories about ethnic and social conflict. Simply put, it tells us that general theories about ethnic and social conflict are necessarily limited in that they *do not* account for the Darfur case (note: this is a purely hypothetical example). And if these theories cannot adequately account for the Darfur case, maybe they do not adequately account for other cases as well. In this sense, "aiming at generalization" does not mean that the researcher will always be on target—sometimes just the opposite may happen. Still, regardless of the outcome, aiming at generalization requires that the researcher be constantly focused on examining his case in light of larger theoretical or conceptual concerns.

This last point is important to remember, but admittedly very difficult to put into practice, especially for the novice comparativist. After all, most students not only are unfamiliar with the history and complexities of specific cases, but also are struggling to make sense of the myriad theories that purport to explain a particular political, social, or economic phenomenon. Just consider the numerous theories purporting to account for or explain ethnic mobilization and conflict. According to Raymond Taras and Rajat Ganguly (2009), there are at least ten distinct theories on these issues; to this list, we can almost certainly add others (for present purposes, details are not necessary). That is a lot to digest even for an expert, much less a beginning student. Regrettably, there is no quick and easy solution to this "problem." Instead, doing a case study in comparative perspective—doing it well, at least—means that the student must not only conduct *intensive* (that is, highly focused) research on the primary case but also carry out *extensive* (that is, broad-based) research on a range of other relevant cases. Moreover, the student must read and be familiar with as much of the relevant theoretical literature as possible. This is not something that most students want to hear—understandably (but mistakenly), many students decide to do a case study precisely because it *seems* to entail less work than explicitly comparative analysis. But knowing about other cases and about the theoretical literature, even for a single case study, is a difficult-to-avoid fact of life in doing comparative politics, or more accurately doing comparative politics well.

*   *   *

The two general rules introduced here provide a very simple, but nonetheless important, foundation for carrying out a case study in comparative perspective or, really, almost any type of comparative analysis, including the other ones discussed in this chapter. Certainly, it would be possible to provide a much longer list of ever more complex or sophisticated rules, but this would probably—and unnecessarily—serve more to confuse than to enlighten. For the key to doing a good case study in comparative perspective is quite basic: think comparatively but deeply and systematically. This maxim applies equally to cases that are original or representative (and everything in between). Indeed, as suggested earlier, a researcher cannot say with any confidence that a case is original unless they first compare it to a range of other cases. This said, doing a single case study in comparative perspective is not without its pitfalls. And, for students, it is vital to recognize both the advantages and the pitfalls of a particular method of analysis, which is the topic of our next section.

Analytical Induction and the Case Study: Some Advantages and Pitfalls

The case study, it is important to understand, represents a significant trade-off. On the one hand, limiting an analysis to a single country or unit has the advantage of allowing the researcher to study a subject in great depth and detail. This allows the researcher, in turn, to achieve a degree of understanding about the case that generally cannot be matched by other comparative models. On the other hand, depth of understanding invariably comes at the expense of explanation or generalization. Thus, although a comparatively oriented case study may aim at generalization, as suggested earlier, it can *never* "hit the bull's-eye." To many scholars, this is a serious if not fatal limitation. That is, if a single case study can never establish general truths or explanatory laws about the social world, then it will always remain of dubious scientific value. There is no denying this point. Still, in the messy real world of political, social, and economic phenomena, a case study sometimes serves as an essential complement to building more comprehensive or encompassing theories. In this regard, individual case studies might best be seen as empirical/theoretical steppingstones. This is the idea behind *analytical induction,* which can be considered a separate, although strongly related, comparative strategy.

Consider a study that makes a general claim about, say, the significance of the middle class in bringing about stable democracy. At first glance, this claim may seem to hold water—if one looks at a broad range of cases, it would be easy to find numerous situations in which the emergence and development of a strong middle class coincided with long-lived democracy. But what if a researcher wanted to test this theoretical claim more thoroughly? How might this be done? Well, one way would be to do a study in which the selected case appears to reflect strongly the main premises of the theory. If an in-depth examination of the case—keeping the existing theory firmly in mind—reveals no inconsistencies, then the case has helped to support (but has not proved) the validity of the theory in question. The case, in short, is one of many useful steppingstones. If, on the other hand, the researcher identifies, or thinks he has identified, a significant inconsistency or exceptional circumstance in their case, this could lead to, and even require, a revision or further refinement of the theory (Dogan and Pelassy 1990). In a sense, this is a negative steppingstone.

In fact, this latter situation is far more likely; that is, in-depth single case studies (especially those expressly based on analytical induction) often bring to light hitherto neglected factors or variables while simultaneously problematizing already-identified causal factors. At the least, they usually provide a more nuanced understanding of these factors and variables than comparative analysis involving multiple cases. In studies of democratization in Latin America, for example, many scholars, to draw from another common argument, contend that divisions within the ruling elite—between so-called **hard-liners** and **soft-liners**—are a major reason for the breakdown of authoritarian regimes, but this was certainly not true in every single case. In other words, there are a few "deviant" cases (especially outside of Latin America) in which divisions within the ruling elite did not play a significant role in the democratization process. And although a researcher may be tempted to discount or ignore exceptional or deviant cases, such cases can often make or break a theory. In this regard, it is useful to note that deviant cases can also play a theoretically important role of **falsification**. As Peters explained it, "The basic argument [regarding falsification] is that science progresses by eliminating possible causes for observed phenomena rather than by finding positive relationships. . . . [T]here is no shortage of positive correlations in the social sciences; what there is sometimes a shortage of [is] research that dismisses one or another plausible cause for that phenomenon" (1998, p. 40). Individual case studies, to put it more simply, often send researchers back to the (theoretical) drawing board. (This, by the way, is a practical strategy to use if you disagree with a particular theory—that is, try to falsify the main claims of the theory by doing a case study!) In this situation, too, an individual case is an important steppingstone, but one that might lead us down a slightly different path. Whatever the situation, however, individual case studies are helping researchers to advance toward stronger and more coherent explanations, which nicely represents the basic goal of analytical induction.

Peters also provided us with another situation in which a case study can serve a central role in the construction of theory. As he wrote, "The second reason for using a single case is that the case may be the hardest one, so that if the theory appears to work in this setting it should work in all others" (1998, p. 64). The particular strategy for this situation is more or less the converse of the one just mentioned; that is, instead of choosing a case that appears to reflect strongly the main features of the archetypal case, you choose one—a **hard case**—that seems to contradict the archetypal case in as many ways as possible. Scholars who want to test theories about political phenomena in Western democracies, for instance, will often choose Japan, because of its particularly distinctive political and social system (at least compared to major Western countries): if the theory works for Japan, the thinking goes, the theory itself likely will have greater general validity (Peters 1998, p. 64). This approach, however, is incremental, since a single case study can only lend additional support to a theory but, again, cannot "prove" it correct.

In sum, despite its undeniable limitations (and trade-offs), the single case study will likely always remain an important and legitimate research strategy in the field of comparative politics. Still, to reiterate a point made earlier, budding comparativists should not choose this strategy only because it appears easier, more convenient, or more manageable to do than a multiunit comparative study. In certain situations, a multiunit study may be a far better choice; it may even be necessary for the purposes of the research project. In the next few sections, therefore, we will take a look at multiunit comparative analysis, beginning with the simplest: the two-unit or binary comparison.

Comparing Two Cases (Two-Unit or Binary Comparison)

I will not say much about the two-unit or binary comparison, since (1) the logic that underlies this specific model is exactly the same logic as that of the MSS or MDS design; and (2) the rules that apply to the single-unit case study apply equally to the binary comparison. Thus, if you follow the suggestions and guidelines from the last few sections, you will already have a good foundation both for understanding and for doing a binary comparison. Still, it is worth reiterating that, in setting up a binary comparison, the selection of cases is an extremely important consideration. It should not be done in an arbitrary or essentially impulsive manner. Of course, this is true of all comparative models, but a binary comparison is (along with the case study) particularly sensitive to **overdetermination** if the units of analysis are not selected carefully. Overdetermination, most simply, is a type of **selection bias** in which the researcher chooses cases that are most likely to support or validate the argument he is trying to test. The problem with overdetermination should be obvious; namely, if you only choose cases that are likely to support your argument, you are, to be blunt, cheating. In more formal terms, you are predetermining (or "overdetermining") the results. This is not always intentional, but it is nonetheless a serious methodological problem.

So, how *should* the cases for a binary comparison be selected? I have already given a good part of the answer: to wit, you must recognize and do your best to avoid overdetermination. This also means that you should adopt an attitude of intellectual honesty or integrity. Choosing hard cases is also very good practice. Of course, this also means that you must "do your research." Selecting appropriate cases for binary comparison requires that you have knowledge of a wide range of possible cases in which you are able to test or assess the variables of interest. At the same time, there should be a (practical) way to narrow down the list of possible cases for a binary comparison. Fortunately, for comparativists, there is. Again, I have already discussed one (controversial) tactic, which is to select cases based on the dependent variable. A comparativist interested in explaining academic achievement, gun violence, suicide, social revolution, or economic development will, not surprisingly, look for cases in which these phenomena are strongest or weakest. (Remember, using the MSS principle, the comparative cases must show wide variance on the dependent variable.)

Another, admittedly more complicated, tactic is based on recognizing that case selection is governed not by methodological logic alone but also by theory. Since we will discuss theory in depth in the following chapter, for now I will only say that good theories often tell us which (independent) variables to focus on in the first place. In so doing, theory also guides our selection of cases. For example, a comparativist doing research on capitalist industrialization might be strongly influenced by a rational-institutional approach (don't worry about what this means for now). This approach tells the comparativist that certain types of states—say, those that have **relative autonomy** from social actors and a clear capacity to implement and enforce public policies—are essential in bringing about and sustaining capitalist transformation. (The approach might also tell the comparativist that other variables are relatively unimportant and, therefore, can be safely ignored.) As a result, the comparativist will, first, select cases in which the aforementioned attributes of the state exist.

One possible example, which I will discuss in Chapter 5, is China. The country is governed by a powerful single-party (ostensibly) *communist* state; yet it is also one of the fastest-growing *capitalist* economies in the world. What about a second case? There are many possibilities, of course, but a comparativist might focus on Russia, which experienced "economic chaos" and near "collapse and failure" between 1991 and 1998 when (among many other events) the former Soviet state, under the "control" of Boris Yeltsin, lost power relative to domestic actors, the so-called oligarchs (Cooper 2008, pp. 2–4). In the case of Russia, the comparativist is especially interested in the fact that the Russian state was in shambles—that it had lost autonomy and capacity. Importantly, though, one could argue that the former Soviet Union and China were otherwise quite similar in that both were large countries that had experienced a communist revolution and a thoroughgoing transformation of their political and social systems along broadly similar lines. Thus we have the makings of a binary comparison based, in this particular instance, on the logic of an MSS design. It is useful noting, too, that the Russian economy made a strong recovery, beginning in 1999, under a new, more authoritative leader: Vladimir Putin. This is a potentially significant development from a methodological perspective. For, in this ostensibly single case, we are able to witness a significant change or variance in the dependent variable. In fact, this is a good example of a special kind of binary analysis—the *within-case comparison.*

Typically, within-case comparisons are done in a tacit or unstated manner; sometimes the researcher does not even realize what he is doing. But the logic is usually quite clear. To wit, in a great many presumably single-unit case studies, the researcher will often divide the study into at least two separate time periods, with the intention of explaining a significant change (in the dependent variable) between the two periods. In the case of Russian economic development after the initial introduction of capitalism, the two time periods can be easily specified: 1989 to 1998 and 1999 to 2008 (in this situation, I am purposely using two equivalent time periods). Each time period can be considered a separate case; thus, instead of one case—say, Russian economic development after the introduction of capitalism, 1989–2007 (or 2015)—we have two cases: (1) Russian economic development, 1989–1998; and (2) Russian economic development, 1999–2008. Importantly, in this research design, it is presumed that all other (significant) variables remain the same from the first period to the second, with the *exception* of the variable or variables that *caused* or brought about the change in the dependent variable (see Figure 2.7 for further discussion). In short, within-case comparisons follow the logic of an MSS design exactly. Indeed, one might argue that a within-case comparison is the nearest one can get to setting up a perfect MSS design, since the two cases can be considered, at least figuratively, identical twins.

Bigger Ns: Comparing Three or More Cases
The next step beyond the two-unit comparison is a comparison of three or more units. Not surprisingly, the same logic that applies to a case study and binary comparisons applies equally to a comparison of three or more units. Generally speaking, though, when a comparison is extended to three, four, five, or even a dozen cases, the prospects for theory-building improve, if only because the claims the researcher makes are based on a bigger N, which ostensibly gives more control over the variables of interest. At the

Figure 2.7 Example of a Within-Case Comparison: Russian Economic Development

The factors shaping Russia's economic development from the collapse of the Soviet empire to today are myriad and complex, and no brief discussion is going to capture even a miniscule amount of the overall story. However, one way to begin getting a grasp of this complexity is through a within-case comparison examining two very distinct periods in Russia's post-Soviet economic development. The first period, 1989–1998, was terrible. As one analyst describes it, "For a fortunate few . . . signs of new wealth began to appear within two or three years of the Soviet collapse. . . . For the rest the price has been horrendous" (Gustafson 1997, p. 5). Unemployment was rampant (exceeding 13 percent), beggars clogged the streets, infant mortality shot up while life expectancy dropped sharply, and, for many ordinary Russians, life was far worse than during the Soviet period (Gustafson 1997). The second period, 1999–2008, by contrast, witnessed a dramatic transformation: real GDP growth increased to 10 percent in 2000 and averaged 6.1 percent between 2001 and 2007. Unemployment declined to the single digits by 2001 and stayed relatively low (it was as low as 6.2 percent in 2007); average real wages also increased significantly. From 2000 to 2006, moreover, the official poverty rate declined from 29 percent to 15 percent.

Case No. 1: Russia, 1989–1998
Dependent variable:
    Economic decline
Independent variable: Weak state?

Case No. 2: Russia, 1999–2008
Dependent variable:
    Strong economic growth
Independent variable: Strong state?

A comparativist will look at these two contrasting periods and ask the simple and obvious question: What happened? More specifically, a comparativist will want to know what else changed during the two periods. Was it, as some might argue, the attributes of the state? Or were there equally, if not more, important factors at play? While I cannot answer these questions here, one thing is sure: a within-case comparison is perhaps the best way to identify the key changes that took place.

same time, as the number of units increases, the level of abstraction and generality increases, too. For many qualitatively oriented comparativists, this is a major (even unacceptable) trade-off if taken too far, since countries become mere "data points" rather than real places with their own histories, cultures, and political/social systems. In practical terms, moreover, when more than a handful of cases are incorporated into a (qualitatively oriented) research design, the analysis becomes empirically unmanageable, especially for an individual researcher. This is because there is simply too much material—too much information and potential evidence—to absorb, organize, and evaluate.

There is, I must emphasize, an obvious and important exception to what I've just said, namely statistical or quantitative analysis. This type of analysis typically aims at "global comparisons"; that is, it is designed to include *all* relevant cases in the same analytical framework. In comparative politics research, this might (but does not necessarily) mean the inclusion of every country in the world. Remember, too, that a case need not refer to a single country. For example, in a study by Barbara Geddes (1999), which I discuss in some detail in Chapter 6, the author defined a case in terms of political "regimes." To Geddes, each time an authoritarian regime breaks down, it constitutes a separate case. Thus, in a given country, there may be multiple "cases" (in fact, in her study Geddes identified 163 individual regime changes or cases). Statistical (or big-N) analysis, however, is distinct from the type of comparative (small-N) analysis we've been discussing thus far. And although the distinction certainly warrants further discussion, I will not cover it here, if only because most political science departments in the United States devote considerable and special attention to this method of analysis.[3] Thus, there is no need to discuss this extremely well-covered ground in this book. Instead, let's return to the main issue of this section by asking the following question: If there are advantages to having more cases, but disadvantages to having *too many* cases, exactly how many cases is optimum for comparative research?

The answer might be clear already: it depends. In other words, it is not possible to pre-specify an optimum number of cases for comparative research, because each situation will be different. But, even if we know the specifics of a situation, we probably still could not specify the most appropriate number of cases to examine, because there simply are no standard criteria for doing so. Suffice it to say, therefore, that you should consider both what is practical and what is minimally necessary given the theoretical scope and ambition of your argument. So what does this mean? For most purposes and for most researchers, this probably means from three to five cases, but a few particularly ambitious researchers have incorporated dozens of cases into their analyses. In subsequent chapters, I give several examples of this. But first another caveat: as with the other forms of comparative analysis, careful case selection based on the logic of comparative analysis is important. This is particularly the case if the researcher is using the method of agreement. Fortunately, with more cases, the problems of selection bias or overdetermination of the dependent variable are reduced, although not, it is important to emphasize, entirely eliminated. For it is still certainly possible to pick-and-choose one's cases in a manner designed to get the results the researcher wants to see. Conversely, selecting cases that *correctly* reflect the MSS or MDS principles makes it harder to "cheat" (even if unintentionally), but finding more than a handful of cases using either the MSS or the MDS principle can be very difficult.

So what is a conscientious comparativist to do? The simple answer is to use a variety of comparative models (and principles) within the context of a single research project. This is the mixed design.

The Mixed Design

In practice, comparativists frequently use a mixed design, and, in general, it is a very useful—and perhaps the best—approach to take. A big reason for this is that a mixed design helps to mitigate the limitations of using only a single comparative strategy based on either MSS or MDS design. In principle, a mixed strategy may be necessary to fully develop an argument when a researcher finds that an MSS, MDS, or MoA alone is clearly inconclusive (which is, not surprisingly, almost always true). A mixed design, in short, may not be a "perfect solution," but it should be used whenever possible, practicable, and feasible. This said, setting up a comprehensive comparative strategy based on a mixed design—as with all comparative models—requires forethought, planning, and a lot of research. Consider the example used earlier, Theda Skocpol's comparison of France, Russia, and China. Recall that the primary logic of this comparison was based on the MDS design. At the same time, Skocpol was very much aware of the need to buttress her primary strategy with other comparative models. Here is how Skocpol explained her overall strategy:

> France, Russia, and China will serve as three positive cases of successful social revolution, and I shall argue that these cases reveal similar causal patterns despite their many other differences. In addition, I shall invoke negative cases for the purpose of validating various particular parts of the causal argument. In so doing, I shall always construct contrasts that maximize the similarities of the negative case(s) to the positive case(s) in every apparently relevant respect. . . . Thus, for example, the abortive Russian Revolution of 1905 will be contrasted with the successful Revolution of 1917 in order to validate arguments about the crucial contribution to social-revolutionary success in Russia of war-related processes that led to the breakdown of state repressive capacities. Moreover, selected aspects of English, Japanese, and German history will be used in various places to strengthen arguments about the causes of revolutionary political crises and peasant revolts in France, Russia, and China. These cases are suitable as contrasts because they were comparable countries that underwent non-revolutionary political crises and transformations in broadly similar terms and circumstances to France, Russia, and China. (1979, p. 37)

The specific details of Skocpol's argument are not important for our purposes. What is important is her rationale for the comparisons she makes. Note, for instance, that Skocpol planned a within-case comparison using Russia. Logically, as we now know, a within-case comparison reflects the MSS principle, which helps to support her original argument by showing that a key change (in the independent variable) occurred between the 1905 and the 1917 revolutions. Although I have already said a little about the within-case comparisons, let me add that, because they allow the comparativist to increase the N without having to analyze a completely different country, within-case comparisons almost always help to strengthen causal analysis. Even more, the within-case comparison reduces the problem of selection bias because, done correctly, it necessarily introduces variance on the dependent variable (Collier 1997).

Skocpol also used three additional cases—England, Japan, and Germany (née Prussia)—to further buttress her argument. In her research design, England, Japan, and Germany (Prussia) were "negative cases" (that is, cases in which a social revolution did *not* occur). Although it is difficult to classify the selection of these cases as unequivocally based on an MDS or MSS design, Skocpol's objective is clear. She wanted to show that, in three "comparable" cases, the *absence* of the key independent variable or set of conditions that was *present* in France, Russia, and China (the three positive cases) resulted in a different outcome. In Figure 2.8, we can get a sense of how Skocpol's comparisons of the three primary and four secondary cases, in a mixed design, supported her overall argument and conclusions.

Skocpol's research design, of course, is not the only way to set up a mixed strategy, but it is a very instructive real-world example. For the sake of clarity, though, let's go through her design one more time. First, she began with a multiunit comparison, based on the MDS principle, using three cases/countries. Second, she singled out one of these cases—Russia—

Figure 2.8 Summary of Skocpol's Comparative Research Design

	Social Revolution	No Social Revolution
Conditions (independent variables) present	France Russia (1917) China	
Conditions (independent variables) absent		Russia (1905) England Japan Prussia (Germany)

From the table, we can see that in those cases where the independent variables assumed to create the basis for social revolution (the dependent variable) were present, a social revolution occurred. By contrast, there were no cases of a social revolution occurring in which the presumed independent variables were absent. Skocpol's basic research design, therefore, seems to offer strong support for her argument.

The limitation, however, is the small-N: Skocpol examined "only" seven cases (which, from a qualitative perspective, is a significant number). Still, for other comparativists, the next question would be: Are there any cases that would contradict Skocpol's findings?

and used a within-case comparison, because there was variance on both the presumed independent and dependent variables. This within-case comparison helped to validate her initial hypothesis. Third, she introduced three secondary and specifically negative cases based loosely on the MDS principle. It is important to note that these three negative cases also differed from the primary cases with regard to the presumed independent and dependent variables. The comparison, therefore, further helped to buttress Skocpol's initial hypothesis/thesis. Finally, in a fourth step not mentioned earlier, Skocpol returned to a deeper empirical examination of her three main cases in an effort (1) to highlight the key similarities, and (2) to account for any significant differences that could weaken her overall argument. This reflected the incorporation of separate case studies or analytical induction into her overall analysis. In sum, Skocpol incorporated the following comparative models into a *single* framework of comparative analysis:

1. MDS design using three primary cases.
2. MSS design/within-case comparison using Russia.
3. Multiple-unit comparison (three or more units), using secondary cases.
4. Individual case studies/analytical induction.

Admittedly, Skocpol's research design and analysis may seem daunting for the beginning comparativist. Still, a basic mixed design strategy is in the grasp of even the most inexperienced comparativist. It really involves little more than a willingness and commitment to "think comparatively." Even if used in a relatively clumsy and cursory manner (which is almost unavoidable in the beginning), a mixed design encourages inexperienced comparativists to adopt a systematic and critical attitude in their analyses, the importance of which should not be underestimated.

Conclusion

Comparative analysis is a second-best strategy, but it is often the only viable strategy open to comparativists. This is especially true of qualitatively oriented researchers who take history seriously. Comparative analysis is also an extremely imperfect strategy, with many limitations and flaws. For this reason, *all* comparativists need to exercise care in their research design and restraint in the conclusions and claims they derive from their research design. This is a simple lesson, but one that is frequently forgotten or ignored. At the same time, comparison is, as noted at the beginning of this chapter, "the engine of knowledge." If we want to better understand the world in which we live, if we want to explain social, political, and economic phenomena, we need to compare. But we need to compare in a logical, systematic, and well-informed manner. If we fail to do this, our "comparisons" may be worthless or, even worse, an engine for distortion, misunderstanding, and falsehood.

Notes

1. I cite a few of these exceptions extensively in this chapter. These include Dogan and Pelassy 1990 and Dogan and Kazancigil 1994. Another useful book focused on comparative analysis is B. Guy Peters's *Comparative Politics: Theory and Methods* (1998).

2. Adam Przeworski and Henry Teune pointed out, though, that the most different systems design generally starts off with a variation of observed behavior below the level of the system (or society as a whole). "Most often," they noted, "this will be the level of individual actors, but it can be the level of groups, local communities, social classes, or occupation. . . . [S]ystemic factors are not given any special place among the possible predictors of behavior" (1970, p. 34).

3. Statistical or quantitative analysis is a major research method used in political science and the social sciences more generally. Indeed, in the United States, a large majority of social science departments require their students to take at least one and sometimes several courses dealing with quantitative methods and statistics (or scope and method). Largely for this reason—and also because there are dozens of good undergraduate textbooks covering quantitative analysis in the social sciences but relatively few covering *qualitative* analysis—I do not discuss statistical analysis in this chapter. It is important to understand, however, that many researchers in comparative politics do use quantitative analysis or cross-national comparisons and that quantitative analysis is clearly an important part of the research methodology in comparative politics.

3

Thinking Theoretically in Comparative Politics

In the social sciences, theory plays an absolutely essential role, although to students and other casual observers it is not always clear what exactly this role is. In comparative politics, unfortunately, the role of theory seems even less clear. One reason is not hard to discern: critics (from both within and without) point out that there is no single or even dominant theoretical approach to distinguish comparative politics. Instead, there has been a proliferation of approaches (especially since the 1970s) "to the point," as one prominent comparativist put it, "where both graduate students and some professional practitioners in the field have at times seen the diversity as anarchy" (Verba 1991, p. 38). Others, such as Peter Evans, see the theoretical eclecticism of the field in a more positive light, arguing that it gives comparativists the freedom "to draw on a mélange of theoretical traditions in hopes of gaining greater purchase on the cases they care about" (Kohli et al. 1995, p. 4). Theory, in this view, is pragmatic: it provides the tools to help frame and explain empirical puzzles, and comparative researchers are "opportunists" who use whatever works (Kohli et al. 1995, p. 46).

Why Study Theory?
The debate over the state of theory in comparative politics is important, but one that need not occupy us here. For now, it is better to focus on how and why theory is necessary in comparative politics (and in the social sciences generally). Let me first say that I realize students are often intimidated by the word *theory*. It not only sounds abstract and therefore difficult to understand, but it also sounds like something only professors, philosophers, or other "intellectuals" would be interested in studying. Thus, as noted in Chapter 1, you might be surprised to learn that we all (including *you*) use theory, every day. We have to. I will come back to this issue shortly, but let me make one more general comment, which is the flip side of the first.

61

Instead of being intimidated by theory, some students tend to think of it as useless, optional, and therefore irrelevant. They equate theory with unsubstantiated and mostly subjective opinion—as in, "It's just a theory"—or worse still, they consider it no more than an abstruse word unrelated to the real world. Theory, in this sense, is considered to be the opposite of or completely separate from fact or, as some might say, the "truth." Although somewhat understandable (in that the term *theory* is often used in a very casual and imprecise manner), this view is misguided and fundamentally misinformed. Indeed, it is important to understand that theory and fact are inextricably connected.

To some scholars—those we might label **positivists**—theory, at least good theory, is an explanation of how "reality (necessarily) works." Positivists believe not only that good theories identify the underlying processes and forces that shape reality but also that, once we identify these processes and forces, we will be able to make predictions and develop "laws" about the social world (in much the same way that natural scientists develop laws about the physical world). To other scholars—in particular, those who embrace the principles of **post-positivism** or **reflectivism**—theory and reality are seen as *mutually constitutive*. Put in very simple terms, post-positivists believe that how we think about the world actually helps to *construct* or make the world in which we live. This particular view of theory, I should note, is especially prevalent among contemporary cultural theorists (whom we will discuss later in this chapter).

The disagreement between positivists and post-positivists (that is, between scholars who emphasize **objectivity** and those who emphasize subjectivity) is another important but complex debate. And although it deserves very serious attention, I will not say anything more on this subject. The main point to remember is that all scholars agree that there is no way to explain *or* understand reality without a firm grasp of theory. Facts and theory are inseparable. At the most general level, this is why we study theory; that is, we study theory because it is part-and-parcel of understanding and explaining the world in which we live. Theory may explain "how things work," or it may explain how the world came to work in certain ways. Theory allows us to understand how and why the world stays the same, but it also enables us to see how and why the world changes. With all this in mind, we can now return to a discussion of the importance and necessity of theory.

How We All Theorize

Earlier I said we all use theory, all the time. There are several ways to interpret this statement. Most generally, if we understand theory as some kind of *simplifying device*—for example, a filter—that allows us to "see" which facts matter and which do not, then "it is at the very point when one starts selecting the relevant details that one begins to theorize" (Rosenau and Durfee 2000, p. 2). Theory, in this case, is clearly not optional. As Steve Smith and John Baylis nicely put it, "It is not as if you can say that you do not want to bother with a theory, all you want to do is to look at the 'facts.' We believe that this is simply impossible, since the only way in which you can decide which of the millions of possible facts to look at is by adhering to some simplifying device which tells you which ones matter the most" (1997, p. 3). Their point should be clear, but an example might help. Consider the question (one that I devote a whole chapter to later in this book) "Why are some countries poor?" A few very quick responses might include the following: (1) "Poor countries are poor because the people are uneducated and lack appropriate skills, are lazy, and have no sense of personal responsibility"; (2) "Poor countries are poor because they lack natural resources or have too few resources given their population size"; (3) "So many countries are poor because the world economic system is inherently unequal and exploitative"; and (4) "Corrupt governments are the reason some countries are poor."

Each of these responses highlights certain *facts*—a generally low level of education and poorly developed (personal) skills, limited resources, overpopulation, large technological and economic disparities, high levels of corruption, massive income inequality, and so on. Yet by choosing to highlight some facts while ignoring (or dismissing) others, you are unavoidably and unequivocally engaged in a theoretical process. Specifically, you are making judgments about what is and is not relevant or important in terms of explaining poverty; you are identifying, albeit implicitly, a specific **level of analysis** and unit of analysis; you are making assumptions about **power**, structure, and **agency**; and you are connecting certain facts with specific outcomes. You are, in short, theorizing. In an important sense, then, you're also doing what any trained researcher or scholar in comparative politics does. A key difference, however, is that most students are generally not aware of the theoretical assumptions they make when stating their answers to certain questions. Students may even assume that their interpretation is the only legitimate one—that is, that the facts they have chosen to focus on "speak for themselves." But, as one set of scholars forcefully put it, facts never speak for themselves: "they only take on meaning as we select some of them as important and dismiss others as trivial" (Rosenau and Durfee 2000, p. 3).

The ways in which researchers select and look at (or evaluate) facts give us another useful way to think about theory. As a number of scholars have explained it, working with theories is like looking through different pairs of sunglasses or, to employ what I think is a much more apt metaphor, using different photographic lenses. Different types of lenses provide different ways to see reality. In our example above, one lens brings into focus *individual* attributes of a person or people—their specific levels of education, technical skills, motivation, ambition, and the like. Another lens may focus on a different set of geographic, demographic, or political attributes, such as a country's natural resource endowment, its climate (in terms of its suitability for agricultural production), or the nature and quality of its political leadership. Some lenses (for example, an infrared lens) may even bring to light otherwise "invisible" elements of reality, such as the "structures of global capitalism" or "relationships of dependence." The possibilities are virtually endless. Some researchers, of course, may feel that their lenses—and pictures of reality—are more appropriate, more reliable, or simply better than others. Researchers using different lenses/theories, in short, do not generally agree on who (or what "lens") is right. This is an important point to keep in mind, for students are often confused about the existence of multiple competing theories. We can make sense of this situation, at least partly, when we recognize that different lenses allow us to focus on different aspects of the same larger reality.

Good and Bad Theorizing

Theoretical disagreements are not only very common but also, at times, seemingly impossible to resolve; this does not mean, however, that all theories of the world are equally valid. This point is even more obvious when we acknowledge the fact that we all theorize, from the most erudite scholar to the greenest student, from the most abstruse pundit to the most hardheaded pragmatist. Yet just because we all theorize does not mean we are equally adept at it, especially when we theorize about broader political, social, and economic phenomena. Some of us, for example, theorize in an extremely superficial or arbitrary manner. We jump to conclusions; we ignore or dismiss facts that don't fit into or don't jibe with our understanding of the world; we fail to see or acknowledge logical contradictions in our thinking; we confuse observation or correlation with causation (see Figure 3.1 for a brief discussion of these two terms); we never (ever) think about the assumptions upon which our views are based; or, worst of all, we regard our theories or theorizing about the world as self-evidently true (meaning we do not need to "prove" or support them with empirical evidence or logic). Each of these tendencies will likely result in inconsistent, problematic, and, quite possibly, completely erroneous understandings about the world. In this regard, even bad theorizing is relevant, for it can help justify, reproduce, and encourage harmful practices and views. Unfortunately, bad theorizing is probably more the rule than the exception, especially outside of academia. Turn on virtually any politically oriented talk show (or "news" program) in the United States, in fact, and you're likely to hear empirically unsupportable, logically inconsistent, and methodologically suspect theories about all aspects of political, economic, and social life in the United

---

Figure 3.1 Correlation and Causation

It may rain whenever I wash my car, but washing my car is not the cause of the rain. The relationship between the two events, in other words, is not based on causation but correlation. *Correlation,* to be clear, describes a relationship or an association between two (or more) different variables. Correlation may be positive or negative, but it can also be spurious, as in the example. In a spurious correlation, it is sometimes the case that a third unidentified variable is actually the deciding influence. Thus, in the example, washing my car may (of course) have nothing to do with the occurrence of rain. Because I wash my car only on cloudy, humid days, however, there might very well be a positive (and nonspurious) correlation between "cloudy, humid days" and rain. Still, the positive correlation between "cloudy, humid days" and rain does not necessarily signify causation.

To establish causality requires a stronger demonstration of a *cause-and-effect* relationship. To do this, other variables need to be eliminated from consideration, which, in turn, requires a proper research design and adequate empirical support. Establishing causation, in short, normally requires systematic observation, analysis, and testing.

Let's consider a more realistic example—the correlation between television viewing and attention deficit hyperactivity disorder (ADHD). Many studies have confirmed that an association between these two variables exists and, from this, many casual observers might assert that excessive television viewing causes or at least contributes to the development of ADHD in very young children. But the casual observer may be jumping to conclusions. After all, it might very well be the case that children prone to ADHD are drawn to television. In this case, television viewing is not the cause but is merely symptomatic of a still unidentified cause. Or the causality could be completely reversed; that is, it may be that ADHD causes excessive television viewing. To determine whether a causal relationship exists or what the direction of causality is, of course, requires a proper research design, observation, and analysis.

States and elsewhere. This tendency, moreover, is not limited to one side of the political spectrum: bad theorizing is an equal opportunity vice.

So how can bad theorizing be avoided? The easy answer is to avoid all the pitfalls I listed in the preceding paragraph. Of course, this is easier said than done, since, for many people, it is difficult to know where or how to begin. More practically, then, a crucial first step toward good theorizing is simply to become much more aware and self-critical of how you think about the world. Think carefully about what informs your views—why you think the way you do in the first place. Do not presume that your views are correct, much less unassailable; instead, assume that you always have something new to learn. Similarly, listen carefully to what others have to say. If you disagree, try to identify clearly the underlying assumptions and the key weakness in the competing view. Obviously, these are basic suggestions, all of which correspond to the dictates of critical thinking discussed in Chapter 1. Good theorizing, however, requires more than critical thinking. You also need to develop a clear understanding of (1) what theory is in general and (2) what the principles of "good theory" are, especially within the context of comparative politics. We will be addressing the rules of or principles for good theory for most of the remainder of this chapter (and throughout this entire book), so I will not say any more on this point here. As for what theory is, perhaps the best place to start is with a basic definition.

Defining Theory

I define theory in the following way: theory is a simplified representation of "reality" and a framework within which facts are not only selected but also interpreted, organized, and fitted together so that they create a coherent whole. Embedded within this simple definition are the following key points:

- Theory necessarily *simplifies reality* but is not separate from reality (even more, theory and reality may be mutually constitutive).
- Theory helps us to determine what facts are important, meaningful, and relevant; that is, theory helps us *select* facts.
- Theory guides our *interpretation* of the facts (what do the facts "mean"?).
- Theory tells us how to *organize* the facts: How do different facts relate to one another? Which are primary and which are secondary?
- Theory allows us to *develop "whole" arguments*—that is, arguments that stick together firmly from beginning to end.

I have already discussed the important elements of this basic definition, but it is worth underscoring a central point, namely that all theories necessarily involve simplification or abstraction. Theories are not reality. They cannot be. On this point, it may be helpful to consider another analogy: theory as a map (Woods 1996). Maps, as we know, are graphical representations of physical reality. They are also extremely simplified versions of that reality. Despite this, almost everyone agrees that maps are valuable and indispensable tools (which, by the way, does not necessarily mean that maps are entirely **objective**: maps can and do reflect the biases and subjective perceptions of those who make them). Using the analogy of the map, we can see that, in the social sciences, theory/theorizing represents an effort to simplify the social world—to map it out, so to speak—by identifying and then interpreting the *key* forces and processes. This is crucial. As we will see in the following sections, the different research traditions in comparative politics can be classified largely in terms of the key forces/processes on which each centers. Moreover, we can "draw" our conceptual maps of the world in many different ways and for many different purposes. Some maps may help us find our friend's house in an unfamiliar city, whereas other maps may help a seismologist locate fault lines. Whatever the shape or purpose of the map, however, it is always an abstraction of a far more complex physical reality.

Theory in Comparative Politics

So far I have discussed theory in very general, essentially generic terms. In this section, I would like to turn to a more concrete but still general discussion of theory in relation to comparative politics. As noted earlier, there is a diversity of theoretical approaches in comparative politics and, except for very short periods, no one theoretical perspective has dominated the field (in the same way, for example, that realism has dominated international relations since the end of World War II). The theoretical diversity that characterizes comparative politics, however, does not mean that the field is completely rudderless. On this point, one very useful volume on theory in comparative politics (Lichbach and Zuckerman 1997) argued that, despite the lack of a single unifying theory, the field is dominated by three strong and well-developed research traditions based on the principles of *rationality, culture,* and *structure.* I will discuss each of these in more detail later—in fact, this chapter and the remainder of this book are largely organized around these three approaches. But first, let's engage in a simple yet instructive exercise.

Thinking About Violent Crime: A Basic Exercise in Theorizing

Consider the following question, which, by now, should be quite familiar: Why are some societies more violent than others? (Unlike our previous discussions, I would like to broaden the issue and not just focus on gun violence, but criminal violence more generally.) How would you answer the question? As an exercise, before you finish reading this paragraph, write down your answer. More specifically, put forward your own *thesis* on (criminal) violence in societies. In so doing, you should clearly identify the key factor or (independent) variable. If you identify more than one factor—a very likely possibility—you should also consider how the different factors you select interact or relate to one another to produce a "violent society" (the dependent variable). You might also want to consider which factors are of primary importance, which are secondary, and so on. Thinking about the question of violent crime, I should emphasize, is a very good way to grasp some of the theoretical issues with which most students, researchers, and scholars in comparative politics must deal all the time. Admittedly, criminal violence is not an issue that comparativists typically examine. But this is precisely why I think it is a useful example: it helps to illustrate the broad utility and applicability of a "comparative politics approach" (plus it is a topic about which most readers are likely to have an opinion). Now that you have written down (or at least thought out) your response, consider the following three arguments.

Argument no. 1. A major source of violent crime lies in "rational" human behavior. In situations where the risks of getting caught are minimal—where, for example, police presence is limited and ineffective—and where the potential rewards are high, individuals are likely to commit more crimes in general to achieve their economic goals—to earn money for their livelihoods. This is particularly true in communities where access to alternative sources of income is restricted—that is, communities in which people may have limited access to jobs, education, and skills training. Violent crime specifically is more likely (1) when the use of violence is a particularly *efficient* or *necessary* "tool"; (2) where the use of violence to achieve one's ends entails relatively limited risk compared to the alternatives; and (3) where attractive and easily accessible alternatives to a (violent) "life of crime" are limited. All of this is clearly demonstrated in the United States (and other countries), where violent crime is disproportionately concentrated in the inner cities. The use of violence, it is important to understand, is a "constrained choice." It is constrained in the sense that the conditions individuals face—conditions that make violent criminal activity more likely—are not generally of their own making. It is a choice, however, in that individual action is never predetermined: all individuals have the capacity to make hard choices—that is, to choose the more difficult path to follow. In fact, we see this all the time: while crime *is* higher in poor inner-city communities, only a small proportion of the population engages in violent crime.

Argument no. 2. Capitalism causes violence—the violence of one individual against another. The violence is not caused directly, but through an unrelenting process that divides societies into the "haves" and "have-nots" and that glorifies competition and efficiency while reducing individuals to abstractions—to anonymous buyers and sellers whose claims on each other are determined solely by their capacity to pay, or to mere commodities themselves. In this way, capitalism alienates people from each other, their families, and their communities, thus setting the stage for antisocial, increasingly violent behavior among ordinary people, against ordinary people. Violence is a response to the soullessness and hopelessness engendered by an inherently exploitative economic system. Of course, violence is not unique to capitalism, nor are all capitalist societies equally violent. Where the most destructive, alienating, and exploitative aspects of the capitalist process are mitigated, intrasocietal violence is lessened. But where the forces of capitalism are unleashed and where vast segments of society are left unprotected, violence thrives. This is why the United States is the most violent capitalist society on the planet.

Argument no. 3. People and societies are responsible for their own actions and decisions, but they do not exist or act in a social vacuum. Their behavior, in other words, is very strongly shaped by the interpersonal environment in which they live. This interpersonal environment may encourage certain practices and values that lead to criminally violent behavior among certain groups of people: it establishes norms that essentially tell people what is right and what is wrong, and how to behave and interact with others. In some places, these norms may sanction and even legitimize the use of violence. In this environment, therefore, members of the community learn to resolve problems and conflicts primarily through the use of violence. Consider, on this point, "gang culture" or, less intuitively, but equally powerful, "military culture." In both cultures, members are *supposed* to commit acts of violence; killing is not only normalized, but also considered a duty. Even more, killing is a noble act. Importantly, as the two examples suggest, cultures of violence are not born, but created. Over time, however, violent cultural practices become deeply embedded within a community, taking on a life of their own. When this happens, the norms themselves become an explanation for behavior.

* * *

Although the foregoing arguments are admittedly (and purposely) very general and highly stylized, they are fairly representative of the type of arguments you will find in the scholarly literature. Indeed, you may even find one or all three to be quite persuasive. If you read each of the arguments above carefully, moreover, you'll note several key, even fundamental differences. These differences can be categorized in a number of ways. For example, the first argument focuses on what some comparativists call *micro-level* factors, whereas the second argument focuses on *macro-level* factors. The third argument, by contrast, fits somewhere in the middle; appropriately, therefore, we can say it concentrates on *meso-level* factors (*meso,* as a prefix, means "in the middle"). At the micro level, explanations of behavior are located within or at the level of the *individual:* the first argument tells us that, ultimately, criminal behavior is the product of individual choice. Meso-level explanations look beyond the individual to broader—but still fairly immediate—social, cultural, political, and institutional circumstances that surround an individual. The basic idea is that the milieu in which individuals exist has a very clear, very powerful influence on their thoughts and attitudes, which in turn shape their behavior in profound ways. The examples of gang and military culture help to illustrate this idea, but we might also consider a countervailing example: in Amish and Mennonite communities we find almost no criminal violence. Many would argue that this has much do with their deeply embedded community norms of peace and nonviolence. Finally, analysis at the macro level looks at the "biggest" or broadest forces and processes that shape not just a single individual, group, community, or society, but numerous societies (even *all* societies) at once or over time. In comparative politics, such forces are distinguished from meso-level forces in that they affect *whole* societies and peoples; they are all-encompassing. Typically, though not necessarily, macro-level forces are international and increasingly global or transnational in scope.

Another, clearly overlapping way to divide the three arguments is through the concepts of *structure* and *agency* (see Figure 3.2 for a more detailed discussion of these two terms). The second of the preceding three arguments, for example, strongly emphasizes structure, as it claims that violent crime is primarily a function of powerful socioeconomic (or structural) forces over which individuals have little control. These "forces" determine how individuals (and whole societies) behave and interact with others. The first argument, by contrast, suggests that individuals, because they exercise

---

Figure 3.2 Agency and Structure

Agency is the capacity of actors to operate independently of externally imposed constraints. Put more simply, agency is the power of human beings to make choices and to impose those choices on the world, rather than the other way around. In this regard, agency implies that the lives we live are primarily of our own making; our lives and choices, in short, are determined *by* us, not *for* us. Certain theories and approaches in comparative politics consider agency primary, whereas others assume just the opposite. Mainstream economic theory, rational choice, and **public choice** (a variant of rational choice), for example, tend to be agent-centered, whereas Marxist theories tend to be structure-centered. *Structure,* in the latter case, refers to an overarching context or framework within which choices are made and actions taken. The existence of a (social) structure implies that human action or agency is not completely undetermined. Indeed, structuralists tend to argue that our choices and actions are often severely constrained, shaped, or otherwise determined by structural factors. It is important to understand, however, that most contemporary researchers reject a completely dichotomous view of agency and structure. Instead, both in theory and in practice, they have embraced an approach that gives weight to both structure and agency. Not only this, but most contemporary researchers understand that structure and agency are interrelated, meaning simply that agency affects structure and vice versa.

choice, are essentially autonomous agents. In this agent-centered argument, structural forces may matter, but they do not ultimately determine the behavior or decisions made by free-thinking individuals. The third argument, again, falls somewhere in between the first two. That is, it assumes that individuals make purposeful decisions (i.e., have agency), but it also assumes that these decisions are strongly, even powerfully, influenced by environmental conditions so that certain decisions or patterns of behavior become very difficult—but *not* impossible—to resist or change. A discussion of the third argument, I should note, helps underscore an important but easy-to-miss point: while it is possible to understand agency and structure as dichotomous or mutually contradictory, it is also possible (and, I would emphasize, advisable) to consider the concepts as existing on a continuum. Most analyses, in fact, contain elements of agency and structure.

Theoretical Divisions: Rationality, Structure, and Culture

Although the foregoing categories are useful, I believe it is more practical to divide the preceding arguments based on the analytically discrete classification of rationality, structure, and culture. This threefold classification has a number of advantages. Most generally, as already noted, it more closely reflects the principal theoretical divisions in comparative politics. The micro/meso/macro and agency/structure divisions, in this regard, are certainly still relevant, but they are better understood as fitting into the categories of rationality, structure, and culture, rather than as clear-cut theoretical categories in and of themselves. A second advantage is this: using a limited number of highly descriptive analytical categories has the advantage of simplifying what would otherwise be an extremely complicated mélange of theoretical approaches. Recall from the beginning of this chapter that comparative politics is a field characterized by tremendous theoretical diversity. In fact, there are scores of specific theories used by comparativists, the sheer number of which can easily overwhelm even the brightest student (see Figure 3.3 for a partial list of theories in comparative politics). A threefold classification provides a very manageable—yet meaningful—set of analytical frameworks for both the beginning researcher and the more seasoned comparativist.

A three-part division, however, is still arbitrary. Certainly, I could include one, two, or even more additional categories. One particularly salient nominee would be **institutionalism**, which can be considered an intermediate, but distinct, analytical/theoretical category that operates primarily at the meso level. Primarily for reasons of space and simplicity, but also because institutionalist approaches not only fit within but have also been explicitly incorporated into the other research traditions, I have opted to stick with a threefold classification. (I will, however, discuss institutionalism separately in this chapter. But, unlike the three main approaches, I will not

---

Figure 3.3 A Sampling of Theories in Comparative Politics

- Bureaucratic authoritarianism
- Corporatism
- Critical development theory
- Dependency
- Elite theory
- Feminism (several variants)
- Imperialism (and new imperialism)
- Instrumentalism
- Marxism (several variants)
- Marxist rational choice
- Modernization
- New dependency

- New institutionalism
- New social movement theory
- Pluralism
- Political culture
- Political systems
- Postimperialism
- Poststructuralism
- Rational choice (several variants)
- Resource mobilization theory
- State-society relations
- Structural-functionalism
- World-systems theory

Students interested in exploring the various theories of comparative politics in more depth should see Ronald Chilcote's *Theories of Comparative Politics: The Search for a Paradigm Reconsidered* (1994) and his related text *Theories of Comparative Political Economy* (2000).

---

integrate a discussion of institutionalism throughout the rest of the book.) With this important caveat in mind, let's turn to a discussion of the three research traditions in comparative politics, beginning with rationality. These discussions, I should note, will be brief and quite general. The remaining chapters in this book will examine concrete issues in comparative politics using each of the three research traditions as a general framework of analysis. The main objective in the discussion that follows, therefore, is to give you a basic and purposefully *nontechnical* sense of what each research tradition is, how they differ, and how they overlap.

Rationality: A Nontechnical Introduction

Comparativists and other political scientists who use rationality as a basis for their research believe that politics—and therefore political analysis—should focus on the behavior of human beings themselves. In other words, the key unit of analysis is the *individual,* and the key level of analysis is the micro level. In rational choice, however, a focus on the individual is only a first step. The second, and far bigger, step is the introduction of a key simplifying assumption about individuals, which is that they are essentially all *self-interested actors.* I will specify what it means to be a self-interested actor in a moment, but before I do it is important to understand the rationale for making such an assumption in the first place. The reason rationalists do this is fairly clear: if the primary motivation for most human decisions and actions can be boiled down to a single characteristic, then it becomes possible to develop powerful generalizations and ultimately predictions, not only about individual action, but also about larger-scale or collective outcomes anywhere, anytime. Understandably, it may not be apparent why this is the case. Think about it this way: the assumption of self-interest suggests that human decisions and behavior are *not* dependent upon the vagaries of culture, gender, race/ethnicity, or specific personal and interpersonal experiences, as well as a slew of other place- and time-specific factors. Thus, faced with the *same set of circumstances,* we can expect all humans to make basically the same decision, whether that human being is a male peasant in **feudal** England, a female slave in seventeenth-century Haiti, the viceroy of colonial-era India, a samurai in Tokugawa Japan, a fighter for Islamic State (also known as ISIS, IS, ISIL, and Daesh), or an ordinary citizen of Russia, Brazil, China, or the United States today. More specifically, if you were in the shoes of, say, Saddam Hussein in 2002—just before the US invasion—rational choice posits that you would have most likely made the same set of decisions as he did, since Saddam was a rational actor just as you or anyone else is a rational actor. To be sure, this example oversimplifies the issue, but the lesson is clear: rationality is a consistent human characteristic across time and space. It is, in short, a *universal* trait.

A skeptical reader may be thinking, "Hold on a minute! Self-interest is important, but people are way more complicated." A rationalist would not necessarily disagree, but the key question is this: "Does the assumption of self-interested action get to the *essence* or core of human behavior?" Not surprisingly, the rational choice answer is yes. Recall, too, that simplifying assumptions are part-and-parcel of any theory. Rationalists, in other words, recognize that people are more complex—that they are not merely rational actors—but they also argue that rational action is ultimately the basis for most, and nearly all, of what people do. *If* true, this allows researchers to use **deductive logic**, which is ostensibly the hallmark of good science. I will have more to say about this later; for now, though, it would be a good time to return to the meaning of self-interest. So what does it mean to say that human beings are self-interested actors? Simply put, it means that people do things to make themselves better off; at a more personal level, it means that I make decisions to make *myself* better off, and that you make decisions to make *yourself* better off. Steven Brams stated it in slightly different terms: "To act rationally [or in a self-interested manner] means . . . to choose *better* alternatives over worse ones" (Brams 1992, p. 313, emphasis added). More formally, rational choice posits that people, in general, are rational maximizers of self-interest "who calculate the value of alternative goals and act efficiently to obtain what they want" (Zuckerman 1991, p. 45).

A still-skeptical reader may ask, "Don't people do things for others all the time? Don't people do things for their families, friends, for their country, and even for complete strangers? We're not all purely selfish creatures, right?" The rationalist will agree, but only up to a point. In fact, a rationalist will argue that much of what seems unselfish, even altruistic, can nonetheless be reasonably construed as self-interested behavior. This is because an actor engaging in seemingly altruistic or unselfish behavior may still derive a personal benefit. Helping one's family or friends, for example, reinforces good relations, which may be an important source of support at some later date. In other words, there is an important, even crucial, element of reciprocity in helping others. Moreover, the benefit from seemingly altruistic action need not be strictly material: helping a stranger typically has no expectation of reciprocity, but it may bring a psychological benefit to the person rendering aid. For example, by helping a stranger, I feel better about *myself.* I do not want to get too far into the weeds here, so suffice it to say that rationalists have at least addressed, and often quite strongly, most of the objections raised to the assertion that human beings are fundamentally self-interested actors. (Among rational choice scholars, however, there is considerable debate on the validity of incorporating nonmaterial or emotional benefits in the rational choice framework.)

Thus far, I have presented the concept of self-interest in largely generic terms. Yet it is important to understand that self-interest, despite its universal nature, is context-dependent. What constitutes an actor's self-interest, in other words, will vary depending on the general context or environment in which decisions are being made. For example, if the context is a stable market economy, where actors are engaged in buying and selling, it is reasonable to assume that self-interest will be defined in terms of maximizing the benefits from economic transactions. More simply, a consumer wants to get the "most bang for her buck," while a seller wants to maximize profit. If the context is a high-risk environment in a poor rural area with no social safety net, self-interest could be defined in terms of maximizing personal survival (Levi 1997). If the context is a political system in which the main actors are politicians and government officials, self-interest would likely be defined in terms of staying in office or in power (think back to the example of Saddam Hussein: rational choice tells us that, as the leader of Iraq, his primary self-interest was to maintain his position of political power). As a student, your self-interest may be to get good grades and to graduate, which can then be used to attain a good career or gain acceptance into graduate school. This last example, I should note, highlights one complicating factor: if you're a student, you may also have a job, a family, and other roles. This means that you don't have a single self-interest, but multiple, often competing, interests. Rational choice recognizes this and posits that rational actors rank order their self-interests as *preferences* such that they choose the best action according to their personal preferences. This is an important but also complicating factor. However, since my goal in this section is to keep things as simple as possible, and since a discussion of preferences is not necessary to understand the basic principles of rational choice, I will leave this for readers to explore on their own.[1]

Once the concept of self-interest is understood, the real work of **deduction** begins. Thus, if we begin with the assumption that individuals generally pursue their self-interests (whether it be wealth maximization, staying in office, or something else), we can come up with a range of testable hypotheses (general claims about political, social, or economic behavior subject to empirical falsification), which can then be used to help explain and predict specific outcomes given a certain set of conditions. Consider the example of crime. If we assume that criminals commit crimes because doing so makes them better off, several hypotheses are possible. A researcher might say, for instance, that policies that rely *solely* on deterrence (for example, more police on the street, a three-strikes law, the death penalty, and so on) will only partly reduce crime. Why? Because in deciding whether or not to commit crimes, individuals respond not just to potential costs, such as being apprehended and punished, but also to benefits and a range of perceived alternatives. If viable job opportunities are extremely limited, to take the most salient example, individuals may commit criminal acts even if the prospects of being caught and severely punished are extremely high. Thus, a researcher might also hypothesize that the most effective way to reduce crime is to combine policies of deterrence with meaningful job-creation programs. This is a simplistic example, but one that should at least give a broad sense of how rational choice analysis "works" in practice.

In the example earlier, another important concept in rational choice was introduced, namely *strategic calculation*. As noted at the outset of this section, an actor's self-interest is based on choosing better alternatives over worse ones, or in *calculating* the value of alternative goals. Both phrases suggest that individuals, when they make decisions, engage in a specific process, namely a cost-benefit calculation, which is the more casual way of saying strategic calculation. (Note: rationalists use the word *strategic* to refer to the self-interested decisionmaking process in general; it does not necessarily have any military connotations.) In applying rational choice principles, then, it is imperative to understand that self-interest is not always self-evident; this is the *choice* part of rational choice, wherein the term is defined, to use a typical dictionary definition, as an act of selecting or making a decision when faced with *two or more possibilities*.

Rationality, Uncertainty, and Bad Choices

Recognizing that decisions are choices helps us understand that not all rational decisions turn out well for the individual. When Saddam chose to defy the United States, for example, it turned out very badly for him: ultimately, his army was crushed, his sons were killed, and he was forced to flee, only to be captured, tried, and executed. Importantly, making such a bad choice does not negate the assumption that Saddam was a rational actor. Why is this? To answer this question, it is useful to both review and add to the preceding discussion. First, we can assume that Saddam's primary self-interest was to stay in power. Second, to determine how best to fulfill his self-interest, Saddam had to engage in a process of strategic calculation. Yet in making his calculation, he had to operate at least partly in the dark: he did not have all the information he needed to make an optimal decision. Most obvious, he did not know the actual intentions of the United States. It was not unlikely, in this regard, that he saw the threat by the United States to invade Iraq as a bluff; after all, Iraq had not directly or even indirectly attacked the United States. If he had known with total certainty what the intentions of the United States were, he likely would have made different choices. In addition, using the same example, Saddam also had to consider how the United States (and other countries) would react to his choices. In a general sense, Saddam was engaged in a (very deadly) game of poker with the United States: in poker, as in real life, the outcome of the game depends on the interaction between (or the choices made by) two or more players. Not surprisingly, rational choice has a name for this situation, too: **strategic interaction**. (More generally, a whole branch of rational choice theory has developed around strategic interaction in what is known as game theory.) Importantly, when more than one player is involved, the decisionmaking process becomes more complex or *uncertain*.

The concept of uncertainty is another central element in the rational choice framework. And it is easy to see why this is the case. After all, if all decisions were made with complete foresight of the consequences or of the trade-offs, there would not be very many interesting—and important—real-world puzzles to solve. But there are. Why, for example, have many societies been wracked by profound and debilitating political violence, as in Darfur, Rwanda, and Bosnia? Why do elites agree to democratize when democracy threatens their economic and political interests? Why do people rise up against repressive and usually quite violent political regimes? Why do people become terrorists or active participants (i.e., killers) in genocide? Answers to these and other questions lie partly in the uncertainty that comes with making rational decisions in a complex world.

To sum up, the reality that people can and do make bad choices does not mean that rational choice is wrong. Indeed, bad choices, or less-than-optimal decisions, are part-and-parcel of the rational choice framework. Part of the researcher's job is to figure out why and even under what circumstances actors are likely to make bad decisions. The key point is understanding that uncertainty adds an element of complexity to the decision-making process. It is up to the researcher to take this into account when analyzing political, social, or economic phenomena. In other words, the researcher must consider the capacity of actors to assess the risks they face, to gauge the potential benefits of their behavior, and to understand the effects their actions are likely to have on other actors (and vice versa).

The Importance of Constraints

Rational choice theory generally takes self-interest or individual preferences as *causes* of the actions people take (Little 1991, cited in Ward 2002, p. 70). At the same time, most rationalists, and especially rational choice comparativists, understand quite clearly that individuals—rational actors— cannot do anything or everything they want to do. Instead, rationalists assume that individual behavior is shaped by a range of *constraints,* which can be economic, social, institutional, and even cultural. Indeed, Margaret Levi argued that the "real action" in rational choice comes from constraints on individual behavior (1997, p. 25). The two most important sources of constraints, according to Levi, are *economic* and *institutional.* Economic constraints have to do with scarcity. Because we do not live in a world of unlimited resources, individuals must "maximize within the confines of available resources" (p. 25). If, for example, you have only $500 to spend on a car, your range of choices will be extremely limited compared to someone with $30,000 or $100,000 or $250,000. Obviously, a researcher cannot afford to neglect the impact of economic constraints on the decisions that individuals make—the next chapter highlights this point.

Institutional constraints are less obvious, but no less important. As Levi also explained it, "Institutions are sets of rules (and sanctions) that structure social interaction and whose existence and applicability are commonly known within a community. Institutions, so defined, structure the individual choices of strategic actors so as to produce **equilibrium** outcomes, that is outcomes that no one has an incentive to alter" (Levi 1997, p. 25, emphasis added). Institutions can be formal or informal; they can be political, economic, cultural/religious, or social; they can be limited to a specific community or place; or they can be national, international, or global in scope. In a broad sense, we might simply say that institutions constitute the *decision- making (or strategic) environment* within which most rational action takes place. For the comparativist using a rational choice framework, it is essential to understand the significance of the decisionmaking environment, which entails, in part, specifying how environmental (or institutional) factors influence or constrain the behavior of rational actors. Failure to do so will likely make one's analysis overly simplistic and even vacuous. (I will come back to some of these points in my extended discussion of institutionalism below.)

Rationality and Comparative Politics

The deductive logic and simplifying assumptions of rational choice mean that it cannot explain everything; nor, as Levi pointed out, "does it unravel all puzzles equally well, but it can illuminate and advance the explanation of a wide range of phenomena in a larger variety of countries and time periods" (1997, p. 33). This makes rational choice a valuable and useful approach even for those researchers who are uncomfortable reducing social and political life to self-interest—uncomfortable because doing so not only ignores the complexity of the world in which we live, but also ignores the many substantive differences that exist among the many countries and societies that make up the world. To embrace rational choice completely, in other words, means rejecting, at least to some extent, the raisons d'être (the purpose of something's existence) of comparative politics. The reason is one I alluded to earlier: if rationality is an unchanging *universal* trait that explains human behavior anywhere and at any time, it implies that those things that define and distinguish individual societies and people—culture, social institutions, historical practices, language, and the like—are unimportant. Put more bluntly, the logic of rationality tells us that the Japanese are ultimately the same as Americans, who are the same as Somalis, who are the same as Swedes, who are the same as Turks, and so on. Needless to say, most comparativists are not willing to concede this point.

Rather than reject rational choice outright, though, many comparativists have developed a compromise based on the premise that self-interest is an unequivocal part of human makeup. At the same time, they assert that rationality is institutionally, culturally, and socially conditioned, shaped, or even defined. This view reflects what is most generally referred to as the "thick variant" of rationality, or simply thick rationality. In subsequent chapters, we will address other important aspects of rationality. For now, just remember that rationality is much, much more than simply asserting that people "act rationally." To rational choice scholars, this is a truism. Far more important is how we can use this basic assumption to better explain the social world. Rationalists believe that the simple concept of rational action can, in fact, explain a great deal, including behavior that, on the surface, appears completely irrational. Indeed, one of the strengths of this research tradition, many scholars argue, is its capacity to provide rational explanations for irrational outcomes, especially at the collective—as opposed to the individual—level. (For a list of basic, but key questions to ask when applying a rational choice framework, see Figure 3.4.) Of course, not all comparativists agree that rationality provides the best answers. Some of the strongest critics are those who are associated with the structural tradition, the subject of our next section.

The Structural Tradition

A structural argument is concerned with *relationships*, which themselves exist within a broader framework or system of action. This suggests that in attempting to understand or explain any social phenomenon, it is never

---

Figure 3.4 Rational Choice Analysis: Key Questions

- Who are the main actors?
- How are their interests or preferences defined?
- What is the nature of the interaction between or among actors?
- What information is available to them?
- What type of constraints do actors face?
- How do constraints influence their actions?
- What are other elements of the strategic environment?

---

enough to look only or even primarily at individual attributes or the behavior of an individual actor. Instead, one must examine the "networks, linkages, interdependencies, and interactions among the parts of some system" (Lichbach 1997, p. 247). Thus, whereas rationalists begin political analysis at the level of the individual, structuralists begin at a more abstract level—for example, the historical system, the international system, the social system. Despite this more abstract starting point, the logic behind the structural view is not all that difficult to understand: structuralists believe that human action and behavior are fundamentally shaped and profoundly constrained by the larger environment, which in turn is the product of dominant economic, political, and social arrangements. One of these arrangements—the international system—has already been discussed. The realist idea that the anarchic international system forces every nation-state to behave in similar ways regardless of its internal makeup or its domestic politics is a structural argument par excellence. It is the structure (or political arrangements) of the international system, in other words, that determines the behavior of individual states.[2]

All structuralists, however, are not the same. Structural realism (or neorealism) in international relations is premised on the notion that the primary structural force governing international relations is *political* and *timeless* (that is, it is defined by a struggle for power and will forever remain the same). In comparative politics, by contrast, most but not all structural arguments are *historical,* which means, in part, that the structures themselves are capable of changing or transforming into something quite different over time, or of simply collapsing (only to be replaced by a new structure).[3] The idea that structures—and the specific relationships they entail—can and do change is an important point to keep in mind. It is also important to understand why and how structural change can occur. One very general reason, according to Fernando Cardoso and Enzo Faletto (1979)—famous for their work on **dependency** in Latin America—is that historical structures, although enduring, are the product of humankind's collective behavior. This implies a mutually dependent relationship between structures and agents. That is, although structures "impose limits on social processes and reiterate established forms of behavior" (p. xi), the **reproduction** of structures requires human agency. Moreover, many structuralists also contend that structures, by their very nature, generate **contradictions** and social tensions, "thus opening the possibilities for social movements and ideologies of change" (p. xi).

The clearest example of a type of structural change, at least to structuralists, is the transformation of **feudalism**, which I will discuss a bit more later. Suffice it to say for now that feudalism lasted for many centuries, but ultimately collapsed. To be sure, there are still vestiges of feudalism today—consider, for example, the royal family in Britain—but these vestiges are just that: a reminder of what once was. With this in mind, it would be useful to provide a more explicit account of what a structure is. My definition, which purposely reflects the foregoing discussion, is as follows: a structure is an enduring pattern of social relationships; it is akin to a framework within which human beings necessarily interact with each other. Importantly, this framework includes embedded political and economic arrangements, norms, and formal and informal institutions, all of which are designed, in part, to preserve the integrity of the structure. It is crucial to understand, too, that a historical structure has the properties of a *system*. On this point, keep in mind that the terms *structure* and *system* are similar and overlapping, but they are nonetheless distinct. Alexander Spirkin (1983) explained it this way: a system is "an internally organized whole where elements are so intimately connected that they operate as one." A structure, according to Spirkin, "is not enough to make a system." He continued: "A system consists of something more than structure: it is a structure with certain properties. When a structure is understood from the standpoint of its properties, it is understood as a system. We speak of the 'solar system' and not the solar structure."

Admittedly, this is a lot to digest. It might help, then, to simplify this discussion by thinking of historical structures (or systems) as deeply embedded games, which are governed by a set of generally unyielding rules and conventions. Significantly, these rules and conventions, like structural forces, define the roles for each player or part of the game: they tell us what the various parts or pieces of the game can and cannot do; they tell us the position that each occupies in the game; and they define how much power individual pieces have. In chess, for instance, the pawn is the lowest-ranking chess piece and may only move forward one square at a time (or two squares in the first move). Pawns do not have much independent power (or agency), and their main purpose is to serve as fodder for the more powerful pieces. The queen, by contrast, has a great deal of power and can move in any direction on the board. And yet, the queen's movements are still governed, not only by the rules and conventions of the game—for example, the queen can only move in a straight line—but also by the limits of the board itself. The chessboard, in this regard, is the framework within which the entire game *must* be played. (Figure 3.5 provides an illustrated depiction of the relationship between chess and structure.) In this very basic sense, games such as chess (not coincidentally, chess is designed to reflect the feudal social structure) are broadly analogous to, although certainly not the same as, complex social structures.

We need to be careful about taking the game analogy too far. Chess, after all, involves the use of inanimate objects, is governed by a clearly spelled out set of rules, and is played on a small board, over a limited period of time, with two players taking responsibility for all the moves and machinations. The pieces in an actual social structure are human beings,

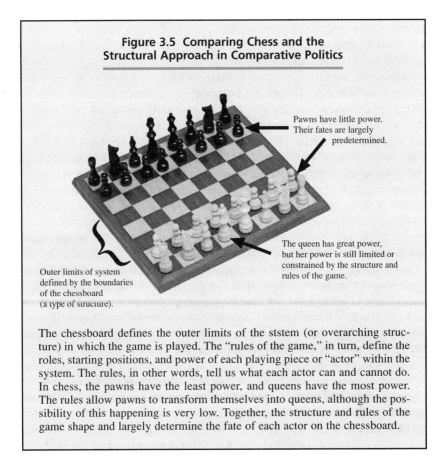

Figure 3.5 Comparing Chess and the Structural Approach in Comparative Politics

Pawns have little power. Their fates are largely predetermined.

The queen has great power, but her power is still limited or constrained by the structure and rules of the game.

Outer limits of system defined by the boundaries of the chessboard (a type of structure).

The chessboard defines the outer limits of the ststem (or overarching structure) in which the game is played. The "rules of the game," in turn, define the roles, starting positions, and power of each playing piece or "actor" within the system. The rules, in other words, tell us what each actor can and cannot do. In chess, the pawns have the least power, and queens have the most power. The rules allow pawns to transform themselves into queens, although the possibility of this happening is very low. Together, the structure and rules of the game shape and largely determine the fate of each actor on the chessboard.

who construct elaborate networks, organizations, and institutions. The rules of the game are often opaque, and there are no godlike creatures moving the pieces around. The board, moreover, is sometimes all-encompassing, and the game can go on for hundreds of years, even a millennium. Thus, in analyzing real-world social structures, the challenge of understanding how everything works and fits together is immense. Fortunately, for the beginning student of comparative politics, none of this needs to be done from scratch. Over the decades and, really, for well over a century, structuralists have figured out many different aspects of the historical social structures that have shaped and governed the modern world. In comparative politics, one particular approach is dominant—historical structuralism—so it would be useful to focus on this perspective.

History, the Economy, and Marx

Historical structuralism is generally concerned with *economic* (or *material*) as opposed to political forces. Indeed, many historical structuralists see political processes as essentially a reflection of economic forces. **Karl Marx** (1818–1883)—upon whose writings most historical structuralist arguments are ultimately based—is perhaps the most famous proponent of this view. Marx argued, for example, that capitalist industrial economies (I will have more to say about capitalism shortly) produced a need for a certain type of political institution, namely the modern state. The modern state, in other words, emerged primarily to serve the needs of an industrial economy, and not the other way around. More precisely, the state serves the needs of those who dominate the industrial economy. Thus, Marx asserted that the state is nothing more than an instrument or tool of the dominant economic class. (This view, however, has been subject to a great deal of criticism and intense debate; today, in fact, even most Marxist scholars agree that the state has relative autonomy or the capacity to act independently of the interests of the dominant class.)[4] Marx took his argument even further: in his view, virtually every political, educational, legal-judicial, social, and religious-cultural institution was a reflection of economic forces. He referred to this mélange of institutions as the **superstructure**, while the economy served as the base or foundation of society. Analytically, the important point is this: because all those institutions are products of the base, the researcher's attention should be primarily focused on the economic forces and processes. Everything else is secondary.

The emphasis on economic forces has other implications as well. One of the most important of these is that societies do not consist *just* of individuals but of individuals who occupy certain economically determined categories or **social classes**. In historical structural analysis, it is the particular category that an individual occupies that is important, not the individual per se. Even more, it is the *relationship* between classes that really matters. To better understand the significance of social class it would be useful to return to the discussion of feudalism, a specific historical structure. Feudal society, in general terms, was organized around a predominantly agricultural mode of production. This meant, among other things, that those who owned or controlled agricultural land—the landlords—necessarily occupied a privileged position in society, whereas those who actually worked the land—peasants or serfs—were in a far different and clearly subordinate position (to use the analogy from chess, we might say that the peasants were pawns and the landlords were knights or rooks). The nature of the relationship between these two categories was all-important. Clearly, occupying one or the other category had a fundamental impact on what an individual could or could not do. The opportunities available to peasants, in particular, were extremely limited if not *predestined.*

The creation of the peasant class and the landlord class, according to Marxist analysis, did not emerge out of thin air. Instead, as just suggested, it reflected the dynamics of an economic *system* built primarily upon agricultural production. Those who controlled the land (how this came to be is another story) needed cheap and plentiful labor, in large part because they needed to generate surplus value to fund their other "needs," including military force. Over time, a rigid class structure was built up, which not only was based upon, but also utterly depended upon the hyper-exploitation of peasants, who, by and large, were held in conditions of bondage or involuntary servitude. Thus, if one was born a peasant during the feudal era, one died a peasant. Even more, generation after generation lived and died as peasants. There was very little chance of upward mobility in feudal society. The reason is obvious: the structure, or feudal system, needed a vast peasant class to function, and the only way to ensure a ready supply of peasant labor was through a coercive, essentially involuntary process that locked peasants, virtually forever, into positions of servitude.

To even the keenest critic of Marxist thought (and there are many), I should note, it is almost undeniable that feudalism was a highly unequal, exploitative *class-based* social structure. Feudalism, then, represents perhaps the best and most powerful illustration of the significance of structure. For structuralists, however, feudalism is not the only historical structure. Today, the historical structure is capitalism, which is organized and operates according to very different principles. This helps explain why the relationship between peasant and lord no longer even exists (with, perhaps, a few exceptions), and why the monarchs, lords, and other rulers of the feudal era have been reduced to fodder for the tabloids and paparazzi of today (especially in the most advanced capitalist countries). Yet, make no mistake, structuralists assert: capitalism also imposes strong, essentially inescapable constraints on human action, although for most of us, these constraints are not always obvious. Beginning in Chapter 4, I will spend considerable time explaining how capitalism works, or, more specifically, how its structural effects and dynamics explain the primary issues covered in this book: poverty, prosperity, democracy, and political violence. Accordingly, I will reserve further discussion until then.

Agency vs. structure. It useful to highlight another implication of the historical structural perspective, one that concerns the relationship between agency and structure. As the term implies, *historical structuralism* posits that structures are difficult to resist, and even more difficult to change through human agency. This does not mean, as already suggested, that structuralists completely discount agency; instead, they understand that historical structures necessarily shape the possibilities for change. As Marx famously put it, "Men make their own history, but they do not make it just as they please; they do not make it under circumstances chosen by themselves, but under circumstances directly encountered, given and transmitted from the past" (Marx [1869] 1994, p. 15). In this view, feudalism did not end because peasants became fed up with being oppressed and decided to do something about it; rather, it ended because broader changes in the economic structure *allowed* or enabled movements against feudalism to succeed.[5] We can make the same sort of argument for social revolutions of all types. Theda Skocpol, whom I've already discussed, is well known for her structural interpretation of social revolutions (an issue of strong interest to comparativists).[6] She argued that, if one wants to understand why social revolutions succeed, it is necessary to examine patterns of relationships among groups and societies (both domestically and transnationally), for this shows us that revolutionary situations "emerge" rather are "made" (Skocpol 1979). What Skocpol meant by this is that successful revolutionary movements never begin merely with a revolutionary intention—that is, a group of people getting together and deciding to overthrow the existing system. Rather, revolutionaries must first wait for the "emergence of politico-military crises of state *and* class domination" (p. 17, emphasis added); it is only within these crisis situations that the possibilities for revolution can be realized. It is important to add, too, that these crises are themselves products of systemic or structural forces.

On the importance of history. It is clear from the foregoing discussion that structural approaches and history are closely connected. Indeed, by definition, historical structuralist approaches are historically grounded. At the most basic level this means, to repeat a point made in Chapter 1, that "history matters." It matters in the sense that the structural relationships that exist in the world today are products of specific historical eras and experiences. This means that structural forces, although they exert similar pressures in all societies, do not always create the same outcome. Indeed, the same structural forces can sometimes create seemingly contradictory outcomes depending on the circumstances: say, communist revolution in one country and capitalist transformation in another. At the end of World War II, for example, the specific historical configuration of the emerging **Cold War** produced a **Stalinist** communist regime in North Korea, and a pro-US, capitalist regime in South Korea. Structuralists also like to say that historical sequence matters too (Rueschemeyer, Stephens, and Stephens 1992). Consider this point: different sequences of industrialization—for example, whether a country began the process of industrialization in the early 1800s, in the late 1800s, or post-1945, or in 1979—may give a very different character to internal changes despite the similar structural effects of capitalist industrialization. Consider the experiences of England, the United States, Germany, Japan, France, Taiwan, and China. Today, these countries share significant similarities with respect to major economic, institutional, and political arrangements—something a structuralist would predict—but there are also meaningful differences, many of which can be attributed to the time each adopted capitalism. The task of the structuralist, in part, is to show how the *homogenizing* effects of structural processes (such as capitalist development) interact with the *heterogeneous* effects of specific historical experiences. The bias, however, is toward discerning the causal patterns that underlie these different paths. Structuralists, therefore, very often do comparative histories in an effort to discover the "historical laws" of structural development (Lichbach 1997). Figure 3.6 offers a summary of key questions to ask when using a structural approach.

The Broad Scope of the Structural Tradition

The structural tradition is a broad one. Within it are "hard structuralists" who see our actions as tightly constrained and almost predetermined as well

---

Figure 3.6 The Structural Approach: Key Questions

- What is the overarching structure or system, and what are the key relationships within that structure?
- How does the structure work or operate? What are the internal logic and basic dynamics of the structure? What are the key forces (political, economic, social) within the structure?
- What are the rules of the game?
- Who are the key players and what are their roles within the structure (or system)? What capacity for agency do the key players have? How are their actions constrained by the structure?
- How is the structure reproduced and sustained over time?

as "soft structuralists" who see a much closer, mutually constitutive inter-action between structures and agents. There are also historical structuralists and structuralists who eschew historical analysis altogether. In addition, there are structuralists who focus their analytical attention on an individual society or state as the primary unit of analysis, and there are others who be-lieve that the main unit of analysis is the system as a whole (for example, **world-systems theory**, a perspective discussed in Chapter 5, argues that the basic unit of analysis should be the historical system, such as the capitalist world-system). In practice, moreover, many comparativists tend to slide back and forth between different positions within the structural tradition. The structural tradition, in short, can be terribly complicated and confusing, especially for the beginning comparativist. It is, nonetheless, a research tra-dition that cannot be ignored. Structuralists have told us a lot about the world and have given us many valuable conceptual and intellectual tools. Even those of you who are uncomfortable with the basic assumptions of structuralism need to understand its utility and value for comparative and social scientific analysis.

The Cultural Tradition

For students, the cultural tradition often makes the most intuitive sense, but it is generally the most misunderstood and misused of the three research traditions. There are good reasons for this, not the least of which is that the concept of culture itself is extremely nebulous. Moreover, in popular usage (and even among some prominent scholars), culture is most typically por-trayed in a simplistic, sometimes crude manner. On this point, consider a January 25, 2004, editorial by Robyn Blumner, a columnist for the *St. Pe-tersburg Times* in Florida (interestingly, the Ivy League–educated Blumner was also the executive director of the American Civil Liberties Union of Florida). In discussing the prospects for democracy in Iraq (and the Arab world more generally), Blumner focused on what she felt were clear and fundamental incompatibilities between democracy and Arab culture. She wrote: "There is a reason political pluralism, individual liberty and self-rule do not exist in any of the 16 Arab nations in the Middle East. Cultural tra-ditions there tend toward anti-intellectualism, religious zealotry and patri-archy, values which provide little fertile ground for progressive thinking." To be fair, Blumner was focused on the near-term prospects for democracy in Iraq, but it is not hard to read another tacit message in her column: even in the long run, Arab culture would represent a near-impenetrable and un-changeable barrier to democratization throughout the region.

This type of argument is common and may even be "right" in a certain, very limited way. Nonetheless, it is seriously misinformed, intellectually crude, and unequivocally ethnocentric. There are four basic reasons for this. First, the argument is based on the mistaken assumption that culture is essentially *static*. Although not explicitly stated, Blumner suggests that Arab cultural traditions are timeless: *once* anti-intellectual, overly "zealous," and patriarchal, so the logic goes, *always* anti-intellectual, overly zealous, and patriarchal. Second, her argument is based on an equally erroneous assumption that culture is *monolithic* or *univocal* (that is, "speaks" with a single voice). To Blumner, it seems, Arab culture across all sixteen Arab nations of which she speaks is identical; Arabs (be they Shia imams or Sunni caliphs, men or women, potentates or ordinary citizens, **Muslims** in the United States, Pakistan, Syria, Indonesia, or Turkey) speak with the same voice, hold the same values and beliefs, and view the world in essentially the same manner. Third, it falsely presumes that the effects of culture are *one-directional* (for example, culture serves either as an obstacle to or as an open path toward certain political, economic, or social developments). On this point, the author clearly implies that there is nothing in Arab Islamic culture—no principle, no value, and no practice—that is compatible with democracy. This was much the same argument, by the way, that scholars and other observers made about "Confucian culture" before Japan, Taiwan, and South Korea democratized. Fourth, the argument suggests that culture exists in a social, political, and economic vacuum; that culture, in other words, is unaffected by other forces in the world. To Blumner, for example, the *only* thing that matters—and the only reason there is no democracy in any of the sixteen Arab nations in the Middle East—is Islamic culture. Blumner's argument, in short, ignores the complex, fluid, and often contingent nature of culture.

More concretely, to see the folly of this type of thinking—or bad theorizing—consider how many of the same charges that Blumner levels against Islamic countries could have been, and still could be, leveled against the United States. After all, in US culture, there is a very strong anti-intellectual element—Americans are supposed to be pragmatic "doers," not pointy-headed, ivory tower intellectuals. The bias against anti-intellectualism is so pervasive that US presidential candidates are required to obscure their academic pedigrees by pretending to be "average Joes." There is also a great deal of religious zealotry in the United States. In fact, surveys tell us that the United States is one of the most strongly religious countries in the world—28 percent of all Americans, for instance, believe in a literal interpretation of the Bible, and another 47 percent consider the Bible to be the inspired word of God (Jones and Saad 2014)—and it is fairly clear that Christian fundamentalism occupies a prominent role in US culture and politics. Last, the United States was a profoundly patriarchal (and racist) society when originally founded; for evidence, one need only recall that women were not allowed to vote until 1920 (and it was only in 1965 that African Americans, with the passage of the Voting Rights Act, were able to effectively exercise their franchise in the deep South). Despite all this, the

United States is a democracy. And to repeat the key point: underlying this transformation were significant, if not profound, cultural shifts. The issue, I recognize, is more complex than I suggest here; however, since the focus of Chapter 6 is democracy or democratization, I will not say anything more for now. My point, however, is not to suggest that the United States and the Arab countries of the Middle East are cultural clones—they obviously are not—but to emphasize the importance of thinking of culture in an open-minded and sophisticated manner. Minimally, the (comparative) experience of the United States tells us that cultural values can and do change. It would be useful, in this regard, to also consider the 2015 US Supreme Court decision to legalize gay marriage: as little as ten years earlier, still less a hundred years ago, such a decision would likely have been considered absurd and "culturally impossible."

What Is Culture?

To understand the significance of culture, it is crucial to know what culture is. One definition is offered by Mark Ross, who defined culture as a "worldview that explains why and how individuals and groups behave as they do, and includes both cognitive and affective [that is, emotional] beliefs about social reality and assumptions about when, where, and how people in one's culture and those in other cultures are likely to act in particular ways" (1997, p. 45). To put it in slightly different (and perhaps easier-to-understand) terms, we can also say that culture is a shared, learned, and symbolic system of values, ideas, beliefs, and practices that shapes and influences our perceptions and behavior—culture is an abstract "mental blueprint" or "mental code" (Dahl n.d.). This definition has several important assumptions and implications, some stated and some unstated, which are described in Figure 3.7. The key element I wish to highlight, however, is this: culture is unavoidably subjective or, more accurately, intersubjective. Most simply, this means culture exists inside our (collective) minds. It is for this reason that culture can never be completely fixed, and why there can be no absolute, unchanging meaning to any culture. With just a bit of reflection, it is not hard to see why this is the case. Consider the other side of the coin: if culture is subjective or intersubjective, it has no objective or concrete existence. It does and cannot exist apart from our minds. Thus, culture is, to a large extent, what we (collectively) *think* it is or *want* it to be.

Even more, culture must be *learned* and constantly *reproduced*. As any student knows, however, learning is an imperfect process no matter how hard one studies. Put another way, human beings are not infallible copy machines, which means there are usually differences between what is taught and what is learned. To be sure, some basic facts and knowledge can be passed on without much if any variation, but when broad systems of meanings (that is, cultures) are reproduced, variations—whether unintentional or

---

Figure 3.7 Definition of Culture: Core Features

- Learned. Process of learning one's culture is called enculturation.
- Shared by the members of a society. There is no "culture of one."
- Patterned. People in a society live and think in ways that form definite patterns.
- Mutually constructed through a constant process of social interaction.
- Symbolic. Culture, language, and thought are based on symbols and symbolic meanings.
- Arbitrary. Culture is not based on "natural laws" external to humans, but created by humans according to the "whims" of the society.
- Internalized. Culture is habitual, taken-for-granted, and perceived as "natural."

Source: Dahl n.d.

---

not, whether small or large—are virtually impossible to avoid. Moreover, in a world of multiple cultures, diffusion (or the passing of specific cultural practices, beliefs, and meanings from one society to another) makes the process of reproduction even less perfect. If it was just a matter of unintended imperfections in the process of transmitting cultural values, principles, norms, and practices, the issue of cultural change and interpretation might be relatively unimportant. But a great deal of cultural change and interpretation is quite clearly intended. Indeed, struggles over the meaning of culture have been a pervasive part of the human condition (I will return to this point later).

The Significance of Culture

Despite its inherently subjective nature, most culturalists agree that culture does have objective *effects*—simply put, culture shapes the behavior and actions of people, at both the individual and collective levels. This is what makes culture especially relevant in an analysis of political, social, or economic phenomena. On the surface, the claim that culture shapes the behavior and actions of people does not sound much different from the argument by Blumner. There is, however, a crucial difference. In the preceding argument, recall that culture is portrayed as essentially static, univocal, and onedirectional. Most culturalists today, as already suggested, regard these assumptions as irredeemably flawed. Instead, they argue that culture must be understood as an inherently fluid system of meaning, with multiple "voices" and a complex influence on social, political, or economic processes. What all this means will become clear in subsequent chapters. For now, suffice it to say that, because of its fluid nature, the manner in which culture shapes behavior is ambiguous, rarely straightforward, and often contradictory. In this regard, it is also important to understand that most contemporary cultural theorists believe that cultural forces rarely, if ever, can be understood without examining them within specific contexts. A researcher, for example, has to ask the question, "Why does religious fundamentalism play such a prominent role in the political landscape of the Arab (or Islamic) Middle East today?" An honest answer to this question almost certainly will bring to fore a number of crucial political and economic factors, such as the role the United States and other Western countries have played in attempting, for most of the twentieth century (and even today), to dominate the region. (In this view, one can argue that the rise of fundamentalism was an attempt to build a collective identity strong enough to stand up to Western domination and power.) Thus, it is more appropriate to see culture as *intersecting* with political, social, and economic forces to produce specific outcomes in specific places and time periods.

With all this in mind, one key to understanding the significance of culture is to recognize that *culture has power.* It not only has the power to shape individual perceptions and behavior but also has the power to unify and mobilize entire societies, sometimes across borders. It is important to note that this is well recognized by those people who wish to harness the power of culture. It is also for this reason that the reproduction of culture is not always or even generally—as common sense might suggest—a neutral or apolitical affair. Indeed, the reproduction of culture is a profoundly political process. Moreover, the power to define culture has become a major source of conflict and political struggle in and across societies throughout the world. This is true even (or especially) in the United States, where various "culture wars" have become a centerpiece of the US political and social landscape. It is important to understand, in case this point is not already clear, that culture wars—whether in (or between) the United States, Western Europe, the Middle East, Asia, or any other part of the world—are often primarily about power. For culture is not *merely* a worldview or set of widely shared beliefs about social reality but also a political resource that can be used to achieve political, social, or economic goals. Part of understanding and assessing the impact of culture, in fact, requires an analysis of how culture is appropriated and manipulated by various groups within society. In Chapter 7, we will focus on this particular aspect of cultural analysis when examining the phenomenon of collective political violence, and specifically genocide and terrorism.

At the same time, it is important to recognize and remember that culture is more than a political resource. One reason for this is obvious: culture is not tangible. It cannot be simply picked up or stored (in the same way that money or a weapon can be). In addition, culture is, by definition, "public." Everyone has access to culture, unlike other types of material resources. Last, despite its intersubjective and malleable nature, there is an enduring or historical substance to almost any culture. Cultures cannot simply be created out of whole cloth. For all these reasons, a comparativist must avoid reducing culture to a mere resource or asset.

The Causal Power of Culture: The Debate

The causal power of culture is subject to debate among social scientists. Indeed, a great many and perhaps most social scientists are extremely skeptical of culture. They consider it to have no *independent* causal power at all. This view is reflected in the relatively scant attention paid to culture in the large majority of social science research (although this has begun to change over the past decade or two). For the beginning comparativist, it is important to understand both the logic behind the skeptical view of culture and the reason why this is an important issue. Indirectly, at least, I have already provided the rationale for the skepticism in my discussion of the rational choice and structural perspectives. For structuralists, culture is typically seen as a reflection or product of more basic economic forces. Recall the historical structural concept of the superstructure; in this view, culture is part of the superstructure, and not necessarily a significant part. The key point is this: if culture only *reflects* deeper forces and processes (that is, if it is a product of those forces), then it need not be taken seriously, or given primary analytical attention. Studying culture, in other words, would be akin to studying a reflection in the mirror, or a shadow, rather than the actual thing. From the rational choice perspective, culture is also considered to be a purely secondary or marginal factor. After all, if human decision-making and action is fundamentally driven by self-interest, which is timeless and universal, then it stands to reason that cultural factors do not and cannot play a central role in explaining behavior. At best, from the rationalist point of view, culture may influence behavior in subtle ways by adding an element to the strategic environment. But this is hardly cause, rationalists assert, for treating culture as an independent variable in its own right.

The case against culture is persuasive. Nonetheless, there are strong reasons to disregard the claims of the skeptics. To begin, the structural argument is, at best, only half right. It is right insofar as culture can be understood as a product of underlying social, economic, or political forces. Many culturalists do not necessarily dispute this view (although some would). Still, once established, cultural systems tend to be perpetuated from generation to generation, even if structural conditions change. Put another way, culturalists argue that, even if cultures *originally* reflect the influence of other forces, once created, cultures begin to take on a life of their own, and begin to operate as a semiautonomous or autonomous force. Culture, in this regard, should most properly be seen as both cause and effect. In Chapter 4, I will provide concrete examples of these points in the discussion of poverty. For now, I will just note that the preeminent structural force and system today—capitalism—has not produced a homogeneous world, even among the most "advanced" capitalist societies. Instead, we see meaningful and sometimes dramatic variation. Culture may not (and admittedly does not) explain all this variation, but it likely does explain a lot of it.

As for rational choice, perhaps the best way to demonstrate the relevance of the cultural response is through another example. Consider the practice of *female* infanticide and feticide, which is still practiced in parts of rural India and China, in particular (see Figure 3.8). The people who engage in this practice, for the most part, are desperately poor, so on the surface one could argue that it is rational for them to kill children who have less "economic value." But why, a culturalist would ask, do girls have less economic value than boys? Where does this idea come from, and why does it continue to hold currency (in some countries and not in others)? Boys may be physically stronger on average, but why should physical strength necessarily be valued more than, say, the ability to bear children (which, of course, no male is capable of doing)? One might also ask, if it is rational for desperately poor Indian and Chinese villagers to kill their female children, why don't we see this practice in every desperately poor country? At the same time, why does female feticide (i.e., selective abortion based on sex) continue to happen in some relatively rich countries or areas such as

---

Figure 3.8　Gendercide and Women

Although female infanticide has been practiced throughout human history and in many parts of the world, the practice is particularly pronounced in India and China today. According to the United Nations Family Planning Agency (UNFPA), China has the most skewed sex ratio at birth among all countries. In 2011, the sex ratio for the country as a whole was 117.8 boys for every 100 girls, one of the highest disparities ever recorded (the natural ratio is about 1.06 to 1.10, males to females). For specific provinces, however, the ratio was even worse: Anhui province stood at the top of the list with a sex ratio at birth of 128.7. India's overall sex ratio at birth was 110.5 between 2008 and 2010. As with China, certain regions have a much higher ratio. Specifically, Punjab state's sex ratio at birth was 120.3 during the same period. More generally, the UNFPA estimated that, in a survey of the fourteen countries with a significantly skewed sex ratio at birth, upward of 117 million women were "missing" in 2010. That is, were it not for female infanticide, the population of women in those fourteen countries would have been 117 million higher (all statistics cited in UNFPA 2012). Significantly, among these fourteen countries and areas are several relatively prosperous ones: Hong Kong (116.2), Taiwan (108.4), Singapore (107.5), and South Korea (106.7).

The huge number of missing women has led some groups to label the process of female infanticide as *gendercide*—the systematic elimination or killing of members of a specific sex.

Hong Kong, Taiwan, Singapore, and South Korea? To answer any of these questions requires going well beyond the issues of self-interest and rationality. Self-interest may be part of the answer, but culture almost certainly plays a role, and perhaps plays a central role. In sum, if there are important questions that *cannot* be answered by rational choice (or by structural) principles alone—and there are many—then it is necessary to look elsewhere, and culture is one of those places to look.

* * *

Culture is complex. It is malleable, and its effects are not always obvious or straightforward. Culture has power, but it is not always or necessarily a causal power. This may all sound confusing, but it need not be. The key is to avoid treating culture as an unambiguous set of unchanging values, norms, and beliefs that define and unproblematically shape—even determine—the social, political, and economic fate of individuals, societies, and countries. Instead, recognize that culture is contested, profoundly political, and inherently fluid. Obviously, this is easy to say but not so easy to do. The next five chapters will provide examples of how to apply the basic principles of the cultural tradition to an examination of real-world problems and issues.

Before concluding our discussion of major research traditions, it would be worth discussing, at some length, an intermediate or hybrid research tradition: institutionalism. As I noted earlier in the chapter, institutionalism can be considered a distinct analytical category and one that could easily be included in this book. One reason for my more limited approach, however, is that institutionalism can be meaningfully incorporated into rational choice, structural, and cultural frameworks. It is in this regard that I refer to institutionalism as a "hybrid" tradition.

A Hybrid Tradition: Institutionalism

For most of the first half of the twentieth century, institutionalism was a dominant tradition in political analysis (Rhodes 1995). However, this early type of institutionalism—what we might call old institutionalism—was static and highly formal. In comparative politics, more specifically, old institutionalism revolved around the same rigidly defined conception of politics discussed in Chapter 1. That is, it focused narrowly on the formal institutions and procedures of the government and of the state. "Comparative analysis" in the old institutional view, moreover, was generally limited to a descriptive comparison of Western institutions. After a short period of decline, however, institutionalism was revived with a new and much broader vision. Institutions were no longer limited to the concrete institutions (or organizations) of government; instead, they were defined as "connected sets of rules, norms and practices that prescribe [and proscribe] roles, constrain activity, and shape the expectations of actors" (Keohane, Haas, and Levy

1993, pp. 4–5). Under this definition, many important elements of the social world came under the "jurisdiction" of institutionalism, from the very big to the very small: states as a whole, markets (and the myriad rules and procedures that govern markets, such as property rights), international agreements, democracy, marriage, patriarchy, religious organizations, codes of conduct (both written and unwritten), and so on. The new conception of institutionalism, one might argue, moved to the other end of the extreme (compared to old institutionalism), as a huge—and perhaps unwieldy— array of economic, social, political, and cultural organizations and practices were swept into the institutional domain.

More pertinent, new institutionalism was a response to the tendency by mainstream scholars and others to dismiss institutions as mere reflections of individual behavior (or of underlying structures), rather than as "autonomous political actors in their own right" (March and Olsen 1984, p. 738). As culturalists did, proponents of institutionalism also challenged the prevailing view. To put it simply, new institutionalists argue that institutions—and not just individuals—have agency. Thus, institutions are not just passive subjects in the political world but are collective actors that have their own interests and goals: most basically, institutions struggle to survive and establish legitimacy. For the beginning comparativist this is a significant argument to keep in mind. For, if institutions do have agency, they not only should be analyzed as a discrete part of the political, social, and economic landscape, but also should be understood as a key (and independent) variable explaining particular outcomes. But what does it mean to say institutions have agency? An example might help to illustrate this point. Consider the "clan," an informal social institution in which actual or putative kinship based on blood or marriage forms the central bond among members. Kathleen Collins (2002) argued that clans are central (and collectively rational) actors in many parts of the world, including Afghanistan and Central Asia. As Collins explained it, clans have played a key role—perhaps *the* key role—in shaping political outcomes in the Central Asia region. In particular, they have *created* a special type of regime, which she calls a "clan hegemony," which is neither a democracy nor a classical authoritarian political order (p. 143). There is, of course, much more to the argument, but the basic point is simple: to understand political development in contemporary Central Asia, it is necessary to focus on the interests, the power, and the role of institutions.

Not all new institutional research is focused on institutions-as-actors; if anything, most of the comparative research in this area has been more restricted: comparativists have tended to focus on the capacity of institutions to constrain, enable, or shape the behavior of other actors, and, through this, to *indirectly* effect larger outcomes. The example of clans can also be used to illustrate this point. Clans are a deeply embedded part of society in Central Asia; thus, all political and economic processes, relationships, and transactions must be mediated through and are therefore profoundly shaped by clans.

It is not just formal institutions that matter; informal institutions can also play a significant role in political outcomes. Consider, on this point, what Gretchen Helmke and Steven Levitsky wrote in "Informal Institutions and Comparative Politics":

> A growing body of research on Latin America, postcommunist Eurasia, Africa, and Asia suggests that many "rules of the game" that structure political life are *informal*—created, communicated, and enforced outside of officially sanctioned channels. Examples abound. For decades, Mexican presidents were selected not according to rules in the Constitution, the electoral law, or party statutes, but rather via the *dedazo* ("big finger")— an unwritten code that gave the sitting president the right to choose his successor. . . . In Japan, the "strict but unwritten rules" of *Amakurdari* ("descent from heaven"), through which retiring state bureaucrats are awarded top positions in private corporations, have survived decades of administrative reforms. . . . And in much of the developing and postcommunist world, patterns of clientelism, corruption, and patrimonialism coexist with (and often subvert) new democratic, market, and state institutions. (2004, p. 725, emphasis in original)

Given all that I have said, albeit in very sketchy terms, about the significance of institutions, the decision to treat institutionalism as a hybrid research tradition may seem strange or problematic. As I have already admitted, the decision is (to some extent) arbitrary, but it is also important to keep in mind that institutional concepts can fit squarely into the three main research traditions discussed in this chapter. For instance, using a rational choice framework, we can think of institutions as an integral part of the larger strategic environment in which individual decisions are made. This corresponds to our earlier discussion about institutional constraints. These constraints can play a powerful role in shaping decisions and actions, but the *guiding principle* is still the underlying rationality of human choice. Michael McGinnis put it this way: "Individuals are presumed to pursue their own self-interest to the best of their abilities, but the options available to them and the ways in which they perceive their own interests are profoundly shaped by the institutions that surround them" (2005, p. 1). This approach, appropriately enough, is called rational choice institutionalism. Even the argument about clans in Central Asia, one can argue, easily fits into a broader rational choice framework, since clans are motivated by collective self-interests.

The structural tradition, too, can subsume institutions into a general framework of analysis that highlights their importance, but that still relegates institutions to secondary status. In Marxist analysis, for example, one can argue that the imperatives of capitalism *as a historical structure* lead to the development and reproduction of certain types of institutions. These institutions are primarily economic, but political, ideological, and cultural institutions (again, these are part of what Marxists refer to as the superstructure) are also understood to play important roles in sustaining and "growing" capitalism. The key point, however, is this: in the structural view, institutions have no power independent of the structure in which they are embedded. Changes to institutions, therefore, will be due more to macrostructural dynamics than to the "agency" of institutions. Finally, in the cultural perspective, we can propose a highly interactive relationship between institutions and culture. We might even consider institutions to be an integral part of a larger culture. Think about the previously mentioned definition of institutions as "connected sets of rules, norms, and practices" (Keohane, Haas, and Levy 1993, pp. 4–5). This is, for all intents and purposes, the same definition of culture, which tells us, perhaps, that institutions are a feature—albeit a very important one—of a larger cultural landscape.

Separation or Synthesis?

My summary of the three research traditions is just that, a summary. It is not intended to be comprehensive or definitive (it certainly is not); rather, I intended to give you a general sense of what each is about—not only to help orient you to the field of comparative politics, but also to allow you to figure out which research tradition best encompasses your *current* views (for it is no doubt the case that you already hold a number of theoretical assumptions). At the same time, I also intended to give you a general sense of how the traditions differ. On this point, though, it is vital that you understand that their differences are not just skin-deep. That is, it is not only a matter of the cultural, rational, and structural (and institutional) traditions having a different emphasis. This is obvious. But each also is premised on fundamentally different assumptions about "reality," about knowledge, and about what it means to do comparative analysis (these are difficult issues requiring far more discussion than can be provided here). It is for this reason that one cannot merely combine elements of the three traditions—as many students are invariably tempted to do. A culturalist, for example, *cannot* accept a version of rationality that posits invariant interests (for example, maximization of wealth, security, or power). For to do so would be to admit that culture has no real significance, that history has no meaning. At the same time, a rationalist must be very careful about incorporating culture (or institutions) into their analysis: although the rationalist can accept the notion that interests are culturally (or institutionally) conditioned, the line must be drawn somewhere. If not, then rationality accounts will themselves become highly particularistic, which is exactly the opposite of what rationalists hope to achieve. Moreover, if a rationalist accepts that culture shapes or determines behavior, then the core assumption of self-interest and individual preferences becomes almost meaningless. By the same token, structuralists cannot give too much weight to cultural factors (or to the concept of rationality) without risk of abandoning their core tenet, namely that structures are "real" and have *primary* causal powers.

None of this is to say, however, that a synthesis or integration of the three traditions is out of the question; as I noted at the outset of this section, there are some comparativists who believe that such a task is not only possible, but also necessary. Mark Lichbach (1997), Margaret Levi (1997), and Doug McAdam, Sidney Tarrow, and Charles Tilly (1997) are some of the more prominent proponents of this view. The latter three, in fact, propose an explicitly integrative approach in their study of social movements (the primary topic of Chapter 8). For this reason, a detailed summary of their argument is not appropriate here; still, a few very general points are worth making. First, it is important to point out, as McAdam, Tarrow, and Tilly did, that simply aggregating variables from the three perspectives will not do (p. 160). Instead, they argued that an integrative approach must show how different variables are *linked together* as part of a coherent *process*. Second, and in a closely related vein, the search for an integrative approach should avoid analyzing each set of cultural, structural, or rational variables in isolation from one another. In their own analysis of the civil rights movement in the United States, McAdam, Tarrow, and Tilly showed that the effects of these variables were *mutually reinforcing* at each stage of the civil rights cycle. As they put it, "There is no substitute for relating all phases of a movement cycle to the three broad classes of factors"—cultural, structural, and rational choice (p. 163). At the same time, at certain stages, one or another set of factors may be more or less prominent. It is up to the researcher to be aware of and extremely sensitive to the changing significance of culture, structure, or rationality. Third, integration, however accomplished, will not be easy. It takes a great deal of careful, well-considered thought to "blend" the three traditions together, and even then, the blendings will undoubtedly be far from perfect or free of contention (p. 159).

Bringing Everything Together

Comparative politics is far more than "studying foreign countries." Nor is it simply about comparing. Instead, it is an extremely diverse field that requires one to grasp a range of—sometimes conflicting, if not contradictory—methodological and theoretical concepts and issues. My main objective in this chapter was to help you to both focus and organize your thoughts for the tasks ahead. This is necessary because understanding what comparative politics is and what it is all about—much less "doing comparative politics"—is *not* easy. To acquire this understanding requires a more disciplined and broader style of thinking than most students are accustomed to. It also requires one to digest a broad range of abstract concepts and methods and apply them to "real-world" cases—which themselves are chock-full of (empirical) complexities and subtleties as well as millions of potentially relevant facts. At the same time, nothing discussed in this chapter is beyond the reach of any student.

Before moving on to the next chapter, it would be worthwhile summing up a few key points about becoming a good comparativist:

- In the most general sense, becoming a good comparativist (and doing comparative politics) means knowing how to use comparisons in conjunction with the use of theory. Theory and the comparative method are necessarily used together to develop and support larger arguments and explanations about the world.
- Becoming a good comparativist means knowing what the limitations of comparative analysis are. This may sound contradictory, but it is critical to recognize both what we can do with comparative analysis and what we cannot do.
- Becoming a good comparativist means being aware of and self-critical about your own theoretical understanding of the world; it also means being able to understand and apply theoretical principles in a consistent, coherent, and informed manner.
- Becoming a good comparativist means knowing how to support your position with adequate, sufficient, and reliable empirical evidence (that is, "the facts").

In short, becoming a good comparativist and doing comparative politics requires the effective integration of method, theory, and evidence. (Figure 3.9

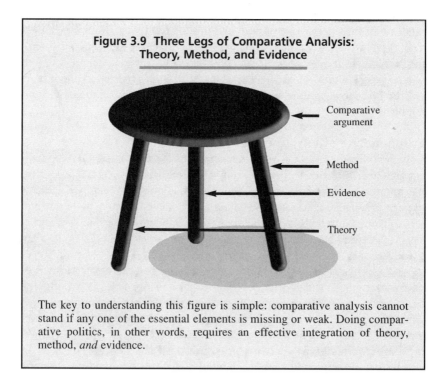

Figure 3.9 Three Legs of Comparative Analysis: Theory, Method, and Evidence

Comparative argument

Method

Evidence

Theory

The key to understanding this figure is simple: comparative analysis cannot stand if any one of the essential elements is missing or weak. Doing comparative politics, in other words, requires an effective integration of theory, method, *and* evidence.

provides a simple graphic representation of this requirement.) Obviously, as already emphasized, this cannot be learned all at once. It takes time, energy, and a genuine commitment. It can be a daunting task, but one that I believe is well worth the effort.

Notes

1. For further discussion of preferences in rational choice, see Levin and Migrom 2004, and Green 2002. For a more general and in-depth discussion of rational choice, students might begin with Jon Elster's *Nuts and Bolts for the Social Sciences* (1989) and *Ulysses and the Sirens: Studies in Rationality and Irrationality* (1984).

2. Although neorealist scholars are clearly structuralists, they also fully embrace the concept of rationality in their analyses. Specifically, they assume that individual states are "rational actors" who respond to the imperatives of the international system in generally predictable ways. In the neorealist framework, though, it is clear that structural forces take precedence, for it is assumed that the actors within the system have no capacity to alter the fundamental dynamics of the system or to otherwise escape from the "logic of anarchy."

3. Another meaning of "historical" derives from the belief, put forward by Marx, that human societies are embedded in their own past (Abrams 1982), such that what happened before necessarily impacts what happens today.

4. The state's relationship to society is another area of deep concern to comparativists. One of the best introductions to this subject is the book *Bringing the State Back In* (1985), edited by Evans, Rueschemeyer, and Skocpol. Another useful and more recent book is *State Power and Social Forces* (1994), edited by Joel Migdal, Atul Kohli, and Vivienne Shue.

5. I am purposefully being vague on reasons for the breakdown in feudalism, since my intention is not to expound a particular argument, only to give a sense of what a structural argument would be at a very general level.

6. Skocpol explored this issue in depth in her 1979 book *States and Social Revolutions.*

Part 2
The Questions

4

Why Are Poor Countries Poor? Explaining Economic Underdevelopment

Why are some countries poor? I asked this question in the preceding chapter to help illustrate how most of us (all of us) already theorize about basic issues in comparative politics. In this chapter, I would like to explore this question in much greater depth, this time paying closer attention to how researchers representing the three major traditions in comparative politics—rationalist, culturalist, and structuralist—deal with or approach the issue of poverty and underdevelopment. There is, as already suggested, deep disagreement among scholars on the issue. Before we get to these disagreements, though, it would be useful to consider (again) the issue at a more casual level, since almost everybody has an opinion.

Many people believe, for example, that the poor are poor solely because of their own *personal* attributes (laziness, lack of ambition, lack of education, irresponsibility, etc.). This opinion, it is important to note, has an important implication: if the poor are wholly responsible for their poverty, this suggests that the poor (from individuals to whole countries) should be left largely on their own to solve the problem of poverty. That is, the poor themselves must create the conditions for their own transformation, which implies, in turn, that any efforts by others to help them may only exacerbate their situation of poverty rather than improve it. This is because helping the poor only "enables" them, whereas forcing them to fend for themselves may lead them to be creative or to work harder or better. The old saying "Give a man a fish and he eats for day, but teach him to fish, and he eats for a lifetime" loosely fits into this line of analysis. In the case of this saying, though, some initial help is provided, but it is still up to the poor to fix their situations of poverty. I should emphasize that this "theory of poverty" is not one to which many scholars subscribe. However, it is a common and even commonsensical argument (at least to some), and one that happens to operate at the micro or individual level.

There are, as just suggested, other types of individual-level arguments on poverty. One of these revolved around welfare reform in the United States during the late 1980s and 1990s. In contrast to the foregoing example, the argument on welfare reform centered squarely on rational choice principles. Proponents of welfare reform, which included both conservatives and liberals, opposed the then-current domestic welfare program for poor people—Aid to Families with Dependent Children (AFDC)—because, it was argued, it made it *irrational* for poor people to do those things that would allow them to break the cycle of poverty that typified their lives. Critics contended, in particular, that AFDC created a perverse system of incentives: it "rewarded" poor people who chose *not* to work full-time, attend college or trade school, have fewer children (or no children at all), or do anything that might help them achieve financial independence and prosperity. In this view, there was a government-based solution, but one designed to change the decisionmaking (or strategic) environment in which poor people made choices. Specifically, the welfare reform movement in the 1990s was premised on "encouraging economic self-sufficiency and more responsible decisions concerning childbearing and family formation" (Weaver 2014, p. 360). The result was the creation of an alternative program called Temporary Assistance for Needy Families (TANF), which was signed into law by President Bill Clinton in 1996 (TANF was part of the Personal Responsibility and Work Opportunity Act). While the details of the welfare reform process are interesting, the more important point is this: proponents of welfare reform, on the surface, seemed to "blame the victims" for making bad choices, but they also recognized that the choices poor people made were not necessarily based on (negative) personal attributes; instead, the choices were based on a rational calculation of costs and benefits. It is also important to recognize, however, that an argument about "the poor" in a rich country such as the United States, and arguments about the poor in poverty-stricken countries, are not fully transferable, a point that will become clear later in this chapter.

Other arguments about poverty take a more "radical" slant. Most of these stress the exploitation, greed, and massive inequality that characterize contemporary capitalism. In this view, the cause of poverty is not to be found in the decisions that the poor make (or their lack of skills, education, or willingness to work hard), but in the positions they occupy within the broader economic structure (or system) at both the national and international levels. A particularly popular—albeit not necessarily sophisticated—version of the radical argument is that the poor are, essentially, helpless victims of a corrupt and evil system. This does not mean that no people (or countries) will ever escape from poverty—there are always a few—but these cases represent exceptions to an otherwise ironclad rule. Indeed, if the exceptions actually became the rule, then we would be witnessing a breakdown or collapse of capitalism as we know it. It is for this reason that radicals see the collapse of the existing structures of capitalism as a *good* thing (this is one reason they are called radicals); for it is only through the collapse of capitalism that genuine equality and social justice can be achieved for the majority of the world's population. This is what Karl Marx predicted would happen a long time ago. The perception that capitalism only seems to be getting stronger (notwithstanding the global financial crisis of 2009), however, has led many people to conclude not only that Marx was wrong about the eventual demise of capitalism but also that his entire argument was fundamentally flawed. We will see, in the discussion that follows, that this is a difficult argument to sustain.

There are several other arguments that we could explore. For present purposes, it is enough to understand that disagreements about the causes of poverty run very, very deep. In this regard, my intention is not to resolve the debate in this relatively short chapter. Instead, this chapter is designed to help you apply the theoretical and methodological tools discussed in Part 1 so that you can learn how to better evaluate existing arguments and, more importantly, to develop your own answer to the question "Why are poor countries poor?" The bulk of this chapter will address the question from the rational choice, cultural, and structural perspectives, respectively. As a preface to this discussion, let me begin with two general points. First, it is important to understand that the discussions that follow are not meant to be comprehensive. I can only present relatively thin slices of each research tradition, since all three are not only broad but also extremely diverse. In other words, there is no single explanation of poverty using the principles of rational choice, nor is there just one cultural or structural interpretation of poverty. To give each research tradition full justice, this chapter would have to be much longer than it already is (entire books have been written on the topic and usually from just one perspective). At the same time, the discussion that follows, I believe, provides a useful representation of each research tradition. When necessary, too, I have included a few slices from the various research traditions, to give you a better sense of important disagreements and debates. Second, it is necessary to say something about the concept of poverty itself, a topic that deserves a slightly extended discussion.

Defining Poverty

At first glance, poverty seems like a clear-cut concept. The most common definitions of poverty center on its material aspects, which makes intuitive sense. Accordingly, poverty is usually defined as the lack of sufficient resources to meet the *basic* necessities of life. Thus, a person without enough food to survive, without access to clean water or to adequate shelter, is considered to be living in poverty. This notion of poverty has the added advantage of being relatively easy to measure. All one needs to do is figure out what minimum level of income is necessary to meet basic needs. Of course, this is easier said than done. Nonetheless, the **World Bank** has developed a measurement that is widely used today, not only by national governments and international organizations, but also by nongovernmental organizations, activists, and scholars. The World Bank measurement is expressed as a simple dollar amount—specifically, $1.25 a day per individual—which is adjusted to account for differences in purchasing power parity (PPP) across countries.

If we accept this figure, however, it raises a number of questions, especially in light of the foregoing discussion on poverty in the United States. One of the more salient questions is this: If $1.25 is the standard, are there any poor people in countries such as the United States? After all, even the poorest people in the United States—including those with absolutely no income—have access to resources from the government programs (e.g., TANF) or charity organizations that provide much more than $1.25 a day in purchasing power. For the working poor in the United States, the issue becomes even muddier. The federal minimum wage is $7.25 per *hour* (as of 2015), and many states have higher minimums. Thus, a $7.25 minimum-wage worker in the United States, working eight hours, makes forty-six times (4,640 percent) more than the World Bank standard for poverty. In the minds of some, this means there are no truly poor people in the United States. Just consider the following title from an article in *Forbes* magazine: "By Global Standards There Are No American Poor; All in the US Are Middle Class or Better" (Worstall 2014). Others have pointed out that most people classified as poor in the United States not only have plenty to eat, but also have televisions, cable or satellite service, refrigerators, air conditioners, computers, Internet service, and the like (Rector and Sheffield 2011). At the same time, still others contend that, in assessing poverty in wealthy countries, a different standard is necessary. Indeed, most analysts, policymakers, and academics presuppose that poverty in wealthy countries differs markedly from poverty in the poorest countries. This has led to a concept known as **relative poverty**, which is based on the idea that poverty can only be assessed relative to the standard of living within a particular area (for a discussion of this view, see Organization for Economic Cooperation and Development 2001). (The question of how to define poverty in wealthy countries is more complex than indicated here; for a basic overview, see Edsall 2015).

The debate over relative poverty serves to highlight an important point: definitions of key concepts should not be taken for granted. It also highlights the fact that generic concepts, such as poverty, often need to be disaggregated. This chapter has already introduced two separate concepts of poverty, one that defines poverty in terms of basic needs, and one that defines poverty in relative terms. The former definition is most commonly referred to as **absolute poverty** (also referred to as extreme poverty), and it is absolute poverty that is the focus of this chapter. Unfortunately, this still does not settle the issue. Critics of the World Bank's standard of $1.25 a day, in particular, argue that reducing poverty to a single statistic is dangerously misleading. One salient and policy-related problem is that this encourages people (governments, international organizations, and others) to conflate absolute poverty with poverty in general. In a 2015 report, for example, the World Bank itself noted that, in 2011, the number of people living in extreme or absolute poverty had been reduced to under 1 billion, which represented about 15 percent of the world's population (down from 1.25 billion and 19 percent in 2008). In the same paragraph, the Bank predicted that the number of people living in poverty (as opposed to extreme or absolute poverty) would reach less than 10 percent by 2020 (2015a, p. xi). While this might seem to be a harmless slip (or a simple editing decision to avoid repetition), it is all too easy to assume that a dramatic reduction in absolute poverty means that poverty, in general, is disappearing. Moreover, the dramatic reduction in absolute poverty begs the question "Where have all these poor people gone?" One conclusion is that they have left poverty altogether. Unfortunately, that's clearly not the case: most have simply moved from one arbitrarily defined category ($1.25 per day) to the next one up. They are still very poor. Indeed, simply earning a penny more per day, $1.26, is enough to move someone out of the category of absolute poverty.

There is, critics assert, another, more conceptual and fundamental problem with the World Bank's standard. Put simply, poverty measured strictly in terms of income provides only a single and overly narrow metric. It is a metric, moreover, that not only fails to "capture the multiple disadvantages that contribute to poverty," but also does not correlate strongly with "trends in other basic variables such as child mortality, primary school completion rates, or undernourishment" (Oxford Poverty & Human Development Initiative 2015b, p. 2). In other words, in considering how to define poverty, it is critical to understand that there are multiple dimensions. One important dimension is, of course, the capacity to meet basic material needs, but other, equally important dimensions include health, education, employment opportunities, sanitation, and political empowerment, as well as freedom from violence, shame, and oppression. To account for these multiple dimensions of poverty, several alternative definitions and measurements have been proposed. One of the first of these, albeit not focused on poverty per se, is the **Human Development Index** (HDI), first introduced in 1990 by the United Nations Development Programme (UNDP). In 2010, a subsidiary measure—this one centered specifically on poverty—was launched by the UNDP, in partnership with the Oxford Poverty & Human Development Initiative (OPHI), known as the Multidimensional Poverty Index (MPI).

The details of each index, while important, need not be covered here. Instead, it is enough to reiterate that they both offer a comprehensive and composite measurement that, at least in part, is explicitly designed to address the limitations of the World Bank's unidimensional income-based metric. (For further discussion of the HDI, see UNDP 2014; for the MPI, see OPHI 2015a.)

Importantly, the application of the MPI, compared to the $1.25-a-day measurement, can yield very different results both generally and for specific countries. According to the MPI, for instance, 2.2 billion people live in multidimensional poverty or near-poverty, a number that is significantly higher than those who live on $1.25 a day or less (UNDP 2014, p. 41). In addition, according to the UNDP, at the country level, "the proportion of multidimensionally poor people is usually higher than the proportion living on less than $1.25 a day," although it depends on the country. "In Cambodia," the UNDP noted, "47 percent of the population were in multidimensional poverty in 2010, but only 19 percent lived on less than $1.25 a day. But in Brazil and Indonesia income poverty is higher" (p. 41). Moreover, while in many countries both multidimensional poverty and income poverty have decreased, the rate of decline in MPI is generally slower.

From the preceding discussion, it should be apparent that how poverty is defined and measured has important implications. It should also be clear that there is more than one way to think about poverty. At the same time, most existing studies—at least the ones that inform the remainder of this chapter—have used, albeit often only tacitly, the World Bank's income-based version. It is for this very practical reason that the discussion that follows incorporates the $1.25-a-day standard as a practical basis for the analysis of poverty. At the same time, I will make use of other indicators, especially the MPI. Given the foregoing discussion, I understand that it may appear problematic, at best, to use the World Bank's one-dimensional metric at all, but this can be justified if used in conjunction with other, more comprehensive measurements. With all this in mind, it is time to see how the question "Why are poor countries poor?" can be answered using the three major theoretical approaches.

To Be Poor or Not to Be Poor?
A Rational Choice Perspective on Poverty

"People," a rationalist might assert, "do not choose to be poor."[1] Yet there are perhaps billions of poor people and, by extension, dozens of poor countries and societies. The question, then, is why does this happen? Why, despite a seemingly unarguable interest in becoming more prosperous, do people (and their societies) remain mired in poverty over long stretches of time? Even more to the point, why are so many societies poor when the route to economic prosperity is well known and well trodden—for example, why do poor countries not simply do the same things that now-rich countries did when they first started to become wealthier? To answer these questions, it is necessary to go back to the basic principles of rational choice. The very first principle in rational choice, of course, is that all of us, including the extremely poor, are rational or self-interested actors. This leads to a simple deductive statement: the very poor behave in a manner meant to make themselves better off. Saying this, however, just raises more questions. For, on the surface, it makes little sense to say that the extremely poor are making rational decisions. How can decisions that leave an individual utterly destitute—day after day, year after year, decade after decade—possibly be rational? Aren't the very poor, in fact, choosing to be poor? Answering this second set of questions also requires that we go back to the same basic principles. Remember, it is not merely self-interest that is important. That is only a starting point. In applying rational choice, the self-interest of the key actors must be specified, which usually means considering the context or strategic environment in which decisions are being made. Applying rational choice principles also requires an understanding that individually rational decisions do not always lead to optimal outcomes, either for the individual or for the organization, community, or society of which that individual is a part. Thus, to properly answer the question "Why are poor countries poor?" it is necessary to delve a little deeper.

Unintended Consequences:
Individual Rationality, Collective Irrationality

To explain national poverty, rationalists often begin with the assumption that a critical disjuncture exists between what is socially or collectively good and what is individually advantageous (Bates 1988b). The key question, therefore, is why this disjuncture exists. The answer, to some rationalists, is fairly simple. Again, we need to begin by considering the interests or preferences of the key actor or actors. If this actor is a poor person living in conditions of absolute poverty (these conditions constitute a critical part of the poor person's strategic environment), then the overarching self-interest of that poor person is quite clear: personal (and familial) *survival*. The reason is easy to see. In a very poor country, the poor must be concerned with having enough to eat, if not every single day, then every week or every month. If they lack the resources they need to buy or, in the case of poor farmers, to grow enough food, they will, bluntly put, die. Even in less dire circumstances, they must be concerned with their continued or longer-term ability to earn an income. If they become injured, sick, or just too old, and cannot afford food, medicine, and other necessities of life, then again, they will die. Note, in this regard, that the primary self-interest of a poor person, living in conditions of absolute poverty, is not the same as the self-interest of a poor person living in a richer country. The poor in the United States, for example, generally need not be concerned with having enough food to survive from week to week or month to month; more formally, the poor in the United States face a dramatically different incentive structure compared to the poor in a very poor country.

With this starting point, the rest of the analysis falls into place fairly easily. To wit, the disjuncture (between what is socially or collectively good, and what is individually advantageous), stems from an individual's need to ensure short- and longer-term survival, on the one hand, and the requirements for national economic growth, on the other hand. Samuel Popkin (1988) explained it this way: in very poor countries, certain economic activities carry a very high risk, especially to those individuals with little or no margin for error. Most individuals (in his study, Popkin focused on peasants engaged in agricultural production) in these destitute countries will therefore engage in practices that minimize their risk of failure—thus ensuring their chances of survival—but this may also result in relatively low levels of productivity. In this view, behavior that "minimizes risk of (personal) failure" is rational and efficient from an individual standpoint, but this same behavior is typically woefully inefficient from the standpoint of the village (and larger economy). A good illustration of this is "the widespread practice of scattering plots [which was once] . . . viewed by many economists as irrational" (p. 248). According to Popkin, however, "the scattering of plots substantially reduces the maximum damage that small local disasters or climatic variations can cause in a given season: mildew or rot in one area of the village, an errant herd, exceptionally light or heavy rains, and similar mini-disasters will be less likely to wipe out a peasant's entire crop when fields are scattered." At the same time, Popkin continued, "scattering also cuts the maximum yield per farmer and for the village as a whole" (p. 248). In other words, the practice of scattering plots represents a trade-off: greater personal security (which, again, maximizes the chances of survival) versus lower productivity and less accumulated wealth. The result at the collective (or national) level, however, is stagnant or very slow economic growth.

Poverty and the rationality of having too many children. The practice of scattering plots, it is important to emphasize, is only one example—albeit a very important one—of how individually rational choices can lead to suboptimal (or bad) collective outcomes in poor countries. Another good example has to do with the relationship between family size and poverty. To the casual observer, there appears to be a strong causal relationship between these two factors: that is, larger family size leads directly to a higher rate of poverty. A cursory look at the basic statistics seems to bear this out. In 2014, the countries with the highest fertility rates (defined as the average number of children a woman gives birth to during her childbearing years), and therefore the largest family size, included, in order: Niger, Mali, Burundi, Somalia, Uganda, Burkina Faso, Zambia, Malawi, Afghanistan, Angola, South Sudan, and Mozambique. In general, all these countries are also very poor, although there is a fairly wide degree of variation (see Figure 4.1 for details). To be sure, the foregoing statistics do not, by any means, prove a causal link, but scholars have used more rigorous quantitative analysis to demonstrate a much stronger relationship between family size and poverty. Aniceto Orbeta Jr. (2005), for example, used multiple regression analysis to discern the effects that additional children had on poor families in the Philippines. His conclusion was clear: additional children, on average, cause a substantial decline in household savings rates and levels, reduce the work participation and wage income of mothers, and reduce the proportion of school-age children attending school. Simply put, having more children makes poor families poorer.

Knowledge of the relationship between large families and increasing poverty, however, is not new. As noted earlier, to many casual observers,

Figure 4.1 Countries with the Highest Fertility Rates, per Capita GDP, and GDP per Capita Rankings, 2014

	Fertility Rate	GDP per Capita ($ adjusted for purchasing power)	GDP per Capita Rank (N = 187)
Niger	6.89	1,048	182
Mali	6.16	1,729	169
Burundi	6.14	911	183
Somalia[a]	6.08	600	197
Uganda	5.97	2,023	164
Burkina Faso	5.93	1,682	172
Zambia	5.76	4,064	135
Malawi	5.66	780	185
Afghanistan	5.43	1,937	165
Angola	5.43	7,203	118
South Sudan	5.43	2,280	161
Mozambique	5.27	1,174	181
Nigeria	5.25	6,031	124
Ethiopia	5.23	1,589	174

Sources: Fertility rate data from Central Intelligence Agency (CIA) 2014; GDP per capita data from International Monetary Fund (IMF) 2015, unless otherwise noted.

Note: a. GDP data for Somalia are for 2010 (estimated), from CIA 2014. The CIA's estimates cover a slightly larger number of countries: 198 compared to the 187 countries covered by the IMF.

the link is obvious. Scholars, too, have long understood the link. Writing almost two decades ago, Nancy Birdsall, a former executive vice president of the Inter-American Development Bank, had this to say:

> The poor and the less educated tend to have more children. As is to be expected in these poor households, spending per child on nutrition, health, and education declines with the number of children. Less spending on the children of the poor creates a new generation in which the number of unskilled workers grows faster than skilled workers, bringing down wages for the former and thus perpetuating the cycle. In societies with high population growth (Africa, for example), the education levels of mothers are a major determinant of fertility rates. As poorly educated mothers have many more children than their well-educated sisters, the cycle of high fertility and poor opportunities for their children continues, helping perpetuate inequality in their societies. (1998, p. 82)

So, again, we are left with an obvious question: "If having more children makes poor families poorer, then why do poor parents decide to have more children?" Certainly, one significant reason is a lack of access to birth control, which reflects a material constraint. On this point, Susheela Singh, Jacqueline Darroch, and Lori Ashford (2014) estimated that more than half of reproductive-age women in developing countries want to avoid pregnancy, but 26 percent of these women (228 million) are not using effective contraceptives. Conversely, the same set of statistics tells us that almost half of reproductive-age women in developing countries—perhaps 850–870 million women—do not want to avoid pregnancy. Thus, at best, the lack of access to birth control can provide a partial answer. To find the rest of the answer, from a rational choice perspective, it is simply a matter of returning to basic principles. Recall that the primary interest of poor people in very poor countries is survival. If so, it is relatively easy to discern the rationale for having lots of children. Children, for example, can provide an essential source of labor (in an agricultural setting) or become extra breadwinners in a poor urban area; they can also provide security when the parents are no longer able to work. Generally speaking, then, more children means more security. On this last point, it is worth noting, too, that having just one or a few children is risky. In poor countries, child mortality rates are high, and children may decide to "abandon" their parents later in life.

To repeat: poor parents living in poverty-stricken countries have lots of children for a variety of *self-interested* reasons. Yet, doing so, as Birdsall made clear, perpetuates a cycle of poverty for the individual, for her family, and for society as a whole. Of course, there may be a host of other reasons for high fertility in developing countries, but it is no accident, a rationalist will assert, that as a society becomes more prosperous (other things being equal), fertility tends to decline dramatically. South Korea is a prime example: in the 1960s (when Korea was still a very poor country), the average

South Korean woman gave birth to six children during her lifetime (Cho and Halm 1968); two generations later (by 2009), that number had decreased to a little over 1.25, giving Korea one of the lowest fertility rates in the world! During that same period, as I discuss in the following chapter, South Korea went through a period of tremendous economic growth. To be sure, there are other factors at play (one of which, quite significantly, was a more interventionist government), but it is almost certain that economic growth led to or created the basis for significant changes in the strategic environment—changes that reduced the incentive for parents to have very large families.

Breaking the Cycle of Poverty

If all this is true, another question arises: How can the cycle of poverty be broken? The general answer is easy enough to see: the incentive structure—which is shaped by the larger strategic environment—that leads poor people to make individually rational but collectively "irrational" decisions needs to change. On the surface, this creates a classic chicken-or-egg argument. That is, what comes first, changes in individual behavior, or changes in the incentive structure? In fact, there is no dilemma. For, while poor people may have very limited, or no, capacity to change the incentive structure on their own (largely because of material constraints), they are not the only actors whose decisions and actions we need to consider. Another very important set of actors is *political leaders*. Indeed, political leaders may be the most important actors in any analysis of the problem of national poverty, given the special position they occupy in society. For, unlike all other actors, political leaders control the preeminent political institution within any country, namely the state. And it is through the state that the incentive structure facing poor people can be reshaped. In other words, the state gives a political leader the organizational capacity to fundamentally change the strategic environment. If, more concretely, poor people engage in economically inefficient practices because they lack security, the state can "simply" provide greater security. Needless to say, this is much easier said than done. Still, in practice, many (albeit not all) rationalists argue that there is no alternative to the state.

Rational Choice and the State

From the rational choice perspective, the importance of the state is hard to exaggerate. Yet it is not at all clear why the state should be assigned such a central role. After all, as Ronald Reagan famously asserted in his 1981 inaugural address, "Government is *not* the solution to our problem; government *is* the problem." By "government," Reagan was referring to the national government—the state; and by "our problem," Reagan was referring primarily to the economic woes the United States was facing at the time.

Although he spoke those words almost four decades ago, his statement still resonates strongly today. Many people, in fact, including many economists and business leaders, are convinced that the state is a major, even *the* major, impediment to dynamic economic growth. But context (or history) matters: the context within which the United States operated in the 1980s, or today for that matter, is very different from the context in which the poorest countries operate. In particular, very poor countries are generally missing or have only partially created the essential building blocks of a national economy, those things that people in wealthier countries (including the United States in the 1970s and 1980s) take for granted, namely **public goods** and **infrastructure**.

The importance of public goods and infrastructure. Public goods and infrastructure are unequivocally essential for economic growth. Consider what would happen to a national economy missing such infrastructural goods as roads, port and rail systems, schools, power lines, and so on. Even more, consider what would happen to the economy and society in the absence of any national security and domestic order (classic examples of public goods). Actually, we don't have to use our imaginations at all. All we need to do is to find a country with limited infrastructure and a lack of essential public goods, and then look at that country's economic situation. While there are many candidates, the Central African Republic fits the bill quite nicely. Its infrastructure is severely underdeveloped. The country has no railroads, a mere 364 miles (587 kilometers) of paved roads out of 15,535 miles of roads, and only a single international airport with deteriorated runways. Despite recent efforts to improve its energy sector, the country's power infrastructure remains "in an embryonic state" with total transmission capacity of 39 megawatts, one of the lowest in **sub-Saharan Africa** (Domínguez-Torres and Foster 2011, p. 24). In addition, there is no sewage network in the country, and just 1.4 percent of the population has access to the Internet, which is less than half the usage rate among all low-income countries combined (all statistics cited in Domínguez-Torres and Foster 2011). Politically and socially, the country has an extremely unstable and insecure domestic environment: since 1992, there have been multiple coups against the central government, the most recent of which took place in 2013 when rebels seized power in the capital and installed a new leader, Michel Djotodia (in January 2014, Djotodia resigned and some small measure of political stability has since been realized, in part through a United Nations peacekeeping mission). Political instability has made it difficult for the government to create and maintain the most basic public goods, especially public security and justice, public health, and education (in the Central African Republic, the mean length of schooling is a paltry 3.5 years).

Not surprisingly, the Central African Republic is among the poorest countries on the planet, and by some measures, it is *the* poorest country.

According to the Multidimensional Poverty Index, in 2014, fully 92 percent of the country's population was either living in poverty or very close to poverty. More precisely, according to the United Nations Development Programme, 76.3 percent of its population was multidimensionally poor, while another 15.7 percent was near multidimensional poverty (UNDP 2014). The Central African Republic also had the lowest per capita GDP in the world in 2014, at approximately $607 when adjusted for purchasing power: this is an astoundingly low figure, as it translates into a daily income of just $1.66 for every man, woman, and child in the country.

While the answer may seem obvious for a country in such sad shape as Central African Republic, a question still must be asked: If public goods and infrastructure are so important, why don't poor countries just create them? That certainly seems like the "rational thing to do." There are two major and interconnected answers to the question just posed, with one, as already noted, being obvious and the other much less so. The more obvious answer is that some countries lack the resources to create public goods and infrastructure. Just as a poor person may not be able to pay for a child to attend school or see a doctor, the leader of a poor country may not have the money to build educational and healthcare systems—or roads, rail and port systems, a communications network, an electrical grid, and so on. Economic constraints are, as we have seen, a very important part of rational choice analysis: don't forget the role of material constraints! The less obvious answer, however, is equally, and maybe even more important. For it tells us *why*—even when there are sufficient resources scattered throughout a country (or available internationally), *and* leaders who desire to use those resources effectively—public goods and infrastructure are still not created. Fortunately, rationalists have a ready explanation. The answer begins with what is known as the **free-rider problem**.

The Free-Rider Problem

In everyday conversation, no one wants to be called a "free-rider." A free-rider is a moocher, even a beggar, and few people want to be around such a person. In rational choice theory, however, free-riding is eminently rational behavior: given the opportunity, *we are all free-riders*. So how does this relate to public and infrastructural goods? To find the answer, we first need some basic definitions, beginning with the notion of a public good. Simply put, a public good is (1) anything that, once created, is available for use by anyone; and (2) something that can be "consumed" or used by one individual without reducing its availability to others. More technically, a public good is nonexcludable and nonrivaled. Infrastructure, while often confused with public goods, refers to "basic facilities, services, and installations needed for the functioning of a community or society, such as transportation and communications systems, water and power lines, and public institutions including schools, post offices, and prisons" (Lukasik, Greenberg, and Goodman 1998, p. 11). One difference between a public good and infrastructure is clear. Once, say, an electrical grid is created, people can be charged for the direct use of electricity. Nonetheless, the more general benefits of having an electrical system do tend to flow to everyone within a particular society regardless of their past or current contributions. Practically speaking, this means that infrastructure has a nonexcludable element. Even more, without certain public goods, especially public security, even those who might want to invest in an infrastructural project will be (rationally) afraid to do so for fear of having their investment destroyed or expropriated by "men with guns."

It is the nonexcludable character of public goods and, to a lesser extent, infrastructure that creates problems, particularly for poor countries. Simply put, while public goods and infrastructure are unequivocally beneficial to everyone, it is irrational for individuals to contribute *voluntarily* to their creation. Individuals, in other words, will seek to free-ride *unless* they can be convinced to do otherwise. As a result, nothing gets created. But how can rational actors be "convinced to do otherwise"? The answer, again, is clear: they must be forced or compelled to do so through some form of collective-action mechanism (Kaul 2000), which refers to any sort of tool that can be used to get a group of individuals to act in their common interest. In almost all countries the primary collective-action mechanism is the state. From here, it is a very short step to understanding the main point of the rational choice explanation of poverty, which is simply this: poor countries are poor because they lack a strong and effective state.

The logic is simple. The state or national government is the preeminent public institution in any modern society, and it is only through a *public* institution that many free-rider or **collective-action** problems can be resolved (i.e., providing public and infrastructural goods). This is because it is only a public institution, such as the state, that has the authority and the capacity to compel whole populations to (involuntarily) contribute to the creation of such goods, typically beginning with the imposition and effective collection of taxes. Only the state, in short, can overcome the free-rider problem. Once this is done, the state will have the resources to create public goods, build the infrastructure, and otherwise create a national framework for sustained and productive economic activity. The state can, in this regard, reshape the strategic environment for the poor; it can create incentives for more economically productive activity. This takes us back to the larger point: it is through a strong, capable state that national poverty can be overcome.

At the same time, rational choice scholars clearly recognize the absolute importance of the (capitalist) market. A well-functioning market creates the private incentives necessary—within society or economy more generally—for sustained and dynamic economic growth to take place. Nonetheless, the rationalist argument presented here posits that markets alone cannot guarantee the development of the public and infrastructural goods necessary for national development—this is a type of **market failure**. What is most needed, in cases of market failure, is political leadership *necessarily* backed up by strong organizational capacity and the "structuring of coercion through . . . public institutions": this set of political elements represents integral parts of the development process (Bates 1988b, p. 242). Yet this is precisely what many poor countries lack.

The State as Solution or Problem?

As suggested in the beginning of this discussion on rational choice, the assertion that poor countries are poor because they lack a strong and effective state is, in some respects, counterintuitive. "Look around the world," many skeptics would say, "and you'll find dozens of corrupt leaders and governments that have done nothing but run their national economies into the ground. The solution is not more government, but less government." This is generally the position of **neoliberal** economists, many of whom subscribe to a variant of rational choice called public choice. Needless to say, advocates of public choice or other schools of liberal economic thought are unconvinced by the need for a strong state; some even dispute the existence of market failures. Unfortunately, this debate is too complex and longstanding to settle here. Suffice it to say that the argument presented earlier represents a "thicker" version of rational choice, which means, in part, that it takes into account the often underdeveloped institutional capacity and seriously deficient authority of the state in poor countries. At the same time, even this thick rational argument recognizes that states can be and are frequently *the* problem, rather than the solution. Comparative checking tells us that this is the case: when one looks at a range of poor countries, it is not at all difficult to find numerous examples of corrupt, unprincipled, and greedy state leaders (and, really, anyone associated with the state, including the police, military, and local officials) who use their positions of power and authority to "line their own pockets," while allowing their countries to fall into economic decrepitude. Yet, recognizing that the state is often the reason poor countries remain poor does not, by any means, rebut the main argument.

Poverty and Corruption: A Rationalist Perspective

It is clear, rationalists admit, that many of the people who command or aspire to command public institutions do not always act in the interests of their country as a whole. Indeed, many literally rob their countries of scarce and extremely valuable resources. Robert Bates (1988a) made this point very clearly in his analysis of agricultural policies in Africa, where political corruption has been a pervasive problem. Bates argued that governments in Africa are driven to spend in ways that are politically rational but that often impose economic costs of "sufficient magnitude to retard development" (1988b, p. 244). As Bates explained it:

> A major reason why politically rational choices are not economically optimal is that expenditures that represent economic costs might well be regarded by politicians as political benefits. Thus price distortions may create opportunities for rationing; although it is economically inefficient, rationing allows commodities to be targeted to the politically faithful. And government regulation may transform markets into political organizations, ones in which too few transactions take place at too high a cost but ones that can be used to build organizations supportive of those in power. (1988b, p. 244)

Bates and others, I should emphasize, provide an even stronger explanation for why national development (or why escaping from national poverty) is so hard to achieve, despite the fact that most individuals in poor countries—from peasants, to small-scale merchants, to the political elite—would *all* benefit from living in a richer country. To wit, those individuals who have the power to implement public policies that can promote national development often have no incentive to do so. In fact, pursuing socially beneficial goals is typically irrational, since it is likely to mean erosion or complete loss of political power—a point Bates made very clearly. Thus the issue is not one of corruption per se (we find corruption everywhere in the world); rather it is about explaining individual behavior within a specific incentive structure, which itself represents a situation of equilibrium (in a situation of equilibrium, no one—or at least no one with the capacity to meaningfully impact policy decisions—has an incentive to make different decisions). This situation of equilibrium, I might note, will be particularly stable if the political leadership has access to economic resources that reduce the necessity to create a strong national economy. These resources can come from other countries or international institutions in the form of foreign aid and loans; or they may be domestic in origin, such as large oil reserves. With a steady source of income not dependent on the efforts of the people the political leaders ostensibly govern, the incentive for corruption is maximized (see Figure 4.2 for an example).

To resolve the problem of corruption requires that we have a clear-eyed understanding of its *underlying rationality,* as opposed to thinking of corruption as a product of personal venality, which then might be solved by simply installing "virtuous" leaders. From a rational choice perspective, of course, virtue is only likely if virtuous behavior equates to self-interested behavior. If virtuous behavior undermines the self-interest of the leader, then it does not matter if that leader is Mother Teresa or Mahatma Gandhi: no matter how virtuous the individual, corruption will emerge if the strategic environment makes corruption the rational choice. This explanation, however, does not necessarily mollify those who are critical of *any* government

---

Figure 4.2 Corruption in Equatorial Guinea

Equatorial Guinea is a small country located in central Africa, with a population of just over 778,000 people. It also happens to be one of the world's top thirty oil producers. On paper, then, Equatorial Guinea is not poor: the per capita income in 2014 was $33,768, more than Spain, Israel, and South Korea, and just behind New Zealand. Yet, according to the World Bank, the percentage of people living in poverty (in 2006) was 76.8 percent (other sources put the poverty rate at 60 percent; the disparity is due to lack of solid data, which is why the country is not included in the MPI). The reason for the tremendous degree of poverty in the midst of great wealth is clear: corruption. Equatorial Guinea is one of the most corrupt countries in the world, according to Transparency International, and has been ruled by the same man for over thirty-five years, Teodoro Obiang Nguema Mbasogo. One indication of the level of corruption came from a court case in the United States targeting President Obiang's son, Teodorín, who currently serves as vice president. Court documents showed that, while Teodorín had a reported salary of less than $100,000 a year, he had amassed a fortune of at least $300 million, including a $30 million mansion in Malibu, California (Phelps 2014). Teodorín settled with the US government for $30 million. It is significant that it was the US government, and not the people of Equatorial Guinea, that was able to hold the country's leadership to account, even if only partially. The people of Equatorial Guinea, unfortunately, have no recourse: the wealth of the country is beyond their control, and their ability to challenge the government is essentially nil. Thus, there is no rational incentive for the president, his son, and their allies to change their corrupt behavior.

---

intervention in the economy, but it at least helps us understand that, in rational choice, apparent contradictions can be relatively easily overcome using the same deductive logic. We know, however, that rational choice is not the only game in town. Another range of explanations can be found in the cultural tradition.

Cultural Explanations of Poverty: The Bad and the Good

Cultural explanations of poverty begin with the assumption that culture is more than just a reflection of economic or political forces. This is a significant assumption, for *if* culture is merely derivative of other, more basic forces, then there would be little reason to begin with or base any analysis on culture itself. Assuming that culture is more than derivative, however, does not mean that it needs to be considered completely autonomous; few, if any, culturalists would go this far. Instead, cultural theorists tend to posit a highly interactive or mutually constitutive relationship among culture, politics, and economy (in this context, the term *mutually constitutive* means, most simply, the cultural factors shape the economy and politics, and vice versa). Max Weber, for example, adopted this position, at least tacitly, when he argued that culture was a significant—but not the only—factor in the rise of Western Europe as the world's first center of capitalism. On this point, Weber surmised that Europeans, notably Protestants, had a particular affinity for capitalism, which was represented in his idea of the "Protestant ethic." (See Figure 4.3 for a discussion of Weber's argument.)

Not surprisingly, Weber's treatment of culture had a major impact on early studies of economic development, especially among US scholars. Beginning in the 1950s, US academics generated a wealth of literature about the cultural roots of "underdevelopment" or of continuing poverty throughout the world. Although other factors, such as a lack of capital, inadequate technology, or low educational levels, were certainly not ignored, studies during this period zeroed in on the cultural (and also institutional and organizational) shortcomings of poorer countries. Thus, according to early cultural theorists (I apply the label very loosely here), explaining why poor countries were poor was as easy as pie: they lacked the appropriate cultural values and practices that made sustained economic development possible. Unfortunately, these early culture-based analyses were, to put it bluntly, crude and irredeemably ethnocentric: most were premised on the assumption that economic development was an *evolutionary, progressive,* and

---

Figure 4.3 Max Weber, the Protestant Ethic, and the Rise of Capitalism

Weber argued that the relatively rapid development of capitalism in Western Europe was due, in no small measure, to the relatively autonomous emergence of Protestantism and rational bureaucratic organization. Specifically, Weber argued—in his well-known work *The Protestant Ethic and the Spirit of Capitalism* ([1930] 1958)—that the tenets of Protestantism played an instrumental role in (1) legitimating individualistic profit seeking by making it a duty willed by God; (2) justifying capitalist exploitation and work discipline by making conscientious labor a sacred duty; and (3) creating a cultural climate in which poverty was seen as a result of individual failing. More generally, Weber suggested that Protestantism contributed to capitalist development by making a "new man"—rational, ordered, diligent, and productive (Landes 2000, p. 12). Weber, I should emphasize, was not saying that Protestantism was necessary for capitalism to survive and thrive, only that there was a particularly strong and mutually constitutive relationship—or affinity—between the two forces. In this view, history is obviously quite important, crucial even. For Weber clearly saw the particular social, political, and cultural context of Western Europe as integral to an explanation of why capitalism originated and thrived there before it did anywhere else in the world. (Here, too, we can see how comparing Europe as a region to other regions of the world would be necessary to support this argument.)

phased process (Comte 1964; Coleman 1968; and Rostow 1960), which was characterized by a progression from a primitive or lower stage of development to an advanced or modern stage of development. Needless to say, Western Europe and the United States represented the most advanced stage (Tipps 1976), and most of the rest of the world represented varying levels of "primitiveness." This original cultural view is referred to as modernization or (classical) **modernization theory**.[2] (Note: I use the term *classical* because modernization theory has undergone many changes over the years and also because there are several versions of modernization theory or modernization, which overlap but also differ from one another; in Chapters 6 and 7, for example, I discuss different versions of modernization.)

According to modernization theory, it was possible for poor countries to follow in the footsteps of the West, but *only* by ridding themselves of their supposedly debilitating and "backward" cultures and embracing modern, Western values. There was little hint, in these early studies, of the complex, fluid, and intersubjective nature of culture; culture was treated as if it was a fixed object that either had to be thrown out entirely, or stubbornly held on to with no chance of change.[3] This description is, admittedly, exaggerated, but hyperbole is sometimes necessary to ensure that the basic point is clear: *not all cultural arguments are good.* Indeed, many cultural arguments—both in the past and today (as noted in the previous chapter)—are downright bad, and a beginning student of comparative politics needs to know the difference. However, even as modernization theory was at the height of its popularity and influence (in the 1950s and 1960s), other scholars using a cultural approach were hard at work developing alternative perspectives. One of the most prominent of these early cultural theorists was Oscar Lewis, whose work on "slum cultures"—or cultures of poverty—in Puerto Rico and Mexico provides an interesting and still very useful perspective on the relationship between culture and poverty. It is to Lewis's work that we turn next.

As a preface to this discussion, I should point out that Lewis's work generated a huge amount of controversy when it was first published—a controversy that continues to generate heated debate even today. In this regard, however, it is also worth noting that many have misread Lewis's argument, imputing political or ideological motives to Lewis and to his writings that were simply not there. It is therefore important to read the following section with great care—and with an open but *critical* mind.

Oscar Lewis's Cultures of Poverty

Cultural factors should always be examined—indeed, *must* be examined—within larger socioeconomic and political contexts. This is exactly what Lewis did in his analysis of poverty. I will come back to this point shortly, but first, let's get right to Lewis's basic argument, the essence of which can be simply stated: individuals who live in poor communities—that is, slums—typically (though not necessarily) share a common set of values, beliefs, and practices that distinguish them from the nonpoor. This distinctive set of values, beliefs, and practices constitutes a "way of life" or a *culture* (more accurately, a subculture), which Lewis dubbed a "culture of poverty." In Lewis's view, a culture of poverty is not merely descriptive of poverty-stricken communities but is also a key force that *reproduces* poverty in that community over time. In other words, Lewis attributed causal power to culture. It is also important to emphasize that, in Lewis's original formulation, cultures of poverty were spatially limited; that is, they did not envelop whole societies, but only relatively small and self-contained urban or rural slums within a larger society. This is why he used the phrase "subculture of poverty" rather than the more inclusive "culture of poverty."

Despite this caveat, Lewis also argued that the culture of poverty "transcends regional, rural-urban, and national differences and shows remarkable cross-national similarities in family structure, interpersonal relations, time orientation, value systems, and spending patterns." "These similarities," continued Lewis, "are examples of *independent* invention and convergence. *They are common adaptations to common problems*" ([1968] 2000, pp. 110–111, emphasis added). In this passage, Lewis made a number of strong claims. First, he stressed that cultures of poverty are *not* idiosyncratic, but instead are part of a much larger pattern that could, presumably, be found across a range of divergent cases. (Lewis, I might note, was tacitly employing a most different systems principle in his analysis. His central methodological strategy, however, was the case study; in his first major book on the subject [1959], for example, he examined five Mexican families—five case studies—in depth.) Second, Lewis contended that cultures of poverty are *made;* they are not, as modernization theory suggested, "genetic" or somehow preformed. Even more, Lewis was suggesting that cultures of poverty are thoroughly modern phenomena, which is precisely why they tend to be broadly similar across a range of "regional, rural-urban, and national differences." Lewis was also careful to point out, however, that there could be significant variations in cultures of poverty depending on local circumstances.

But what exactly are the "cross-national similarities" to which Lewis was referring? Surprisingly, perhaps, Lewis formulated a very long list of "some seventy interrelated social, economic, and psychological traits" ([1968] 2000, p. 111), which included the following: apathy, fatalism, hedonism (that is, pleasure-seeking), present-time orientation, extreme provincialism, illiteracy, a tendency toward authoritarianism, and a propensity for violence. One of the most crucial characteristics of the culture of poverty, however, was the "lack of effective participation and integration of the poor in the major institutions of the larger society" (p. 112). This translates into "a critical attitude toward some of the basic institutions of the dominant classes, hatred of the police, mistrust of government and those in high positions, and a cynicism that extends even to the church" (p. 112). One additional and very important characteristic, according to Lewis, is a very low level of organization—a level that rarely extends beyond the nuclear and extended family. More concretely, people with a culture of poverty are generally unwilling to take part in or to support organized, collective activities of any sort; they do not join unions or voluntary organizations or participate in social movements. Lewis was careful to point out that none of these traits *by itself* is distinctive of a culture of poverty; instead, it is their conjunction, their function, and their patterning that define the subculture.

It is precisely the characteristics enumerated in the foregoing paragraph that are responsible for the general misunderstanding of his argument. In particular, many critics of Lewis felt he was "blaming the poor" for their own conditions of poverty (Harvey and Reed 1996). But this was decidedly not Lewis's intention. Instead, he argued, quite emphatically, that the "culture of poverty is both an *adaptation* and a *reaction* of the poor to their marginal position in a class-stratified, highly individuated, *capitalist* society" ([1968] 2000, p. 111, emphasis added). To Lewis, the culture of poverty was an expression of agency, albeit one that was highly constrained by the (structural) power of capitalism. As Lewis explained it, "many of the traits of the culture of poverty can be viewed as attempts at local solutions for problems not met by existing institutions and agencies" (p. 111). Moreover, the link with capitalism (Lewis also singled out colonialism) is what marks the culture of poverty as an essentially modern, as opposed to traditional, phenomenon. It is in this respect, too, that a culture of poverty is "made"; that is, it is *produced* as a response to dominant social, political, and economic forces.

At the same time, Lewis argued that culture is not only an adaptation to a set of objective conditions and forces, for "once it comes into existence, it tends to perpetuate itself from generation to generation because of its effect on children" (p. 111). The subculture itself develops mechanisms for reproduction. The perpetuation (or reproduction) of these values, in turn, means that poor people may continue to engage in practices that keep them poor, even if the "objective conditions" of their poverty change. That is, even if the people in a culture of poverty have viable opportunities to increase their wealth and productive powers, they may continue to be poor because their values and beliefs systematically lead them to make the "wrong" decisions. Culture, therefore, is both cause and effect (or, first, an effect of the capitalist system, and second, a cause of continued poverty in poor communities).

To give a somewhat simplistic but still meaningful example to illustrate this point, consider a poor person who wins $500,000 in the lottery. This money could be used for a wide range of wealth-producing purposes: it could, for example, be invested in real estate or the stock market; it could be put into the bank; it could be used to start a small business; or it could be used to obtain a better education or vocational skills. Instead, the money is spent on expensive cars and clothes, more gambling, drugs, vacations, lavish gifts, and other nonproductive, or non-wealth-producing, activities. After a year or two, the money is all gone, and the "winner" is, once again, poor. (Figure 4.4 provides a real-world example.) Culturalists suggest that, to fully understand this behavior (and outcome), we need to take account of the cultural milieu in which the individual exists. For it is not just a matter of the person engaging in rational, self-interested behavior, as a rationalist might argue, but also of the impact of cultural forces on the individual's understanding of and behavior in the world. This cultural milieu, to repeat, *explains* why the individual would rather consume than invest, but the milieu itself is the product—or an effect—of broader forces in society and the world.

**Figure 4.4 Why Professional Athletes Go Broke:
A Cultural Explanation?**

A 2009 article in *Sports Illustrated* magazine (by Pablo Torre) detailed how (and why) many highly paid professional athletes "go broke." A good part of the explanation, according to the article, stemmed from extraordinarily poor investment decisions, costly divorces, unexpected injuries, lawsuits, and outright theft (by "trusted advisers"). In many cases, however, it is difficult to understand how millions of dollars could "disappear" without reference to the mind-set of the individual athlete.

A culturalist might argue that many athletes—a large number of whom come from relatively impoverished backgrounds (i.e., a culture of poverty)—share a similar set of ingrained values, attitudes, and practices that make it possible (even likely) to lose huge fortunes and return to a situation of (relative) poverty. Consider Kenny Anderson, a former National Basketball Association (NBA) guard, who filed for bankruptcy in 2005 after a career in which he earned approximately $60 million. Anderson, the article tells us, "bought eight cars and rang up monthly expenses of $41,000, including outlays for child support, his mother's mortgage and his own five-bedroom house in Beverly Hills, Calif.— not to mention $10,000 in what he dubbed 'hanging-out money.' He also regularly handed out $3,000 to $5,000 to friends and relatives."

Anderson was not alone. As a number of in-the-know financial advisers have noted, highly paid athletes often suffer from the "problem of the $20,000 Rolex." The problem is described this way: "If a 22-year-old spends $20,000 on a watch or on a big night out at a nightclub, that money is either depreciating or gone. 'But if they invested in a five percent, Triple A insured, tax-free municipal bond for a period of 30 years . . . that $20,000 would be worth $86,000 . . . [a]nd needless to say, they buy more than one $20,000 Rolex.'"

The conclusion that culture is both cause and effect, it is crucial to add, is also what sets Lewis's argument apart from structural explanations, which would assign almost no causal power to culture. It is also what separates Lewis's argument from the relatively crude assumptions of classical modernization theory. On the first point, the astute reader may have already noticed that Lewis's argument initially portrayed culture as derivative of other, more basic forces. In this view, the structural basis of his argument is easy to discern: he acknowledges the profound effects that capitalism has on communities and societies around the world. Capitalism is a quintessentially structural force, in Lewis's view. Unlike pure structuralists, however, he argued that, once created, subcultures of poverty take on a life of their own. These subcultures of poverty, in other words, become independent causal forces: they act to reproduce poverty for members of a community, generation after generation. Pure structuralists, on the other hand, do not ascribe any independent causal power to culture.

Many have misunderstood Lewis's argument, I should reemphasize, because they gloss over his discussion of how cultures of poverty are made, or why they exist in the first place. Again, cultures of poverty are products of—reactions and adaptations to—an oppressive, unequal, and class-stratified system of exploitation (i.e., capitalism). Lewis was not blaming the poor for their poverty; instead, if anything, he was blaming the overarching system in which they lived. At the same time, he wanted to explain why poverty could persist in communities (or whole countries) even when or if the objective conditions of exploitation and oppression changed. There is, of course, much more to Lewis's analysis than I have presented here. Indeed, his analysis is extraordinarily rich and thick in detail, and interested readers should peruse his two major works, *Five Families: Mexican Case Studies in the Culture of Poverty* (1959) and "A Study of Slum Culture: Backgrounds for *La Vida*" (1968).

Comparing Two Cultural Accounts

From the preceding discussion, the differences between Lewis's approach and the modernization approach should be readily apparent. In general, Lewis treated culture in a much more nuanced manner. He understood, for example, that culture is not a fixed object, and he understood that, even in a single society, there could be multiple cultures existing side by side. From a methodological perspective, moreover, Lewis also took history and especially *historical particularity* more seriously than did modernization theorists. Thus, although he acknowledged that the "culture of poverty" is an abstract, highly generalized concept (which is similar to the modernization view), Lewis was careful to note that the "profiles of the subculture of poverty will probably differ in systematic ways with the difference in the national cultural contexts of which they are a part" ([1968] 2000, p. 117).

In other words, not all "slum cultures" are alike, and sometimes the differences are significant. In a similar vein, Lewis was careful to distinguish between poverty itself and the culture of poverty. "In making this distinction," as he explained it,

> I have tried to document the broader generalization; namely, that it is a serious mistake to lump all poor people together, because the cause, the meaning, and the consequences of poverty vary considerably in different sociocultural contexts. There is nothing in the concept that puts the onus of poverty on the character of the poor. Nor does the concept in any way play down the exploitation and neglect suffered by the poor. Indeed, the subculture of poverty is part of the larger culture of capitalism, whose social and economic system channels wealth into the hands of a relatively small group and thereby makes for the growth of sharp class distinctions. (p. 117)

The distinction Lewis made between poverty and the culture of poverty is a critical one. For, within (classical) modernization theory, there is an unstated assumption that they are one and the same—that all poor societies by definition have cultures (i.e., a traditional or premodern culture) that both explain why they are poor to begin with and also why they stay poor. The distinction between poverty and a culture of poverty also tells us that, even in objective conditions of poverty, a culture can be "rich" in history, in traditions, in religious and ethical values, in education, in community organization, and so on. This "cultural richness," in turn, can help explain how and why some formerly poverty-stricken communities (or whole societies) are able to quickly transform into major industrial powers—an argument that could be applied to the East Asian countries, which I discuss in the next chapter. In sum, Lewis follows a path of cultural analysis that not only provides important and useful insights into the issue of poverty, but can also serve as a model for students and other researchers to emulate. Yet, even if you find Lewis's argument convincing, there is still one more research tradition to consider, and one that relegates cultural analysis to a clearly subordinate if not completely marginal position.

Keeping the Poor Down? Structural Explanations of Poverty

Rationalists, as we have seen, focus primarily on explaining poverty as a product of individual decisions made within a framework of institutional and material constraints. In this sense, rationalist arguments are not entirely nonstructural, as many critics claim. Indeed, Keith Dowding and Andrew Hindmoor (1997) argued that rational choice is as structural as it is individualistic. What they meant by this is that rational choice models functionally define actors in terms of the roles they play; actors, for example, are "voters," "capitalists," "workers," and so on. Structuralists are also very concerned with constraints; some might even say they are obsessed with them.

But, unlike rationalists, structuralists believe that the most severe constraints are *externally* imposed and sustained. This is a significant distinction, and one that has extremely important implications in explanations of national poverty. In particular, in rationalist explanations of poverty, it is generally assumed that the rational actions of the poor produce a suboptimal (or "bad") outcome at the collective level. However, it is possible for the framework of incentives to be dramatically altered, most commonly by a domestic actor using the power of the state. Thus it is possible for poor countries *themselves* to overcome their conditions of poverty. At least, this is the clear logic of the rationalist position.

Structural explanations of poverty, by contrast, might argue that it simply does not matter what most of the world's poor do or, by extension, what leaders of poor countries do. They are still going to be poor. Thus, poor people can save money for the future, learn new and valuable skills, invest wisely, have smaller families, and otherwise do everything they can to improve their lives. Similarly, political leaders can change the incentive structure; they can build infrastructure, create public goods, and encourage economically efficient behavior. Yet none of this will guarantee a better, more prosperous life—especially at the collective level. Why? The answer is clear: because the fate of individuals and of individual countries is primarily determined by forces and factors beyond their control. This is not to say that structural explanations completely rule out the possibility of a few "exceptions to the rule." Perhaps, through dint of hard work, wise and prudent decisions, and maybe a little luck, some *individuals* (mired in poverty) can achieve economic success and long-term prosperity, and perhaps even a few poor countries can. But—and this is a key assumption in structural analysis—what is true for the part is not necessarily true for the whole. That is, what one individual (or country) can achieve *cannot* be achieved by all at the same time. The basic reason for this is because capitalism as a system (or structure) depends, to a large extent, on the existence of the poor.

Poverty and Dependency

Structural explanations of national poverty began, for the most part, with the emergence of a school of thought known simply as dependency (see Figure 4.5 for a discussion of dependence). Early dependency researchers were particularly skeptical of modernization theory, especially its assumptions about the evolutionary and Eurocentric character of economic development. Indeed, as suggested earlier, most argued that it was precisely because of Europe that Latin America, Asia, Africa, and other parts of the world were poor. In 1957, for example, Paul Baran argued that the economic backwardness of India was caused by the "elaborate, ruthless, systematic despoilation of India by British capital from the very onset of British rule" (p. 145). According to Baran, India's postcolonial poverty was

---

Figure 4.5 What Is Dependence?

Theotonio Dos Santos, one of the leading scholars in the dependency school, defined dependence as "a situation in which the economy of certain countries is conditioned by the development and expansion of another economy to which the former is subjected" ([1970] 1996, p. 166). According to Dos Santos, dependence typically results in a condition of exploitation, but this does not mean that dependence necessitates a complete lack of economic growth or industrialization in the subordinate country. Continuing, he explained the situation this way: "The relation of interdependence between two or more economies, and between these and world trade, assumes the form of dependence when some countries (the dominant ones) can expand and be self-sustaining, while other countries (the dependent ones) can do this only as a reflection of that expansion, which can have either a positive or a negative effect on their immediate development" (p. 166). In sum, then, dependence represents a clear and unequivocal constraint on "subordinate" countries, but it does not imply absolute or permanent destitution.

---

due not only to Britain's plundering of the land but also to the destruction of India's native industrial base, the long-term distortion of its economy (for example, toward reliance on imported British goods, many of which were once produced more efficiently in India), and the disastrous reordering of Indian society. It is this last factor that is perhaps the most important. For, even though the other factors could be overcome (albeit with difficulty) once British rule ended, the creation of a new social and political order that was purposefully based on dividing Indian society—essentially pitting different groups against one another in a zero-sum game—was a legacy that has proven to be extraordinarily difficult to root out. The result, according to Jawaharlal Nehru, has been that "nearly all [of India's] . . . major problems have grown up during British rule: . . . the princes; the minority problem; various vested interests, foreign and Indian; the lack of industry and the neglect of agriculture; the extreme backwardness in the social services; and, above all, the tragic poverty of the people" (cited in Baran 1957, p. 149).

Baran's argument, I might point out, is compatible with rational choice explanations: that is, given the framework of incentives imposed on India by British colonial rule, the actions of individuals in different competing groups were eminently rational. In principle, then, India's postcolonial problems were amenable to internal or endogenous changes. This seemingly contradicts the structural position. Baran's argument, however, was one of the first studies in a now vast literature on dependency; it also tended to focus on the *enduring* significance of past colonial practices, which the modernization literature largely dismissed (if anything, modernization researchers saw colonialism as a good thing, since it exposed "primitive" societies to modern values). For this reason alone, Baran's study was an essential, but far from adequate, corrective. It was up to later dependency researchers to show that, just because formal colonialism was abandoned, the old structures of exploitation did not necessarily disappear. One of the most influential writers, in this regard, is André Gunder Frank ([1966] 1988), who argued that the past *and* current development of the West was and is premised on the underdevelopment of the third world—a notion that he summarized quite nicely in his pithy concept "the development of underdevelopment."

As Baran did, Frank focused on the historical significance of colonialism, but he pointed out that, from an economic perspective, it never really ended. For after the French, the British, the Spanish, and so on had withdrawn their governors, administrators, and soldiers, the transfer of national wealth from the former colonies to their erstwhile oppressors continued largely unabated through a constellation of what Frank called metropolis-satellite relationships. (Frank's concept of the metropolis and satellite was later supplanted by the similar notions of "core" and "periphery," which I will adopt for present purposes.) These core-periphery relationships, it is important to note, were said to exist not just between poor and rich countries at the international level, but also *within* the poor countries themselves, at the national, regional, and local levels.

The main function of these relationships was to *extract* economic surplus from the poorer, less powerful areas (the periphery) to the richer, more powerful areas (the core). The core accumulated, by far, the lion's share of surplus, while the periphery retained just enough to survive and reproduce itself—"reproduce" here is meant literally, as the core needed people in the periphery to have children, thereby increasing the number of future workers on a consistent basis. This process of extraction, it is important to note, required a local presence. That is, the political and economic elite in the core needed local allies to ensure the efficient extraction of economic surplus; after all, this was a coercive and often violent process that could not be done at arm's length. In return for their help, local allies were generously "paid" (that is, given positions of privilege and power); this led to the creation of a core within the periphery. Because the relationship between the core and the periphery was meant to be inherently unequal and exploitative, moreover, there was little to no chance that the poor would become more prosperous through a "trickle-down" process. Instead, just the opposite was the case, since the longer the relationship persisted, the more the basis for autonomous economic growth in the periphery was degraded, a point that is reflected in Frank's notion of the development of underdevelopment.

Other dependency scholars continued to work on and refine the concept of dependency. Among these was Theotonio Dos Santos ([1970] 1996), who argued that there are at least three distinct historical types of dependence:

colonial dependence, financial-industrial dependence, and technological-industrial dependence. According to Dos Santos, it is the third type of dependence (together with a fourth type, which he also simply called the "new dependence") that exemplifies the period after World War II (and up to the present day), when many former colonies began to experience a degree of industrial growth. To modernization researchers, the incipient industrialization of former colonies signified the beginning of a process toward full modernization and eventual parity with the West. To scholars such as Dos Santos, however, it signified a change in the dynamics and underlying nature of dependence, but not of dependence itself. Consider, for example, what is necessary to industrialize: poor countries require industrial machinery or capital goods and technology, which are produced only in the advanced capitalist economies. To purchase these goods and technology, however, poor countries need hard currency (typically US dollars, euros, or Japanese yen). Significantly, though, there are only two ways to obtain hard currency: to borrow (usually from Western financial institutions) and to export.

A Key Mechanism of Poverty: International Debt

Borrowing, it is important to emphasize, is invariably tied to exporting, for the only way to pay back an international loan is to export. Herein lies the trap in which most poor countries were and are ensnared, according to dependency theorists. In principle, exporting allows poor countries, or any country, to earn foreign exchange by selling their products and services in global markets. Fair enough, one might say. There is a problem, though, for poor countries in particular: the global trading and financial systems are utterly dominated by the advanced capitalist economies. This means, among other things, that "trade relations take place in a highly monopolized international market, which tends to lower the price of raw materials [the primary export of developing countries] and to raise the prices of industrial products, particularly inputs [controlled by the richer countries]" (Dos Santos [1970] 1996, p. 169). The upshot is this: developing countries almost always find themselves with a highly unfavorable **balance of trade** (that is, they import more than they export). Imports, moreover, include not only capital goods and technology, but also a full range of products and services, much of which is absolutely essential—such as food, medicine, petroleum, and raw materials needed for manufacturing. Consider the Caribbean economies: twenty-two of twenty-three ran trade deficits in 2013. The same pattern was evident in most other regions, as well: in Central America, all eight economies had deficits in 2013; in Africa, forty-one of fifty-one; and in South Asia (which includes Iran), eight of nine—and Iran was the one exception in South Asia, but only because of its possession of large oil reserves.

There is, unfortunately, more to the story. For, over time, a persistently unfavorable balance of trade leads to mounting national debt, which makes it necessary for poor countries to borrow even more foreign currency. This creates a perverse situation in which poor countries are forced to borrow more to pay back what they already owe. Even more perversely, the debt has grown so large and unmanageable that poor countries, as a whole, now send more financial resources every year to the core than they receive (see Figure 4.6). One reason for this is the cost of borrowing for most countries, which is many multiple times higher than the cost of borrowing for richer countries. For example, the lending interest rate for private sector loans to Bangladesh, a poor country in South Asia, averaged around 13 percent between 2010 and 2014; for the United Kingdom, by contrast, the average lending rate was a scant 0.5 percent. Even worse, at one point, the cost of borrowing for the Democratic Republic of Congo, another very poor country, was an astoundingly high 56.5 percent in 2010 (World Bank 2015b). Figure 4.7 has additional data.

More to the point, in 2014, the *negative* net transfer of financial resources from poor countries to the core amounted to a staggering $971 billion (see Figure 4.6). To be fair, 2014 was an exceptional year, but the negative net transfer has been going on since the early 1990s, and for the most part has been growing bigger and bigger. The casual observer might agree that the situation is perverse, but might also ask: "Why don't poor countries just declare bankruptcy and refuse to pay back the money they owe?" The answer is simple: in the global *system* of capitalism, financial capital is akin to blood. Blood provides the essential nutrients and elements the body needs to survive, just as capital is the medium through which an economy is nourished and protected. Blood is not optional, and neither is capital. Any country that refuses to pay back its loans will have its blood-supply cut, and

---

Figure 4.6 Net Transfer of Financial Resources from Poor Countries to Rich Countries, Selected Years ($ billions)

	2005	2006	2007	2008	2009	2010	2014
Developing economies (all)	−597.2	−807.8	−881.1	−876.4	−545.1	−557.0	−970.7
Least-developed countries	1.3	−7.9	−5.2	−4.5	26.3	16.8	—

Sources: United Nations Department of Economic and Social Affairs (UN/DESA) 2011, p. 71, table III.1; and, for 2014, UN/DESA 2015, p. 64.

Figure 4.7 Lending Interest Rates in Selected Countries, 2010–2014 (percentages)

	2010	2011	2012	2013	2014
Low lending interest rate					
United Kingdom	0.5	0.5	0.5	0.5	0.5
Japan	1.6	1.5	1.4	1.3	1.2
Canada	2.6	3.0	3.0	3.0	3.0
United States	3.3	3.3	3.3	3.3	3.3
High lending interest rate					
Brazil	40.0	43.9	36.6	27.4	32.0
Uganda	20.2	21.8	26.3	23.3	21.5
Honduras	18.9	18.6	18.5	20.1	20.6
Democratic Republic of Congo	56.5	43.8	28.4	19.4	18.7
Peru	19.0	18.7	19.2	18.1	15.7

Source: World Bank 2015b.

the blood will no longer flow; this is tantamount to committing national suicide.

In sum, financial-industrial-technology dependence creates a coercive vise. But from the outside it does not appear to be coercive at all. After all, poor countries are not forced to take out loans at gunpoint; nor are they forced to engage in international trade. Right? Yet, understanding that poor countries exist within a broader framework or system of action helps us understand that they have little choice. The near-absolute need for capital, combined with their structurally disadvantaged position in the global trading system, ensures that poor countries, eventually, have no choice but to take out loans. Moreover, what little choice (or agency) they might have has been and continues to be systematically undermined or eliminated by the major capitalist or core economies. In the past, core economies would simply use military power and naked aggression to get what they wanted. To see this, one need only consider the era of colonialism, when the core—using its superior military power—took direct control of societies in the periphery. Today, by contrast, the primary mechanism of control is, as should already be apparent, international debt, and the field marshals are international banks and financial institutions. The **International Monetary Fund** (IMF), in particular, plays a central role (see Figure 4.8 for further discussion) in ensuring that the periphery becomes thoroughly integrated into global capitalism. For instance, when a poor country turns to the IMF for a

---

Figure 4.8 The International Monetary Fund and Its Critics

The International Monetary Fund and companion institution, the World Bank, were established in 1944; together, they are known as the **Bretton Woods** institutions. The IMF was initially designed to promote international monetary cooperation, and it still fulfills that role. But it also engages in short-term lending to countries experiencing financial difficulties. In principle, IMF loans (and loan guarantees) are meant to solve temporary balance-of-payment problems faced by member countries that cannot otherwise obtain sufficient financing. In this sense, the IMF is an international lender of last resort. This, too, is a very important role, which has brought a great deal of stability to the international financial and economic system.

At the same time, the IMF has been subject to intense criticism. Critics are mainly concerned with the conditions imposed on borrower countries. These conditions typically require borrowers to liberalize their economies and cut government spending. The problem, critics charge, is that **liberalization**, in particular, is not primarily designed to return a country to economic health, but instead is meant to make poorer or emerging economies more dependent on the core. Conditionality, in this regard, is often portrayed by Marxist scholars as a tool of neoimperialism. The constantly growing debt of developing economies—and the huge negative net transfer of financial resources to the core—suggest that Marxists are not necessarily wrong.

---

loan, the IMF typically requires that this country—as a condition for the loan (referred to as **conditionality**)—"liberalize" it markets; that is, to open its markets to free trade. Doing so enables the core to tighten its control even more. Indeed, in the present era, armies have become, to some extent, an anachronism. It is far more effective and far cheaper to use debt to exercise control over the periphery, although, when necessary, force is still used. It is also important to understand, with regard to the last point, that major capitalist economies used all their collective power to ensure that the one historical alternative to the capitalist system—the communist system created by the former Soviet Union—could not survive.

From the "Development of Underdevelopment" to "Dependent Development"

Although the foregoing discussion is a highly simplified account, it provides a good sense of the dependency perspective. The basic point is clear: poor countries occupy a structurally disadvantaged position in the world economy such that there are very strict limits on the level of economic autonomy and prosperity they can achieve. There is, however, one big hole in the account I have presented thus far: the dependency model seemingly leaves no room for poor countries to ever break the bonds of poverty. Yet just a little comparative checking makes it clear that there have been more than a few exceptions. As the next chapter vividly demonstrates, the economies of Japan, South Korea, Taiwan, and China are all major exceptions to the assertion that poor countries must remain stuck in poverty: all four East Asian economies have made very decisive moves out of the periphery (although the case of Japan is more complicated). There have also been success stories in Latin America, South America, Eastern Europe, Africa, and elsewhere. These successful cases present a challenge to **dependency theory**: the strongest theories should, even must, be able to account for both typical and atypical cases. That is, if atypical or anomalous cases cannot be explained in a manner consistent with the theory, then the theory as a whole becomes suspect. Thus, even though this chapter is centered on the question "Why are poor countries poor?" it is important to see if dependency theory, or the structural approach more generally, is able to explain anomalous cases. Since I will provide a full structural account for the economic rise of East Asia in Chapter 5, however, a very simple explanation here should suffice.

To deal with anomalies, dependency scholars had to be sure that they did not jettison their concept of dependency altogether. They did this, most generally, by specifying the conditions under which "development" in the periphery was possible, while still arguing that there were clear structural limits. One of the first to take on this challenge was Fernando H. Cardoso (a onetime sociologist, political activist, and, perhaps most surprisingly, former president of Brazil, from 1995 to 2002). Cardoso (1973) introduced the concept of "associated-dependent development," which was based on the argument that, under certain conditions, it was in the interest of core countries and their corporations to promote economic development in the periphery. As labor costs rise in core economies, for example, it makes economic sense to relocate production into lower-cost areas. A country in the periphery with an ample supply of the right kind of labor, as well as an "attractive" environment for investment (e.g., low tax rates, minimal health and safety regulations, a stable political system), could be one of those areas. Significantly, another important criterion was the existence of a highly capable authoritarian state, which was needed to keep tight control over labor and ensure that the interests of foreign capital would not be challenged. Under *these* conditions, Cardoso posited, "the interests of foreign corporations [could] become compatible with the internal prosperity of the dependent country. In this sense, they help promote development" (p. 149). Not surprisingly, though, this is, in principle, a very limited type of development; at best, it allows for the emergence of a small middle class (in addition to a very wealthy elite class). The large majority of the population, however, remains destitute. Even more, because the country's development is, in this view, *dependent* upon foreign investment—and, by extension, foreign technology and foreign equipment—if that investment is suddenly withdrawn, the country as a whole may end up back where it started: in the periphery.

There are, it is important to add, other structural accounts that have sought to explain the possibility of development, or strong economic growth, taking place in the periphery. One of these comes from a structural theory known as world-systems theory, which shares many assumptions and principles with dependency theory, but also differs from dependency in that it offers a more dynamic explanation of economic development in the world economy, in part by emphasizing the *systemic* as opposed to strictly structural aspects of capitalism (although world-systems theory has its own specific structural model too). The emphasis on systemic elements suggests a stronger focus on process. In world-systems theory, capitalism never rests, but is instead in constant motion: expanding and contracting both on a short- and long-term basis; shifting from one center of accumulation to another; constantly incorporating and integrating new areas and markets; creating and transforming organizational forms and practices; and so on. This unremitting movement allows for a relatively wide degree of change at the national level. During periods of contraction, for example, the core tends to weaken its control over the periphery as a whole (in part because of the need to refocus on internal needs), which gives a few countries in the periphery a limited chance to pursue autonomous, and not merely dependent, development. Only a very few poor countries, however, are likely to be in a position to take advantage of these limited openings—those countries with some combination of valuable natural resources, a cohesive society, and a strong and highly competent state. (In this regard, world-systems theory finds some common ground with rational choice regarding the significance of a strong state and of agency.) As I will discuss in Chapter 5, moreover, specific historical circumstances can play an outsized role: during the Cold War, in particular, when the Soviet Union threatened to permanently remove large parts of the world from the reach of global capitalism, core capitalist powers, led by the United States, actively promoted development in parts of the periphery. Today, however, the situation is reversed: increasingly intense global competition within the core has led to ever stronger pressure to heighten the exploitation of the periphery, albeit with some exceptions.

Despite some not insignificant differences between world-systems theory and dependency theory, both hold fast to the principle that capitalism is a powerful structure or system, one that absolutely requires a periphery in order for capitalism as a system to survive. In the end, then, the simple answer to the question "Why are poor countries poor?" is basically the same for most, if not all, historical structuralists: poor countries are poor because of the unavoidably exploitative nature of capitalism. While the foregoing discussion has already provided some insight into this conclusion, it would be useful to wrap up with a brief summation on the general logic of the structural argument.

To begin, capitalism, as a system, is premised on the capacity to accumulate profits, but to do so, workers must be exploited. In other words, to turn a profit, capitalist enterprises need to pay workers less than the value of the goods or services the workers produce (this is, in very basic terms, the Marxist definition of exploitation). The greater the difference between the value of goods and services produced by workers and their wages, the higher the profit. In this view, one might argue, exploitation does not necessarily lead to poverty, but this can only be true in the absence of competition. As with profit accumulation and exploitation, competition is an integral part of capitalism. One of the most salient consequences of competition is that it puts constant downward pressure on wages, since, in a competitive environment, firms must continually find ways to undercut their rivals. The stronger the competition, the stronger the pressure to reduce wages to the lowest possible point. For evidence, just look at the massive and still ongoing relocation of production from the core to the periphery—or **semi-periphery** (an intermediate zone posited by world-systems theory)—over the past fifty years or so. Importantly, though, only those areas with the right kind of workers, the necessary infrastructure, and a compliant but strong state qualify. Moreover, just as labor is exploited, so is everything and anything else that undermines profit accumulation. The end result, again, is continued poverty on a global scale.

Conclusion

In this chapter we have looked at several ways in which the three major research traditions of comparative politics approach the question of poverty in the world today. I have tried to treat each tradition evenhandedly (albeit not comprehensively), so that you can decide for yourself which provides the best explanation or understanding of world poverty. Of course, it is not necessarily the case that you must choose one tradition over the others. Each, as we have seen, has its own strengths and weaknesses. In fact, I hope that you, as a beginning student of comparative politics, keep as open and critical a mind as possible. It is almost certain that you can learn more by *taking seriously* what culturalists, rationalists, and structuralists all have to say about the issue of world poverty (and other questions of interest to comparativists). After all, each of these traditions represents the work of a great many very intelligent, very insightful individuals over many decades; it is therefore unlikely that any one of the traditions is completely or even mostly wrong. Even in those situations where the initial assumptions and methods of analysis turned out to be flawed (as with classical modernization theory and dependency theory)[4], the original insights were often quite important and difficult to dismiss. In such cases, it would be not only imprudent but also downright unscientific to "throw the baby out with the bathwater."

Before ending this chapter, let me make one final note. Except for a few brief comments, I did not talk explicitly about methods of comparison in discussing the research on poverty. One reason for this was just practical: this is already a lengthy chapter, so to have included separate discussions on methods would have been too much. But another reason is less obvious: I want *you* to make the connection between theory and method on your own. When thinking about the rational choice argument, for example, did you consider what sort of comparisons would have helped researchers validate or invalidate the basic claims? In a similar vein, in the discussion of dependency theory, did you consider the importance of anomalous cases and how comparative analysis could deal with these? If these sorts of questions did not cross your mind, you would do well to consider them now. Put yourself in the shoes of a researcher representing one of these traditions, and ask yourself: If I want to emphasize the role of culture, rationality, or structure, what should I compare? How should I compare? What conclusions can I legitimately draw from the comparisons I make? If you do all this, you'll be well on the way toward becoming a good comparativist and doing comparative politics.

Notes

1. The perspective portrayed in this section, I should stress, represents the "thicker" variant of rational choice—one that gives much greater prominence to the institutional context in which rational action takes place. This thicker variant is generally referred to as rational choice institutionalism, which itself is part of a broader trend in institutional approaches simply called "new institutionalism."

2. Samuel Huntington (1971), one of the most prominent modernization theorists of the time and still an influential figure today, added that modernization is an evolutionary process that changes societies in a revolutionary manner (cited in Roberts and Hite 2000, p. 9).

3. Alvin So (1990, pp. 53–59) provided a nice summary of the main criticisms against early modernization studies. Critics, for example, also challenged modernization's (1) evolutionary assumption of unidirectional development; (2) assumption that traditional and modern values are mutually exclusive; (3) implicit justification of US intervention in the third world; and (4) neglect of the issue of foreign domination.

4. Lawrence Harrison, for example, asserted that "neither colonialism nor dependency has much credibility today" (2000, p. xx). According to him, "the statute of limitations on colonialism as an explanation for underdevelopment lapsed long ago. . . . Dependency is rarely mentioned today, not even in American universities where it was, not many years ago, a conventional wisdom that brooked no dissent" (p. xx). But Harrison was only partly right. *Classical* dependency theory has largely disappeared, but so too has classic modernization theory. (Harrison, by the way, demonstrated an extremely strong bias in asserting that dependency "brooked no dissent"; remember, modernization theory was also a very powerful school of thought that itself "brooked no dissent" in many university departments.) The basic

point is simply that offshoots of classic dependency, especially world-systems theory, have taken strong root in the intellectual community today. This means that elements of the original theory are still relevant today, and the same could be said for classical modernization theory. In this regard, dependency is by no means a moribund tradition.

5

Why Has East Asia Prospered? Explaining Economic Growth in Japan, South Korea, Taiwan, and China

In the preceding chapter, I asked the question "Why are some countries poor?" This deceptively simple question, we discovered, can be answered in a number of very different ways. It should come as no surprise, then, that the question "Why is East Asia rich?" also has a number of divergent answers. (See Figure 5.1 for a discussion of economic growth in East Asia.) Indeed, the postwar economic success of East Asia (beginning in the 1950s and extending to the early 1990s) has been the subject of intense debate for decades. Until fairly recently, the debate centered on the success of the three main "miracle economies": Japan, South Korea, and Taiwan (and to a lesser extent, the much smaller economies of Singapore and Hong Kong). More recently, attention has shifted to China, which has witnessed an extraordinarily rapid pace of economic growth since the late 1980s, but especially since the turn of the twenty-first century. It should be noted, however, that China's status as a "rich" country is a bit premature: while its overall GDP adjusted for purchasing power made it the second largest economy in the world in 2014 (or first, using the World Bank's estimate), its per capita GDP of $12,880 ranked it 89th of 187 countries that same year. Moreover, according to the Multidimensional Poverty Index, 5.5 percent of China's population was multidimensionally poor in 2012 (OPHI 2015a), a relatively low proportion, but still a significant number in terms of people: with a population of about 1.3 billion, 5.5 percent comes out to around 72 million individuals.

This chapter will discuss all four larger countries in East Asia, although my initial focus will be on the Japanese, South Korean, and Taiwanese cases. (See Figure 5.2 for a map of the region.) For these three cases, the theoretical controversy surrounding their economic ascendance started a long time ago. On one side are those who, like David Henderson, argue that

Figure 5.1 How "Rich" Is East Asia?

"Since 1960 Asia," noted IMF economist Michael Sarel (1996), "the largest and most populous of the continents, has become richer faster than any other region of the world." Much of Asia's economic growth, however, has been concentrated in just a few countries located in the northeastern part of Asia, with Japan leading the pack. Japan's early postwar economic growth, in fact, has been extraordinary by almost any measure. Ardath Burks described it this way: "in bald figures, the results were almost unbelievable" (1981, p. 157). In the case of Japan, the country's "gross national product in current prices actually increased 1.9 times in a five-year period (1955–1960), jumped another 2.1 times in the next five-year period (1960–1965), and increased another 2.5 times in the succeeding five-year period (1965–1970)" (p. 157). In concrete terms, this meant that Japan's per capita income increased from $200 in the early 1950s to almost $2,000 by 1971, which made Japan the fifth richest country in the world in terms of per capita income and third richest in terms of gross domestic product (pp. 157–158). In 2014, Japan had a purchasing power–adjusted GDP of over $4.6 trillion (fourth in the world) and per capita GDP of over $36,223 (based on World Bank data).

In South Korea and Taiwan (known collectively, along with Hong Kong and Singapore, as the Four Tigers), the economic performance has been equally impressive. According to Sarel (1996), "The Tigers have had annual growth rates of output per person well in excess of 6 percent. These growth rates, sustained over a 30-year period, are simply amazing. While the average resident of a non-Asian country in 1990 was 72 percent richer than his parents were in 1960, the corresponding figure for the average Korean [for example] is no less than 638 percent." In raw figures, Taiwan's per capita income increased from $50 in 1970 to $2,500 in 1984, and in South Korea (which started its accelerated economic growth a little later), the comparable figures were $87 in 1962 and $1,709 in 1983 (all figures cited in Hamilton and Biggart 1997, p. 115). By 1998, in terms of purchasing power parity, per capita income in Taiwan and South Korea was $16,500 and $12,600, respectively. Ten years later, in 2008, purchasing power–adjusted per capita income had almost doubled to $30,881 in Taiwan, and more than doubled to $27,647 in South Korea (figures from IMF). In 2014, Taiwan's purchasing power–adjusted per capita GDP climbed to almost $46,000, just a step behind Germany and ahead of Canada. In South Korea, for that same year, the comparable figure was $35,277.

GDP, however, is only one (somewhat crude) measure of wealth and development. Using the more comprehensive Human Development Index from the United Nations Development Programme, Japan and South Korea, along with forty-seven other countries, were ranked as "very high" in human development, with both countries showing incremental but steady progress since the measure was first introduced in 1980. In 2013, South Korea's rank actually surpassed that of Japan for the first time (UNDP 2015). Taiwan is not included in the HDI (for reasons that have to do with international politics), but it is fair to surmise that Taiwan would also be ranked as very high in human development.

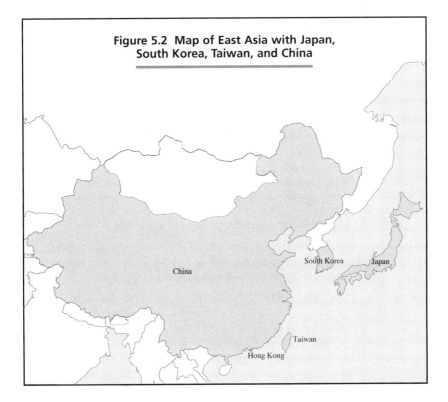

Figure 5.2 Map of East Asia with Japan, South Korea, Taiwan, and China

the success of East Asia's main capitalist economies has been based on close adherence to market principles in general and to "low government intervention or to reductions in government intervention" more specifically (2000, p. 74). On the other side are those who claim just the opposite, namely that the state has played a central and pervasive role in first creating and then promoting, through carefully conceived and efficiently implemented economic strategies, rapid capitalist growth. Still others argue that East Asia's economic growth was a product of external linkages and the broader systemic forces of world capitalism, over which individual states exercised little or no control. To this mix, we can also add culture-based arguments, the most common of which focused on the region's "Confucian heritage" and related aspects of East Asian culture that ostensibly emphasize a reverence for education, respect for authority, group-oriented norms, and so on. (Many cultural arguments, unfortunately, are overly simplistic and specious.)

In this chapter, we will look closely at a few of the more prominent arguments—both good and bad—concerning East Asia's economic success.

And, as I did in Chapter 4, I will divide these arguments roughly along rationalist, culturalist, and structuralist lines. At the same time, I should emphasize, not all of the explanations that follow fit easily into a single research tradition. But this is not necessarily a bad thing, since it gives you an opportunity to think seriously about how researchers must draw from different research traditions in order to construct their arguments. In this sense, the discussion that follows will also give you an opportunity to think seriously about the question of *theoretical synthesis*. Remember, though, theoretical synthesis is easier said than done, for it is not simply a matter of combining seemingly compatible aspects of different explanatory accounts. This may seem fine on the surface, but if the underlying assumptions of the various arguments contradict one another, then your synthesis will likely be unable to stand on its own.

An examination of East Asian economic growth also gives us an opportunity to revisit some important methodological issues. Specifically, in a large number of studies on East Asian economic growth and industrialization, there has been a strong tendency to treat Japan, South Korea, and Taiwan as "most similar systems" (for now, I will leave China out). Even more, many researchers have used these countries' similarities—and *only* their similarities—as a basis for drawing hard-and-fast conclusions about the key factor or factors responsible for their rapid economic growth (the dependent variable). At first glance, this makes sense: after all, if we can find the same key factor in all three cases, then "logic" tells us that the factor we have identified explains the rapid growth in each of the cases. Recall from Chapter 2, however, that *differences* are crucial to the logic of the MSS design. A most similar systems design, to recap quickly, requires significant variance on the dependent variable among all cases—without this variance, the search for the independent variable is short-circuited. Unfortunately, this has not prevented both casual observers and seasoned researchers from making logically flawed comparisons of Japan, South Korea, and Taiwan. It is important to add, though, that a focus on the three most similar systems is not always what it appears to be. Many times, in fact, Japan, South Korea, and Taiwan are tacitly treated as single-unit case studies, where the other cases are used in an essentially secondary capacity (that is, a case study in comparative perspective or analytical induction). Less frequently and sometimes unwittingly, comparativists carry out within-case comparisons while examining the three cases. Done correctly, as I also noted in Chapter 2, a within-case comparison is a near-ideal means of conducting a binary comparison using an MSS design. Finally, some researchers have compared the three countries using the method of agreement, which is not unreasonable. Still, when using the MoA, it is crucial to keep in mind its methodological limitations, especially in drawing hard-and-fast conclusions based on a comparison of three and only three units (with no negative cases).

Whatever the situation, however, it is crucial for the beginning (and seasoned) comparativist to cultivate a clear-eyed understanding and awareness of proper research design. For example, if you are going to conduct a within-case comparison or a series of case studies (in comparative perspective), then you should be explicit and systematic in your approach; if not, you greatly increase the risk of making serious, even fatal, methodological mistakes. With this in mind, as you read the various explanations of East Asian prosperity put forth in this chapter, think carefully about the strengths and weaknesses of the comparisons being made. In particular, consider what additional types of comparisons would help support the argument. What specific cases would you choose? Why? There is no need, moreover, to limit your geographic focus to East Asia. Good comparisons—and sometimes the best ones—can be made on a cross-regional basis, too. Constantly asking and reflecting on such questions will help you develop the mind-set for doing comparative politics and becoming a good comparativist. I should emphasize that I will not leave you completely to your own devices; throughout the chapter (including in the next section), I will highlight important methodological points to assist you in the process of developing your comparative analytical skills.

Let me make one final point before we begin our examination of rationalist, culturalist, and structuralist arguments on East Asian prosperity. In keeping with my previously stated position that "history matters," in the remainder of this chapter more attention will be paid to integrating history into the various analyses; this will be particularly apparent in the next section (this discussion of history, however, will be applicable to all succeeding sections as well). My intention is to demonstrate, albeit in a sometimes unavoidably cursory fashion, *how* history matters in explaining recent and contemporary events and processes.

Rationality, the Strong State, and Rapid Economic Growth in East Asia

In the preceding chapter, I introduced a simple contention in the rational choice tradition regarding national poverty: poor countries are poor, in large measure, because they lack a strong and effective state. It would make sense, therefore, to argue that the reason for the relative prosperity of East Asia's economies—from a rational choice perspective—must be that they have such a state. In essence, this is exactly what (some) rational choice scholars argue. Robert Bates, for example, was very clear on this point. In his edited book *Toward a Political Economy of Development: A Rational Choice Perspective* (1988b), he pointed to the critical importance of the state—as the preeminent public institution—in creating and sustaining the basis for capitalist industrialization and growth. (A capitalist economic system, as noted in the previous chapter, constitutes an essential context for this discussion. In other words, a strong state and effective state in a *non*capitalist system will almost certainly not produce the same results. A good comparative example is North Korea—a country with a very strong and capable state, but also with a command economy: economically, North Korea is a veritable basket case, and has been so since the 1980s.) Bates (1988b) suggested, moreover, that the most effective and efficient allocation of resources often required less market and more state intervention. The emphasis on the state is important, recall, because people in general will attempt to free-ride on the contributions of others unless a public institution/organization exists that can compel their participation. Without the coercive capacity of the state, to repeat another key point, public and infrastructure goods would not be created. States, we also know, can play a key role in altering the strategic environment in very poor countries by making "individually rational but socially irrational" behavior far less likely.

The existence of a strong state, though, is only part of the rational choice equation. The other part of the equation centers on the following questions, also raised by Bates (1988b): What makes it in the private interests of those in power to implement policies designed to secure public and infrastructure goods? More to the point, what makes it in the interests of the holders of political power to adopt policies that promote economic growth and industrialization? According to Bates, the answers to both questions are linked to a number of factors, which may include political **ideology**, the economic interests of the political elite, and the political elite's need for public revenues. Bates gave some credence to all three factors, but for leaders of an authoritarian system, the most important reason Bates gave was the following: holders of power are likely to adopt policies that promote economic development when doing so allows them to *retain political power.* The reason, rationally speaking, is clear: retaining political power generally constitutes *the* key self-interest for state leaders. The problem, of course, is that, in most poor countries, especially nondemocratic ones, the conditions under which the pursuit of power (e.g., staying in office) by the political elite leads to collectively or socially beneficial outcomes, such as the growth of the national economy, are not at all common. Instead, as I also covered in the last chapter, a more common (self-interested) goal for the political elite is to engage in corrupt behavior. The reason is simple: corruption has relatively limited costs—at least to political leaders—but a great deal of benefits for those in power in authoritarian regimes.

Based on the foregoing discussion, the core principles underlying the rational choice explanation for East Asia's economic prosperity should be apparent. In case they are not, let me summarize. First, the existence of a strong public institution/organization capable of overcoming collective action and free-rider problems is a necessary, though not sufficient, factor for national economic growth. Second, among those who control the state apparatus, there must be a clear private incentive (for example, maintaining political office or power) for acting in a socially beneficial manner. In examining the economies of Japan, South Korea, and Taiwan (we can also include China on this list), both of these core principles seem to have empirical validation—a point I will discuss in the following sections. Remember, though, that validation is relatively easy, and therefore inconclusive from a strict, or even loose, methodological standpoint. As just noted, we especially know that finding one similarity among many is not at all decisive when similar systems (e.g., Japan, South Korea, and Japan) show no meaningful variance on the dependent variable. Still, the *deductive logic* of rational choice theory points us directly to a specific variable, namely a strong, effective state. In this regard, a strategy of analytical induction is ideal: this is because, theoretically, it is already clear what the potential independent variable is or should be, each case can serve as a theoretical steppingstone. Still, relying on a single comparative strategy is almost always problematic. Thus, a better methodological approach would be to combine different principles and strategies into a mixed design. In this particular situation, the method of agreement and within-case comparisons can also be used. Keep these methodological points in mind as we proceed.

The East Asian State: Strong and Developmental

To rational choice analysts, two features immediately stand out when looking at Japan, South Korea, and Taiwan during their periods of most rapid economic growth. First, all had strong, very effective, and highly interventionist states. Second, in all three cases, the political leadership was clearly committed to maximizing industrial development over almost anything else—I say "almost" because there was one exception, which was achieving the parallel goal of building a strong military (a point to which I will return later). This *combination* of state capacity and dedication to rapid industrialization led scholars to create a special name for the East Asian states: the **developmental state**. The developmental state is more than just a strong and effective state. It is also a state in which there is a solid, even unwavering commitment to economic development among the political leadership; thus the term *developmental* state. Actually, the developmental state is composed of much more than just these two elements, but for present purposes, our focus will be on state capacity and commitment to national economic development (I discuss the developmental state in more depth in another book, *Politics in East Asia* [Lim 2014]).

To begin, it is important to understand that the East Asian developmental state did not materialize out of thin air. Instead, it is a product of the specific history of the region. The precise origin is difficult to pinpoint, but most East Asia scholars will take us back to the latter part of the nineteenth century, when Japan first emerged as an industrial power. Indeed, some will take us back much, much further, to the origins and development of Japan's feudal system. The historical details, while certainly important, are much too complex and intricate for us to deal with here. Suffice it to say that Japan developed the basis for a strong, centralized political system in the premodern era, which set it apart from almost all other non-Western countries at the time. To put it in rationalist terms, the premodern or preindustrial Japanese state clearly had the strength and capacity, at least potentially, to overcome the collective action and free-rider problems on a national scale—and to pursue a full range of policies designed to promote national economic development. And, beginning in the mid-1800s, that power was used quite effectively, when a coalition of five *daimyo* (powerful territorial lords) took control of the central government and ushered in a new period in Japanese history, known as the Meiji era or the **Meiji Restoration** (1868–1912).

It was during this period, contrary to popular perceptions, that Japan witnessed its first economic "miracle." Consider a few of the key steps taken by the new government that laid the foundation for this miracle. In transportation and communication, the first railroad was constructed from Tokyo to Yokohama in 1870–1872 (and 2,000 miles of track were added to the system over the next twenty years); the first steamer service (between Yokohama and Nagasaki) was inaugurated in 1866; and 4,000 miles of telegraph line were strung by 1893 (Lockwood 1968, p. 14). The new government also invested heavily in industrial development: it played a key role in building or expanding iron and steel works, munitions plants, shipyards, textile mills, cement factories, mining (of copper, coal, and precious metals), and so on. Perhaps most important, given the discussion from Chapter 3, the taxation and finance systems were also thoroughly revamped, all with an eye toward maximizing national economic wealth and industrialization. Significantly, the revenue systems created a strong burden on farmers, merchants, and others, but these individuals had little choice but to abide by the dictates of the state. In other words, free-riding was not an option.

It is also worth noting that investment in education (another very important public good) increased significantly during the Meiji era: it amounted to a "hefty third of Meiji state expenditure" and allowed Japan's system of compulsory education to surpass "that of most Western countries in terms of rationalisation and centralisation" (Bouissou 2002, p. 21). The Meiji state, in sum, did those things that a rationalist would consider essential to turning a relatively poor country (by Western industrial standards) into a wealthy one. Of course, this may help to explain what happened in prewar Japan, but how does it explain the subsequent postwar industrialization of Japan, South Korea, and Taiwan? Fortunately, using a rational choice framework, the answer to this question is also fairly easy to discern, for Japan's first period of rapid industrialization also prompted the country's leaders to pursue another "Western practice," namely colonialism.

Rational Choice, the Strong State, and the Importance of Colonialism

Colonialism was a deliberate state policy whereby industrially and militarily weak territories in Asia, Africa, and the Americas were essentially made into economic and political appendages of the major European powers and of the United States. Typically, subjugation of a territory involved the projection of military force, followed by the creation of a colonial structure that institutionalized an unequal and highly exploitative relationship between the colonial "master" and the native population. It was not unusual, however, for the colonial power to **co-opt** local elite and other members of the native population once the colonial structure had been created. Japan proved to be no exception to this general rule, as it used its superior industrial (and military) power to subjugate its closest neighbors, Korea and Taiwan (and also parts of China). For rationalists, the most relevant aspect of Japan's domination of Korea and Taiwan was the imposition of a *common* (albeit not identical) set of economic, political, and social institutions and arrangements that, to a significant extent, came to characterize *postwar* capitalist development in all three countries. One of the most important of these institutions was a highly articulated, disciplined, and penetrating bureaucracy that constituted the core of the so-called strong state in Japan's colonial empire (Cumings 1984).

Another important and integrally related element of the strong (colonial) state derived from a particular *model* of state-directed economic development (Woo 1991). This model was designed to mobilize, in a top-down fashion, the entire population for the purpose of achieving rapid industrialization. The model, moreover, was a highly intrusive, repressive, and coercive one. To ensure compliance with state goals (especially in the colonies), it was necessary for the state to maintain strict control over the economic activities of workers, ordinary citizens, and capitalists. To control workers and the general population, the state invested a great deal of attention to ideological indoctrination, surveillance, and, when necessary, violent repression: the colonial state was a police state (Chen 1984). For capitalists, control was exercised through less direct and repressive means. One of the most effective of these was the creation of a sophisticated but tightly controlled financial structure, which required capitalists to come to the state for any major investment project (for further discussion, see Woo 1991).

Japan's colonial domination of Korea and Taiwan ended in 1945. This year also marked the demise of Japan's military-authoritarian state and the emergence of a new democratic political system. Yet the core characteristics of the colonial state (in Japan and its colonies) did not simply disappear. Indeed they remained quite strong—even if sometimes dormant—in all three countries. A major reason for this stemmed from conditions following the end of World War II. In Japan, years of total war had left the economy in shambles and the society enervated. In Korea, the sudden withdrawal of Japanese forces created a political vacuum that was, in one respect, quickly filled by the Soviet Union and then the United States; unfortunately, this served to divide the country into a procommunist north and a pro-US south. Domestically, the political vacuum took longer to fill due to internecine political battles between different groups vying for political control. In Taiwan, the Japanese surrender led to a different type of division: pro-US nationalists from mainland China, known as the **Kuomintang** (KMT, also spelled Guomindang), took complete control of the island after losing a civil war in 1949 against communist forces led by **Mao Zedong** (also spelled Mao Tse-Tung). This takeover created a division between the KMT and its 2 million followers and the local, indigenous population, who had suffered for decades under Japanese rule. The KMT, I should note, had been exercising political control over Taiwan since shortly after the Japanese surrender, and antipathy between local Taiwanese and the KMT had already been running very high prior to 1949.

In all three countries, in short, there was a significant degree of political, social, and economic tension in the few years following the end of the war. Added to these difficulties was the emergence of a strong leftist or radical influence, especially in Japan and South Korea. For the US government—the newly dominant player in the region—these developments were ominous, and US officials were therefore loath to dismantle or even weaken the apparatus of state capacity and control that had been built up and repeatedly reinforced during the era of colonialism. Doing so would have invited political chaos or, worse still, given an opening for leftists to exert control. The US government, it almost goes without saying, had its own self-interest in ensuring strong, US-aligned countries in East Asia—a point on which structuralists also agree, and which I will discuss later. The upshot is clear: US efforts in Japan, South Korea, and Taiwan had the effect of ensuring that the basic structures of the strong state would remain intact and in operation in all three countries long after the colonial period ended.

These "basic structures of the strong state" enabled postwar Japanese leaders to continue along a political economic path similar to the prewar period; and, more important, this also allowed leaders in South Korea and Taiwan to follow closely in their footsteps. There is not enough space in this chapter to cover this issue in any depth, so let me just make two general but important points. First, it is fair to say that in postwar Japan, South Korea, and Taiwan, the state possessed the capacity (or power) to compel private actors—from farmers, to urban workers, to powerful capitalists—to contribute to national economic goals. In Japan, this power was manifested in a range of policy instruments designed, as in the first period of rapid industrialization, to overcome the free-rider problem. As a fledgling democracy, however, Japanese officials needed to build a more cooperative strategic environment compared to the prewar period, one in which all actors, but especially the most powerful ones, were motivated more through incentives than fear. The national government, therefore, used a range of "carrots"—for example, tax incentives, research and production subsidies, **infant industry** and home market protection, government financing, export promotion, and so on (Okimoto 1989)—to spur behavior that would maximize capitalist growth and development. Where stronger encouragement was needed, the state (through its very capable bureaucracy) exercised **administrative guidance**, an informal method of controlling economic actors. In South Korea and Taiwan, the same policy instruments were generally used, but in a nondemocratic political environment the "stick" was used much more liberally. This was especially true in South Korea, which not coincidentally experienced its most rapid economic growth only after an iron-fisted, military authoritarian government took control in 1961 (I will return to this point later). In Taiwan, the state relied more strongly on direct control of key industries and therefore was less reliant on the cooperation of powerful business leaders (Amsden 1988).

Second, and in a strongly related vein, the state has frequently played a leadership role in industrial development and planning in all three economies—this has led some scholars to describe industrial development in East Asia as "bureaucratic capitalism," "guided capitalism," or some variant thereof (Amsden 1988; Cumings 1999; Johnson 1982). The reason for this terminology is clear: in the three countries, bureaucratic agencies were directly involved in targeting certain industries or industrial sectors for development and expansion; they directly shaped the pattern of investment, production, and international trade; and did many things that are supposedly left in the hands of the private sector in other capitalist economies. (I should note that this is not a position without some controversy; many scholars, myself included, argue that the state's leadership role in East Asia has been overstated.)

Why Did East Asia's Leaders
Focus on National Development?

As suggested earlier, the question "Why did East Asia's leaders focus on national development above all else?" is crucial. Rationalists must demonstrate, in other words, that state leaders in East Asia had a *private incentive* for action focusing on national economic development. If the rationalists cannot do so, then the deductive principles of their theory fall flat. Fortunately, it is not difficult to find evidence that the actions of political leaders in East Asia were essentially self-interested. To see this, one must understand that, in the particular context of postwar East Asia, the power to rule and political legitimacy were intimately, if not inextricably, tied to national economic development. There are many reasons for this, but one of the most important has to do with the profound awareness of *national vulnerability* found in all three countries. What this means, in a basic sense, is the objective fear of domination or destruction by outside or cross-border enemies: the proverbial "existential threat" (that is, a threat to one's very existence or survival). In this regard, national vulnerability is clearly not just a postwar phenomenon in East Asia. Indeed, the fear of outside domination or destruction is precisely what drove Japan's leaders in the mid-1800s to abandon a centuries-old system and rush headlong into capitalist industrialization.

Japan and the threat from the West. In Japan, the specific threat was the continuing and seemingly unstoppable expansion of Western imperialism across the globe. In fact, prior to the Meiji era, the Japanese *shogunate* (a type of military-led government) had already been forced to sign "unequal treaties" with Westerners; these were widely seen as a prelude to Western domination. The turning point, however, occurred in 1853, when a naval fleet commanded by Matthew C. Perry sailed into Edo Bay. Although Perry's visit was an outwardly peaceful one meant to establish trade relations between the United States and Japan, Perry was prepared to use force if his mission was refused by the Japanese—he even sent white flags to the Japanese negotiator indicating that, if his demands were not met, he would "bring on a war that Japan would most assuredly lose, and in that case, the white flags of surrender would be useful" (Jansen 2000, p. 277). The almost certain threat of foreign control or domination, to make the point clear, provided the rational impetus for *individual* Japanese political leaders to pursue policies designed to bring about rapid industrialization. For it was only by building and industrializing the economy as a whole that they could hope to maintain their positions of power. In this regard, Japan's Meiji leaders understood quite well the inextricable connection between industrialization and military strength, a point that can be seen clearly in a major slogan of the seen Meiji era: *fukoku kyō hei,* which translates as "enrich the nation, strengthen the military," or more simply, "wealthy nation, strong military." Fortunately for Japan, political leaders had access to material resources and institutional capacity that allowed them to meet the challenge from the West—a luxury that few, if any, other non-Western countries had.

Following World War II, of course, the threat of colonial domination disappeared, but national economic development remained an important goal toward which (conservative) postwar political leaders were obliged to strive. There are two closely interrelated reasons for this. First, and more generally, Japan's postwar leaders now presided over a democratic political system. Minimally, this required that they run for and be elected to office. This meant that they were now directly accountable to the citizenry. Second, in the highly radicalized political context of the immediate postwar period, the policies and tactics used to repress the left (which included a significant segment of Japan's population) required a quid pro quo: in return for electoral support, the conservative political leadership was required to formulate and effectively implement policies that would serve the interests of the voting public. The most obvious path was to grow the national economy (along nonmilitary lines). Thus the conservative leaders promised that they would rebuild and restrengthen the national economy, and help Japan catch up with the industrialized West (Pempel 1982). In this way, the authority to govern, on the one hand, and national economic development, on the other hand, had become strongly and unequivocally connected in Japan's postwar political environment.[1] Of course, failure to achieve the goal of national development would have resulted in, at worst, electoral defeat rather than in national subjugation. Yet, from a rational choice perspective, both were essentially equal: either outcome would still have meant a loss of political power for individual leaders.

Assessing the threats facing South Korea and Taiwan. In South Korea, the experience with colonialism, one might argue, contributed to a profound sense of national vulnerability among the leaders and the entire population (note, though, that during the colonial period, there was only one Korea, not a north and south). Virtually every adult in South Korea understood that the country's colonial subjugation was a product of a lack of industrialization and economic development. By itself, however, an experience with colonialism does not provide a sufficient explanation. After all, looking around the world (that is, engaging in simple comparative checking), we can find plenty of former colonies that continued to wallow in economic misery decades after liberation; we can also find many profoundly corrupt political leaders in these same countries. For the first fifteen years following liberation, in fact, South Korean political leaders conformed to the same pattern of "politically rational" but economically destructive practices common to so many other poor countries. To put it bluntly, South Korea was an economic basket case into the early part of the 1960s. And there is good reason for this, particularly from a rational choice perspective: the political and social environment of postliberation South Korea—which was deeply divisive as would-be political leaders representing different regions and different ideologies scrambled for power—made corrupt and narrowly self-serving political choices almost necessary for those who wished to gain and retain power (more on this point later).

In Taiwan, the situation was quite different. From the very beginning (1949), the regime was united and sharply focused. This had a lot to do with the historical experiences of the KMT, which had a long history on mainland China prior to taking over Taiwan, and which had developed an exceptionally strong organizational base (ironically, modeled along the lines of the Soviet Union's Communist Party). Indeed, the organizational strength of the KMT was such that it likely did not need, nor necessarily benefit from, the legacy of Japan's colonial rule on Taiwan. Be that as it may, the rationalist argument on the importance of a strong and effective state still holds true. Before I digress too far, though, let me return to the key point: despite their different starting points, the regimes in South Korea and Taiwan ended up being very much on the same page, and, again, from a rationalist perspective, the reason is clear: both were eventually united by an overriding concern with national vulnerability.

For Taiwan, the threat was crystal clear: China. The communist leadership in the newly formed People's Republic of China (PRC), despite forcing the KMT to flee, did not consider the matter settled. Taiwan, in the eyes of the PRC leadership, belonged to China; the KMT leadership, for its part, harbored the hope of regaining control of the mainland. Thus, tensions between the KMT and the PRC remained extremely high, as did the threat of renewed hostilities. Taiwan, however, gained some relief in 1950, when US president Harry Truman deployed the US Seventh Fleet to the straits between the mainland and Taiwan, effectively precluding an invasion, at least for a short time. To this day, the communist Chinese leadership considers Taiwan to be a "renegade province" rather than a sovereign country. There is, of course, a whole lot more to the PRC-Taiwan (and US) relationship. But the most salient point, in terms of the rational choice argument, is that the threat posed by China compelled the KMT leadership to do everything possible to build a strong, industrial economy as quickly as possible. And this is precisely what happened. Almost from the moment they landed in Taiwan, the KMT leaders launched an ambitious industrialization plan. Whether this was strictly for national survival is open to debate—one prominent scholar, Robert Wade (1990), suggested that the motivation for rapid industrialization was less self-preservation than a desire to recapture the Chinese mainland. Still, as Wade put it, "recapturing the mainland—which remained a central preoccupation of the government through the 1950s—required the development of some upstream industries" (p. 77). Whatever the case, then, the motivation of Taiwan's early political leadership clearly fit within a rational choice framework.

South Korea: A within-case comparison. In South Korea, the situation was more complicated. In sharp contrast to Taiwan, as I alluded to earlier, in the years following the end of Japanese colonialism there was an intense struggle for power in South Korean society among a number of hostile factions. The main targets for each of these competing factions were the institutions and agencies of the state, which were understandably perceived as the key to political and social power. In this environment, gaining and keeping control of the state led to the use of ostensibly irrational tactics and policies (from the standpoint of national economic development). These included financial policies that created negative real interest rates (that is, interest rates below 0 percent with inflation factored in), unsustainably high levels of government spending (especially for the police and military forces), extremely biased lending practices (to supposed allies of the government), and so on.[2] Over time, the less than optimal nature of South Korea's postliberation economic policies had predictable results: by 1960, the economy was close to collapse. Between 1955 and 1960, for example, nominal per capita gross national product (GNP) had increased from $79 to only $86 (cited in Woo 1991, p. 58), and the per capita rate of GNP growth was a mere 1.5 percent between 1953 and 1962 (Mason et al. 1980, p. 187). But even this figure was exaggerated by the fact that South Korea had been receiving high levels of foreign aid from the United States—according to one estimate, it is likely that per capita GNP would have decreased by as much as 1.6 percent per year in the absence of US aid (Mason et al. 1980, p. 187). All of this raises an obvious, and fundamentally comparative, question: What changed? That is, what happened within South Korea that created the basis for rapid economic growth?

The short answer is this: a new, very strong leadership took over. In 1961, General Park Chung Hee led a coup d'état that toppled the existing government. Park almost immediately began an ambitious program of economic reform, which laid the basis for South Korea's "miraculous" transformation. His first order of business was to vastly improve the country's infrastructure, which also meant increasing government revenues. He did the latter in part by sending Korean workers abroad—thousands of men were sent to German mines, and thousands of women to German hospitals to work as nurses (Kamppeter 2008). A large portion of the hard currency they earned was repatriated back to South Korea. Citizens were also exhorted to save, and he quickly normalized relations with Japan, which led to the infusion of hundreds of millions of dollars in the form of reparations (for Japan's colonial rule). Almost all the capital coming into the country, or saved domestically, was used to invest in infrastructure or industrial projects, including the construction of a highway between South Korea's two largest cities (Seoul and Pusan) and a huge new factory (Pohang Iron and Steel).

From a practical perspective, the contrast with the previous regime could not have been starker. Just as clear, from a methodological perspective, was the stunning turnaround in the economy, which, for all intents and purposes, corresponded exactly with the change in political leadership. The causal link is hard to deny. Indeed, the contrast between the two periods (i.e., South Korea from 1948 to 1961 and from 1961 to 1979) provides near-perfect conditions for a within-case comparison. Methodologically, the comparison tells that the new leadership—presiding over an effective state apparatus—almost certainly played a central role in the country's economic transformation. After all, in these two most similar systems the most salient *difference* was the leadership.

Again, though, it is essential to understand *why* this new leadership pushed national economic development, whereas the former regime did not. From a rational choice perspective, we would expect the answer to be found in a decisionmaking environment that compelled the new leaders to equate national economic development with their chances for political survival. And this is largely what happened. First, the previous regime, to a significant extent, lost the legitimacy to rule because of the lack of economic development. In this regard, the relative lack of public protest when the coup took place is notable: people had become fed up and were willing to give the new leaders a chance, even if they took power in nondemocratic fashion. Still, the new regime, led by Park Chung Hee, could only establish legitimacy if it effectively and efficiently reversed the economic direction in which the country was headed. In addition, it is important to note another critical contextual factor that helps account for the overriding importance the South Korean populace placed on a strong national economy. Simply put, it was the existence of a hostile and militarily powerful enemy situated right next to South Korea—the Democratic People's Republic of Korea, or North Korea. The threat posed by North Korea could not be ignored, particularly because the two countries had already engaged in a vicious and highly destructive war between 1950 and 1953 (even now, in 2016, South and North Korea exist in a technical state of war). North Korea was the quintessential existential threat, a threat that has arguably grown over time because of its development of nuclear weapons: in January 2016, North Korea successfully tested what it referred to as a "hydrogen" nuclear bomb.

Given this ever-present and very real threat, a government that failed to build a strong national economy—one that could provide a material foundation sufficient to counter the North Korean threat—could hardly expect to stay in power. And while it is true that the previous regimes also faced the same existential threat, internal rivalries for political power were much greater and more pervasive in the 1950s than in the 1960s after the military coup. In this respect, the military coup itself had a material effect on altering the strategic (decisionmaking) environment within South Korea. One other absolutely crucial element of the strategic environment was a decline (both real and perceived) in the level of US commitment to defend South Korea. South Korean military leaders (including Park Chung Hee), in particular, were extremely wary of counting on the United States too heavily, especially as the Vietnam War swung into full gear in 1961 (the sense was that the United States would become preoccupied with the war in Vietnam and begin to put less emphasis elsewhere). They understood that their lives and careers depended on building a strong and at least partially independent industrial economy. General Park himself was very clear about the connection between economic development and national security, as two of his favorite sayings were "Steel equals national power" (cited in Woo 1991) and "Savings is national strength" (cited in Kamppeter 2008).

Rational Choice and East Asian Development: Conclusion and a Caveat

The foregoing analysis is, I readily admit, quite broad. Certainly, it is not sufficient to clearly establish the empirical (much less theoretical) validity of the rational choice perspective. But this decidedly is not my intention. Instead, my goal is simply to provide you—as a student new to the study of comparative politics—a general sense of how the basic principles and concepts of rational choice could fruitfully be used to analyze capitalist development in East Asia. I hope I achieved this. At the least, you should understand how a core assumption of the rational choice school—that is, that people are rational maximizers of self-interest—can provide a plausible account or explanation of how the three East Asian economies became prosperous. If you are interested in further exploring this issue, however, it is up to you to develop a more systematic, more rigorous, and deeper plan of action. The same can be said for the alternative theoretical analyses that follow.

An Alternative View of the State

Before we move on to other theoretical perspectives, though, it is necessary to reemphasize that the rational choice account just offered is only one of several versions. Some rational choice variants, as I noted in Chapter 4, utterly reject the general premise that a strong, highly interventionist, developmentally oriented state is needed to overcome **collective-goods** problems in capitalist economies. Instead, proponents of these competing rational choice arguments argue that *limited* state intervention is required only in situations of widespread market failure or imperfection. State intervention in the market must be limited, because any interference in the market process tends to inhibit economic efficiency (and growth). This happens because state policies invariably create barriers or other obstacles to the free flow of goods, capital, labor, and information (all of which are needed to maximize economic gains through rational or self-interested action on the part of economic agents). Thus, from a mainstream economic perspective, the success of East Asia can be directly traced to minimal or very selective state intervention based on reducing market "imperfections." One set of economists, for example, has argued that the key to East Asian economic success was the adoption of "outward-looking development strategies," or **export-oriented industrialization**. This involves (1) a market- or private sector–oriented approach, where business activities are mainly left to the private sector and "the allocation of resources is basically left to the market"; (2) the correction of price distortions (i.e., bringing prices in line with market forces); (3) cautious financial management; (4) state support for education and human resource development; and (5) flexibility (James, Naya, and Meier 1989, pp. 17–21). The logical conclusion of this explanation, I should emphasize, is that once market imperfections are corrected, even limited state intervention will no longer be necessary.

Although we should not discount this mainstream economic argument out of hand, it is important to understand that it is based not only on a more deductive and highly abstract set of principles, but also, and more importantly for our purposes, on a noncomparative method of analysis. In contrast, the (thick) rational choice explanation (discussed earlier)—which is sometimes referred to as rational choice institutionalism—although also deductive, adopts a much more historically grounded, concrete, and comparative method. In other words, rational choice institutionalists examine how public institutions (or organizations), such as the state, *actually* behave and interact with markets. In this regard, they explicitly link theory, method, and evidence together to support their arguments as opposed to putting forth axiomatic claims that, in essence, have little or no comparative-historical and empirical foundation. This said, other comparativists might argue that the rational-institutional perspective is still too general, that it does not look closely enough at the specific histories and cultures of particular societies. This criticism is particularly evident in the cultural approach, to which we turn next.

Culture and Capitalist Development in East Asia

There are few, if any, scholars who argue that cultural factors *alone* can explain the economic rise of East Asia. There are, however, an increasing number of scholars who assert that completely ignoring or dismissing cultural factors is equally misguided. This latter view, generally speaking, is based on the belief that economic activity (and the institutions that sustain it) does not and cannot occur in a historical and cultural vacuum. With this as a starting point, some scholars argue that culture helps to shape the *specific* patterns and modes of economic activity and organization that differentiate one country (region or location) from another. This, in turn, can have a very large effect on how a national economy develops. Under certain conditions, moreover, specific types of cultural practices or patterns of cultural activity may in fact lead to rapid economic growth. In Japan, for example, some culturalists argue that the widely held Japanese belief in *wa,* or harmony, has led to a highly efficient but culturally specific form of cooperative economic behavior (e.g., see Abegglen and Stalk 1985, and Benedict 1946, both cited in Biggart 1997, p. 12). Regarding Taiwan, by contrast, some scholars argue that the Taiwanese business environment is "inspired by the heterodoxy of **Taoism**," which has led to an entrepreneurial class dominated by "rebels" and "bandits," figuratively speaking. It is this spirit of rebellion, these scholars suggest, that has led to Taiwan's economic success.

I will discuss these and other culture-specific views in more detail, but before doing so, it is important to say a few words about the most common cultural approach to capitalist development in East Asia, namely the idea that **Confucianism** is a common ingredient in *all* East Asian societies and is therefore a central factor explaining the region's economic success. Students should view this type of approach with extreme caution. I will explain why in the next section; for now, though, let me state the basic problem: those who use a Confucian argument typically commit the sin of dehistoricizing and decontextualizing culture. What I mean by this is that some scholars remove culture from its specific historical, social, and political context and then, worse still, assume that a broad range of societies can be classified, in essence, as cultural clones. This type of "cultural" analysis will almost always lead to superficial and distorted conclusions, since treating culture as a generalized, even generic, variable is almost always a fundamental mistake.

Still, viewing the Confucian argument (and similar approaches) with skepticism does not mean that we should abandon all culture-based interpretations of East Asian capitalism. Nor does it mean that Confucianism is irrelevant in any account of East Asian capitalism. This is decidedly not the case. For, as suggested earlier, there *are* valuable and valid interpretations of East Asian capitalism using a cultural approach, which I will discuss shortly. It might be useful, however, to first take a quick look at the traditional Confucian argument as an exemplar of bad cultural analysis. The point of doing so, however, is not to belittle a particular cultural approach (and the scholars and others who still use it), but to help you understand what to avoid in your own cultural analysis.

The Bad Confucian Argument

Most arguments based on East Asia's shared cultural heritage claim that a "Confucian ethic" is the key to understanding the region's economic success. Some scholars argue, for example, that core values of Confucianism—which are usually identified as respect for authority, faith, loyalty, filial piety (that is, deference to and respect of elders), harmony, and intellectualism—have been instrumental in promoting economic development in East Asia. The impact of these values on capitalist development, though, is not necessarily direct. Instead, Confucian ethics are said to help build those institutions (e.g., the state) and relationships (e.g., state-business, state-labor, and business-labor) that are important for rapid industrialization. In this view, therefore, the prominent role of East Asian governments can be traced to the importance Asians place on respect for authority or obedience to superiors. This supposedly explains, for instance, why East Asian business leaders have generally deferred to government officials—that is, because government officials are, by definition, superior in a Confucian society, their authority to lead is not subject to challenge. The same pattern of patriarchal deference can be found in business-labor relationships. Workers, moreover, are supposedly willing to give up personal gains because of their strong culturally rooted sense of self-sacrifice, loyalty to the larger group, and discipline. One scholar explained it this way: "The Confucian cultural inheritance meant that the authority and benevolence of a business leader could be anticipated on the basis of authority and benevolence traditionally expected of the head of a family. Similarly, cultural expectations anticipated that employees would perform their jobs at the direction of their superiors without question or debate" (Park 1999, p. 131). This clearly defined and respected hierarchy, so the argument goes, has allowed the East Asian countries to function as a single, strongly focused, tightly disciplined, and highly efficient economic unit. Hence the terms "Japan, Inc." and "Korea, Inc." have often been used to suggest that each of East Asia's economies is essentially a single, but massive, corporation, with the government as chief executive officer, the companies as departments or divisions, and the citizen-workers as loyal employees. The capacity to act as a monolithic economic unit, according to advocates of this view, has given East Asian countries a critical edge in the increasingly competitive and cutthroat milieu of global capitalism.

Variants of the Confucian argument see a more direct cause-and-effect relationship. Some writers, for instance, see Confucianism as a substitute for the "Protestant ethic," which supposedly unleashed the forces of capitalism in the West. The Protestant ethic, recall from Chapter 4, is based on the idea that capitalism thrived in the West when economic acquisition became solidly linked, as happened with the rise of **Puritanism** (in the sixteenth century), with the idea of salvation and service to God. In the Confucian version of the Protestant ethic, it is not believed that hard work and self-sacrifice will bring salvation in the afterlife, but the core values of Confucianism do encourage East Asians to behave in ways that have proven to be extremely helpful to rapid capitalist development in the postwar era. For instance, Confucianism preaches thriftiness. Thus Asians are supposedly more prone to save than, say, Latin Americans (and increased national savings leads to a greater availability of investable and cheap financial capital, which is necessary for rapid economic growth). Self-sacrifice is another Confucian value; thus Asians are, again, supposedly more willing to give up personal gains if this means contributing to a broader, collective good. Perhaps the most important Confucian value, many argue, is education. In East Asia, as one proponent of this view clearly put it, there is "enormous prestige of education, with the concomitant motivation to provide the best education for one's children. . . . [There are also] severe (some would say, brutally severe) meritocratic norms and institutions, which, while egalitarian in design, serve to select out elites when they are at an early age" (Berger 1998, p. 5, cited in Chan 1993, p. 40). This "enormous" emphasis on educational achievement not only has given East Asian societies a huge advantage over less educated and less skilled societies but also has allowed East Asia to catch up with the West much more quickly than would otherwise have been the case.

Problems with the bad Confucian argument. On the surface, the Confucian argument, in all its various forms, makes sense, which is one reason why the argument remains popular today. If we look under the surface, however, a number of problems immediately pop up. The basic problem, to reiterate, is this: advocates of the Confucian argument assume that Confucianism has played an essentially similar role throughout East Asia generally, but as even the most cursory *comparative analysis* will show, this just is not true. Thus, although most critics of the Confucian argument agree that Japan, South Korea, and Taiwan share a Confucian (and, to a lesser extent, **Buddhist**) heritage, it is equally clear that this has not created a bunch of cultural clones. Quite the contrary. In Japan, South Korea, and Taiwan (not to mention China, Singapore, Hong Kong, and other so-called Confucian societies), Confucianism not only is incorporated into different contexts, but also occupies dramatically different positions within each respective society. Some of these differences will become clear as we proceed.

The main point, however, is not to say that Confucianism is irrelevant in defining East Asian culture. It is not. Rather, the point is that Confucian values do not have the same impact or influence in every country or society. These values, for example, may be more or less accepted by the general population, or they may be accepted by only the economic or political elite of that society. Confucian values may also be modified or dramatically transformed (usually by the elite) in order to fit in with or to legitimize other dominant social, economic, or political arrangements. By the same token, the imposition of Confucian values may spur active resistance within society and encourage the development of strong and dynamic *countercultures.* Confucian values, too, generally must coexist with other strong cultural values. In South Korea, for example, Christianity is a strong, if not dominant, religion: almost one-third of South Koreans say they are Christian. Contrast this with Japan, where a mere 0.7 percent of the population is Christian. What, if anything, does this difference mean? Indeed, once we recognize these possibilities and differences, we must admit that an *all-encompassing* Confucian argument cannot adequately explain the economic success of Japan, South Korea, and Taiwan.

Confucianism in Context: An Updated View
In place of an all-encompassing Confucian argument are approaches that examine the relationship between culture and economy with careful regard

to specific contexts. This is what the better studies using a culturalist perspective do. A good example of this is the work of Greg Ornatowski (1996), who argued that, although Confucianism was an important part of Japan's economic rise (both prewar and postwar), there was no ready-made fit. In fact, at the beginning of the industrialization process, according to Ornatowski, traditional Confucianism was more of an obstacle to Japan's capitalist development than it was a help. This was largely because an important element of traditional Confucianism in Japan (or, more accurately, "elite" Confucianism) was strongly antagonistic toward merchant life and to the very idea of profit making. Partly for this reason, Japan's Meiji leaders at first rejected traditional Confucian values as anachronistic, belonging as they did to the previous and decidedly noncapitalist era. (On this last point, I should also emphasize that, while Ornatowski and others focus only on Confucian values, Japan's traditional culture included strong elements of **Shinto** and **Buddhism**.) Instead, the Meiji leadership advocated an embrace of Western values and culture. After all, so the thinking went, those values helped the West to achieve its economic, political, and military dominance, so they should also help Japan.

The attempt to Westernize Japanese society and culture, however, met with failure. The problem was not so much a clash of cultural values, but rather the fact that the more individualistic values of modern Western societies clashed with the demands of accelerated, **late industrialization**: late-industrializing countries, in general, suffer from a significant competitive disadvantage relative to early industrializers; thus there is intense pressure to keep the costs of production as low as possible, while maintaining high levels of worker productivity. In Japan, this translated into extreme hardship for workers—working long hours for little wages in dirty, difficult, and dangerous conditions. The requirements of late industrialization, in more practical terms, called for a disciplined, loyal, obedient, and self-sacrificing work force. Yet modern Western values encouraged a very different mindset. This was manifested in a strong propensity for Japanese workers to hop from one job to another in search of higher wages or better working conditions; or to engage in strikes, work stoppages, and other forms of "labor radicalism."

According to Ornatowski (1996), by the 1890s, some leaders in the Meiji government began to call for a Western-type national labor law as a way to create a more stable industrial environment, but Japan's industrialists were adamantly opposed to this. Instead, they advocated a culture-based solution premised, not surprisingly, on traditional Confucian and other traditional values. Some industrialists, for example, appealed to the "'special' relationships they said existed between management and labor in Japan as one reason why such a labor law was unnecessary. These relationships [between workers and factory owners] were based upon 'affection,' they claimed, and were similar to that between 'parent and children' or 'master and retainer'" (p. 576). The reference to "master and retainer," it is useful to note, suggests another very strong traditional cultural element: **Bushido**, or the "way of the warrior." Bushido, in other words, was the code of conduct for Japan's famous samurai. Indeed, it is fair to say that Japan's industrialists made a very strong—and partly successful—effort to transfer *selected* principles of Bushido to the industrial work force (as with Confucianism, many values of traditional Bushido were not compatible with capitalism). Put somewhat facetiously, they wanted to turn ordinary workers in "samurai salarymen."

Overall, Japan's industrialists began to build the basis for a new industrial culture, one that made factory work the equivalent of duty to the nation as a whole, and to the emperor. Consider the following statement by the presidents of the Industrial Bank in Japan: "The master—the capitalist—is loving toward those below, and takes tender care of them, while the employee—worker—respects those above and will sacrifice himself to his work. The spirit of loyalty and love of country . . . is by no means limited to the relationship between the sovereign and subject" (Marshall 1967, p. 58; cited in Ornatowski 1996, p. 576). Of course, such statements are only meaningful, from a cultural perspective, insofar as they become broadly accepted. In Japan, this acceptance did not, by any means, come quickly, easily, or uniformly. Importantly, though, the efforts by industrialists to create (or re-create) a new cultural system compatible with the demands of accelerated capitalist development were reinforced by Meiji leaders. Some Meiji leaders had their own reasons for reemphasizing Confucian values, while others (perhaps most) were in full agreement with the country's capitalist leaders on the need to create a more compliant, loyal, and disciplined work force. Indeed, since rapid industrialization was the raison d'être of the Meiji government, there was very strong support for reshaping culture as a way to maximize industrial growth. Whatever the rationale, the effort by the Meiji leaders to reincorporate Confucian values into Japanese society was crucial.

The effort began, as Ornatowski pointed out, in the educational system, as Japanese schoolchildren were required—in accordance with the first Imperial Rescript on Education (1890)—to learn and recite Confucian ideals regarding loyalty, filial piety, harmony, and the common good. Although these ideals were not necessarily tied to economic goals, in 1908 a second imperial rescript on education referred "more directly to the moral duty of subjects to perform economically on behalf of the Emperor" (1996, p. 575). Embedding Confucian values into the educational system was a critical step. For, while it can be very difficult to bring about profound cultural change for adults, it is much easier to do so for children. Nonetheless, it is fair to say that Japanese schoolchildren were not the only ones whose cultural viewpoints changed in the Meiji era.

To repeat: the construction of a culture that linked Confucian values to the demands of accelerated capitalist development was a long, difficult, and uneven process. Labor strife was pervasive in Japan into the 1930s, which meant that significant segments of Japan's labor force never fully bought into the Confucian (industrial) order. At the same time, it is fairly clear that the effort was at least partially successful in promoting industrial development by "encouraging sacrifice toward national goals as well as obedience to superiors within the workplace" (Ornatowski 1996, p. 580). Importantly, this self-sacrificing and obedient behavior was much more strongly evident in the early *postwar* period, a time when Japanese workers were renowned around the world for their willingness to work extraordinarily long hours for low wages, often sacrificing their social and family lives for the sake of their company and the country as a whole. This makes sense, as those who were inculcated with Confucian values as children in the prewar era had come of age in the early postwar period (I will return to a discussion of the postwar period shortly). Regarding the prewar period, it is also important to note that Confucian industrial culture proved to be a double-edged sword. Thus, while it helped to create a hardworking and disciplined work force, it "also limited innovation by tending to focus moral effort upon upholding company traditions and respecting the thinking of older generations rather than looking for innovative responses to new economic circumstances" (Ornatowski 1996, p. 581).

In sum, in the prewar period, Confucianism both helped *and* hindered capitalist development in Japan. It helped by compelling self-sacrificing behavior, especially on the part of workers and ordinary citizens, but it hindered capitalist development by wrapping Japanese capitalism in a moral and highly nationalistic straitjacket, so to speak. The two-edged aspect of Confucianism is important to highlight, for it illustrates two other general points about contemporary culturalist approaches. First it tells us that culture is complex and often has multiple, and unanticipated, effects in society (i.e., its causality was not unidirectional). Second, it tells us that culture is always more than merely a political resource: once (re)created, it can and does take on a life of its own.

Confucian values in the postwar period. In the postwar period, as suggested earlier, Confucian (and other traditional) values continued to play an important and very similar role: the idea of the "samurai salaryman" was still very strong in the postwar period. At the same time, changes in Japan's political and social context led to significant modifications in the moral-cultural code that governed Japanese capitalism. Thus, while Japan's industrial culture still extolled the virtues of hierarchy, self-sacrificing behavior, loyalty, and obedience in the workplace, even greater emphasis was put on the idea of Japan as a meritocratic society. This was particularly evident in the educational system, where meritocratic entrance exams—along with a student's cumulative grade point average—were the primary basis for determining entrance into Japan's public universities, as well as the country's public high schools. To a significant degree, performance on a single entrance exam would determine the fate of many Japanese workers. The economic effect was clear: it produced keen, if not extreme, competition throughout Japanese society to get into the best schools, which in turn prepared future generations of workers for the similarly intense competition they would face in a modern capitalist economy (Ornatowski 1996). In fact, even after finishing college, students who wished to enter government service were required to score well on another meritocratic test (some private sector corporations also had their own "entrance exams"). Importantly, along with the development of a hypercompetitive culture was the development of an equally strong emphasis on *fairness*. In the Japanese system, everyone had an opportunity to reach the top because there was one primary standard for measuring achievement. "Such a feeling of fairness," according to Ornatowski, "has an economic benefit in that it encourages people to participate rather than to drop out of the system or protest against it" (1996, p. 582).

To many cultural analysts, including Ornatowski, the combination of intense competition and fairness is a key to understanding the dynamism of postwar Japanese capitalism (as opposed to the prewar period). One of the strongest advocates of this position is Ronald Dore, who has written extensively on the relationship between culture and capitalist development in Japan. Specifically, Dore argued that Japanese economic and social arrangements—which are a reflection of both cultural (primarily Confucian) influences *and* rational responses to market pressures—have generated a sense of fairness within the context of intense competition that enables people to work "cooperatively, conscientiously and with a will" (1987, p. 18). This melding of competition and fairness, in Dore's view, not only made Japan unique, but also is a large part of what gave the country its competitive edge in the international economy for much of the postwar period.

It would be useful to consider a concrete example of how cultural influence and rational responses to market pressures have led to a unique business environment in Japan. Consider a well-known element of Japan's postwar employment system: lifetime employment. The premise of lifetime employment is simple: once a worker is hired, the company makes a commitment to never fire or layoff that worker—regardless of the worker's performance in the company (when lifetime employment was first introduced in the prewar period, it was limited to managerial or white collar workers; in the 1950s, however, most of Japan's largest corporations extended lifetime employment to regular employees). It is clear that one reason for the creation of lifetime employment was to secure a stable supply of skilled labor by dissuading workers from job-hopping. Market pressures were clearly at play, but lifetime employment also fit seamlessly with the Confucian ideal of benevolence and loyalty: adopting lifetime employment made corporations appear as good moral or Confucian citizens in the eyes of ordinary Japanese (Dore 1987). Significantly, once the practice of lifetime employment became embedded in Japan's employment system, it served to reinforce intense competition between and among the major corporations within the economy. The reason is fairly simple: when workers became tied to a single company for the rest of their working lives, they began seeing other companies as implacable rivals. This intense competitive environment helped make large Japanese corporations stronger and more productive.

The postwar story, I should emphasize, is vastly more complicated—and more extensive—than what I present here. Suffice it to say that culture continued to play an important and even central role in Japan's economic success. Keep in mind, however, that culture can explain only part of the reason for Japan's economic success. Keep in mind, too, that Japan's traditional culture was significantly and *selectively* transformed to fit with the demands of late capitalist development in Japan.

Finding Differences: Taiwan in Comparative Perspective

From the perspective of Ornatowski, Dore, and others, one can say that Confucian values were effectively integrated into the social and economic arrangements of Japan. It is easy to see, then, why so many scholars have been keen to embrace a (bad) Confucian argument, not just for Japan but also for all of East Asia. After all, if Confucianism helped Japan develop, the thinking goes, then it must have helped South Korea and Taiwan develop, since both these countries draw even more deeply from a Confucian heritage. But this is precisely why in-depth, historically based comparative analysis is so important. For when we look below the surface, it is usually not very difficult to find important differences or dissimilarities (this is often a goal among scholars who use a cultural approach). Consider the case of Taiwan. In Taiwan, as Danny Lam, Jeremy Paltiel, and John Shannon (1994) point out, Confucian orthodoxy *is* the dominant culture, or rather the culture of the dominant elite. But it is not the only, or necessarily the most important, dimension of culture in Taiwan. There is also a diverse and dynamic heterodox culture, which includes **Taoist**, Buddhist, and other subcultures or countercultures. Indeed, in Taiwan's case, Lam and colleagues argue that it is the very dominance of Confucianism—which is premised on "stifling restrictions and on stereotyped behavior" (p. 208)—that has spurred the development of Taiwan's strong and long-standing underground counterculture. More important, these authors contend that it is this counterculture, for the most part, and not the dominant Confucian culture, that defines and governs Taiwanese capitalism. According to Lam and colleagues, the standard "Confucian argument" unequivocally does not apply to Taiwan, because Confucian values have played only a minor role in the country's economic success. If they are right, then the Taiwanese case, by itself, would be enough to put to rest the grander and even not-so-grand claims made by advocates of the traditional Confucian argument.

So, are they right? Lam and colleagues made a compelling case. They began by pointing out an "indisputable fact," namely that small- to medium-size enterprises have played the major role in Taiwan's economy. At first glance, it may not be clear why this fact is important. Its importance, though, becomes apparent when we consider the obverse situation—that is, an economy dominated by large-scale firms. Large-scale firms, to put this issue in the simplest terms, are highly bureaucratic; they generally require strong, often rigid hierarchies, and operate in a top-down manner with obedience and discipline at the "lower levels" being crucial. In other words, large-scale firms typically reflect traditional Confucian values. Smaller-scale firms, by contrast, typically operate in a looser, more personal manner; they are, bluntly put, less "Confucian." I will come back to this point shortly, but a few comparative points are in order. To begin, it would be incorrect to say that small- to medium-size enterprises are unimportant in Japan (or South Korea), but it is clear that their role in Taiwan is far more significant. On this point, for example, Lam et al. noted that firms with 200 employees or fewer account for 50 to 70 percent of Taiwan's exports. In Japan and South Korea, by contrast, super-large firms utterly dominate the export market. Second, the authors argued that the outsized role of small- to medium-size enterprises in Taiwan did not necessarily begin solely as a cultural phenomenon. Instead, the growth of these enterprises reflects the particular political and social context of Taiwan. As Lam and colleagues explained it: "One factor that has engendered the proliferation of small-scale enterprise and reinforced its heterodox character in Taiwan is the social distance between the majority Taiwanese and the minority mainlanders who monopolized state power through the KMT [the dominant political party in Taiwan]" (Lam, Paltiel, and Shannon 1994, p. 211). The interaction between politics and culture, in other words, has helped to create unique economic arrangements in Taiwan. The same could be said of Japan.

Unlike the situation in Japan, however, the glorification of Confucian values did not encourage cooperation and social harmony, much less provide the basis for rapid economic growth. Rather, in the context of Taiwan's postwar society, the attempt by the elite to inculcate a Confucian orthodoxy in the "hearts and minds" of the Taiwanese people led to widespread contempt and distrust of impersonal and patriarchal authority. In other words, it led to the growth of an *anti*-Confucian attitude in the general population. Indeed, as Lam and colleagues argued, to fully understand the prevalence of small- to medium-size enterprises in Taiwan, one must take into account the strong anti-Confucian bias among entrepreneurs and ordinary citizens. As they explained it:

> As a firm begins to expand beyond the family, hires more distantly related persons, and forms partnerships with friends and even "outsiders," tensions and cracks begin to appear in the organizational structure of the firm. The classical Confucian reaction to these tensions is for the firm's "patriarch" to begin to act much like the Emperor in the state by replacing strictly personal, face-to-face loyalty with the more abstract loyalty of orthodoxy and punishing "unorthodox" or innovative behavior within the firm as "disloyalty," especially where it involves nonfamily members. Patriarchal behavior in the firm typically exacerbates underlying factional tensions and leads talented and innovative individuals to vote with their feet and form their own firms. . . . The tendency for talented individuals to exit larger firms as the firms' competitiveness declines partially explains why there is a large number of small-scale enterprises in Taiwan. (Lam, Paltiel, and Shannon 1994, p. 209)

More than encouraging the growth of small- to medium-size enterprises, Taiwan's strongly anti-Confucian bias helped to create a freewheeling, hypercompetitive domestic market that has imbued the Taiwanese economy with dynamism and resiliency. The underlying strength of the Taiwanese economy, the reason for the country's prosperity, to reiterate, is not Confucianism but the opposite: the *rejection* of Confucian values, combined with the embrace of heterodox, primarily Taoist, values. Lam and colleagues went even further than this. They claimed that where Confucianism is strongest in Taiwan's economy—in the largest, often state-owned firms—dynamism and entrepreneurialism are weakest. In this regard, they argued that, in Taiwan, Confucianism has been a largely *dysfunctional* ideology insofar as capitalist development is concerned.

Revealing the anti-Confucian foundation of the Taiwanese economy, however, is not enough to account for the country's economic success. There must also be, from a cultural perspective, something that creates a positive (economic) dynamic. According to Lam and colleagues, this is not difficult to find. Simply put, it is the complex webs or networks of tightly integrated but independent firms. These are a product of anti-Confucianism generally, but more specifically are a reflection of **guanxi**, or (very roughly translated) "personal connections." Lam, Paltiel, and Shannon argued that Taiwanese firms have put great effort into establishing "close personal ties of *guanxi* between people as a way of subverting the orthodox Confucian order. Because of the unique relationships between firms in Taiwan, networks are created that facilitate challenges to the orthodoxy" (1994, p. 212). On this point, it is important to understand that these networks do far more than facilitate "challenges to the orthodoxy"; they also have allowed Taiwan's small- to medium-size enterprises to create a functional substitute for large, hierarchically organized firms that, despite their drawbacks, provide a critical economic advantage, namely economies of scale. Indeed, in international competition, size often is the key advantage to defeating rivals and dominating markets. Taiwan's small- to medium-size enterprises have been able to overcome their size disadvantage, however, precisely because they are part of a large but highly flexible network of firms. In fact, Lam and colleagues argued that these networks, in many cases, are better thought of as constituting "group corporations." If one wants to understand the reasons for Taiwan's prosperity, then the place to look most carefully is in the structure and dynamics of the country's business networks and group corporations. The key point to remember, though, is that these structures have a unique cultural foundation.

Culture and Capitalist Development: A Few Methodological Issues

From this brief summary of two cultural accounts, one thing should be clear: Confucian values have played very different roles in East Asian capitalism. This should not be a surprise. After all, to a culturalist, it is natural to expect societies—even those that seemingly share many traits—to differ in substantial and pervasive ways. This does not mean that we should automatically ignore or gloss over similarities between societies. Rather, it means that, in assessing the impact of cultural variables, we should be extremely wary of efforts to generalize across cases, particularly without engaging in careful, in-depth comparative-historical research. Indeed, in the cases of Japan and Taiwan, just a little careful comparative analysis allowed us to see that Confucianism, as a *generic* concept, explains little, if anything, about the nature of capitalist development in the two countries. That is, just knowing that Japan and Taiwan are "Confucian societies" (a very problematic term, I should emphasize) does not tell us if Confucian values contributed to or undermined capitalist development in both countries. It certainly does not tell us *how* Confucian values impacted capitalist development (whether positively or negatively), even at the most general level. Instead, we learned that understanding the *context* of Confucianism is critical for a meaningful culture-based argument. In this regard, it is never enough to say that "Confucianism matters" or, more broadly, that "culture matters." Instead, it is crucial to examine, in as much depth and specificity as possible, the relationship between cultural factors and the broader political economy. Failing to do this will likely result in a specious or vacuous argument. This is, I hope, a simple lesson you will keep in mind. At the same time, although cultural theorists tell us to avoid overgeneralizing, structuralists adopt, as you already know, a strongly contrasting approach. We will look at this research tradition next.

Global Capitalism and the Rise of East Asia

Up until the 1990s or so, many structural analysts still firmly believed that, with the exception of Japan, the structure and dynamics of global capitalism would prevent the smaller East Asian economies—South Korea and Taiwan—from achieving a significant degree of autonomous economic growth. Writing in 1984, for example, Bruce Cumings was convinced that South Korea and Taiwan were on the brink of an economic collapse due to their inability to "break into the system of economic exchange at a point other than comparative advantage in labor, that is, in marketing, better technology, or better organization" (p. 35). Cumings also posited that the two countries would be unable to keep ahead of poorer states and therefore would be shut out of the export game both from above (by the more technologically advanced or core economies) and from below (by poorer or peripheral economies with lower labor costs). Cumings's pessimistic assessment for continued economic ascent on the part of South Korea and Taiwan was primarily based on his evaluation of regional and world-systemic dynamics (i.e., a structural analysis), which, in his view, were inexorably squeezing these two economies from all directions. As for Japan, structuralists were forced to acknowledge not only its rapid economic growth, but also the country's capacity to catch up and even exceed the hitherto more advanced Western economies in many critical industries. Still, there was a widely (but not universally) shared assumption among structural analysts that Japan's economic ascent would continue to be constrained by systemic forces.

Cumings's main conclusion, of course, was way off the mark: instead of collapsing, South Korea and Taiwan moved very rapidly ahead in exactly those areas that he and others thought impossible, namely technology-intensive industries. In fact, it is fair to say that both countries, once firmly rooted in the periphery, are among the most technologically advanced economies in the world today: they have reached core status. South Korea's leading companies—which include Samsung, Hyundai, and LG—occupy top spots in the global hierarchy of transnational corporations. Samsung, in particular, is one of the largest and most sophisticated producers of high-tech electronics for both the consumer and business markets. It is also simultaneously the top *rival* for Apple (generally considered one of the most innovative companies in the world), and a major *partner*. Apple, for example, chose Samsung to supply the mobile processors (the A9 chipset) for the next-generation iPhone 6 model (Arce 2015) and will also rely on another Korean company, LG, to supply displays—the 2016 version of the Apple Watch will use P-OLED displays designed and manufactured by LG (Burlacu 2015). More generally, *Bloomberg Businessweek* (2014) named South Korea the "most innovative" country in the world for 2014. Taiwan is certainly no slouch, either. In the same survey, Taiwan was listed as the tenth most innovative country (while Japan was third). Taiwan's top technology companies are less well known, but they have a major presence in world markets. Taiwan Semiconductor Manufacturing, for instance, was the world's third largest semiconductor company in 2014. Another prominent example is Hon Precision Industry, better known as Foxconn, which is one of the largest electronics manufacturers in world. Hon Hai produces a range of the most advanced consumer electronics, including most of Apple's products (the iPhone, iPad, and iMac), as well as products for Sony, Blackberry, Amazon, Nintendo, and others.

Does this mean that structural arguments, in general, are wrong? The short answer is an unequivocal no. To be sure, some of the bolder predictions may have been (dead) wrong, but the basic principles—at least according to structural analysts—remain valid. In particular, they argue that economic growth in Japan, South Korea, and Taiwan was clearly spurred and sustained by systemic processes and forces over which the individual East Asian countries had little, if any, control. It was not, in other words, their adherence to market principles, their developmental states, or their unique cultural characteristics that put them on the path of economic growth; instead, it was their advantageous position in the postwar system of global capitalism.

A First Step in Structural Analysis: Systemic Interaction in the Capitalist World-System

Although Cumings was clearly wrong about the long-term prospects for South Korea and Taiwan, other structuralists argue that he was right in his main assertion. To wit, any effort to portray capitalist development in East Asia as solely a state-based or national-level phenomenon is fundamentally misguided. It is no accident, for example, that Japan, South Korea, and Taiwan all ascended in more or less lockstep fashion: their economic growth was part of a larger process. Thus, in place of discrete, country-by-country analyses, Cumings suggested (demanded, even) that analysts adopt a dramatically different approach, one "that posits the *systemic* interaction of each country with the others, and of the region with the world at large" (1984, p. 4, emphasis added). More concretely, Cumings argued, first, that Japan played a key role in the *region's* economic ascendance by linking the three economies together, beginning in the colonial period. That is, Japan created an *integrated regional economy,* whereby economic growth in Korea and Taiwan directly reflected Japan's economic progress and needs in both the colonial and postwar periods. Second, Cumings further argued that the region as a whole fulfilled a critical function as part of the global system of capitalism, which meant that regional growth was largely a function of system-level dynamics and requirements.

The foregoing discussion provides a good basis for understanding the rest of the structural argument, or at least one structural argument: *world-systems theory.* I briefly introduced world-systems theory in Chapter 3, and my discussion here will also be fairly brief. This is because the key elements of the world-systems argument are not all that complicated. The starting point is the "systemic interaction" among and between countries and regions. This interaction is driven by the requirements of the capitalist world-system, both for the system as a whole and for the major parts of the system: the core, semiperiphery, and periphery (see Figure 5.3 for further discussion). One of these systemic requirements is the need for capitalism to *constantly expand.* Expansion is necessary, to put it in the simplest terms, because all markets eventually become sated. That is, they reach a point where the capacity to fulfill demand (i.e., supply) exceeds demand. Or, in

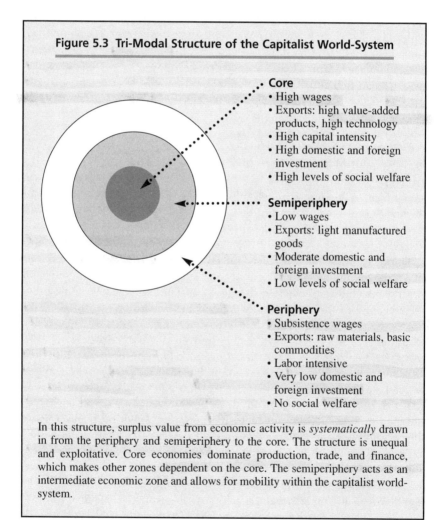

Figure 5.3 Tri-Modal Structure of the Capitalist World-System

Core
- High wages
- Exports: high value-added products, high technology
- High capital intensity
- High domestic and foreign investment
- High levels of social welfare

Semiperiphery
- Low wages
- Exports: light manufactured goods
- Moderate domestic and foreign investment
- Low levels of social welfare

Periphery
- Subsistence wages
- Exports: raw materials, basic commodities
- Labor intensive
- Very low domestic and foreign investment
- No social welfare

In this structure, surplus value from economic activity is *systematically* drawn in from the periphery and semiperiphery to the core. The structure is unequal and exploitative. Core economies dominate production, trade, and finance, which makes other zones dependent on the core. The semiperiphery acts as an intermediate economic zone and allows for mobility within the capitalist world-system.

the case of labor markets, they reach a point where the demand for labor exceeds the available supply. In both (and other) situations, profit making becomes more and more difficult to sustain.

The solution is to find or open new markets on a more or less constant basis. This does not necessarily require geographic expansion—for example, developing a brand new product, such as the tablet computer, is one way to open a new market—but geographic expansion is the most reliable method, especially in the case of labor markets. It is for this last reason that core economies, in general, depend on the periphery: the periphery enables sustained profit accumulation because of its vast supply of cheap labor. This means, then, that those economies hoping to join the core must, in essence, make or find their own periphery. These two factors explain why Japan—in the prewar period—almost immediately took control of Korea, Taiwan, and parts of China. (Japan really had its eyes set on all of China, but for present purposes, this section will focus on Korea and Taiwan.) Both colonial-era Korea and Taiwan were used to fulfill the economic interests of Japan first and foremost; thus, the exploitation was intense—a classic case of the "development of underdevelopment."

"Flying geese" and regional integration. The close integration of the three East Asian economies came to an abrupt end following Japan's surrender to the United States in 1945, but, for reasons I will discuss later, the economies were reintegrated after the 1950s. Not surprisingly, the same hierarchical and exploitative relationship that existed in the colonial period seemed to reemerge. Interestingly, it was a Japanese economist, Akamatsu Kaname (1935), who first identified this relationship during the colonial period, and famously likened it to a "flying geese" formation. As Akamatsu explained it, in the "flying geese" model a specific division of labor is created whereby the dominant economy, the lead goose so to speak, relies on cheap labor in the follower economies to accelerate its industrial progress by relocating mature industries in subordinate economies (see Figure 5.4). In this manner, industries in the lead economy continue to accumulate relatively large profits, which can then be invested in new products, new technology, more capital equipment, and so on. In principle, this should allow follower economies to achieve a certain degree of dependent development, but under colonial rule, Japanese firms owned most of the factories located in Korea and Taiwan. As a result, the profits stayed with Japanese capitalists even as production moved to the colonies, and Korea and Taiwan stayed very poor and underdeveloped. In the postcolonial period, however, indigenous capitalists were able to play a more active role, and thus both South Korea and Taiwan were able to make incremental economic progress, thus moving to a condition of dependent development.

Cumings and other structuralists, as suggested at the outset of this discussion, assumed that dependent development would be the end-stage for

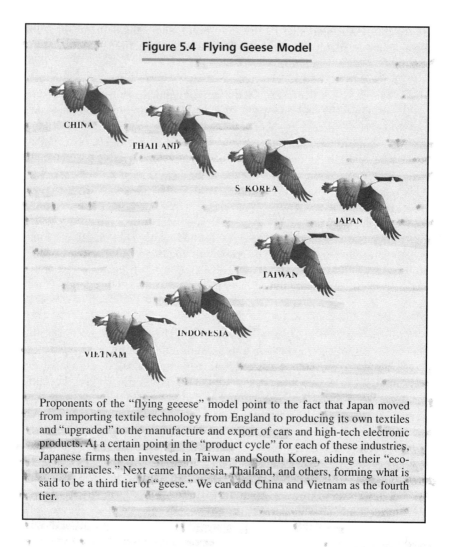

Figure 5.4 Flying Geese Model

Proponents of the "flying geeese" model point to the fact that Japan moved from importing textile technology from England to producing its own textiles and "upgraded" to the manufacture and export of cars and high-tech electronic products. At a certain point in the "product cycle" for each of these industries, Japanese firms then invested in Taiwan and South Korea, aiding their "economic miracles." Next came Indonesia, Thailand, and others, forming what is said to be a third tier of "geese." We can add China and Vietnam as the fourth tier.

South Korea and Taiwan. What they may have failed to fully appreciate, however, was that there were other forces at play in the capitalist world-system that would open wide a window of opportunity, first for Japan to move relatively quickly to the core, and second for South Korea and Taiwan to follow several decades later. (Actually, it is more likely that they failed to appreciate, as "hard structuralists," the significance of agency.) These "other forces" were contingent in nature—that is, they were not part of the normal dynamics of the capitalist world-system. Nonetheless they had a profound impact for the East Asian economies.

Windows of opportunity in the postwar era. In the postwar period, the basic requirements of the capitalist world-system remained the same. However, the growing strength of the communist world—led by the Soviet Union and, a little later, China—created serious complications. Most salient, the emergence of a communist world created a zero-sum game: the geographic expansion of **communism** meant a corresponding shrinkage in the territory or markets available to capitalism. In this context, rebuilding and expanding the capitalist world-system in the years following the war was clearly not an option, but a necessity. This was particularly the case because the communist world-system presented what seemed, at the time, to be a viable (ideological and practical) alternative to the capitalist world-system. This was especially true for the dozens of "new" countries that began to emerge after 1945 due to the delegitimation of colonialism: after decades and even centuries of domination by Western nations, many former colonies were understandably averse to joining the capitalist world. Even more, the major communist power, the Soviet Union, was willing to use its military power to force neighboring countries into its communist orbit. At the same time, within the core, the major economies have historically tended toward conflict and competition rather than cooperation or collaboration. Indeed, World Wars I and II can be seen, in part, as a struggle for dominance among the core economies.

Thus there was a clear problem: the capitalist world-system *had* to be reinvigorated, but that could not take place spontaneously. In this sense, world-systems theory shares common ground with rational choice: despite an understanding that a particular outcome would be desirable for all the core capitalist economies (e.g., a stable and growing capitalist system), in an environment in which the major players compete against one another, there is no incentive for any player to take action. In rational choice, recall, this is referred to as a collective-action problem (and is similar to the free-rider problem). The key question, then, was this: How would the rebuilding and expansion of capitalism take place? Structuralists, of course, *should* have an answer to this question for their explanation to hold water. And, not surprisingly, they do. The answer can be found in the concept of **hegemony**.

The importance of hegemony. The structure of the capitalist world-system, as alluded to above, is a triad, with the core at the center. The core is composed of the most advanced, wealthiest, and strongest capitalist economies. Yet within the core itself is another two-tiered **hierarchy**, with a single predominant actor sitting at the pinnacle of power. That actor or country is known as the hegemon. The hegemon, as William Robinson explained it, is the "leading core state that exercises its political domination and control over the system and imposes rules and norms that bring it disproportionate benefits" (2011, p. 9). It is the existence of a hegemon that resolves the collective action problem. In an important sense, the hegemon is similar to how rational choice scholars think of the state at the domestic level. That is, because of its preeminent position—its overwhelming dominance—the hegemon is the sole entity capable of overcoming collective-action problems in the capitalist world-system. More specifically, in the early postwar period, only a hegemon would have had the capacity to rebuild and create the conditions for the further expansion of capitalism, and, more importantly, the *incentive* (or interest) to do so. Robinson already suggested why the hegemon would have this incentive, namely that it has the most to gain (disproportionately benefit) when the capitalist system expands.

For structuralists, the hegemon is not just an abstract concept. It is a real-world actor, and the hegemon throughout most of the postwar period has been the United States. (There is, I should note, a long-standing debate among scholars as to whether the United States continues to be the hegemon—some have argued that US hegemony ended as early as the mid-1970s—but that debate is not crucial for present purposes.) Having taken the basic step of identifying the United States as the actual hegemon, the crux of the structural or world-systems argument can now be addressed. Thus, the answer to the question "Why is East Asia rich?" boils down to the crucial role played by the United States acting as the hegemon. In this role, the United States provided East Asia with guaranteed security, capital, technology, and, very importantly, one-way access to the vast and growing US market (in the first few decades of the postwar period). It is because of this extraordinary "largesse," according to structuralists, that East Asia was able to achieve the economic growth and success that it did. In other words, if the United States had not focused so much of its attention on the region— and especially Japan—the world would never have witnessed the so-called East Asian miracle, which was really no miracle at all. It was, in fact, a clear reflection of the power and interests of the United States in the early postwar period. As one world-systems scholar, Giovanni Arrighi put it, US support for East Asian capitalism in general, but for Japan specifically, made possible a phenomenal structural transformation and upgrading of the Japanese economy, and "it was this phenomenal upgrading of the Japanese economy that became the main factor of the industrial expansion and economic integration of the entire East Asian region" (1996, pp. 14–15).

The role of the United States as hegemon: "Capitalist-in-chief." So why did the United States create the so-called East Asian miracle? This question has already been answered, at least in general. Still, it would be useful to consider the logic of the world-systems answer both in more detail and in broader terms. To begin, it is worth repeating that the capitalist world-system was essentially without a hegemon for the first half of the twentieth century. The resulting instability, which was manifested in the

Great Depression and two major wars, forced US policymakers to come to terms with the role that their country had to play in the postwar period. That is, by the end of the war, they understood quite clearly that the smooth functioning of the capitalist world-system depended on the willingness of the United States to underwrite (accept responsibility) for the capitalist world-system as a whole. To put it in simpler terms, it was clear to everyone that the United States had to become "capitalist-in-chief."

As the capitalist-in-chief, the United States was obviously not just concerned with East Asia. Indeed, as hegemon, the first order of business for the United States was to construct a new financial order designed to prevent the sort of breakdown that led to the worldwide depression of the late 1920s and 1930s (the Great Depression). To this end, after the end of World War II, the United States established the gold exchange system, as well as arguably the two most prominent international financial institutions in world history, the IMF and the World Bank. (While undoubtedly important, the details of the gold exchange system, the IMF, and the World Bank—known collectively as the Bretton Woods system—are better discussed elsewhere. See, for example, Steil 2013.) As noted earlier, the United States was also vitally concerned with rebuilding Western Europe as quickly as possible, which it did primarily through the **Marshall Plan**, officially known as the European Recovery Program. The Marshall Plan earmarked $13 billion in economic support to Europe, which is roughly equivalent to $120 billion today. This was a hitherto unheard of amount of foreign aid, which speaks to the absolute priority US policymakers had put on reestablishing a firm foundation for capitalism in Europe.

Yet, even while East Asia was not the first priority of US policymakers, there was no doubt that the region was viewed as a critical part of the capitalist world-system. Originally, though, the United States was more focused on China. In the eyes of US policymakers, China represented the logical first choice given its huge population and historically central position in Asia. Of course, that choice was taken away from the United States when Mao Zedong led the Chinese Communist Party (CCP) to victory in 1949. The "loss of China" (a phrase used repeatedly by US policymakers and the US media after the communist victory) meant that a replacement had to be found, and Japan was the only viable candidate. In fact, fears of communist victory had compelled the United States to "reverse course" in Japan prior to 1949. On this last point, it important to understand that the original US policy in Japan was meant to *prevent* Japan from becoming a major industrial power. Thus, while US policy was not punitive, the United States "leaned toward a strategy that would contradict Japan's comparative advantage. Japanese industry would be decentralized and scaled down through the break-up of the prewar monopolies and the forfeit of industrial reparations to its wartime Asian victims" (McCormick 1995, p. 57). Much more attention, instead, was given to political and social reforms designed to democratize Japan.

By 1948, however, US policymakers realized that an "impoverished and enfeebled Japan . . . would not serve America's strategic interests" (Allen 1981, p. 189). Thus the decision was made to rebuild and reindustrialize Japan. In fact, this became a *prime objective* of US policy (US Department of State 1948, p. 694). Significantly, key US policymakers such as George Kennan and Dean Acheson not only advocated the economic revival of Japan, but also argued that achieving this goal would require creating an economic hinterland for the Japanese ("hinterland," in world-systems terms, means periphery). Ironically, this meant that US policy was designed to reestablish Japan's regional economic dominance—something the Japanese fought so hard to do in the first half of the twentieth century, but which was now being handed to them on a silver platter by the hegemon. The United States took this goal so seriously that it fought one of the most traumatic wars in US history just so Japan would have continued access to its own economic hinterland.[3]

The last sentence is likely somewhat perplexing. Just what war did the United States fight on Japan's behalf? The answer may come as a surprise: the Vietnam War. It is surprising since, for many if not most Americans, the reason the United States entered the war in Vietnam was to prevent the spread of communism. Certainly, there is more than just a little truth to that belief. But structuralists and world-systems analysts, specifically, tell us that there is more to the story. For the issue was not so much the implied military-security threat that communism represented, but its *economic* threat to the capitalist world-system: as noted earlier, as communism expanded, the space for capitalist expansion necessarily diminished. The threat that a communist victory in Vietnam posed to the capitalist world-system, in this view, had little to do with Vietnam itself: that country's economic footprint was exceedingly small. The real threat was the idea that a communist victory in Vietnam would embolden communists in neighboring countries—Malaysia, Thailand, Laos, Cambodia, Burma, Indonesia, and the Philippines. In other words, US policymakers were deeply afraid that communist victory in Vietnam would lead to subsequent communist victories throughout Asia.

This fear was articulated in the "falling domino" principle, which was first introduced by President Dwight Eisenhower in 1954. But what does this have to do with Japan? Interestingly, it was Eisenhower himself who provided the answer. In responding to a reporter's question during a press conference on April 7, Eisenhower first talked of the "broader considerations" of Vietnam (or Indochina as it was then called): "You have a row of dominoes set up, you knock over the first one, and what will happen to the last one is the certainty that it will go over very quickly. So you could have a beginning of a disintegration that would have the most profound influences." And here is where we get to the crux of the matter. For in Eisenhower's view, the "most profound influences" were not future threats to the US homeland, but were instead, as he put it, centered on the elimination of the "region that Japan must have as a *trading area* or Japan, in turn, will have only one place in the world to go—that is, toward the Communist areas in order to live" (Eisenhower 1960, p. 383, emphasis added). To repeat, Eisenhower justified fighting a war in Vietnam to protect Japan, and more specifically to protect Japan's trading area!

Development by invitation. From the world-systems perspective, the importance of the geopolitical context that characterized much of the postwar period—especially the first few decades, when the threat of international communism was at its height—cannot be understated. In particular, it made US hegemony far more beneficent than it might otherwise have been. Consider, again, a major part of US largesse for Japan: one-way access to US markets. In other words, US policymakers allowed Japanese manufacturers to export as much as they wanted to US markets, but the United States did not demand that Japan open its market to US-made goods. In retrospect, this is almost as astounding as the US willingness to wage a war in Vietnam on Japan's behalf. Beginning with the Korean War, moreover, the United States tapped Japan to be a major supplier for the US military, which was a huge boon to Japanese industry and to the country's early economic growth. Ironically, Japan directly profited from the Vietnam War, too, by producing war supplies, including as much as 92 percent of the napalm used by the United States (Havens 2014, p. 98). For a long time, the United States also backed a fixed exchange rate of 360 yen to the dollar, which gave Japanese exporters an even bigger advantage in US and international markets (by making Japanese products relatively less expensive). To top off all of this, the United States forced its European allies to admit Japan to the General Agreement on Tariffs and Trade (GATT) and to accept Japanese exports. In an important sense, the United States showered Japan with a huge array of invaluable gifts.

The notion that the United States bestowed gifts on Japan is, for world-systems scholars, particularly apt. For they contend that Japan was "invited to develop" by the system hegemon, the United States (Arrighi 1996; Cumings 1984; Wallerstein 1974). And just as Japan was invited, so too were South Korea and Taiwan. Their invitations came a little later, but they ended up showered with many of the same gifts received by Japan, including security guarantees, economic and military aid, privileged access to US markets, and (especially in the case of South Korea) military procurement benefits. For example, as South Korea was a chief ally to the United States during the Vietnam War, the United States helped the country's development of its fledgling electronics industry by purchasing military radios and radar (So and Chiu 1995, p. 196). In fact, US military and economic aid to South Korea and Taiwan was even more than Japan received: between 1946 and 1978, South Korea alone received $13 billion and Taiwan $5.6 billion (cited in Arrighi 1996, p. 17).[4]

World-Systems Theory and East Asia's Economic Rise: Criticisms and a Conclusion

It is fairly easy to see that the interpretation of East Asian prosperity from the perspective of world-systems theory gives limited credit to the countries themselves. If anything, the economic rise of Japan, South Korea, and Taiwan is portrayed as almost entirely a function of forces and factors beyond the control of strong states, capable entrepreneurs, visionary political leaders, hardworking (and well-educated) populations, or any other domestically based factor. And this is precisely the point that world-systems analysts, in general, wish to make. World-systems theory analysts, however, do not discount domestic factors completely. Indeed, they agree with rationalists to a certain extent: to take the best advantage of the opportunities presented (or the invitations extended), strong and capable states do matter. They also agree that particular social relationships, institutional arrangements, economic policies, and so on, might make some difference in national outcomes. Nonetheless, world-systems researchers clearly believe that agency is constrained and, ultimately, of only secondary importance. Critics, of course, would argue that the structural view is too narrow. Constraints—almost everyone agrees—do matter, but by themselves they do not *determine* which countries thrive and which do not. Japan, South Korea, and Taiwan may have occupied privileged positions in the capitalist world-system, but even tremendous advantages can be frittered away. Remember, for more than a decade prior to the military coup, South Korea's economy was in serious decline. Relying on a within-case comparison, we can surmise with reasonable confidence that this trend would have continued were it not for the sudden and dramatic change in leadership.

The macrodynamics of the world-system, it is also worth noting, cannot fully account for the rise of Japan as a viable competitor to the United States. That is, although world-systemic dynamics tell us why Japan pursued the path it did in the middle to late 1800s (that is, to avoid being incorporated into the capitalist world-system as a peripheral territory) and why Japan was "chosen" to develop after the end of World War II (to further the geopolitical goals of the United States), they do not tell us—except in a very general manner—how Japan achieved its status as a global economic "superpower." Again, to answer this question, we must turn to an analysis of regional- and domestic-level factors, some of which we have already discussed, and others not. These might include Japan's industrial and financial policies, its unique business structure (e.g., networks of vertically or horizontally linked companies known as *keiretsu*), its culturally based pattern of industrial (i.e., labor-management) relations, and its strategic deployment of foreign investment throughout Asia. To be sure, in assessing the importance of regional and domestic factors, most would agree that it is useful (even necessary) to do so with a keen appreciation of how broader systemic and geoeconomic forces helped or hindered Japan's economic ascendancy. But again, it is clear that system-level forces do not explain everything—and perhaps do not explain nearly enough.

Critics might argue that structural or system-level approaches do a particularly poor job in explaining the recent economic rise of China. For one thing, it is clear that China does *not* enjoy a special relationship with the United States; instead, the relationship has been marked more by hostility, anxiety, and suspicion than amity. Neither does China's enormous presence in the capitalist world-system explain the timing of its sudden but sustained capitalist growth. China, after all, has been around for centuries, but it is only fairly recently (since the 1950s) that it has had a highly centralized, very powerful, and cohesive national state. And it is even more recently that the Chinese state has embraced capitalism. From this perspective, then, one might argue that the rational choice approach provides the best framework for explaining China's economic emergence. As we shall see in the next section, however, structuralists are not willing to concede much, if anything, to the rationalists or anyone else. Instead, they argue that China's recent experience clearly confirms the most basic elements of a structural approach. With all this in mind, let us conclude this chapter with a brief discussion of China.

Explaining China's Economic Rise

On the surface, it is hard to ignore the strikingly similar trajectories of China's economic rise, on the one hand, and the rise of Japan, South Korea, and Taiwan, on the other hand. One aspect of this similar trajectory is the rate of growth. Over a thirty-five-year period, from 1960 to 1995, South Korea and Taiwan experienced annualized, and at the time unprecedented, average growth rates of more than 8 percent (Japan's was lower, but only because its economy was already quite large). Since 1980, China has grown at an even faster pace, averaging almost 10 percent per annum between 1980 and 2014. For one five-year period, between 2005 and 2009, moreover, China's growth rate averaged a historically unprecedented 11.4 percent per year (see Figure 5.5). Of course, a comparison of GDP growth rates tells us very little—*except* that there is definitely something quite unusual about China. In other words, China (like its East Asian neighbors) has not just successfully navigated a path toward capitalist industrialization, but it has also done so in a way that has been largely unmatched from a historical perspective.

**Figure 5.5 China's Average
Annual Real GDP Growth Rate, 1960–2014**

	Annual Growth Rate (percentage per year)
1960–1978 (pre-reform)	5.3
1980–1984	9.6
1985–1989	9.9
1990–1994	10.9
1995–1999	9.12
2000–2004	9.18
2005–2009	11.4
2010–2014	8.6

Source: World Bank n.d., "GDP Growth (Annual %)."

Another Developmental State?

A second, much more important similarity, many might argue, is the role the state has occupied and played in all four Asian societies and economies. (A methodological word of caution: remember that we cannot compare China, Japan, South Korea, and Taiwan based on an MSS design, although MoA can be applied.) I have already discussed this point in relation to Japan, South Korea, and Taiwan, but it bears repeating that, prior to their developmental thrusts, each country had a (very) strong state. Each East Asian state also had a significant degree of *autonomy* from societal interests (that is, the states were not mere instruments or tools of dominant groups in society).

In China, the strength and autonomy of the state was, if anything, much greater prior to that country's developmental takeoff. Decades of iron-fisted, essentially totalitarian communist rule under Mao Zedong, after all, had served to crush societal (interest) groups. When the transition to a market-based economic system began in 1979, therefore, it was primarily a matter of *loosening* the state's viselike grip on society so that nonstate actors could have not only some breathing room but also the capacity to pursue their own economic interests in a more decentralized environment (Unger and Chan 1995). Loosening its grip, however, did not mean abandoning control of the economy. Indeed, from the very beginning of the reform process, the Chinese state played a central role in assiduously managing the transition from a command economy to a market-based one. According to Barry Naughton (2007), the Chinese state took a measured, gradualist approach designed to spur rapid growth while minimizing major disruptions. The first step was to dismantle the command economy while maintaining economic growth. Second, markets were introduced in a phased (but comprehensive) manner, ownership was diversified, and competition created, all within the framework of existing institutions. Third, beginning around 1993, "the emphasis on reform shifted as it became more fundamental and thorough [but still controlled by the state]. The main accomplishments of this phase have been the remaking of the institutional setup to make it compatible with a market economy, the dramatic shrinkage of the state sector, and the creation of conditions enabling fair competition among all market participants. This . . . stage is still ongoing," but thus far, it has been a clear success, at least according to Naughton (2007, p. 86).

At a general level, then, China's state seems to have followed the same basic economic and institutional path as the other East Asian states. Of course, there are also marked differences, particularly since China had to first make the transition from a rigidly planned socialist economy to a market economy. Still, the principle of a state-directed or state-guided market economy in China is not fundamentally different compared to the other East Asian countries. Yet, from a rationalist perspective, we know that a strong state is often the problem, not the solution. So the question arises: Why did the individuals controlling the Chinese state (i.e., officials in the Chinese Communist Party) use the might of the state to spur and sustain national economic development *instead* of promoting their own narrow economic or political interests? Actually, this is the wrong question to ask. For, since 1979, the CCP has followed two separate paths. On one, it has demonstrated an extraordinarily strong commitment to national economic development (especially, but certainly not solely, in the form of massive public investments in infrastructural and public goods). On the other, hundreds of thousands of local-level CCP and government officials have engaged in rampant and massive corruption and **rent-seeking** activity. (See Figure 5.6 for further discussion of both these issues.)

The Janus-faced character of the Chinese state, however, does not necessarily surprise rationalists. The key to understanding why a state can be both strongly "developmental" and intensely "predatory" (i.e., exhibiting extreme corruption by the state or state officials) at the same time is found, in part, in an examination of the strategic environment. In the case of post-1979 China, this environment is, at a very general level, defined by a combination of still unaccountable political power (especially at the local and regional levels, but also at the national level) *and* an overriding incentive to catch up economically and militarily with, or to surpass, core industrial powers and potential military rivals. On the last point, it is fair to say that China's national leadership perceives the United States and its allies as a long-term existential threat—a fear that is not entirely unfounded given the West's heavy-handed intervention in China during the nineteenth and much

Figure 5.6 The Contradictions of Chinese Development? Strong Public Investment and Runaway Corruption

Since the 1990s, in particular, the Chinese state has poured massive amounts of capital and labor into creating or re-creating infrastructural and public goods and expanding the capacity of essential upstream industries, such as steel. In the early 1990s, for example, intercity travel in China was, as *The Economist* ("Rushing by Road, Rail, and Air" 2008) explained it, "often a choice between slow, crowded trains or a perilous journey by car or bus on narrow rural roads. . . . But since the 1990s China has built an expressway network criss-crossing the country that is second only to America's interstate highway system in length. By the end of 2007, some 53,600km of toll expressways had been built." A new terminal at the Beijing Capital International Airport (BCIA)—to cite another prominent example—was completed in 2008. This terminal cost $2.7 billion (part of a $3.8 billion overall expansion) and took four years and 50,000 workers to build. It more than doubled the capacity of the BCIA, from 35 million to 82 million passengers annually, thereby fulfilling a critical infrastructural need for more air transport capacity. Significantly, the expansion of the BCIA and of the expressway network were only parts in a much larger transportation infrastructure program: between 2001 and the end of 2005, in fact, "more was spent on roads, railways, and other fixed assets than was spent in the previous 50 years" ("Rushing by Road, Rail, and Air" 2008). Perhaps the most well-known infrastructural project is the $30 billion Three Gorges Dam, which is the world's largest hydroelectric power station, producing 100 terawatts of electricity annually (a terawatt is equal to 1 trillion [10^{12}] watts).

Closely linked to infrastructural investments are investments in basic upstream industries. (An upstream industry is an industry that produces inputs for other industries.) On this point, the Chinese state has also played a central role. In particular, it has been in charge of a massive expansion of China's steel industry: Chinese steel production increased from 40 million tons in 1980, to 151 million tons in 2001, to a government-capped 460 million tons in 2009. Despite that cap, China's steel production grew to an astounding 800 million tons in 2015 (Tan 2015). It is also worth noting that the Chinese state has expended considerable resources on developing the country's human capital, especially in the realm of primary, secondary, and tertiary education (Holz 2008).

At the same time, corruption is rampant in China and has been particularly serious since 1979, when the economic transition to a market-based system was first implemented. Each year since the 1980s, according to Minxin Pei, between 100,000 and 175,000 members of the Chinese Communist Party have been subject to "disciplinary action" by the Central Discipline Inspection Committee, the CCP's top anticorruption agency (cited in Pei 2008, p. 231). And each year, "Chinese courts prosecute more than 30,000 cases of corruption involving 'large sums of money'" (p. 229). These numbers, however, are likely only the tip of a very large iceberg. Significantly, infrastructural projects account for a large proportion—as much as one-quarter or more—of all corruption scandals. Most of these cases involve kickbacks of between 10 and 20 percent of the total costs of an infrastructural project. Obviously, corruption has not (yet) derailed China's economy, but it almost certainly has increased the costs of commerce, led to large-scale waste and inefficiency, exacerbated inequality, damaged public safety (both in China and abroad via Chinese exports), and—most important perhaps—eroded the legitimacy of the CCP and the authority/power of the state (pp. 229–230). As Pei put it, "Given the corrosive effects of corruption, it would be hard to imagine how China could confront its manifold economic, social, and political challenges in the decade ahead without waging a more committed and effective campaign against official corruption" (p. 230).

of the twentieth century. The strategic environment, of course, is much, much more complicated than this, but even at this high level of generality, the basic point remains: the Chinese state has played a key role in *remaking* the Chinese economy.

The theoretical bias of the analysis thus far should be crystal clear: rational choice institutionalism. It is almost impossible to ignore the central role the Chinese state has played in the country's economic transformation over the past thirty years. Even the many critics of state intervention— those who believe that excessive meddling by the state will ultimately ruin the Chinese market economy—generally adopt a rational institutionalist approach. John Lee, for example, concurred that the Chinese state has been responsible for the country's rapid growth, but he warned (in contrast to Naughton) that the economy has become far too biased toward the state sector, especially in terms of domestically funded fixed investment: fully 70 percent of all bank lending goes to state-controlled enterprises, which produce only one-quarter to one-third of all output in the country (2009, p. 11). Lee argued that this "massive bias towards the state sector would be acceptable if the state-controlled enterprises could learn to innovate and adapt. Unfortunately . . . this is not the case" (p. 12). In this view, the state is still portrayed as the key player, and rational self-interest is still understood to govern the behavior of individuals who control the state. So, is this the end of the (theoretical) story? That is, is the rational institutionalist explanation the obvious and only choice to explain China's economic rise? The short answer is no. As already noted, structuralists are not willing to concede the explanatory high ground. At the same time, this does not mean that there is no area of agreement. This said, let's see what the structuralists have to say about China's economic rise.

Global Capitalism and China's Economic Ascendance

The first thing to note about China's economic ascendance, *as a capitalist economy,* is this: for about three decades, the country's leaders attempted to chart an intentionally noncapitalist path. Obviously, their efforts failed. To casual observers, this failure was primarily, if not entirely, the product of an inherently inefficient and unproductive socialist system that was destined to collapse. To structuralists, this observation is not entirely wrong, but it misses the larger point, which is that China's socialist economy was, from the very beginning, firmly situated within the dominant capitalist world-system. As a potential (and potentially essential) part of the capitalist world-system, China's attempt to withdraw from that system *necessarily* provoked efforts to undermine and eventually reverse this decision. Not surprisingly, these efforts were led by the core powers, and especially by the United States (as hegemon). For example, immediately following the communist victory in China, the United States sent warships to patrol the Taiwan Strait and attempted to undercut the new government in China by freezing Chinese assets in the United States, imposing an embargo on Chinese products, and waging an intense ideological war against the Chinese (and Soviet) "menace" (So and Chiu 1995, p. 142). This was done, it is important to understand, not because communist China represented a military threat to the United States or other core powers; instead, it was done because China's attempted withdrawal represented a threat to the continued and future expansion of global capitalism. To see this, consider President Eisenhower's "falling domino" argument again. In referring to China, Eisenhower made this point: "Asia . . . has already *lost* some 450 million of its peoples to the Communist dictatorship, and we simply can't afford greater losses" (1960, p. 383, emphasis added). Of course, no Chinese were lost: Eisenhower and everyone else knew exactly where they were. What he obviously meant was that China's immense market was lost to US and world capitalism, and making sure that this did not happen in other places justified the use of massive military force. The failure of China's socialist system, in sum, was predetermined (in the view of structuralists); however, it had more to do with the imperatives of the capital world-system than with the deficiencies of socialist economics.

China's initial socialist failure also helps explain its subsequent capitalist success. The capitalist world-economy, to put it very simply, *needed* China to become an integral and integrated part of the overall system. The early stages of this integration, for example, invariably provided opportunities for wealth creation, as quite literally hundreds of millions of as yet unexploited, low-paid workers became part of the global production process. The very low labor costs in China, combined with low costs for other factors of production (land and capital), also made China an extremely attractive location for what Paul Ciccantell and Stephen Bunker (2004) called "generative sectors" (generative sectors are those industries—such as steel, shipbuilding, transportation, raw materials—that generate change in other sectors and, in general, create more dynamism and growth in a national economy). China, because of its advantageous position in the capitalist world-system, was *selected* to become the host for many of these sectors. This first happened in the steel industry. It is important to note, on this point, that the expansion and technological advancement of the Chinese steel industry has been strongly reliant on Japanese capital and technology; other core economies have also played a role (Ciccantell and Bunker 2004). Without this "help," it is not at all clear that China would have become the leading steel producer that it is today, for, as late as the mid-1990s, China's steel industry suffered from extremely low levels of productivity. Chinese steel mills produced 37 tons of steel per year, per employee, compared to a per employee output of about 400 tons in the United States, Europe, and Japan (cited in Ciccantell and Bunker 2004, p. 580).

While no one can dispute China's tremendous overall economic growth over the past thirty years, structuralists will also point out that, in keeping with the inherently exploitative nature of capitalism, China's growth has been tremendously uneven. As Naughton described it, "Since the 1980s . . . inequality in China has increased steadily and inexorably" (2007, p. 217). Indeed, in the course of two decades (between 1981 and 2002), China experienced a virtually unprecedented deterioration of income equality—or as Naughton succinctly put it, "there may be no other case where a society's income distribution has deteriorated so much, so fast" (p. 218). All of this tells us that China is reproducing a core-semiperiphery-periphery structure within its borders. Thus, while a new, relatively prosperous middle class has emerged—along with the rise of a class of economic elite—a huge and almost assuredly *permanent underclass* of hyperexploited, low-skilled workers has also been created. Capitalism, after all, requires inequality.

In this regard, structuralists will also tell us that the central role the Chinese state has played in the country's transformation was utterly predictable. The reason is clear: in global capitalism, sustained capitalist development at the national level requires a strong state. A strong state is necessary because it provides a "buffer" against the power of core economies, who would otherwise dominate weaker economies and their societies. (Strong states are also necessary in the early stages of capitalist industrialization to suppress workers and keep wages and other costs of production as low as possible.) Moreover, since the "mechanisms of domination" are well known, states that have the capacity to challenge or stand up core economies will generally employ the same policies and approaches. This is the primary reason for the similarity between China and the other East Asian "success stories." Fortunately for China, the state had this capacity and the opportunity—given its advantageous position in the capitalist world-economy—to achieve a significant degree of capitalist growth.

Global Capitalism and China's Economic Descent?
One final point: despite all of its economic success, China's economic future is far from certain. Since 2007, for example, public and private debt in China has skyrocketed. According to *The Economist* (2015), in an article titled "Deleveraging Delayed," China's overall debt-to-GDP ratio climbed from 160 percent of annual output (that is, total outstanding debt was 1.6 times the country's GDP) to more than 240 percent or $25 *trillion* in 2015. Just between 2012 and 2015, China's debt increased by nearly 50 percent. China's stock market has also become far more volatile and uncertain: on January 7, 2016, to cite just one instance, the Chinese market (the Shanghai index) experienced a 7.0 percent drop in just fourteen minutes of active trading. While day-to-day volatility in the stock market is not, by any means, indicative of deeper economic problems, it is fairly clear that the "real" Chinese economy is facing a number of serious interconnected issues, one of which is its massive debt, but another is serious overcapacity. Consider, on this last point, that China manufactured more cement from 2010 to

2013 than the United States produced over the entire twentieth century (Hutton 2015).

China's huge productive capacity is a boon as long as robust economic expansion, both domestically and globally, is taking place. However, when expansion slows or reverses on a long-term basis, especially globally, the results can be disastrous. China is already beginning to witness this, as its double-digit or near double-digit growth rates between 1990 and 2010 are likely over: in the third quarter of 2015, its economy grew at a more than realistic 6.9 percent, but that rate is likely a harbinger of much slower growth for the future. The problem for China is that combined with its very high national debt and overcapacity, even moderate growth may lead to serious difficulties. As noted in Figure 5.6, for example, China's annual production of 800 million tons of steel as of 2015 is becoming a major burden as steel consumption in China has declined; some factories have suspended production, while others have shut down completely (Tan 2015).

The main issue facing China, to be clear, is structural. China occupied an extraordinarily advantageous position in the global economy for the first thirty years of its rise as a new capitalist power, but those advantages have begun to disappear (at least in the structural view): its vast reserve of labor has diminished considerably, which has raised the costs of production; decades of unregulated industrialization have decimated China's domestic environment and threaten the global environment; its firms are facing increasingly intense competition from both below and above (rising labor costs mean China is losing its competitive edge over other developing economies, and rapid technological development means China must increasingly compete "at the cutting edge"); among other issues. None of this means that the Chinese economy will necessarily collapse, but it does mean that maintaining, still less improving upon, its present position in the global economy will be more and more difficult.

As usual, there is much more to the story than presented here. The key point, though, is that a structural account of China's economic rise is no less coherent and empirically supported than the rational institutionalist explanation. However, this does not mean that we are left where we started: a good comparativist will carefully consider both accounts and will assess their strengths and weaknesses through an appeal to both evidence and method.

Conclusion

It should be apparent that there is no easy answer to the question "Why is East Asia rich?" Saying this, however, does not mean that the question is unanswerable. Far from it. Indeed, one can argue that there are a number of plausible, even compelling, explanations for East Asian prosperity. Certainly, each of the major research traditions provides valuable insights into the process of "successful" capitalist development, although perhaps none provides a fully satisfactory account. This is not uncommon, nor is it necessarily surprising. For real-world capitalist development is a complex and—many would argue—highly contingent phenomenon, which is something you would be well advised to keep in mind. That is, the lack of a single, overarching explanation for capitalist development in all places, for all times, may be due to the possibility that no such explanation exists. There may be, to put it in slightly different terms, multiple explanations and multiple truths about the process of capitalist development.

At the same time, students must recognize that not all explanations are equally valid. The better theories of capitalist development need to be supported, as just noted, by an appropriate method and by evidence. In this regard, as emphasized at the outset of this chapter, a comparison of *only* Japan, South Korea, and Taiwan is problematic. This is especially true if the researcher is not even aware of the logical pitfalls of comparing three "most similar systems" that do not vary on the dependent variable. One way to mitigate this problem, as also noted, is to use within-case comparisons. In principle, this is an excellent strategy to use in conjunction with an MSS design in which the choice of cases is extremely limited. Unfortunately, this strategy is not always available. Of the three cases, for instance, South Korea is the only one in which a within-case comparison is unequivocally appropriate, since there is a clear demarcation between two periods: (1) a period of stagnant and declining economic development (dependent variable X_1) and (2) a period of rapid economic development (dependent variable X_2). In addition, between the two periods, there was also a major change in the political regime (an independent variable) while a range of other factors remained essentially the same. If we add China into the mix, we do have another potentially useful within-case comparison: the pre-reform period and the post-reform period. Significantly, the Chinese case tells us immediately that a strong state, *by itself,* is not a sufficient condition for rapid economic growth. You should ask yourself why this is true.

Even when within-case comparisons are possible, however, a good research design will also incorporate other, completely separate cases. To "test" or further buttress the structural argument, for example, a researcher might find other cases that seem to have the same geopolitical advantages of the Japanese, South Korean, and Taiwanese cases. In this view, the Philippines might be a good candidate, since it was also a bastion of anti-communism, with a "special relationship" with the United States. In addition, the Philippines also had a strong state, composed of highly trained and well-educated bureaucrats (often called technocrats). Unlike South Korea and Taiwan, however, the Philippines did not experience a comparable period of rapid industrialization, nor was its economy integrated into a regional economy led by Japan. Perhaps this was the critical difference. Or not. Only additional research and investigation can tell us the answer. We could use the Philippines, too, to test the rational choice argument, which focuses more heavily on the state itself. The key question here might be how and why did the Filipino state significantly differ from the East Asian states. A culturalist might have something to add, too, since the cultural foundation of the Philippines and its historical experience are very different from those of Japan, South Korea, and Taiwan. Admittedly, using the Philippines also raises methodological issues, since, as a most different system, it would be better if the dependent variable did not differ from Japan, South Korea, and Taiwan. On this point, however, we are faced with the practical problem of simply not having enough cases to fulfill the strict requirements of our research design—that is, the small-N problem.

Notes

1. One can argue that this basic context remained unchanged for the roughly twenty-year period between the early 1950s and early 1970s. But in the early 1970s, as one well-regarded scholar noted, things began to change. "Public readiness to sacrifice present for future economic rewards turned to insistence upon a reexamination of priorities. Individual and collective demands for improved living conditions, even at the expense of lower growth rates, recurred constantly. The opposition parties were outspoken in their challenges to the policies of high growth. As a result of all these changes in the context of economic policy, a substantial shift took place in both the agenda and the process of Japanese economic policy" (Pempel 1982, p. 52).

2. For further discussion, see Woo 1991, especially chap. 3.

3. Cumings argued that US policymakers originally designated Southeast Asia as the "preferred candidate for Japan's hinterland" (1984, p. 19). The idea was that Southeast Asia would provide markets for Japan's textiles and light industrial exports, and Japan would have access to badly needed raw materials. "The problem," however, "was that France and Britain sought to hold the countries in the region exclusively, and nationalist movements resisted both the Europeans and a reintroduction of the Japanese" (p. 62).

4. By today's standards these amounts may not seem like much, but they represent a staggering amount in comparative terms. Consider, for example, that the amount of grants and loans received by South Korea alone from 1946 to 1978 equaled almost 90 percent of aid received by all African countries combined during the same period, and about 40 percent of total economic aid to Latin America (Cumings 1984).

6

What Makes a Democracy? Explaining the Breakdown of Authoritarian Rule

As recently as the early 1990s, but especially since the mid-1970s, the so-called third world was still dominated by military governments, one-party regimes, and personal dictatorships (Pinkney 2003). Since then, however, the situation has changed dramatically. Indeed, as Robert Pinkney described it:

> Virtually all the governments of Latin America . . . [are now] chosen by means of competitive elections. Asia, South Korea, Bangladesh, Thailand, Nepal, the Philippines, and Indonesia, have all emerged from authoritarian, military, or personal rule, and single party domination in Taiwan has ended with the main opposition party winning a free election. In sub-Saharan Africa the vast majority of countries have held competitive elections since 1990, even though many authoritarian tendencies persist and political violence continues. (2003, p. 1)

To this list, we can also add much of Eastern Europe, including: Croatia, the Czech Republic, Estonia, Latvia, Lithuania, Poland, Slovakia, Bulgaria, and Romania. Impressive as the global trend toward democracy has been, it is still important to recognize that (1) major parts of the world are still, by and large, nondemocratic; and (2) many democratic or partially democratic countries have been or are in constant danger of being pulled back out to sea, so to speak. On the first point, the major exceptions to the democratization trend are most of North Africa (although Tunisia is an important and recent exception), the Middle East, a number of "postcommunist" countries (e.g., Russia, Belarus, Kazakhstan, Tajikistan, Turkmenistan, and Uzbekistan), and parts of Asia, including Vietnam and China, the latter of which is a major exception all by itself. As for the danger of being pulled back out to sea, it is clear that, even though a sizable number of countries seemed to have achieved a more or less permanent democratic transformation (often referred to as consolidated democracy), many others continue to struggle. In fact, according to Arch Puddington (2015) of Freedom House, 2014 not only marked the ninth consecutive year of decline in global freedom (or democracy), but was an exceptionally grim year, as "nearly twice as many countries suffered decline as registered gains, 61 to 33, with the number of gains hitting its lowest point since the nine-year erosion began" (p. 1). Some of the most notable countries that witnessed a slide in democratic standards included Russia, Venezuela, Egypt, Turkey, Thailand, Nigeria, Kenya, Azerbaijan, and Hungary, the latter of which is a **European Union** member state.

This initial discussion on the ebb and flow of "democracy," I should emphasize at the outset, presupposes a clear-cut definition of the term. After all, we cannot reasonably talk about democracy as emerging, advancing, or declining without first knowing what democracy is. Similarly, we cannot reasonably talk about how many democracies exist in the world unless we can distinguish between democratic and nondemocratic political systems. And, of course, we cannot *explain* democracy (or the democratization process) unless we can define the term. Yet, adequately defining democracy is a serious challenge; even more, there has been a long-standing and quite intense debate over the meaning of democracy. Thus, the first major task of this chapter is to examine the main issues of the definitional debate, with a view toward providing a practical meaning of the term. At the same time, the primary focus of this chapter, as usual, is how the three research schools have sought to explain the process of democratic transition.[1] As you might guess, there is also sharp disagreement among the various perspectives; yet there is a great deal of overlap and, therefore, perhaps even greater potential for meaningful theoretical synthesis.

Defining Democracy: A Never-Ending Debate?

"To take democracy seriously," Charles Tilly warned us, "we must know what we are talking about" (2007, p. 7). That is, we are required to *define* the term. In the academic literature, democracy is often (although certainly not always) defined in terms of procedures (such as elections) and constitutional provisions and principles. From this perspective, the definition of democracy *is* straightforward. Here is one definition offered by Anthony Giddens (2000), an eminent sociologist: "I would say democracy exists where you have a multiparty system with political parties competing with one another, free and non-corrupt voting procedures to elect political leaders, and an effective legal framework of civil liberties or human rights that underlie the mechanisms of voting processes." If we break down this definition, we have three readily discernible components of democracy:

1. A competitive multiparty system.
2. Free and noncorrupt elections.
3. An effective legal framework of civil liberties or human rights.

To this list it would be useful to add a fourth component: universal and equal suffrage (suffrage is simply the right or privilege of voting). These four components constitute what many scholars would consider the minimum or *core requirements* for democracy; it is a definition that they use to guide their research. But this raises an important question: Are the minimum requirements enough? That is, is a country that has a competitive multiparty system, free and noncorrupt elections, an effective legal framework of civil liberties or human rights, and universal or near-universal suffrage a *real* democracy? Or is something else—something more substantive—required? Not surprisingly, the answer, to other scholars (and perhaps to many students reading this book), is crystal clear: something more is required. Entailing much more than laws and procedures, democracy is instead, these scholars tell us, all about the *quality* or the *substance* of political, social, and economic life. Definitions that highlight the quality of democracy are generally referred to as substantive definitions. In this view, democracy revolves around issues of human welfare, individual and social freedom, security, equity, social and economic equality, public deliberation, peaceful conflict resolution, and so on.

Substantive definitions of democracy are important. Analytically, however, they present two basic problems (Tilly 2007). The first raises a question about trade-offs, namely: How are trade-offs handled between and among the various—and presumably coequal—substantive principles? For instance, achieving *greater* social/economic equality and equity—which typically requires a government-enforced redistribution of wealth within a society—may require *less* individual choice. Yet many Americans see this as "socialism," which they (wrongly) equate to a form of government tyranny, and therefore as the opposite of democracy. However, outside of the United States, especially in Western Europe, many fewer people believe that democracy and **socialism** are incompatible (Janda et al. 2012, p. 21). Perhaps an even more pertinent example, though, is the trade-off between security and individual freedom. Since September 11, 2001, in particular, the quest for greater security in the United States and other countries has meant a diminution of civil rights and liberties. Many critics see this as an untenable trade-off that necessarily degrades democracy. But, taken to the extreme, no security could easily mean limited freedom of movement, the complete elimination of civil rights and liberties, heightened surveillance, and so forth. So, again, where should the line be drawn? This is a difficult, maybe even impossible, question to answer (especially when we consider every substantive principle or aspect of democracy): this is precisely the analytical problem we face. That is, if we cannot specify how to handle such trade-offs, substantive definitions of democracy become exceedingly tricky.

The second problem is equally if not more important: focusing exclusively on "possible outcomes of politics undercuts," as Tilly put it, "any effort to learn whether some political arrangements . . . promote more desirable substantive outcomes than other political arrangements" (2007, p. 8). In other words, with a focus primarily on substantive outcomes we lose sight of how specific types of political arrangements (e.g., democracy, communist dictatorship, military authoritarianism) might differ with regard to promoting or retarding human welfare, equity, social equality, security, and so on. For this reason, as Tilly suggested, there is value in studying and comparing different political arrangements in and of themselves. We want to know, for example, if procedural democracy (scholars also use the phrases "formal democracy" or "minimal democracy") makes the achievement of social equality, to cite just one substantive outcome, more or less likely, or whether it provides a better way to deal with trade-offs compared to other types of political systems. More concretely, do democratic procedures make the achievement of social equity more likely in South Korea (a democracy) than in North Korea (a dictatorship)?

The Case for a Formal Definition of Democracy

The foregoing debate should be taken quite seriously. However, for our purposes, using a procedural or formal definition of democracy has merits in its own right. Georg Sørensen explained it this way: A substantive definition "does not give us much guidance in determining whether specific countries are democratic. For that purpose we need a precise concept that provides a clear identification of what democracy *essentially* is" (1993, p. 11). It is necessary, therefore, "to cut through the debates in order to find a *tool* with which we can identify democracy by its *core features,* as a form of government in which the people rule. Most helpful would be a *narrow concept* that focuses on democracy as a specific type of political system" (p. 11, emphasis added).

Sørensen, to be clear, is not an apologist—he is not making the case for a narrow definition of democracy in order to justify the less-than-ideal democracies that exist throughout the world, including the United States (as some critics would charge). Instead, he is asserting that, in studying the phenomenon of democracy, and especially the related phenomenon of democratic *transition* (or authoritarian breakdown), we need to set forth minimal and clearly identifiable boundaries for what *is* and what *is not* a democracy. Comparativists and other researchers who fail to do this will face serious analytical difficulties, not the least of which is that democracy as a dependent variable ends up being anything we want it to be or nothing at all. Still, many people remain uncomfortable with and even hostile to Sørensen's position. This is especially true if you believe that a procedural definition of democracy is nothing but a sham, nothing but a way to mollify the "masses" into believing they have political power when, in fact, they do not (a position held by many Marxist and progressive scholars). In this case, Sørensen's argument would be far less defensible, perhaps indefensible. The key question, therefore, is this: Does a formal definition of democracy have any meaning beyond its "operational" precision?

To many scholars who study and think about democracy, the answer to this question is an unequivocal, albeit often implicit, yes. One set of scholars who address this question explicitly are Dietrich Rueschemeyer, Evelyne Stephens, and John Stephens. In their 1992 book *Capitalist Development and Democracy,* this trio asked: "Why do we care about formal [procedural] democracy if it considerably falls short of the actual rule of the many?" (p. 10). Their answer was simple: "We care about formal democracy because it tends to be more than merely formal. It tends to be real to some extent" (p. 10). In other words, Rueschemeyer and colleagues believe that procedural democracy matters. It matters because, once the most basic institutions, practices, and components of democracy are established in a society, they almost invariably create a "promising basis for further progress in the distribution of power and other forms of substantive equality" (p. 10). Specifically, the authors contend, "the same factors which support the installation and consolidation of formal democracy, namely the growth in the strength of **civil society** in general and of the lower classes in particular, also support progress towards greater equality in political participation and towards greater social and economic equality" (pp. 10–11). Whether or not you agree with Rueschemeyer and colleagues, it is important to carefully consider their points and the questions they raise. Does the initial establishment of certain institutions of democracy create the basis for substantive change in society (for example, toward greater social and economic equality)? Do these institutions, no matter how weak they may be or become, ultimately provide the promise of political power for ordinary citizens—power that citizens would otherwise not have? Are real-world democracies, in this regard, qualitatively different than the nondemocratic systems that preceded them?

The answers to these questions are admittedly debatable. Nonetheless, a strong case can be made that formal democracy can be and invariably is more than an empty shell—that it has its own substance and meaning, even if largely and often unrealized, imperfect, or transitory. If we accept this premise, however, we need to return to the starting point of this section, namely offering a practical or **operational definition** of democracy. The minimal definition provided by Giddens earlier is, for the purposes of this chapter, sufficient. But it would be useful to at least consider other minimal requirements. In this regard, one standard point of reference is Robert Dahl's classic definition. Among the requirements for democracy, Dahl argued that eight institutional guarantees are required: (1) freedom to form and to join organizations; (2) freedom of expression; (3) the right to vote; (4) eligibility for public office; (5) the right of political leaders to compete for support and votes; (6) alternative sources of information; (7) free and fair elections; and (8) institutions for making government policies depend on votes and other expressions of preference (1971, pp. 1–3).[2]

Other scholars, although agreeing with Dahl's basic list of guarantees, argue that it is insufficient because it lacks, for example, the requirement for a "constitution that itself is democratic in that it respects fundamental liberties and offers considerable protections for minority rights" (Stepan 2000, p. 39). Still others—in particular, Charles Tilly (2007)—argue that any *static,* either-or definition of democracy is problematic; instead, he asserts that we need a process-based definition, one that conceptualizes democracy as a *movement.* In this view, with which I largely concur, emphasis is put on whether a country is becoming more democratic (democratizing) or less democratic (de-democratizing).

Whichever (procedural) definition you choose, it is important to remember the main purpose: a *procedural* definition of democracy is designed, first and foremost, to provide a clear-cut basis *for analysis.* More specifically, it is used for determining, at a minimum, the basic dividing line between (real-world) democracies and nondemocracies. Conversely, a procedural definition is *not* necessarily meant to be a normative statement. A normative statement expresses a value judgment about whether something is good or bad, desirable or undesirable, superior or inferior (to something else). Many critics of procedural definitions of democracy, at base, believe that anything less than a pure or ideal form of (substantive) democracy should not and cannot be called democracy. However, if we understand democracy to simply be a political system that includes certain core characteristics that other political systems do not possess, it is possible to find common ground. Democracy, in this regard, is not necessarily an admirable political system—Winston Churchill famously defined democracy as "the worst form of government, except for all those other forms that have tried from time to time"—nor is it automatically superior to other political systems. It is merely different. Thus, in terms of its political system, the United States is different from China, just as Germany's political system under the leadership of Angela Merkel is different from Germany's system under Adolf Hitler, or as Iran's theocracy is different from Turkey's secular democracy. Value judgments do not need to be made.

Admittedly, in practice, it is difficult to strip away the normative belief that democracy is supposed to be better than other political systems. It is, perhaps, even more difficult to accept the notion that democracy does not have to be an ideal political system. I should point out, though, that the strongly held belief that democracy represents a better or ideal political system—from a cultural perspective—is an important factor leading to democracy (I discuss this point later). Nonetheless, without a willingness to accept a "stripped down" definition, there is little reason to even attempt an analysis of how and why countries democratize *in a concrete sense,* which is the topic of this chapter. After all, if a definition of democracy essentially excludes all real-world cases, then any analysis of "democracy" will be empirically empty.

Explaining or accounting for changes in the democratization process, of course, is the main topic of this chapter and our next subject of discussion. Unlike the previous two chapters, however, we will begin with the structural tradition.

Economic Development and Democracy: A Necessary Relationship?

It is virtually impossible to dispute, from an empirical perspective, the strong positive relationship between democratization and economic development. (Here the concept of economic development is used in its narrowest sense—the accumulation of economic wealth as measured through increases in per capita income.) Most knowledgeable observers recognize, in other words, that economic development (and more specifically, capitalist development) is related to, but not necessarily a direct cause of, democratization. Agreeing that there is a relationship between economic development and democracy, to be clear, is not the same as agreeing on the reasons for or the exact nature of this relationship. Indeed, within comparative politics (and the social sciences more generally), sharp and even fundamental differences exist among researchers who have attempted to explain this relationship. One school of thought—which derives from early research made most famous by Seymour Lipset—argues that democratization is the final stage in a general process of social change brought about by modernization (modernization, in this reading, is largely synonymous with capitalist development).[3] As explained by Adam Przeworski and Fernando Limongi:

> Modernization consists of a gradual differentiation and specialization of social structures that culminates in a separation of political structures from other structures and makes democracy possible. The specific causal chains consist of sequences of industrialization, urbanization, education, communication, mobilization, and political incorporation, among innumerable others: a progressive accumulation of social changes that ready a society to proceed to its culmination, democratization. (1997, pp. 156–157)

Modernization Theory: A Defective Structural Explanation?

In modernization accounts, then, the relationship between economic development and democratization is not strictly one-dimensional. It is not, to put it very simply, just a matter of a country reaching a certain level of wealth and then magically transforming into a democracy (although popular accounts, to some extent, are based on this simplistic premise); rather, the transition to democracy happens because modernization creates new economic, social, technological, and political *conditions* that "primitive" or premodern political systems (for example, dictatorships or monarchies) are simply unable to handle over the long run. One less obvious but very important product of these conditions is a viable civil society—that is, the set of social institutions, organizations, and associations that stand apart from the state. In modernization theory, the development of a civil society leads inexorably to democracy. The transition to democracy, in sum, may not always be smooth and completely predictable, but it is largely *irresistible* once (capitalist) economic development gets under way.

As should already be apparent, modernization theory offers a structural—and largely deterministic—account of democratic transformation or authoritarian breakdown. From the perspective of other structuralists (especially historical structuralists), however, it is a very limited and inadequate account. It is limited and inadequate, in part, because many of its advocates presume that the key to understanding democratic transformation can be found in the inability of nondemocratic political systems to deal with rising social, economic, and technological complexity. But as a few exceptional cases clearly show—Singapore, which is an advanced capitalist country, is perhaps the best contemporary example—authoritarian regimes not only are concretely capable of maintaining control over complex, "modern" societies, but also are capable of managing these complexities in an effective and efficient manner over relatively long periods of time. Of course, if Singapore is *truly* exceptional, modernization theory might be only dented, rather than crushed. Unfortunately, there are a plethora of other exceptions.

These exceptions include relatively poor, underindustrialized or industrializing democracies, such as India, Ghana, Indonesia, and Lesotho; and relatively wealthy authoritarian regimes, especially the so-called **rentier states**: Qatar (the richest country on the planet in terms of per capita GDP), the United Arab Emirates, Kuwait, Brunei, Saudi Arabia, and others. Even China—which despite its still relatively low per capita wealth—might be included in this list. After all, the most "developed" parts of China are now thoroughly modern, and yet the ostensibly communist authoritarian regime seems to be handling the economy and society with a great deal of skill and aplomb (although there is much debate on this issue). With so many exceptions, many argue that modernization theory, at best, is too generic; thus, while it might seem to explain some cases, it does not explain many others.

Another criticism is this: modernization theory is unable to explain why countries at roughly similar stages of economic development have very different experiences with democracy. Consider, for instance, the following seven countries with roughly similar per capita purchasing power–adjusted GDPs in 2014: Suriname ($16,623), Iran ($17,114), Botswana ($16,036), Venezuela ($17,685), Azerbaijan ($17,618), Libya ($15,706), and Mexico ($17,881). Despite their very similar levels of wealth, there are significant differences in political status: in 2014, Suriname and Botswana were ranked as "free" (or democratic) by Freedom House (freedomhouse .org); Venezuela and Mexico were ranked as "partly free"; and Iran, Libya, and Azerbaijan as "not free." In these seven cases, in short, there is no clear relationship between wealth (as a rough proxy for modernization) and democracy. Yet any good theory needs to be able to explain significant variations on the dependent variable when the presumed independent variable is consistent across all cases.

Perhaps the most damaging criticism, however, is the almost antiseptic manner in which modernization portrays the transition to democracy. In modernization theory, political change just seems to happen as a product of "progressive accumulation of social changes." Yet, as critics have pointed out, the transition to democracy is often extremely "messy" and highly contingent. Transitions can be bloody and violent, and even in cases in which violence is limited, there is almost always an underlying power struggle. Indeed, one might argue that modernization theory sees democratization as an apolitical process. To many, this is a fatal limitation.

Capitalist Development and Democracy: A Historical-Structural Explanation

But if modernization theory is limited, how do the critics—especially those who embrace a historical-structuralist approach—explain the relationship between capitalist development and democratization? There is, of course, no single answer to this question. But one thought-provoking and particularly powerful argument is provided by a set of authors mentioned earlier—Rueschemeyer, Stephens, and Stephens—in their book *Capitalist Development and Democracy* (1992). We will focus on their argument for the remainder of this section.

In laying out their explanation of the relationship between economic development and democracy, Rueschemeyer and colleagues began with a simple but telling observation (an observation, by the way, that researchers in the rational choice school also generally accept): the people (or the social class) who have predominant control over economic resources in society are generally not friends of democracy. Indeed, for the dominant groups in society, democracy represents a concrete threat to their own interests, since, by its very nature, democracy gives power to subordinate classes who constitute the large majority of any society's population. Think of it this way: if the majority of people in a society are poor and exploited (which is often the case), would they not be immediately tempted, in a democratic system, to use their newfound and overwhelming voting power to redistribute economic resources and, ultimately, to undermine permanently—if not destroy—the position and privileges of the wealthy (or political and economic elite)? More to the point, would not the elite be well aware of this potential threat and, therefore, do whatever they could to prevent democracy from taking hold? The answer to both questions is clear: a resounding yes. It is largely for this reason that Rueschemeyer and colleagues argued that political democracy "inevitably stands in tension with the system of social inequality" (p. 41).

Given the almost undeniable tension between democracy and social inequality, Rueschemeyer and colleagues made a basic assertion, one that undergirded their entire argument: democracy is above all a matter of power (p. 5). By this they meant that democracy is not the product of altruism or of morality. It is not a "gift" given to the masses. Neither, as we have already discussed, does democracy emerge merely because society has become "too complex" or modernized. Instead, it is almost always a product of *political struggle*—a result of one or (more likely) several hitherto excluded groups assiduously fighting to break down barriers to their more complete participation in the political process. The struggle for democracy, however, is also *highly conditioned*. What this means is that transitions to (and consolidations of) democracy are conditioned—that is, constrained and enabled—by broad *structural changes* that reorder the balance of power among different classes and class coalitions in society. These structural changes, in turn, are primarily—although not exclusively—an inexorable product of capitalist development. As the authors explained it:

> Capitalist development is associated with the rise of democracy primarily because of two *structural effects:* it strengthens the working class as well as other subordinate classes, and it weakens large landowners. The first of these must be further specified: capitalist development enlarges the urban working class at the expense of agricultural laborers and small farmers; it thus shifts members of the subordinate classes from an environment extremely unfavorable for collective action to one much more favorable, from geographical isolation and immobility to high concentrations of people with similar interests and far-flung communications. (p. 58, emphasis added)

It is worth emphasizing that Rueschemeyer and colleagues were not merely dressing up modernization's structural argument in new clothes. It is not, for example, a generic and uniformly prodemocratic civil society that creates the basis for democratic transformation. Instead, it is a historically shaped civil society, within which class interests can and do play out in very different ways. In other words, the concrete role of various classes in various societies—with regard to the issue of democracy or any other social issue—will differ according to the particular historical circumstances in which they emerge and develop. "History matters," therefore, even in the face of large-scale structural change. At the same time, the authors argued that a specific segment of civil society—the *urban* (that is, nonagricultural) *working class*—almost always stands at the center of the struggle for democracy. The centrality of the urban working class is, to reiterate, no accident. As suggested in the preceding passage, this class not only is a direct product of the capitalist process—a process that necessarily creates an unequal and exploitative class division—but also is the most consistently and most important prodemocratic force within capitalist societies.

Democracy and the working class. The foregoing discussion raises important questions: *Why* does the urban working class support democratization, and more important, *how* does it bring about democratic transformation? The answer to the first question should already be clear: the urban working class supports democratic transformation because it is this class that has the most to gain from democracy, in both the short and long run (Rueschemeyer, Stephens, and Stephens 1992). On this last point, it is important to recognize that, in authoritarian regimes, the working class is typically subject to harsh and unrelenting repression by the capitalist class and the state (which usually work hand-in-glove). The repression is itself a reflection of the imperatives of capitalism. Specifically, in the early stages of capitalist industrialization, developing countries almost always occupy a disadvantaged position in the global economy. To compete in foreign markets, therefore, production costs needs to be kept as low as possible, and since the price of labor is a main cost of production, repression is used to prevent workers from organizing, from demanding higher wages and better working conditions, and so on. Workers understand that the only way to ensure a better life for themselves is through political change—democratization.

Rueschemeyer and colleagues were careful to assert that class interests, and working-class interests in particular, are not given or objectively determined. Interests, instead, are **socially constructed**. By this they meant that class interests are variable and subjective—they are shaped by a large number of factors, including leadership, organizational dynamics, race, ethnicity, "history," and so on. Still, according to Rueschemeyer and colleagues, for the most part (and from a concrete historical perspective), the urban working class consistently and systematically favors democracy because democratic change gives members of this class greater control of economic and other resources in society, which ultimately gives members of this class greater control over their own lives.

The answer to the second question (How does the urban working class bring about democratic transformation?) is less clear, but it goes to the heart of the authors' argument. To begin, it is important to reemphasize two points made earlier. First, the capacity of the urban working class to bring about democratic transformation is, to a significant extent, a function of a changing "balance of power" within society. Second, shifts in the balance of power are the product of capitalist development, which simultaneously erodes the (relative) power of some social groups/classes while fortifying the power of others. In this regard, and just to underscore the main point here, it is not capitalism (or wealth creation) per se that creates the basis for democracy but capitalism's largely unintended and unavoidable effect on class structure—or as Rueschemeyer and colleagues put it: "It was not the capitalist market nor capitalists as the new dominant force, but rather the *contradictions* of capitalism that advanced the cause of democracy" (p. 7, emphasis added).

The main contradiction is this: although capitalism as a system is not designed to empower ordinary workers (in fact, capitalists, for the most part, are positively hostile to this outcome), this is exactly what it does. And it does so because capitalist development *necessarily* creates subordinate classes with the capacity for *self-organization*. The basis of this self-organization is explained by the authors: "Capitalism brings the subordinate class or classes together in factories and cities where members of those classes can associate and organize more easily; it improves the means of communication and transportation facilitating worldwide organization; in these and other ways it strengthens civil society and facilitates subordinate class organization" (pp. 271–272). Still, this does not tell *how* the urban working class actually brings about democratic transformation.

How the working class brings about democracy. Here is where the answer becomes more complicated. This is largely because the working-class role in democratization is highly *contingent* or context-dependent (that is, dependent on particular historical, social, and geopolitical circumstances). This is a crucial point, and one that must not be underestimated. For it means, in part, that there is, according to Rueschemeyer, Stephens, and Stephens, no single or homogeneous causal sequence in the process of democratic transition (1992, p. 284); instead, there are (potentially) innumerable and innumerably divergent paths to democracy (or continued authoritarian rule, as the case may be). On the surface, this makes the process of democratization very messy, theoretically speaking (a bane to many social scientists). But underlying this ostensible messiness is a key similarity: an overall balance of power between classes (and between civil society and the state) that gives the urban working class the potential strength to challenge the status quo. From a methodological or comparative perspective, I might note, the challenge is to find and demonstrate the importance of this "key similarity" across as many (divergent) cases as possible. With this in mind, then, the very broad contours of how the urban working class brings about democratic transformation are as follows.

First, once the urban working class develops a sufficient level of organizational strength, pressures and demands for greater political inclusion are brought to bear on the dominant class. This pressure, not surprisingly, is manifested through a variety of forms: radical mass political parties, organized labor unions, and broader-based labor movements (a type of social movement; social movements are discussed in Chapter 8) are the most common. Sometimes the demands of the working class are met through **co-optation**, whereby the state or dominant classes accommodate some working-class interests without opening up the political system in a meaningful way. One of the best examples of this is in Mexico (according to Rueschemeyer and colleagues), where the subordinate classes, including the urban working class, have been effectively co-opted into state-sponsored and elite-controlled organizations for a long time. This helps to explain why Mexico is not a full-fledged democracy today. At other times, demands by the working class are met with violence and repression (as noted above, this is the rule)—this is especially likely when the organizational strength and ideological radicalism of the working class are particularly high and, therefore, particularly threatening to the dominant classes. We can see evidence of this throughout the developing world. In most situations, however, even a well-organized urban working class is not strong enough to achieve an expansion of political and democratic rights *on its own;* this was generally the case in the countries that underwent capitalist industrialization early on (for example, in Western Europe, the United States, and Commonwealth countries) and is even more significant for the late-industrializing countries of the twentieth century. For this reason, the working class has invariably had to rely on establishing *alliances* across class boundaries.

This establishment of alliances is the second, and more salient, part of the answer of how the working class, in concrete terms, brings about democratization. These alliances, as with the interests of the working class itself, are not predetermined. That is, the allies of the working class are not always the same. Historically, for example, it was the urban and the rural **petty bourgeoisie** (merchants, craftsmen, farmers, and other self-employed groups) who were the most significant allies of the working class in Europe. In Latin America and East Asia, however, the most important ally has been the employed middle classes (including the "intellectual class," which is primarily composed of professors and university students). Because of the variable nature of class alliances—and because working-class power itself is a highly variable phenomenon—the specific role the working class plays in the process of democratization also varies across time and space. Sometimes (in fact, quite often) this role will be subtle and seemingly secondary, and sometimes it will be quite obvious and important. Nonetheless, in virtually all cases, the working class constitutes an essential *foundation* for democratic change. On this latter point, it is important to note that, even when the middle class (or other allies of the working class) plays the leading role in pushing for democratic rule, the middle class "commitment to democracy [has] tended to be instrumental and contingent, aimed at their own exclusion and subject to abandonment in the face of militant lower-class pressures for radical reforms which [might affect] . . . the material conditions of middle-class life" (Rueschemeyer, Stephens, and Stephens 1992, p. 282). To put it more bluntly, one can never count on the middle class (or any other potential class ally of the working class) to support democracy; indeed, absent an alliance with the working class, the middle class tends to be antidemocratic (or favors only a highly exclusionary form of democracy). If this is true, though, why does the middle class (or any other social class) ally with the urban working class in the first place? The answer becomes obvious when we realize that, just as the working class is sometimes too weak to bring about political change on its own, other excluded social classes are also too weak to accomplish their goals acting alone. Thus, when democracy is in the *interest* of middle-class actors, they will forge an alliance with the working class.

Alliances and the balance of power among social classes within a given society obviously play a central role in the framework put forth by Rueschemeyer and colleagues. It is not surprising, then, that balance of class power constitutes the first and main configuration of power in their analytical framework. It should also be noted, however, that the authors put strong weight on two other broad configurations of power (or, as the authors put it, "clusters of power"): (1) the structure, strength, and autonomy of the state apparatus and its interrelations with civil society (i.e., state-society relations); and (2) the impact of transnational power relations. Both factors deserve in-depth discussion, but for the sake of brevity and because they are explicitly not the analytical focal point of Rueschemeyer, Stephens, and Stephens, I will not cover them here (a complete summary of the authors' argument, however, is available in their 1993 article "The Impact of Economic Development on Democracy"). Suffice it to say that the three clusters of power—largely because they are inextricably interrelated—all play an integral role in the process of democratic transformation and consolidation. Even more, each is generally a product of or deeply affected by long-established social patterns. For this reason, according to Rueschemeyer, Stephens, and Stephens, we must, without exception, avoid "presentist" explanations of democracy (that is, explanations of democracy that ignore history) or, in a similar vein, any "mechanical account of the impact of class, state, and transnational power on constitutional form" (1992, p. 7). In sum, to understand the process of democratic transition (and consolidation), we must engage in "comparative *historical* analysis, which can take . . . persistencies into account and respond sensitively to alternative paths of causation" (p. 7, emphasis in original).

Structure, Agency, and Method in
Capitalist Development and Democracy

It is clear that the structural account of democratization does not completely dismiss the importance of agency. If anything, just the opposite may seem to be the case, as the urban working class—which must make a series of purposeful decisions to achieve its goals, including, but not limited to, creating strategic alliances with other classes—is accorded primacy as an agent of democratization. It is equally clear, however, that structural factors are at the core of their analysis. For it is only through an inexorable process of structural change that the conditions for working-class strength can be realized. Thus, to understand the prospects for democracy in a particular society, any analysis must start with an examination of underlying structural conditions and processes (which, as Rueschemeyer, Stephens, and Stephens assert, must include comparative *historical* analysis as well). Ignoring these conditions and processes—believing that democracy is possible "anywhere, anytime" as long as people "want it"—is analytically foolish and extremely naive. Consider, for example, what happened in Egypt after massive popular protests overthrew a long-lived dictator, Hosni Mubarak. Many Egyptian citizens clearly wanted democracy. They fought for it, and they seemed to get it when Mohammed Morsi was elected president in 2012. Yet a year later, Morsi was ousted by a military coup d'état led by General Abdel Fattah el-Sisi. Sisi himself was later elected president with 96.9 percent of the vote—a result that almost screams "Fraud!" The upshot is clear: wanting democracy is not enough when the structural conditions that would allow democracy to take root are missing.

Before I conclude this section, one last point on the issue of method is in order. The structuralist account just presented is abstract and empirically limited. (This is not to imply, however, that the analysis by Rueschemeyer and colleagues is empirically limited; in fact, the authors go into great depth and detail in their book. It is my summary of their argument that lacks empirical depth.) The historical reality of democratization is, of course, in empirical terms, messy and complex. Rueschemeyer and his coauthors not only recognized this but also carried out a methodological strategy—much of which was based on the specific comparative strategies we discussed in Chapter 2—designed to deal head-on with this complexity. Their strategy, more specifically, was based on the concept of analytical induction. To refresh your memory, analytical induction is based on the idea of discerning general theoretical principles from only a few cases (a process called induction) and then testing and retesting these general principles through other detailed case studies (in comparative perspective). In the authors' words, "analytical induction builds its arguments from the understanding of individual histories" (p. 37).

At the same time, recall, this sort of approach, no matter how meticulously carried out, has shortcomings. Rueschemeyer and colleagues acknowledged this. As they put it, "the speculative element, and even arbitrariness, can never be fully eliminated from such case-based theory building" (p. 37). It is important to note, however, that the authors did not rely solely on individual case studies. Instead, they used multiple and overlapping comparative strategies (or a mixed research design), including inter- and intraregional comparisons of three or more units, across broad stretches of history. Each of these comparisons, in turn, involved analyses of "most similar systems" and "most different systems." We don't have the time or space to cover this ground, but it is important to understand that no matter how persuaded or, conversely, no matter how unconvinced you are by their theoretical argument (or any theoretical argument), you must pay careful attention to the quality, depth, and comprehensiveness of the researchers' methods and evidence. When authors use multiple and overlapping strategies and do so with great care, all of which Rueschemeyer and colleagues did, then you are well advised to take the argument seriously. Of course, it is important, from a methodological point of view, always to consider what is left out. In *Capitalist Development and Democracy,* the authors have very little empirical and no systematic analysis of Asia, sub-Saharan and North Africa, the Middle East, or—most pertinent today—postcommunist Russia, Eastern Europe, and Central Asia. (To be fair, their book was written before many changes in these areas occurred.) Yet as we will see later, leaving out these major regions from their comparative study might very well weaken, if not seriously undermine, the theoretical generalizations they put forth. This point is taken up in our next section, which looks at actor-centric and rational choice explanations of democratization.

Agents of Democratization:
Rational Choice and Democratic Transition

For many comparativists and other researchers, the structural approach just outlined offers a compelling portrait of democratization. It is theoretically coherent, methodologically rigorous, and empirically rich. Still, for others, the idea that democracy—and, more to the point, that the people who live under oppressive political regimes—must somehow "wait" for the conditions to produce it is simply untenable. In reflecting on his discomfort with old-fashioned structuralists, this is exactly what Adam Przeworski argued. As he put it: "We [want] . . . to know what movements in different countries could do to bring dictatorships down rather than simply wait" (1997, p. 6).[4] Michael McFaul, in even blunter terms, stated: "Inert, invisible structures do not make democracies or dictatorships. *People do.* Structural factors such as economic development, cultural influences, and historical institutional arrangements influence the formation of actors' preferences and power, but ultimately these forces have causal significance only if translated into human action" (2002, p. 214, emphasis added). It is significant that neither McFaul nor Przeworski discounted structural factors completely, just as Rueschemeyer, Stephens, and Stephens did not completely discount agency; instead, they suggested that such factors are contributory to, as opposed to determinative of, democracy. The issue, then, may be one not necessarily of choosing between a structure-based and agent-centric approach but rather one of determining the relative importance of each in explaining democratic transition (and consolidation).

Elite-Centered Explanations

For researchers wedded to a rational choice perspective, of course, the overriding emphasis will always be on the role that individual actors play in the democratization process. Even so, this does not mean that all rational or actor-centric explanations are the same. At the risk of oversimplification, we might say that there are two main variants: elite-centered (top-down democratization), and mass-based mobilization (democratization from below). Elite-centered explanations themselves compose a relatively broad and diverse category of rationality-based approaches. As the name implies, this school of thought focuses on the role that the ruling elite plays in the process of democratization. The basic position in this school is that the transition to democracy (from an authoritarian regime specifically) is primarily the product of divisions or splits among elites. Guillermo O'Donnell and Philippe Schmitter (1986) made this point very clearly and unequivocally in their highly influential book, *Transitions from Authoritarian Rule: Prospects for Democracy.* There is, they categorically asserted, "no transition whose beginning is not the consequence—direct or indirect—of important divisions within the authoritarian regime itself, principally along the fluctuating cleavage between hard-liners and soft-liners" (pt. 4, p. 19).

The reference to "hard-liners" and "soft-liners" among the ruling elite in this view needs to be highlighted, for transitologists (as they are sometimes called) argue that these are *the* key choice-making actors in the large majority of democratic transitions. It is their decisions, generally arrived at through strategic calculation and interaction, that either lead to democracy or stop it in its tracks; it is their decisions and actions that provide the basis for democratic consolidation or that lead to a breakdown and reversion to authoritarian or some other nondemocratic form of governance. It is also important to understand, however, that there is a third set of actors we need to consider—actors who exist *outside* the established elite: these are moderates or radicals who want or demand political change. Although nonelites are not the main agents of change, the role of such outsiders is important because it is their challenge to the regime that brings about pressure for political change to begin with. That is, without the existence of challengers, the elite generally have no incentive to even consider bringing about political change. Once demands for change arise, however, the established elite are pressured to react. If the elite are united and surmise that the challengers have little power, they will simply crush the opposition, or more likely its leadership.

A concrete and salient example of the importance of elite unity was the crackdown on prodemocracy protestors in Tiananmen Square in Beijing in 1989. Despite a protest that eventually drew upward of 1 million supporters, when the Chinese regime decided to end the protest it did so with brutal and deadly efficiency. More recent examples include the 2009 election protests in Iran (known as the Green Movement), and of course the series of protests throughout the Middle East and North Africa (the Arab Spring), which began at then end of 2010. (See Figure 6.1.) In Iran, large-scale and sustained street protests, while impressive, did not succeed in undermining the power of the fundamentalist regime, which remained strong and unified. During the Arab Spring, the situation was more complicated. In four countries—Tunisia, Egypt, Libya, and Yemen—a long-lived dictator was forced from power, but a close examination of the four cases will reveal divisions among the elite. This was perhaps most evident in Egypt, when the military elite decided to distance themselves from the then-president, Hosni Mubarak. In another six cases—Syria, Algeria, Jordan, Morocco, Saudi Arabia, and Sudan—the results and state responses were mixed. In some countries (Syria, Sudan, and Bahrain) the state cracked down hard on protests, while in others the state offered economic and, in some cases, limited political concessions to mollify protestors (Morocco, Saudi Arabia, Algeria, and Jordan). In all cases, though, transitologists assert that it was elites ultimately calling the shots.

As the diversity of outcomes during the Arab Spring suggest, if the elite are divided and the challengers have some degree of power, then the prospects for a *compromise* arise. In this view, a democratic transition is most likely when soft-liners in the regime have relatively equal power to hard-liners *and* when opposition (outside the regime) is moderate, as opposed to radical. The relative equality of power is an important feature of this argument, for when one side within the elite has preponderant power, it will use that power to impose its will on everyone else. It is only when both sides within the elite realize that they cannot prevail unilaterally that they settle for compromised solutions. Even in this case, however, the dominance of the elite means that democracy is not *taken by* but, instead, is *given to* the masses in a manner designed to protect the interests of the elite. Ironically, this implies that elite-driven democratization generally is a product of people who do not believe in—or are outright hostile to—the idea of democracy. It is a situation encapsulated in the well-known aphorism that a country can become a "democracy without democrats."

Figure 6.1 Major Prodemocracy Protests:
From China to MENA

China (1989). The largest antigovernment protest in China occurred in the spring of 1989 and was centered in Tiananmen Square in Beijing. Initially, Chinese citizens, mainly students, began to congregate in Tiananmen Square to commemorate the death of Hu Yaobang, a high-ranking Communist Party official, but also a soft-liner very popular with students. When he died in 1989, thousands of students poured into Tiananmen Square, at first to mourn his death. The gathering, however, soon morphed into an antigovernment protest, which elicited widespread support throughout the country. At one point, it is estimated that more than 1 million citizens were involved in the movement. While the Chinese leadership did not immediately crack down—there was a debate between hard-liners, led by Li Peng, and soft-liners led by Zhao Ziyang—eventually the hard-liners won and heavily armed military units, supported with tanks, were sent in to crush the protest. Hundreds and perhaps thousands of civilians were killed or wounded. Since then, China has not seen a similar large-scale antigovernment movement.

Iran (2009). In Iran, an unprecedented series of antigovernment protests was triggered by the disputed results of the Iranian presidential election held on June 12, 2009. In that election, the incumbent, Mahmoud Ahmadinejad, was declared the winner with over 60 percent of the vote. His closest rival was Mir-Hossein Mousavi (a moderate political leader), who soon became the symbol of the antigovernment protests. The initial response by the government was harsh and violent: Iran's security forces were sent in to "launch brutal attacks against the ringleaders of the reform movement" (Coughlin 2009), and potential soft-liners, such as former Iranian president Ali Akbar Hashemi Rafsanjani, were subject to intimidation (six members of his family were arrested). Despite the harsh crackdown, the movement remained viable for many months. Still, the hard-line Iranian government eventually suppressed the movement.

Middle East and North Africa (2010–2012). The Arab Spring can be traced back to a single act of defiance: on December 17, 2010, a vegetable vendor named Tarek Mohammed Bouazizi set himself on fire to protest his humiliation and harassment by a municipal official (Ryan 2011). The act of self-immolation was the catalyst, first, for large-scale protests within Tunisia, which in less than a month led to the ouster of Zine El Abidine Ben Ali (who had been in power for more than twenty years). Second, and equally important, it set in motion similar popular protests in Egypt, Libya, Yemen, Bahrain, Syria, Algeria, Jordan, Morocco, Saudi Arabia, and Sudan. In three of the cases, long-lived dictators were forced from power, but as of 2016, Tunisia remains the only country in the region to have successfully democratized. The Arab Spring will be examined in more depth in Chapter 8.

Thus, in strong contrast to the position espoused by Rueschemeyer, Stephens, and Stephens, advocates of elite-centered explanations portray democracy as always being imposed on society from above or, alternatively, as being created through **pacts**—that is, through negotiated agreements and bargaining (i.e., compromise) among contending elites that establish formulas for power sharing. This difference—between structuralists and elite-centered transitologists—raises a simple but very interesting question: Who is right? After all, Rueschemeyer, Stephens, and Stephens and most transitologists are examining many of the same cases, yet their interpretations of the facts are quite different. I cannot and do not want to definitively answer this question here, but I raise the question to underscore a point made much earlier in this book: different theoretical "lenses" can and do lead to very different interpretations of the same empirical evidence. I should also say that it is not just structuralists who disagree with the argument that democratization is always a top-down, elite-determined process. Within rational choice, as noted at the outset, there are many scholars who see the democratization process as largely shaped by mass movements—that is, by ordinary citizens willing to fight for their political freedom. Certainly, in looking at the events surrounding the Arab Spring—the toppling of long-standing and repressive dictators by mass movements—it does seem difficult and imprudent, at least on the surface, to dismiss this view.

Democratization from Below:
An Alternative Rational Choice Explanation

Importantly, though not surprisingly, the democratization-from-below approach did not get its start with the Arab Spring. Instead, it was the experience with the post-Soviet and postcommunist countries—the former Soviet republics and **satellite states**—that arguably had the greatest impact. Beginning in the late 1980s and accelerating with the collapse of the Soviet Union toward the end of 1991, there was a frenzy of political activity among the then-Soviet republics and satellites. Much of this activity was spurred and sometimes dominated by popular protests or civil unrest—in 1987 and 1988, for example, there were major protests in Latvia, Estonia, Armenia, Azerbaijan, Georgia, Moldova, and Ukraine. Much of this activity was directed toward independence, but the struggle for independence invariably raises questions about the type of political system that will follow when or if independence is achieved. In this regard, it is significant that there was, in fact, a diversity of political outcomes among the postcommunist countries once the dust settled. Some countries moved relatively strongly toward democracy (Estonia, the Czech Republic, Hungary, Latvia, Lithuania, Poland, Bulgaria, Romania, Slovakia, and Slovenia), while others moved toward authoritarian rule, "clan hegemony" (recall the discussion from Chapter 3), or something in between authoritarian and democratic rule (Tajikistan, Belarus, Kazakhstan, Kyrgyzstan, Turkmenistan, Uzbekistan, Armenia, Bosnia-Herzegovina, Moldova, Ukraine, Albania, and others).

Methodologically, the postcommunist cases were something of a godsend to comparativists. The reason, as Michael McFaul put it, was unmistakable: "Clear variation on the dependent variable with a finite set of independent variables would seem to offer a unique laboratory to isolate causal patters" (2002, p. 212). So what did close comparative examination of this "unique laboratory" tell us? McFaul's answer was fairly straightforward. In those countries that successfully democratized, "societal mobilization was critical." It was critical because it "produced transitional leaders—Walesa [in Poland], Havel [in Czechoslovakia], Landsbergis [in Lithuania]—who were not previously members of the elite and who became important actors only because of their widespread societal support." Even more, McFaul continued, "when the balance of power became clear, these new political actors, aided by the support of society, *imposed* their will on the weak elites, whether soft-liners or hard-liners, from the **ancien régime**" (p. 228, emphasis added). To repeat: according to McFaul and others, democratic transformation in the postcommunist world was *not* primarily a top-down process, or a product of internal divisions among contending elites. Instead, mass protests played a key role in bringing about democratization. (McFaul, I should emphasize, also pointed out that, when elites from the ancien régime—leaders of the "old order"—held preponderant power, they imposed their will over the rest of society by reestablishing a dictatorial system. Moreover, when there was a relative balance of power between the old guard and those advocating for democracy, a stalemate resulted, which meant a political system with elements of democracy and authoritarianism—Russia prior to 2004 was a good example of this.)

From a rational choice perspective, the significance of mass mobilization (as opposed to elite-centered strategic interaction) is not necessarily mysterious. As Valerie Bunce (2003) explained it, mass-based political protests signal a breakdown of authoritarian order; they create a widespread understanding of alternative political arrangements; they push authoritarian leaders to the bargaining table; they give opposition leaders a resource advantage when bargaining with authoritarian elites; and they create a mandate for radical change. Mass-based protests, to put it in language you should now be quite familiar with, change the strategic environment of decisionmaking. In this regard, too, it can be argued that mass mobilization reduces "uncertainty" among those who both advocate for and oppose political change (Bunce 2003). When the mass mobilization is unequivocally strong—even if only potentially—opponents of political change have little choice but to negotiate for an end to authoritarian or nondemocratic rule. Alternatively, they may accede to a "partial opening" or liberalization of the political system. If they fail to take either step, they face the dim prospect of a mass uprising that will forcefully remove them from office. Even with less certainty about the eventual outcome, mass mobilizations create a viable and all but impossible-to-ignore threat to the status quo, which opposition leaders can then exploit to their advantage. It is significant that this implies a situation quite different from what Rueschemeyer, Stephens, and Stephens posited, for it is not a *balance of power* per se that leads to change but a *highly unequal* distribution of power that produces political transformation—and one that is not necessarily the product of capitalist development. In the postcommunist cases, in particular, relatively equal distributions of power often "resulted in protracted confrontation, yielding unconsolidated, unstable partial democracies and autocracies" (McFaul 2002, p. 214).

Elites or Masses?

The division of rationality-based and actor-centric explanations into two categories is, of course, a simplification. It can also be an analytically dangerous one if taken to extremes. Przeworski argued along just these lines when he stated: "Short of a real revolution—a mass uprising that leads to the disintegration of the apparatus of repression—decisions to liberalize [which are precursors of democracy] combine elements from above and from below" (1991, p. 56). From this perspective, a more reasonable or "realistic" rational choice approach *might* be to recognize and incorporate both mass-based mobilization and elite-centered strategic interaction into the same general framework. Intuitively, this makes sense. Empirically (and comparatively), however, the issue is far from clear, in large part because analyses of different regions give us very different results. As just discussed, the experiences of postcommunist countries underscore the importance of mass protests. This conclusion is also strongly supported by many cases in sub-Saharan Africa. In a study of forty-two cases there, for example, Michael Bratton and Nicolas van de Walle noted that "transitions in Africa seem to be occurring more commonly from below" (1997, p. 83). At the same time, as Barbara Geddes (1999) and others pointed out, there is little evidence of popular mobilization having played a major, still less causal, role in other places or regions, including, most prominently, much of Latin America. A little comparative checking, in other words, tells us that the two major rationality-based explanations of democratic transition might both be right.

Differing Authoritarianisms and Transitions to Democracy

So where does this leave us? Can the rational choice approach provide a theoretically coherent and empirically comprehensive explanation of democratic transition? If so, how might this be possible? One potential solution is offered by Geddes (1999), to whom I have referred several times already.

Geddes argued, in part, that a basic problem in much of the then-existing literature (back in the 1980s and 1990s, and still today to some extent) had been the tendency to treat authoritarianism as a generic concept—to portray all authoritarian political systems as basically alike. Although seemingly innocuous, this generally unacknowledged practice, Geddes suggested, is largely responsible for the inconsistent results among different rational choice models of democratic transition. Specifically, because "different kinds of authoritarianism differ from each other as much as they differ from democracy" (p. 121), it makes little sense to assume that transitions will all play out in the same general manner, even if all the relevant actors are acting strategically. As Geddes explained it: "Because comparativists have not studied these differences systematically, what theorizing exists about authoritarian regimes is posed at a highly abstract level, and few authors have considered how characteristics of dictatorship affect transitions. These differences, however, cause authoritarian regimes to break down in systematically different ways, and they affect transition outcomes" (p. 121). The necessary analytical step, therefore, is clear: develop a meaningful classification of different ("pure") types of authoritarian regimes. Geddes, of course, did this. In her research, she proposed three basic categories of authoritarian rule, plus a fourth mixed one: personalist, military, single-party, and "amalgams of pure types."

Each category reflects different institutional conditions and historical circumstances. In other words, each represents a different strategic environment or decisionmaking context. And as any good comparativist knows, context matters. Thus, within each type of authoritarian regime, according to Geddes, we can expect the main actors to define their interests and preferences in particular ways. With this starting point, Geddes provides an easy-to-understand application of rational choice principles that corresponds to the basic steps I laid out in Chapter 3.

Consider the military authoritarian regime. The main actors in this type of regime are obvious: the military elite. Next, the interests of the military elite must be identified. In Geddes's analysis this is an easy step too. The military elite in a military-authoritarian regime are primarily concerned with the survival and efficacy of the military. Why this is so is not immediately apparent, but for Geddes, the reason is not difficult to discern: the military elite generally see holding political office primarily as a *means* to better protect the integrity and power of the military itself. In this regard, it is important to note that military leaders most often take power when domestic instability threatens to undermine the military (or the security of the country), or when civilian leaders directly threaten the autonomy and power of the military. In this view, once stability is returned, or once the military elite are confident that civilian leaders will respect their autonomy, holding political power becomes unnecessary.

Of course, this does not mean that military leaders will automatically give up political power. Usually, there must be something that prompts them to do so. One common issue involves rivalries or policy differences that invariably emerge, often because the regime is unable to deal effectively with economic or social problems. Major disagreements can lead to factionalism, which can threaten the cohesiveness, or integrity, of the military as a whole. This situation, it is important to recognize, represents a constraint built into the regime type: in military-authoritarian regimes, there is no single leader or dictator; power is shared among senior military commanders (Geddes 1999). Thus, when rivalries or factionalism become significant, "a return to the barracks becomes an attractive option for most officers" (p. 127). After all, if ensuring the survival and efficacy of the military is paramount and if "returning to the barracks" (the traditional way of referring to the voluntary relinquishment of control of the government by military leaders) will help prevent factional splits from further harming military cohesion, then this becomes the optimal or rational choice. Moreover, as Geddes noted: "For officers, there is life after democracy, as all but the highest regime officials can usually return to the barracks with their status and careers untarnished" (p. 131).

By contrast, in personalist regimes, which are based on the dominance of a single individual and the cliques that form around that individual, the overriding interest of the ruling elite is the survival of the regime itself—and more specifically, of the dictator in power. Significantly, the cliques are often based on family relationships, which ties them even more strongly to the dictator-in-power. Other forms of identity can also play a role—for example, clan, ethnicity, religion, region, or some combination thereof. But the key point is that "membership" in the ruling clique is severely circumscribed; that is, it is open to only a very small portion of the population who must share some preexisting relationship to the ruler. One of the most vivid examples of this type of system was the regime of Saddam Hussein, prior to his ignominious defeat and capture by US forces (and subsequent trial and execution on December 30, 2006). In personalist regimes, voluntary reform or splits within the ruling elite are extremely unlikely—the potential costs are simply too high, as the loss of political power or position typically means personal calamity, imprisonment, and even death for the entire clique (or to anyone who unsuccessfully opposes the clique). The high costs are largely due to the relative narrowness of the support base and the violent repression typically used by such regimes. This means, however, that when change does come, it is typically violent and extreme (this point will be taken up again shortly).

Finally, in single-party authoritarian regimes, the preference of party leaders and **cadres** is quite simple: to stay in office. In this type of system, a little surprisingly perhaps, splits within the ruling elite are even less likely than in personalist regimes. As Geddes explained it, although "factions form in single-party regimes around policy differences and competition for leadership positions . . . everyone is better off if all factions remain united and in office" (1999, p. 129). This is true even during periods of leadership struggles and succession crises, for the ordinary cadres understand that the best way to ensure their privileged positions within the regime is simply to support whoever wins. Another reason single-party systems remain highly cohesive is their capacity to co-opt potential opponents. For, quite unlike personalist regimes, single parties are "more likely to be open to all loyal citizens . . . and are less likely to limit their clientele to particular clan, regional, or ethnic groups" (p. 134). Those who are excluded, however, have a great deal to lose, since the hegemony of single parties gives them near-total control over the allocation of educational opportunities, jobs, and positions in government.

Explaining variations in democratic transition. Combined with the basic assumptions of rational choice analysis, this relatively simple schematic of different types of authoritarian regimes (see Figure 6.2), according to Geddes, provides a powerful way to explain democratic transitions across a wide range of cases. In transitions from military rule, as noted earlier, factional splits within the regime are relatively common, and, in an effort to preserve the integrity of the armed forces, military rulers are more likely to *negotiate* orderly—albeit top-down, elite-centered—transitions. This, in fact, is the modal (that is, the value or item occurring most frequently in a series of observations or statistical data) pattern of transition, according to Geddes, and was especially prevalent in Latin America. For a personalist regime, however, the situation is quite different: because it is far more resistant to endogenous instability—that is, instability located *within* the regime itself—*exogenous* (external) factors are likely to play a stronger role in bringing about democratic transition. Exogenous factors may include such things as the oil crisis of the 1970s, the debt crisis, regionally centered financial crises, the collapse of the Soviet Union, and (as we have seen most recently with the US-led war against Iraq) a foreign invasion.

To put it in less formal terms: some outside "nudge," or perhaps more accurately "shove," is usually necessary to bring about the breakdown of personalist regimes (a key but fairly obvious exception is the death of the leader). **Exogenous shocks** typically precipitate a particular event or process—for example, a coup, an insurgency, an assassination, a popular uprising—that directly brings down the regime. Some of these events or processes are top-down (coups and assassinations), and some are bottom-up (popular uprisings, insurgencies). Whatever the exact dynamics, breakdowns of personalist authoritarian regimes are usually *not* negotiated. Instead, they

Figure 6.2 Authoritarian Regime Types and Democratic Transition

Type of Authoritarian Regime	Likelihood of Democratic Transition	Primary Basis for Transition	Primary Mode of Transition	Examples
Personalist	Low	Exogenous shock (especially economic crisis); death of incumbent	Violent overthrow (coup, assassination, popular uprising)	Iraq/Hussein; Uganda/Amin; Argentina/Perón
Military	High	Factional split (among ruling elite)	Negotiated pact; top-down transition	Brazil (1964–1985); Argentina (1976–1983); El Salvador (1948–1984)
Single-party	Very low	Exogenous shock (often severe and multiple)	Mass-based pressure; negotiated "extrication"	China/CCP; Mexico/PRI; Tanzania/CCM
Amalgam	Depends on nature of amalgamation	Depends on nature of amalgamation	Depends on nature of amalgamation	Indonesia/Suharto; Chile/Pinochet

Source: Adapted from Geddes 1999.
Note: CCP = Chinese Communist Party; PRI = Institutional Revolutionary Party; CCM = Party of the Revolution.

are forced and most often violent. And they are violent primarily because members of the personalist clique have a lot to lose and almost nothing to gain once they no longer are in power. They will therefore generally fight to the bitter end. A prominent contemporary example is Syria, which was part of the Arab Spring. Syria's regime, led by Bashar al-Assad, can be described as largely personalist (Heydemann and Leenders 2013) and has been engaged in a bitter and extraordinarily violent conflict since mid-2011. By March 2015, according to the BBC, an estimated 220,000 people have died and 11 million others have been forced to flee their homes (*BBC News,* "Syria: The Story of the Conflict" 2015), and yet there are no signs that the regime will ever voluntarily back down.

On first glance, one might assume that the logic of breakdowns in single-party regimes would be the same as in personalist regimes. But this is not necessarily the case, because single parties frequently try to co-opt their critics when faced with serious opposition or a crisis situation. This is possible, Geddes explained, because the institutional arrangements of single-party regimes make it relatively easy to allow for greater participation and popular influence on policy without giving up control of the political system. For this reason, it is no surprise (at least to Geddes) that single-party authoritarian systems tend to survive the longest: of the single-party regimes that either existed in 1946 or were formed after that date, according to analysis by Geddes, 50 percent still existed in 1998—by contrast, only 11.4 percent of military regimes and 15.7 percent of personalist regimes survived over this same period. So, what brings an end to single-party regimes? Not surprisingly, the same thing that knocks down personalist regimes: exogenous shocks. As in any authoritarian system, exogenous shocks undermine the regime by impeding the distribution of benefits to supporters and allies and, in some cases, destroying coercive capacity. Still, in single-party regimes, even long-lived regimes, serious crises can be overcome. Indeed, as the statistics just cited demonstrate, single-party transitions are relatively uncommon; in fact, as Geddes and others have noted, most occurred as a direct result of the Soviet collapse—one of the most profound exogenous shocks of the twentieth century.

When exogenous shocks do lead to single-party breakdowns, moreover, it is often a combination of factors. The collapse of the Soviet empire, for example, not only caused widespread economic distress throughout the Soviet trading bloc but also destroyed coercive capacity in most of Eastern Europe (since most Eastern European regimes were dependent on Soviet power for domestic enforcement). On top of this double-barreled shock, postcommunist countries became more dependent on financial and technical support from major Western countries and Western-dominated institutions, which typically demanded a quid pro quo of aid for political reform (that is, democratization). In this situation, popular uprisings and bottom-up pressure—because they cannot be easily repressed or resisted—often play an important role in the breakdown of single-party authoritarian systems. Single-party regimes, in short, are faced with a clear choice: continue to resist or negotiate an "extrication" with *mass-based* opposition forces (as opposed to negotiating exclusively with other factions within the ruling elite). As Geddes noted, extrication through democratization is often the best alternative. This is so because single parties are almost always better off in a democracy than in some other form of authoritarianism. After all, "previous **hegemonic** parties have remained important in political life wherever countries have fully democratized, but they have been outlawed and repressed in several that did not. Consequently, they have good reason to negotiate an extrication rather than risking a more violent ouster" (1999, p. 141).

Geddes's comparative strategy: A quantitative approach. Methodologically, Geddes provided empirical support through a broad-based comparison of a very large number of cases (to be precise, she included 163 regime *transitions* in her data set). Her basic methodological strategy, in this regard, was clearly more quantitative than qualitative; that is, rather than examining a few carefully selected individual cases in depth, she essentially fit all post-1946 authoritarian regimes into one of the three categories discussed earlier (plus amalgam-types). Through a fairly simple statistical analysis, Geddes then showed how the results—such as the survival rates of different types of authoritarian regimes, discussed earlier—confirmed her various hypotheses. When Geddes did compare or refer to individual cases, she did so at a very general level. For example, she noted that, of the fifty-one personalist regimes included in her data set, "only four survived more than a short time after the dictator's death or ouster: Salazar's in Portugal, Somoza's in Nicaragua, Tubman's in Liberia, and Duvalier's in Haiti" (1999, p. 18). These cases, she argued, were exceptions that "underscore the importance of the elimination of able potential rivals as an explanation for why personalist regimes so seldom last longer than their founders" (p. 132). Except for a few brief words about each case, though, Geddes was content to let the cases largely speak for themselves. Although this approach is much too "thin" for many comparativists, it is important to recognize that behind her quick references to concrete cases lay not only a comprehensive statistical analysis but also a solid knowledge of important empirical details in dozens of individual cases.

Structure and Rationality: Competition or Synthesis?

In sum, Geddes provided a theoretically coherent and empirically comprehensive explanation of democratic transition based on rational choice principles. She seemed to account for a full range of variations in regime-change dynamics (for example, in transitions to democracy) within a single and fairly parsimonious analytical framework. Does this mean that she offered a better explanation than the structural argument provided by Rueschemeyer, Stephens, and Stephens in *Capitalist Development and Democracy*? In considering this question, it is worth noting that Geddes had nothing to say about the role—pivotal or otherwise—of the urban working class and very little to say about the importance of a balance of *class* power as a *prerequisite* to democratic transition and transformation. Indeed, Geddes had very little to say—at least directly—about power at all, although the logic of her argument suggests that distributions of social power are at least relevant (for example, the stability of single-party regimes must be due, in part, to the power that comes from their capacity to limit serious factional splits; she also suggested that exogenous shocks are important only insofar as they undermine the power of authoritarian regimes). Conversely, Rueschemeyer, Stephens, and Stephens did not say much about the *independent* causal power of different types of authoritarian regimes (or the strategic environment that different types of authoritarianism entail). Yet, to use their own standards for evaluating quantitatively oriented arguments, the strong correlation among different types of authoritarianism, regime survival, and democratic transition cannot be ignored.

The debate between structuralists and rational choice comparativists is clearly important, but not one that I intend to resolve here—even if this were possible. Suffice it to say that the arguments are not necessarily incompatible. They may, instead, be two sides of the same coin (as suggested at the beginning of this chapter). Structuralists, for example, seem to provide a better account of the crucial conditions or prerequisites for authoritarian breakdown, whereas rational choice scholars appear to offer a better explanation of how the structural *potential* for democracy is actually realized. In this regard, a synthesis of the structural and rational choice models may be appropriate. Again, this is not an issue that can or really should be resolved here. It is, however, an issue that students of comparative politics would be well advised to contemplate. On this point, it is crucial to avoid overly simplistic remedies, which typically involve merely combining the two approaches in serial fashion—first one, then the other. As Gerardo Munck warned us, this is not enough. Instead: "What is needed is a theory of regime transition and formation that incorporates the simple yet theoretically complex notion that actors make choices but not in the circumstances of their choosing" (1994, p. 371). This requires us to consider how structure shapes "choices" and how choices influence structures (or more generally, how structure and choices interact), how the same choices may lead to different outcomes in different structural contexts, and so on. This is not easy, but it is necessary if we want to develop a fuller understanding of the complexities of democratic transition.

This said, we already know that structural and rational choice explanations are not the only games in town. Culturally oriented studies of democratic transition, although far less prominent (even marginalized), provide yet another set of variables to consider. The more recent culturally oriented studies, however, do not purport to provide a generalized, still less universal (and parsimonious), account of democratic transition and transformation (as structural and rational choice models do). Nor do most of these studies even claim that certain sets of cultural values and practices are necessary "preconditions" for the initiation of democracy, which many early culture-based studies did (Diamond 1994). Instead, as I noted in Chapter 3, cultural theorists have tended to focus on how cultural factors *intersect* with political, social, and economic forces to produce specific outcomes in specific places and time periods. With this general point in mind, let us examine the relationship between culture and democratization.

A Missing Link? Culture and Democracy

On the surface, structural and rational choice models of democratic change account for a wide variety of cases. For this reason alone, it would be foolish to discount the hundreds (if not thousands) of well-supported, well-argued, and meticulously analyzed studies done by scholars in both research schools. And certainly few cultural theorists are willing to discount this vast body of literature. Still, for all the theoretical power of structural and rationality-based models, important questions remain largely unanswered (at least to the satisfaction of many). Why, for example, do some areas of the world seem so resistant to democracy? Was Samuel Huntington (1996)—one of the most outspoken observers of democracy—right when he suggested that the principles of democracy are simply, and forever, incompatible with the culture of many societies in the world? Conversely, how have some places in which the foundation for democracy seemed especially bleak (theoretically speaking) been able to effectively break away from authoritarian rule? Do these "exceptional" places—for example, India, Mauritius, Costa Rica[5]—possess special societal attributes, derived from unique historical or cultural experiences, which set them apart? To most cultural theorists, the answers to these and other questions—some of which are addressed in the following section—cannot be found strictly by peering through a cultural lens. At the same time, they believe the concept of culture cannot be divorced, much less extirpated, from studies of democratization. Culture, in short, does matter in the democratic process and not only in exceptional cases. The question, then, is how?

How Culture Matters in the Democratization Process

To understand the relationship between culture and democracy, it is important to first dispense with the naive notion that certain cultures possess deeply rooted traits, characteristics, and practices that *automatically lead to* or, conversely, *permanently block* the democratization process. On the latter point, for example, many political leaders, commentators, religious leaders, and even professors have argued that the teachings, values, and practices of **Islam** are antithetical to democracy (recall the example of this in Chapter 3). Nor is it only those in the West who hold this view: many Islamic fundamentalist leaders explicitly speak against democracy. Abed Shehadeh, leader of the Salafic Jihadi movement in Jordan, to cite just one such leader, asserted that the democratic concept "ruling of the people by the people . . . should be forbidden in Islam," and that **sovereignty** and government belong to Allah alone and not to the people (cited Toameh 2013). But, as Alfred Stepan pointed out, the view that Islam and democracy are incompatible is empirically unsupportable. According to his calculation (writing in 2000), upward of half of all the world's Muslims, 435 million people (or more than 600 million when Indonesia is included), live in democracies, near-democracies, or intermittent democracies (2000, p. 48). Regular surveys demonstrate, too, that the large majority of Muslims worldwide do not see a conflict between Islam and democracy. A 2006 survey by Gallup, for instance, found that most Muslims, when asked what they most admired about the West, frequently mentioned political freedom, liberty, fair judicial systems, and freedom of speech. The results suggested, according to Dalia Mogahed (who interpreted the results of the survey for Gallup), that Muslims "do not believe they must choose between Islam and democracy, but rather, that the two can co-exist inside one functional government" (2006, p. 1).

In a similar vein, many observers used to argue that "Confucian cultures" were also inherently inhospitable to democracy. Indeed, as late as 1991, Samuel Huntington, who was considered one of the most prominent scholars of democracy, had this to say: "Almost no scholarly disagreement exists regarding the proposition that traditional Confucianism was either undemocratic or antidemocratic" (p. 24). This argument, too, turned out to be incorrect, as the democratic transformations of Japan, South Korea, and Taiwan demonstrate (although, as I emphasized in the previous chapter, defining any of these three countries, but especially Taiwan, as strictly Confucian is wrongheaded). One of the basic problems in these ostensibly culture-based arguments, to repeat a point made earlier, is clear: they all portray culture as univocal, essentially fixed (or at least as practically impervious to meaningful change), and unidirectional with regard to causation. One additional, and related, problem is the tendency to view cultures as completely shielded from one another, as if the barriers among different cultures are so thick and impenetrable that there is no possibility for values, principles, and ideas to intermix or commingle. As many culturalists today argue, such assumptions are irredeemably flawed.

Keeping the foregoing caveats in mind, as a starting point for understanding how culture matters in the democratization process, it is useful to recall another basic point from Chapter 3: the ideas, beliefs, values, and identities that societies embrace and by which they define themselves—among both the leaders and the masses—have power. These ideas, beliefs, values, and identities have power at both the individual and the collective levels. They can compel individuals and whole peoples to act and behave in certain ways, to make profound sacrifices, and even to give up their very lives for the sake of a larger good. Consider, for example, Tarek Mohammed Bouazizi (see Figure 6.1), mentioned earlier in the chapter. While it is difficult to say with certainty what motivated Bouazizi at a personal level, there is no doubt that his act of self-immolation—which ultimately and predictably led to his death—served as an extraordinarily powerful symbol. His act inspired hundreds of thousands, even millions, of people across the Middle East and North Africa (**MENA**) to stand up figuratively at once against violent and repressive authoritarian regimes. Many, albeit not all, of those demonstrating explicitly sought social justice, dignity, freedom, and, it is important to emphasize, democracy. Standing together, in a few countries the people succeeded in toppling repressive regimes. Most uprisings, however, failed. Yet the relative lack of success—the fact that failure was clearly a possibility—highlights another key point, which is that many of those demonstrating did so at great risk to themselves.

The high risk and limited prospects for "reward" further suggest that the decisions by hundreds of thousands or millions of people to stand up against repressive regimes were, in a word, irrational. After all, there is a public-good element in struggles against repressive regimes: if the protestors win, the benefits from a less repressive and more socially just society will flow down to everyone, including those who did not participate (i.e., the benefits are nonexcludable). And given the risk that participants face—such as death, imprisonment, or torture—the *only* rational thing to do is to free-ride. For this reason alone, rational choice theory is extremely hard put to explain the series of events that rocked MENA beginning in 2010, and which continue to impact parts of the region in 2016. (To be fair, there are alternative rationalist explanations, which are discussed in Chapter 8, also in relation to the Arab Spring.) Structuralists, too, have trouble explaining events in MENA. The first problem is in explaining the suddenness of the Arab Spring. Structurally speaking, it makes little sense that so many countries, at different levels of capitalist development, experienced massive and sustained popular movements at roughly the same time. Second, while structural principles are likely helpful in explaining why, say, the social uprising in Tunisia has thus far succeeded in establishing democracy, while the uprising failed to do the same in Egypt—for example, Tunisia has a larger middle class, a much higher level of urbanization, and a more developed capitalist economy compared to Egypt—it is still hard to deny the central role that cultural factors played in those two countries and in the region more generally.

Ironically, perhaps, the most obvious cultural factor at play in MENA and in the Arab Spring more specifically was and is the influence of Islam. Consider, on this point, what Kat Eghdamian wrote:

> In order for protests to occur and be sustained, collective action requires that the number of activists increase rapidly. Such growth in participation *cannot* occur without a strong motivation of a critical mass to sustain their activity, regardless of the costs involved to them and their family. An examination of the **discourses** and language used by its actors during the Arab Spring reveals the role that Islamic discourse played in inspiring, motivating, and sustaining activists. Through *reinterpretations* of the **Quran**, Islamic leaders in mosques and Islamic organisations and charities mobilised resources and networks that combined ideological commitment with human and social capital. Bridging divisions of class, Islamic groups and leaders would connect professional and middle classes with lower class citizens as volunteers and activists. Gathering people together in prayer during demonstrations, mosques were also used to spread the message of reform through sermons, ushering in new supporters and encouraging them to continue their involvement in the opposition movements, reinforcing and affirming their ideological commitment. (2014, emphasis added)

Reflecting good cultural analysis, Eghdamian is careful to acknowledge that a range of other factors—institutional, technological, and structural—played important roles in the Arab Spring. He also acknowledges that religion, and Islam specifically, was not the only cultural factor at play. This last point bears repeating: the subjective/cultural forces that propelled the Arab Spring were not merely Islamic. Instead, they reflected a close blending of values, principles, and ideas from both inside and outside the region. "Democracy" was clearly one of the most important of those ideas. (I use scare quotes to indicate that the interpretation of democracy among participants in the Arab Spring likely varied widely.) It is easy to forget that democracy is not merely a concrete set of institutional practices and procedures, but is also, perhaps equally importantly, a set of essentially subjective or normative values, which many people have accepted as the proper way to organize a country's political system. In this regard, democracy is something that people come to "believe in."

As already pointed out, however, not everyone believes in democracy. Indeed, there are many who find the *idea* of democracy repugnant and antithetic to the values and principles that define their lives and the world around them. At the same time, there are others whose objections to democracy are less cultural or ideological than they are material. That is, many see the practice of democracy as a threat to their political or material self-interests. In either case, it is clear that once the idea of democracy is introduced into a society, and once it becomes an important part of the cultural milieu, it cannot help but to have an impact on the political, economic, and social dynamics of that society, too. The most salient political impact is easy to discern: the belief in democracy creates a demand for democracy. More broadly, the belief in democracy creates a demand for political change, particularly if the regime in power is an authoritarian one. In a related vein, the belief in democracy undermines the legitimacy and authority of authoritarian regimes, whether secular or theocratic. The belief in democracy, in short, has become a very powerful force in its own right for political and social change.

Again, though, I need to emphasize that a good cultural argument cannot hang its hat on a single factor. Culture does not stand alone, and neither does any cultural factor (e.g., a belief in democracy) stand alone. Good cultural analysis is integrative and inclusive (to the extent called for); it endeavors to highlight the significant cultural variables. Sometimes culture is absolutely crucial to an explanation, and sometimes it plays a less prominent role. Whatever the case, though, it is likely always part of any explanation of significant outcomes in the social world. To get a better sense of what all this means, its necessary for us to examine the relationship between culture and democratization in more concrete terms. An especially useful example is provided by Daniel Philpott, who, in two articles (2004 and 2007) has endeavored to show how the Catholic Church contributed to democratization in a range of countries in Western and Eastern Europe, Latin America, and Asia.

Briefly put, Philpott's argument centers on the premise that, unless and until the Catholic Church was able to undergo a cultural transformation—a transformation that reconciled the Church's centuries-old opposition to the idea of the sovereign state (as something that could exist separately from the authority of the Church and of God), to liberal values, and to democracy—the prospect for democratization in predominantly Catholic countries would remain dim. However, once the transformation was accomplished, the Church could and did become a key agent of change. It could use its moral authority and legitimacy, as well as its institutional power, to bring an end to authoritarian rule, which had dominated much of the Catholic world. Indeed, so dramatic and wide-ranging was the political change brought about by this cultural transformation that Philpott dubbed it the "Catholic Wave." More specifically, the Catholic Wave refers to the period of time between 1974 and 1990 when, of the thirty countries that made a transition to democracy, three-fourths were predominantly Catholic (this period is more commonly referred to as democracy's "Third Wave" [Huntington 1991]). As Philpott wrote, "It is a striking finding: why would countries the majority of whose population belong to a particular religious community, especially one that has historically distrusted democracy, compose the motor of a global trend in democratization?" (2007, p. 510). This is a question very much worth exploring.

Christian Culture, the Catholic Church, and Democratization

"It's not uncommon for Christians in America," wrote Austin Cline (n.d.), "to ask whether Islam is compatible with democracy. People do not, as a rule, ask this about Christianity; on the contrary, some claim that Christianity is required for democracy." Cline highlights a common assumption about the relationship between Christianity, in general, and democracy. To wit, the two share a natural and even indestructible affinity. As Philpott made clear, however, this affinity did not exist for a very long time between Catholicism—one of the most important denominations within Christianity—and democracy. As he concisely put it, "Historically, the two have clashed" (2004, p. 32). Others have been more loquacious. Writing in 1959, the eminent political scientist Seymour Martin Lipset wrote:

> The linkage between democratic instability and Catholicism may also be accounted for by elements inherent in Catholicism as a religious system. Democracy requires a universalistic political belief system in the sense that it legitimates different ideologies. And it might be assumed that religious value systems which are more universalistic in the sense of placing less stress on being the only true church will be more compatible with democracy than those which assume that they have the only truth. The latter belief, held much more strongly by the Catholic than by most other Christian churches, makes it difficult for the religious value system to help legitimate a political system which requires, as part of its basic value system, the belief that "good" is served best through conflict among opposing beliefs. (pp. 92–93, n. 40)

Lipset, in the same article, referred to another scholar, Kingsley Davis, who argued, in 1942 (the years in which these statements were written is important to keep in mind), that a Catholic state church tends to be *irreconcilable with democracy* since "Catholicism attempts to control so many aspects of life, to encourage so much fixity of status and submission to authority, and to remain so independent of secular authority that it invariably clashes with liberalism, individualism, freedom, mobility, and sovereignty of the democratic nation" (cited in Lipset 1959, p. 93, n. 40). It should be noted, however, that the Church's opposition to liberalism and democracy was not strictly theological or doctrinal: during the nineteenth century, in particular, the authority of the Church was directly challenged by "partisans of the French revolution, republicanism, socialism, and Bismarck's *kultursampf*" (Philpott 2007, p. 511), the latter of which refers to German policies—some quite draconian (Bell 2008)—expressly designed to reduce the role of the Roman Catholic Church in Prussia. In other words, the Church's rejection of liberal values can also be construed, at least partly, as a rational reaction to external efforts by state leaders to undermine and even eliminate the (political) power and authority of the Church. This eminently rational reaction is also reflected in the fact that the Catholic Church adopted a somewhat tolerant position toward those countries, specifically the United States, that guaranteed religious freedom (Philpott 2004). At the same time, and equally rationally, the Church showed even more tolerance for authoritarian and totalitarian systems: in July 1933, most famously, the Church signed a concordat (treaty or agreement) with Hitler's Nazi regime. The concordat obligated the Nazi regime to accept the Church's Code of Canon Law, while the regime, in turn, promised to guarantee Catholic rights in Germany (Bell 2008).

There is little doubt that the Catholic Church, or leaders of the Church, have been motivated by rational concerns. But it is equally certain that the principles and values—the cultural elements—of Catholicism are not simply ornamentations. Catholic doctrine has a deep, albeit (and this is a very important point to keep in mind, too) *not* unvarying substance. Thus, the culturally based antipathy toward the tenets of liberal democracy were, according to Philpott, very real. Given the Catholic Church's long-standing and seemingly ingrained opposition to liberal democracy (and liberal states), it comes as no surprise that the Church did not support democratization efforts anywhere in the world for almost its entire history. As I noted earlier, though, the Church's staunch opposition to the values of liberal democracy, to liberal culture, one might say, did come to a fairly abrupt end in the mid–twentieth century. Philpott marked the end of this opposition with the **Second Vatican Council** (also known as Vatican II), which opened under Pope John XXIII on October 11, 1962, and closed under Pope Paul VI in 1965. It was during Vatican II that the Church finally reconciled its teaching and doctrine with the principles of liberal democracy. This was, according to Philpott, the endpoint of a very long process, a process that he referred to as the "long rapprochement." The most pertinent change was contained in Pope Paul VI's encyclical *Dignitatis Humanae* (Of the Dignity of the Human Person), which declared that religious liberty is a fundamental right based in the God-given dignity of the human person (Philpott 2004, p. 35).

It was this cultural change or shift within the Catholic Church that set the stage for the Catholic Wave. The shift allowed for the Church to adopt a "political theology"—Philpott defined this as "the set of ideas that a religious body holds about legitimate political authority" (2007, p. 507)—that placed importance not just on religious freedom, but also on human rights, democracy, and economic development. Following Vatican II, subsequent popes and, equally important, many (but not all) bishops became vigorous and often outspoken advocates of democracy and human rights. John Paul II (who served as pope from 1978 to 2005) was a particularly vigorous papal advocate. He once declared, "I am not the evangelizer of democracy; I am the evangelizer of the Gospel. To the Gospel message, of course, belong all the problems of human rights; and if democracy means human rights, it also belongs to the message of God" (cited in Philpott 2004, p. 35).

Democratization, though, is a national-level phenomenon, so it was up to the bishops in individual countries to spur concrete change by forcefully challenging the legitimacy of authoritarian regimes that governed in ways that violated the principles of human rights and democracy. This did not happen everywhere, but where it did happen, the Church often played a pivotal role in the democratization process. Among the most prominent examples cited by Philpott were in Poland, Lithuania, Ukraine, South Korea, Brazil, Chile, El Salvador, Spain, Portugal, and the Philippines. Philpott is careful to point out that, in some of these countries, a liberal political theology emerged prior to Vatican II, but "virtually every Catholic effort to promote democracy gained vigor and explicitness once Rome had pronounced it officially" (2007, p. 511).

Among the countries where the new political theology of the Church played an especially crucial role, Spain stands out. Prior to Vatican II, the Spanish Catholic Church provided strong support to the authoritarian regime led by Generalissimo Francisco Franco. In fact, the relationship was extraordinarily close, so close that many people during that period referred to the relationship between the Church and the state as "clerical fascism" (Casanova 1983, p. 949). At the same time, the Spanish Catholic Church was also "devoutly loyal to Rome" (Philpott 2004, p. 37). Thus, following Vatican II, the Spanish Catholic Church was faced with a difficult decision: stand firm with the authoritarian state, with which it had developed a long-standing and mutual beneficial (i.e., self-interested) relationship, or embrace the cultural shift espoused by Rome. It could not do both. Ultimately, the Spanish Catholic Church decided to embrace the new political theology of Rome, which meant disentangling itself from the regime. This decision, it is important to add, was laden with serious risks for the Church, given the coercive power that all authoritarian states possess. In other words, Church leaders could not be sure of their own safety—indeed, in the last days of the regime, right-wing forces "publicly shouted to put Cardinal Tarancón [the Archbishop of Madrid from 1971 to 1983; his full name was Vicente Enrique y Tarancón] and 'the red priests' 'up to the wall'" (Casanova 1983, p. 965). Once the decision was made to part ways with the regime, however, the underpinning of authoritarian rule quickly began to crumble. One reason is clear. As José Casanova, writing in 1983, explained it: "the role of the Church and of Catholicism was . . . crucial in providing the main ideological support of the regime" (p. 949). For this reason too, the Church was the regime's main source of mass popular mobilization; thus, "the progressive distancing of the Church from the regime and the final break between the two opened the way for a severe crisis of legitimation" (p. 964).

There is, of course, much more to the story of democratization in Spain and elsewhere. Philpott and others who use a cultural framework all acknowledge this. In his own work, for example, Philpott emphasizes the importance of "differentiation," which he defined as "the degree of *mutual autonomy* between religious bodies and state institutions in their foundational legal authority" (2007, pp. 506–507, emphasis added). Differentiation is not a cultural phenomenon, although in the case of Spain it was the embrace of a liberal democratic political theology that led the Spanish Catholic Church to seek a more autonomous or differentiated role in the first place. In some countries, though, differentiation emerged many decades before Vatican II, and in others it never did. In countries in which the Catholic Church remained closely tied to or integrated with the authoritarian state—such as Czechoslovakia, Angola, Cameroon, Uganda, and Rwanda—cultural change within Catholicism at large did not have any impact on the political process.

Most, if not all, contemporary culturalists, too, will readily acknowledge that regime type, underlying economic processes (both domestic and transnational), particular institutional arrangements unrelated to cultural dynamics, and other "objective" factors play key roles in conditioning political outcomes. Philpott himself was quite clear on this point: "if the Church's new teachings corresponded in timing and form to the Catholic wave, the extent of Church influence on any of the far-flung new democracies is hard to know." Even more, he wrote, "in degrees difficult to measure, this influence has had to compete with economic advancement, changing popular attitudes, the decay of authoritarian regimes, the role of secular actors, and the influence of powerful external democracies such as the United States" (2004, p. 36). Nonetheless, any analysis that does not account for the significance of subjective or intersubjective factors (i.e., culture) will be incomplete at best—and perhaps seriously if not fatally flawed at worst.

Culture and Democracy: Concluding Remarks

The foregoing discussion is far from sufficient to prove the significance of culture as a key variable in transitions to democracy among so-called Catholic Wave (or Third Wave) countries. Even the full articles by Philpott, from a methodological perspective, lack the in-depth empirical examination *and* systematic comparative analysis required to accept the conclusions he draws on the causal relationship between the cultural shift in the Catholic Church and democracy. Still, Philpott's conclusions are hard to dismiss. At the very least, it is clear that a shift to a liberal democratic political theology—standing in stark contrast to the principles and practice of authoritarian rule—provided a hitherto missing source of inspiration for popular movements. It is equally clear that, in those predominantly Catholic countries where bishops actively supported movements against the regime, the Church played a pivotal role in galvanizing and mobilizing social forces. The People Power movement in the Philippines during the 1980s is, perhaps, the best example of this. Within many countries, moreover, the

Church served as an institutional counterweight to the repressive authoritarian state, a counterweight that simply could not have materialized until a cultural transformation had taken place within the Church.

An examination of the Catholic Wave also helps highlight three general lessons about culture—lessons that are particularly important to reiterate for the beginning student of comparative politics. First, the unfolding of the Catholic Wave provides a clear indication of how even seemingly bedrock cultural values can change in dramatic fashion. It is clear, on this point, that the transformation of the Catholic Church's political theology was not a minor shift in doctrine, but instead represented an almost complete about-face. On this point, recall the opening discussion on how the Church's values and teachings were once viewed, both inside and outside the Church, as inherently antithetical to democratic principles. Yet the seemingly unshakable cultural position of the Church suddenly became quite pliable. Second, it is important to understand that cultural change does not simply emerge out of the blue. Most typically, cultural change is the product of *multiple voices*—that is, of competing discourses and interpretations. Philpott (2004), on this point, emphasized the critical role played by Catholic intellectuals beginning in the 1930s in laying the groundwork for the Church's ultimate endorsement of liberal democracy. He and others noted, too, that elements of a liberal democratic political theology emerged in other parts of the Church prior to Vatican II. Most notably, in Latin America, an early version of a liberal democratic theology, which came to be known as **liberation theology,** was first formally articulated in 1955 (Edmonds 2010, pp. 46–47). The key point, to repeat, is this: even an ostensibly single and rigidly hierarchical culture can be and is multivocal.

The third lesson is embedded in the following quote by Philpott: "Religion devastates not only New York skyscrapers but also authoritarian regimes; it constructs not only bellicose communal identities but also democratic civil society" (2007, p. 505). In other words, as a primary component of culture, religion's effects can cut in multiple and seemingly contradictory directions, as intersubjective forces are wont to do. For most of its modern history, the culture of the Catholic Church put it on the side of authoritarianism, but since the mid-1960s it has been largely on the side of democracy. In retrospect, as we have seen, it is not difficult to understand how this causal turn came about, but it is very easy to lose perspective. To a significant extent this is precisely what is happening today in debates about Islam. Many well-educated and well-meaning people believe very firmly that Islamic culture is inherently incompatible with democracy. Again, as noted earlier, this belief is held by those both inside and outside Islamic culture, by ayatollahs and *Fox News* pundits. Yet Islamic culture shares a fundamental similarity with Catholic culture, as well as with Hindu culture, Judeo-Christian culture, Buddhist culture, and so forth. The fundamental similarity among all these cultures, to repeat, is their subjective or intersubjective foundations.

Taking the Next Step

The study of democratization from a comparative perspective is complex and, in some respects, confusing. For despite the huge amount of research and writing on the subject, no definitive explanation of democratization exists. Nonetheless, a lot of immensely valuable work has been done, the best of which relies on a strong and sophisticated melding of theory, method, and evidence. Students who wish to better understand or explain the process of democratization are well advised to keep this basic lesson in mind. By this point in the text, however, you should have moved beyond simply understanding the importance of bringing theory, method, and evidence together: you should be ready to conduct your own analysis; that is, you should be ready to *do* comparative politics. The issue of democracy is, in this respect, a particularly appropriate subject on which to focus your efforts, for there are a number of extremely interesting and relevant contemporary real-world cases on which you can practice.

We have already touched on a wide range of cases. Among these is Russia, which has seen an especially rocky path of democratization (immediately after the collapse of the Soviet regime), followed by de-democratization under the leadership of Vladimir Putin (president of Russia from 1999 to 2008, and from 2012 to the present). What factors led to Russia's democratization (and the collapse of the old Soviet regime), and what factors led to the rollback of democracy? Were these factors primarily economic, cultural, institutional, or something else? How do you know? That is, what sort of comparative design can you set up to test your theory or explanation about the process of democratization/de-democratization in Russia? On this last question, it is useful to repeat a point made much earlier in this chapter: Russia can be considered to be part of a set of most similar systems, the postcommunist countries. Among this set of countries, according to Freedom House (see Figure 6.3), were several consolidated democracies (e.g., Latvia, Poland, Lithuania, Czech Republic, and Slovenia), a number of nondemocracies (Azerbaijan, Belarus, Turkmenistan, Uzbekistan), and many in between (Albania, Armenia, Macedonia, Kosovo, Georgia). With a score of 6.29, Russia was ranked by Freedom House as decidedly nondemocratic. Knowing that Russia is one of the least-democratic states among a roughly similar set of states is a potentially very important comparative-methodological asset. Don't forget, too, the utility of a within-case comparison: a comparison of Russia before and after the ascendance of Vladimir Putin could be quite useful.

China is another monumentally important case. Is the country destined to become democratic after decades of rapid and sustained capitalist growth? Will China, in other words, follow the path of other high-growth capitalist

**Figure 6.3 Freedom House's Democracy Score
for Postcommunist Countries, 2014**

	Democracy Score
Slovenia	1.93
Estonia	1.96
Latvia	2.07
Poland	2.18
Czech Republic	2.25
Lithuania	2.36
Slovakia	2.61
Hungary	2.96
Bulgaria	3.25
Romania	3.46
Serbia	3.64
Croatia	3.68
Montenegro	3.86
Macedonia	4.00
Albania	4.18
Bosnia-Herzegovina	4.43
Georgia	4.68
Moldova	4.86
Ukraine	4.93
Kosovo	5.14
Armenia	5.36
Kyrgyzstan	5.89
Russia	6.29
Tajikistan	6.32
Kazakhstan	6.61
Azerbaijan	6.68
Belarus	6.71
Turkmenistan	6.93
Uzbekistan	6.93

Source: Freedom House 2014, https://freedomhouse.org/sites/default/files/NIT2014%
20booklet_WEBSITE.pdf.

Note: Countries are rated on a scale of 1 to 7, with 1.0 representing the highest level
of democratic progress, and 7.0 representing the least progress. The democracy score is a
composite score that includes seven individual categories: electoral process, civil society,
independent media, national democratic governance, local democratic governance, judicial framework and independence, and corruption.

economies in East Asia, namely South Korea and Taiwan? Even if structure
"isn't everything," as might appear to be the case in China, does this mean
that it is reasonable to discount structural forces completely? The answer is
most likely no. Indeed, since it is essentially beyond question that capitalism has reshaped significant elements of China's economy and society in

profound ways since 1979, these (structural) changes are most likely impacting China's political dynamics. It is up to the researcher to discern what this impact is, and why, for now, it has not entailed a breakdown of authoritarian rule. In this regard, though, the rationalist focus on the resilience of single-party systems may also be a relevant, and perhaps central, factor. And what of culture? Is China's lack of democracy simply a reflection of Confucian culture, as some have argued? As I have already tried to emphasize, however, that sort of argument is deeply flawed. Yet rejecting a crude Confucian argument does not mean culture is unimportant. Consider, on this point, the extraordinary lengths the Chinese Communist Party has gone to control the flow of information to most Chinese citizens. Try a Google (or Yahoo! or Bing) search on "Tiananmen Square massacre" while in China: you will not find any information about what happened in 1989 (Flanagan 2014). Similarly, during the height of the Arab Spring, Chinese officials made sure that keyword searches for terms such as "Egypt" and "Cairo" were blocked, while official coverage portrayed the uprisings in MENA in a negative manner (Rizzo 2011). China's leaders, it seems, are deathly afraid of ideas and symbols that might inspire a far-reaching change in political culture.

Finally, what of the Islamic countries in MENA, which despite the turmoil of the Arab Spring remain almost completely nondemocratic in 2016? Indeed, why has Tunisia thus far been the only country to experience a significant degree of democratization? Can something be learned from comparing Tunisia to Egypt and Yemen, the two other MENA countries where uprisings led directly to the collapse of the then-existing regime? What would a broader-based comparison of all or most of the countries in the region tell us? Granted, answering any of these questions would be a difficult task, but even a relatively cursory comparative and empirical analysis—the type of analysis that is within the grasp of any beginning student of comparative politics—might yield important insights.

"Taking the next step" (or, more accurately, "steps") does not have to be hard. But it does require an explicit effort. First, you need to think theoretically, which means that you need to consider how principles from rational choice, structural, and cultural approaches can help shed light on complex processes, such as democratization. The preceding brief discussion gives a concrete sense of how to do this. Importantly, thinking theoretically usually means asking a lot of questions from the get-go and then figuring out how those questions might best be answered. Taking the next step also requires that you make a strong effort to support your answers with method and evidence. For our purposes, of course, a key method is comparison. Again, the foregoing discussion provides examples of the sorts of comparisons that can be made. Doing good comparisons, in turn, requires that you "do your homework." That is, good comparisons are based not just on logic, but also on facts or empirical evidence. If you compare Tunisia to Egypt and Yemen, for example, you need to know something about all three countries. You can begin with their "vital statistics"—for example, purchasing power–adjusted GDP per capita, levels of urbanization, type of government, poverty rates, and so on. But statistics require context, which means learning the social, political, and cultural histories of the cases you are comparing. Admittedly, acquiring in-depth, qualitative knowledge about a number of countries requires effort. Thus, while taking the next step isn't hard, it's not always easy, either.

Notes

1. In this chapter, the focus will be on democratic transition, which is the initial stage in the process of democratization. A second important stage is democratic consolidation. Although the two stages are obviously connected, the key factors or variables in each stage are not necessarily the same. In other words, analyses of democratic transition and consolidation can be regarded as two separate endeavors.

2. Dahl himself was hesitant to classify any real-world political system as a democracy. Instead, he used the term "polyarchy" for concrete systems and reserved "democracy" for the nonexistent, ideal-type. Few scholars today, however, stick to the distinction made by Dahl.

3. In Chapter 4, we placed modernization theory into the cultural camp, whereas in this chapter, modernization is placed in the structural camp. Although confusing, the discrepancy lies primarily in the fact that modernization theory treats culture as an exogenous variable that acts to inhibit or prevent modernization from unfolding in the first place. In this regard, culture helps explain why the modernization process has taken so much longer to get started in some societies; however, once the modernization process gets under way, culture is subject to the same structural imperatives as all other aspects of society.

4. Elsewhere Przeworski has expanded on this point. In a coauthored article, Przeworski and Limongi wrote: "The emergence of democracy is not a by-product of economic development. Democracy is or is not established by political actors pursuing their goals and it can be initiated at any level of development. Only once it is established do economic constraints play a role the chances for the survival of a democracy are greater when the country is richer" (1997, p. 177).

5. For a discussion of democracy in Mauritius, see Laville 2000, Srebrnik 2002, and Miles 1999. For a discussion of democracy in Costa Rica, see Wilson 1998 and Booth 1998. Wilson offered a primarily institutional argument, whereas Booth argued that Costa Rican democratization was best explained by structuralist and elite settlement approaches.

7

Why Do People Kill? Explaining Genocide and Terrorism

This chapter focuses on two types of collective political violence: genocide and terrorism. There is little doubt that both phenomena are worthy of serious attention and study, although, in the Western world, most attention, since September 11, 2001, has been on terrorism. Indeed, one might argue that terrorism has become an obsession and fetish, especially in the United States (Ali 2004). One reason is clear: Americans (and Europeans) see the West as the primary, or at least the most important, target of terrorists. And while the number of terrorism-related deaths is relatively low, the only thing that has prevented more 9/11s, many assume, are the extraordinary protective measures that Western countries have implemented. Even more, seen through a Western lens (albeit one that reflects only a partial view), terrorism is frequently portrayed as an essentially irrational and illegitimate, if not evil, method of violence used by disgruntled and fanatical groups (usually composed of religious zealots) in pursuit of impossible goals. To be sure, such views are not entirely without merit, as leaders of terrorist organizations, including **al-Qaeda**, have not only engaged in gruesome violence, but also have called for the killing of Americans and their allies everywhere, civilian and military, as the duty of all Muslims (cited in Gunaratna 2002, p. 1). Even more, they have pledged to impose a fundamentalist version of **sharia** on the entire world (Habeck 2012)—a fruitless objective. Given such seemingly irrational behavior, it is also not difficult to understand why there is generally little concern with explaining or understanding contemporary terrorism. Instead, the overwhelming focus (among Western scholars and other analysts) is on how to *eliminate* it.

Despite the perception that Western countries and societies are the main targets of terrorists, the countries at highest risk of terrorism not only lie outside the West but also are primarily (although not universally) Islamic. According to the US government's own National Counterterrorism

233

Center, the countries with the largest number of deaths from terrorism include, in order (for 2013): Iraq, Afghanistan, Pakistan, Nigeria, Syria, Somalia, India, Lebanon, the Philippines, Yemen, and Thailand. In Iraq alone, some 6,395 people died in terrorist attacks during 2013—more than 35 percent of all deaths (18,066) from terrorism that year (cited in Statista 2015a). More generally, between 2006 and 2014, a total of 161,834 people worldwide died as a result of terrorism (cited in Statista 2015b). These figures are certainly significant, and they help us understand why so much attention has been paid to terrorism. Yet, in terms of lives lost, terrorism pales in comparison to genocide. Specifically, scholars estimate that genocide has been responsible for more than 100 million deaths—of innocent victims—between 1915 and 2015. In this regard, it is easy to conclude that genocide is vastly more important than terrorism, and as important as war. Indeed, from the standpoint of lives lost, as Daniel Goldhagen succinctly put it, genocide is even "worse than war": the death toll from genocide over the past century is "more than all the combat deaths in all the wars fought during that time everywhere in the world" (in DeWitt and Goldhagen 2009).

Significantly, while the human devastation of genocide is undeniable, it garners little general attention compared to terrorism. This is partly because people, especially people who occupy positions of power in national governments, purposely divert their eyes. To put it bluntly, they do not want to see or acknowledge genocide. There is obvious reason for this behavior: genocide is viewed as a problem of other people. Thus, as terrible and as heart wrenching as it may be, genocide can be safely ignored, since the killing is generally confined to the borders of a single country and carried out by states against their own people. For other countries, then, not seeing genocide, or pretending that it is not actually happening, provides an excuse to do nothing. When not seeing isn't an option, genocide will be called something else—"primordial ethnic conflict" or "acts of genocide"—with the barely disguised intent to avoid responsibility to intervene. The need for such subterfuge, it is important to point out, originally stems from the most widely known of all genocides, the Holocaust.

During the Holocaust, as many as 6 million Jews and 5 million others (including Slavs, Roma, the disabled, and homosexual men) were systematically killed by Germany's Nazi Party. The monstrous violence committed against these groups led the international community to promise that it would "never again" allow another genocide. Unfortunately, this has not been the case. At all. Certainly, the world stood by in 1994 when upward of 1 million people, most identified as Tutsi, were killed in the space of only a hundred days by the dominant Hutu population in Rwanda. The world also stood by two decades earlier in the 1970s when the Cambodian regime, known as Khmer Rouge, killed 1.5 to 3 million of its own people. But these are the most well known genocides. There have been many other genocides of which the general public, at best, has only a vague knowledge. Before the Rwandan genocide in 1994, for example, it was the Tutsi who carried out smaller-scale, but no less significant, massacres against the Hutu: in 1972, between 150,000 to 300,000 Hutu were slaughtered by the Tutsi-dominated army in neighboring Burundi (Lemarchand 2008); in 1988, Tutsi forces killed another 20,000 Hutu; and in 1991—just a few years before the Rwandan genocide—3,000 more Hutu were killed. Moreover, following the Rwandan genocide, which was stopped when the Tutsi-led militia, the Rwandan Patriotic Front (RPF), defeated the Hutu movement, as many as 2 million Hutu fled to neighboring countries, including the Democratic Republic of Congo (DRC), to avoid retribution. Unfortunately, crossing borders did not provide a safe haven, as many were hunted down and killed. Worse still, since 1996, the DRC has been the site of some of the worst violence since World War II: as many as 6 million people have died as a direct or indirect result of the conflict there, although it is not possible to attribute all these deaths to genocide. Darfur (in Sudan) is another scene of mass violence and genocide. The conflict there started in 2003, and has ebbed and flowed since then, resulting in 300,000 to 400,000 "excess" deaths, and 2.5 million displaced people (United Human Rights Council 2015). As late as 2014, Human Rights Watch documented two campaigns of killing and mass rape carried out by the Sudanese government.

It is also important to note that, while sub-Saharan Africa is the primary site of the most recent genocides, the Holocaust was carried out by a Western European state, Germany, "the land of Beethoven, Goeth, and Schiller, where Kantian philosophers and university professors inculcated generations in the virtues of Bildung [which refers to the German tradition of philosophical self-cultivation] and humanism" (Levene 2009, p. 260). Historically, in fact, the West has been responsible for many genocides, especially of indigenous peoples—for example, Australia's destructive policies toward Aborigines, the systemic violence directed toward Native American tribes in the United States and Canada, and Belgium's "murderous exploitation" of the Congolese in the late nineteenth and early twentieth century. Asia, too, has seen its share of genocides, including Japan's slaughter of 200,000 Chinese men and mass rapes of Chinese women in 1937, immortalized in the 1997 book *The Rape of Nanking,* by Iris Chang. The list of genocides is, unfortunately, much longer—including those in Armenia, Bosnia, Kosovo, the Soviet Union, China, and East Timor, to name just a few more—but the main point, to repeat, is this: genocide is not a problem of the past, nor is it a rare or geographically (or culturally) limited phenomenon. It has happened throughout history, in every corner of the world, and remains with us today. The stubborn persistence of genocide makes the close and serious study of the phenomenon as important today as ever.

Still, it is not immediately clear why an introductory book on comparative politics would include a discussion of terrorism and genocide. After all, neither topic has, arguably, ever been a major or even minor focus of research in the field. Even more, some might assert, the examination of these two forms of collective political violence is better left to experts in other disciplines, such as international relations, psychology, and sociology. My answer, though, is simple: even a basic comparative politics approach can tell us a lot about both phenomena. One can even argue that a comparative politics approach is essential to a full explanation and understanding of terrorism and genocide. Significantly, many specialists in terrorism and genocide studies already understand and accept the importance of comparative analysis, although this is far truer for studies of genocide than of terrorism. Consider, on this last point, what Adam Jones (2006) had to say in his comprehensive introduction to the subject of genocide. In his discussion of the earliest studies on the Holocaust, he noted that, while most scholars were Jewish and while the empirical focus was on a single case, "still, rereading these pioneering works, one is struck by how inclusive and comparative their framing is" (pp. 15–16). Beginning in the 1970s, moreover, one could begin to talk of the field of "comparative genocide studies." (There is, I should note, no well-developed counterpart in terrorism studies; that is, there is no distinct field of "comparative terrorism studies.")

With the foregoing discussion in mind, it is (almost) time to turn to the heart of this chapter, which is to explain, or at least try to explain, genocide and terrorism from the perspectives of rational choice, culture, and structure. Of course, given the immense amount of research and analysis devoted to both issues, in a single chapter it is only possible to scratch the surface, or perhaps a little below the surface, of explanation and understanding. Still, the comparative politics approach I apply in the remainder of the chapter provides a strong basis for further research and analysis, which is something I encourage of all readers. Before beginning with our theoretical discussion, however, it is, once again, essential to discuss definitions. Understandably, you may find another (fairly long) discussion about definitions to be tiresome, unnecessary, and even annoying. But it is not a discussion that a good comparativist or social scientist can just skip.

Definitions: Genocide and Terrorism

At the most basic level, to see why skipping a discussion of definitions is ill-advised, think about the almost perfunctory assertion I made earlier, that genocide was committed against Native American tribes in the United States. Some people in the United States would find the foregoing claim absurd, and even offensive; while others, at the very least, would find the claim highly debatable. Even more contentious are the claims, made by some, that the US war in Vietnam was not only a war, but also a genocide (Sarte 1968), and that "the lynching and other forms of assault on the lives and livelihoods of African Americans from 1945 to 1951 . . . amounted to genocide" (cited in Docker 2010). While debates over what was and what was not genocide are often little more than (intellectual) parlor games—albeit often highly charged and extremely emotional ones—they underscore a deeper issue: without first establishing definitional clarity it is impossible to move forward, whether in a debate or in a causal analysis of the issue at hand. This is not to suggest that it is a simple matter to agree on a definition. It is not. Indeed, even scholars of genocide cannot agree on single definition. The same can be said for efforts to define terrorism: as I will discuss below, there are multiple and not always consistent definitions.

While universal agreement or consensus may be unachievable, for the purposes of this chapter, definitional clarity is certainly possible. It is not only possible, but, to repeat an oft-made point in this book, also necessary: if you intend to say something meaningful about an issue or subject of study, then you had better be able to define that subject, which, I should add, means being able to differentiate or separate it from other, especially similar, phenomena. In this regard, it is important to understand that this chapter presupposes that genocide and terrorism are distinct—albeit strongly related—phenomena. This means, too, that we should expect explanations of each to be different in at least a few (causally) significant respects, but we should also not be surprised to see a good deal of theoretical overlap.

Defining Genocide

From the standpoint of international law, there *is* a single, authoritative definition of genocide (reproduced in Figure 7.1), which comes from the 1948 United Nations Convention on the Prevention and Punishment of the Crime of Genocide. The existence of a legal definition of genocide raises an obvious question: "Why not simply accept that definition and move on?" The question is certainly reasonable, but critics have pointed out seemingly major flaws in the convention or, more simply, the UN definition. (Keep in mind that, because international organizations are rife with political maneuvering among states, they typically are not the best places to develop analytically neutral definitions.) For example, in the minds of most people, what makes genocide such a heinous violation of human rights is the mass slaughter of innocent human beings. Yet, by the standards of the UN definition, as Jones emphasized, "one does not need to kill anyone at all to commit genocide!" (2010, p. 14). This is because, in the UN definition, genocide is defined explicitly as an intent to destroy a national, ethnical, racial, or religious group, not just by killing, but also by "causing serious bodily or mental harm," or by "imposing measures to prevent births," or by "forcibly transferring children of the group to another group." The latter three acts may be repugnant, but in the absence of large-scale death, critics argue that the essence or core meaning of genocide can be entirely lost.

Another major flaw or criticism of the UN definition is that it fails to include groups of people who do not fit into the category of a national,

---

**Figure 7.1 Definition of Genocide from the Convention
on the Prevention and Punishment of the Crime of Genocide**

The Convention on the Prevention and Punishment of the Crime of Genocide
was adopted by the United Nations General Assembly on December 9, 1948, as
General Assembly Resolution 260. Included as an integral part of the convention was a detailed and technical definition of genocide, as follows:

Article 2. In the present Convention, genocide means any of the following acts
committed with intent to destroy, in whole or in part, a national, ethnical, racial
or religious group, as such:

(a) Killing members of the group;
(b) Causing serious bodily or mental harm to members of the group;
(c) Deliberately inflicting on the group conditions of life calculated to bring
    about its physical destruction in whole or in part;
(d) Imposing measures intended to prevent births within the group;
(e) Forcibly transferring children of the group to another group.

Source: UN General Resolution 260 can be found at http://www.un.org/ga/search
/view_doc.asp?symbol=a/res/260(III).

---

ethnical, racial, or religious group. On the surface, this may not seem to be
particularly important. But consider campaigns waged against socioeconomic groups. In the former Soviet Union, for example, individuals known
as kulaks were the targets of systemic oppression under Soviet dictator
Joseph Stalin. Originally, kulaks were defined as "wealthy peasants," which
meant that they owned their own land, but as landowners they were considered class enemies by the Soviet regime. Ultimately, though, a much wider
range of peasants was classified a kulak, including isolated farmers, widows, and the elderly—that is, the most vulnerable (Jones 2010). The details
of their oppression cannot be covered here (for more discussion, see Conquest 1987); suffice it to say, the kulaks were subject to "liquidation" primarily through mass deportations. While most were not killed outright, the
conditions of their transport and the appalling circumstances in which they
were forced to live meant that the elderly and children "died like flies"
(Jones 2010, p. 192), while the able-bodied were literally forced to work,
usually in **gulags**, until they dropped dead (Werth 2008). As many as 1.8
million individuals labeled as kulaks were deported, and at least 500,000
died in a two-year period between 1931 and 1933 (Werth 2008). To exclude
the kulaks and or other socioeconomic as well as political groups from a
definition of genocide, many argue, is simply not defensible.

Since the Convention on the Prevention and Punishment of the Crime
of Genocide was adopted in 1948, then, multiple alternative definitions of

genocide have been offered. Jones (2010) listed twenty-two of the most in-fluential of these definitions and classified them into two broad groups: "harder" and "softer" positions (citing Rudolph 2001), although he noted that a given definition could have both hard and soft elements. A harder definition is one that defines genocide fairly rigidly. Thus, such a definition might consider only the near-total physical destruction of a group to be genocide. It would also severely restrict the types of groups or people that could be classified as victims of genocide. On this second point, for exam-ple, a harder position might assert that victims must be defined by their "es-sential defenselessness" (Charny 1994) or that they be "innocent and help-less" (Midlarsky 2005). Conversely, harder definitions also have a restrictive view of the perpetrators of genocide. Most typically, these definitions are state-centric; that is, they consider only the state or agents of the state (which might be private citizens acting at the behest of the state) to be capa-ble of committing genocide.

Softer positions, according to Jones, "reflect concerns that excessively rigid framings . . . rule out too many actions that, logically and morally, de-mand to be included" (2010, pp. 20–21). Some of these other actions are spelled out in the UN definition—for example, the imposition of measures designed to prevent births within the targeted group, or the forcible transfer of children from the targeted group to another group. Another example, suggested above, is the forced deportation or movement of individuals under conditions that lead to a disproportionately large number of foresee-able deaths. Softer positions also adopt a more open position with regard to victims and perpetrators. Thus, victims might include any civilians whether or not they are essentially defenseless or completely innocent; they could also include captured soldiers and other combatants who are systematically slaughtered after being disarmed. As for the perpetrators, this group could include nonstate actors who wield significant political power and influence over a given territory. One emerging example of the latter group is ISIS, also known as Islamic State, IS, or ISIL. Although typically thought of as a terrorist organization, in some areas of the Middle East and North Africa, ISIS has become a quasi-state and has targeted certain ethnic groups—the Yazidi minority in Iraq—for elimination (Cumming-Bruce 2015). The ques-tion of whether ISIS is a perpetrator of genocide or a terrorist organization, it is worth emphasizing, is not merely a matter of terminology. Indeed, the discussion in this section is based on the assumption that there is an impor-tant analytical distinction. (ISIS, in fact, can be defined as both; the key point to consider is the context within which ISIS uses violence.)

There are a number of other factors embedded in most definitions of genocide: *goals, scale, strategies,* and *intent* (Jones 2010). Each of these is important, but I will focus on just two: scale and intent. The issue of scale, bluntly put, has to do with the number or proportion of people killed (or otherwise harmed) within a targeted group. Is it genocide if, say, 1 percent of the targeted group is killed? Does it matter whether that 1 percent translates into only a few hundred people? What if it is 20,000 or 200,000 people? Harder positions assert that if the proportion or absolute number is very small, then it is not genocide. Softer positions, by contrast, suggest that genocide is possible even if the scale is very limited, in both relative and absolute terms. More important, in this view, is *intent*. That is, it matters if the perpetrators carry out acts that are intended to destroy or liquidate the targeted group. In this respect, genocide requires a significant degree of planning, organization, and sustained effort. A primarily spontaneous and haphazard outbreak of violence, even if targeted toward a specific group, therefore, would not be genocide. A good example of this is the massacre of Koreans living in Japan following the Great Kanto earthquake of 1923, which destroyed half the homes in Tokyo and almost all homes in Yokohama and caused upward of 140,000 deaths (Lee 2008). In the immediate aftermath of the earthquake, false rumors spread that Koreans were setting fires, poisoning wells, and looting in preparation for an uprising. This led to a spasm of spontaneous violence—carried out by ordinary Japanese citizens, soldiers, and police—that resulted in the killing of 6,000 Koreans. It is important to stress that, in saying the "spontaneous" massacre of 6,000 individuals is not genocide, researchers are not suggesting their deaths are less significant or less meaningful. Rather, it suggests (again) that there are analytical distinctions between the two types of collective violence (just as there are analytical distinctions between genocide and terrorism).

I realize that I have not yet provided "definitional clarity." I will try to do so now, although I will not provide my own definition, if only because I am a neophyte when it comes to genocide studies. For definitional clarity, then, I will rely on Jones, whose work I have referenced repeatedly in this section. He defined genocide as follows: "actualization of the intent, however successfully carried out, to murder in whole or in substantial part any national, ethnic, racial, religious, social, gender or economic group, as these groups are defined by the perpetrator, by whatever means" (2006, p. 22). It is important to underscore a few elements of his definition. First, in Jones's definition, the victims of genocide include a very broad range of groups (he explicitly adds social, gender, or economic groups); he also emphasized that the identity of the targeted group is defined by the perpetrator, not by the victims. Second, his definition is premised on intent to *kill* or *murder* members of the targeted group. In other words, it is not enough to prevent births or transfer children. Third, Jones's definition does not require total physical destruction of the group, only of a *substantial part* of the group (he purposely left the meaning of "substantial" ambiguous). Fourth, with regard to intent, Jones emphasized the necessity of "actualization," meaning that concrete steps toward physical destruction have to take place in order to qualify as genocide. Finally, Jones did not specify who the perpetrator must be—although, on this last point, it is fair to say that genocides, in general, are carried out by state actors or agents of the state.

Defining Terrorism

As noted earlier, in the minds of many if not most people, terrorism is an illegitimate and irredeemably evil act committed by irrational fanatics. Some analysts have gone so far as to define terrorism in essentially those terms. One example is Paul Johnson, a terrorism expert, journalist, and recipient of the Presidential Medal of Freedom (awarded by George W. Bush in 2006). Johnson defined terrorism as the "deliberate, systematic murder, maiming, and menacing of the innocent to inspire fear in order to gain political ends. . . . Terrorism . . . is intrinsically evil, necessarily evil, and wholly evil" (cited in Whittaker 2012, p. 4). While few if any scholars would define terrorism in such a vehement and overtly normative way, the foregoing definition likely strikes a strong cord with many people outside the academic world. For this reason, it is worthwhile exploring, *from a scholarly perspective,* the potential problems embedded in (the second part of) Johnson's definition. After all, many people might wonder, isn't terrorism actually evil, and isn't it just "political correctness" that prevents scholars from calling terrorism what it really is? My answer to both questions is not necessarily. Even if terrorism can be reasonably described as evil in many instances (and I certainly believe it can be), defining it as evil from the get-go creates a strong bias in explanatory or interpretive accounts. Keep in mind, in this regard, that "terrorism" is the dependent variable in many analyses; that is, it is the outcome that researchers are trying to explain. Thus, if terrorism is equated with evil, then research on terrorism can easily be transformed into an explanation *of* evil. This is shaky ground for a political or social scientist, although not necessarily for a theologian, philosopher, or psychologist. (Some scholars, I should note, disagree. Paul Formosa [2007] and Susan Neiman [2001], for example, both make a case that evil can be addressed at a political rather than just theological level.)

There is another, perhaps more important problem with definitions that have a strong normative bias: whether intentionally or not, they can preclude and occlude (i.e., obstruct or shut off) certain types of theoretical analysis. For instance, in defining terrorism as *intrinsically* evil, Johnson's definition could easily (although not necessarily) preclude or occlude rational choice analysis. To see why, think about the following two scenarios. In the first, a terrorist kills because there are few other methods available to achieve a larger political goal, such as challenging a powerful and dominant state. (Importantly, the first part of Johnson's definition suggests the possibility of just such a scenario.) In the second scenario, the terrorist is interested in the act of killing itself. Even more, the terrorist—for his/her own twisted pleasure—wants the victim to suffer and to die a slow, miserable death. In the first scenario, killing is strictly instrumental; that is, it is a strategic (and therefore rational) action taken to achieve a specific goal. Killing, in this scenario, is no different from a state that uses its military to conquer new territories, control resources, or, as the United States did in 2003, overthrow an uncooperative political regime. All these state-led goals require killing. In the second scenario, the killing, one might argue, is simply evil. This further suggests—by definition—that the killing is done to satisfy some base, perverse, or pathological need of the killer. This need could be the product of childhood trauma or abuse, or it could be from some sort of genetic defect. Whatever the case, the reason for killing is fundamentally irrational.

The issue, of course, is actually far more complicated than presented here, but my intent is simply to highlight a few potential problems in normatively biased definitions (although, admittedly, eliminating any normative bias is likely an impossible task). To repeat the basic point, though: the first scenario is amenable to rational choice analysis (as well as structural and cultural analysis), while the second is much less so. (Johnson's entire definition further confuses the issue by including the possibility that terrorism is a rational choice, but then essentially negates that possibility with his assertion that terrorism in "evil.") Structural analysis, as I noted, could be applied in the first scenario, too, but probably not in the second—since childhood trauma and abuse or idiosyncratic psychopathologies are generally considered to be the product of psychological processes (as opposed to macro-level structural processes), especially if those affected represent only a small part of a given society's population. None of this means that "evil" is unexplainable. Psychological explanations, as already suggested, would likely be an appropriate approach to the study of evil (for an example, see Allen 2007). Indeed, psychological approaches are likely quite valuable (and even partly compatible with rational, structural, and cultural analyses), but for comparativists, explanations of terrorism—a complex sociopolitical phenomenon—cannot be reduced to mental and physiologic processes. In this regard, definitions should be agnostic with regard to theory, although this is easier said than done.

This relatively lengthy critique of a single definition, it is important to emphasize, is meant to underscore a more general point: definitions cannot be taken for granted. As I have tried to make clear, a definition can push researchers—especially novice researchers—toward certain (biased) positions. Sometimes this "push" is unintentional, but other times it is fully intended. On this last point, it is important to recognize that some definitions are purposely designed to make a political or ideological statement, as opposed to serving as a social scientific concept. In crafting the second part of his definition, for example, it is likely that Johnson had just such a polemical purpose in mind: he wanted to condemn terrorism and terrorists *by definition.* This underscores another important issue with the term *terrorism:* it is ideologically, rhetorically, and emotionally loaded, and is often used as a political tool. In particular, national governments of all stripes use the term *terrorism* as a rhetorical weapon that, once successfully deployed, can serve to mobilize, accumulate, and justify the use of vast resources in an ostensible effort to wipe out the terrorist threat. Still, this does not mean that we should not or cannot attempt, as Martha Crenshaw (1995) argued, to transform the concept of terrorism "into a *useful analytical term* rather than a polemical tool" (p. 7, emphasis added).

So, how should terrorism be defined? Again, I will not pretend to be an authoritative source on this question. As with genocide, among the many experts on the subject, debates over the best way to define terrorism have produced a plethora of definitions that, as David Brannan, Philip Esler, and N. T. Strindberg observed, have "led to a rather perverse situation where a great number of scholars are studying a phenomenon, the essence of which they have (by now) simply agreed to disagree upon" (2001, p. 11). By one reckoning in the early 1980s, there were at least 109 different definitions of terrorism used in the scholarly literature (Schmid and Jongman 1983, pp. 5–6). Today, no doubt, there are probably dozens more definitions (see Figure 7.2 for a sampling of definitions, both from official sources—governmental agencies and international organizations—and from scholars). Given this definitional morass, the search for conceptual clarity might seem to be an impossible task. David Whittaker (2012), however, provides a fruitful approach. The key is to *distinguish* terrorism from other forms of violent activity, such as interstate war, guerrilla or insurgent warfare, genocide, and ordinary criminality. The main point, however, is not to legitimize or delegitimize different types of violence (or to say one type of violence is evil, while another is not). Rather, the point is to show, in analytical terms, that *not* all collective political violence is the same. This is especially important for types of violence that appear, on the surface, to be synonymous, such as terrorism, guerrilla warfare, insurgency, and violent crime. Whittaker did that (for our purposes it is not necessary to provide details), and thus (pp. 9–10) "by distinguishing . . . terrorism from other forms of crime and irregular warfare . . . [it becomes possible] to appreciate that terrorism is":

- ineluctably political in aims and motive;
- violent—or equally important, threatens violence;
- designed to have far-reaching psychological repercussions beyond the immediate victim or target;
- conducted either by an organization with an identifiable chain of command or conspiratorial cell structure (whose members wear no uniform or identifying insignia) or by individuals or a small collection of individuals directly influenced, motivated, or inspired by the ideological aims of some existent terrorist movements and/or its leaders;
- perpetrated by a subnational group or nonstate entity; and
- designed to create power where there is none or to consolidate power where there is very little.

Figure 7.2 Some Definitions of Terrorism

1. The unlawful use of force or violence against persons or property to intimidate or coerce a government, the civilian population, or any segment thereof, in furtherance of political and social objectives (Federal Bureau of Investigation).
2. The calculated use of violence or the threat of violence to inculcate fear, intended to coerce or intimidate governments or societies as to the pursuit of goals that are generally political, religious, or ideological (US Department of Defense).
3. Contributes the illegitimate use of force to achieve a political objective when innocent people are targeted (Walter Laqueur).
4. A strategy of violence designed to promote desired outcomes by instilling fear in the public at large (Walter Reich).
5. [International terrorism is] the threat or use of violence for political purposes when (1) such action is intended to influence the attitude and behavior of a target group wider than its immediate victims, and (2) its ramifications transcend national boundaries (Peter Sederberg).
6. Terrorism is a political label given to people who are perceived to be planning or carrying out acts of violence for political objectives. The violence may be directed against individuals and sometimes property. The violence may not always be that of individuals or groups. A government's armed forces may be labeled terrorist, as they often are, by the party at the receiving end of that violence (Jamal Nassar).
7. Criminal acts intended or calculated to provoke a state of terror in the general public, a group of persons or particular persons for political purposes are in any circumstance unjustifiable, whatever the considerations of a political, philosophical, ideological, racial, ethnic, religious or any other nature that may be invoked to justify them (UN General Assembly Resolution 51/210).
8. Terrorism is defined as political violence in an asymmetrical conflict that is designed to induce terror and psychic fear (sometimes indiscriminate) through the violent victimization and destruction of noncombatant targets (sometimes iconic symbols). Such acts are meant to send a message from an illicit clandestine organization. The purpose of terrorism is to exploit the media in order to achieve maximum attainable publicity as an amplifying force multiplier in order to influence the targeted audience(s) in order to reach short- and midterm political goals and/or desired long-term end states (Carsten Bockstette).

Sources: Definitions 1–5 are from Whittaker 2012, pp. 3–4; definition 6 is from Nassar 2004, p. 17; definition 7 is from United Nations General Assembly 2010; and definition 8 is from Bockstette 2008, p. 8.

The foregoing list provides the basis for Whittaker's definition of terrorism "as the deliberate creation or exploitation of violence or the threat of violence in pursuit of political change. . . . Terrorism is specifically designed to have far-reaching psychological effects beyond the immediate victim(s)." In addition, according to Whittaker, terrorism "is meant to instill fear within, and thereby intimidate, a wider 'target audience' that might include a rival ethnic or religious group, an entire country, a national government or political party, or public opinion in general." Last, Whittaker's assertion that terrorism is "designed to create power where there is none or to consolidate power where there is very little" is important to highlight: it suggests that terrorist organizations are relatively weak, albeit in relation to their ultimate, as opposed to proximate, targets. Thus, part of the study of terrorism revolves around why relatively weak nonstate actors turn to violence. In this regard, too, the foregoing definition tells us that terrorism is analytically distinct from genocide, the latter of which is perpetrated by relatively powerful and mostly state actors.

In sum, Whittaker's definition endeavors, even if imperfectly, to provide a "useful analytical" rather than polemical definition. Still, there is little doubt there are many who will not agree with his effort, if only because any attempt to define terrorism definitively is destined to fail. One reason, as I have already noted, is because the term itself is simply too emotionally, politically, and ideologically charged. In this respect, Brannan, Esler, and Strindberg (2001) suggested that we should dispense with the word *terrorism* altogether and replace it with a more neutral term: *violent substate activism.* The notion of violent substate activism has many advantages, not the least of which is its discursive distance from terrorism. Another important advantage is the obvious connotation of "activism" in the phrase. In a general sense, activism can be described as an intentional act to bring about social, political, economic, or environmental change. And while the word *activism* is often used synonymously with *nonviolent protest* or *dissent,* activists can use a wide variety of tools to achieve their goals, including violence. As we will see later in the chapter, activism may also unfold in a series of steps: from campaigning, to nonviolent protest, to aggressive confrontations, to violence. In this regard, it makes analytical sense to view terrorism as a violent (and extreme) *type* of activism. There is, however, one problematic aspect of the phrase "violent *substate* activism." To wit, many (but not all) of the most important "activists" are not strictly substate actors, but instead operate on a transnational basis. Thus it might be better to replace "substate" with "nonstate." (To avoid confusion—and also because the term by Brannan and colleagues never caught on—this chapter will stick with the term *terrorism.*)

Strategic Killers? Rational Choice Explanations of Genocide and Terrorism

Rational choice explanations of genocide and terrorism begin with a simple assumption: *killing is a rational act.* The choice of targets (i.e., victims), the methods of violence (e.g., bombing, shooting, poisoning or gassing, decapitating, stabbing or hacking to death), and the scope and scale of killing are all part of a conscious and purposeful process. Those who direct or lead this process, in particular, are strategic or rational actors. That is, they weigh the costs and benefits of their choices (which means, in part, that killing is one of many possible choices), and they have a larger goal they hope to achieve. They do not kill for the sake of killing, or to satisfy their internal demons. Nor do they kill, rational choice analysts would assert, because they are megalomaniacs or religious zealots or are suffering from a psychopathology—they might be, but their megalomania, religious zealotry, or psychopathology are not the reason they kill. As rational actors, most simply, those who organize and participate in collective political violence, whether genocide or terrorism, do so because it is a *means toward an end.*

Understandably, the foregoing characterization will likely strike many people, including scholars, as wrongheaded. One example of this view can be found in the book *The Roots of Evil: The Origins of Genocide and Other Group Violence,* by Ervin Staub (1989). Staub did not mince words, as he summarily rejected the idea that "genocides and mass killings [are] ever 'rational expressions of self-interest'" (cited in Jones 2010, p. 62, n. 142). Given the title of Staub's book (and in light of our foregoing discussion on terrorism), his conclusion is hardly surprising. But equally strong arguments—those not based on defining certain types of violence as evil—can be found in studies of terrorism. This is particularly the case for contemporary or "new" terrorism, which increasingly revolves around the use of *suicide* attacks (more on this below). Here the logic is clear: an individual who successfully commits suicide in the ostensible pursuit of an earthly political goal simply cannot benefit from his or her actions. Thus, the decision and the actor must be irrational. As Robert Nalbandov put it, "The thought of exchanging individual lives for a greater common good is quite problematic to accept since sacrificing one's life for the unknown and, thus, the unquantifiable outcome, is far from being rational" (2013, p. 96).

Those who argue that neither genocide nor terrorism are or can be rational make a compelling prima facie case. Before we accept such arguments, however, we need to look below the surface, which the rational choice framework allows us to do. To understand their position, rationalists tell us to think carefully about whom the central actors are in situations of terrorism and genocide. This is easy enough to do. As I have already suggested, there are two basic types: those who make the decisions that lead directly to killing—that is, the *leaders* of terrorist organizations or the leaders of states (or those who occupy positions of significant political power)—and those who carry out the violence, the actual killers or perpetrators. While some rationalists argue that the actions of both leaders and perpetrators reflect rational choices (e.g., Crenshaw 1998), others admit, even if only tacitly, that rational choice principles do best in explaining decisions by leaders. When the focus is on leaders, in particular, it is not difficult to discern their self-interests; nor is it difficult to explain how and why they choose mass violence as the best means to achieve their self-interested goals. This said, it is important to keep in mind one of the analytical distinctions between genocide and terrorism: in genocide, violence is generally used by those already *in* (political) power, while in terrorism, violence is used by those *aspiring* to greater positions of power.

Genocide and Power: Killing the Helpless

For those occupying positions of power and authority, their primary goal, as with most any political leader, is to stay in power or to further consolidate political power. Under certain conditions—most generally "difficult life conditions" (Staub 1999)—leaders may choose to instigate mass violence (genocide) against targeted groups. Sometimes the targeted group is seen as a direct threat, a situation that might, albeit quite arguably, describe the targeting of Tutsi (and moderate Hutu) by the Hutu leadership in Rwanda during 1994. On this point, recall that Tutsi leaders in neighboring countries had carried out mass slaughters of Hutu in the years prior to the 1994 genocide, and that an army led and composed of Tutsi, the Rwandan Patriotic Front, in particular, was created with the specific goal of overthrowing the Hutu-led regime in Rwanda. In most cases, though, the targeted group is initially *scapegoated*, as the Jews were scapegoated for the Nazi regime, or as the Armenians were scapegoated for the "difficult life conditions" faced by the Ottoman Turks. (There is, I should emphasize, a long-standing and intense debate on the concept of scapegoating in genocide studies; see Newman [2002] for further discussion.) For leaders, finding a scapegoat serves at least three useful, self-interested purposes. First, it deflects actual or potential criticisms for any difficulties the country is facing from the leadership to a largely defenseless group. Second, it creates a basis for sustained popular mobilization, which can be manipulated to reinforce the political power of the leadership. Third, it can serve as a pretext for eliminating political rivals or other oppositional threats.

Still, this does not answer the question "Why genocide?" That is, why would leaders facing difficult life conditions choose mass violence over some other, less extreme policy? Rationalists have one answer: as a policy choice, genocide is not typically the first choice. Instead, it often represents a last resort—that is, an action when other policies have failed to achieve a desired result. As Staub argued, genocide is often the endpoint of "steps [or stages] along a continuum of destruction" (1999, p. 307). From a rational choice perspective, this is expected, as it gives leaders a chance to evaluate the effectiveness of various policies in terms of fulfilling their larger goals. In other words, if a less extreme policy does not prove effective, another policy may be used, eventually leading up to mass killings or genocide. Even if genocide is a first step, however, it can still be viewed as a rational policy choice insofar as leaders see it as an efficacious and viable option. In other words, if political leaders know that mass killings help them achieve their political goals, and if they know they can "get away" with genocide—not just domestically, but also, even more importantly, internationally—then it will always remain as one of many political choices on the table, so to speak. Conversely, if they know that the choice of genocide will invariably result in serious and unacceptably damaging repercussions from the international community (i.e., other states), they will take it off the table. Unfortunately, history has demonstrated, time and time again, the stubborn unwillingness of the international community to respond strongly to genocide, or, in some cases, to even acknowledge that it happened in the distant past. Even worse, history has shown that the international community would rather close its eyes to genocide—to simply pretend that it is not taking place in order to avoid any "responsibility to protect" (I will return to a discussion of this phrase shortly) a people from mass slaughter.

A textbook case of international indifference to genocide is Rwanda. At first, the international community turned a blind eye to the fairly obvious buildup toward genocide in late 1993 and early 1994. As Samantha Power explained it, "The signs of militarization in Rwanda were so widespread that even without much intelligence-gathering capacity, Dallaire [the general in charge of a UN 'peacekeeping' force in Rwanda at the time] was able to learn of the extremists' sinister intentions" (2001). Despite Roméo Dallaire's desperate pleas that he be allowed to act, he was forbidden by his "political masters" at the UN to do anything—in part because of US resistance to any sort of "aggressive peacekeeping" (see Figure 7.3 for a discussion of and background on the peacekeeping operation in Rwanda). Once the mass killing started, more importantly, the international community—"led" by the United States—not only did nothing, but also, in a manner, facilitated the killings by quickly withdrawing almost all UN forces. Here is how Power, in her scathing critique of US policy during the genocide, explained the role of the United States specifically:

> The United States did much more than fail to send troops. It led a successful effort to remove most of the UN peacekeepers who were already in Rwanda. It aggressively worked to block the subsequent authorization of UN reinforcements. It refused to use its technology to jam radio broadcasts that were a critical instrument in the coordination and perpetuation of the genocide. And even as, on average, 8,000 Rwandans were being butchered each day, U.S. officials shunned the term "genocide," for fear of being obligated to act. The United States did virtually nothing to "try to limit what occurred." Indeed, staying out of Rwanda was an explicit U.S. policy objective. (2001)

Since Rwanda, the international community has vowed to take a stronger and more consistent stance toward genocide, which was manifested in the Responsibility to Protect (R2P) principle. Unanimously adopted by

---

Figure 7.3 The UN Peacekeeping Operation in Rwanda

Prior to the genocide of 1994, Rwanda had been beset by a civil war, which began in 1990, when the Rwandan Patriotic Front, a rebel army composed of 4,000 mostly Tutsi soldiers, invaded Rwanda from neighboring Uganda. The RPF's main target was the Rwandan government, then led by President Juvénal Habyarimana, who had been in power since 1973. Despite its small size, the RPF seriously threatened the Rwandan regime, which was saved in large part by the intervention of French troops. A stalemate ensued, which led to the signing of peace accords, known as the Arusha Accords, in 1993. Among other things, the agreement established a broad-based transitional government, which was a power-sharing agreement between the RPF and the Rwandan government, and led to the United Nations Assistance Mission for Rwanda (UNAMIR). UNAMIR was meant to assist in ensuring the security of the capital city of Kigali, monitor the cease-fire agreement, and establish a demilitarized zone. To carry out its mission, a peacekeeping force was sent to Rwanda: initially Belgium and Bangladesh each contributed 400 troops, and later Ghana and Tunisia sent troops. Brigadier-General Roméo Dallaire, a Canadian, served as the first force commander of UNAMIR.

---

heads of state at the 2005 UN World Summit and codified in the World Summit Outcome Document (paragraphs 138 and 139), R2P obligates the international community—both the UN *and* individual member states—to protect groups threatened by genocide. Not surprisingly, implementation of R2P has been, at best, uneven. As Mónica Serrano put it, "If the Responsibility to Protect was to be expected to lead to an overhaul of domestic and international human rights structures guaranteeing the physical integrity of the individual, this is all still a pending matter" (2011, p. 13). In other words, the rhetoric is strong, but the action has still been limited (for further discussion, see Bellamy 2010). This is not surprising: after all, just as those leaders who are responsible for genocide are acting in their self-interests, so are the leaders of countries that have the capacity to intervene to stop genocides. For the latter, in their self-interested views, as long as the mass slaughter of human beings "somewhere else" does not represent a threat to the security or interests of their own countries (or their own political positions), there is absolutely no rational reason to act. So they don't.

There is, it is important to note, a crucial implication that flows from the foregoing analysis. If genocide is a rational act made by rational actors, then it is clear that it can be prevented or stopped by raising the "costs." John Mueller (2000), for example, argued that in Rwanda, a small contingent of lightly armed UN peacekeepers easily stopped Hutu "murder squads" from slaughtering thousands of Tutsi refugees in a Kigali stadium merely by forbidding the killers entry into the stadium. More significant, consider, too, how the Rwandan Patriotic Front, a relatively small but organized military force, was able to end the genocide shortly after moving into Rwanda. Indeed, the RPF encountered "little opposition except around Kigali [the capital city of Rwanda]. . . . As RPF soldiers advanced south down the eastern side of the country and then swept west, they even stopped the killers in the act of attacking or preparing to attack Tutsi at several churches or camps for the displaced. More often they rescued Tutsi with no dramatic confrontation" (Des Forges 1999, p. 1052). The relative ease by which the RPF stopped the mass killings, to repeat, reinforces the assertion that the Rwandan genocide was a rational policy choice made by leadership: once it was clear that it was no longer an effective policy, it was abandoned. Even more, it suggests that the actual killers—not just the leaders—were also rational actors who weighed the costs and benefits of their decisions and actions. When confronted by an adversary capable of fighting back, the killers backed down almost immediately.

Obviously, this cursory analysis is far from sufficient to establish the validity of the rational choice perspective on genocide. It does, however, provide food for thought, which is ultimately all I can hope to do in this section. It also provides a useful analytical contrast with rational choice explanations of terrorism, which is a form of collective political violence that typically involves killing on a much smaller scale. The reason, though, is not due to a stronger aversion to the use of killing as a tool to achieve a political goal. Instead, the reason is based on the much weaker positions that terrorist organizations occupy.

Terrorism: Weapon of the Weak?

Even the strongest and most well-known terrorist organizations tend to be very small and underequipped in relation to their avowed enemies. Consider al-Qaeda, perhaps the most prominent and dangerous terrorist organization in the world. (Others might point to ISIS, but as I noted above, ISIS is both a terrorist organization and a political authority or semi-state.) Despite al-Qaeda's deadly reputation, estimates from a dozen terrorism scholars put its core membership (in 2011) at anywhere from just 200 individuals to, at most, 1,000. In addition, there may be between 2,000 and 20,000 "affiliated fighters or funders" (Bialik 2011). Compared to the size of the US military—the United States is one of the main targets of the organization—even the highest estimates of al-Qaeda's numbers are, to put it bluntly, puny: the United States has 1.4 million frontline personnel and 1.1 million active reserve personnel (Global Fire Power 2015). In addition, of course, the United States possesses massive and largely unmatched military firepower, which includes a nuclear arsenal comprising 7,100 intact nuclear warheads, of which 2,080 are actively deployed (Kristensen and Norris

2015). While the United States stands largely alone in overall military power, other major targets of terrorist organizations—including, most significantly, Israel—are quite formidable in their own right. Most military analysts agree that Israel's battle-tested defense force is one of the best trained in the world, but it is also very well armed, with 160,000 frontline personnel, 630,000 reserve personnel, 4,170 tanks, 10,185 armored fighting vehicles, 242 fighter jets, and an annual defense budget of $17 billion (Global Fire Power 2015).

Facing demonstrably more powerful adversaries, leaders of terrorist organizations have limited options (put another way, there are serious *constraints* on what they can do). In particular, *direct* and *sustained* attacks against their enemies' military forces are doomed to failure; such attacks would be irrational. Seen in this light, it is predictable and rational that terrorist organizations tend to attack civilian targets primarily, or, given the right set of circumstances, to launch one-off or hit-and-run attacks against military targets. It also helps explain why suicide attacks have become a dominant mode of terrorist violence. That is, while suicide attacks may make little or no sense from the perspective of the individual bomber, it makes very good sense from the perspective of an organization's leadership. Consider the 1983 suicide attacks launched by Lebanon's **Hezbollah** (literally, "the party of God") against US and French military contingents stationed in Beirut. This was a one-off attack against a military target that was, in retrospect, very poorly protected and unprepared. The attack itself was meticulously planned and skillfully executed. At the same time, it posed little risk to Hezbollah's leadership, since it involved only a couple of "expendable" individuals driving trucks laden with explosives. Yet the suicide attack met with "astonishing success" (Kramer 1998, p. 141), not because it killed a lot of people (as it did), but because it enabled Hezbollah to achieve a clear political objective, namely the withdrawal of foreign forces from Lebanon. (See Figure 7.4 for a brief discussion of this incident.) The success of that attack, in turn, demonstrated to Hezbollah and other terrorist organizations that suicide attacks were an effective and relatively low-risk "tool" to use against much stronger opponents. This is a major reason why suicide bombings have become, for all intents and purposes, the weapon of *choice* for terrorist organizations. On this point, it is useful to note that stronger (usually state) actors largely eschew this tactic, since they have more effective means to achieve their goals.

As with genocide, however, the question arises, "Why choose terrorism at all?" More to the point, why choose an obviously very risky strategy that is likely to elicit a very strong and violent reaction on the part of the real target or targets (usually a state)? Terrorism is, in this respect, likely more dangerous to the terrorists than it is to the entities to whom their actions are ultimately directed. On this point, not surprisingly, rationalists will again

**Figure 7.4 The Suicide Terrorist Attack
Against US Forces in Lebanon**

On October 23, 1983, around 6:20 A.M., a Mercedes delivery truck drove to Beirut International Airport, where the US Marines had their headquarters. The driver turned onto a road leading to the compound and circled a parking lot; he then gunned his engine, crashed through a barbed-wire fence, passed between two sentry posts, crashed through a gate, and barreled into the lobby of the Marine headquarters building. The suicide bomber detonated his truck, which contained 12,000 pounds of TNT. The force of the explosion collapsed the four-story cinder-block building into rubble, ultimately killing 241 US Marines and naval personnel (and injuring sixty others). At almost the same moment a similar explosion blew up the French military barracks a few kilometers away, killing fifty-six French troops.

The US Marines were originally in Beirut as part of a multinational force (MNF) composed of 800 French, 800 US, and 400 Italian troops (the United Kingdom also joined a few months later). The MNF was an integral part of a cease-fire agreement designed to end the conflict between Israel and Lebanon, which also involved the Palestine Liberation Organization (PLO) (which was using Lebanon as a base for attacks against Israel). The first deployment of the MNF was generally successful, but later incidents brought the MNF back to Beirut. The second deployment turned out to be much more politically complicated, as US forces, in particular, were involved in a number of incidents that made it appear as if the United States had taken a side in what had now become a largely internal struggle within Lebanon. Rather than a neutral arbiter, therefore, the United States became identified as a key player on the side of the Christian-dominated central government, which also had a friendly relationship with Israel. This made the MNF, in the eyes of those who opposed Israel, an unequivocal enemy. The attack against US forces, which was meant to drive the United States out of the country, achieved its goal: US Marines were moved offshore in February 1984, and the MNF operation essentially came to an end. All of this took place, moreover, despite a pledge by then-president Ronald Reagan that the United States would stay in Lebanon. Vice President George H. W. Bush was even clearer. After touring the bombing site on October 26, he said, "We will stay." He also asserted that the United States would not be cowed by terrorists, which, in essence, proved not to be the case.

Sources: "1983 Beirut Barracks Bombing," http://en.wikipedia.org/wiki/Marine_Barracks_Bombing; John H. Kelly, "Lebanon: 1982–1984," Rand Conference Report: US and Russian Policymaking with Respect to the Use of Force, www.rand.org/publications/CF/CF129/CF-129.chapter6.html.

point to the tendency for terrorism to be a last, as opposed to a first, resort. Indeed, the turn to terrorism is often part of a longer process, whereby ordinary individuals become political activists, usually in response to objectively oppressive, unequal, or unjust conditions. The conditions may not be deep or pervasive enough to create a societywide movement (although this certainly is not always the case), but are still strong enough to compel individuals to form groups or organizations designed to challenge the status quo. Once these organizations are formed, they will press for change through a variety of tactics but are likely to be continually frustrated. As a result, the group gradually turns toward more and more extreme measures, ultimately leading to terrorist violence. For small, relatively weak groups, it is important to add, terrorism has a very clear benefit: most simply, as Martha Crenshaw noted, it is able to "put the issue of political change on the public agenda" (1998, p. 17). In other words, terrorist acts attract attention, and by "attracting attention [terrorism] makes the claims of the resistance a salient issue in the public mind" (p. 17). This, in turn, may build or coalesce a critical mass of "popular support" (not necessarily from the public at large, but from other disaffected members of the public), which would be the main ingredient for future success.

The key point from the foregoing discussion is simple: terrorism is a choice based on reason and logic. Even if its consequences are evil, its use is instrumental. If we accept this argument, moreover, we must accept a clear implication, which is that terrorism does not arise out of thin air: terrorists do no just wake up one day and decide to kill (innocent people). Nor do they wake suddenly and begin, with no reason, to hate Americans, other Westerners, or anyone or anything else. Instead, from a rational choice perspective, terrorism must be understood as a response or reaction to external (as opposed to psychological) forces and conditions. This means, in turn, that terrorism is very unlikely absent conditions of oppression, repression, severe discrimination (including religious and ethnic discrimination or subordination), exploitation, deep inequality, or any number of other hard felt social, economic, or political injustices. Thus, from a rational choice perspective, we would expect to see greater incidences and more intense levels of terrorism in those areas where repression, oppression, inequality, and the like, are strongest. There are at least a couple of other criteria as well. First, terrorism is likely to be strongest in those places where other forms of nonviolent political activism have proven to be largely, if not completely, ineffective. Second, terrorism will tend to be strongest where the capacity of the state (or other political authority) is relatively weak or hamstrung.

Consider the list of countries with the most (domestic) terrorist activity (the following list is slightly different than the one introduced at the beginning of the chapter): Iraq, Afghanistan, Pakistan, Nigeria, Syria, India, Somalia, Yemen, the Philippines, Thailand, Russia, Kenya, Egypt, and Lebanon (*Global Terrorism Database* 2015). At first glance, it is fairly evident that each of these countries suffers from a combination of serious economic, political, and social problems. In each country, moreover, certain groups likely find it difficult to effect change through nonviolent activism. And, with a few exceptions (most notably Russia), the capacity of the state to monitor or stamp out terrorist organizations and to prevent terrorist attacks is limited. In

Iraq, the group al-Qaeda in Iraq (AQI) has been particularly successful in carrying out high-profile attacks against civilians (both foreign and Iraqi), police and security forces, and government officials, all with the aim of destabilizing the Iraqi government, fomenting a larger civil conflict (along sectarian lines), combating the US presence in Iraq, and creating safe havens and sanctuaries. AQI's power has ebbed and flowed since it was established in the aftermath of the US invasion of Iraq in 2003, but it has proven to be a resilient and effective organization. Importantly, both before and since it was almost wiped out in 2007 (largely due to a surge in US military forces and the creation of US-supported militias), AQI has demonstrated a capacity to actually achieve its goals. This suggests quite clearly that terrorism can work as a rational means of achieving a political goal. Thus, it is no surprise at all—and perhaps even predictable—that Iraq has suffered the most from terrorism.

Why "They" Hate "Us"

While the rationality of domestic terrorism is easy enough to discern, what explains the rise in global or cross-border terrorism since the early 1990s? More specifically, why is terrorism also directed against the United States and Western European countries? The answer, at least with regard to motivation, is also fairly easy to discern: Western countries have used, and continue to use, their overwhelming economic and military capacity to dominate poorer countries, to sustain repressive and dictatorial regimes, to exploit local labor and resources (e.g., oil in the Middle East), and to project military power to all corners of the world. While these practices have been going on for many decades, terrorist organizations have only relatively recently developed the capacity to launch attacks on a cross-border or global basis against Western targets. Still, it is extraordinarily difficult to carry out such attacks, and the risks to the organization are exceedingly high. Thus, cross-border attacks have been very few and far between. At the same time, some of these attacks have arguably been effective, including the 9/11 attacks. On this point, it is important to understand what the concrete goals of terrorist organizations are, as opposed to the rhetorical bluster (i.e., establishing a global caliphate or Islamic government). For the 9/11 attacks, the concrete goals were fairly clear: (1) to push US military bases out of Saudi Arabia (after the Gulf War in 1991, the Saudi government allowed the United States to establish bases in the country); (2) to compel the United States to devote massive spending and other resources to counterterrorism activities; and (3) to raise the global profile of al-Qaeda. Arguably, all three goals were achieved, and perhaps they could only have been achieved with the "spectacular acts of terrorism" (Robertson 2007).

Why a relative handful of individual terrorists—the leaders of terrorist organizations—would be willing to assume the risks of attacking the most powerful and capable states on the planet, however, is still unclear. What is clear, though, is the efforts they take to protect themselves, which reflect a concern with self-preservation (certainly a rational interest). It took the United States, for example, almost a full decade to find and kill Osama bin Laden. In the meantime, he likely benefited greatly from his reputation as the mastermind of 9/11, as well as other prominent attacks against the United States, including the 1998 bombings of the US embassies in Nairobi (Kenya) and Dar es Salaam (Tanzania) and the 2000 attack on the *USS Cole*. Perhaps his stature as the "world's greatest terrorist" was enough?

Rationality, Mistakes, and Constraints: A Closing Point

Arguing that terrorist leaders act rationally does not mean that their decisions are always or even mostly effective or productive. Indeed, as Crenshaw (1998) pointed out, terrorist organizations often make miscalculations and even huge blunders. But this is primarily (albeit not completely) a product of limited or imperfect information and not of an insufficient or distorted grasp of reality. As Crenshaw aptly put it, "Perfect knowledge of available alternatives and the consequences of each is not possible, and miscalculations are inevitable" (p. 9). In addition, as I have already emphasized, the decisions that terrorist organizations make are constrained by a lack of resources and viable alternatives. In the case of Hezbollah's opposition to the United States, for example, suicide bombings represented one of the few means available to confront the overwhelming military advantage enjoyed by US (and Israeli) forces. As one Hezbollah cleric put it, "If an oppressed people does not have the means to confront the United States and Israel with the weapons in which they are superior, then they possess unfamiliar weapons. . . . Oppression makes the oppressed discover new weapons and new strength every day" (quote by Sayyid Muhammad Husayn Fadlallah; cited in Kramer 1998, p. 144).

Assessing the Rational Choice
Argument for Genocide and Terrorism

The rational choice approach begins at a high level of generality or abstraction. That is, it begins with an overarching assumption regarding the *rational* motivations of those who direct collective political violence, whether from positions of relative strength or positions of relative weakness. That assumption is then applied, in deductive fashion, to a range of concrete and specific cases and actors to see if it can provide a reasonable and accurate basis for explanation. As we have seen, there is good reason to believe that it does. Thus, we reach the conclusion that both genocide and terrorism are rational, albeit extreme, means of pursuing interests in the political arena. As a caveat, though, few rational choice analysts will claim that the principles of rational choice explain everything significant about genocide and terrorism, or that those principles are always and necessarily the important factors when it comes to decisions to kill. "But," as one rational choice scholar put it, "it is [always] critical to include strategic reasoning as a possible motivation, at a minimum as an antidote to stereotypes of 'terrorists' [or leaders of genocide] as irrational fanatics" (Crenshaw 1998, p. 24).

While the rational choice approach is, to put it gently, counterintuitive to many people—especially to those who consider both genocide and terrorism to be evil—a dispassionate analysis, to repeat, strongly suggests there is an undeniable logic to both forms of collective political violence. This does not mean, I should emphasize, that there is anything admirable or courageous in purposely targeting often defenseless and innocent victims. The killing of defenseless and innocent human beings is, in the eyes of rationalists, just as vile and despicable as it is in the eyes of most other people. Yet, recognizing the underlying and *universal* rationality of such violence provides a crucial insight: given the right set of circumstances, genocide and terrorism can emerge from *any* society—whether Western or Islamic, Buddhist or secular, fascist or democratic—or from any group of people. In other words, the logic and principles of rational choice tell us that neither genocide nor terrorism is or ever has been the product of a specific culture or a specific set of social values—and comparative checking easily confirms this. To put the issue in very blunt terms, rational choice asserts that anyone reading this chapter is, in principle, capable of killing (or at least condoning killing), either as a *génocidaire* ("one who commits genocide") or as a terrorist.

I emphasize this point here as earlier in the chapter because, especially in the West, many people are convinced that only a few "barbarous" cultures and societies are capable of producing genocide and terrorism. This is a naive and arrogant attitude, which is supported neither by (rational choice) theory nor by the facts. After all, from a historical perspective, the West was the primary perpetrator of genocide, and continues, to this day, to sanction the killing of tens and even hundreds of thousands of innocent and defenseless human beings in the form of another prominent type of collective political violence: war. (In the case of war, however, the deaths of the defenseless and innocent are referred to as "collateral damage"; they are usually not the intended targets, but their deaths are frequently foreseeable and equally as tragic.)

So, is the rational choice argument correct? That is, is strategic reasoning a key element of genocide and terrorism? Are *génocidaires* and terrorists, in fact, rational actors doing rational things? In my foregoing analysis, I cite a few illustrative examples, but are these sufficient to confirm the rational choice approach? Conversely, can you think of any cases that would undermine or invalidate this approach? More generally, from a broader methodological and comparative perspective, what is necessary to establish a strong and compelling case? Asking these questions, I should emphasize, is simply meant to refocus *your* attention on a crucial, but often neglected, aspect of doing comparative politics, namely using comparisons (and the evidence on which those comparisons are based) to both evaluate arguments made by others and support your own arguments. Of course, if you have limited to no knowledge about cases of genocide and terrorism—or if your knowledge is superficial and purely anecdotal—using comparisons may not be helpful. This is why it is important not only to do your own research, but also to endeavor to apply the principles or logic of comparative analysis in a manner that can help you overcome (rather than confirm) bias and unscientific analysis.

The Culture of Killing: Cultural Approaches to Explaining Collective Political Violence

Rational choice provides a useful and, perhaps, invaluable way to think about the motivations behind genocide and terrorism. Yet even if that argument is accepted without any reservations, crucial questions still remain. Thus, while rational choice seems to provide a reasonable explanation for the behavior of leaders, what explains the actions of rank-and-file killers? That is, how can we account for the behavior of the ordinary *génocidaire* and terrorist? After all, without the "soldiers" of genocide and terrorism, neither form of collective political violence is possible. Another question, but one for terrorism in particular, is this: "Why is there no shortage of people willing to give up their lives to carry out suicide attacks?" Since such attacks have become more the rule than the exception, suicide terrorism cannot be simply dismissed as a tangential or insignificant phenomenon. If anything, it has become a defining feature of contemporary terrorism, and thus must be explained. Fortunately, cultural analysis provides an almost ready-made framework for answering the two preceding questions, as well as many others. As usual, though, it is important to emphasize, from the outset, that even the most compelling cultural analysis cannot explain everything. Culture, as I have repeatedly emphasized, is frequently a crucial and even necessary part of an explanation about social, political, or economic phenomena, but it never stands alone.

Keeping the foregoing points in mind, in an examination of collective political violence, cultural analysis generally emphasizes the significance of culture as a meaning-making medium that influences or shapes—to a potentially profound extent—the *behavior* of individuals, communities, or even whole societies. The term "meaning-making medium," I realize, may sound a bit "too academic." So, at the risk of grossly oversimplifying the issue, let me make the point more bluntly: cultural analysis asserts that social, ideological, and religious beliefs (all of which, recall, are part-and-parcel of culture) can turn normally peaceful people into compliant and even bloodthirsty killers. It is important to reemphasize, very strongly, that this transformational power is *not* limited to only certain cultures or societies. On this last point, culturalists are in full agreement with rationalists: pretty much any individual from any place in the world—whether in the Middle East, North America, Asia, Africa, Western Europe, and so on—can become a *génocidaire* or terrorist under the right conditions. As I suggested at the outset, too, culturalists also find common ground, at least to some extent, with rational choice regarding the motivations of the leaders who make the decisions to kill. That is, in general, both culturalists and rationalists agree that individual leaders are keenly aware of the consequences of choosing to instigate and pursue a campaign of wanton killing, yet do so to further their own political, social, or economic goals. Even on this point, however, cultural analysts may assert that culture plays a central role in shaping the actions of the leaders themselves.

To repeat the central point: cultural analysis suggests, on the one hand, that two parallel explanations for genocide and terrorism may be necessary, one that explains the decisions and actions of leaders, and another that explains the decisions and actions of the followers, or, more bluntly, the killers. Having two parallel, but completely separate, explanatory accounts, however, is potentially problematic. Thus, on the other hand, it is important to discuss how the two accounts (of leaders and followers) can be brought together into an integrated or coherent explanation. The discussion that follows will endeavor to address both issues, although the emphasis will be on the first. Before moving forward, though, it would be useful to take one step back. I began this section with the assertion that individuals from *any* society or culture can be transformed into killers. This assertion requires some explanation. The reason is clear: since at least the 1990s, and particularly since 2001, "Islamic culture" has been singled out (at least in the West) not only as the primary source of collective violence in the world today, but also as *the* source of the most savage and barbaric violence.

Islamic Culture Is Not Uniquely Violent

At first glance, there appears to be good reason for the foregoing view, particularly with the emergence of ISIS, which has become infamous for its cruelty and depraved violence. The followers of the organization do not just kill their victims: they behead them, burn them alive, mutilate and torture them, and otherwise engage in extreme acts of brutality. Even more, ISIS films many acts of violence and proudly posts the videos online for the world to see. Predictably, this has led observers, especially in the West, to posit that the brutality of ISIS is not just the product of "ordinary" zealots, fanatics, and psychopaths, but is instead deeply rooted in the Islamic faith (and culture) itself. They suggest, too, that Islam is essentially *unique* among all the world's cultures in condoning and inspiring such depravity.

In a widely read article in *Atlantic Monthly,* for example, Graeme Wood argued that ISIS fighters are *"authentic* throwbacks to early Islam and are *faithfully reproducing* its norms of war" (2015, emphasis added). This throwback behavior includes slavery, crucifixion, and (of course) beheadings, all of which, Wood asserted, are integral to Islam's sacred texts. To Wood and others, therefore, ISIS is not merely an authentic representative of Islam, but is instead perhaps the *most* authentic representative. (Significantly, Wood suggested that members of mainstream Muslim organizations who denounce ISIS are not true representatives of Islam. Approvingly citing Bernard Haykel, a professor of Near Eastern Studies at Princeton University, Wood implied that mainstream Muslims who condemn ISIS as un-Islamic have a "cotton-candy view of their own religion" and are willfully ignorant of "what their religion has historically and legally required.")

There are two glaringly obvious problems with the view expressed by Wood, Haykel, and others. First, as I have emphasized multiple times throughout this book, culture as a whole is a fluid, unavoidably (inter)subjective system of values, beliefs, principles, and practices. So, too, are the major elements of culture, including, most saliently, religion. In simpler terms, culture, and especially the religious principles upon which many cultures are based, is what people believe it to be *in the here and now.* Ironically, Haykel acknowledged this very point, asserting, as he did, that there is no such thing as Islam per se; instead, Islam is "what Muslims do, and how they interpret their texts" (cited in Wood 2015). But he also strongly implied, in a thoroughly contradictory manner, that the interpretation by followers of ISIS is somehow more Islamic than the interpretation by mainstream and moderate Muslims. Back to the main point: saying that culture is fluid and subjective does not mean, as I noted in Chapter 3, that cultures can be invented and reinvented out of whole cloth—there *is* an enduring substance to any culture or system of belief. Still, to argue that there is and can be only one essentially fixed and authentic meaning of culture and religion—across hundreds or thousands of years—is simply and profoundly wrong. Unfortunately, when thinking about collective political violence today, this point is lost on many people outside the Islamic world (and, to be fair, within the Islamic world, too). They see only the connection between Islam and the atrocities committed by groups such as ISIS (and al-Qaeda), who, to further confuse the matter, claim to represent the "true Islam." Yet, for the vast majority of Muslims, ISIS does not represent Islam any more than the Christian *génocidaires* of the 1994 Rwandan genocide represented Christianity.

It is worth noting, on the last point, that both Catholic and Protestant churches in Rwanda, according to Timothy Longman (2010), helped make the genocide possible by giving moral legitimacy to, and in some cases directly facilitating, the killings of tens of thousands of Tutsi. It is also worth noting that "Christian anti-Semitism has a long and terrible history, as does Christian aggression against Islam during the Crusades and against fellow Christians during the Wars of Religion" (Beverly 2002). In addition, Catholic and Protestant churches punished heretics by burning them at the stake and by drawing and quartering, the latter of which involved being dragged by a horse to the gallows, hanging almost to the point of death, live disemboweling, burning of the entrails, beheading, and pulling the arms and legs off the body (sometimes by tying each of the four limbs to a different horse and spurring them in different directions). I emphasize the grisly details of drawing and quartering to underscore the point that gruesome violence is a characteristic of many, if not most, long-standing cultures at one point in their histories. Keep in mind, too, that the Christian leaders who condoned such violence, at the time, undoubtedly believed that they represented the only "true Christianity."

Culture and the Legitimation of Killing

In light of the foregoing discussion, the second problem with the view that Islam gives rise to a uniquely violent and cruel culture should be glaringly clear. To wit, it has been very common for cultures—especially long-established, religiously based ones—to condone and encourage killing of outsiders and nonbelievers, often in extremely brutal ways. One does not have to look to the past, however, to find cultures that sanction massive violence against outsiders. The most salient is the culture of nationalism, which is a pervasive feature of the contemporary world. To be sure, most people do not associate nationalism with culture, but the association is not hard to see. Nationalism, as with any other "ism," is a set of values, principles, beliefs, and practices; it is, in the words of Jack Snyder, a doctrine adopted by a people "who see themselves as distinct in their origins, culture, history, institutions, or principles," and who believe they "should rule themselves in a political system that expresses and protects those distinctive characteristics" (2000, p. 23). For present purposes, the important point is this: nationalism *permits* the state to use violence against whole societies and peoples who are deemed enemies or threats. Importantly, though, those deemed enemies or threats are often defenseless noncombatants who have never engaged in any violence. And, while there are, in principle, restrictions on the targets and types of violence that can be used by states against those deemed enemies, in practice these restrictions are often ignored.

Thus, in World War II, it was "permissible" for all sides to firebomb whole cities, which unavoidably resulted in tens or hundreds of thousands of civilian deaths. Also in Vietnam (as well as World War II), it was permissible to use napalm—a highly flammable liquid designed to stick to the skin—against both military and civilian targets. Indeed, in war, it is permissible to use all sorts of extremely lethal weapons—such as flamethrowers, antipersonnel mines, cluster bombs, among others—that are arguably inhumane even when used solely against enemy combatants. The most lethal and inhumane of all weapons, of course, is the nuclear bomb. In the Pacific War, the United States—both the country's leaders and the large majority of US citizens—deemed it permissible to drop atomic bombs on two Japanese cities, Hiroshima and Nagasaki, instantly killing tens of thousands of noncombatants, but also condemning thousands more civilians, including many infants and children, to agonizing and exceedingly cruel deaths from burns and radiation (it is estimated that the atomic blasts killed between 60,000 to 80,000 people immediately and 135,000 over time). The US government—and other nuclear powers—still consider the use of nuclear weapons a legitimate option. The point, however, is not to condemn the United States or any country for hypocrisy; rather, the point is to underscore the fact that no culture has a monopoly on legitimizing brutal violence against outsiders, including those who are personally innocent of any transgression or who pose no actual or even potential threat.

The Power of Culture:
Making Genocide and Terrorism Possible

The capacity for culture—*any culture*—to provide the basis for the legitimation of violence and killing makes it an extremely powerful force in human society. This point is not lost on those who stand to benefit from harnessing such power for their own purposes. This is true both for those who already occupy positions of power (i.e., leaders of genocide), and for those who aspire to positions of greater power (i.e., leaders of terrorist organizations). They understand that the use and manipulation of culture can evoke deep emotions, can unify otherwise disparate followers, and can compel people to act in ways they would normally, and under most conditions, entirely eschew. The conditions under which culture is used successfully to legitimate, trigger, and sustain collective political violence in general, and genocide and terrorism more specifically, can and do vary significantly from case to case, suggesting the need, methodologically speaking, for in-depth case studies. At the same time, in terms of identifying the key elements of the legitimation process itself, there is a fairly easily discernible and oft-repeated pattern. Gregory Stanton (1998), for example, listed eight general stages in the genocidal process (although Stanton's focus was on genocide, what he wrote applies, it is fair to say, equally well to terrorism and other forms of collective political violence). The first three stages speak specifically to the significance of culture: (1) classification, (2) symbolization, and (3) dehumanization. (Dehumanization, according to Jonathan Maynard [2014] is only one aspect of the process that legitimates violence. He listed several more, including guilt-attribution, threat-construction, "deagentification," "virtuetalk," and future-bias. To keep things simple, however, my analysis will focus primarily on dehumanization because of its dominance in the literature.)

Classification is common to all cultures; it is a way to distinguish between "us" and "them," or between insiders and outsiders, or believers and nonbelievers. Often, classification may be based on racial or ethnic categories, but it may also be based on religion, language, place of birth, socioeconomic status, occupation, or any one of dozens if not hundreds of perceived differences. *Symbolization* refers to the act of naming differences. Thus, as Stanton put it, "we name some people Hutu and others Tutsi, or Jewish or Gypsy, or Christian or Muslim. Sometimes physical characteristics—skin color or nose shape—become symbols for classifications. Other symbols, like customary dress or facial scars [or tattoos], are socially imposed by groups on their own members" (1998, n.p.). Classification and symbolization can be and usually are innocuous cultural practices. But they become absolutely crucial steps toward genocide and terrorism when *combined with dehumanization*. As Stanton explained it, dehumanization involves the

> denial of the humanity of others [and] is the step that permits killing with impunity. The universal human abhorrence of murder of members of one's own group is overcome by treating the victims as less than human. In incitements to genocide the target groups are called disgusting animal names—Nazi propaganda called Jews "rats" or "vermin"; Rwandan Hutu hate radio referred to Tutsis as "cockroaches." The targeted group is often likened to a "disease," "microbes," "infections" or a "cancer" in the body politic. Bodies of genocide victims are often mutilated to express this denial of humanity. (1998, n.p.)

Of course, simply listing stages in a general process does not tell us all or even most of what we need to know. Among the (many) other things we need to know are, first, why the fateful transition from classification and symbolization to dehumanization is made. Second, we need to know why the killers decide to act on their beliefs, and more specifically, why they decide to kill. After all, people's minds are not like software programs: they will not simply and unthinkingly follow, in algorithmic fashion, instructions to kill other human beings, especially those who are innocent and defenseless. These two concerns, I should note, take us back to the starting point of this section, which posited the existence of two parallel explanations for genocide and terrorism, one that explains the decisions and actions of leaders, and another that explains the decisions and actions of the followers. It is on these two parallel explanations that I will focus next.

Making the Call to Kill: Beliefs, Ideology, and the Role of Leaders

Leaders are critical, even essential, actors in *initiating* collective political violence. Without the role played by these "entrepreneurs of death," it is quite possible that neither genocide nor terrorism would or could ever transpire.

This does not mean that genocide and terrorism can be made possible by leaders alone. Most, if not all, cultural analysts would readily acknowledge there are almost certainly a range of structural, economic, or sociopolitical factors that create the necessary conditions for, or significantly increase the probability of, either type of violence. Still, no set of social conditions, as Daniel Goldhagen put it, "singly or in combination, inexorably produces such assaults" (2009, p. 68). This is true even when a group has already been subject to dehumanization. In Germany, for example, antisemitism long predated the rise of Hitler, but it was only when Hitler decided to mobilize and organize a program of hate and killing directed against the Jews (and other groups) that the Holocaust could unfold. Goldhagen explained the issue as follows: "we must accept that different paths lead to mass murder and that the patterns that exist are partial. We must treat politics as central in the genesis of mass murder. We must specify the source and character of people's motivation to slaughter others. Perhaps most important, we must acknowledge that *only one or a few people initiate a mass annihilation or elimination*" (pp. 68–69, emphasis in original). Goldhagen was talking specifically about genocide, but, as with the points made by Stanton (1998), the same basic logic equally, and perhaps even more strongly, applies to terrorism. Terrorism, after all, is a phenomenon that requires fierce commitment by a relatively small group of people willing to organize against a vastly superior foe.

The fact that leaders of genocide and terrorism are willing to make the call to kill, however, begs the question "Why do they see the killing of usually innocent and defenseless people—including small children, infants, and even fetuses—as a choice at all?" Is the call to kill simply a reflection of a rational cost-benefit calculation, or is there something else at play? For cultural analysts, the answer is clear: there has to be something else at play. This "something else" can be boiled down to a belief, or, more accurately, a coherent set of ideas or *ideology* (see Figure 7.5 for a further discussion of ideology). This ideology typically, and most generally, sees the existence of certain groups as intolerable threats that must be eliminated or expunged. Importantly, targeted groups do not have to be a present-day threat. Nor must they pose an actual physical threat. Indeed, as Jonathan Maynard (2014) noted, it is not uncommon for ideologies to be based on a vision of a utopian future, one in which the world is ostensibly restored or brought to its pure form—this was clearly evident in the ideologies of Nazi Germany, the Khmer Rouge (in Cambodia), the Soviet Union under Stalin, and China during the Maoist Cultural Revolution, to name a few. The importance of this "future-biased" ideological view, according to Maynard, is profound: because the restoration of a pure future will bring so much good, "no means in the present is sufficiently terrible as to be unjustifiable given the confident assertion of huge benefits multiplied into the infinite future. This creates an extraordinarily permissive moral logic" (p. 832).

Figure 7.5 Defining Ideology

Jonathan Maynard (2014) argued that, while most scholars agree that ideology is a key factor in explaining genocide (and terrorism), those same scholars usually define the term vaguely or not at all. Obviously, for reasons I have already discussed, the lack of conceptual clarity can lead to serious analytical issues. To rectify the problem, Maynard focused on the need "to engage more seriously with the specialist contemporary literature on ideology, regarding two points in particular. First, atrocity-theorists should heed the increasing agreement amongst ideological analysts that a broad definition of ideology is the most analytically productive one." Second, scholars of genocide (and terrorism) should view ideologies as "rich and multifaceted phenomena" that not only reflect a "handful of core principles and beliefs" but also represent "elaborate and burgeoning cultural edifices—historically sculpted networks of values, meanings, narratives, assumptions, concepts, expectations, exemplars, past experiences, images, stereotypes, and beliefs about matters of fact." With these two points in mind, Maynard defined ideology in the following manner: "an ideology is a distinctive system of normative, semantic, and/or reputedly factual ideas, typically shared by members of groups or societies, which underpins their understandings of their political world and shapes their political behaviour" (p. 824).

Asserting the centrality of ideology is admittedly difficult, if not impossible, to prove, as it requires the researcher to get inside the minds of those leaders—that is, to know what they actually believed, as opposed to what they publicly espoused. It also requires the researcher to be able to find a clear causal link between ideology and action. Despite these difficulties, among scholars there is fairly wide consensus that beliefs or ideologies are an absolutely crucial part of any explanation of genocide, terrorism, and other forms of collective political violence. But what do leaders believe? What ideology do they embrace that inspires them to initiate and plan for the slaughter of innocent human beings? Of course, the specific content of the ideologies that drive individual leaders varies, sometimes to a significant extent. Still, there are discernable and recurring ideological themes. Goldhagen, for example, asserted that leaders of genocide in particular have almost always been "radical antipluralists, seeking purity or homogenization, or to forfend [i.e., prevent or avert] the apocalypse, or bring about their vision of utopia" (2009, p. 83). Eric Weitz (2003), to cite another example (that concurs with both Goldhagen and Maynard), emphasized that leaders who commit genocide are frequently motivated by utopian visions based on highly exclusionary conceptions of race and nation. They harness the state in an effort to create their vision of a future society composed of a pure, homogeneous population (cited in Straus 2012).

It is not difficult to find these same ideological characteristics in leaders of terrorist organizations, many of whom, especially in the postwar era, have expressed an intention to rid the world of nonbelievers. This is certainly and most saliently evident in pronouncements by Islamist terrorist organizations, such as Hezbollah (Kelly 2014) and al-Qaeda, that sanctify the killing of infidels in their quest (at least in principle) to build a caliphate, or Islamic state. But it is also true of some supposedly modern-day Christian organizations, especially in the United States. Although fragmented and diverse, many of these militant Christian organizations—such as the Aryan Nations, the Order, the Covenant, the Sword and Arm of the Lord, and Posse Comitatus—subscribe to a branch of Christianity known as Christian Identity. Although obviously and completely at odds with the theological doctrine of Islamist terrorist organizations, Christian Identity ironically (but not surprisingly) ends up in much the same place: its theology creates an unbridgeable separation between believers and nonbelievers, and, in fact, goes further than Islamist organizations in asserting that only white "Aryans" are capable of doing "God's work" (Barkun 1997). As with Islamist organizations, too, Christian Identity activists yearn for a revolution that will establish a theocratic society governed by religious law (Jurgensmeyer 2003). And most important, Christian Identity groups—while they have only been involved in sporadic terrorist activity in the United States—see violence and killing as a necessary and fully justifiable extension of their beliefs. On this point, it is likely that their violence is limited primarily by the fact that the United States has a strong and effective state, which makes it extremely difficult for Christian Identity *groups* (as opposed to "lone wolves," such as Timothy McVeigh, who is believed to have been influenced by Christian Identity)—or any terrorist organization, foreign or domestic—to successfully carry out terrorist attacks within the United States in a sustained manner. Last, and interestingly, as with Islamists, Christian Identity activists also display an "obsessive concern for movement martyrs, including those who died at Waco, Texas" (Barkun 1997, p. vii). The similarity between Islamist and Christian Identity groups is useful to highlight: again, it tells us that no religion (or culture) has a monopoly on political violence.

The foregoing discussion provides a basic answer to the question "Why is the fateful transition from classification and symbolization to dehumanization made?" For leaders, the transition is the product of strongly held beliefs and ideas about the world (i.e., their ideology), which convinces them that their plans to kill or murder the innocent are subjectively good, necessary, and just (Goldhagen 2009, p. 83). The origin of their ideologies may go back many years or decades, or it may be fairly recent; yet the decision to organize and carry out genocide, or to wage a campaign of terrorism, ultimately hinges on their beliefs. This does not mean that ideology is sufficient, by itself, to explain genocide and terrorism. Ideological factors, as Maynard wrote (and as I have repeatedly emphasized), "sit alongside psychological, personal, institutional, situational, economic, and political ones." At the same time, continued Maynard, "they are central in their own right, and are also entangled with these other factors, since few forces can shape human behaviour unmediated by the worldviews and schemas of meaning which ideologies provide" (2014, pp. 833–834). The second question—"Why do the killers decide to act on their beliefs, and more specifically, why do they decide to kill?"—still must be answered. Let me address that question now.

Following the Leader: Why Do Perpetrators Kill?

Are followers motivated to act by the same ideological constructs as those of the leaders? Are those who carry out acts of violence willing or voluntary killers? Or do the killers kill only because they must? Indeed, many analysts have argued and continue to argue that, especially in genocides, there is a crucial element of coercion. That is, perpetrators kill, not because they believe their victims deserve or need to die, but rather because they are *forced* to do so. In explaining the Holocaust, this was a prevalent argument, which was, as Goldhagen (2009) put it, "concocted and eagerly accepted by those wishing to absolve Germans of criminal culpability." Yet, according to Goldhagen, not a single German perpetrator was ever punished, much less killed, for refusing to participate in the Holocaust. Indeed, "many knew they did not have to kill, because their commanders explicitly told them so"; more important, for the few who decided not to participate in the killings, "nothing happened to them" (p. 149). In other genocides, especially Rwanda, one might make a case that a small proportion of killers were coerced, but for the most part the *génocidaires* killed willingly, according to candid testimony from the killers after the genocide ended. Equally important, as Goldhagen and many others have thoroughly documented, perpetrators often seem to revel in their murderous behavior. Thus, they do not merely kill their innocent victims, but instead seem to take great pleasure in brutalizing them, which again does not reflect reluctant or involuntary action. In Guatemala, for example, the *génocidaires* called themselves "killing machines": they bayoneted pregnant women, beat babies and small children against walls and the ground until they died, amputated limbs and decapitated their victims, doused them in gasoline and set them on fire, and disemboweled fellow human beings while still alive. The Guatemalan genocide, unfortunately, is no exception: the same behavior can be found almost everywhere that genocides have occurred or are currently taking place. ISIS, in this regard, is only the most recent example.

Goldhagen pointed out that other rationalizations also fail to provide an adequate explanation for the killers' behavior. There is little evidence, more specifically, that *génocidaires* only kill as a product of obedience, "peer pressure," personal benefit, or a bureaucratic mind-set (wherein killing becomes simply part of one's job). Instead, Goldhagen asserted that the killers are, ultimately, motivated by the same ideological (and cultural) constructs as leaders. As he put it, "When leaders are ready for elimination and the kill, they activate people's otherwise inert eliminationalist beliefs by announcing . . . that the onslaught is about to begin. Depending on how much people have contemplated what to actually do to the targeted groups, different reactions greet the eliminationalist announcement and notification" (2009, p. 216). These "inert eliminationalist beliefs" may derive from some objectively based historical or fairly recent wrong—as in the case of Hutu-Tutsi relations—or they could be entirely imagined, or anything in between. The key, however, is that they provide the basis for animosity and hatred that enables the perpetrators to believe, with little to no doubt, that their actions are good, necessary, and just (Goldhagen 2009). This also explains the killing of the most innocent of victims, infants and small children. Children represent the future; thus, if the targeted group *needs* to be eliminated, then it becomes crucial that no member of that group—no matter how small, innocent, and defenseless—be allowed to survive. After all, if the children are spared, the "problem" will simply reappear later.

It is important to understand, too, how these beliefs or larger ideologies are both communicated and rendered persuasive. As Maynard (2014) strongly argued, it is decidedly not a matter of "brainwashing"—a crude term that suggests either a coercive psychological process or, in almost opposite terms, a highly gullible and weak-minded audience. Instead, Maynard emphasized that the communication of an ideology is typically part of a process that may involve everyday social interactions, long-term institutionalized programs (that, for example, can take place in schools), outright propaganda and sustained media campaigns, organized public demonstrations (aimed at leaders), short-term calls to violence, or any combination thereof. "Effective ideological dissemination will usually rely on multiple channels, and involve a combination of 'top-down,' 'bottom-up,' and 'horizontal' communication. This is important, as it demonstrates the error in assuming that a lack of explicit indoctrination in blatant political organisations indicates the weakness of ideological motives or beliefs" (p. 827).

As to why individuals accept and even embrace "atrocity-justifying ideologies," as Maynard put it, one general answer can be found in the idea of *epistemic dependence* (Hardwig 1985, cited in Maynard 2014). While a bit jargony, the meaning of epistemic dependence is not hard to grasp (a rough synonym for *epistemic,* by the way, is *knowledge*). Consider the following: almost all of what we know and believe necessarily comes from others—from politicians, corporate or business leaders, political pundits, journalists and reporters, professors and teachers, scientists, parents, clergy and church leaders, coworkers, friends, and so on. Most of what all these people know, in turn, comes from still other sources; in fact, most of the knowledge people possess is pure hearsay. This is especially the case for "common knowledge." Thus, anyone's knowledge and beliefs are ultimately *dependent* on communal or shared sources. Importantly, some sources of knowledge or information have greater authority or legitimacy than others; they are trusted sources or "epistemic authorities" (Maynard 2014). When these epistemic authorities speak, therefore, people listen. Of course, accepting and acting upon an ideology that justifies wholesale slaughter of men, women, and children does not just happen. The larger political, social, cultural, and economic context within which such an ideology is propagated is extremely important. Still, it is fairly clear that beliefs, in general, must precede action, especially when the primary victims of violence pose no objectively determined threat.

Culture and the Rise of Suicide Terrorism

Suicide terrorism, as I noted earlier in the chapter, has become a prominent characteristic of contemporary terrorism—that is, terrorism in the post–Cold War period. Data from the *Suicide Attack Database* (Chicago Project on Security and Terrorism 2015), makes this last point clear. Between 2000 and 2015, there were 3,908 suicide terrorist attacks worldwide, resulting in 33,204 deaths and 83,329 injuries. Although these figures represent a relatively small minority of total attacks, deaths, and injuries from terrorism over the same period, they are undoubtedly significant both for their psychological or fear-inducing impact, and also for the media attention they generate. Indeed, the most spectacular, headline grabbing, terrorist actions—such as the 9/11 attack—are typically suicide attacks. These types of attacks, to repeat, have an influence well beyond the number of deaths and injuries they cause. They bring a huge amount of attention and publicity to the terrorist organizations that carry them out, and therefore are considered a crucial tool. This means that we cannot simply dismiss suicide terrorism as a marginal or tangential aspect of contemporary terrorism. An explanation is required.

From a rational choice perspective, as previously discussed, the emergence and increasing prominence of suicide terrorism is difficult to explain, especially in trying to account for the actions of *individual* terrorists (remember: in rational choice, the individual actor is the focus of analytical attention). For example, Bryan Caplan, in his evaluation of the rational choice model's relevance to terrorism, admitted, "suicidal terrorists are probably simply irrational" (2006, p. 101). At the same time, he pointed out that suicide terrorists are "outliers," meaning that they fall far outside the norm. Importantly, in statistics, an outlier usually indicates that some sort of error was made in analyzing data—that is, an outlier does not actually exist. Yet in terrorism, suicide attackers are clearly *not* the product of a measurement error: they are a very real and significant part of contemporary terrorism. Caplan's main (albeit implied) point, though, was this: suicide terrorists do not represent terrorists in general; thus their actions do not have to be explained using rational choice principles. He put it this way: "if standard rational choice models did not roughly apply to the *typical devout Muslim,* suicide attacks would be orders of magnitude greater" (p. 92, emphasis added).

It is fair to say that Caplan has a point. Still, even if suicide terrorists are outliers—even if they are not "typical devout Muslims" (or devout Christians, Buddhists, or something else)—they are also not, by any means, unique or even extraordinarily rare. In fact, the data show a dramatic increase in suicide attacks since the early 2000s: prior to 2000, there were never more than 15 suicide attacks in a given year, but since 2005, there have been at least 254 every year, with a peak of 489 in 2007 (Chicago Project on Security and Terrorism 2015). The "explosion" in the number of suicide terrorist attacks suggests an increasingly important trend or pattern of social behavior, one that further suggests a more general cause or reason. So, how can this increase in suicide terrorism, and suicide terrorism more generally, be explained? From a cultural perspective, the answer is not complicated, and it parallels very closely the argument made in the first part of this section. Nalbandov, while not necessarily endorsing the cultural view, put it this way: "A possible explanation for the irrational behavior of the actors is the factor of identity, which varies in different actors. Specific identity constructs force [or at least, push] them to choose different options not based on the objective **utility calculations** but on their subjectively constructed assessment of the objective reality" (2013, p. 94).

More concretely, a cultural analyst would almost certainly agree with rational choice scholars who argue that suicide terrorists are outliers, and perhaps extreme outliers. Yet the rise in suicide terrorist attacks suggests that a profound cultural shift has taken place, one that not only justifies killing innocent victims, but also justifies taking one's own life to more effectively kill others. On this point, it is significant that suicide terrorism—in the Islamic world specifically—was completely unheard of before the Beirut bombing by Hezbollah in 1983. It is significant, in large part, because the accepted theological view of suicide among Muslims, according to Franz Rosenthal (1946), has always been unequivocal: "Suicide is a grave sin, and the person who commits suicide is doomed to continual repetition in Hell of the action by which he killed himself" (quoted in Kramer 1998, pp. 142–143). The Quran puts it this way: "Whoever kills himself with an iron weapon, then the iron weapon will remain in his hand and he will continually stab himself in the belly with it in the fire of hell eternally, forever and ever; whoever kills himself by drinking poison will eternally drink poison in the hellfire, and whoever kills himself by falling off a mountain will fall forever in the fire of hell."

Given the unequivocal prohibition against suicide, it is no surprise that the vast majority of devout Muslims would reject taking the path of suicide terrorism. Recognizing this, "epistemic authorities" in the Islamic world sought to reconcile suicide attacks with Islamic theology. In Lebanon, the solution relied on an appeal to the "special context" of the conflict in that country. Sayyid Muhammad Husayn Fadlallah, the spiritual leader of Hezbollah, explained it this way: When an enemy cannot be attacked through conventional means, then the combatant must fight with "special means," which includes purposefully sacrificing one's own life. But "such an undertaking differs little from that of a soldier who fights and knows that in the end he will be killed. The two situations lead to death; except that one fits in with the conventional procedures of war, and the other does not." In this regard, Fadlallah concluded, "There is no difference between dying with a gun in your hand or exploding yourself" (quoted in Kramer 1998, p. 145). This and other justifications were promulgated by a range of epistemic authorities (Freamon 2003) such that, over time, suicide not only ceased being a grave sin, but also became a heroic act. It was also explicitly linked to the concept of martyrdom, which was interpreted by many of the same epistemic authorities to include the oft-heard promise that those who die fighting for Islam will be rewarded with seventy-two virgins in Paradise. The reinterpretation—that is, equating suicide terrorism with martyrdom within the context of a "holy war"—has been "deeply influential," and "the methodologies it has spawned," according to Freamon, "have swept the Islamic world, such that they now dominate the conceptions of military *jihad* and martyrdom for *jihadists*, whether Wahhabist, Palestinian, Islamist, mainstream Sunni, or [**Shiite**]" (2003, p. 360).

To be clear, the rise of suicide terrorism, in the Islamic world specifically, can clearly be tied to a cultural shift, to a reinterpretation of supposedly bedrock principles in Islamic culture. The fact that only a tiny fraction of "devout Muslims" decide to become suicide terrorists or martyrs is far less important than the fact that the ideological reinterpretation has been embraced, even if very unevenly, throughout the Islamic world. The shift made it possible for the leaders of terrorist organizations to use suicide terrorism on a *sustained,* as opposed to ad hoc or one-off, basis; without that shift, in other words, it is doubtful that suicide terrorism would or could be the strategic tool that it has become.

Culture as a Meaning-Making Medium: Concluding Remarks

The foregoing example demonstrates the power of culture to shape, in profound ways, the choices people make, including, most significantly, choices that have deadly consequences. It also underscores the malleability of culture. In the example, the malleability of Islamic culture specifically was the center of attention. But to repeat a point that I have made numerous times throughout this section (and in the entire book), *any* culture, *any* system of beliefs, is subject to change, whether intended or not. Cultural change, of course, does not necessarily, nor even usually, lead to the legitimation of violence and killing. But when it does, the effects can be catastrophic both for individuals and for whole communities of people. Understanding the power and effects of culture, therefore, is an extremely important task, not just for students of comparative politics, but also for anyone interested in the question "Why do people kill?" For many people, moreover, answering that question is not merely an academic or intellectual exercise, but is instead a matter of great urgency. For their hope is to prevent or at least minimize the deadly effects of genocide and terrorism. The cultural approach does not necessarily provide the key to prevention, but it does provide crucial insights into the complex and *subjective* aspects of both forms of collective political violence.

Choice or Fate? A Structural View of Genocide and Terrorism

In general, structural analysts have had relatively little to say, at least directly, about genocide and terrorism—although there are certainly a number of important structurally themed studies, especially of genocide (I will return to this point shortly). It is not difficult, however, to apply structural principles to an explanation of both forms of collective political violence. Albert Bergesen and Omar Lizardo (2004), for example, noted that structural concepts such as the "globalization backlash" can be linked directly to the rise of terrorism. Here the logic is simple: the past century or so has witnessed a continued expansion and deepening of Western-based economic, social, and political models based on "rationalized action" and "universal standards" (p. 44). In many societies, however, the imposition of these Western models represents a serious and profound challenge to traditional or existing social, political, and economic relations. Where traditional relations of power have remained the strongest and most deeply rooted—as in many parts of the Middle East, North Africa, and South and Southeast Asia—the backlash can be expected to be extremely violent, often manifesting itself as terrorism. This helps to explain why there is seemingly such a strong connection between religious fundamentalism and terrorism, a point that a number of scholars and other observers have noticed. Tariq Ali (2002) went one step further: he portrayed contemporary terrorism as a "clash of fundamentalisms." In this clash, Islamic fundamentalism is one obvious part, but the other, equally important, part is market fundamentalism or, more simply, capitalism. As the author put it, "Capitalism has created a single market, but without erasing the distinctions between the two worlds that face each other across a divide that first appeared in the eighteenth and became institutionalized in the nineteenth century" (p. 3).

The Clash of Fundamentalisms

The clash of fundamentalisms, however, is not (in the structural view) an essentially ideological or cultural conflict. Instead, it primarily reflects an objective process of subjugation and domination by major capitalist powers over the rest of the world. Capitalism, in this regard, must be understood as a *system of domination* that disempowers large swaths of humanity. It imposes economic and political arrangements throughout the world designed to perpetuate unequal and highly exploitative class-based relations. The upshot, according to Ali (and other structuralists) is clear:

> A disempowered people is constantly reminded of its own weakness. . . . [P]eople become flustered, feel more and more helpless and nervous. Anger, frustration and despair multiply. They can no longer rely on the state for help. The laws favour the rich. So the more desperate amongst them, in search of a more meaningful existence or simply to break the monotony, begin to live by their own laws. Willing recruits will never be in short supply. The propaganda of the deed—the homage paid by the weak to the strong—will endure. It is the response of atomised individuals to a world that no longer listens, to politicians who have become interchangeable, to corporations one-eyed in the search for profits and global media networks owned by the self-same corporations and locked into a relationship of mutual dependence with the politicians. *This is the existential misery that breeds insecurity and fosters deadly hatreds.* If the damage is not repaired, sporadic outbursts of violence will continue and intensify. (2002, pp. 3–4, emphasis added)

Given the foregoing analysis, it should not be surprising that the Islamic world has become a main source of terrorism in the world today. The reason is crystal clear: although Western powers have a long history of intervention in the Middle East (Ismael 1986), the discovery of large reserves of oil in the region—in the 1920s and 1930s—dramatically intensified both Western interest and efforts at domination. More simply, the Middle East became a prime target for Western capitalists and their states. Indeed, to a significant extent, the history of the Middle East throughout the entire twentieth century is a history of Western efforts to control the region's oil. Oil, of course, is the lifeblood of industrial capitalism. Significantly, for the vast majority of people in the Middle East, the physical possession of this vital resource did not lead to riches. Instead, it led to their impoverishment and subjugation as Western oil companies—backed by the military power of Western states—simply snatched control. By the 1930s, a handful of Western oil companies were able to assume virtually total control of Middle East oil, a situation that lasted into the 1970s (Ismael 1986). In the 1970s, however, the oligopolistic hold of the major oil companies was broken, in part by increasing competition from other oil companies, but largely by the ability of oil-producing countries to forge an alliance through the Organization of Petroleum Exporting Countries (OPEC). The story here is immensely complex, so, at great risk of oversimplification, suffice it to say that OPEC finally enabled those countries that had physical possession of oil to reap a large portion of the profits from that resource.

Still, all was not well. In the capitalist system, the nationality of those sitting at the top of the economic hierarchy is largely irrelevant to the question of inequality and exploitation. Thus, despite a partial transfer of control from Western capitalists to Middle Eastern capitalists—who were often state elites—the vast majority of people in the Middle East did not benefit. After the formation of OPEC, in fact, the West (with the United States in the lead) looked for new ways to exert control. This was partly done by forging alliances with brutal, but *vulnerable,* autocratic regimes, which were made dependent on US weapons and military training (Jones 2012). Keep in mind, too, that the United States had an earlier history of undermining nascent efforts at democratization in the region: in 1953, for example, the US Central Intelligence Agency (CIA) played an instrumental role in organizing a coup that overthrew Mohammed Mossadeq, the democratically elected prime minister of Iran. He was replaced by a US-backed and brutally oppressive dictator, Mohammed Reza Shah Pahlavi. More to the point, though, US support of autocratic regimes helped to ensure that the profits from the sale of crude oil would accrue primarily to a handful of increasingly powerful rulers (who became one and the same with the capitalist elite). To be sure, the rulers in the most oil-rich states did redistribute some of the wealth by funding modernization projects and cradle-to-grave social services in an effort to placate their own citizens (Jones 2012). Yet, to ensure they would never lose control, these rulers also employed any means necessary—including imprisonment, torture, and murder—to prevent any challenges that might undermine their positions of political and economic advantage.

The predictable result, at least according to structural analysts, has been the sort of sporadic but increasingly common and organized outbursts of violence, directed both at the West, but also—and much more frequently—at autocratic regimes in the Middle East (as discussed at the beginning of this chapter). To repeat, this violence can be viewed as the direct outgrowth of a profoundly exploitative and oppressive system. Importantly, though, the most powerful regimes had the capacity to minimize domestic terrorism through iron-fisted rule and the development of a "security state," funded by oil revenues and often supported with US-made arms and equipment.

For those countries without the wealth provided by oil, however, the situation was very different. Indeed, the very forces that enriched countries such as Saudi Arabia, Kuwait, Iran, Iraq, and Libya had a devastating impact on the oil-*importing* countries in the region. This is because higher oil prices—which were made possible by the formation of OPEC—meant dramatically higher import costs since much more money was being spent just to import the same amount of oil. At the same time, high oil prices cut global demand for other products: many countries simply had less money, or almost no money, to spend on non-oil imports. The result was predictable. To wit, oil-importing countries in the Middle East and elsewhere suffered from a severe "balance-of-payments crisis," that is, a situation in which so much money flows out of a country that it has difficulty earning or borrowing enough to sustain essential services or to import essential goods. That was bad enough, but the United States and other Western countries used that as an opportunity to pry open Middle Eastern markets to Western goods. This was done, first, by providing "food aid," which had the effect of destroying local producers. After all, how could local farmers compete with "free" or heavily subsidized food? Adam Hanieh (2013) argued that was the intention of the United States and other Western nations. As he explained it, the long-term US goal was to lay the basis for the neoliberal transformation of agrarian relations in the Middle East in order to increase the region's dependence. Thus, "instead of relying on farmers to produce food for domestic consumption, countries across the region became increasingly reliant upon imported grain and other food" (p. 30). This was particularly apparent in Egypt, which saw its food self-sufficiency ratio (domestic production in relation to consumption) drop from 70 percent in 1960 to 23 percent in 1980 (Hanieh 2013).

Faced with lower export earnings, a continued need for oil, and an ever-increasing need for food imports, Middle Eastern countries also became dependent on Western capital in the form of loans. This "debt dependence" was key: in return for financial support, the West demanded that countries "agree to lift restrictions on trade, begin the privatization of state-owned enterprises, deregulate labor markets, and . . . drop barriers to capital flows" (Hanieh 2013, p. 40). Needless to say, these economic changes were not designed to help the average citizen or worker; instead they did just the opposite by creating the "existential misery" of which Tariq Ali spoke. "Existential misery," however, is not sufficient to explain the turn to terrorism.

There are many people around the world living in conditions of severe poverty, yet very few become terrorists. In fact, the leaders of terrorist organizations and even many of the individuals who carry out terrorist attacks are neither poor nor oppressed; many are well educated and come from relatively privileged backgrounds (Pratt 2006). It is here that the "clash of fundamentalisms" is most clearly felt: in the struggle against market fundamentalism, those opposed must find an alternative basis for developing a coherent and sustainable countermovement, which, it is important to add, directly and necessarily draws on the "existential" *and* objectively based misery caused by capitalism. Fundamentalist religious beliefs—whether Islamic, Christian, Buddhist, or something else—have proven to be the most reliably effective of the alternatives (but not the only one). This is perhaps because such beliefs provide the sharpest distinction between the secular and the theistic, between the imperatives of capitalism and the imperatives of fundamentalism. This distinction magnifies the challenge, defines the enemies, mobilizes supporters, and provides a framework for action. There is, structural analysts might agree, an important subjective or cultural element here. Nonetheless, the motive force is an essentially structural-economic process: the unfolding of capitalism on a global scale. This last point underscores a key assertion in the structural view: capitalism, with the US acting as its key agent, has been both the prime cultivator of Islamic fundamentalism (Achcar 2002) and the primary factor behind the rise of contemporary terrorism.

The Capitalist World-System and Genocide

As I noted at the outset, genocide has not been a focal point of structural analysis. Still, there are a few genocide scholars—most notably Mark Levene—who have used a structural framework to explain the stubborn persistence of genocide in the *modern* era. On this last point, it is important to understand that most structural accounts do not purport to explain a particular type of phenomenon—such as genocide or terrorism—*throughout* history. Instead, structural analysis is concerned with explaining certain phenomenon in relation to specific historical structures, such as global capitalism. This said, structural explanations of genocide begin with the premise that genocide is *not* to be explained primarily, much less solely, by focusing on the direct perpetrators, whether leaders and followers, or on the unique circumstances surrounding individual cases of genocide. As Levene put it, even "if the economic, political or cultural characteristics or configurations peculiar to a given polity society are the necessary building blocks for understanding modern genocides, they are rarely sufficient" (2004, p. 161). Instead, Levene argues that, as a recurring and global phenomena, genocide almost certainly reflects the influence and power of broader economic and political dynamics in the world. So what are these broader dynamics? The answer is clear enough: modernization. (Note: the term *modernization* here overlaps with, but is not exactly the same as, the use of the term in other chapters.)

Modernization is based on two interrelated processes. The first is the rise of the nation-state (Levene 2005), which also presupposes the parallel development of an international system composed of those selfsame nation-states. The second is the capitalist system, which is integrally associated with the emergence of the nation-state. The connection between the modern state and capitalism has been subject to intense academic scrutiny, but there is general agreement that the early development, deepening, and expansion of capitalism—which often meant a drastic reconfiguration of then-existing social, political, and economic arrangements—required the institutional and organizational power of the state, and vice versa. On this point, too, there is general consensus that the nexus between the modern state and capitalism was propelled forward by the imperatives of war-making. This is because capitalism "massively increases the technical base of warfare" (Scott 2008). Most simply, political leaders understood that the most effective way to build a strong, indomitable military was to build a capitalist economy. Importantly, this tells us that, from the very beginning, there was an intimate connection between collective political violence, on the one hand, and state-building, the international system, and capitalism on the other hand. This connection, in the structural view, never went away. It has, however, transformed itself over time. While the war-making capacity of capitalism continues to play an absolutely central role in the world, many nation-states, especially newer ones, have struggled just to maintain their sovereign viability. This has had crucial implications with respect to genocide. Citing Levene (2005), A. Dirk Moses explained in the following manner:

> Genocide, then, is explained . . . by the pressure that a competitive, indeed Darwinistic, system of state economies places on national leaderships to establish and maintain sovereign viability. In some cases, usually among the second tier late-comer states (postcolonial) to the club established by Westerners, desperate shortcuts had been taken to accelerate and institutional[ize] modernization: by exterminating a native people who live in an area desired for economic exploitation, or by exterminating a minority associated with an external enemy that is held responsible for endangering the nation in a security crisis, or holding back the country's independent development by effectively representing the interests of a competitor. (2008)

None of this is to say that individual instances of genocide—whether in Germany, China, Soviet Russia, Rwanda, Cambodia, Bosnia, Guatemala, or elsewhere—are wholly determined by structural or macro-level forces. They are not. Individual circumstances and choices matter, and they matter a great deal. However, the "micro-level of radicalized state violence cannot in the twentieth century be isolated from the macro-context in which it occurs anymore than a perpetrator society's possibly historic hatred against a particular group or groups can be disentangled from hegemonic, globalizing pressures which may finally and fatally push it over the genocidal precipice" (Levene 2004, p. 162). What this also means, it should be emphasized, is that genocide is part-and-parcel of the modern international system, a system that has been and continues to be dominated by the United States, Western Europe, and few other capitalist powers. In this regard, "modernization" is not the cure for the barbarism of genocide; instead and again it is the primary cause.

A Few Closing Remarks on Structure and Genocide

The shortness of the foregoing discussion does not mean that the structural approach has limited applicability to the issues of genocide. That is not the case. But it is the case that a structural explanation of genocide, as Levene put it, is best at establishing the macro-level context within which particular, but related, events play out. While the same can be said of structural accounts for other phenomena (e.g., poverty, prosperity, and democracy), for genocide in particular it is fairly clear that a much sharper and more in-depth focus on micro- and meso-level factors and processes is warranted. After all, while genocide is a recurring phenomenon, it is also sporadic. This suggests that macro-level forces, while important, play a very general, nondeterminative role. In other words, while larger economic and political dynamics set the stage for genocide, those forces cannot tell us where and when a genocide will occur, or even why it occurs when it does. In this regard, consider what Daniel Goldhagen had to say: "Setting eliminationist slaughters in motion is a quintessential act of choice, freely taken, neither determined by abstract forces or structures, nor brought about accidentally by circumstances. In this case, the *great man* view of history—if 'great' means *powerful*—has enormous credence in the sense that a man who can set the state in motion is necessary" (2009, p. 83, emphasis in original).

Conclusion

Terrorism and genocide are complex, multidimensional issues. None of the three theoretical approaches, it is fair to say, can provide a complete or satisfactory explanation of either phenomenon. This suggests, quite strongly, that an integrative approach is necessary. In other words, to explain either form of collective political violence, it is necessary to draw insights from the rational choice, cultural, and structural perspectives. This is harder than it sounds, because it is not simply a matter of picking and choosing whatever "sounds good" from each approach. Minimally, it involves bringing together insights from the three approaches in a coherent manner. This requires figuring out how different factors relate to or influence one another, and how they interact in specific ways. Put another way, the main task is to figure out how to fit all the (theoretical) pieces together so that they create a complete or recognizable picture. The jigsaw puzzle is frequently used as a metaphor to illustrate this process (Gozzi 1996). While metaphors can only take us so far, the jigsaw puzzle is an apt metaphor in that it requires the puzzle master to bring order out of chaos. More specifically, the puzzle master begins with a large collection of seemingly random pieces, which must then be slowly and methodically fit together until the puzzle has been solved.

For comparativists, phenomena such as genocide and terrorism are particularly complex jigsaw puzzles. Nonetheless, the three theoretical approaches provide a ready way to bring order out of chaos. Consider, first, the structural approach, which emphasizes the significance of the macro-level context of genocide and terrorism. This macro-level context provides the basic framework of action. Importantly, the framework is not fixed or static. It pushes and pulls individuals, societies, and states in various directions; it squeezes some "pieces" to the breaking point, while allowing other pieces to prosper and thrive. Identifying the key features and dynamics of the macro-level context allows the researcher to see the general conditions that make genocide or terrorism more or less likely—or more rational. As other chapters have highlighted, and as this last point suggests, structural arguments generally incorporate rationality: structures themselves create opportunities, impose constraints, and otherwise shape and perhaps even define the *broadest parameters* of the strategic environment. However, for genocide and terrorism, it is almost certain that structural forces do not determine what specific actors do or don't do. Agency matters, and it matters a great deal. The next task, then, is to determine the key elements that shape the decisions and actions of actors. This will likely require, as this chapter has demonstrated, a very careful melding of rational and cultural principles (as well as psychological and institutional factors). Again, this is easier said than done, but the discussion in this chapter has given you a basis for doing so.

8

Why Collective Action? Explaining the Rise of Social Movements

Emily Acevedo and Atsuko Sato

Scholars first began to study mass mobilization and social movements in the middle to late nineteenth century. Today, the study of mass mobilization and social movements spans several social science disciplines including anthropology, history, political science, and sociology. As the progression of the social movement literature (which subsumes studies of mass mobilization) shows, scholars were influenced not only by theoretical developments in the social science disciplines, but also by domestic and global events. The dominant paradigm that guided scholars' understanding of mass mobilizations and social movements (see Figure 8.1 for a brief discussion of these two terms), at least until the middle of the twentieth century, was collective behavior. Interestingly, most scholars interpreted collective behavior—or mass mobilization—as something "deviant." There were two basic reasons for this. First, mass mobilizations occurred outside traditional or established institutions. Second, and more important, they were assumed to be the product of irrationality. On this last point, the underlying assumption was that individuals who participated in mass mobilizations were primarily motivated by shared grievances (or discontent) and generalized beliefs—that is, psychological and ideological factors.

By the 1970s, however, both the understanding and the perception of social movements had begun to change. Within the United States, in particular, the shift reflected the growing prominence of rational choice theory within the US social sciences more generally, but also (and perhaps more importantly) deeper empirical research that failed to show a "close link between preexisting discontent and generalized beliefs in the rise of social movement phenomena" (McCarthy and Zald 1977, p. 1214). There was also growing recognition that traditional explanations of mass mobilization—which tended to portray participants as alienated and disconnected from

---

**Figure 8.1 The Distinction Between
Mass Mobilization and Social Movements**

The terms *mass mobilization* and *social movement* are very closely related. Depending on the circumstances, the two terms can be used interchangeably, but there is an important analytical distinction. First the similarities: both terms refer to the collective mobilization of the civilian population as part of a process designed to make a political point or to bring about or resist political or social change (this is also known as contentious politics). Both a mass mobilization and a social movement can assume various forms, such as nonviolent mobilization (parades, demonstrations, or marches), violent mobilization (riots or uprisings), or institutional mobilization (voting). The key difference, however, is that while a social movement is typically a product of a grassroots organization, mass mobilization can also take place at the behest of elite groups, such as dominant political parties or national governments. For example, the Nazi Party relied on mass mobilization techniques, such as mass meetings and parades, to gain support for its policies.

---

mainstream society—simply did not capture the reality of many, if not most, social movements in the postwar era. Many participants in social movements from the 1960s onward, for example, could hardly be described as "socially unstable and alienated," as those pressing for the expansion of civil rights, social justice, and political equality in the civil rights and women's movements, especially in the United States and Western Europe, were often highly educated and economically well off.

From the 1960s through the 1980s, therefore, new theoretical explanations emerged that not only altered the then-prevailing understanding of what social movements were, but also altered how to study them. Soon the traditional explanations, known by such names as "social strain," "grievances," and "relative deprivation," gave way to structural and cultural explanations for movement mobilization. While scholars in the United States focused on structural and rational perspectives, scholars in Western Europe primarily followed a cultural path—in sharp contrast to early European studies, which were often based on the "structural reductionist" approach. This latter approach, which is strongly associated with traditional Marxism, generally portrayed social movements as a product of class dynamics. However, newer studies acknowledged that social movements did not necessarily center on conflict over material interests (based on economics and class); instead, these studies recognized that nonmaterial issues such as gender, race and ethnicity, or other forms of identity could and did play an important role in mass mobilization. This shift led to the development of the *new social movement* approach, which took account of the broader context within which social movements emerged and developed, and which also considered other factors such as culture, ideology, and identity as independent variables in their own right. The new social movement theory did not gain much resonance among US scholars, particularly since US researchers did not see anything "new" about these movements. Instead, US scholars began to expand on their own approaches, most prominently resource mobilization theory (Snow and Soule 2010), which will be discussed in depth later.

In this chapter, we will review how the social movement literature has evolved. At the same time, as in the other chapters, we will examine the study of social movements from the rationalist, structural, and cultural perspectives. As you proceed through the chapter, you might notice that there is not a completely clear distinction among these three perspectives; you might also notice that an examination of social movements requires an integrative approach (a point that the previous chapter also emphasized). Indeed, from the outset, it is fair to say that none of these approaches alone can fully explain social movements. This suggests that explanations for movement emergence, tactics, survival, and outcomes are best understood by blending or integrating these approaches. Thinking about an integrative approach will allow you to see how different variables, such as movement actors, institutions, and cultural forces, are linked together in one coherent process. In the last section of this chapter, in fact, we will discuss an example—the Arab Spring—from a more comprehensive, at least partly integrated, perspective. As usual, before discussing the various theoretical explanations, it is important to examine, in more depth, the definition of a social movement.

What Is a Social Movement?

What exactly does the term *social movement* mean? Unfortunately, as with many concepts in the social sciences, we can find a number of competing and not always compatible definitions. One reason for the lack of a strong consensus is clear: researchers using different theoretical approaches do not always share the same assumptions and goals. This is not always an insurmountable obstacle—for example, in studies of democracy, as we have seen, there is a considerable degree of consensus among scholars from all three research schools. Still, it is not unusual for definitions within different research schools to emphasize different properties, aspects, and characteristics of key concepts. This is the case with social movements: in general, research representing the three theoretical perspectives holds different assumptions about actors, motivations, and the environment. Furthermore, the questions each theoretical perspective seeks to address vary, ranging from explaining individual motivations for movement participation, to understanding the structural conditions that explain movement emergence, to assessing the impact of shared identities that explain movement solidarity.

With the foregoing points in mind, let's consider how one prominent scholar, Doug McAdam, defines social movements. McAdam sees social movements as "organized efforts, on the part of excluded groups, to promote or resist changes in the *structure* of society that involve recourse to noninstitutional forms of political participation" (1982, p. 25, emphasis added). As his definition illustrates, the reasons for the emergence of a social movement, and its ability to effect an outcome, are both contained in the definition itself—that is, social movements are the product of dynamics in the societal structure. McAdam is a proponent of the political process model, also known as political opportunity structure (discussed below). As the name implies, the political opportunity structure approach is largely structural in orientation. The cultural approach, by contrast, stresses the role of **framing**, collective identity, context, and institutions in shaping social movement behavior. This perspective leads to a very different way of conceptualizing social movements. Håkan Thörn, for example, described a social movement as "a process of action and interaction involving as a fundamental element the construction of a collective identity, or a sense of community, of 'us,' sharing a set of values and norms, and 'others,' i.e., antagonistic actors or 'enemies'" (2006, p. 294). As should be apparent, the foregoing definition stresses cultural factors (collective identity, norms, and values) over objective factors. While there is certainly room to debate the strengths and weaknesses of each definition, for present purposes this is not necessary. Instead, the main point, to repeat, is that, in the literature, there are many contrasting definitions of or ways to conceptualize social movements, some of which can be seen in Figure 8.2.

Although there are many definitions of a social movement, and although not all are fully compatible, for the purposes of this chapter a practical approach—one that identifies common features or characteristics found in most definitions—will suffice. Fortunately, this is not difficult to do, as there are three fairly common and readily identifiable characteristics recognized in the literature. First, all social movements are seen as reflections or products of *collective mobilization.* This means that social movements are not about individual deeds of activism, but instead are about the combined and concerted efforts of myriad individuals. Thus, for example, while there may be many individuals engaged in separate or disconnected protests against animal cruelty, their actions do not constitute a social movement unless they join together in common cause. Second, social movement scholars all agree that *intent* is crucial: a social movement is meant to influence or bring about political, social, or cultural change. This is, not coincidentally, similar to the definition of terrorism, which includes, as one of its core characteristics, an effort to achieve a political goal. It is not coincidental for one simple reason: a social movement and terrorism are both types of political activism. Third, social movement scholars agree that the participants in a social movement

---

Figure 8.2 Selected Definitions of a Social Movement (and Mass Mobilization)

- Social movement actors are engaged in political and cultural conflicts meant to promote or oppose social change (De la Porta and Diani 2006, p. 21).
- [Social movements are] instances of collective action with clear conflictual orientations to specific social and political opponents, conducted in the context of dense inter-organizational networking, by actors linked by solidarities and shared identities that precede and survive any specific coalitions and campaigns (Diani and Bison 2004, p. 283).
- Social movements can be viewed as collective enterprises to establish a new order of life. They have their inception in the condition of unrest and derive their motive power on one hand from dissatisfaction with the current form of life, and on the other hand, from wishes and hopes for a new scheme or system of living (Blumer 1939, p. 199).
- [A social movement is a] set of opinions and beliefs in a population which represents preferences for changing some elements of the social structure and/or reward distribution of a society (McCarthy and Zald 1977, pp. 1217–1218).

---

are, at least initially, *political outsiders*. They are not, in other words, an integrated or influential part of dominant political or economic institutions, or otherwise considered to be (organized) mainstream actors. Social movements, therefore, do not include established political parties or interest groups. The rationale for excluding mainstream actors and organizations is straightforward: organizations or groups that are acknowledged political and social actors have the tools at their disposal to *effectively* challenge the status quo (or to pursue grievances) within the established political process. Actors in social movements, by contrast, are compelled to operate outside the mainstream institutional process. This means that they must rely on unconventional strategies and tactics, such as political protesting, demonstrations, or boycotts to raise awareness of their issues.

Taken together, the three aforementioned characteristics lead to a basic definition of social movements as "collectivities acting with some degree of organization and continuity, partly outside institutional or organizational channels, for the purpose of challenging extant systems of authority, or resisting change in such systems, in the organization, society, culture or world system in which they are embedded" (Snow and Soule 2010, pp. 6–7). Using this definition, several examples of social movements can be readily identified:

- The anti-apartheid movement (within South Africa) that opposed the system of racial segregation in South Africa. (Apartheid was a political system designed to keep the majority of Africans and other ethnic groups under the control of the Dutch Afrikaner minority by excluding them from mainstream political, economic, and social institutions.) Within South Africa, the anti-apartheid movement began as a grass-roots movement in 1948 revolving around civic issues, such as rent increases, fees for basic services, and forced relocations. Activists first mobilized local communities to engage in demonstrations, to refuse (collectively) to pay rent, and to picket and boycott services and service providers. Over time, it developed into a broad international movement (involving governments, nongovernmental organizations, and businesses).

- The civil rights movement (1954–1968) in the United States, which sought to end racial discrimination and segregation and to secure full recognition and federal protection of rights granted through the passage of the Fourteenth and Fifteenth Amendments to the US Constitution. (This movement will be discussed at length later in the chapter.)
- Ecological/environmental movements focused on conservation and protection of natural resources, such as land, water, and forests.
- The environmental justice movement, which, unlike the environmental movement, focuses on the plight of low income and people of color who live in the most polluted environments and are often forced to live with a lower quality of life due to exposure to harmful chemicals and pollutants, as well as placement of waste sites and industrial plants. Environmental justice groups refer to this as environmental racism.
- The lesbian, gay, bisexual, and transgender (LGBT) movement, which fights for the equal treatment of LGBT in the workplace and in society. The LGBT movement has taken shape in many countries throughout the world.
- Islamic State (commonly referred to as IS, ISIS, or ISIL), which is a self-proclaimed militant movement that emerged from al-Qaeda in Iraq (AQI), the latter of which formed shortly after the US invasion of Iraq in 2003 under the leadership of Jordanian militant Abu Musab al-Zarqawi.

As the preceding list illustrates, real-world social movements are truly diverse, not just in the goals that they seek, but also in their geographic concentration, and in the types of tactics and methods employed. The list also helps to dispel a commonly held misperception that all social movements are peaceful, progressive, and nonviolent. To be sure, most social movements are peaceful and advocate for reform that is progressive in nature, but there are violent and reactionary movements, or movements that mobilize to prevent change. ISIS, of course, is one of these, but there are many others. The Ku Klux Klan (KKK), for instance, was the vanguard of a reactionary and racist movement in the United States that saw "as its mission the preservation of the institutionalized caste pattern of the South and the promotion of patriotic ideology" (Schaefer 1971, p. 143). The KKK and the movement it propelled (the KKK was founded by six college students, all former Confederate soldiers, in 1865) emerged in response to the post–Civil War Reconstruction Era policies that sought to establish political and economic equality for African Americans. The KKK not only became the symbol of white resistance to these policies in the South, but also became a symbol of intolerance, bigotry, and intimidation, as it used brutal violence—especially lynching—in an effort to prevent legal and institutional change from taking root.

The KKK movement, it should be noted, grew into a vast, nationwide organization with up to 5 million members, in 4,000 chapters, at its peak in the early 1920s (Wilson 2013). In fact, it is not unusual for social movements to become national in scope, as the KKK did, or to even develop a global reach. One example of the latter is the Indigenous Movement of First Peoples Worldwide, which began in 1997 and, according to the movement's website (http://www.firstpeoples.org), is focused on helping indigenous peoples everywhere in the world to "protect their territories and stop the 'asset stripping' that robs them of their livelihoods, and the foundations of their cultures." Other social movements, however, remain highly localized, such as the Mothers of East Los Angeles (MELA), which started in 1986 as a group of Latina mothers focused on fighting the proposed construction of a state prison in their neighborhood (since then, MELA has remained tightly focused on neighborhood issues, including opposition to the construction of an incinerator).

Whether local, national, or global, a key area of concern and interest is, for scholars and others, first, why collective action emerges in the first place, and second, why collective action—in the form of social movements—is sometimes "successful" (see Figure 8.3 on the challenges of measuring social movement outcomes) and other times not. Answering these two related questions, of course, is the primary focus of this chapter. And again, to find the answers, we will examine social movements through an application of each of the three theoretical approaches: rational, structural, and cultural. Let us begin with the rational approach.

Social Movements and Rationality

How do social movements emerge, develop, and change? Why do some social movements, but not others, result in successful political or social outcomes? To answer these questions from a rationalist perspective, we must, as usual, begin with the basic assumptions of rationality, one of which is a focus on individual-level action. That is, from a rationalist perspective it is

Figure 8.3 Measuring Social Movement Outcomes: Success or Failure?

Determining whether a social movement has succeeded or failed is not a simple task, as a number of studies have demonstrated (Amenta et al. 2010; Earl and Schussman 2004; Earl 2000; Giugni 2008, 1999). In general, though, scholars often define success in terms of a movement's ability to accomplish its stated objective (Gamson 1990). While this is a seemingly commonsensical way to measure success, it creates a larger problem in the way we think about social movements. One reason for this is clear: a single social movement is not usually a homogeneous thing, since any movement involves a diverse group of individuals. For some participants, achieving a certain stated objective may be the one and only goal, whereas other participants may view the initial objective as little more than a steppingstone, or they may not view it as an important goal at all. Consider, too, another scenario: a social movement may start off with a very specific goal, such as preventing a prison from being built, or a waste transfer station from being put in a community. After achieving the primary objective, however, there may be unintended consequences that make it difficult to determine success or failure. A good example of this is the movement started by the Anti-Saloon League of America (ASLA). The ASLA emerged in 1895, and, as its name implies, was focused on eliminating the distribution and sale of alcohol in the United States. In this regard, "the League was unlike many reform movements of its time . . . in that it retained a singled-minded focus, avoiding entanglement in related problems and issues of other causes" (Lamme, 2004, p. 66). The ASLA was successful in its stated objective with the passage of the Eighteenth Amendment, which legally forbade the sale and distribution of alcohol in US territory. An unintended consequence of the ASLA's success, however, was a rise in criminal activities that emerged during prohibition, including bootlegging and, more important, organized crime. Even more, after the passage of the Eighteenth Amendment, there was a public backlash and disillusionment. Eventually, the amendment was repealed—a scant thirteen years after it passed. Was the movement a success or failure?

Measuring success in terms of "objectives," it must also be emphasized, implies that something tangible, such as a concrete change in legislation or government policy, must take place. However, a focus on tangible goals may obscure less tangible, but no less important, forms of success (Burstein 1985; Rochon and Mazmanian 1993). Some social movements, for example, are successful at bringing about underlying cultural changes, or they can lead to significant changes in how an issue is framed by the media—think about how same-sex marriage can be framed as an issue of "religious freedom" or as an issue of "civil rights." Cultural change has been a particularly prominent feature of the LGBT movement in the United States. To be sure, the LGBT movement has focused and continues to focus on concrete objectives—such as fighting against discriminatory laws and practices—but the movement has also sought to change what has hitherto been a profoundly negative image, among the mainstream population, of the LGBT community as a whole. Arguably, the movement has had great success in changing public perceptions: in 2013, the proportion of Americans who had a favorable view of gay men (specifically) stood at 55 percent, an 18 percentage point increase from a decade earlier; for lesbians, the respective figures were 58 and 19 percent. Despite these figures, cultural shifts or shifts in media framing can mark a major achievement (or success), but their impact, in both the short and the long run, can be very difficult to measure.

important to remember that social movements—even if they are defined in terms of *collective* action—must still be understood as the product of decisions made by individual actors. After all, there can be no movement without people, or individual actors. Understanding how social movements arise, therefore, requires that we identify the determinants of individual participation. A key question in this regard is whether or not individuals gain new advantages or benefits from a decision to participate in or join a social movement. For rationalists, of course, individual motivation and strategic calculation are the *basic* keys to explaining the emergence, development, and success or failure of social movements.

Unlike the collective-goods problem discussed in Chapters 4 and 5, however, participation in social movements does *not* ultimately hinge on the capacity of political or social institutions to coerce or otherwise compel participation from reluctant free-riders. Indeed, a distinguishing aspect of social movements is that participation is essentially voluntary. In this regard, many rationalists understand social movements as a form of cooperative or collective self-help designed to achieve material gains (or other individual benefits) that would be difficult, if not impossible, to achieve through individual action alone. It is easy to see, for example, that individuals who are not happy with their working conditions will join a labor movement to pursue material advantages, such as higher wages, increased health benefits, greater job security, and reduced workloads (although unions are able to use coercion to reduce free-riding). More generally, some researchers argue that, given situations of **relative deprivation**, people across society are more likely to develop grievances and, therefore, are more likely to participate in social movements to address their grievances. Moreover, for individuals experiencing severe economic deprivation, doing nothing (that is, nonparticipation) is already very costly; therefore, joining a social movement that promises to improve their situation is rational, even if the rewards are relatively diffuse and uncertain. Deprivation and grievances, it is important to understand, are not necessarily based on economic or material considerations alone. The gay pride movement, the civil rights movement, the feminist (or women's) movement (including, for example, the political struggle for the Equal Rights Amendment) all revolved or revolve around questions of social alienation and political marginalization, although, even here, economic concerns may be an underlying factor.

Social Movements and the Free-Rider Problem: A Rational Conundrum?

On the surface, then, a rationality-based approach seems to offer an exceedingly simple yet compelling explanation for the emergence of social movements. Yet if we delve only slightly below the surface, it is clearly a very limited explanation, as many critics have pointed out. To understand why, it is important to reemphasize a point made earlier: social movements, in general, are geared toward achieving collective, as opposed to private, goals. That is, social movements (especially contemporary social movements) typically produce broad political, economic, and social changes that, by their very nature, are nonexclusive. The success of the civil rights movement in the United States or the anti-apartheid movement in South Africa, for example, brought essentially the same expansion of rights to every member of black society in both countries, whether or not they participated in the struggle. It is worth noting, too, that participating in the struggle for civil rights or against apartheid entailed huge potential costs—for example, imprisonment, extreme harassment, torture, and even death. As suggested earlier, analysts are therefore faced with a serious free-rider problem, which is significantly different from the free-rider problem discussed in Chapters 4 and 5. To repeat: without the existence of a political or social institution that can coerce or compel participation in the creation of a public good, how can the free-rider problem be overcome? This is a conundrum for the rational choice approach.

This issue (or conundrum), not surprisingly, has not gone unnoticed by rationalist scholars. It is ironic, though, that many seemed to offer only an explanation, at least in earlier studies, for why people do *not* participate in social movements. Mancur Olson (1932–1998), one of the leading figures in the field of public choice and an eminent economist, for example, came right to the point in his seminal work *The Logic of Collective Action* (1965). As Olson put it, "unless the number of individuals is quite small, or unless there is coercion or some other special device to make individuals act in their common interest, *rational self-interested individuals will not act to achieve their common or group interests*" (1965, p. 2, emphasis in original). Writing much earlier, Eric Hoffer (1951), another prominent scholar working under the collective behavior tradition, described the seemingly irrational human behavior of participation in mass movements in much more colorful terms: "For men to plunge headlong into an undertaking of vast change, they must be intensely discontented yet not destitute. . . . They must also have an extravagant conception of [or be] wholly ignorant of the difficulties involved in their vast undertaking. Experience is a handicap" (p. 7).

The basic assumption of rationality, once again, leads to a paradox: guided by self-interest, participation in collective action based on voluntary, cooperative group behavior is seemingly irrational; yet there are hundreds of significant, dynamic, and large-scale social movements throughout the world. Indeed, given the singular logic of self-interest, many social movements should not even exist, still less develop the collective force necessary to bring about significant political or social change. Without resolving the free-rider puzzle, therefore, rationalist theories might very well have little or nothing meaningful to say about social movements.

The problem is made even more serious in the case of so-called new social movements, which tend to be more altruistic (that is, less materially motivated) than traditional social movements (see Figure 8.4). To appreciate the significance of this point, consider environmental movements. In these movements, the effort by participants to protect the ozone layer, combat climate change, save endangered species, or preserve tropical rainforests is based on achieving an unequivocal public good. Even more, since "successful" environmental movements may actually raise the economic costs for individuals living in the most industrialized societies (from which many of the most vocal and active participants in the environmental movement come), the rational basis for participation is undermined even further. Other types of new social movements, such as animal rights, are even more problematic from a rationalist perspective, since it appears that individuals in such movements are motivated exclusively by nonmaterial and normative considerations. Moreover, new social movements present at least one additional and no less important complication: many of the participants come from high-status as opposed to low-status groups. We will discuss later why this is important.

Figure 8.4 New Social Movements

Most simply, *new social movements* can be defined as those that have arisen since the late 1960s; they include the ecology, gay rights, animal rights, anti–nuclear energy, New Age, peace, and women's movements (Kriesi et al. 1995). What separates "new" social movements from "old" social movements, according to Hank Johnston, Enrique Laraña, and Joseph Gusfield (1994, pp. 6–9), are eight basic characteristics. New social movements

1. Are not generally class-based; instead, the "structural roots" of these movements tend to be based on a diffuse social status, such as gender, sexual orientation, or profession.
2. Are characterized by a pluralism of ideas and values rather than a clear-cut ideological position.
3. Often involve the emergence of new or formerly weak dimensions of identity, often ethnically or historically based.
4. Blur the distinction between the collective and the individual.
5. Are concerned with a range of ostensibly noneconomic issues: abortion, alternative medicine, opposition to smoking, sexual behavior, and so on.
6. Tend to use "radical" mobilization strategies of disruption and resistance.
7. Reflect, to some degree, skepticism toward conventional channels for democratic participation.
8. Tend to be segmented, diffuse, and decentralized.

Resource Mobilization Theory: Solving the Conundrum

Not surprisingly, rationalist scholars did not just give up. Instead, they worked hard to develop an explanatory framework that was consistent with the basic principles of rational choice. The most prominent framework is known as resource mobilization theory. Unlike prior social movement theories that emphasized grievances, relative deprivation, or system breakdown, this approach focuses on the ability of participants in a social movement to acquire and mobilize *resources* (McCarthy and Zald 1977); thus the name of the approach. Resources include human resources (e.g., people's time, skills, expertise, and leadership), access to mass media, and a range of material goods such as money, property, technology, and equipment (Kendall 2006). Also important, even crucial, in resource mobilization theory is the social movement organization (SMO). SMOs are necessary because the aggregation and mobilization of resources requires a significant level of organizational capacity. Resources, in other words, do not just coalesce on their own; instead, they must be managed. Similarly, an SMO does not just emerge out of thin air: it is a conscious creation, typically formed by a relatively small group of (rational) actors who use it as a vehicle to achieve their self-interested goals. It is on this point that resource mobilization theory addresses the free-rider problem head on. The theory asserts that the goal of a social movement is *not* merely or primarily to achieve a collective good; instead, the approach assumes that social movements are, at base, the product of "issue entrepreneurs" who use SMOs for personal resource gain (McCarthy and Zald 1977).

Issue entrepreneurs (or the leaders of SMOs), in other words, play a central role in galvanizing a social movement, and they do so, to underscore the main point, because they stand to benefit personally from taking a leading role. Issue entrepreneurs, a bit more specifically, identify and define grievances, develop a group sense, devise strategies, and facilitate mobilization by reducing its costs and taking advantage of opportunities for collective action (Canel 1997). Of course, their success or failure is never a sure thing, and this is where the availability of resources comes back into play: issue entrepreneurs and the SMOs they create must have access to resources, some of which are used to bring in more and more participants. John McCarthy and Mayer Zald (1977), it is useful noting, used a supply-and-demand model to describe the general process by which SMOs succeed (or fail). In this view, an SMO can be viewed as part of a social movement industry, which produces a good just like any other industry. The good is, ostensibly, the larger goal of the social movement. To reach that goal the SMO relies on individuals "buying" the good that the SMO is "selling." Buying is represented, for example, by individuals contributing their own time, skills, and money toward achieving the larger goal of the social movement. The more the SMO can "sell," the more successful it becomes for the leaders of the organization. They control more resources and they develop more power and influence; in short, they become better off. Consider how the leaders of SMOs can become minor or even major celebrities, and how this status provides a very clear personal benefit. Ironically, this model suggests that leaders of SMOs are not primarily concerned with achieving the larger goal of the social movement; instead, their primary goal is preserving the SMO itself (Crawford 2005).

For any given social movement, it is important to add, there may be several different SMOs at work, each of which endeavors to maximize its control over resources. This makes good sense from a rational choice perspective. After all, for any particular issue, there will likely be many issue entrepreneurs who believe that they can benefit by creating their own SMO, for while the overarching "good" is the same, for each SMO within a social movement the methods of producing that good may differ "depending on the extremity of the solution, the means, and the efficiency of the organization" (Crawford 2005).

Social Networks and Mass Participation in Social Movements

Although the foregoing discussion is quite general (and, admittedly, over-simplified), it is fair to say that resource mobilization theory has made strong contributions to the understanding of social movements and social movement organizations, especially with regard to their internal and organizational dynamics. Still, as presented, the resource mobilization model of political action fails to account for the behavior of ordinary citizens (or the "buyers") who participate in social movements—a phenomenon that cannot be overlooked. After all, even a strong, rationally motivated issue entrepreneur who creates an SMO still requires some sort of mass base in order to be successful. Not surprisingly, there are many studies that address this issue, too.

We have already suggested one simple explanation, namely that individuals with little or nothing to lose may have a rational basis for joining social movements. Indeed, as Marc Dixon and Vincent Roscigno noted, this is the basic position in a large body of literature grounded in rationality that holds, in very general terms, "that individuals of markedly low status or those with greater autonomy from institutional or political constraint will be more likely to participate, since the costs of involvement (be they social, political or economic) will be lower and rewards arguably higher" (2003, p. 1294). But as we also noted, it is not only individuals from low-status groups that join new social movements; instead, there is increasing participation from members of high-status groups—for example, highly educated, upper-middle-class whites. This is clearly evident in women's movements, environmental movements, and peace movements, especially in the United

States and other well-off countries. The reason why this is a concern is simple: high-status individuals have much less to gain from participation (at least in material terms), and the "costs" of participation (even if only opportunity costs) are generally higher. In short, their participation has a weaker rational basis.

To account for the participation of individuals from high-status groups in particular (but for all individual actors in general), some rationalists have focused on the idea of social ties or social networks (concepts, it is important to note, that are also used by structuralists). The basic argument here is that social networks, which are generally based on friendships or community relationships, serve to condition the decisions individuals make. More specifically, rationalists argue that individuals are more likely to join social movements when they have social ties to other joiners (Gould 2003). But why is this rational behavior? David Gould explained it this way: "people who expect future interaction with movement participants should be more likely, all else [being] equal, to join." "Such people," Gould continued, "are more likely to view joining as beneficial to themselves because their 'ties' to other joiners give the latter an opportunity to reward (or punish) their decision to join (or not to join)" (2003, p. 241). This account, moreover, helps explain why social movements that are directed to the benefit of a third party (for example, child workers in foreign countries, endangered animals, young women subject to female circumcision in Africa) are still able to attract participants; to repeat, so long as the other joiners can reward other participants with their continued "friendship" or other benefits of an ongoing social relationship, the participation is rational (p. 241).

The process just described is, in more formal terms, similar to reciprocity in the logic of an iterated or repeated game. In a repeated game, the behavior of actors is dependent on or conditioned by the prospect of continued interaction. Put simply, since all actors understand that they will meet again, all have an incentive to be "nice" to each other: if you are nice to me, I'll be nice to you, because I know that, if I'm not nice today, you'll "punish" me tomorrow and thereafter (Gould 2003; Axelrod 1984). Thus, if my friend wants me to join a social movement, I will cooperate ("be nice") by joining the movement, but I will expect a sustained friendship (my reward). Of course, my friend also realizes a (reciprocal) gain. This is a key point, for, as Robert Axelrod argued, "once cooperation based on reciprocity is established in a population, it can protect itself from invasion by uncooperative strategies" (1984, p. 173).

In short, the free-rider problem is overcome in a repeated game. Other research has reinforced this view. Anthony Oberschall (1973), for example, demonstrated that individuals were more likely to join a social movement based on how connected they were to social organizations within the community. Oberschall identified two forms of preexisting social organizations that could help facilitate recruitment and mobilization: communal and associational organizations. Communal organizations are those that are based on culture, religion, or ethnicity, whereas associational organizations are more formal organizations that reflect common interests. Members of such organizations, Oberschall pointed out, were more likely to participate in social movements than those who were isolated, marginalized, or displaced. In this regard, too, Oberschall's analysis challenged the traditional "mass society approach," which viewed movement participants as isolated, alienated individuals who were most likely to be recruited by a social movement, particularly extremist movements.

Resource mobilization theory and the civil rights movement. The civil rights movement of the 1950s and 1960s provides a strong example of how a social movement "rises." It is also a particularly worthy case to study, for the civil rights movement, as Aldon Morris put it, was "clearly one of the pivotal developments of the twentieth century" (1999, p. 517), and it has served, and continues to serve, as a model for other social movements both domestically and internationally. In explaining the success of the civil rights movement it is of course important to understand the larger context and history of black oppression in US society, which Morris covers in his article. For our purposes, however, the focus will be on Morris's theoretical account, one that uses resource mobilization theory to explain the development and success of the civil rights movement (Morris, we should note, discusses the importance of structural prerequisites or "preconditions," too).

To begin, Morris pointed out that protests against racial inequality had been going on throughout the first half of the twentieth century, but they tended to be localized and restricted in scope. There were a few exceptions, but these were short-lived and relied heavily on elites external to the black community. The first inkling that collective action, or mass mobilization, could be an effective strategy came with the Montgomery bus boycott of 1955, a boycott that involved large numbers of black participants, and a protest that lasted for over a year. "The boycott revealed the central role that would be played by social organization and a Black culture rooted in protest tradition" (Morris 1999, p. 524).

Significantly, the first highly visible social movement organization emerged from the bus protest, the Montgomery Improvement Association (MIA). And, as resource mobilization theory predicts, it was created by a small group of black community and church leaders, led by Martin Luther King Jr. (acting as an issue entrepreneur). It is equally significant that the MIA was both "church based and structurally linked to the major community organization of the Black community" (Morris 1999, p. 525); in other words, it was part of and able to tap into a larger social network. This connection to a social network allowed the MIA to develop a significant base of human resources; in addition, it was able to "sell" its product by creating an effective strategy of nonviolent collective action (primarily through boycotts), which simultaneously helped to increase the MIA's supply of moral resources (e.g., legitimacy).

Of course, the MIA was not the only significant SMO. The success of the Montgomery bus boycott (in 1956, the US Supreme Court ruled that the law mandating bus segregation in Montgomery, Alabama, was unconstitutional) inspired others to follow suit. One example is the Student Nonviolent Coordination Committee (SNCC), which became a social movement organization and, among other actions, mobilized a number of sit-ins at segregated lunch counters throughout the South. As the name implies, the SNCC was a student-based organization, started by Ella Baker in 1960 (Baker had been involved in the struggle for racial equality for several decades). Other important SMOs included the Southern Christian Leadership Conference (SCLC), the Congress of Racial Equality (CORE), and the National Association for the Advancement of Colored People (NAACP, which was established long before the civil rights movement), along with numerous local movement organizations.

While the details of the activities and influence of these SMOs is too much to cover in this chapter, suffice it to say that this played an absolutely central role in the emergence and success of the civil rights movement. Morris explained it in the following way:

> Each of the major SMOs of the civil rights movement shaped collective action by carving out its own spheres of organizational activity and producing the leaders, organizers, and tactics that provided the movement with its power and dynamism. At the interorganizational level, these organizations engaged in competition, cooperation, and conflict. What has been learned from this interorganizational standpoint is that when SMOs compete and cooperate they can produce greater volumes of collective action by sharing knowledge, and resources by triggering tactical innovations. (1999, p. 532)

The rise of multiple SMOs thus reinforces a key lesson in resource mobilization theory, which is that successful social movements require an organizational base or structure. That organizational structure, in turn, requires issue entrepreneurs or leaders, such as Martin Luther King Jr., Ella Baker, Baynard Rustin (cofounder of the Southern Christian Leadership Conference), Gloria Richardson (cofounder of the Cambridge Non-Violent Action Committee), James Farmer (cofounder of CORE), among others. Morris's analysis did not demonstrate clearly that these leaders created and then used SMOs for personal resource gain, or that they were more interested in preserving their own SMOs than in pursuing the larger objective of the civil rights movement, but he did provide at least indirect evidence. In particular, he noted that there were instances of "intense conflict" between civil rights SMOs that undermined the general struggle against racial discrimination. In one instance, a conflict between the SCLC and the SNCC led to failure of the Albany Movement, which was an effort to end all forms of racial segregation in the city of Albany, Georgia (in 1961). A *New York Times* article at the time pointed to "competition for financial support and power" between the SCLC and the SNCC as the primary reason for the lack of success; even more, the article, written by Claude Sitton, suggested that the rift between these two SMOs would have "important implications for the future of the civil rights movement throughout the South" (Sitton 1961).

Limitations of the Rational Approach

Rational choice has contributed greatly to understanding social movements. Resource mobilization theory, in particular, does a very good job of showing that many social movements can be, and most likely are, motivated by rational considerations and by rational actors. The theory also provides crucial insight into the organizational basis and dynamics of social movements—an insight that matches extremely well with real-world cases, such as the civil rights movement. Still, as Stu Crawford (2005) pointed out, "there are a few problems with [resource mobilization theory] when it is applied to certain social movements. One problem is that [it] focuses almost solely on social movement organizations." And this is a problem because many contemporary social movements—so-called new social movements (refer to Figure 8.4)—lack the sort of organizational basis that resource mobilization theory takes for granted. Instead of an expected core of social movement organizations, new social movements have what some scholars have called a social movement *community* (Buechler 2011). The social movement community is typically highly decentralized and thus does not fit into the SMO framework (Crawford 2005). A recent example (and one that will be the focus of analysis at the end of this chapter) of a decentralized social movement is the Arab Spring, which some scholars have referred to as a "leaderless social movement" (Sutherland, Land, and Böhm 2014).

A second problem, which also comes from the new social movement literature, is the assumption that individual participation—whether on the part of leaders or rank-and-file participants—is determined primarily, if not solely, by material or calculable interests. The assumption of rationality, critics contend, not only overemphasizes individual incentives and material gains, but also, and perhaps more importantly, fails to examine qualitative values, such as a sense of solidarity or commitment to a cause, which cannot be reduced to a cost-benefit analysis (Ferree 1991–1992).

Structural Accounts of Social Movements

Rational choice analysts, as you well know by now, believe that individual motivation and human agency are key to explaining most, if not all, significant outcomes in the social world. Social movements are no exception. They do not completely discount underlying social, political, or economic forces, but it is clear that rationalists do not consider these nearly sufficient to account for the emergence, still less the success, of social movements. Indeed, for many rational choice scholars, social movements appear to be quintessentially nonstructural or "voluntary" phenomena. Structuralists, meanwhile, argue that micro-level factors, even though relevant, are unequivocally secondary in that the rise, development, and success (or failure) of social movements must be understood as conditioned—constrained and enabled—by forces or structures largely beyond the control of even the most capable leaders and individual activists.

With these basic points in mind, it is useful to note that the macro or structural foundation for examining social movements—or contentious politics—has a relatively long (scholarly) history, although that history has not followed exactly the same path. Doug McAdam, Sidney Tarrow, and Charles Tilly, on this last point, noted that US scholars "were first off the mark with a largely structural approach to movements that centered on several versions of the concept that has come to be known as 'political opportunity structure'" (1997, p. 145), a concept that will be examined in more depth later. Western European scholars, by contrast, "developed a different kind of structuralism—post-Marxism" (p. 145), which came in several different varieties. Both the US and European approaches, however, were "resolutely structural" in that they focused on conditions that could not be molded to the actors' preferences. It is important to point out, though, that more recent structural accounts of social movements are generally based on a "soft" structuralism—that is, a structuralism that is contingent rather than strictly determined, and one that is sensitive to the "nuances of the political process" (McAdam, Tarrow, and Tilly 1997). This makes sense, especially for those scholars who focus most of their intellectual energy on the study of social movements. For embedded in the very concept of social movements is an understanding that agency matters. Social movements, after all, are agents of change; they are the manifestation of people working collectively and with purpose to bring about change within societies.

Political Opportunity Structure

This softer structural position is certainly evident in one of the main structural approaches to the study of social movements, which is based on a concept alluded to earlier: the political opportunity structure. Sidney Tarrow explained this term in the following manner: "By political opportunity structure, we refer to consistent—but not necessarily formal, permanent or national—dimensions of the political environment which either encourage or discourage people from using collective action. The concept of political opportunity emphasizes resources external to the group—unlike money or power—that can be taken advantage of even by weak or disorganized challengers" (1994, p. 18).

According to Tarrow, it is the political opportunity structure itself, or rather changes in the structure, that creates the impetus for social movements. As he put it, "Social movements form when ordinary citizens, sometimes encouraged by leaders, respond to changes in opportunities that lower the costs of collective action, reveal potential allies and show where elites and authorities are vulnerable" (p. 18). In other words, Tarrow and others posit that changes in the underlying political process (or structure) create "openings" that enable the mobilization of resource-poor actors into new movements. In this view, then, the analytical focus clearly shifts away from the individual or individual leader. But rather than shifting to a largely abstract structure such as the capitalist system or to a concrete entity such as the social movement organization, the political opportunity structure approach identifies the political system as the key structures. The political system, according to Hanspeter Kriesi (1995), is composed of three broad properties: (1) a formal institutional structure; (2) informal procedures and prevailing strategies with regard to challengers; and (3) the configuration of power relevant for a confrontation with the challengers. On the surface, this makes the political opportunity structure approach very similar to an institutional approach (or institutionalism). Yet with a stronger deterministic element, there is a reasonable basis for classifying political opportunity structure as a structural approach. The deterministic bias of political opportunity structure is readily apparent in Tarrow's conceptualization. But he is not alone: other proponents speak of the manner in which the timing and fate of movements are largely dependent upon the opportunities afforded to activists by changes in the broader political system or structure (see, for example, Lipsky 1970; Jenkins and Perrow 1977; McAdam 1982). Subsequent studies have continued along the same general track, although there have been efforts to incorporate rationalist assumptions into the political opportunity framework (for example, McAdam 1982).

With the foregoing discussion in mind, it would be useful to turn to a more concrete discussion of the political opportunity structure approach by looking at a specific example: the Zapatista movement.

Exploring Mexico's Shifting Political Opportunity Structure

On the morning of January 1, 1994, the Zapatista Army of National Liberation (Ejército Zapatista de Liberación Nacional [EZLN]) seized four towns in the southern Mexican state of Chiapas. The seizure was in response to the deteriorating economic conditions faced by the indigenous people of the region. The EZLN, or Zapatistas as they came to be known, consisted of several hundred indigenous (Mayan) people from the Chiapas highlands, as well as a leadership and support network comprised of nonindigenous, university-educated Mexicans. The EZLN can trace its roots to the National Liberation Forces (Fuerzas de Liberación Nacional [FLN]), a Marxist-Leninist group formed in 1969, which advocated a revolutionary platform emphasizing class-conflict and anticapitalist rhetoric. The emergence of liberation theology in the 1970s, and Marxist guerrilla movements in other Latin American countries, further shaped the EZLN's ideological preferences. It November 1983, six FLN members founded the EZLN in the Lacandon Jungle of Chiapas.

At first, the EZLN largely parroted the Marxist, anticapitalist ideology of the FLN and spoke of liberating the exploited indigenous population through a classic revolutionary guerrilla war. Over time, however, the rhetoric and strategy of the group changed, largely due to the influence of indigenous Mayan beliefs. Still, the group was led by a non-Mayan known as Subcomandante Marcos (later he changed his name to Subcomandante Insurgente Galeano). Most important, while the EZLN began as a classic guerrilla group determined to overthrow the government, it transformed into a social organization that sought justice, democracy, and freedom for indigenous people. In this regard, when the Zapatistas declared war on the Mexican government on January 1, 1994, the group maintained that the uprising was due to the state's historical discrimination and neglect of Mexico's indigenous communities, the authoritarian practices of Mexico's ruling political party—the Institutional Revolutionary Party (Partido Revolucionario Institucional [PRI])—and the unfettered pursuit of neoliberal policies.

The transformation of the EZLN into a social movement needs to be highlighted. Keep in mind, on this point, that the EZLN started off as an armed insurrection—not a social movement—but after its initial use of force, the Zapatistas suspended the use of armed insurrection and began to use nonviolent means to achieve the group's objectives. In 2001, in particular, the Zapatistas led a peaceful march across Mexico to the capital. The march was designed to force the Mexican congress to live up to the San Andrés accords, signed in 1996, which granted autonomy, recognition, and rights to the indigenous population of Mexico. The march was impressive, but it failed to force the Mexican government to act. In 2005, the Zapatistas launched the "Other Campaign," which was an effort to mobilize a country-wide alliance of resistance groups across Mexico. This campaign, too, largely failed to achieve its objectives. Despite these "failures," the Zapatistas have survived for more than two decades and have managed to establish de facto autonomous indigenous communities that operate quite well (Wallerstein 2008). Perhaps more important, at least according to Immanuel Wallerstein, the Zapatistas have succeeded in raising consciousness and inspiring similar movements across the globe. As Wallerstein simply put it, "there is no question that the Zapatista insurrection of 1994 became a major inspiration for antisystemic movements throughout the world" (2008).

In thinking about the Zapatista movement, especially from a structural perspective, several questions immediately arise. First, why did the Zapatista movement take place when it did? After all, discrimination against indigenous groups had been going on for a very long time, and the EZLN, as noted, first emerged (albeit in different form) in the 1960s. So, did the timing reflect changes in the political structure, or was it entirely happenstance? Second, despite the lack of clear-cut "victory," it is obvious that the Zapatistas were not instantly and summarily crushed by the Mexican government. Thus, while the government used its vastly superior military force against the Zapatistas—and, in fact, launched an immediate counterattack to take back Osocingo, one of the cities the Zapatistas seized—it also agreed to a cease-fire on January 12, 1994 (although the cease-fire agreement was not fully observed by the government). But why agree to a cease-fire at all against a weak, resource-poor organization, which had only days earlier declared war against the entire Mexican state? Consider, on this point, that during the initial uprising in Chiapas many of the indigenous people carried wooden rifles, instead of actual weapons, a clear demonstration that the "rebels" had very limited capacity to actually fight against the Mexican government.

Not surprisingly, the answer to these questions can be found through an application of the political opportunity structure approach, which focuses on the "political openings" (or opportunities) that made it possible, or at least more probable, for the Zapatistas to declare a "war" against the Mexican state in 1994 and then to survive and even thrive as a social movement for decades following that declaration. To begin, it is important to recognize that the political opportunities were products of changes in both the domestic and international (or global) environments, although it is perhaps more accurate to say that the changes were due to the intersection between these two environments. José Muñoz provides a nice summary:

> The EZLN . . . uprising in Chiapas, Mexico, in 1994 took advantage of many political opportunities in an economic and politically liberalizing state. Most significantly, the negotiation and passage of the **North American Free Trade Agreement** (NAFTA) generated issues over which to mobilize and created political openings in the system to support mobilization. While NAFTA highlighted the dark side of globalization with its negative effects on living conditions in southern Mexico, it also ushered in political reforms that protected human rights and brought great international attention to Mexico. Many nations were watching to see whether Mexico had reached economic and political maturity. Taken together, these political opportunities provided the foundation for the EZLN to mobilize as a political movement. (2006, p. 251)

Prior to NAFTA, however, PRI governance—the bedrock of Mexican government—had already been under strain. In particular, the debt crisis of the 1980s led to the implementation of austerity measures that forced a reversal of economic policies that had long helped to ensure PRI dominance. In particular, the debt crisis forced the Mexican government, under President Carlos Salinas, to privatize many state-owned companies, which in turn required the government to significantly scale back on social policies (since the state had fewer economic resources at its disposal) or, in the words of Tilly (1995), "commitment-producing mechanisms" (cited in Muñoz 2006, p. 262). In other words, external forces in the system of global capitalism forced changes in Mexico's hitherto **clientelist** system, a system designed to provide material incentives in exchange for political patronage. Little by little, these economic reforms contributed to the destabilization of the PRI's political power and reach. Eventually, the partial breakdown of the PRI's grip on the political system created pockets of democratic openings (or opportunities), especially in the urban areas, that permitted ordinary Mexicans, including the Mayans of Chiapas, to challenge PRI hegemony.

This still does not explain the (relative) success of the Zapatistas. Thus it is crucial to find other changes in the political opportunity structure. Muñoz identified several of these. First, he noted that the Mexican government had become increasingly vulnerable to economic and social pressure, including pressure from transnational financial elites and institutions that wanted the Mexican government to end the Zapatista conflict and to secure investments. Pressure from the financial community reflected the more general impact of global economic integration on Mexico. Pressure also came from external human rights groups, which made it difficult for the Mexican government to use overwhelming military force to put down the uprising, or to dismantle the Zapatistas. This latter source of pressure points to a second change in the political opportunity structure: the formation of international human rights norms, to which the Mexican government had become increasingly beholden. Adherence to international human rights norms, it must be emphasized, was not necessarily a reflection of a newfound normative commitment, but was instead a reflection of "Mexico's new international position, highlighted by NAFTA, [which] required it take a stand on human rights befitting a country laboring to situate itself as a regional and hemispheric economic power" (Muñoz 2006, p. 252). In this regard, the Mexican government's commitment to human rights was primarily instrumental, but it was also a product of Mexico's shifting position within the global economic and political system.

The changes in the political opportunity structure help to explain the timing of the Chiapas uprising, although not in a completely straightforward manner. That is, the uprising did not occur on January 1, 1994, simply because that was the same day that NAFTA came into force. NAFTA was a pretext, or a symbol, of the actual concerns of the movement and reflected only one of the many grievances between the Zapatistas and the Mexican government (Muñoz 2006). Instead, as Muñoz suggested, the timing was related to the fact that the negotiations over NAFTA, and the agreement itself, forced the Mexican government to adopt a more tolerant stance toward political opposition groups. The political and economic context of NAFTA also provides an explanation for (1) why the uprising was not immediately and decisively crushed, and (2) why the Zapatista movement survived. On the first point, Muñoz noted that US intelligence services were aware of the EZLN months before NAFTA's implementation, but the "delicate nature of the NAFTA negotiations made it difficult for the government to deal with Zapatistas militarily given the international attention to Mexico" (p. 266). On the second point, Muñoz argued that competing interests created rifts among different elite groups, which resulted in an incoherent and ineffective policy toward the Zapatistas. In 1995, for example, the Mexican government launched a major offensive against the EZLN in hopes of capturing the group's leadership, but the operation was called off due to domestic and international opposition. Subsequently, the government pursued a policy of low-intensity conflict and militarization, which was designed, in part, to allay the concerns of transnational capital (and others), without, at the same time, provoking too much opposition. It was a fine line that the Mexican government had to walk, but the line itself was drawn by a range of economic and social-structural shifts in and around Mexico.

Limitations of the Structural Approach

Despite its many strengths, the political opportunity approach is not free from criticism. Perhaps the most salient is this: as with resource mobilization theory, the political opportunity structure approach does a poor job of demonstrating the passage from condition to action. As one social movement researcher put it, "expanding political opportunities . . . do not, in any simple sense, produce a social movement. . . . [Instead] they only offer insurgents a certain objective 'structural potential' for collective action. Mediating between opportunity and action are people and the subjective meanings they attach to their situations" (McAdam 1982, p. 48). In the example of the Zapatista movement, the basis for this criticism is readily apparent. After all, regardless of the expanded opportunities for the Zapatistas to act, the decision to carry out an uprising in Chiapas on January 1, 1994, was not made for the group. It was a decision that both the leaders and the participants had to make for themselves. It is also significant that the prior actions—actions taken long before the political opportunity structure was supposedly amenable to a successful social movement—were integral to the events that transpired on January 1, 1994, and for many years following. What if the FLN were never created? Would the events in Chiapas have occurred when they did? Would they have ever occurred? It's not possible to answer the last two questions, but they highlight an important gap in the structural perspective.

Even more, the political opportunity structure approach seems to shortchange the agency of movement actors in maximizing the potential and

effectiveness of their actions. In the case of the Zapatistas, again, the movement could have easily faltered or collapsed. Every step required planning
and a powerful will, as well as careful strategizing. Indeed, one of the great
achievements of the Zapatistas was the capacity to build a support network
virtually from the ground up. To his credit, Muñoz also recognized this in
his analysis. As he explained it:

> Part of the explanation for the success of the Zapatista support network is the
> use of the Internet and other types of media reporting. These resources played
> a part in creating a communication infrastructure, which worked to mobilize
> external support for the movement. The Zapatista support network's ability to
> take advantage of improved technologies and communication structures in-
> creased its ability to mobilize transnationally and provide information about
> the movement's conflict with the government. These technologies allowed for
> organizations within Mexico, such as the Center for Economic and Political
> Research, to send communiqués through the network during a period of mili-
> tary aggression in 1995. It is through information politics that the EZLN has
> received attention from activists in France, Australia and the US as well as in-
> ternational agencies such as Amnesty International, the United Nations High
> Commissioner for Human Rights and Global Exchange. (2006, p. 259)

Muñoz went on to explain how the Zapatistas carefully, and quite consciously, constructed an image and how the organization used that image to
build both domestic and international support—support that proved decisive to the longevity and success of the movement.

In sum, structural approaches to the study of social movements, although undoubtedly valuable, also appear not to give us all the answers. To
fill in the gaps, it may be necessary to again turn to culture.

Culture and Social Movements

For many observers, it is difficult to dismiss completely the idea that culture and cultural factors matter in the study of social movements. After all,
participants in social movements invariably, perhaps even necessarily, subscribe to a set of values and beliefs that are distinct from the population at
large. Furthermore, as Nick Crossley put it, "those who subscribe to those
beliefs must feel some degree of affinity with others [that is, solidarity] . . .
at least if they hold those beliefs with any degree of passion" (2002, p. 6).
Many cultural theorists, however, argue not only that culture does matter,
but also that it is a crucial element to understanding how collective mobilization emerges in the first place. Yet as you know, culture is often quite
fluid, which means that both its "meaning" and impact are hard to pin down.
These issues have already been discussed in other chapters, so we will not
cover the same ground here. Suffice it to say that, in research on social
movements, there are generally two broad views of culture that, although not
necessarily irreconcilable, have moved off in very different directions.

The Traditional Approach: Culture from the Inside Out

The first, more traditional, view can be called the inside-out approach (Swidler 1995). This approach stems, at least in part, from the ideas of Max Weber. In one of his most famous works (discussed in Chapter 4), *The Protestant Ethic and the Spirit of Capitalism,* Weber explored religious doctrine to understand why a relatively wealthy individual would choose to live a frugal lifestyle. Weber's conclusion was simple: the decision to live a life of asceticism was based on the concept of "a calling," which refers "to the idea that the highest form of moral obligation of the individual is to fulfil his duty in worldly affairs" (Giddens 2005, p. xii). As Anthony Giddens explained it, in his introduction to Weber's original work, "this projects religious behaviour into the day-to-day world, and stands in contrast to the Catholic ideal of the monastic life, whose object is to transcend the demands of mundane existence" (2005, p. xii). Weber argued that the calling, while originally introduced many centuries ago by the German theologian Martin Luther (1483–1546), became more rigorously developed in the various Puritan sects (Puritanism is part of the larger Protestant tradition): Calvinism, Methodism, Pietism, and Baptism (Giddens 2005). The upshot is this: the belief in and devotion to the calling served as a powerful influence in shaping the behavior and actions of the individual.

To understand why Weber's argument is interpreted as an "inside-out" view of culture, consider the basic logic: culture acts as a driving force that "shapes actions by defining what people want and how they imagine they can get it" (Swidler 1995, p. 25). In other words, the inside-out approach presumes that our internalized views of the world (that is, the "inside") come to have an independent—and therefore explanatory—influence on social action: people find themselves constrained, or enabled, by they very ideas they use to understand and describe the world in which they live. In this view, the connection with social movements is fairly clear. Specifically, social movements are presumed to be a product, at least in part, of cultural processes located entirely within the minds of the people who constitute the movement. Thus the analytical focus is on how the preexisting "stock" of cultural symbols—again, already internalized by activists and others—is used to accomplish key processes in mobilization (Johnston and Klandermans 1995, p. 14). Culture's influence, therefore, is presented in fairly unproblematic terms; that is, it either is an obstacle to or a resource (or "tool kit") for mobilization, depending on the nature of values and beliefs individual actors in a society already hold.

The Outside-In or Global Approach to Cultural Analysis

The second view largely rejects the Weberian, inside-out image of culture and, according to Ann Swidler (1995), rightly so. The problem is not that inside-out treatments of culture are all wrong but that they are incomplete.

Instead, Swidler and others (for example Wuthnow 1987; Sewell 1985; Melucci 1995) have suggested that social movement researchers need to adopt an outside-in or global approach to the study of culture and its relationship to social movements. But what exactly does it mean to say that culture should be understood from the outside in? To answer this question, consider, for example, the work of Emile Durkheim, one of the most prominent sociologists and philosophers of the late nineteenth and early twentieth centuries. As Swidler (1995) noted, Durkheim viewed culture as shared or "collective representations," rather than as ideas developed and held by individuals or groups pursuing their own interests. In this view, culture (or the symbols that represent culture) is the vehicle of a "fundamental process in which publicly shared symbols constitute social groups while they constrain and give form to individual consciousness" (p. 26). Culture, in short, does not merely reflect group life, it constitutes it (Swidler 1995). There were, of course, other very important developments in cultural analysis, including the pathbreaking work of Clifford Geertz (1973), who fundamentally broke from the traditional Weberian approach by arguing that culture should be studied for its meanings rather than its effect on actions.

Geertz's analysis of culture is, for the beginning comparativist, quite abstract and even obtuse; for present purposes, then, we will eschew further discussion except to say that many of the concepts introduced by Geertz (including "publicness," practices, and power) have helped to transform cultural analysis. More concretely, these concepts have helped lead to practical suggestions about how culture might be applied to develop a better understanding of social movements. Swidler (1995) provides a basic four-point summary:

1. It is critical to "entertain the possibility that culture's power is independent of whether or not people believe in it" (p. 39). This may not make much sense on the surface, but consider how we often do things we don't "believe in"—for instance, giving Christmas presents even though we may deplore the commercialization and secularization of Christmas (p. 32). Yet in engaging in the practice of exchanging gifts, people absorb important elements of Christian culture. In understanding social movements, this means that, for example, we need to dispense with the idea that culture only matters insofar as individual actors consciously believe in the values of the movement or even in the value of activism.

2. It is equally important to understand that the influence of culture is not only dependent on shaping or reshaping the beliefs of individuals per se; instead, culture's influence is also premised on shaping their knowledge of how others will interpret their actions. The example of Christmas gift giving works here, too: we give gifts, in part, because of our knowledge of how others interpret this action (pp. 32–33).

Thus, if you receive a gift from a friend, you will likely reciprocate because you do not want your actions to be misinterpreted by your friend (e.g., your friend may believe that you dislike him or her or that you did not appreciate the gift). In this regard, the success of a social movement should not be judged purely in terms of its capacity, for example, to influence public policy, but also in terms of its ability to transform aspects of the prevailing culture and dominant public discourse.

3. Swidler suggested "that students of culture in general, and social movement scholars in particular, need to pay close attention to the public contexts in which cultural understandings are brought to bear" (p. 39). In other words, it is essential to recognize that culture influences action much more powerfully in some contexts and historical moments than in others. Consider a local council meeting to discuss the issue of homelessness. Or imagine yourself in a large group meeting discussing what action to take against a government policy, say, outlawing the construction of mosques in your city. Before attending the meeting you may have been completely indifferent to the issue. However, as you hear various arguments, you may find yourself aligning strongly with one side or the other. Suddenly, and perhaps unconsciously, you are galvanized to take action. As Swidler put it, "reminding ourselves of the power that meetings and other group forums have to crystallize ideological splits and recode public speech and action, I suggest that culture can have consistent, coherent effects on action in particular contexts even if individuals and groups are divided and inconsistent in their beliefs" (p. 39).

4. Swidler reminded us to recognize that cultures of social movements are shaped by the institutions that the movements confront. As she explained it, "Different regime types and different forms of repression generate different kinds of social movements with differing tactics and internal cultures. Dominant institutions also shape the movements' deepest values" (p. 37).

Admittedly, this is a lot to digest. But you should already be familiar with most of the ideas expressed by Swidler, since they have been discussed, in one form or another, throughout this book. The task, then, is to see how we might use the suggestions given to us by Swidler (as well as other modes of cultural analysis) to make sense of social movements in a concrete and meaningful manner. Unfortunately, this is easier said than done. It is difficult, in part, because the social movement literature that might, in one way or another, be classified as culturalist is extremely diverse and often more conceptual than empirical. There is, however, a very simple lesson: social movements are not just the product of objective conditions, or of cost-benefit calculations. There is always an important cultural or intersubjective element. With this exceedingly simple lesson in mind, in this next section we will examine a concrete case of nationalist movements in Canada.

Collective Identity, Names, and Social Movements: Nationalist Movements in Canada

Culturalist approaches to social movements frequently stress the **social construction** of collective identity as an essential part of collective action. At the most basic level, collective identity can be defined as a shared sense of "we-ness." Francesca Polletta and James Jasper explained it this way: "It is a perception of a shared status or relation, which may be imagined rather than experienced directly, and it is distinct from personal identities, although it may form part of a personal identity" (2001, p. 284). In addition, although a collective identity is often self-defined, it may, the authors noted, "have been first constructed by outsiders (for example, as in the case of 'Hispanics')" in the United States. When imposed by outsiders, a collective identity is often meant as a basis for discrimination, marginalization, or subordination. Whether imposed from the outside or self-defined, collective identities are usually based on and expressed through "cultural material," which may include narratives, symbols, verbal styles, rituals, clothing, and so on. A collective identity, therefore, is not preformed or objectively determined (in the way a classical Marxist understands class identity) but arises through an interactive, intersubjective, and largely purposeful process that sometimes develops in unintended ways.

Often, as Jane Jenson argued, a collective identity—and the social movements it defines—hinge on a name (a type of "cultural material"); "movements," as she put it, "struggle over names and seek recognition of the one they prefer, both within and outside the community" (1995, p. 107). More broadly, this can be seen as a competition for "discursive space," the construction of which allows social movements to demarcate their boundaries—that is, the line between their collective self and a collective other; or more simply, the line between "us" and "them" (Hunt and Benford 2004). The (culture-based) demarcation of boundaries, therefore, is a critical step in the formation, maintenance, and even success of a social movement. It is clear, however, that choices "are never unconstrained. . . . They are made in particular structural and institutional contexts, traversed by relations of power" (Jenson 1995, p. 108). This means that dominant groups and institutions invariably limit the ability of subordinate communities to define and name themselves, for a name is more than just a word; it is, instead, an exercise and expression of power.

On the last point, some cultural analysts also speak of a "discursive opportunity structure" (in addition to the political opportunity structure). Ruud Koopmans and Paul Statham (1999) used the term "discursive opportunity structure" to identify the ideas in the broader political culture believed to be "sensible," "realistic," and "legitimate," and whose existence would therefore make it easier for specific forms of collective action framing (cited in McCammon 2013). This model was used, for example, to show how violence against asylum seekers in Germany was related to newspaper coverage. As Christian Bröer and Jan Willem Duyvendak explained it, "If newspapers report about right-wing violence more favorably, the number of violent attacks increases; right-wing activists interpret the newspaper coverage—the discursive opportunity—as proof of the legitimacy of an antimigrant position, shifting the normative limits of acceptance of their violent behavior" (2009, p. 339). In many societies, the discursive opportunity structure may severely limit the possibilities for social movements to develop, but this structure—constituted as it is by intersubjective forces—is subject to significant change and is itself a target of social movements, which understand the importance of reshaping this structure.

Naming, to return to the basic point, is more than just attaching a unique label for one's group or movement. It can provide a basis for mobilization, for the definition of interests, and for the elaboration of strategies, all of which have real, material consequences (Jenson 1995). Consider, in this regard, the struggle over the representation of Canada. For nearly a century, as Jenson argued, Canada was officially represented as a society with two distinct languages (English and French), two cultures, and equal rights of recognition and cultural expression for the two groups. In the 1970s, however, the federal government began pursuing a "pan-Canadian" project based on redefining (or reimagining) Canada as a liberal and multicultural nation, where individual, as opposed to collective, rights would take center stage. The effort by the federal government to create a new collective and cultural identity for all Canadians, however, generated strong resistance among women, visible minorities, aboriginal peoples (a self-defined collective identity), and French-speaking nationalists within Quebec. In particular, among many (but not all) groups within the province of Quebec, the effort reinvigorated a long-standing social movement based on nationalism that, despite a number of strong factional differences, coalesced around "Quebec" as a collective name. Indeed, as Jenson argued, "the imagery of the Quebec nation [has become] . . . hegemonic both in Quebec and in the rest of Canada" (1995, p. 110). Moreover, the "pan-Canadian idea of a single country defined around a linguistic duality has virtually disappeared" (p. 110). Thus, although it may seem natural now to think of Quebec as distinct from the "rest of Canada," it is important to understand that this was not always the case. Indeed, prior to the 1960s, the name "Québécois" did not, strictly speaking, exist (p. 110; see also p. 125, n. 8).

It is significant that a great deal of meaning and a number of concrete implications are attached to the seemingly innocuous name "Quebec" (there is also a lot of dispute). Christopher Jones (2000) explained one implication: "The choice of Quebec as a collective name and territorial definition of francophone Canada . . . denies equal recognition to francophones living in Ontario, Manitoba and New Brunswick, while at the same time diminishing the rights of indigenous peoples and anglophones living within Quebec borders." In fact, Quebec was never a homogeneous French-speaking province but was composed of at least fourteen ethnic groups with hundreds of thousands of residents who spoke only English (since the 1970s, according to some estimates, 100,000–400,000 English-speaking residents have left Quebec). The name, in this regard, creates an imagined identity, where the Québécois share a common culture, history, and language. Even more, the name necessarily implied an "other," which stood in direct opposition to the imagery of Quebec. The "other" is English (or anglophone) Canada. Yet as Jones (2000) asserted, the "Anglo/French opposition represents a necessary myth—part of the foundation of contemporary Quebec nationalism—but the historical reality on which it is based is more complex."

The "historical reality" is indeed complex and, for this reason, something we cannot delve into in this chapter. Suffice it to say, then, that the construction of an identity based on the collective name "Quebec" was designed to mobilize and give substance to a broad-based but focused social movement. As a movement defined by a particular language and culture, it is not surprising that language and culture became the primary basis by which the movement identified its collective interests. Thus, although the political goal of the movement was to assert francophone control of the economy in Quebec, one of the chief means used to accomplish this was a campaign to change public and private institutions through laws establishing the primacy of the French language (Jones 2000). This was certainly the most visible aspect of the Québécois social movement (or Quebec nationalism), at least to those living outside of Canada, but it was probably one of the most perplexing as well. After all, if the Québécois were primarily interested in changing their socioeconomic status, why did they not just attack the problem directly? To the Québécois, however, the problem was not just economic, but cultural. It was not just that Quebec had lagged behind all other Canadian provinces in terms of economic performance (and still does), but also that francophone residents were near the bottom of the economic ladder in Quebec. According to several studies, in fact, francophones ranked twelfth among fourteen ethnic groups in Quebec in terms of economic prosperity, and Canadian corporations systematically excluded French-speaking employees from the management ranks. Even bilingual French and English speakers suffered from wage discrimination. Culture, therefore, was the issue, which is why the Québécois were insistent on demanding that the sites of provincial social and commercial power become francophone (Jones 2000).

A focus on naming and the construction of a collective identity, however, does not explain everything about the Québécois movement (or Quebec nationalism). As we have learned throughout this book, most contemporary culturalists do not insist that a cultural approach tells us all or even most of the story. Jenson (1995), for example, suggested that we must avoid making a false choice between culture and structure, between culture and rationality, and so on. Indeed, she argued that an integrative approach is not only advisable but also necessary. In her own analysis, she brought together "identity" and "opportunities." As she explained it, "the configuration of the political opportunity structure cannot be analyzed without first inquiring about who the actors are. The names with which movements represent themselves in seeking representation are one of the ways that opportunities can be made, and the names may contribute to a reconfiguration of the political opportunity structure" (p. 114). What Jenson was saying, in part, was that the very act of naming—of self-defining a collective identity—generates resources, solidarity, alliance possibilities (and opposition), and "routes to representation" (that is, institutional access). In other words, naming helps to "make opportunities" within the prevailing political and discursive opportunity structure. But it is not only a matter of "making opportunities," for Jenson also suggested that, although we cannot do whatever we want (that is, structural and institutional constraints—including structured relations of power—do exist), political structures and the larger social environment are not fixed entities "into which social movements must enter" (p. 115). Instead, structures and institutions are dynamic and can themselves be "changed actors struggling in the universe of political discourse," a crucial dimension of which is the activity of self-naming (p. 115).

So, what does all this tell us about the Québécois movement? On the one hand, it tells us that culture was an integral, perhaps indispensable, element of the movement. It also tells us that culture, expressed through a self-defined collective identity, can create new openings in the political opportunity structure. On the other hand, it tells us that, although cultural politics can help "make" opportunities in the prevailing political structure, it can also, unintentionally, close off future opportunities. Jenson argued that this, in fact, happened to the Québécois movement. The success of the Québécois movement, for example, invited other groups to press their claims for representation and collective rights as well. Chief among these groups were the aboriginal peoples, who insisted that they be recognized as nations within Canada. Moreover, as Jenson explained it, "they learned from the nationalists in Quebec that claims to nation building and national identity were powerful tools in the Canadian universe of political discourse" (p. 119). In "naming" themselves, the aboriginal groups created their own opportunities in the political opportunity structure and were eventually included in constitutional negotiations over the distribution of political power in Canada. The expansion of the constitutional agenda, however, was a direct blow to the Québécois nationalists, who had always claimed that their needs took precedence over the concerns of any other group (p. 117). Ironically, though, it was their own success at transforming political discourse, which opened up the political opportunity structure, that led to a diminution of their power. In this regard, too, we can see how context matters.

The Three Perspectives and the Arab Spring

As we have suggested throughout this chapter, none of the three perspectives provides, on its own, a complete explanation for the emergence and development of many or most social movements. To complete this chapter, then, it would be useful to take a look at another social movement—the Arab Spring—this time from a more comprehensive perspective. Of course, Chapter 6 (on democracy) also had a somewhat extensive discussion of the Arab Spring, but, in a number of ways, it is a more useful focus on analysis here. This is true, in part, because only a single one of the Arab Spring countries—Tunisia—has thus far been able to democratize in a sustained manner (as of January 2016). This chapter, of course, is not concerned with democratization per se; for this reason, the Arab Spring gives us a lot of material to study, as it was composed of a range of separate social movements. It is also very useful to look at the Arab Spring again, for present purposes, because the conditions that gave rise to it were, to put it very simply (if not tritely), highly complex. Even a cursory glance suggests that no single theoretical perspective is capable of providing a full or adequate explanation of that complexity.

On the last point, it is worth repeating that the Arab Spring was composed of many separate movements in a range of countries. For the comparativists, that is both a hindrance and a benefit. On the one hand, it makes analysis more difficult because there is so much more (empirical) material to cover. On the other hand, the existence of multiple, related movements allows us to more easily make use of comparative analysis. In the Arab Spring, some movements generated massive public participation and support and succeeded in removing long-ruling dictatorial leaders from power (Tunisia, Egypt, and Yemen), while other movements led to only minor changes (Kuwait, Morocco, Jordan, and Oman). Still others devolved into internecine civil war (Libya and Syria; in the case of Libya, the government of Muammar Qaddafi was overthrown in August 2011, while in Syria the fighting was still going strong at the beginning of 2016, more than four years after it started). It is also significant that, in a few places in the Middle East and North Africa, an antigovernment *social movement* (as opposed to sporadic and unorganized protests) never clearly emerged; this was the case in Saudi Arabia and the United Arab Emirates. In short, the Arab Spring presents researchers with a diversity of outcomes (i.e., variance on the dependent variable), which is, recall, a necessary condition for comparisons based on the most similar systems principle. The researcher should not merely assume, however, that MENA countries are all "most similar systems," but given geographic, cultural, demographic, economic, and other similarities, there are likely more than a handful of potentially good MSS comparisons. In addition, the diversity of the Arab Spring cases provides a good foundation for the application of the method of agreement—that is, the diversity of outcomes in the region allows analysts to look for commonalities in both "positive" and "negative" cases. (Recall that the discussion of the MoA in Chapter 2 used the Arab Spring as an example.)

Admittedly, in the analysis that follows, we will not be able to provide complete answers, but that would be impossible in a short section. Rather, the intent is to provide a basic framework for you to begin to develop your own answers. (We also encourage you to do additional reading; one good place to start is the book *The Arab Uprisings Explained: New Contentious Politics in the Middle East* [2014], edited by Marc Lynch.) This said, a little background on the Arab Spring would be helpful.

Brief Background on the Arab Spring

The Arab Spring began in Tunisia when Tarek Mohammed Bouazizi, discussed briefly in Chapter 6, set himself on fire outside the municipal headquarters building in the town of Sidi Bouzid on December 17, 2010. That day, he had gone to the same building to complain to local officials after Faida Hamday, a council inspector, confiscated his unlicensed vegetable cart and goods. He was turned away. That rejection spurred his act of self-immolation. Not surprisingly, there was much more behind Bouazizi's desperate act of suicide. Bouazizi, who was twenty-six years old at the time, was the breadwinner for his family of eight, and the cart represented his sole means of earning a living. Bouazizi had also been subject to police harassment before. Indeed, only six months prior to his death, he was fined 400 dinars ($280), roughly equivalent of two months' earnings. On the day of Bouazizi's death, moreover, Hamday purportedly "slapped him and, with the help of her colleagues, forced him to the ground" (Ryan 2011): that humiliating treatment reinforced the deep resentment and profound frustration that Bouazizi no doubt felt. Bouazizi's act of self-immolation, though, was not unique: at the time, self-immolation had become a relatively common act in Tunisia, accounting for 15 percent of all burn cases in Tunis hospitals; in addition, in the six months following Bouazizi's death, more than a hundred Tunisians set themselves on fire, and "scores more around the Arab world, from Morocco to Saudi Arabia and Iraq, had also set themselves on fire" (Addala and Spencer 2015). Still, for whatever reason, it was Bouazizi's act of self-immolation—witnessed by friends and passersby—that became the catalyst for a large-scale uprising in Tunisia, and for the Arab Spring more widely.

The Arab Spring, in general, as Marc Lynch put it, "*was massive,* incorporating sectors of society that had not previously joined protests and linking together protest sectors that had previously remained isolated from one another" (2014, p. 7, emphasis in original). Even more:

> It was *surprising,* often shocking both the regimes and the protest organizers themselves. It was *fast,* with protests going from minimal to overwhelming national convulsions seemingly overnight. They were often (though not always) driven by new protest *actors,* a self-conscious "youth" category of social action that used distinctive means (social media, SMS [i.e., texting], popular coordinating committees) to challenge the rules and red lines of traditional political engagement. In addition, they mobilized previously non-mobilized sectors into the streets, particularly the urban middle class, which had previously remained sullenly aloof from political protest. (p. 7, emphasis in original)

As noted earlier, though, the outcomes varied across MENA. Thus, while a few dictators lost power with relatively little bloodshed, others fought back with brutal force. In Libya, Qaddafi "unleashed the full force of his army on peaceful protestors, triggering a virtually unprecedented international military intervention to prevent a slaughter of rebels in the city of Benghazi" (Lynch 2014, p. 1). Ultimately, Qaddafi was captured while hiding in a culvert, and unceremoniously killed by rebel fighters. In the tiny island state of Bahrain, by contrast, the government successfully cracked down on the movement using overwhelming military force, and then by systematically purging political opponents. In other places, a compromise of sorts was reached. In Morocco, for instance, the king offered limited, preemptive concessions, while Saudi rulers combined harsh repression with lavish public spending designed to co-opt political opponents (Lynch 2014).

Explaining the Arab Spring

So, how can the Arab Spring be explained? Admittedly, this is hardly a question we can satisfactorily answer in a short section, but we can provide some important ideas. We will begin by considering the question from the rational choice perspective. In resource mobilization theory, recall, the availability of resources increases the opportunity for collective action to take place. To be effective, however, resources have to be organized or managed. That requires both organizational capacity (the SMO) and leadership. In the case of MENA, a number of scholars have pointed to one particularly important resource: social or digital media (e.g., Facebook, Twitter, YouTube, blogs). Social media, as Philip Howard and colleagues (2011) demonstrated, was used heavily to conduct political conversations, to spread democratic ideas across and within borders, and to organize protests. The widespread availability and easy accessibility to social media is particularly important in authoritarian regimes, which typically control traditional sources of mass media, and which are more willing to use coercive measures to quell dissent (compared to democratic regimes). The emergence of social media, then, perhaps for the first time in many MENA countries, allowed for latent networks of political opponents and other dissatisfied citizens to organize effectively and in a sustained manner.

On this last point, it is worth emphasizing that public protests and smaller-scale social movements had been going on in several MENA countries, most notably Egypt, well before the beginning of the Arab Spring. None of these earlier movements, however, were enough to undermine the governments in power. Nonetheless, they contributed to the establishment or reinforcement of social networks and helped to develop community leaders and activists, all of which were important for subsequent social mobilization. Where the prior basis for social mobilization was strongest, as in Tunisia and Egypt, the Arab Spring movements tended to be strongest. In areas where social networks were weakest, by contrast—say, Saudi Arabia and Bahrain—the Arab Spring seemed to have little effect.

The availability of resources and latent organizational capacity, however, are only part of the equation according to resource mobilization theory. A third critical component is effective leadership. On this point, though, some scholars have pointed out that the Arab Spring was a largely leaderless movement (Sutherland, Land, and Böhm 2014). While there is certainly truth to that observation, one can also argue that the Arab Spring saw many issue entrepreneurs at work: prominent individuals who served to rally and mobilize protestors. In Egypt, for example, a former police officer by the name of Omar Afifi helped to coordinate the protest efforts while sitting at his desk in Washington, D.C. Importantly, he used Skype, Facebook, Twitter, and his cell phone to communicate with protestors in Egypt (Presutti 2011). Afifi also wrote a book instructing ordinary citizens how to avoid police abuse or, more bluntly, to how avoid getting "hit on the back of the head" (Noha 2008). Another prominent individual is Rami Nakhle, also known by his pseudonym Malath Aumran. Nakhle is a Syrian pro-democracy activist who also used Skype, Twitter, and Facebook, in the earlier stages of the Syrian uprising, to raise awareness about the way Syrian security forces were mistreating demonstrators. His posts were critical in ensuring that the Western media knew what was happening in Syria.

There were likely dozens if not hundreds (or more) of issue entrepreneurs involved in the various movements throughout MENA during the Arab Spring. Significantly, though, these entrepreneurs, for the most part, failed (or more accurately, did not even attempt) to create social movement *organizations.* Many worked as individuals or as part of a relatively small team; there was a major effort to connect with and mobilize others, but not in a manner that built a cohesive organization. Yet, surprisingly perhaps, some were quite effective—even those operating from thousands of miles away. Were these issue entrepreneurs rational actors hoping to derive a personal benefit for their "leadership"? It is certainly possible, but it is also possible that there were other, equally important factors at play. We will return to this issue later, but there is another question that must be addressed. Earlier, we noted that, *prior* to the Arab Spring, there had been many antigovernment protests—none of which succeeded in toppling a government—in various countries throughout the region. Why did these previous protests fail? Why did large-scale and sustained social movements fail to materialize? One possible answer is simply that Facebook, Twitter, and Skype were still relatively new technologies—all three were introduced around 2005–2006. But it is fairly clear that technology is not sufficient. If it were, it is likely that Egypt would be a democracy today. Instead, after Hosni Mubarak was overthrown in 2011, the country returned to authoritarian rule after a very short-lived "flirtation" with democracy: in 2013 the democratically elected president of Egypt, Mohammed Morsi, was removed from power by the military through a coup. The prevalence of social media obviously did not prevent the return to authoritarianism, nor has it had much impact in Egypt since 2013. It is also worth emphasizing that there are likely no fewer issue entrepreneurs in Egypt in 2016 than there were in 2010–2011.

None of what we've just said is meant to imply that social media (as a resource) and issue entrepreneurs were unimportant in the Arab Spring. They almost certainly played a key role, but we need to consider the larger political context within which those roles were played. It is on this point that we need to consider the political opportunity structure. As we learned earlier in the chapter, mass mobilization is often, if not always, contingent upon "opportunities" that decrease the cost of collective action, on the one hand, and, especially in authoritarian regimes, increase the costs of repression on the other hand. The first lesson in this view is simple: the structural opportunities for political change were not equal across MENA. In this regard, it is no surprise that some movements failed to bring about change, while others did so with relative ease. The critical variable, perhaps, was the unity of the ruling elite at the time the Arab Spring unfolded. As Eitan Alimi and David Meyer noted:

> The willingness of presumed supporters of the challenged regime to defect and throw their support to elements of the challenging coalition—or at least to refuse to cooperate in violent repression—was one critical factor in shaping these political outcomes. And of course, each event affects the constellation of possibilities in the future: as the numbers and diversity in the streets grew, repression would be more difficult and costly; as the visibility of regime defectors increased, more diverse elements in society saw their interests served by throwing in with the protestors. (2011, p. 477)

In the cases of Tunisia and Egypt, the unity of the elite proved to be quite fragile. As protest demonstrations began to spread throughout Tunisia, for example, President Zine El Abidine Ben Ali called on the police and national guard to quell the uprising. The protestors were violently suppressed and arrested en masse. Still, the movement against the government persisted. President Ben Ali then announced on national television that he would step down at the end of his term (which was in 2014). The following day, however, Ben Ali declared a state of emergency and called on the military to help support the police and national guard (Hanlon 2012, p. 2). To Ben Ali's surprise, General Rachid Ammar, chief of staff of the army, refused "to fire on the demonstrators" and "left Ben Ali with no means to forcibly quash the demonstrations, and he fled to Saudi Arabia that same day" (Hanlon 2012, p. 2). In Egypt, the process unfolded in much the same way, except that the military went one step further: not only did the army decide that it "would not fire on the protesters, [but also] the Supreme Council of the Armed Forces staged a coup d'état that removed Mubarak from power" (Galvin 2015, p. 68).

The fall of the Ben Ali government, more generally, shifted the political opportunity structure throughout MENA. For citizens, it signaled the basic fact that, through collective mobilization, they had the power to effectively challenge long-standing authoritarian regimes. Thus, hundreds of thousands and even millions of citizens across the region, perhaps for the first time, grew emboldened at the possibility that regime change was possible. For governments, the fall of the Ben Ali government signaled—also for the first time—their vulnerability to popular unrest. This helps to explain why, in many countries where protests broke out, the governments offered economic concessions and promised political reforms; this was the case, for example, in Algeria, Jordan, Oman, Bahrain, Morocco, and Saudi Arabia. In thinking about the political context (or opportunity structure), moreover, it is equally important to consider the larger "international structure of political alliances, based on interests, values, norms, or prejudices" (Alimi and Meyer 2011, p. 477). Since the end of the Cold War—a structure, it is important to emphasize, that played an instrumental role in creating and embedding authoritarian regimes throughout the world—factors and processes at the international level have, on balance, created more opportunities for social movements to emerge, especially in authoritarian systems. The dynamics of the international or global structure are too complex to cover here; suffice it to say, then, that authoritarian governments, in general, have been less likely to find support from major international powers (especially the United States and the European Union) over the past two decades than at any other time in the postwar era. There are, of course, exceptions—including, most prominently, Saudi Arabia—but for the most part, social movement activists can often count on support (or at least not active resistance) from the international community, governments, nongovernmental organizations, international organizations, and foreign citizens.

The political opportunity approach, it is fair to say, explains key elements of the Arab Spring. Yet, even combining these insights with equally important insights from resource mobilization theory, the dynamics of the

Arab Spring are still not entirely clear. To complete our "theoretical puzzle," then, it is important to consider the role that cultural and ideational factors played. Particularly key are the concepts of shared identity and solidarity. As already discussed, though, "new technology" (referring primarily to social media, but also to mobile phones, alternative online news sources such as Al Jazeera, and the Internet more generally) played a central role in the Arab Spring: they were crucial resources that had a profound impact on social movement formation. New technology, most simply, made the construction of a widely shared identity, both domestically and regionally, possible. Consider on this point that, in MENA, the "number of mobile cellular subscriptions . . . almost tripled from 2006 to the end of 2011, from 126 million to 350 million. As of the end of 2011, mobile cellular penetration in Arab countries . . . [reached] 97 per 100 people, 19 points higher than the world average" (Zuehlke 2012). While pervasive ownership of mobile phones was the physical infrastructure for an interpersonal network, social media made it possible for individuals to broadcast their observations and thoughts to millions of people quickly and easily, and at virtually no cost. In this regard, "social media introduced a novel resource that provided swiftness in receiving and disseminating information; [it] helped to build and strengthen ties among activists; and increased interaction among protesters and between protesters and the rest of the world" (Eltantawy and Wiest 2011, p. 1218). Together, mobile phones and social media made it far easier, to emphasize the basic point, to create a shared identity and forge the solidarity needed to challenge authoritarian regimes.

Phones and social media *alone,* however, do not make a movement. What is said, written, and posted via technology is obviously quite significant, too. Very simply put, people unite—especially against great odds—because of language, albeit only in part. Language itself can create the opportunities needed to build a social movement. On this point, it is important to note that, during the Arab Spring, it was not traditional Islamist, opposition parties, or other organized actors that led the various movements. In Egypt, for example, liberal and civil society voices were the strongest and loudest, and these voices created a cascade of messages about freedom and democracy across MENA (Howard and Hussain 2013). The same was true in Tunisia, where "conversations about liberty, democracy, and revolution on blogs and Twitter often immediately preceded mass protests" (O'Donnell 2011, based on an interview with Philip Howard, professor at the University of Washington). The last point bears repeating: much of the public discussion came *before* the first protests of the Arab Spring. This suggests that the Arab Spring was, to some extent, created by discourse. (There is, as pointed out in Chapter 2, some debate on this point.)

The cultural explanation, however, is more usefully applied when it accounts for the social, political, and economic context in which identity is formed. There are, of course, myriad elements of this larger context, so we will cite a single but important one of these: the emergence of Al Jazeera (literally, "The Peninsula"), a satellite television channel launched in 1996 and based in the tiny oil-rich country of Qatar (the emir of Qatar provided $140 million in capital for the station to get started). The story behind Qatar's funding and hosting of Al Jazeera is complicated (see Bakshian 2012), but it is clear that an editorially independent satellite news organization based in the Middle East could not have existed in the 1970s or 1980s. (In the 1990s, a precursor to Al Jazeera, BBC Arabic Television, was set up, but it almost immediately ran into trouble with its principal financial backer: the Saudi royal family. After an unflattering report aired, the royal family withdrew its funding and the station collapsed [Seib 2005]). Moreover, while originally dismissed by many Westerners as a propaganda tool or "Islamist stalking horse," this was and is not the case. As one commentator, Aram Bakshian (2012), wryly put it, Al Jazeera is a "not-for-Prophet as well as not-for-profit news operation"; indeed, Al Jazeera has proven to be a highly professional and moderate news organization committed, for the most part, to humanistic and democratic values.

The larger point, though, is this: the rise of Al Jazeera helped lay the groundwork for the emergence of the Arab Spring. As Lin Noueihed and Alex Warren explained it:

> For the first time, Arabs were able to watch commentators, activists, and politicians offering conflicting points of view on the news rather than guests carefully selected to cheerlead for the government or, on opposition stations, parrot an incendiary opposition line. . . . Through its controversial political talk shows, the station had, over the years, played a significant role in eroding the cult of personality that Arab dictators had so carefully tried to construct among their domestic populations. (2012, p. 48)

The fact that Al Jazeera is an Arab-run news organization has been an important cultural asset, too: as an Arab organization, it likely had greater credibility than any Western news organization. Al Jazeera's credibility increased with the quality of its reporting, which in turn increased its constituency. It was this credibility and constituency that helped Al Jazeera play a decisive role during the Arab Spring by "linking together disparate national struggles into a coherent narrative of popular Arab protests against both foreign intervention and domestic repression" (Lynch 2012, p. 56).

Conclusion

The foregoing, albeit quite cursory, examination of the Arab Spring is designed to emphasize the utility of rational choice, structural, and cultural approaches in explaining or making sense of social movements. Even more, it is designed to underscore the need for an integrative approach. After all, ᴏvements are complex and seemingly contradictory affairs. They ᴀneous, but also organized. They reflect a significant imbalance in ᴡer, but they also have the potential to fundamentally alter that balance. They provide opportunities for a few individuals to promote their own self-interests, but they also require many thousands more to act in a largely selfless manner. It is fairly clear, in other words, that no one perspective can adequately answer the question "Why collective action?"

I hope, however, that this chapter provides the basis for developing one's own perspective for explaining and understanding social movements, which have long been and remain a vital part of the world in which we all live. Indeed, while some of the other issues discussed in this book may seem far removed from our daily lives (especially for those of us who live in wealthy, capitalist democracies), it is likely that we have encountered social movements at a personal level.

Part 3

The Future of Comparative Politics

9

Globalization and the Study of Comparative Politics

Comparative politics, as we have seen throughout this book, tends to pay close attention to specific times and places. There is, in other words, a bias toward particularity, or in-depth understanding, as opposed to generalization or explanation (the distinction between the goals of understanding and explanation are discussed in Chapter 1). Even in those approaches that ostensibly emphasize general theory over particularity (that is, rational choice and structuralism), the tension between understanding and explanation is strong. Indeed, the ongoing tension between understanding and explanation is one reason, and perhaps the most important one, why the concept of globalization is so important to the field. The reason is clear: "globalization" is typically portrayed as an economically, politically, socially, and culturally homogenizing force. This means that, as individual societies, cultures, and countries are "exposed" to globalization—whether voluntarily or involuntarily—they are compelled to act in a similar, if not identical, manner. Over time (and perhaps after a great deal of conflict, struggle, and violence), this will result, some argue, in a world where every society, every country, and every person will be basically the same. From a certain perspective, we can already see this happening: go to almost any major city in the world today, and you can find many of the same shops, many of the same products, and many of the same services. But globalization means much more than superficial changes in where we shop and what we buy. Benjamin Barber, writing about two decades ago, put it this way:

> Every demarcated national economy and every kind of public good is today vulnerable to the inroads of transnational commerce. Markets abhor frontiers as nature abhors a vacuum. . . . In Europe, Asia, and the Americas . . . markets have already eroded national sovereignty and given birth to a new class of institutions—international banks, trade associations, transnational lobbies like OPEC, world news services like CNN and the BBC, and multinational institutions that lack distinctive national identities. (1996, p. 13)

321

According to Barber, these trends will only intensify and broaden as time goes by. Moreover, the expansion of markets does not just mean far-reaching economic change but also equally profound political, cultural, and social change: a global market creates a global culture based on "MTV, Macintosh, and McDonald's." In this new "McWorld," using Barber's now-famous term, the study of individual countries, societies, and cultures becomes largely irrelevant—or, at best, fodder for historians and anthropologists studying a defunct way of life. Although this is obviously an exaggeration, the basic point is clear: globalization portends a serious erosion of the raison d'être of comparative politics and comparative analysis. That is, if the world truly does become a big McWorld, then there will be very little left to compare and even less reason to compare, since studying one country or society will be pretty much like studying any other country or society. (Recall from Chapter 1 that comparison requires both similarities *and* differences between and among units.) In a world of no meaningful differences, politics and political science will still matter, although it will likely be a politics of the "whole" rather than of the "parts." (See Figure 9.1 for additional discussion of Barber's argument.)

Needless to say, most comparativists are not ready to throw in their towels. Certainly, even though most will concede that globalization is an important force in the world today, most also believe that differences will continue to matter a great deal. James Mittelman put it this way: "Globalization is not flattening civil societies around the world but, rather, *combining with local conditions* in distinctive ways, *accentuating differences,* and spurring a variety of social movements seeking protection from the disruptive

---

Figure 9.1 Benjamin Barber's "McWorld"

Benjamin Barber, it is important to understand, is not an enthusiastic or uncritical proponent of "McWorld." Rather, he sees it as an unremitting and *undiscriminating* juggernaut: the logic of McWorld is simply too strong, too overwhelming to stand up to. Herein lies the danger. According to Barber (1998), McWorld displaces not only reactionary critics—the zealots and fundamentalists of the world—but democratic rivals as well, those who dream of a genuinely internationalized civil society made up of free citizens from many different cultures. As he put it, "McWorld . . . does little for consumer autonomy, less for competition, and nothing at all for the kinds of liberty and pluralism essential to political freedom. But perhaps more dangerous to liberty, McWorld has encroached upon and helped push aside public space. Its greatest victory—and here it has been mightily assisted by the antigovernmental privatizing ideology that has dominated its politics in recent years—has been its contribution to the eradication of civic space" (p. 40).

and polarizing effects of economic liberalism" (1996b, cited in Crawford 2000, p. 69, emphasis added). This is a useful and reasonable perspective. Mittelman is also almost certainly right. Still, the questions remain: How does (and how will) globalization impact the study of comparative politics? Will globalization, for example, require all comparativists to become hyper-structuralists? After all, globalization fits into a structural framework quite nicely, even ideally. Or will globalization become simply another element in a broader context (and not necessarily the most important one) that needs to be factored into any analysis of domestic politics? Or does the answer depend on the particular circumstances of an individual case or issue?

This chapter will not endeavor to answer these and other pertinent questions in a definitive manner. Rather, like the general approach in this book, my intention is to get you to think about the issue in an open-minded and critical manner. To begin, though, it is important to take another look at the basic question: What is globalization? The concept is not at all clear-cut. At a minimum, therefore, we need to establish a common basis of understanding, or else we risk not talking about the same phenomenon. This does not mean that everyone must agree on a single definition, only that we have a common point of reference. Rather than merely repeat what was already covered, however, we will consider a few additional, but important, aspects of defining globalization.

What Is Globalization?

Most scholars who study globalization agree that it is a multidimensional concept. Ulrich Beck, for example, argued that the economic, social, cultural, and other dimensions of this process are, it is important to recognize, concrete processes "through which sovereign national states are criss-crossed and undermined by transnational actors with varying prospects of power, orientations, identities and networks" (2000, p. 11). It would be wrong to assume, however, that the various processes of globalization—no matter how much of their complexity we detail—are all there is to a comprehensive conceptualization of the term. For, as Beck pointed out, there are other analytically distinct aspects of globalization that are not adequately captured by these various dimensions alone. He identified two additional distinctions, which he called "globality" and "globalism." The first term refers to the "conjuring away of distance." Or, as Beck put it, globality means "that *we have been living for a long time in a world society,* in the sense that the notion of closed spaces has become illusory" (p. 10, emphasis in original). The point to remember is this: globality and globalization are tightly related aspects of a larger whole, but they are *not* identical. There is a good reason why it is important, if not necessary, to maintain this analytical distinction. As Beck explained it, on the one hand, globality is, for the most part, here to stay. That is, the gradual disappearance of closed-off spaces—time-space compression, as other scholars like to say—cannot be reversed, at least barring a catastrophic event that literally destroys most of the world as we know it. On the other hand, globalization (or, more accurately, the globalizing process) *is* reversible; at least, globalization is not an inexorable, impossible-to-manage, and overwhelming force majeure. Rather, it is a multitude of "various autonomous logics . . . the logics of ecology, culture, economics, politics and civil society [that] exist side by side and cannot be reduced or collapsed into one another" (p. 11). Each logic, moreover, can be independently "decoded" or understood, and through this understanding, Beck argued, it is possible to envision and create alternative paths or directions. What this means, in more understandable terms, is that the various globalizing processes are subject to human agency—or to political action. Indeed, Beck suggested that globalizing processes can move or unfold in very different ways, all depending on the (political) actions—or inactions—that people take or are *able* to take. Breaking "globalization" down into separate logics, moreover, provides a better way of seeing how it may not be as homogenizing a force as it is often portrayed to be.

The third analytical distinction that Beck made, and one that is more controversial than the other two, is "globalism." By this he meant "the view that the world market eliminates or supplants political action—that is, the *ideology* of rule by world market, the ideology of **neoliberalism**" (p. 9, emphasis added). This is a critical point, in large part because most people, when they hear the word "globalization," do not think of it as an ideology at all—Marxism and even capitalism might be ideologies, but not globalization. If we take a moment to reflect, however, Beck's point is not all that difficult to see. Consider, for example, the definition of ideology from the 1988 edition of the *Oxford Paperback Encyclopedia:*

> A political belief-system that both explains the world as it currently is and suggests how it should be changed. . . . Some have sought to reserve the term for political outlooks that are seen as rigid and extreme in contrast to those that are more pragmatic and moderate. It seems better, however, to recognize the pervasiveness of ideology as the means by which people order their perceptions of the social world, whether or not they consciously subscribe to a political creed.

Underlying most popular portrayals of globalization is the notion, although often only implied, that it is a technological/economic process leading toward the eventual creation of a global market, where people will be free not only to exchange goods and services but also to participate in an environment of unlimited individual choice, prosperity, and genuine democracy. In this view, markets are *inherently* democratic, voluntary (that is, noncoercive), and apolitical. The unfolding of this process, moreover, is generally portrayed as a simple but hard "fact of life," where those who express any doubt, opposition, or resistance are seen as either naive or stupid or both.[1] Opponents of globalization are naive or stupid, so the thinking goes, because they just "don't get it"—that is, they fail to understand that globalization is both inevitable *and* beneficial. In this way, then, the popular understanding of globalization clearly tells us how the world currently is and how it will be. But how is this a political belief system? After all, isn't it possible that globalization *is* an inevitable and ultimately beneficial process? On this question, unfortunately, there is far less agreement. Suffice it to say, therefore, that Beck offered one of many competing perspectives (one that I support).

With this caveat in mind, Beck contended that globalism is a political belief system in that it assiduously promotes a particular view of politics based on the idea that the market is essentially the solution to all our problems. We must therefore all put our faith in the market, because the "market knows best." This means, most tellingly, that nonmarket actors—states, churches, trade unions, nongovernmental organizations, and civil society more generally—need to either accept and adapt to this "new reality" or get out of the way. This is a political belief system par excellence. The real keys to understanding globalization as an ideology, however, are to recognize, for one thing, that the market is not simply an abstraction where, if left alone (by nonmarket actors), the forces of supply and demand will *always* ensure an optimal (and socially acceptable) distribution of scarce economic resources. A second thing is that markets are populated not by millions of equally empowered individuals and companies but by some very large, extremely rich, and disproportionately powerful corporate actors. In this critical view, then, the "marketization of politics" means the empowerment of corporate actors in general and of large, rich, and transnational corporate actors in particular.

In Chapter 1, I discussed an admittedly crude measurement of corporate power—the sheer economic size and muscle of Wal-Mart compared to a number of countries and all of the individual actors that exist within their borders. In fact, if Wal-Mart were a country, it would be more than twice as large as Ireland or almost three times the size New Zealand (comparing total revenue to GDP; see Figure 1.3). While such a comparison is admittedly problematic, the key point is this: as an ideology, globalization is a political belief system designed to build acceptance of a world where corporate decisionmaking and interests are given precedence over all other types of decisionmaking and all other interests. As an ideology, however, globalization is at least partly an intersubjective (as opposed to a strictly objective) phenomenon. This means, in turn, that globalization, or globalism, can unfold and develop in a number of divergent ways depending on the interests and concerns of people. Moreover, according to Beck, neoliberal globalization is only one form of globalism, although it is, by far, the most dominant form. There are also competing globalisms that confront, undermine, and interact in a variety of ways, all of which make globalization a more problematic process than it may appear to be on the surface.

To sum up thus far: globalization is an important concept. It is important whether one agrees that it signifies a fundamental change in the world today or whether one believes that it is nothing new. For even if globalization is not entirely new—that is, if it reflects centuries-old processes of (uneven) integration, incorporation, or expansion—it is virtually undeniable that these processes (of integration, incorporation, and expansion) are taking place today and that they are having a meaningful impact on the world in which we live. In this sense, perhaps the one point on which almost everyone can agree is simply this: the world is more closely bound together—spatially and temporally—in more ways and in more areas (with both positive and negative results) than ever before. Moreover, most might also agree that the *pace* of change has been faster and the *scope* of change more extensive than at other times in history. Given all this, it is not difficult to understand why more and more observers—whether of a progressive, radical, or conservative persuasion—also agree that globalization is a dialectical process of homogenization *and* differentiation.

Implications of Globalization in Comparative Politics

The foregoing discussion of globalization is, I readily admit, clearly one designed to leave plenty of space for the "survival" of comparative politics as a distinct field of study. Still, we should not gloss over or simply dismiss the potentially profound impact that globalization may have on the study of comparative politics. To repeat: as time and space become more and more compressed and as globalizing processes create a more homogenized world—economically, politically, socially, and culturally—differences among countries and societies, on the surface at least, will become less pronounced and perhaps less meaningful. Consider, too, that in just the past several decades—a period of intense globalization—we have witnessed a worldwide breakdown in the legitimacy of authoritarianism, dictatorship, and political repression and a corresponding rise of a global and widely shared discourse on human rights, democracy, and individual freedom. In a similar vein, consider the massive movement away from centrally planned or socialist economies to economies based on the (universal?) principles of capitalism and free markets. *If* all these trends continue, as Benjamin Barber and many others believe they will, we will see not only a continuing erosion of differences among countries, societies, and cultures but also the emergence of a single or borderless world where spatial (and to a lesser extent, temporal) barriers to the cross-border movement of information, capital, ideas, values, people, and goods will have all but disappeared and where regions and individual countries will have shed their cultural parochialisms for more global orientations.

At this point, some might argue, the dialectical process of homogenization and differentiation will have reached its endpoint. Or, in the now immortal words of Francis Fukuyama ([1989] 1999), we will have reached "the end of history."

In the meantime, of course, differences will still matter, and they will matter a great deal. Indeed, it is possible, if not likely, that tens of thousands if not millions of lives will be lost as the forces of differentiation attempt to stave off the inevitable. But this is exactly the point to some: ultimately, the forces of differentiation are doomed to failure. To those who subscribe to this "story of globalization," then, comparative politics as a distinct field of study would also seem to be doomed (although it may be many decades before the field becomes completely irrelevant).

Globalization and Heterogeneity

As I have already suggested, however, this particular story is based on a one-dimensional and (probably) overdetermined conception of globalization. The more analytically distinct and multidimensional conception of globalization just discussed, conversely, allows us to see that comparative politics will likely remain a relevant and dynamic field for a long, long time. Not only is the world still quite heterogeneous, but also, in the interactive or dialectical process of homogenization and differentiation, *new forms* of heterogeneity or difference are likely to emerge. These, in turn, may be transformed into something else, and into something else again and again. The point is clear: even as the world becomes more similar in some ways, it becomes more different in other, often unanticipated ways. As it becomes more democratic, for instance, democracy itself is likely to take more and more different forms. So, too, with capitalism, with nationalism, with environmentalism, or with any other symbol or force of homogeneity. On this point, consider this simple observation by Jeffrey Kopstein and Mark Lichbach: "The source of globalization, the West, is also frequently the source of the challenges to it: Liberalism, democracy, **fascism**, and socialism, for example, are all Western innovations" (2000, pp. 7–8).

The Global Context

So what does all this mean? At a minimum, it means that comparative politics is clearly not dying as a field of study. But it also means that comparative politics, or comparativists, must pay increasingly serious attention to the global context within which all political, economic, social, and cultural change takes place. Comparativists, of course, have been doing this for a long time—long before the idea of globalization was even around. Still, a great deal of previous research in comparative politics had a tendency to take the global (and international) context for granted, which means that it was generally treated implicitly or as a part of the background. Still other research has, in effect, treated domestic units as self-contained entities, where "outside" forces were considered largely, or at least analytically, separate. In future research, either type of approach will become less and less viable. From now on, in other words, comparativists—including students new to the study of comparative politics—will need to think explicitly, rigorously, and systematically about the *interrelationship* between the global context and local conditions. This means, too, cultivating an understanding that globalization is not, as I have repeatedly stressed, a monolithic, primarily technological-economic force but a highly diverse and contradictory (or dialectical) force that includes nonmaterial (for example, ideological) as well as material processes.

This position, I should stress, would probably not be embraced by all comparativists. Still, as Martha Finnemore and Kathryn Sikkink put it, "the processes of globalization have made even the most passionate country specialists aware of the increasing influence of international factors, both material and ideational, on domestic politics around the globe. Comparativists are becoming increasingly attentive to the interpenetration of international affairs and domestic politics" (2001, p. 411). One concrete example of this, the authors pointed out, is the tendency for researchers interested in social movements to be

> attentive not only to domestic social movements but also to transnational movements and to the linkages between domestic and transnational movements. Social movement theorists are increasingly aware that social movements operate in both a domestic and an international environment; they speak of "multi-layered" opportunity structures including a "supranational" layer, or a "multi-level polity," or highlight how international pressures influence domestic opportunity structures. (p. 411)

The main warning here, to repeat, is that comparativists be sensitive to and keenly aware of the potential significance of globalizing forces and processes in their analyses. This does *not* mean, however, that globalizing forces and processes will always or necessarily be at the center of the analysis. It is certainly possible that they may not be. In other words, how important globalization is in any situation will still depend on the circumstances of the individual case or issue under study. On some issues and in certain places, careful analysis may show that global and international forces have played, at best, a marginal role. On other issues and in different places (or sometimes on the same issue in different places), global and international forces may prove to be absolutely central. In all cases, however, it would be dangerous to simply assume that globalization is irrelevant.

Globalization and the Three Research Traditions

Now that we have discussed the connection between globalization and the study of comparative politics in very general terms, it would be useful to ask ourselves: How can a *beginning* comparativist think more explicitly, rigorously, and systematically about the interrelationship between the global context and local conditions? Not surprisingly, there is no simple, step-by-step way to answer this question. We can, however, use the same general framework we have been using throughout this book to help develop a useful approach. That is, in thinking about how local conditions both shape and are shaped by the global context, we need to consider this interrelationship from the perspective of rationality, culture, and structure.

Rational Choice in a Global Context

Globalization does not affect the basic premises of rational choice. Globalization can certainly have a profound impact, however, on the *environment* in which strategic calculations are made. At times, the impact of globalization on the environment of strategic calculation is obvious, but often the impact is likely to be quite subtle and complex. Consider, for example, how economic globalization—as many scholars argue—has fundamentally changed the strategic environment for a whole range of actors, from ordinary workers to entire nation-states. Certain aspects of this changed environment are easy enough to discern—for example, the transborder expansion of production and the increasing spatial and temporal mobility of capital. From the standpoint of rational choice, then, the question becomes how these processes or changes impact the strategic calculations made by certain actors. This is not difficult to discover. For example, beginning in the early 1990s, the American Federation of Labor–Congress of Industrial Organizations (AFL-CIO) and many smaller US labor unions put their support behind a project called the Coalition of Justice in the Maquiladoras. The idea behind this project was to improve working conditions (via a campaign for a corporate code of conduct) for Mexican workers employed in the maquiladoras along the United States–Mexico border. On the surface, this would seem to be a strange event—after all, for decades, US unions had been, if anything, vehemently antiforeign and almost totally unconcerned with the conditions facing workers outside of the United States. Yet to a rational choice researcher, the source for this turnabout is quite simple: economic *constraints* created by economic globalization. More specifically, the ongoing—and seemingly irreversible—trend toward the internationalization or globalization of production made it clear to US unions that it was in their economic interests to pursue cross-border alliances with foreign workers *and* with groups that support those workers. This also explains why, in supporting the Coalition of Justice in the Maquiladoras, the AFL-CIO and affiliated unions formed working relationships with dozens of religious and community-based organizations, the Canadian Auto Workers, and even the radical and anti–AFL-CIO United Electrical Workers (which had long been a pariah in top AFL-CIO circles [Moody 1997, pp. 239–242]).

The same logic underlies a series of loosely connected protests—and broad-based social movements—beginning in the late 1990s. The most well known of these was the "Battle in Seattle," a major protest timed to coincide with the 1999 **World Trade Organization** (WTO) Ministerial Conference. In this and other protests, the target was ostensibly globalization, although it is more accurate to say that the target was global neoliberalism. The WTO meeting was chosen because the WTO, along with the IMF and the World Bank, are generally considered to be the primary mechanism through which neoliberal economic policies are embedded in countries around the world, as well as in the global economic system itself. While the dynamics of the antiglobalization movement are extremely complicated, for present purposes there is one point to highlight: the movement, in general, made for a long list of "strange bedfellows," including the Teamsters, the National Lawyers Guild, the Ruckus Society, the Sierra Club, the Zapatistas, Friends of the Earth, the AFL-CIO, South Korean labor activists, and so on. The odd conglomeration of protestors was puzzling. What possibly could bind them together? Of course, understanding the dramatically changed strategic environment provides us with a ready-made explanation.

As I said, however, the changes to the strategic environment wrought by globalizing processes are not always going to be obvious and easy to discern. Yet if the researcher stays sharply focused on the key tenet of rationalist approaches (that is, that individual actions are motivated by self-interested behavior or determined by a particular set of preferences), eventually that researcher will be "rewarded." On this point, let us consider another real-world example: **anarchy** and brutal violence in the sub-Saharan African countries of Angola, Sudan, Sierra Leone, Liberia, Somalia, and Rwanda—an issue that I touched on in Chapters 2 and 7. On the surface, it would seem hard to connect either rationality or globalization to the "anarchic violence" in what many people consider to be the least-globalized region of the world. Looking a little below the surface, however, some possibilities become immediately apparent. William Reno (1995, cited in Hoogvelt 1997), for instance, argued that economic "globalization"—specifically, the imposition of neoliberal economic reforms on many weak states in Africa—has led to the disintegration of state-civil relations, which in turn has created the basis for anarchy and immense bloodshed in a number of countries. In particular, Reno argued that neoliberal reforms—pushed by the international financial institutions and leading Western governments—have seriously undermined, if not destroyed, the one basis for relative peace in these countries, namely the patrimonial state.

In the patrimonial state, according to Reno, leaders use the state's resources to "buy off" the opposition. This is necessary because, following the end of colonialism, there were few other bases of authority or legitimacy. In addition, fledgling state leaders needed a way to counterbalance formidable coalitions of tribal-based "strongmen." (In this regard, the "patrimonial state" itself can be explained easily via a rational choice framework.) This particular state form, unfortunately, is inherently "corrupt" and inefficient, at least from an economic standpoint. Thus, when these African countries began to experience serious economic difficulties, the first target of neoliberal reformers (that is, of the IMF and the World Bank) was the corrupt and inefficient state apparatus. In attacking the patrimonial state, however, the IMF and World Bank did nothing to replace, much less institutionalize, an alternative form of centralized authority. As a result, any semblance of central authority collapsed in these countries.

With the collapse of a central authority, the strategic environment changes considerably. Moreover, the collapse of central authority in an economy with few prospects makes "anarchic violence" a far more understandable phenomenon. Reno noted that in Sierra Leone "much recent fighting, especially its territorial spread, is directly related to the elimination of opportunities for powerful strongmen under 'reform' [imposed by the IMF] and the efforts of these strongmen to strike out on their own for *personal gain*" (cited in Hoogvelt 1997, p. 176, emphasis added). And what of ordinary civilians? Why do they engage in brutal, seemingly senseless violence? According to Paul Richards, the reason is clear: "They [primarily teenage fighters in Sierra Leone] see their violence not as anarchic bickering over scraps, but [as] a life-and-death struggle against a political elite pursuing global riches at the expense of domestic improvement. . . . If rebels burn the UN compound it is because the UN is full of successful educated West Africans who have abandoned their countries (so the fighters believe)." Or, in the words of one teenage fighter, "Everybody just has to fight for themselves" (1999, p. 17). They need to fight for themselves, I might note, because fighting is one of the few ways to pursue their self-interests. As Richards pointed out, "Many young combatants report they took up arms as a substitute for non-existent schooling. It was better than nothing. Learning to service a heavy machine gun is access to modern technology of a sort. But they also know war is a zero-sum game" (p. 17).

It is important to underscore the point that this globally oriented, rationalist interpretation of the violence in sub-Saharan Africa does not emerge automatically. Instead, it derives from an analytical framework that is explicit with regard to assumptions (about rationality, for example), systematic with regard to tracing the process by which the global context shapes and is shaped by domestic forces, and rigorous with regard to the matching of theory with evidence. This is not to say that the rationalist perspective on violence in sub-Saharan Africa is necessarily right: from my brief summary earlier, it would be impossible to say this with any certainty. But this is one reason why *comparative analysis* is so important. It is through comparative analysis that one can "test" one's theoretical claims and the assumptions upon which these claims are based.

Globalization and Culture

Culture, as we have learned, is understood from a variety of perspectives. Some comparativists see culture as an unchanging, or at least highly stable, system of beliefs, values, and practices that is passed on, more or less intact, from one generation to the next. Others see culture as a societal resource—which is one way of saying that some cultures are impoverished or backward, whereas others are rich or advanced; or that some cultures are weak or dysfunctional, whereas others are strong and highly adaptive. This second view of culture is often combined with the first to produce a *hierarchy of cultures*—for example, if some cultures are not only weak and dysfunctional but also unchanging, then those cultures are inherently inferior to others. It is possible, therefore, to rank cultures from the "best" to the "worst." In stark contrast to this view, still other comparativists see culture as merely a label for values and commitments generated in the process of making social life happen—that is, "we produce culture as we go" (Richards 1999, p. 17). The importance of this is that "cultures" are not only mutable—that is, capable or subject to change—but also adaptive and highly porous.

Culture and globalization: The traditional view. In the first and second views, the relationship between "culture" and "globalization" is straightforward and could be characterized in the following (albeit simplistic) way. Cultures are like self-contained ships. Those cultures with enough passengers and an able crew will likely continue to survive for some time to come, but almost all are destined to disappear in an era of globalization. This is true because globalization is essentially a project of Western culture—the biggest, most powerful "ship" of them all. Thus, as the forces of globalization continue to expand and intensify, smaller ships (or cultures) will simply be overwhelmed. In this process, of course, some cultures will not go down easily—they may strike out at the dominant culture or retreat even further into themselves. That is, they may become ever more isolated and closed off from the rest of the world (consider North Korea). In an era of *globality,* however, we know this is not possible. The forces of globalization will seep—or, more likely, flood—into these cultures no matter what they do to stop it. To some scholars—especially those who see cultures as part of a global hierarchy—this is both a positive and a negative process. It is positive because, after the "flood" is over, only the "best" culture will survive. Not surprisingly, according to these scholars, the "West is the best" among all the world's cultures: not only will it survive, but it *should* survive (see, for example, Rothkopf 1997).

Conversely, the process can be negative, as I have already suggested, because it will likely lead to pervasive conflict and violence between and among "cultures." This is a prediction made, for example, by Samuel Huntington. In his provocative—and highly criticized—article (and subsequent book published in 1996) "The Clash of Civilizations?" (1993), Huntington asserted that cultures (he uses the term "civilizations") are fundamentally different and that these differences "will not soon disappear" (1996, p. 70). And although cultural differences do not have to lead to conflict, Huntington argued that globality and globalizing processes make the "clash of civilizations" increasingly likely. In particular, he argued, first, that because the world is "becoming a smaller place" (that is, globality), people are more likely to become aware of cultural differences, which in turn "invigorates differences and animosities stretching or thought to stretch back deep into history" (p. 70). Second, he contended that because economic globalization is weakening the nation-state as a source of identity, cultural (as opposed to national) identities will most likely fill the void. This reinforces the first factor and when combined with a number of other processes that Huntington identified—including Western dominance and increasing economic regionalism—means that a violent clash of civilizations is almost inevitable. Huntington and his supporters would probably point to 9/11 and the string of terroristic violence since then as significant "proof" of this thesis, for the attacks were carried out not simply by an isolated group of anti-American fanatics but by a group representing the civilization of Islam against the symbol of Western civilization.

Problems and issues with the traditional view. This is not the place to engage in a detailed critique of specific arguments, but it would be useful to note that those who subscribe to the preceding views tend to look at culture from an extreme distance. That is, they tend to make broad generalizations not only about cultures but also about how cultures shape people's thinking, sense of identity, and behavior—for example, Confucianism makes all Chinese think and act basically the same; it makes them all, in short, Chinese; Islam does the same to Muslims (no matter where they live); and so on. Looking at a culture from an extreme distance also encourages the observer to miss real and basic intracivilization differences. Not all Muslims, for example, are alike, and not all Muslims like each other; as Fouad Ajami succinctly put it, "The world of Islam divides and subdivides" ([1993] 1999, p. 100). These divisions and subdivisions, Ajami and others might argue, are no less real and no less basic than the divisions between "civilizations." Finally, looking at a culture from a distance means that the subtler (but not always less important) aspects of the interplay between cultural values and identities, on the one hand, and globalizing processes and global identities, on the other hand, will likely be missed.

Needless to say, looking at culture from afar, especially while imputing to it causal powers, is not something I would recommend. I would not recommend it, in large part, because far-off observers of culture may only be observing what they *think* exists, rather than what actually does. They cannot be sure, because they never do the on-the-ground research necessary to find out. This is not to say, however, that observers who get "up-close and personal" are immune from making mistakes. They are not. On this point, let me return briefly to the issue of "anarchic violence," a subject about which one journalist, Robert Kaplan, has written a great deal. Looking at Sierra Leone, Kaplan argued that the cause of violence there is simple: a "weak" culture unable to withstand the pressures of rapid urbanization and population growth. Kaplan quoted approvingly from a West African "friend" (an unidentified government official):

> In the poor quarters of Arab North Africa, there is much less crime, because Islam provides a social anchor: of education and indoctrination. Here in West Africa we have a lot of superficial Islam and superficial Christianity. Western religion is undermined by animist beliefs not suitable to a moral society, because they are based on irrational spirit power. Here spirits are used to wreak vengeance by one person against another, or one group against another. (1994, p. 46)

This all sounds fine until Kaplan finds a country that does not quite fit his (theoretical) vision of the world: Cambodia. Cambodia is neither overpopulated nor "culturally backward"; indeed, it has an ancient and long-admired cultural heritage. But, as Paul Richards (1999) noted, "it is uncannily like anarchic Sierra Leone." Kaplan not only recognized this but readily admitted: "I was light-headed. It was not the fear of crime that I felt or disease, but the deeper writer's fear of having oversimplified something—in this case, the idea of culture, which now seemed like a greater mystery to me than at the beginning of my journey in West Africa" (quoted in Richards 1999, p. 17). Kaplan could have avoided this light-headedness, of course, if he had simply engaged in good comparative analysis from the very beginning.

Culture and globalization: A processual view. This brings us back to the third view of culture and its relationship to "globalization." Not surprisingly, in this view the relationship is less straightforward than in the others. One reason is clear: since culture is understood as "processual" (that is, culture is defined and redefined in the ongoing process of "making social life happen"), its relationship with globalization is likely to be more complex, interactive, and mutually constitutive. In other words, when culture and globalization "collide," it is not like two solid objects hitting one another (where the bigger and heavier object invariably smashes the other). Instead, it is more like multiple streams coming together. Even if one stream is larger and more powerful than the others, not only do they all survive but also the quality of each is altered, sometimes subtly and sometimes dramatically. They may also combine together into a new stream or streams, which can move off in unanticipated directions. I do not want to take this imagery too far, for as James Rosenau usefully pointed out, "metaphoric analysis can extend understanding only so far. It can be suggestive but not incisive, hinting at relationships but not revealing their workings" (1995, p. 48). So it is with the metaphor of two streams. Still, the basic point should be clear: when culture is understood as processual, its relationship and interaction with globalization will not be a simple matter of the latter destroying or completely absorbing the former.

A good way to illustrate this point is to focus on the issue of *identity*, which is not only a central part of cultural approaches but also an issue integrally related to globalization. We have already discussed (in Chapter 3) some reasons identity is central to cultural interpretations of politics, but a brief recap might be useful. As Jeffrey Kopstein and Mark Lichbach explained it:

> Politics is . . . about identity. Although evidence shows that people all over the world often pursue common goals, and thus can be said to share certain interests, people also frequently define what is in their interests differently. Based on particular sets of beliefs and values that we often refer to as culture, they will even define their material interests differently. What people are willing to give their life for, how much hardship they will bear during war, or how many hours on weekends people are willing to work varies across societies. Likewise, the kind of ideas, political language, and even physical demeanor that people expect from their politicians also varies across nations and states. (2000, p. 12)

Identities, moreover, are not usually singular, but multiple: a person who lives in Northern Ireland is not just Irish, but Irish Catholic. A Muslim woman living in Iran is not just an Iranian Muslim, but also a Shiite woman who supports moderate political reform (and therefore voted for Mir-Hossein Mousavi in the 2009 Iranian election). These multiple identities may exist side by side, but they are not always compatible, nor are they necessarily stable. This latter point is key. For although identities can be powerful forces in shaping human (and political) behavior, they can also be manipulated. Consider the case of Iran—that society's particular "Islamic" identity today is not merely a product of a centuries-old devotion to Islam but also very much a product of the late 1970s and 1980s, when a "revolutionary" Islamic regime "pursued an active program of Islamization of culture, media, education, and social conduct" (Tehranian 2000, pp. 362–363). In other words, the now-dominant identity of Iran was consciously created—that is, socially constructed—by those who opposed the secularization of Iranian society. This was not an easy process, nor was it automatic; but once achieved, the Islamization of Iran gave the new fundamentalist leadership tremendous power and authority. (At the same time, we should not expect this newly fashioned cultural identity to stay the same; it, too, will change and is, in fact, in a constant state of change—the turmoil leading up to and following the reelection of Mahmoud Ahmadinejad in June 2009 helps illustrate this.) But what does this have to do with globalization? According to Frank Lechner and John Boli, the connection is fairly clear: "While globalization was by no means the sole cause of Iranian fundamentalism, it helped and provided targets for the Islamic program. Fundamentalists also took a stand on two questions raised by globalization as challenges for any society: What does it mean to live in a world society? What is any one group's place in it? Globalization, in other words, challenges groups and societies to 'identify' themselves" (2000, p. 319).

It is important to understand, as Lechner and Boli also pointed out, that fundamentalism is but one of many possible responses to globalization—which means that the interaction between globalization and local cultures is not likely to lead to a single, undifferentiated "global culture" but to dozens, if not thousands, of "globalized local cultures." It is also important to understand, as already suggested, that globalization in all its various dimensions is also affected by local cultures, which become part of an overall "global flow." Consider this admittedly trite but telling example: globalization was once almost completely defined in terms of the Westernization—even Americanization—of the entire world. Increasingly, however, globalization includes strong influences from Asia. Hello Kitty, feng shui, karaoke, Pokémon, anime, tai chi chuan, shiatsu, yoga, and so on, have all become a significant portion of the global flow. The influences from local cultures, of course, run much deeper than Hello Kitty. Much of the environmental movement today, for example, is based at least partly on "traditional" cultural understandings of the proper relationship between human society and "nature." (Environmentalism, I might note, is itself another type of identity.)

For a student researcher, it is critical to understand, first, the multidimensional and processual nature of culture and, second, the myriad and complex ways in which culture and globalization interact. For if we take seriously the idea that culture affects politics—that it "shapes what people want out of politics, what they are willing to do, and how they define their interests" (Kopstein and Lichbach 2000, p. 13)—then to do otherwise would invite gross oversimplification and misunderstanding. Unfortunately, it is not possible to provide a blueprint for how best to do this. Suffice it to say, therefore, that the methods and principles of comparative analysis provide a solid foundation for research incorporating culture and globalization.

Globalization and Structural Approaches

For many, but not all, historical structuralists the effects of globalization might be summed up in the following manner: "The more things change, the more they remain the same." By this, I mean that for historical structuralists—that is, Marxists and others who view capitalism as part of a still-unfolding historical process—globalization is simply the continuation of "trends that have long accompanied the expansion of capitalism" (Chase-Dunn 1994, p. 97). To be sure, as John Bellamy Foster (2002) succinctly put it, "capitalism has become more extreme." Still, this does not change the fundamental nature of the problem, which is that the capitalist system still "operates" as it always has. Perhaps the most significant novelty of economic globalization is that the expansion and deepening of capitalist integration are more widely recognized—by an increasingly diverse audience—than they have ever been. In this regard, too, concerns or questions about the structural effects and implications of the capitalist system have, in many ways, reached the mainstream, not only in academia but also in the mass media, in the popular consciousness, and even within the institutions of neoliberalism. In the opening pages of its 1996 *World Development Report,* for example, the World Bank quoted approvingly from *The Communist Manifesto* by Marx and Engels: "Constant revolutionizing of production, uninterrupted disturbance of social conditions, everlasting uncertainty and agitation. . . . All fixed, fast frozen relations, with their train of ancient and venerable prejudices, and opinions, are swept away, all new-formed ones become antiquated before they can ossify. *All that is solid melts into air*" (cited in Foster 2002, emphasis added). The quote was used by the World Bank to emphasize how the transition from planned to market economies, as well as the entire thrust of economic globalization, is an inescapable, elemental process, lacking any visible hand behind it (Foster 2002).

This does not mean, of course, that the World Bank has converted to Marxism. It definitely has not. Instead, it means that the World Bank—or rather the elites who ultimately control it—understand that the structural imperatives of globalization can no longer be ignored or hidden from plain view, so to speak. So, rather than cling to an obvious lie, the World Bank and others are attempting to co-opt Marxism and other historical structuralist perspectives. In other words, in recognizing that economic globalization is an ineluctable structural force, the World Bank and others implicitly reject the fundamental liberal view on the centrality of agency. In so doing, however, they are also implying that there is no discernible center of power behind economic globalization and that the processes of globalization are primarily progressive. This, in short, is the ideology of globalization, *globalism.*

Ironically, but not surprisingly, a notable exception to this trend toward greater recognition of the structural imperatives of globalization/global capitalism can be found in the so-called antiglobalization movement. Foster (2002) suggested that this is primarily a reaction (or perhaps overreaction) to the portrayal of globalization as an overwhelming structural force that erases any prospect of agency. As he put it, "the movement against the neoliberal global project has chosen to exaggerate the role of the visible instruments of globalization at the expense of any serious consideration of historical capitalism. Radical dissenters frequently single out the WTO, the IMF, the World Bank and multinational corporations—and even specific corporations like McDonald's—for criticism, while deemphasizing the system, and its seemingly inexorable forces." Both viewpoints, according to Foster, are wrong. The former is wrong because it presents a hyperstructural argument, and the latter is wrong because it overplays (or distorts) the role of agency.

This brings us back, albeit via a somewhat circuitous route, to the main question of this section: How does globalization affect the study of comparative politics from a structural perspective? The basic answer should already be clear: very little. The reasoning is simple: because globalization is "nothing new" (or at least nothing fundamentally new), the study of comparative politics from a structural perspective can remain basically the same. The focus must still be on the structure and logic of global capitalism, on the importance of (structural) relationships, and on the continuing relevance of class.

This said, given the "extremeness" of the present era of capitalism and the efficacy of capitalism's new globalist ideology, it would still be useful to highlight a number of pertinent issues about which a beginning comparativist should take special heed. The first is the most obvious: the nature of the relationship between structure and agency. Not surprisingly, there is no agreement on just what the nature of this relationship is; nonetheless, there is widespread agreement on the need to "join structure and agency in a compelling manner" (Mittelman 1996a, p. 232). There are many ways to do this, but one of the most important is to understand that there actually *is* agency behind globalization. The key agents, however, are not a new breed of supranational organizations such as the World Trade Organization, still less international institutions such as the World Bank and the IMF, but instead the "usual suspects": globalized monopoly capital and "advanced" capitalist states. (With regard to states, there are many structuralists who argue that state power is on the decline, but that the loss of sovereignty or control is primarily found among states in the periphery rather than among states in the "core.")

Understanding where power resides—or how power is configured—in the current capitalist system is crucial, especially for those who wish to understand the prospects for agency among subordinate actors—for example, social movements, peripheral states and their societies, labor unions, and so on. It is crucial, in part, because there is no way to pose a viable alternative—theoretical or practical—to neoliberal or economic globalization unless one knows how power is exercised in the system as a whole and from what sources. Recognizing that the state remains a center of power is particularly important in this regard, for despite its key role in the "international constitutionalization of neoliberalism . . . there is no prospect whatsoever of getting to more egalitarian, democratic, and cooperative world order beyond global competitiveness, without a fundamental struggle with domestic and global capitalists over the transformation of the state" (Panitch 1996, p. 109). In other words, the *system* of global capitalism cannot be effectively challenged if the political source of capitalist power is essentially left alone or ignored.

Another way to "join structure and agency in a compelling manner" is to understand that, despite its seemingly overwhelming nature, global capitalism is not a monolithic force but, instead, is permeated by unavoidable contradictions. Put more simply, this means that economic globalization, as it unfolds, creates not only strong tensions but also the conditions for its own destruction. It is the job of the historical-structuralist comparativist, in part, to identify and trace—in a concrete and historically specific manner—these tensions and contradictions. It is also the job of the comparativist to examine the impact of and response to the tensions/contradictions of global capitalism, whether at the local, regional, or transnational levels. This, in fact, is an area in which a great deal of research has already been done. Comparativists, for example, have examined how the centralizing tendencies of globalization have given rise to an increase in religious or nationalist fundamentalism (an issue we discussed earlier) in Iran, India, Pakistan, Lebanon, Northern Ireland, and even the United States. For structuralists, it is important to reiterate, the rise of fundamentalism is not a "cultural" phenomenon per se but a reflection of structurally created tensions inherent in capitalist expansion.

Comparativists have also studied how the imperatives of global capitalism have created increased rivalry, conflict, and violence within states or political communities: throughout Africa, the Middle East, Eastern Europe, South and Southeast Asia, Latin America, and, really, the entire world. At the same time, an understanding of the logic and contradictions of capitalism has helped comparativists explain, for instance, the reemergence of stronger—and reconstituted—labor movements in South Africa, South Korea, Venezuela, Brazil, Colombia, and so on (see Alder 1996; Moody 1997).

* * *

All of this, I hope, gives you a good sense of the "issues about which a beginning comparativist should take special heed." Let me conclude this chapter, however, with one important methodological caveat regarding another "tension." This tension, as James Mittelman (1996a) pointed out, is the one between "top-down" and "bottom-up" approaches. As Mittelman explained it: "Although it would be wrong to present a dichotomy between top-down and bottom-up perspectives, or between macro- and microlevels of analysis, one cannot simply posit that in work on globalization there is room for views from both above and below." Instead, Mittelman continued, "the task is to determine how various aspects of globalization merge and interpenetrate under concrete and varied conditions. One way to do so is to examine a series of interactions that constitute the globalization process" (p. 234). This is a little abstruse, but Mittelman's basic point is clear: for a structural argument to hold water, a researcher must be able to connect seemingly discrete political, social, and economic phenomena into a single process.

Conclusion

This chapter has covered a lot of ground in only a limited amount of space. It is probably likely, then, that you still have many unanswered questions. But, for the most part, this is desirable. It is also unavoidable, for comparative politics remains an immensely diverse, immensely challenging field of study (notwithstanding the "homogenizing" effects of globalization). No matter how hard I try, moreover, I can only present a limited perspective. It is up to you, therefore, to take what I have written in this chapter—and in the entire book—and begin charting your own intellectual path. Indeed, this is my primary objective; that is, I wrote this book as a theoretical and methodological—but decidedly *not* empirical—primer to the study of comparative politics. On many topics of discussion, including globalization, you will no doubt need to consult other sources. This is not only good practice but also necessary to doing comparative politics.

Note

1. Mittelman (2001) argued that we need to be very careful when we talk about those who "oppose" globalization, for opposition implies only two choices: for and against. Yet this twofold division is highly simplistic in that it obscures "the varied complaints about globalising trends that have emerged from different locales and diverse points on the political spectrum" (p. 214). Moreover, it suggests that "opponents" have nothing affirmative or positive to say; yet, as Mittelman nicely put it, many critics of globalization "oppose" it because "they are imagining possibilities for a more inclusive, participatory and democratic globalisation" (p. 214). Mittelman, therefore, suggested an alternative concept: resistance. This concept should not be considered a mere change in vocabulary but should, instead, be understood as a much more accurate and meaningful way to conceptualize the antithesis of (neoliberal) globalization. Resistance implies not opposition, but transformative potential, protection from "disease," and refusal to obey unjust and immoral conditions (as in the civil rights movement in the United States or resistance to the Nazi occupation in France).

Glossary

Many of the definitions in this glossary are adapted from three main sources: David Jary and Julia Jary, *The HarperCollins Dictionary of Sociology,* 2nd ed. (New York: HarperPerennial, 1991); "Wikipedia: The Free Encyclopedia," http://en.wikipedia.org; and Graham Evans and Jeffrey Newnham, *The Penguin Dictionary of International Relations* (London: Penguin, 1998). Items printed in SMALL CAPITALS are cross-references to main glossary entries.

*   *   *

absolute poverty. Absolute poverty, as defined by the World Summit for Social Development, "is a condition characterized by severe deprivation of basic human needs, including food, safe drinking water, sanitation facilities, health, shelter, education and information. It depends not only on income but also on access to social services" (http://www.un.org/esa/socdev/wssd/text-version/agreements /poach2.htm).

administrative guidance. Typically used in reference to DEVELOPMENTAL STATES, administrative guidance is an informal directive put forth by state agencies designed to give private firms "guidance" on certain economic issues and policies. These directives do not have the force of law, but they are not easily ignored.

agency; agent. Often contrasted with the concept of STRUCTURE, agency implies that actors, whether acting individually or collectively, have an ability to affect or shape the larger (social) environment in which they live. Although a seemingly commonsense assertion, many scholars argue that all human action is, to at least some degree, constrained or otherwise shaped by broader forces, which can derive from INSTITUTIONS, culture, the economic system, or other overarching structures.

al-Qaeda. Arabic for "the foundation." Al-Qaeda is an Islamist paramilitary movement widely regarded as a terrorist organization, especially in the West. The organization, led by Osama bin Laden and Ayman al-Zawahiri, was responsible for the attack against the World Trade Center buildings and the Pentagon on September 11, 2001.

341

analytical induction. Analytical induction is a specific research strategy based on the case study. The basic idea behind analytical induction is to use individual case studies as a way to build a stronger theoretical EXPLANATION. Cases are used in a step-by-step manner, with each case contributing to the development of a general theory.

anarchy; anarchic. In INTERNATIONAL RELATIONS, anarchy refers to the absence of a central or ultimate authority within a POLITICAL SYSTEM. In general, IR scholars consider the international system to be anarchic because there is no institution or political entity vested with the authority and capacity to resolve conflicts between individual states. In other words, there is no authority that exists beyond the level of the sovereign STATE.

ancien régime. A French term that means "old order." Although it technically refers to the political and social system of France prior to the French Revolution, it is used more generally to refer to any long-standing political system.

area studies. In the humanities and social sciences, area studies are a type of research that focuses on a particular geographical region or country. Common fields of area studies include Middle East studies, Asian studies (which can include East Asian, Southeast Asian, and South Asian studies), African studies, Latin American studies, and Caribbean studies. Although seemingly a "natural fit" for comparative politics, area studies research is a heterogeneous field, with no common methodological or theoretical approach.

authoritarianism. A nondemocratic political regime in which decisionmaking authority is highly centralized and exclusionary. Typically, authoritarian regimes are ruled by a single dictator, or by a small elite, who makes decisions in top-down fashion. Authoritarian systems are characterized by limited individual freedoms, minimal civil liberties and rights, excessive reliance on violence and coercion (including imprisonment, torture, and murder) against political opponents, and limited accountability on the part of government officials.

balance of trade. The balance of trade is the difference between what a country imports and what it exports. For example, if a country exports $10 billion worth of goods and services, and imports $8 billion dollars worth of goods and services, its balance of trade would be $2 billion. It is also possible to have a negative balance of trade. In the same country in the example, with imports of $12 billion worth of goods and service, its balance of trade would be –$2 billion.

binary analysis. In the context of comparative methodology, binary analysis refers to a comparison of two distinct units or CASES. For example, a researcher might compare the United States and Canada. See Chapter 2 for a more detailed discussion of this term.

Bretton Woods. Bretton Woods itself is the name of a resort area located in New Hampshire, but it was also the site of an important set of meetings that took place in July 1944 among 730 delegates from forty-four Allied countries. The meeting, however, was thoroughly dominated by the views of the United States and Great Britain. It was during these meetings that the framework for a new international financial system was developed and agreed upon. The main objective was to develop an international monetary regime whereby participating states bound themselves to an exchange rate mechanism with all major currencies tradable for US dollars, which in turn were convertible to gold at a fixed rate. This system broke down in 1971 when President Richard Nixon unilaterally abrogated the US commitment. Nonetheless, key elements of the Bretton Woods system remained: the INTERNATIONAL MONETARY FUND, the WORLD BANK, and the WORLD TRADE ORGANIZATION.

Buddhism; Buddhist. A Buddhist is a follower of Buddhism, which is a major religion of Asia. There are an estimated 300 million followers worldwide. Buddhism is based on the teachings of Siddhartha Gautama, but there are many forms, including Theravada Buddhism (Way of the Elders), Mahayana Buddhism, Zen Buddhism, Pure Land Buddhism, Nichiren Buddhism (Lotus Sect), and Tibetan Buddhism (Lamaism).

Bushido. Bushido, which can be translated as the "way of the warrior," refers to the code of conduct that governed the lives of Japan's samurai class during Japan's FEUDAL era. Bushido is not a fixed set of values. Indeed, it has been influenced by broader cultural currents over the many centuries of its existence—its origins can be dated back to the Kamakura period (1192–1333). In very general terms, though, it espouses obedience to authority, obligation, absolute loyalty, and fearlessness.

cadre. A cadre is an elite or select group—or a member of such a group—that forms the core of a larger organization.

case; case study. These are frequently used, but vague, terms. In general, though, a case may be said to be based on (1) a specific issue or concern (for example, terrorism, industrialization, revolution); (2) a delimited geographic space (Japan, France, Italy); and (3) a certain period of time (although this is sometimes implicit). Thus, we may talk about the case of postwar Japanese industrialization or the case of the Russian Revolution of 1917. In addition, cases do not have to involve whole countries or societies but can focus on specific INSTITUTIONS, policies, events, or even people. A case study is simply research or analysis that focuses on a single case.

causation; causal relationship. A relationship in which change in one or more factors or VARIABLES leads to, results in, or "forces" changes in one or more other factors or variables.

civil society. An ambiguous term generally defined as the multitude of organizations in a *democratic* society that operate independently of the state. These include nonprofit organizations, nongovernmental organizations (NGOs), SOCIAL MOVEMENTS, trade unions, churches, policy institutions (for example, think tanks), the news media, universities, and so on. Many scholars also consider business firms to be separate from civil society, although the distinction is not always clear-cut (consider, for example, the mass media, which are all owned by large corporations).

class. A hierarchical and relatively permanent division between individuals and groups within society, usually defined by occupation, income, or education. In Marxist thought, classes are economically determined and inherently conflictual divisions based on ownership and nonownership of property or the means of production.

clientelist. Refers to a relationship between individuals of unequal social, political, or economic status—that is, a relationship between a "boss" and their "clients." In the social sciences, clientelist relationships are understood to entail a reciprocal (but unequal) exchange of goods or services based on the *personal* link between the boss and client. Such relationships, many scholars argue, invariably lead to corruption, especially in electoral politics. In the case of elections, for example, the boss may ask clients to vote for a particular candidate in return for a small payment or reward.

Cold War (circa 1945–1989). Describes the relationship between the United States and its noncommunist allies, on the one hand, and the Soviet Union and its satellites, allies, and other COMMUNIST regimes, on the other hand. In contrast to a "hot" war, the Cold War did not involve direct combat between the two superpowers, although the relationship itself was characterized by ongoing hostility, high levels of distrust, suspicion, and rivalry for influence throughout the world. The rivalry for influence often led to armed conflict in which the superpowers fought each other indirectly.

collective action. In the context of rational choice, collective action is concerned with the provision of COLLECTIVE GOODS through the cooperation or collaboration of two or more individuals. More generally, collective action or collective behavior refers to the nonroutine or out-of-the-ordinary actions of people in groups or crowds.

collective good (also public good). Commodities or services—for example, national defense, clean air and water, law enforcement, and highways—that, when made available to one person, are available to all. In short, a collective good is a *nonexclusive* commodity or service. The nonexclusive nature of collective or public goods leads to the FREE-RIDER PROBLEM in that consumers of the public good have no incentive to contribute voluntarily to its cost.

colonialism. A system in which one STATE claims SOVEREIGNTY over a territory and people outside its own established boundaries. The most common motivation for colonial expansion was to take control of the economic resources, labor, and often markets of the colonized territory. This was typically accomplished through military force. Historically, colonialism is most closely associated with the period from the fifteenth to nineteenth centuries, when the major European powers (Britain, France, Holland, Portugal, and Spain) steadily expanded their reach into Africa, Asia, and Latin America. The European powers were joined in the late nineteenth and early twentieth centuries by Belgium, Germany, Italy, the United States, Japan, and Russia. Colonialism, it is fair to say, has been a major force in shaping the political and economic character of the modern world.

communism; communist. Communism is both a theory and a practice. As a theory, communism rests on the ideas of historical materialism proposed by KARL MARX and developed and implemented by Vladimir Lenin. In Marxist theory, communism denotes the final stage of human historical development in which there is no STATE, and people rule both politically and economically. Ironically, as a practice, communism represented a totalitarian system of government in which a single party controlled state-owned means of production with the professed aim of establishing a stateless society (as in the former Soviet Union).

complex causality; causal complexity. This concept suggests that political, social, and economic phenomena are rarely the product of a single cause but instead are the product of combinations of conditions that intersect in various and interdependent ways. In addition, there are usually several different combinations of conditions that may produce the same change. For further discussion, see Ragin 1987, chap. 2.

conditionality. Refers to the conditions a bank or lending institution places on the borrower in exchange for a loan. More commonly, however, it refers specifically to the conditions placed by the IMF or World Bank on individual countries in return for a loan provided or approved by the IMF. Despite its seeming reasonableness, IMF conditionality is extremely controversial, as many developing countries view the IMF as an institution controlled by the major Western economies, and especially the United States. In this view, conditionality is seen as a way for the US and other major economies to gain control over poorer countries.

Confucianism; Confucian. An East Asian ethical and philosophical system developed mostly upon the teachings of Confucius (traditionally 551–479 B.C.E.). Confucianism remained the mainstream Chinese orthodoxy for 2,000 years, until the beginning of the twentieth century, when the Chinese Communist Party first began to exert influence in Chinese politics. Outside China, Confucian ideas have influenced a variety of Asian societies, including Korea, Japan, Taiwan, Singapore, and Vietnam.

contradiction. Key in Marxist and other historical-structuralist analysis, contradictions are thought to be an inherent aspect of most social or economic processes. In capitalism, for example, the imperatives of competition and accumulation necessarily generate exploitation and oppression, which create conflict between workers and capitalists. Eventually, this conflict will lead to a revolutionary struggle that will destroy the system.

control. In an experimental design, "to control" means to limit the factors influencing a VARIABLE under observation. In comparative politics, researchers use different forms of comparative analysis, such as the MOST SIMILAR SYSTEMS design or the MOST DIFFERENT SYSTEMS design, to loosely control for a wide range of variables.

control variable. Control variables are additional variables in a research design that might affect the relationship between the independent and dependent variables. When control variables are used, the researcher wants to ensure that these variables are not, in fact, responsible for variations observed in the dependent variable.

co-optation; co-opt. A political strategy designed to neutralize or win over subordinate groups through accommodation. Unlike *poser sharing,* a policy of co-optation is fundamentally designed to limit or undermine the power of weaker, but potentially significant, groups by accommodating some demands for inclusion while deflecting more radical demands.

correlation. Correlation describes a relationship between two different VARIABLES. If one increases when the other increases (or vice versa), then there is a correlation between them. For example, there is a well-established correlation between the per capita level of GROSS DOMESTIC PRODUCT and democracy. The fact that there is a correlation, however, does not necessarily mean that one *causes* the other; a third (still unidentified) variable could be involved. In other words, correlation does not necessarily indicate a CAUSAL RELATIONSHIP.

country. A country is a fixed geographical area that includes an independent political entity with its own GOVERNMENT, regulations and laws (generally codified in a constitution), judicial system, police/military force, and population. The terms *country* and STATE are generally interchangeable, but there are a few exceptions. Political entities that have a distinct history or culture, such as England, Scotland, and Wales, can be considered separate countries but part of a single state, namely the United Kingdom.

deduction; deductive logic. Deduction is a "top-down" approach. It begins with a general principle (for example, rational action) or theory, then draws conclusions about specific cases. Rational choice theory is based on deductive logic.

dependence. When comparativists use the term *dependence,* they are usually referring to the inability of poor and weak societies (or subordinate social classes) to control their own economic and political fates. They argue, instead, that the economic and political fate of poorer societies—primarily former colonies—is largely determined by exploitative and unequal relationships.

dependency; dependency theory. Dependency theory—which was most influential in the 1970s—is a theory that attempts to explain the continuing poverty and political and social instability of many poor countries in the world. An explicitly structural theory, dependency focused on the exploitative relationship between advanced capitalist societies and the third world. More specifically, dependency scholars argued that the nature of this relationship, rather than internal conditions,

was the primary cause of poverty and underdevelopment. There is a huge litera-
ture on dependency, but some of the leading figures are Fernando Cardoso and
Enzo Faletto (1979), André Gunder Frank ([1966] 1988), and Theotonio Dos
Santos ([1970] 1996).

dependent variable. In a causal or social scientific analysis, the dependent variable
is that variable the researcher seeks to explain. It is the *result* or *effect* in a CAUSAL
RELATIONSHIP. For example, if a researcher argues that economic deprivation
causes an increase in violent crime, "violent crime" is the dependent variable. See
INDEPENDENT VARIABLE for further explanation and an additional example.

developmental state. The developmental state is a particular type of STATE distinguished by its high capacity to promote and facilitate rapid industrial development. The concept has been around for several decades, and one of the most influential early works was Chalmers Johnson's *MITI and the Japanese Miracle*
(1982). For a more recent discussion, see Woo-Cumings 1999.

discourse. In academia, the term *discourse* refers to much more than a "conversation" or "words"; instead, discourse is considered to be an institutionalized way
of thinking and UNDERSTANDING. Discourses, many scholars (especially REFLEC-
TIVISTS) argue, shape our views of the world and provide a framework for action.
Discourses, in this view, can have a profound impact on society.

equilibrium. In rational choice theory, and especially game theory, equilibrium represents an optimum strategy for all players in a game, in the sense that no one
player can benefit by changing their strategy while all other players keep theirs
the same.

ethnocentrism. The problem or tendency of assessing different cultures and societies by one's own standards, values, and expectations. Ethnocentrism can lead
to misunderstanding and biased research.

European Union (EU). An international organization of twenty-seven European
STATES (as of March 2010), established by the Treaty on European Union (also
known as the Maastricht Treaty). The European Union has many activities, the
most important being a common single market, consisting of a customs union; a
single currency, called the euro (though some member states retain their own national currency); a common agricultural policy; and a common fisheries policy.
Arguably, the EU is the most powerful regionally based international organization in the world today and represents, in an important respect, a completely new
type of international organization.

exogenous shock. The dictionary definition of *exogenous* is "of, relating to, or developing from external factors." This provides a basic way of defining the term
exogenous shock—a shock (or crisis) that is external to the political system or
regime. Another characteristic of an exogenous shock is that it is not predictable.

experimental method. A research design in which the researcher has complete or
near-complete control over the INDEPENDENT VARIABLE, the UNITS OF ANALYSIS,
and the overall environment. Under experimental conditions, the researcher is
able to manipulate one or more variables, while controlling other factors, to determine the effects on one or more other variables. In comparative politics, the
experimental method is rarely used or used in only a very limited fashion.

explanation. In the social sciences, explanation is generally concerned with identifying the cause or causes of a particular event or general phenomenon. Typically,
explanations involve specifying the CAUSAL RELATIONSHIP between two or more
VARIABLES—for example, "the existence of or a change in x causes y." In comparative politics, researchers often use case-based research to build a theoretical explanation in a step-by-step manner. This is also referred to as ANALYTICAL INDUCTION.

export-oriented industrialization. As the term suggests, export-oriented industrialization is an industrialization strategy—typically associated with the East Asian newly industrializing countries—that gives priority to export-based growth. To encourage export-based growth, a government will typically provide domestic manufacturers with subsidies or other incentives to export their products. "Export-oriented industrialization" and "export-led growth" are often used interchangeably.

falsification. Falsification is a procedure used in science to test the validity of a hypothesis or theory by finding refuting evidence. For example, a single black swan refutes the general hypothesis that "all swans are white." For Karl Popper, a renowned philosopher, falsification provided the decisive criterion of demarcation between science and nonscience. Many scholars, however, reject this view, since a single refutation does not necessarily imply that theories are wrong; indeed, some commentators argue that the procedures suggested by Popper fail to fit the actual practice of science and, if used strictly, would likely cripple the scientific endeavor.

fascism. A political philosophy or movement—most closely associated with Italy and Germany of the 1920s and 1930s—that places the nation or the race above the individual. Fascism is also premised on the need for a highly centralized government led by a dictator; belief in militarism, racism, and nationalism; and opposition to liberal capitalism and democracy.

feudalism; feudal. Although subject to a variety of definitions, feudalism can be generally thought of as a political, economic, and social system in which all the aspects of life were centered on "lordship." In feudal systems, lords (overlords and vassals) controlled the land. Serfs were required to work the central manorial farm and to provide the lord with produce and money payments in return for their own rights to land use. The lord was obligated to provide for the social welfare of peasants, however minimal that may have been.

formalism/legalism. In the context of comparative politics, the term *formalism* is generally used to denote the study of the formal political system—that is, the main INSTITUTIONS and agencies of the state. These may include the legislature, the executive branch, the judiciary, and the bureaucracy. *Legalism* refers to the formal laws and lawmaking processes of the state.

framing. Framing presupposes that the communication of knowledge is shaped in particular and selective ways, and is often designed to elicit certain understandings, responses, and emotions. Framing is found everywhere, but those who control the major modes of mass communication generally have the most influence over how information and knowledge are framed.

free-rider problem. To free-ride is to receive or benefit from a PUBLIC GOOD (or COLLECTIVE GOOD), such as national defense or clean air, without contributing to its cost. The free-rider problem, therefore, refers to the problem preventing free-riding from taking place, or at least limiting its effects.

globalization. A complex term referring, very broadly, to the acceleration and deepening of processes of technological, economic, political, social, and cultural change throughout the world. See Chapter 9 for a more detailed discussion of this concept.

government. A government is the agency or apparatus through which a body exercises authority and performs its functions. In this definition, governments need not be part of a STATE; moreover, multiple governments may exist within a single state. Indeed, we can find governments in all sorts of places—in a university or school (that is, the student government) or in sovereign NATIONS (for example, a

Native American tribal council)—and at many levels. Cities, counties, provinces, and whole regions (for example, the EUROPEAN UNION) can also have their own separate governments.

Great Depression. The Great Depression was a period of severe economic difficulties in the decade preceding World War II. In the United States, the official beginning of the Great Depression was October 29, 1929, the day the stock market crashed. The Great Depression, however, was not limited to the United States: countries around the world, but especially Western European countries, were also hit very hard. Germany, which was already suffering from serious inflation (really hyperinflation as a result of the large debts it was required to pay back after losing World War I), was in a particularly precarious position since it had borrowed large sums of money from the United States in order to repay its European debts.

gross domestic product (GDP). A measure of the total flow of goods and services produced by an economy over a specific period of time, normally one year. GDP is often used as a measure of an economy's overall size and prosperity, but it is only a very rough measure. Today, researchers prefer other measurements, including, more prominently, PURCHASING POWER PARITY and the HUMAN DEVELOPMENT INDEX.

guanxi. In general, *guanxi* refers to a system of social networks and strong personal relationships based on mutual commitment and reciprocity that exist in Chinese societies. Literally, *guanxi* can be translated as "relationships" or "connections," although this simple translation cannot do proper justice to the term.

gulag. A Russian term referring to the specific government agency (the *Glavnoe Upravlenie Ispravitel-no-trudovykh Lagerei,* translated as "chief directorate of prison camps") responsible for administering a system of forced labor camps during the Soviet era. More casually, *gulag* is used as a synonym for a *forced labor camp* housing political prisoners.

hard case. A CASE that appears least likely to confirm the theory or hypothesis being tested. The rationale behind selecting or using hard cases is straightforward: the researcher hopes to show that if a theory *cannot* be falsified or invalidated with a particularly difficult case, then the theory is more likely to be right. B. Guy Peters explains it this way: "This strategy can be seen at work in many contemporary analyses of Japan. The mystique of Japan as a distinctive political system has grown to the point that it is being used as the most difficult test case for a variety of political theories with the assumption that they will not work in that setting" (1998, p. 64). To put it simply, if it (the theory) works there, it will work anywhere.

hard-liner. The dictionary definition of a hard-liner is a person who advocates an uncompromising course of action. In the context of an AUTHORITARIAN regime, the definition is essentially the same. That is, a hard-liner is a ranking member of the regime who is rigidly opposed to political liberalization or any compromise with opponents of the regime. A hard-liner will typically advocate the use of violence, including deadly force, to quell political dissent.

hegemony; hegemonic. A term used in a variety of ways but generally meaning primacy or leadership. More specifically, hegemony implies complete dominance—politically, economically, militarily, and even culturally. An important aspect of hegemony is that the dominance of the leader (that is, the hegemon) is typically exercised without the use of force per se but instead is based on consent.

Hezbollah. A militant SHIITE political party in Lebanon. Hezbollah—whose name means "Party of God"—began as a guerrilla group fighting against the Israeli occupation in southern Lebanon. It maintains an active militia known as the Islamic Resistance.

hierarchy; hierarchic. In general sociological terms, hierarchy refers to an asymmetrical relationship or a set of such relationships in which those at the top have power over those at the bottom. In studies of formal political processes, however, hierarchy has a slightly different meaning: it refers to the existence of a state or governmental authority that has the legitimate power to impose public order. Domestically, most political systems are hierarchic, whereas the international system, according to many INTERNATIONAL RELATIONS scholars (especially those who subscribe to REALISM), is considered to be ANARCHIC.

Human Development Index (HDI). In 1990, the United Nations concluded that aggregate economic data, such as GROSS DOMESTIC PRODUCT, were inadequate to measure the concept of development. In place of GDP, the HDI was developed. The HDI consists of three aspects of development: (1) standard of living (measured on the basis of per capita income in PURCHASING POWER PARITY; (2) knowledge (measured on the basis of adult literacy and combined enrollment ratio); and (3) longevity (that is, life expectancy at birth). HDI scores range from 0 to 1. The closer to 1 the score is, the higher the level of human development. Since its inception in 1990, the HDI has been supplemented with a number of other measures, including the Gender-Related Development Index and the Human Poverty Index. Additional information is available at http://hdr.undp.org.

hypothesis. A statement proposing a relationship (usually a CAUSAL RELATIONSHIP) between two or more VARIABLES.

ideology. Any system of ideas underlying and informing social and political action. Traditionally, ideology was clearly distinguished from THEORY; the latter was assumed to present an objective or scientifically based explanation of the world.

independent variable. An independent variable is one that influences another variable, called a DEPENDENT VARIABLE. In the statement "Poverty is responsible for an increase in violent homicides," "poverty" is the independent variable, and "increase in violent homicides" is the dependent variable—in other words, poverty is said to influence the rate of violent homicide.

indirect method of difference. Based on the work of J. S. Mill, this method involves a comparison of at least three CASES. The first two cases should be compared on the basis of the METHOD OF DIFFERENCE; the third case should be similar to the first in a number of respects and to the second in a number of other respects.

infant industry. In an already-established and internationally competitive industrial sector, an infant industry is one that emerges relatively late. As a newcomer, the infant industry normally cannot operate on the same scale and, therefore, at the same level of competitiveness and efficiency as its more established international competitors. Thus, some argue that STATES should be allowed to protect and nurture their infant industries until they have time to mature.

infrastructure. Refers collectively to the roads, bridges, rail lines, water supply, sewers, power grids, telecommunication systems, and similar public works that are required for an industrial economy, or a portion of it, to function efficiently and effectively. Viewed functionally, infrastructure facilitates the production of goods and services; for example, roads enable the transport of raw materials, intermediate goods, and so on, to a factory, and also the distribution of finished products to markets. In many contexts, the term may also include basic social services such as schools and hospitals.

institution. Traditionally, institutions were equated with concrete public and private organizations or agencies, such as a legislature, the presidency, the STATE as a whole, a university, and so on. The traditional definition is certainly still relevant and frequently used (including in this book), but recently scholars have adopted a more expansive definition. Specifically, the term *institution* is used to refer to "a stable, recurring pattern of behavior" (Goodin 1996, p. 21), which may be either formalized/codified (for example, the institution of marriage) or informal/unwritten (for example, the "code of silence" among police officers can be considered an informal but powerful institutional practice). The key is the existence of "rules" that govern or influence, either directly or indirectly, the behavior of actors.

institutionalism. A concept that includes a diverse and complex array of approaches (too many to discuss here). A common theme among the different approaches, however, is a focus on how INSTITUTIONS determine (enable or constrain), shape, or influence the behavior of actors. See Chapter 3 for a more detailed discussion of institutionalism.

International Monetary Fund (IMF). An international financial institution established in 1946 to (1) provide international liquidity on a short- and medium-term basis and (2) encourage liberalization of exchange rates. The IMF has been subject to intense controversy in recent years, largely because of its policy of requiring debtor countries (mostly in the developing world) to implement sometimes painful NEOLIBERAL policy reforms.

international relations (IR). The academic study of relations between and among STATES or NATION-STATES. Although a diverse and heterogeneous field, IR has long been dominated by a particular theoretical perspective known as REALISM. Traditionally, comparative politics and IR have been considered separate fields of study, with the former focusing on domestic political, social, and economic dynamics. Recently, however, the separation between the two fields has begun to break down.

intersubjective. Most basically, intersubjectivity refers to the experiences, understanding, and knowledge *shared* among people and whole societies. REFLECTIVISTS and other POST-POSITIVISTS believe that intersubjectivity provides the basis for understanding how "reality" is socially constructed.

Islam; Islamic. Arabic word meaning submission (to God), and the name for the religion founded under the leadership of the prophet Muhammad; it also denotes the MUSLIM community. There are an estimated 1.6 billion followers of Islam worldwide.

Kuomintang (KMT). The Chinese Nationalist Party (DMTW) ruled Taiwan for most of the postwar era under the leadership of Chiang Kai-shek. The KMT, however, was founded much earlier on mainland China (in 1919) and was originally led by Sun Yat-sen. After being defeated by the Chinese Communist Party, the KMT and its supporters fled to Taiwan, where it established a single-party AUTHORITARIAN system that lasted into the 1990s.

late industrialization. Late industrialization, as the term implies, has a temporal meaning: late as opposed to early. The early industrializers include, most prominently, England, which began the industrialization process in the eighteenth century. Other European countries—France and Belgian in particular—began the industrialization process a bit later, while Germany and Eastern European countries lagged much further behind. Still, all countries that began the industrialization process by the end of the nineteenth century are usually considered early industrializers. Countries that began in the twentieth century, especially in the second half of the century, are considered late industrializers. The issue is not just temporal. Late industrializers, according to some scholars, most prominently Alice Amsden (1989), believe that the challenges faced by late industrializers require active and pervasive state intervention in the economy, if the country is to have any hope of prospering or catching up with earlier industrializers.

level of analysis. In the social sciences, the term *levels of analysis* is both used and categorized in different ways. Most commonly, though, scholars define levels of analysis as a source of explanation. If analysis, for example, seeks to explain political, economic, or social phenomena by focusing primarily on individual motives and characteristics, the source of explanation is the micro-level or the individual level. Other analyses may focus on, say, the larger institutional or cultural environment, which reflect the meso-level. Still others will pay most attention to the even larger global or transnational environment—the macro-level.

liberalization. Has several meanings, depending on the context. Political liberalization refers to the movement toward democracy, individual rights and liberties, and personal freedom. Economically, liberalization generally refers to increasing privatization, which is the economic process of transferring property from public ownership to private ownership. Another important element of economic liberalization is the promotion of a "freer" framework for market activity through deregulation.

liberation theology. A twentieth-century religious or social movement in Latin America centered on the needs of the poor. Advocates argued that the Bible could only be understood when read and interpreted from the perspective of the poor. The ideas of liberation theology were the basis for a political struggle against social injustice and inequity and against the oppressive power structures—which often included the Catholic Church—that characterized much of Latin America in the 1960s and 1970s.

macrosocial. As a prefix, *macro* means "very large in scale, scope, or capability." Macrosocial, therefore, refers to large-scale social structures or to whole societies. For example, the United States is a macrosocial unit.

Mao Zedong (also Mao Tse-tung). Mao, or Chairman Mao, was the founding father of the People's Republic of China and presided over the country from its founding on October 1, 1949, to his death on September 9, 1976. His rise to power began as one of the founders of the Chinese Communist Party (CCP) in 1921. He gradually rose through the ranks of the CCP and became part of the top leadership in 1934–1935 during the Long March (the 6,000-mile military retreat by the CCP's Red Army to evade the pursuit of the KUOMINTANG). Despite a number of severe missteps while ruling China, including the Great Leap Forward and the Cultural Revolution, Mao remains a revered figure.

maquiladora. A specific type of assembly plant in Mexico, primarily located near the United States–Mexico border. Typically, in the *maquiladora,* foreign materials and parts are shipped in and assembled, and then the finished product is returned to the original market (usually in the United States). This allows US and other non-Mexican firms to take advantage of lower production costs in Mexico while avoiding duties and other taxes.

market failure. Refers to situations in which the market, operating in a free or unfettered manner, fails to provide an efficient allocation of resources. One type of market failure is associated with monopolies. When one economic actor is able to dominate a market (e.g., Microsoft), this makes it possible for that entity to block mutually beneficial gains from trade from occurring. Market failure is often the justification for political intervention in the marketplace. Among economists, there is not universal consensus that market failures (1) can be addressed adequately through government intervention, or (2) even exist.

Marshall Plan (also known as the European Recovery Plan). The Marshall Plan, which ran from April 1948 to December 1951, was a US foreign aid program designed primarily to aid in European reconstruction following the end of World

War II. The plan disbursed about $13 billion—an extraordinarily large amount at the time—to sixteen European countries, including Germany, but excluding European countries then under the military occupation by the Soviet Union (the Soviet Union and its satellite countries were, however, eligible to receive aid; but when the Soviet Union refused to participate, the Eastern European countries under its influence also withdrew).

Marx, Karl (1818–1883). A German scholar of the nineteenth century and the founder of Marxism, the fundamental theory of COMMUNISM. Much of his work, including *Das Kapital* (volume 1 published in 1867, and volumes 2 and 3 published posthumously) and *The Communist Manifesto* (1848), was done with Friedrich Engels. Marx lived outside Germany most of his life, notably in London, where he wrote *Das Kapital.*

Meiji Restoration. A turbulent period of Japanese history that saw the fall of a long-lived feudal system, known as the Tokugawa *shogunate* (1600–1869), and the rise of a new Western-oriented regime that oversaw rapid industrialization, modernization, and far-reaching social change throughout Japan. It was during this period that imperial rule was "restored" to Japan with the emperor assuming a supreme position (during the earlier period, by contrast, the shogun or "great generals" ruled). The new emperor took the name *Meiji,* which means "enlightened rule." The Meiji era lasted from 1868 to 1912, when the Meiji emperor died.

MENA. An acronym for a region encompassing about twenty-two countries in the Middle East and North Africa—roughly the area from Morocco in northwest Africa to Iran in southwest Asia and down to Sudan in Africa (there is some debate as to which countries should be included). The following countries are usually included in MENA: Algeria, Bahrain, Djibouti, Egypt, Iran, Iraq, Israel, Jordan, Kuwait, Lebanon, Libya, Malta, Morocco, Oman, Qatar, Saudi Arabia, Syria, Tunisia, the United Arab Emirates, West Bank and Gaza, and Yemen. Ethiopia and Sudan are sometimes included (http://www.investopedia.com/terms/m/middle-east-and-north-africa-mena.asp).

method of agreement (MoA). Based on the work of John Stuart Mill (1806–1873), this method is based on the idea that, when several observations of the same phenomenon (that is, the DEPENDENT VARIABLE) have only one of several VARIABLES in common, then the common variable is the cause of the phenomenon. The MOST DIFFERENT SYSTEMS design is based on this method. See discussion in Chapter 3.

method of difference. Based on the work of John Stuart Mill (1806–1873), this method involves studying two very similar cases that differ only with respect to the relationship between the INDEPENDENT and DEPENDENT VARIABLES. The MOST SIMILAR SYSTEMS design is based on this method.

middle class. In modern capitalist societies, the middle class is composed of nonmanual occupational groups (small-business owners, white-collar professionals, managers, and so on). The middle class is considered important insofar as the interests of those who compose this class differ from the interests of those in the upper and working classes.

mixed design. Combines a minimum of two comparative research strategies, such as the CASE STUDY (including a WITHIN-CASE COMPARISON), BINARY ANALYSIS, and multiunit analysis using three or more units. See Chapter 2 for a more detailed discussion.

modernization theory. Theory based on a particular model of societal development in which the decisive factor in modernization is the overcoming and replacement of traditional values and practices considered antithetical to progressive social change and industrialization. It is important to note that there are different versions of modernization theory.

most different systems (MDS). The MDS design is based on finding key *similarities* between or among very dissimilar units. See discussion in Chapter 2.

most similar systems (MSS). The MSS design is based on finding key *differences* between or among very similar units. See discussion in Chapter 2.

multiple causation. Related to the idea of COMPLEX CAUSALITY, multiple causation implies that social phenomena are rarely the product of a single cause or condition but rather the product of multiple causes or conditions.

Muslim. A believer in or follower of Islam. The word *Muslim* means "one who submits" and implies complete submission to the will of God. Muslims believe that nature is itself Islamic, since it follows natural laws placed by God.

nation. Although often confused with the concept of the STATE, nation refers to a social collectivity, the members of which share one or more of the following characteristics: a common identity (which may be based on ethnicity, race, religion, or a similar identifier) or a common history, culture, language, or economic life. Multiple nations, therefore, can exist within a given country or territory (for example, the Sioux nation) and can also cross borders (the Islamic nation).

nation-state. The term *nation-state* or *national state,* although often used interchangeably with the term STATE, refers more properly to a state composed of a single NATION. By this definition, there are few, if any, nation-states in the world today. A looser definition of nation-state, however, is frequently used. Most scholars, for example, assert that a nation-state exists when a single nation is merely dominant. Yet even with this looser definition, places such as the United States, Canada, Belgium, Iraq, Spain, China, and Indonesia might not be considered nation-states. Typically, though, a common national identity has been constructed in most modern states to create a sense of unity. A better term than *nation-state,* therefore, might simply be *national state.*

neoliberalism; neoliberal. Loosely associated with neoclassical economics, neoliberalism is a school of economics based on the premise that GOVERNMENTS or STATES in general lack the capacity to manage complex industrial economies. Hence, except for core responsibilities of creating and maintaining an infrastructure, a system of justice and national defense, and a few other related COLLECTIVE GOODS, governments should shrink and privatize. Neoliberalism puts great emphasis on unregulated or "free" markets as the best way to build prosperity in any economy or society. The neoliberal doctrine, it is useful noting, is also a subset of the so-called Washington Consensus, a set of specific policy goals designed for Latin American countries to help them recover from the "lost decade" of the 1980s.

neorealism. See REALISM.

norm. Any standard or rule, formal or informal, that regulates, shapes, or governs behavior in a social setting. A normative position is any position that holds certain rules, values, or practices as preferable to others.

North American Free Trade Agreement (NAFTA). A comprehensive but controversial trade agreement linking Canada, the United States, and Mexico into a free trade sphere. NAFTA went into effect on January 1, 1994. The agreement immediately ended tariffs on some goods; on other goods, tariffs were scheduled to be eliminated over a set period of time.

objectivity; objective. In the social sciences, objectivity implies that the existence of an entity, process, or structure does not depend on human awareness. The computer used to type this sentence exists "objectively," because it would still exist in exactly the same form whether or not I was aware of it. In studying the social world, however, objectivity is not as clear-cut. Do social CLASSES, for example, have a purely objective existence? Or are they partly a product of our awareness? Many scholars, especially REFLECTIVISTS, reject the idea that our accounts of the world can be purely objective. Instead, they argue that the world we perceive is INTERSUBJECTIVE.

operational definition. A process that involves defining a concept empirically so that it can be measured. In QUALITATIVE ANALYSIS, the emphasis on empirical specification is not strictly followed, but the key to operationalizing a concept is the ability to translate it into a consistent measurement of some kind.

overdetermination. Overdetermination is most apparent in the MSS design: it occurs whenever there are a large number of potentially relevant INDEPENDENT VARIABLES, but only a limited number of CASES. The basic problem is that the researcher does not have enough cases to know with confidence that the particular independent variable being examined is the one and only cause.

pact. In the context of research on democratization, a pact refers to a negotiated settlement (or agreement), typically among a country's elite, for limited political change toward democracy. Some scholars, especially rationalists, believe that such settlements are essential to democratic transition and consolidation.

per capita. A term meaning "for each person." It is most often used as a measurement of relative wealth as measured by GROSS DOMESTIC PRODUCT. For example, a country such as China may, at first glance, appear to be extremely wealthy: its GDP is the second highest in the world, just behind that of the United States. On a per capita basis, however, China ranks only about eighty-eighth in the world due to the country's very large population of over 1.3 billion. On the other hand, Qatar (population 2.1 million) has by far the highest per capita GDP in the world, but is ranked fiftieth on the basis of GDP alone.

petty bourgeoisie. The class of small-business owners, artisans, and (middle-class) professionals. KARL MARX originally coined this term to distinguish between large capitalists and small shopkeepers, on the one hand, and small shopkeepers and the proletariat (that is, workers), on the other hand.

political system. The political system includes the sum total of organizations and INSTITUTIONS within a COUNTRY that influence or are influenced by the political process. This is an inclusive concept that covers the agencies of the STATE and GOVERNMENT; political parties; interest and pressure groups; the media of communication (newspapers, radio, television, the Internet, and so on); and a host of ostensibly nonpolitical institutions, including the family, the community, schools, churches, corporations, foundations, think tanks, and the like.

positivist. A positivist subscribes to the principles of positivism, which is a doctrine formulated by Auguste Comte (1798–1857). Comte asserted that the only true knowledge is scientific knowledge; that is, a knowledge based on empirical observation. Positivists generally hold two strong positions: (1) a belief in the (methodological) unity of all sciences, which is to say that the methods of the physical sciences can be carried over into the social sciences; and (2) an assumption that the "objective" world exists independently of any perspectives of the researchers. A distinguishing feature of positivism, in other words, is the absence of any distinction between reality (as things that exist) and knowledge of reality (as things that are recognized).

post-positivism; post-positivist. The rejection of the idea that science and knowledge can be grounded in entirely objective observations of the social world, as suggested by those who are POSITIVISTS.

power. There is no simple definition of power; it is an extremely complex and contested concept. Suffice it to say, therefore, that power has many dimensions and can both constrain (for example, through coercion) and enable action. It is also important to understand that power has both material and nonmaterial sources, neither of which necessarily has primacy.

presidential system. Refers to a type of democratic political regime in which the chief executive (that is, the president) is elected by popular vote and in which the terms of office for the president and the assembly are fixed. In addition, in a "pure" presidential system, the president has authority over the cabinet. The presidential system is often contrasted with the parliamentary system.

public choice. Public choice theory is a branch of economics that developed from the study of taxation and public spending. The key principles of public choice draw from rational choice theory, but unlike many of the arguments discussed in this book, public choice is focused on the conditions for "government failure" rather than "market failure." In this sense, public choice theory has a strong normative position, which is that government intervention be strictly limited.

public good. See COLLECTIVE GOOD.

purchasing power parity (PPP). A method that attempts to more accurately compare incomes across countries than do traditional statistics, such as GROSS DOMESTIC PRODUCT. PPP converts income in each country from that country's domestic currency to US dollars. At the PPP rate, therefore, one dollar has the same purchasing power over domestic GDP that the US dollar has over US GDP. PPP rates are designed to allow a standard comparison of real price levels between countries, just as conventional price indexes allow comparison of real values over time; otherwise, normal exchange rates may over- or undervalue purchasing power.

Puritanism. The Puritans were a group of radical Protestants who emerged in England after the Reformation (around the sixteenth century). The central tenet of Puritanism was based on a belief in God's supreme authority over human affairs, and followers advocated strict religious discipline along with simplification of the ceremonies and creeds of the Church of England.

qualitative analysis. Qualitative research places strong emphasis on understanding and interpreting data or information that cannot be adequately or meaningfully quantified (or expressed in numbers). An interview of a high-ranking official or peasant farmer, for example, is generally nonquantifiable. An analysis of historical records, events, and documents, too, often cannot be meaningfully expressed in numbers. CASE STUDIES and comparative-historical approaches are generally based on qualitative analysis.

quantitative analysis. In the social sciences, quantitative analysis refers to the use of numerical data and statistical techniques rather than the analysis of qualitative material. In its simplest form, quantitative analysis includes the analysis, reporting, and summary of aggregate data; but in its more sophisticated form, it includes the use of contingency table analysis, analysis of variance, and correlation and regression analysis.

Quran. The Islamic holy book of Allah (the Divine, that is, God). Believers in ISLAM believe that the Quran is the eternal, literal word of God, revealed to the prophet Muhammad over a period of twenty-two years. The Quran consists of 114 *suras* (chapters) with a total of 6,236 *ayats* (verses).

realism; realist. Realism, in the most general terms, refers to a type of theoretical argument in INTERNATIONAL RELATIONS that portrays the STATE as the preeminent actor in world affairs. Realism also emphasizes the overriding importance of POWER, defined primarily in terms of military capacity, as the driving force behind international politics. Indeed, to realists, international politics is defined primarily as a "struggle for power" among self-interested states. Realism, it is important to note, is not a single coherent theory; instead, it is a diverse school with many important cleavages. The dominant version of realism, however, is neorealism, which is based on the assumption that international politics is essentially the product of an anarchic structure. ANARCHY—not to be confused with chaos—locks all states into a "self-help" system that requires all states to do whatever they can to achieve national security.

reflectivism; reflectivist. A very broad concept, reflectivism refers to a broad range of POST-POSITIVIST approaches or theories. A very basic, and perhaps overly simplistic, way to define reflectivism is to say that it is premised on the idea that there is no clear-cut distinction between reality and our knowledge (or theories) of reality. To put it even more simply, reflectivists believe that our theories or knowledge actually help construct the world or reality in which we live.

relative autonomy. Refers to the notion that the STATE can and does play a *limited independent* role in the maintenance and stabilization of capitalist society. This contrasts sharply with the classical Marxist view, which saw the state almost purely as a tool of the capitalist (or dominant) class.

relative deprivation. When an individual believes that he or she has been deprived of something based on a comparison to others. Feelings of relative deprivation can lead to frustration and anger.

relative poverty. In contrast to ABSOLUTE POVERTY, relative poverty is defined by the standards of the society in which an individual lives; that is, poverty is relative to individual countries and their economic conditions. For example, in the United States, the poverty level for a single person in 2014 was set at $11,770 a year (and is higher for the state of Alaska). Compare this figure to the World Bank's purchasing power–adjusted $1.25 a day standard for determining absolute poverty: on an annual basis, that would amount to $456.25.

rentier state. Refers to a STATE that derives all or a substantial portion of its national revenue from rents; rents, in turn, can be considered income or earnings derived from control over "rare natural gifts"—the best example is rents earned from oil resources (although rents can be earned from a variety of natural resources). Thus, rentier states include Saudi Arabia, Qatar, the United Arab Emirates, Libya, and Venezuela.

rent-seeking. In economics, rent-seeking occurs when an actor seeks to extract uncompensated value (that is, rent) from others by nonmarket or political manipulation of the economic environment. In everyday usage, rent-seeking is often associated with corruption, whether by private or public sector actors. The word *rent* in this context stems from Adam Smith's division of incomes into profit, wage, and rent. Rent-seeking behavior is distinguished from *profit-seeking* behavior, in which economic actors seek to extract value by engaging in mutually beneficial transactions.

reproduction. When applied to studies of culture or societies, reproduction refers to the process by which aspects of culture are passed on from person to person, from generation to generation, or from society to society. Reproducing culture, however, is not the same as reproducing a memo on a copy machine (Wilkins and Hull 2014). The reproduction of culture is instead a continuous, highly interactive, and often contested process. As culture is reproduced, therefore, it is subject to change.

satellite state. During the COLD WAR, a satellite state referred to a country that was formally independent or SOVEREIGN, but that was heavily influenced—politically, economically, militarily, and ideologically—by another very dominant country. Typically, however, this term was only applied to states in the "orbit" of the Soviet Union, and not to states that were heavily influenced by, say, the United States. Soviet satellite states included Albania, Poland, East Germany, Romania, Czechoslovakia, and Hungary.

Second Vatican Council. The Second Vatican Council was the twenty-first ecumenical council of the Roman Catholic Church, held between 1962 and 1965. Pope John XXIII announced the Second Vatican Council on January 25, 1959; it was designed to be a means of spiritual renewal for the Church and an occasion for Christians separated from Rome to join the search for reunion. An ecumenical council, in today's Catholic Church, is an assembly of patriarchs, cardinals, bishops, abbots, male heads of religious orders, and other juridical persons (nominated by the pope). In assemblies or ecumenical councils, the members meet to discuss matters of faith and Church discipline.

selection bias. In QUALITATIVE ANALYSIS or comparative research, selection bias refers to the tendency of researchers to "focus on certain outcomes of exceptional interest." In other words, selection bias occurs when a researcher chooses only those cases that clearly illustrate or support the argument being made. Although oftentimes unavoidable in comparative, SMALL-N research, this practice can seriously distort a study's findings, especially if the researcher is unaware of the biases in his or her selection of CASES.

semiperiphery. In WORLD-SYSTEMS THEORY, the semiperiphery is one of the three "zones" in the capitalist world system (the other two are the core and periphery). The semiperiphery is an in-between zone, needed to help stabilize the capitalist world-system in that it facilitates interaction between the low-income areas of the periphery and the high-income areas of the core. As an in-between zone, the semiperiphery is both exploited (by the core) and exploiter (of the periphery). Much of South America, Central America, South and Southeast Asia, and parts of the Middle East and North Africa are in the semiperiphery.

sharia. A basic understanding of this concept is provided by the Southern Poverty Law Center: "Sharia stands for Islamic or sacred law. It is an Arabic word meaning 'the way' or 'the path to water.' For centuries, Muslim scholars have given a broad definition of Sharia reflecting the diversity of interpretations on how Muslims have attempted to best understand and practice their faith." One interpretation is as follows: "Sharia represents how practicing Muslims can best lead their daily lives in accordance with God's divine guidance. It may be generally defined as the Islamic law revealed by God to the Prophet Muhammad. That divine law was then interpreted by Muslim scholars over the centuries. Among the primary aims of the Sharia are the achievement of justice, fairness and mercy" (http://www.tolerance.org/publication/sharia).

Shiite. Shiites make up the second largest sect of believers in ISLAM, Shia Islam, constituting about 10–15 percent of all MUSLIMS worldwide. The largest sect, the Sunni Muslims, make up about 85 percent of all Muslims.

Shinto. Meaning "Way of the Gods," Shinto is a native religion of Japan. Shinto stresses the importance of harmony between humans and nature and involves the worship of *kami*, which can be translated to mean "gods" or "nature spirits."

small-N. Refers to a situation in which the researcher has only a small number of relevant cases to analyze or compare. In QUANTITATIVE ANALYSIS (statistical analysis), a small-N represents a serious, even fundamental, problem because the small sample size may yield biased results. In comparative politics, however, researchers often have only two or three relevant cases; thus, the small-N problem represents a large and inherent obstacle to the development of general theories. Despite this problem, the comparative method allows for in-depth and systematic comparison that, if appropriately utilized, can contribute to the assessment of alternative explanations and THEORY development.

social class. See CLASS.

social construction; socially constructed. The concept of social construction suggests that the world in which we live reflects an ongoing and INTERSUBJECTIVE process, whereby reality is produced (that is, constructed) and reproduced by people and societies acting on their interpretation and their knowledge of it.

socialism. Despite its prevalent usage, the term *socialism* is defined in a number of not always compatible ways. According to the World Socialist Movement, to cite one example, the central meaning of socialism is common ownership, but this does not literally mean that everyone must own part of everything. Instead, in practice, "common ownership will mean everybody having the right to participate in decisions on how global resources will be used. It means nobody being able to take personal control of resources, beyond their own personal possessions" (http://www.worldsocialism.org/english/what-socialism). In this regard, socialism always means democratic control of resources.

social movement. A broad-based alliance of people seeking to effect political or social change. Unlike political parties or other organized political interest groups, social movements typically begin as informal organizations but may, over time, develop a strong institutional basis. Social movements are most generally associated with such issues as democratization, labor rights, environmental protection, civil and human rights, and world peace. For fuller discussion, refer to Chapter 8.

social revolution. For KARL MARX, a social revolution involved the overthrow of one class by another, producing a qualitative change in society. Revolutionary change is not to be confused with a coup d'état (replacement of one leader by another) or with reform (change that does not challenge the position of the class that holds power in the existing system).

society. In the broadest terms, society refers to any grouping of people living in a country or region and having a shared culture and a distinctive way of life (which may be defined through family relations, economic practices, and political institutions). Among scholars in comparative politics, society (or civil society) is often distinguished from the STATE.

soft-liner. A soft-liner is a ranking member of a political regime (typically an AUTHORITARIAN regime) who espouses a moderate stance toward opponents of the regime. They generally eschew violent repression and are willing to engage in negotiation and compromise with the opposition. Soft-liners are willing to support limited political liberalization as long as their core interests are protected.

sovereign; sovereignty. In international law, sovereignty suggests, first, that every state has *supreme* decisionmaking and enforcement authority over the population, resources, and territory it controls or is responsible to; and second, that no higher authority exists to regulate relations among states. In practice, however, the concept of sovereignty is more problematic than it appears. Some scholars argue that sovereignty has become anachronistic as a result of increasing GLOBALIZATION and interdependence, and others argue that sovereignty is a SOCIAL CONSTRUCTION, designed to preserve the privileges of the most powerful actors in world politics.

Stalinism; Stalinist. A colloquial term for the totalitarian political and economic system implemented by Joseph Stalin (1879–1953) in the Soviet Union.

state. Perhaps the simplest definition of state is a political entity or INSTITUTION possessing SOVEREIGNTY (that is, not being subject to any higher political authority). Most scholars agree, moreover, that another fundamental characteristic of the state is its monopoly on legitimate violence in a particular geographic area. In casual usage, the terms STATE, COUNTRY, GOVERNMENT, and even NATION are often regarded as synonymous. Although such usage is understandable and sometimes permissible, it is important to recognize the difference in meanings, which can be quite substantial. For further discussion, see Figure 1.1 in Chapter 1.

statistical analysis. See QUANTITATIVE ANALYSIS.

strategic interaction. Refers to situations in which rational decisions made by two or more actors involve an assessment of the other actor's knowledge and also of what the other actor knows about the first actor's knowledge state.

structure. The everyday meaning of structure is akin to the framework of a building or some other artifact. Structure also refers to the interrelation or arrangement of parts in a complex entity. In comparative politics, both meanings are reflected in the concept of social structure, which might be most easily defined as any relatively enduring pattern of social relationships. The existence of a social structure implies that human action (or agency) is at least partly constrained and enabled by the structure within which that action takes place.

sub-Saharan Africa. The region of the continent of Africa south of the Sahara, ranging west from Sierra Leone to Somalia and south to South Africa.

superstructure. The dictionary definition of superstructure is a structure built on top of something else. In the structural view, the meaning of superstructure is essentially the same, except that the "structure built on top of something else" consists of all the political, social, educational, religious, and cultural institutions, norms, and practices of society. The "something else," in turn, is the economic base or foundation of that society. In the contemporary world, the base is the capitalist mode of production and the superstructure is everything else. It is important to understand that the base determines the superstructure, not the other way around.

Taoism; Taoist. A spiritual belief system developed in ancient China, based on the harmonization of counterbalancing forces (that is, *yin* and *yang*), such as dark and light, male and female, strong and weak. The aim is to achieve the *tao*, which is comparable to the idea of enlightenment. Translated literally, *Taoism* means "Teaching of the Way" or "Path."

theory. There are many complex ways to define the term *theory*. For the purposes of this book, the following definition will suffice: theory is a simplified representation of "reality" and a framework within which facts are not only selected, but also interpreted, organized, and fitted together so that they create a coherent whole. See discussion in Chapter 3.

totalitarian. A totalitarian system is a nondemocratic political system in which citizens are almost completely subject to the control of a governing authority in all aspects of day-to-day life. It goes well beyond an AUTHORITARIAN system and involves pervasive surveillance, control, and indoctrination. Perhaps the closest real-world example of a totalitarian system today is North Korea.

understanding. In common usage, the terms *understanding* and EXPLANATION are used interchangeably, but it is worth distinguishing between them. The basic difference revolves around the question of causality. Researchers interested in explanation are most concerned with discerning specific CAUSAL RELATIONSHIPS that hold across time and space. Researchers interested in understanding (or interpretation), by contrast, prefer to investigate a particular event or state of affairs in its own right. The objective is to develop an account that is keenly sensitive to the particular historical, social, cultural, and political context of the event or state of affairs being examined. Not surprisingly, culturalists are generally more interested in understanding, whereas rational choice scholars and structuralists are more concerned with developing causal explanations. In practice, however, explanatory and interpretative accounts often overlap.

unit of analysis. The main actor—for example, individual, group, INSTITUTION, STATE, system—specified in a particular hypothesis or argument. The unit of analysis may be either observational or explanatory.

utility calculation. In economics, utility is a measure of the happiness or satisfaction gained from a good or service. Utility can be assessed, in the most basic manner, by simply asking an individual how they rank different options. As Jon Elster (1989) explained it, if the individual prefers three oranges to four apples, but chooses five apples over three oranges, we can use this list of pairwise comparisons to create a preference ordering. "Using a mathematical trick, [this] preference ordering can be converted to a utility function, which is a way of assigning numbers to options so that the more preferred options receive higher numbers. We can then say that the person acts so as to maximize utility" (p. 23).

variable. A term used in statistics and other social scientific analysis to describe the factor that is to be studied.

Weber, Max (1864–1920). A German economist and sociologist, considered one of the founders of modern sociology and public administration. Weber is known for a wide range of intellectual contributions, including his development of the "ideal-type." He also wrote *The Protestant Ethic and the Spirit of Capitalism*. This was a seminal essay on the differences between religions and the relative wealth of their followers.

within-case comparison. A type of comparative strategy in which the same CASE is examined over two different periods of time. The key difference between the two time periods is a change or variation in the DEPENDENT VARIABLE.

World Bank. Originally known as the International Bank for Reconstruction and Development (IBRD), the World Bank is a group of related international financial institutions designed to provide long-term development loans. The World Bank is considered a companion institution of the INTERNATIONAL MONETARY FUND, which provides short-term loans. Like the IMF, the World Bank has been subject to a great deal of criticism.

world-systems theory. A Marxist-influenced theory of global capitalism, world-systems theory is a holistic theory, not only of capitalism but of world history in toto. With respect to the *current* world-system, however, advocates of this theory argue that capitalism is its defining characteristic and that the logic of capitalism has created a particular spatial and temporal structure. Spatially, the capitalist world-system is divided into three zones—the core, the SEMIPERIPHERY, and the periphery—which are linked together in an inherently exploitative relationship. Temporally, the system is characterized by three basic processes: cycles, CONTRADICTIONS, and crisis. World-systems scholars argue that analyses of any social, political, or economic phenomenon must begin with an understanding of the spatial relationships and temporal dynamics of the system.

World Trade Organization (WTO). An international organization created to manage and oversee international trade agreements. The WTO was established in 1995 as an outgrowth of the General Agreement on Tariffs and Trade (GATT). Recently the WTO has been a main target of so-called antiglobalization protestors.

Selected Bibliography

Abegglen, James C., and George Stalk Jr. *Kaisha: The Japanese Corporation.* New York: Basic, 1985.

Abrams, Elliot, and James Turner Johnson, eds. *Close Calls: Intervention, Terrorism, Missile Defense, and "Just War" Today.* Washington, DC: Ethics and Public Policy Center, 1998.

Abrams, Philip. *Historical Sociology.* Ithaca: Cornell University Press, 1982.

Achcar, Gilbert. *The Clash of Barbarisms: September 11 and the Making of the New World Disorder.* New York: Monthly Review Press, 2002.

Addala, Radhouane, and Richard Spencer. "'I Started the Arab Spring; Now Death Is Everywhere, and Extremism Is Blooming.'" *The Telegraph,* December 17, 2015.

Ajami, Fouad. "The Summoning." In *The New Shape of World Politics: Contending Paradigms in International Relations,* edited by Foreign Affairs, 92–100. New York: Foreign Affairs, [1993] 1999.

Alder, Glenn. "Global Restructuring and Labor: The Case of the South African Trade Union Movement." In *Globalization: Critical Reflections,* edited by James H. Mittelman, 117–143. Boulder: Lynne Rienner, 1996.

Ali, Amir. "Terrorism and Genocide: Making Sense of Senselessness." *Economic and Political Weekly* 39, no. 6 (February 7–13, 2004): 521–524.

Ali, Tariq. *The Clash of Fundamentalisms: Crusades, Jihads, and Modernity.* London; Verso, 2002.

Alimi, Eitan Y., and David S. Meyer. "Seasons of Change: Arab Spring and Political Opportunities." *Swiss Political Science Review* 17, no. 4 (2011): 475–479.

Allen, G. C. *A Short Economic History of Modern Japan.* New York: St. Martin's, 1981.

Allen, Jon G. "Evil, Mindblindness, and Trauma." *Smith College Studies in Social Work* 77, no. 1 (2007): 9–31.

Amenta, Edwin, Neal Caren, Elizabeth Chiarello, and Yang Su. "The Political Consequences of Social Movements." *Annual Review of Sociology* 36 (2010): 287–307.

Amsden, Alice H. *Asia's Next Giant: South Korea and Late Industrialization.* Oxford: Oxford University Press, 1989.

———. "Taiwan's Economic History: A Case of *Etatisme* and a Challenge to Dependency Theory." In *Toward a Political Economy of Development: A Rational Choice Perspective,* edited by Robert H. Bates, 142–175. Berkeley: University of California Press, 1988.

Arce, Nicole. "Samsung Will Be Main Supplier of A9 Chip for Next Apple iPhone: Report." *Tech Times,* January 26, 2015.

Arrighi, Giovanni. "The Rise of East Asia: World Systemic and Regional Aspects." *International Journal of Sociology and Social Policy* 16, nos. 6–7 (1996): 6–44.

Axelrod, Robert. *The Evolution of Cooperation.* New York: Basic, 1984.

Bakshian, Aram, Jr. "The Unlikely Rise of Al Jazeera." *Atlantic Monthly,* January 10, 2012.

Ban Ki-moon. "A Climate Culprit in Darfur." *Washington Post,* June 16, 2007.

Baran, Paul. *The Political Economy of Growth.* New York: Monthly Review Press, 1957.

Barber, Benjamin. "Democracy at Risk: American Culture in a Global Culture." *World Policy Journal* 15, no. 2 (1998): 29–41.

———. *Jihad vs. McWorld.* New York: Ballantine, 1996.

Barkun, Michael. *Religion and the Racist Right: The Origins of the Christian Identity Movement.* Chapel Hill: University of North Carolina Press, 1997.

Bates, Robert H. "Governments and Agricultural Markets in Africa." In *Toward a Political Economy of Development: A Rational Choice Perspective,* edited by Robert H. Bates, 331–358. Berkeley: University of California Press, 1988a.

———. "Toward a Political Economy of Development." In *Toward a Political Economy of Development: A Rational Choice Perspective,* edited by Robert H. Bates, 239–244. Berkeley: University of California Press, 1988b.

Baylis, John, and Steve Smith. Introduction to *The Globalization of World Politics: An Introduction to International Relations,* 6th ed., 1–14. Oxford: Oxford University Press, 2014.

Baylis, John, Steve Smith, and Patricia Owens, eds. *The Globalization of World Politics: An Introduction to International Relations.* 6th ed. Oxford: Oxford University Press, 2014.

BBC News. "Syria: The Story of the Conflict." March 12, 2015.

Beck, Ulrich. *What Is Globalization?* Cambridge: Polity, 2000.

Bell, Edward. "Catholicism and Democracy: A Reconsideration." *Journal of Religion & Society* 10 (2008). https://dspace.creighton.edu.

Bellamy, Alex J. "The Responsibility to Protect—Five Years On." *Ethics and International Affairs* 24, no. 2 (2010): 143–169.

Benedict, Ruth. *The Chrysanthemum and the Sword: Patterns of Japanese Culture.* Boston: Houghton Mifflin, 1946.

Berger, Peter L. "An East Asian Development Model?" In *In Search of an East Asian Development Model,* edited by Peter L. Berger and H. H. M. Hsiao, 3–11. New Brunswick, NJ: Transaction, 1998.

Bergesen, Albert J., and Omar Lizardo. "International Terrorism and the World-System." *Sociological Theory* 22, no. 1 (March 2004): 38–52.

Beverly, James A. "Is Islam a Religion of Peace?" *Christianity Today,* January 7, 2002.

Bialik, Carl. "Shadowy Figure: Al Qaeda's Size Is Hard to Measure." *Wall Street Journal,* September 10, 2011.

Biggart, Nicole Woolsey. "Explaining Asian Economic Organization: Toward a Weberian Institutional Perspective." In *The Economic Organization of East Asian*

Capitalism, edited by Gary G. Hamilton, Nicole Woolsey Biggart, and Marco Orrù, 3–32. Thousand Oaks, CA: Sage, 1997.

Birdsall, Nancy. "Life Is Unfair: Inequality in the World." *Foreign Policy* 111 (Summer 1998): 76–93.

Bloomberg Businessweek. "Most Innovative in the World 2014: Countries." *Bloomberg Rankings,* 2014. http://images.businessweek.com/bloomberg/pdfs /most_innovative_countries_2014_011714.pdf.

Blumer, Herber. "Collective Behavior." In *An Outline of the Principles of Sociology,* edited by Robert E. Park, 219–280. New York: Barnes and Noble, 1939.

Blumner, Robyn E. "Why Democracy Will Fail in Iraq." *St. Petersburg Times,* January 25, 2004.

Bockstette, Carsten. "Jihadist Terrorist Use of Strategic Communication Management Techniques." Occasional Paper no. 20. George C. Marshall European Center for Security Studies, December 2008. http://www.marshallcenter.org /mcpublicweb/MCDocs/files/College/F_Publications/occPapers/occ-paper_20 -en.pdf.

Booth, John A. *Costa Rica: Quest for Democracy.* Boulder: Westview, 1998.

Bouissou, Jean-Marie. *Japan: The Burden of Success.* Boulder: Lynne Rienner, 2002.

Brams, Steven J. "The Study of Rational Politics." In *Approaches to the Study of Politics,* edited by Brian Susser, 312–317. New York: Macmillan, 1992.

Brannan, David W., Philip F. Esler, and N. T. Anders Strindberg. "Talking to 'Terrorists': Towards an Independent Analytical Framework for the Study of Violent Substate Activism." *Studies in Conflict and Terrorism* 24 (2001): 3–24.

Bratton, Michael, and Nicolas van de Walle. *Democratic Experiments in Africa: Regime Transitions in Comparative Perspective.* Cambridge: Cambridge University Press, 1997.

Braudel, Fernand. "History and Social Science." In *Economy and Society in Early Modern Europe: Essays from Annales,* edited by P. Burke, 11–42. New York: Harper and Row, 1972.

Bröer, Christian, and Jan Willem Duyvendak. "Discursive Opportunities, Feeling Rules, and the Rise of Protests Against Aircraft Noise." *Mobilization: An International Journal* 14, no. 3 (2009): 337–356.

Buechler, Steven M. *Understanding Social Movements: Theories from the Classical Era to the Present.* London: Routledge, 2011.

Bunce, Valerie. "Rethinking Recent Democratization: Lessons from the Postcommunist Experience." *World Politics* 55 (2003): 192–197.

Burks, Ardath W. *Japan: Profile of a Postindustrial Power.* Boulder: Westview, 1981.

Burlacu, Alexandra. "Apple Watch 2 Reportedly Coming Out in 2016 with LG as Sole P-OLED Display Supplier." *Tech Times,* June 12, 2015.

Burstein, Paul. *Discrimination, Jobs, and Politics: The Struggle for Equal Employment Opportunity in the United States Since the New Deal.* Chicago: University of Chicago Press, 1985.

Canel, Eduardo. "New Social Movement Theory and Resource Mobilization Theory: The Need for Integration." In *Community Power and Grassroots Democracy: The Transformation of Social Life,* edited by M. Kaufman and H. Dilla Alfonso. International Development Research Centre, 1997. http://web.idrc.ca /en/ev-33847-201-1-DO_TOPIC.html.

Caplan, Bryan. "Terrorism: The Relevance of the Rational Choice Model." *Public Choice* 128 (2006): 91–107.

Cardoso, Fernando H. "Associated-Dependent Development: Theoretical and Practical Implications." In *Authoritarian Brazil,* edited by Alfred Stepan, 142–176. New Haven: Yale University Press, 1973.

Cardoso, Fernando H., and Enzo Faletto. *Dependency and Development in Latin America.* Berkeley: University of California Press, 1979.

Casanova, José. "Modernization and Democratization: Reflections on Spain's Transition to Democracy." *Social Research* 50, no. 4 (Winter 1983): 929–973.

Central Intelligence Agency (CIA). *The World Factbook.* 2014. https://www.cia.gov/library/publications/the-world-factbook/index.html.

Chan, Steve. *East Asian Dynamism: Growth, Order, and Security in the Pacific Region.* 2nd ed. Boulder: Westview, 1993.

Chang, Iris. *The Rape of Nanking: The Forgotten Holocaust of World War II.* New York: BasicBooks, 1997.

Charney, Israel W. "Toward a Generic Definition of Genocide." In *Genocide: Conceptual and Historical Dimensions,* edited by George Andreopoulos, 75–94. Philadelphia: University of Pennsylvania Press, 1994.

Chase-Dunn, Christopher. "Technology and the Logic of World-Systems." In *Transcending the State-Global Divide: A Neostructuralist Agenda in International Relations,* edited by Ronen P. Palan and Barry Gills, 84–105. Boulder: Lynne Rienner, 1994.

Chen, Ching-Chih. "Police and Community Control Systems in the Empire." In *The Japanese Colonial Empire, 1895–1945,* edited by Ramon H. Myers and Mark R. Peattie, 213–239. Princeton: Princeton University Press, 1984.

Chicago Project on Security and Terrorism. *Suicide Attack Database.* 2015. http://cpostdata.uchicago.edu/search_new.php.

Chilcote, Ronald H. *Theories of Comparative Political Economy.* Boulder: Westview, 2000.

———. *Theories of Comparative Politics: The Search for a Paradigm Reconsidered.* Boulder: Westview, 1994.

Cho, Lee-Jay, and Man Jun Halm. "Recent Changes in Fertility Rates of the Korean Population." *Demography* 5, no. 2 (1968): 690–698.

Christiansen, Jonathan. "Four Stages of Social Movements." *EBSCO Research Starters: Academic Starters.* 2009. https://www.ebscohost.com/uploads/imported/this Topic-dbTopic-1248.pdf.

Ciccantell, Paul S., and Stephen G. Bunker. "The Economic Ascent of China and the Potential for Restructuring the Capitalist World-Economy." *Journal of World-Systems Research* 10, no. 3 (Fall 2004): 564–589.

Cline, Austin. "Christianity vs. Democracy: Is Christianity Compatible with Democracy?" N.d. http://atheism.about.com/od/aboutchristianity/a/Christianity-Democracy-Compatible.htm.

Coleman, James S. "Modernization: Political Aspects." In *International Encyclopedia of the Social Sciences,* edited by David L. Sills, 395–402. New York: Macmillan, 1968.

Collier, David. "The Comparative Method." In *Theory, Case, and Method in Comparative Politics,* edited by Nikolaos Zahariadis, 35–46. New York: Harcourt Brace College, 1997.

Collins, Kathleen. "Clans, Pacts, and Politics in Central Asia." *Journal of Democracy* 13, no. 3 (July 2002): 137–152.

Comte, A. "Modernization: Political Aspects." In *Social Change: Sources, Patterns, and Consequences,* edited by Amitai Etzioni and Eva Etzioni, 14–19. New York: Basic, 1964.

Conquest, Robert. *The Harvest of Sorrow: Soviet Collectivization and the Terror-Famine.* Oxford: Oxford University Press, 1987.

Cooper, William H. "Russia's Economic Performance and Policies and Their Implications for the United States." *CRS Reports for Congress* (November 2008): 1–27.

Coughlin, Con. "The Hardliners Are Winning in Iran's Green Revolution." *The Telegraph,* June 22, 2009.

Crawford, Darryl. "Chinese Capitalism: Cultures, the Southeast Asian Region, and Economic Globalisation." *Third World Quarterly* 21, no. 1 (2000): 69–86.

Crawford, Stu. "Resource Mobilization Theory and New Social Movements." Unpublished paper. 2005. http://web.uvic.ca/~stucraw/Lethbridge/MyArticles/ResourceMobilization.htm.

Crenshaw, Martha. "The Logic of Terrorism: Terrorist Behavior as a Product of Strategic Choice." In *Origins of Terrorism: Psychologies, Ideologies, Theologies, States of Mind,* edited by Walter Reich, 7–24. Washington, DC: Woodrow Wilson Center, 1998.

———. "Thoughts on Relating Terrorism to Historical Contexts." In *Terrorism in Context,* edited by Martha Crenshaw, 3–26. University Park: Pennsylvania State University Press, 1995.

Crossley, Nick. *Making Sense of Social Movements.* Buckingham, UK: Open University Press, 2002.

Cumings, Bruce. "The Origins and Development of the Northeast Asian Political Economy: Industrial Sectors, Product Cycles, and Political Consequences." *International Organization* 38, no. 1 (1984): 1–40.

———. "Webs with No Spiders, Spiders with No Webs: The Genealogy of the Developmental State." In *The Developmental State,* edited by Meredith Woo-Cumings, 61–92. Ithaca: Cornell University Press, 1999.

Cumming-Bruce, Nick. "United Nations Investigators Accuse ISIS of Genocide over Attacks on Yazidis." *New York Times,* March 19, 2015.

Dahl, Kathleen. "Culture." N.d. http://www2.eou.edu/%7Ekdahl/cultdef.html.

Dahl, Robert A. *Polyarchy: Participation and Opposition.* New Haven: Yale University Press, 1971.

Dalton, Russell J., Manfred Kuechler, and Wilhelm Bürklin. "The Challenge of New Movements." In *Challenging the Political Order: New Social Movements and Political Movements in Western Democracies,* edited by Russell J. Dalton and Manfred Kuechler, 3–20. New York: Oxford University Press, 1990.

Davis, Diane E. "The Power of Distance: Re-Theorizing Social Movements in Latin America." *Theory and Society* 28, no. 4 (1999): 585–638.

Deaton, Angus. "Measuring Poverty." In *Understanding Poverty,* edited by Abhijit Vinayak Banerjee, Roland Bénabou, and Dilip Mookherjee, 3–16. New York: Oxford University Press, 2006.

De la Porta, Donatella, and Mario Diani. *Social Movements: An Introduction.* 2nd ed. Malden, MA: Blackwell, 2006.

Des Forges, Allison. *Leave None to Tell the Story: Genocide in Rwanda.* New York: Human Rights Watch, 1999. http://www.hrw.org/reports/pdfs/r/rwanda/rwanda993.pdf.

DeWitt, Mike (director and writer), and Daniel Jonah Goldhagen (writer). *Worse Than War.* Video. JTN Productions and WNET.org, 2009.

Diamond, Larry. "Causes and Effects." In *Political Culture and Democracy in Developing Countries,* edited by Larry Diamond, 229–249. Boulder: Lynne Rienner, 1994.

————. *Developing Democracy: Toward Consolidation.* Baltimore: Johns Hopkins University Press, 1999.

Diani, Mario, and Ivano Bison. "Organization, Coalitions, and Movements." *Theory and Society* 33, no. 3 (2004): 281–309.

Dixon, Marc, and Vincent J. Roscigno. "Status, Networks, and Social Movement Participation: The Case of Striking Workers." *American Journal of Sociology* 108, no. 6 (2003): 1292–1327.

Dobson, Charles. "Social Movements: A Summary of What Works." In *The Citizen's Handbook,* edited by Charles Dobson. Vancouver: Vancouver Citizen's Committee, 2003. http://www.vcn.bc.ca.citizens-handbook.

Docker, John. "Raphaël Lemkin, Creator of the Concept of Genocide: A World History Perspective." *Humanities Research* 16, no. 2 (2010). http://press.anu .edu.au//apps/bookworm/view/Humanities+Research+Vol+XVI.+No.+2.+2010 /5271/docker.xhtml.

Dogan, Mattei, and Ali Kazancigil. *Comparing Nations: Concepts, Strategies, Substance.* Oxford: Blackwell, 1994.

Dogan, Mattei, and Dominque Pelassy. *How to Compare Nations: Strategies in Comparative Politics.* 2nd ed. Chatham, NJ: Chatham House, 1990.

Domínguez-Torres, Carolina, and Vivien Foster. "The Central African Republic's Infrastructure: A Continental Perspective." *Africa Infrastructure Country Diagnostic: Country Report* (May 2011). http://infrastructureafrica.org/system/files /CAR%20country%20rpt%20Web.pdf.

Dore, Ronald. *Taking Japan Seriously: A Confucian Perspective on Leading Economic Issues.* Stanford: Stanford University Press, 1987.

Dos Santos, Theotonio. "The Structure of Dependence." In *International Political Economy: State-Market Relations in the Changing Global Order,* edited by C. Roe Goddard, John T. Passé-Smith, and John G. Conklin, 165–175. Boulder: Lynne Rienner, [1970] 1996.

Dowding, Keith, and Andrew Hindmoor. "The Usual Suspects: Rational Choice, Socialism, and Political Theory." *New Political Economy* 2, no. 3 (1997): 451–463.

Doyle, Michael W. "Correspondence: On the Democratic Peace." *International Security* 19, no. 4 (1995): 180–184.

Durkheim, Emile. *The Elementary Forms of the Religious Life.* New York: Collier, [1915] 1961.

Earl, Jennifer. "Methods, Movements, and Outcomes: Methodological Difficulties in the Study of Extramovement Outcomes." *Research in Social Movements, Conflicts and Change* 22 (2000): 3–25.

Earl, Jennifer, and Alan Schussman. "Cease and Desist: Repression, Strategic Voting, and the 2000 U.S. Presidential Election." *Mobilization* 9 (2004): 181–202.

The Economist. "Deleveraging Delayed." October 24, 2015.

Edmonds, Amy. *Authoritarianism and the Catholic Church in Latin America.* Dissertation, Department of Political Science, Baylor University, 2010. https:// baylor-ir.tdl.org/baylor-ir/handle/2104/7966.

Edsall, Thomas B. "How Poor Are the Poor?" *New York Times,* March 25, 2015.

Eghdamian, Kat. "What Was the Role of Religion in the Arab Spring." *OpenDemocracy,* July 28, 2014.

Eisenhower, Dwight D. "Dwight D. Eisenhower: 1954—Containing the Public Messages, Speeches, and Statements of the President, January 1 to December 31, 1954." *The Public Papers of the Presidents of the United States.* Washington, DC: Government Printing Office, 1960. http://name.umdl.umich.edu/4728402 .1954.001.

Eley, Geoff, and Ronald Grigor Suny, eds. *Becoming National: A Reader.* Oxford: Oxford University Press, 1996.

Elster, Jon. *Nuts and Bolts for the Social Sciences.* New York: Cambridge University Press, 1989.

———. *Ulysses and the Sirens: Studies in Rationality and Irrationality.* Paris: Maison des Sciences de l'Homme, 1984.

Eltantawy, Nahed, and Julie B. Wiest. "Social Media in the Egyptian Revolution: Reconsidering Resource Mobilization Theory." *International Journal of Communication* 5 (2011): 1207–1224.

Evans, Graham, and Jeffrey Newnham. *Penguin Dictionary of International Relations.* London: Penguin, 1998.

Evans, Peter B., Dietrich Rueschemeyer, and Theda Skocpol, eds. *Bringing the State Back In.* Cambridge: Cambridge University Press, 1985.

Faris, Stephan. "The Real Roots of Darfur." *Atlantic Monthly,* April 2007.

Ferree, Myra Marx. "Institutionalizing Gender Equality: Feminist Politics and Equality Offices." *German Politics & Society,* nos. 24–25 (1991–1992): 53–66.

Finnemore, Martha, and Kathryn Sikkink. "Taking Stock: The Constructivist Research Program in International Relations and Comparative Politics." *Annual Review of Political Science* 4, no. 1 (2001): 391–416.

Flanagan, Ed. "What Happens When You Google 'Tiananmen Square' in China?" *NBC News,* June 3, 2014.

Formosa, Paul. "Understanding Evil Acts." *Human Studies* 30, no. 2 (2007): 57–77.

Foster, John Bellamy. "Monopoly Capital and the New Globalization." *Monthly Review* 53, no. 8 (2002). http//:www.monthlyreview.org.

Fowler, Barbara. *Critical Thinking Definitions.* Critical Thinking Across the Curriculum. Longview Community College, n.d. http://www.kcmetro.cc.mo.us /longview/ctac/definitions.htm.

Frank, André Gunder. "The Development of Underdevelopment." In *The Political Economy of Development and Underdevelopment,* edited by Charles K. Wilber, 109–120. New York: Random House Business, [1966] 1988.

Freamon, Bernard K. "Martyrdom, Suicide, and the Islamic Law of War: A Short Legal History." *Fordham International Law Journal* 27 (December 2003): 299–369.

Freedom House. *Nations in Transit 2014: Eurasia's Rupture with Democracy.* Washington, DC, 2014. https://freedomhouse.org/sites/default/files/NIT2014% 20booklet_WEBSITE.pdf.

Friedman, Milton. *Essays in Positive Economics.* Chicago: University of Chicago Press, 1953.

Fukuyama, Francis. "The End of History?" In *The New Shape of World Politics: Contending Paradigms in International Relations,* rev. ed., 1–25. New York: Foreign Affairs, [1989] 1999.

———. "Social Capital, Civil Society, and Development." *Third World Quarterly* 22, no. 1 (2001): 7–20.

Galvin, James L. *The Arab Uprisings: What Everyone Needs to Know.* New York: Oxford University Press, 2015.

Gamson, William. *The Strategy of Social Protest.* 2nd ed. Belmont, CA: Wadsworth, 1990.

Geddes, Barbara. "What Do We Know About Democratization After Twenty Years?" *Annual Review of Political Science* 2 (1999): 115–144.

Geertz, Clifford. *The Interpretation of Culture: Selected Essays.* New York: Basic, 1973.

Giddens, Anthony. *Director's Lectures: Runaway World—The Reith Lectures Revisited.* Lecture 5. 2000. http://www.lse.ac.uk/Giddens/pdf/19Jan00.pdf.

———. "Introduction by Anthony Giddens." In *The Protestant Ethic and the Spirit of Capitalism* by Max Weber, trans. Talcott Parsons, vii–xxiv. London: Routledge, 2005 (1930).

Giugni, Marco G. "Introduction: How Social Movements Matter: Past Research, Present Problems, Future Developments." In *How Social Movements Matter,* edited by Marco G. Giugni, Douglas McAdam, and Charles Tilly, xiii–xxxiii. Minneapolis: University of Minnesota Press, 1999.

———. "Political, Biographical, and Cultural Consequences of Social Movements." *Sociology Compass* 2 (2008): 1582–1600.

———. "Was It Worth the Effort? The Outcomes and Consequences of Social Movements." *Annual Review of Sociology* 24 (1998): 371–393.

Global Fire Power. "Countries Ranked by Military Strength." 2015. http://www.globalfirepower.com/countries-listing.asp.

Global Terrorism Database. 2015. http://www.start.umd.edu/gtd.

Goldhagen, Daniel Jonah. *Worse Than War: Genocide, Eliminationism, and the Ongoing Assault on Humanity.* New York: PublicAffairs, 2009.

Goodin, Robert E. "Institutions and Their Design." In *The Theory of Institutional Design,* edited by Robert E. Goodin, 1–53. Cambridge: Cambridge University Press, 1996.

Gould, David. "Why Do Networks Matter? Rationalist and Structuralist Interpretations." In *Social Movements and Networks: Relational Approaches to Collective Action,* edited by Diani Mario and Doug McAdam, 233–258. Oxford: Oxford University Press, 2003.

Government of Canada. "Firearms and Violent Crime in Canada, 2012." 2014. http://www.statcan.gc.ca/pub/85-002-x/2014001/article/11925-eng.htm#a3.

Gozzi, Raymond, Jr. "The Jigsaw Puzzle as a Metaphor for Knowledge." *Etc.: A Review of General Semantics* 53, no. 4 (1996): 447–451.

Green, Steven L. "Rational Choice Theory: An Overview." Baylor University Faculty Development Seminar on Rational Choice Theory, May 2002.

Gunaratna, Rohan. *Inside Al Qaeda: Global Network of Terror.* New York: Columbia University Press, 2002.

Gustafson, Thane. *Capitalism Russian-Style.* Cambridge: Cambridge University Press, 1997.

Guyuron, Bahman, David J. Rowe, Adam B. Weinfeld, Yashar Eshraghi, Amir Fathi, and Seree Iamphongsai. "Factors Contributing to the Facial Aging of Identical Twins." *Plastic and Reconstructive Surgery* 123, no. 4 (April 2009): 1321–1331.

Habeck, Mary. "What Does Al Qaeda Want?" *Foreign Policy,* March 6, 2012.

Hamilton, Gary G., and Nicole Woolsey Biggart. "Market, Culture, and Authority: A Comparative Analysis of Management and Organization in the Far East." In *The Economic Organization of East Asian Capitalism,* edited by Gary G. Hamilton, Nicole Woolsey Biggart, and Marco Orrù, 111–150. Thousand Oaks, CA: Sage, 1997.

Hanieh, Adam. *Lineages of Revolt: Issues of Contemporary Capitalism in the Middle East.* Chicago: Haymaker, 2013.

Hanlon, Querine. "Security Sector Reform in Tunisia: A Year After the Jasmine Revolution." Special Report no. 304. Washington, DC: US Institute of Peace, 2012. http://www.usip.org/sites/default/files/SR304.pdf.

Hardwig, Johh. "Epistemic Dependence." *Journal of Philosophy* 82 (1985): 335–349.

Harrison, Lawrence. "Introduction: Why Culture Matters." In *Culture Matters: How Values Shape Human Progress,* edited by Lawrence E. Harrison and Samuel P. Huntington, xxii–xxxiv. New York: Basic, 2000.

Harvey, David L., and Michael H. Reed. "The Culture of Poverty: An Ideological Analysis." *Sociological Perspectives* 39, no. 4 (Winter 1996): 465–495.

Havens, Thomas R. H. *Fire Across the Sea: The Vietnam War and Japan, 1965–1975.* Princeton: Princeton University Press, 2014.

Helmke, Gretchen, and Steven Levitsky. "Informal Institutions and Comparative Politics: A Research Agenda." *Perspectives on Politics* 2, no. 4 (December 2004): 725–740.

Henderson, David. "Lessons of East Asia's Economic Growth: Fresh Perspectives on East Asia's Future." In *Stand! Global Issues,* edited by Timothy Lim, 74–83. Boulder: Coursewise, 2000.

Heydemann, Steven, and Reinoud Leenders. *Middle East Authoritarianisms: Governance, Contestation, and Regime Resilience in Syria and Iran.* Stanford: Stanford University Press, 2013.

Hoffer, Eric. *The True Believer: Thoughts on the Nature of Mass Movements.* New York: Harper and Row, 1951.

Holz, Carsten A. "China's Economic Growth, 1978–2025: What We Know Today About China's Economic Growth Tomorrow." *World Development* 36, no. 10 (October 2008): 1665–1691.

Hoogvelt, Ankie. *Globalization and the Postcolonial World: The New Political Economy of Development.* Baltimore: Johns Hopkins University Press, 1997.

Hopkin, Jonathan. "Comparative Methods." In *Theory and Methods in Political Science,* 2nd ed., edited by David Marsh and Gerry Stoker, 249–267. Basingstoke: Palgrave Macmillan, 2002.

Howard, Philip N., Aiden Duffy, Deen Freelon, Muzammil Hussain, Will Mari, and Marwa Mazaid. "Opening Closed Regimes: What Was the Role of Social Media During the Arab Spring?" Working paper. Project on Information Technology and Political Islam, 2011.

Howard, Philip N., and Muzammil M. Hussain. *Democracy's Fourth Wave? Digital Media and the Arab Spring.* Oxford: Oxford University Press, 2013.

Hunt, Lynn. "Charles Tilly's Collective Action." In *Vision and Method in Historical Sociology,* edited by Theda Skocpol, 244–275. Cambridge: Cambridge University Press, 1984.

Hunt, Scott A., and Robert D. Benford. "Collective Identity, Solidarity, and Commitment." In *The Blackwell Companion to Social Movements,* edited by David A. Snow, Sarah A. Soule, and Hanspeter Kriesi, 433–457. Malden, MA: Blackwell, 2004.

Huntington, Samuel P. "The Change to Change: Modernization, Development, and Politics." *Comparative Politics* 3 (April 1971): 283–322.

———. "The Clash of Civilizations?" *Foreign Affairs* 72, no. 3 (1993): 22–49.

———. *The Clash of Civilizations and the Remaking of World Order.* New York: Simon and Schuster, 1996.

———. "Democracy's Third Wave." *Journal of Democracy* 2, no. 2 (Spring 1991): 12–34.

Hutchinson, Nick. "'Climate War' Darfur?" *GeoDate* 21, no. 4 (August 2008): 10.

Hutton, Will. "The World Economic Order Is Collapsing and This Time There Seems No Way Out." *The Guardian,* October 10, 2015.

International Monetary Fund (IMF). *World Economic Outlook Database.* 2015. https://www.imf.org/external/pubs/ft/weo/2015/01/weodata/index.aspx.

Ismael, Tareq Y. *International Relations of the Contemporary Middle East: A Study in World Politics.* Syracuse: Syracuse University Press, 1986.

James, William E., Seiji Naya, and Gerald M. Meier. *Asian Development: Economic Success and Policy Lessons.* Madison: University of Wisconsin Press, 1989.

Janda, Kenneth, Jeffrey Berry, Jerry Goldman, and Deborah Schildkraut. *The Challenge of Democracy: American Government in Global Politics.* Boston: Cengage Learning, 2012.

Jansen, Marius B. *The Making of Modern Japan.* Cambridge: Belknap, 2000.

Jary, David, and Julia Jary. *The HarperCollins Dictionary of Sociology.* New York: HarperPerennial, 1991.

Jenkins, J. Craig, and Bert Klandermans. "The Politics of Social Protest." In *The Politics of Social Protest: Comparative Perspectives on States and Social Movements,* edited by J. Craig Jenkins and Bert Klandermans, 3–13. Minneapolis: University of Minnesota Press, 1995.

Jenkins, J. Craig, and Charles Perrow. "Insurgency of the Powerless: Farm Worker Movements (1946–1972)." *American Sociological Review* 42 (1977): 429–468.

Jenson, Jane. "What's in a Name? National Movements and Public Discourse." In *Social Movements and Culture,* edited by Hank Johnston and Bert Klandermans, 107–126. Minneapolis: University of Minnesota Press, 1995.

Johnson, Chalmers. *MITI and the Japanese Miracle: The Growth of Industrial Policy, 1925–1975.* Stanford: Stanford University Press, 1982.

Johnston, Hank, and Bert Klandermans. "The Cultural Analysis of Social Movements." In *Social Movements and Culture,* edited by Hank Johnston and Bert Klandermans, 3–24. Minneapolis: University of Minnesota Press, 1995.

Johnston, Hank, Enrique Laraña, and Joseph R. Gusfield. "Identities, Grievances, and New Social Movements." In *New Social Movements: From Ideology to Identity,* edited by Enrique Laraña, Hank Johnston, and Joseph R. Gusfield, 3–35. Philadelphia: Temple University Press, 1994.

Jones, Adam. *Genocide: A Comprehensive Introduction.* 1st ed. New York: Routledge, 2006.

———. *Genocide: A Comprehensive Introduction.* 2nd ed. New York: Routledge, 2010.

Jones, Christopher. "Song and Nationalism in Quebec." *Contemporary French Civilization* 24, no. 1 (2000). http://ml.hss.cmu.edu/facpages/cjones/QuebecSong1.pdf.

Jones, Jeff, and Lydia Saad. "Gallup Poll Social Series: Values and Beliefs." *Gallup News Service,* May 8–11, 2014.

Jones, Toby Craig. "America, Oil, and War in the Middle East." *Journal of American History* 99, no. 1 (2012): 208–218.

Jurgensmeyer, Mark. *Terror in the Mind of God: The Global Rise of Religious Violence.* Berkeley: University of California Press, 2003.

Kamppeter, Wener. "Dictatorship, Democracy, and Economic Regime: Reflections on the Experience of South Korea." Friedrich Ebert Stiftung, January 2008. http://library.fes.de/pdf-files/iez/05399.pdf.

Kaname, Akamatsu. "Waga Kuni Yomo Kogyohin no Boekisusei" [Trend of Japanese Trade in Wool Goods]. *Shogyo Keizai Ronso* [Journal of Nagoya Higher Commercial School] 13 (1935): 129–212.

Kaplan, Robert. "The Coming Anarchy." *Atlantic Monthly,* February 1994.

Kaul, Inge. "What Is a Public Good?" *Le Monde Diplomatique,* June 2000.

Kelly, Mike. *Bus on Jaffa Road: A Story of Middle East Terrorism and the Search for Justice.* Guilford, CT: Lyons, 2014.

Kendall, Diana. *Sociology in Our Time: The Essentials.* 5th ed. Belmont, CA: Thomson Wadsworth, 2006.

Keohane, Robert O., Peter M. Haas, and Marc A. Levy. "The Effectiveness of International Environmental Institutions." In *Institutions for the Earth: Sources of Effective Environmental Protection,* edited by Robert O. Keohane, Peter M. Haas, and Marc A. Levy, 3–26. London: Massachusetts Institute of Technology Press, 1993.

KNOEMA. "World GDP Ranking 2015: Data and Charts." 2015. http://knoema.com/nwnfkne/world-gdp-ranking-2015-data-and-charts.

Kohli, Atul, Peter Evans, Peter J. Katzenstein, Adam Przeworski, Susanne Hoeber Rudolph, James C. Scott, and Theda Skocpol. "The Role of Theory in Comparative Politics: A Symposium." *World Politics* 48, no. 1 (October 1995): 1–49.

Koopmans, Ruud, and Paul Statham. "Ethnic and Civic Conceptions of Nationhood and the Differential Success of the Extreme Right in Germany and Italy." In *How Social Movements Matter,* edited by Marco Giugni, Douglas McAdam, and Charles Tilly, 225–251. Minneapolis: University of Minnesota Press, 1999.

Kopstein, Jeffrey, and Mark Lichbach, eds. *Comparative Politics: Interests, Identities, and Institutions in a Changing Global Order.* Cambridge: Cambridge University Press, 2000.

Kramer, Martin. "The Moral Logic of Hizballah." In *Origins of Terrorism: Psychologies, Ideologies, Theologies, States of Mind,* edited by Walter Reich, 131–157. Washington, DC: Woodrow Wilson Center, 1998.

Kriesi, Hanspeter. "The Political Opportunity Structure of New Social Movements: Its Impact on Their Mobilization." In *The Politics of Social Protest: Comparative Perspectives on States and Social Movements,* edited by J. Craig Jenkins and Bert Klandermans, 167–198. Minneapolis: University of Minnesota Press, 1995.

Kriesi, Hanspeter, Ruud Koopmans, Jan Willem Duyvendak, and Marco G. Giugni. *New Social Movements in Western Europe: A Comparative Perspective.* Minneapolis: University of Minnesota Press, 1995.

Kristensen, Hans M., and Robert S. Norris. "US Nuclear Forces, 2015." *Bulletin of the Atomic Scientists* 7, no. 12 (2015): 107–119.

Lam, Danny, Jeremy T. Paltiel, and John H. Shannon. "The Confucian Entrepreneur? Chinese Culture, Industrial Organization, and Intellectual Property Piracy in Taiwan." *Asian Affairs: An American Review* 20, no. 4 (1994): 205–227.

Lamme, Margot O. "Tapping Into War: Leveraging World War I in the Drive for a Dry Nation." *American Journalism* 21, no. 4 (2004): 63–91.

Landes, David. "Culture Makes Almost All the Difference." In *Culture Matters: How Values Shape Human Progress,* edited by Lawrence E. Harrison and Samuel P. Huntington, 2–13. New York: Basic, 2000.

Lane, Ruth. *The Art of Comparative Politics.* Boston: Allyn and Bacon, 1997.

Laraña, Enrique, Hank Johnston, and Joseph R. Gusfield, eds. *New Social Movements: From Ideology to Identity.* Philadelphia: Temple University Press, 1994.

Laville, Rosabelle. "In the Politics of the Rainbow: Creoles and Civil Society in Mauritius." *Journal of Contemporary African Studies* 18, no. 2 (2000): 277–294.

Lechner, Frank J., and John Boli. "Introduction (Part 8)." In *The Globalization Reader,* edited by Frank J. Lechner and John Boli, 319–321. Malden, MA: Blackwell, 2000.

Lee, Jinhee. "The Enemy Within: Earthquake, Rumors, and Massacre in the Japanese Empire." Faculty Research & Creative Activity Paper no. 58. Eastern Illinois University, 2008. http://thekeep.eiu.edu/history_fac/58.

Lee, John. "Is China Really an 'East Asian Success Story'?" *Policy* 25, no. 2 (Winter 2009): 9–13.

Leftwich, Adrian. *Redefining Politics: People, Resources, and Power.* London: Methuen, 1983.

Lemarchand, René. "Case Study: The Burundi Killings of 1972." *Online Encyclopedia of Mass Violence,* June 2008. http://www.massviolence.org/the-burundi -killings-of-1972#citation.

Levene, Mark. "Connecting Threads: Rwanda, the Holocaust, and the Pattern of Contemporary Genocide." In *The Genocide Studies Reader,* edited by Samuel Totten and Paul R. Bartrop, 258–284. London: Routledge, 2009.

———. "A Dissenting Voice: Or How Current Assumptions of Deterring and Preventing Genocide May Be Looking at the Problem Through the Wrong End of the Telescope, Part I." *Journal of Genocide Research* 6, no. 2 (2004): 153–166.

———. *Genocide in the Age of the Nation-State.* 2 vols. London: Tauris, 2005.

Levi, Margaret. "A Model, a Method, and a Map: Rational Choice in Comparative and Historical Analysis." In *Comparative Politics: Rationality, Culture, and Structure,* edited by Mark Irving Lichbach and Alan S. Zuckerman, 19–41. Cambridge: Cambridge University Press, 1997.

Levin, Jonathan, and Paul Migrom. "Introduction to Choice Theory." Unpublished paper. September 2004. http://web.stanford.edu/~jdlevin/Econ%20202/Choice %20Theory.pdf.

Lewis, Oscar. *Five Families: Mexican Case Studies in the Culture of Poverty.* New York: Basic, [1959] 1975.

———. *A Study of Slum Culture: Backgrounds for* La Vida. New York: Random, 1968.

———. "A Study of Slum Culture: Backgrounds for *La Vida.*" In *From Modernization to Globalization: Perspectives on Development and Social Change,* edited by J. Timmons Roberts and Amy Hite, 110–118. London: Blackwell, [1968] 2000.

Lichbach, Mark I. "Social Theory and Comparative Politics." In *Comparative Politics: Rationality, Culture, and Structure,* edited by Mark I. Lichbach and Alan S. Zuckerman, 239–276. Cambridge: Cambridge University Press, 1997.

Lichbach, Mark Irving, and Alan S. Zuckerman, eds. *Comparative Politics: Rationality, Culture, and Structure.* Cambridge: Cambridge University Press, 1997.

Lim, Timothy C. *Politics in East Asia: Explaining Change and Continuity.* Boulder: Lynne Rienner, 2014.

Lipset, Seymour Martin. "Some Social Requisites of Democracy: Economic Development and Political Legitimacy." *American Political Science Review* 53, no. 1 (March 1959): 69–105.

Lipsky, Michael. *Protest in City Politics.* Chicago: Rand McNally, 1970.

Little, Daniel. *Varieties of Social Explanation.* Boulder: Westview, 1991.

Lockwood, William W. *The Economic Development of Japan: Growth and Structural Change.* Princeton: Princeton University Press, 1968.

Longman, Timothy. *Christianity and Genocide in Rwanda.* Cambridge: Cambridge University Press, 2010.

Lukasik, Stephen, Lawrence T. Greenberg, and Seymour E. Goodman. "Protecting an Invaluable and Ever-Widening Infrastructure." *Communications of the ACM* 41, no. 6 (June 1998): 11–16.

Lynch, Marc. *The Arab Uprising: The Unfinished Revolutions of the New Middle East.* New York: PublicAffairs, 2012.

———. Introduction to *The Arab Uprisings Explained: New Contentious Politics in the Middle East,* edited by Marc Lynch, 1–28. New York: Columbia University Press, 2014.

MaCammon, Holly. "Discursive Opportunity Structure." In *Wiley-Blackwell Encyclopedia of Social and Political Movements* (online), edited by David A. Snow, Donatella Della Porta, Bert Klandermans, and Doug McAdam. January 2013.

Macionis, John J. *Sociology*. 8th ed. Upper Saddle River, NJ: Prentice-Hall, 2001.

Macridis, Roy C., and Richard Cox. "Research in Comparative Politics." *American Political Science Review* 47 (June 1953): 641–657.

Mahler, Gregory S. *Comparative Politics: An Institutional and Cross-National Approach*. 3rd ed. Upper Saddle River, NJ: Prentice-Hall, 2000.

March, James G., and Johan P. Olsen. "The New Institutionalism: Organizational Factors in Political Life." *American Political Science Review* 78 (1984): 734–749.

———. *Rediscovering Institutions: The Organizational Basis of Politics*. New York: Free Press, 1989.

Marshall, Byron K. *Capitalism and Nationalism in Prewar Japan*. Stanford: Stanford University Press, 1967.

Marx, Karl. *The Eighteenth Brumaire of Louis Bonaparte*. New York: International Publishers, 1994 [1869].

Mason, Edward S., Mahn Je Kim, Dwight H. Perkins, Kwang Suk Kim, and David C. Cole. *The Economic and Social Modernization of the Republic of Korea: Studies in the Modernization of the Republic of Korea, 1945–1975*. Cambridge: Harvard University Press, 1980.

Maynard, Jonathan L. "Rethinking the Role of Ideology in Mass Atrocities." *Terrorism and Political Violence* 26, no. 5 (2014): 821–841.

McAdam, Doug. *Political Process and the Development of Black Insurgency, 1930–1970*. Chicago: University of Chicago Press, 1982.

McAdam, Doug, Sidney Tarrow, and Charles Tilly. "Toward an Integrated Perspective on Social Movements and Revolution." In *Comparative Politics: Rationality, Culture, and Structure*, edited by Mark I. Lichbach and Alan S. Zuckerman, 142–173. Cambridge: Cambridge University Press, 1997.

McCammon, Holly H. "Discursive Opportunity Structure." *The Wiley-Blackwell Encyclopedia of Social Movements and Political Movements* (online). 2013. http://onlinelibrary.wiley.com/book/10.1002/9780470674871.

McCarthy, John, and Mayer N. Zald. "Resource Mobilization and Social Movements: A Partial Theory." *American Journal of Sociology* 82, no. 6 (1977): 1212–1241.

McCormick, Thomas J. *America's Half-Century: United States Foreign Policy in the Cold War*. Baltimore: Johns Hopkins University Press, 1995.

McFaul, Michael. "The Fourth Wave of Democracy and Dictatorship: Noncooperative Transitions in the Postcommunist World." *World Politics* 54 (2002): 212–244.

McGinnis, Michael D. "Rebellion, Religion, and Rational Choice Institutionalism: Towards an Integrated Framework for Analysis." Paper presented at the Annual Meeting of the Midwest Political Science Association, Chicago, April 2005.

Melucci, Alberto. "The Process of Collective Identity." In *Social Movements and Culture*, edited by Hank Johnston and Bert Klandermans, 41–63. Minneapolis: University of Minnesota Press, 1995.

Midlarsky, Manus I. *The Killing Trap: Genocide in the Twentieth Century*. Cambridge: Cambridge University Press, 2005.

Migdal, Joel S., Atul Kohli, and Vivienne Shue, eds. *State Power and Social Forces: Domination and Transformation in the Third World*. Cambridge: Cambridge University Press, 1994.

Miles, William F. S. "The Mauritius Enigma." *Journal of Democracy* 10, no. 2 (1999): 91–104.

Mill, John Stuart. *A System of Logic: Ratiocinative and Inductive.* Toronto: University of Toronto Press, [1843] 1967.

Miller, Frederick D. "The End of SDS and the Emergence of Weatherman: Demise Through Success." In *Waves of Protest: Social Movements Since the Sixties,* edited by Jo Freeman, 303–324. Lanham: Rowman and Littlefield, 1999.

Mittelman, James H. "How Does Globalization Really Work?" In *Globalization: Critical Reflections,* edited by James H. Mittelman, 229–242. Boulder: Lynne Rienner, 1996a.

———. "Mapping Globalisation." *Singapore Journal of Tropical Geography* 22, no. 3 (2001): 212–218.

———. "Rethinking the 'New Regionalism' in the Context of Globalization." *Global Governance* 2 (1996b): 190–197.

Mogahed, Dalia. "Islam and Democracy." *Gallup World Poll,* 2006. http://media .gallup.com/WorldPoll/PDF/GALLUPMUSLIMSTUDIESIslamandDemocracy 030607.pdf.

Moody, Kim. *Workers in a Lean World: Unions in the International Economy.* London: Verso, 1997.

Morris, Aldon. "A Retrospective on the Civil Rights Movement: Political and Intellectual Landmarks." *Annual Review of Sociology* 25 (1999): 517–539.

Moses, A. Dirk. "Toward a Theory of Critical Genocide Studies." *Online Encyclopedia of Mass Violence,* 2008. http://www.massviolence.org/Toward-a-Theory -of-Critical-Genocide-Studies#citation.

Mueller, John. "The Banality of 'Ethnic War.'" *International Security* 25, no. 1 (2000): 42–70.

Munck, Gerardo L. "Democratic Transitions in Comparative Perspective." *Comparative Politics* 26, no. 3 (1994): 355–375.

Muñoz, José A. "International Opportunities and Domestic Protest: Zapatistas, Mexico, and the New World Economy." *Social Movement Studies* 5, no. 3 (2006): 251–274.

Nalbandov, Robert. "Irrational Rationality of Terrorism." *Journal of Strategic Security* 6, no. 4 (Winter 2013): 92–102.

Nassar, Jamal R. *Globalization and Terrorism: The Migration of Dreams and Nightmares.* Lanham: Rowman and Littlefield, 2004.

Naughton, Barry. *The Chinese Economy: Transitions and Growth.* Cambridge: Massachusetts Institute of Technology Press, 2007.

Neiman, Susan. "Theodicy in Jerusalem." In *Hannah Arendt in Jerusalem,* edited by S. E. Aschheim, 65–90. Berkeley: University of California Press, 2001.

Newman, Leonard S. *Understanding Genocide: The Social Psychology of the Holocaust.* New York: Oxford University Press, 2002.

Noha, el-Hennawy. "Egypt: Insider How-To on Avoiding Police Abuse." *Los Angeles Times,* June 15, 2008.

Noueihed, Lin, and Alex Warren. *The Battle for the Arab Spring: Revolution, Counter-Revolution, and the Making of a New Era.* New Haven: Yale University Press, 2012.

Oberschall, Anthony. *Social Conflict and Social Movements.* Englewood Cliffs, NJ: Prentice-Hall, 1973.

O'Donnell, Catherine. "New Study Quantifies Use of Social Media in Arab Spring." *UW Today,* September 12, 2011.

O'Donnell, Guillermo, and Philippe C. Schmitter. "Tentative Conclusions About Uncertain Democracies (Part 4)." In *Transitions from Authoritarian Rule:*

Prospects for Democracy, edited by Guillermo O'Donnell, Philippe C. Schmitter, and Lawrence Whitehead, 3–78. Baltimore: Johns Hopkins University Press, 1986.

Okimoto, Daniel I. *Between MITI and the Market: Japanese Industrial Policy for High Technology.* Stanford: Stanford University Press, 1989.

Olson, Mancur. *The Logic of Collective Action: Public Goods and the Theory of Groups.* Cambridge: Harvard University Press, 1965.

O'Neil, Patrick. *Essentials of Comparative Politics.* 5th ed. New York: Norton, 2015.

Orbeta, Aniceto C., Jr. "Poverty, Vulnerability, and Family Size: Evidence from the Philippines." Discussion Paper no. 2005-19. Philippine Institute for Development Studies, 2005. http://www.eaber.org/sites/default/files/documents/PIDS _Orbeta_2005_04.pdf.

Organization for Economic Cooperation and Development (OECD). *OECD Employment Outlook 2001.* Paris, 2001.

Ornatowski, Greg K. "Confucian Ethics and Economic Development: A Study of the Adaptation of Confucian Values to Modern Japanese Economic Ideology and Institutions." *Journal of Socio-Economics* 25, no. 5 (1996): 571–590.

Oxford Poverty & Human Development Initiative (OPHI). "Global MPI Data Tables for 2015." 2015a. http://www.ophi.org.uk/multidimensional-poverty-index/mpi -2015/mpi-data.

———. *Measuring Multidimensional Poverty: Insights from Around the World.* Oxford, 2015b.

Panitch, Leo. "Rethinking the Role of the State." In *Globalization: Critical Reflections,* edited by James H. Mittelman, 83–113. Boulder: Lynne Rienner, 1996.

Park, Tae-Kyu. "Confucian Values and Contemporary Economic Development in Korea." In *Culture and Economics: The Shaping of Capitalism in Eastern Asia,* edited by Timothy Brook and Hy V. Luong, 125–136. Ann Arbor: University of Michigan Press, 1999.

Pei, Minxin. "Fighting Corruption: A Difficult Challenge for Chinese Leaders." In *China's Changing Political Landscape: Prospects for Democracy,* edited by Cheng Li, 229–250. Washington, DC: Brookings Institution Press, 2008.

Pempel, T. J. *Policy and Politics in Japan: Creative Conservatism.* Philadelphia: Temple University Press, 1982.

Peters, B. Guy. *Comparative Politics: Theory and Methods.* New York: New York University Press, 1998.

Phelps, Timothy M. "Foreign Official Gives Up Malibu Home in Federal 'Kleptocracy' Probe." *Los Angeles Times,* October 10, 2014.

Philpott, Daniel. "The Catholic Wave." *Journal of Democracy* 15 (April 2004): 32–46.

———. "Explaining the Political Ambivalence of Religion." *American Political Science Review* 101, no. 3 (August 2007): 505–525.

Pinkney, Robert. *Democracy in the Third World.* 2nd ed. Boulder: Lynne Rienner, 2003.

Polletta, Francesca, and James M. Jasper. "Collective Identity and Social Movements." *Annual Review of Sociology* 27 (2001): 283–305.

Popkin, Samuel L. "Public Choice and Peasant Organization." In *Toward a Political Economy of Development: A Rational Choice Perspective,* edited by Robert H. Bates, 245–271. Berkeley: University of California Press, 1988.

Power, Samantha. "Bystanders to Genocide." *Atlantic Monthly,* September 2001.

Pratt, Douglas. "Terrorism and Religious Fundamentalism: Prospects for a Predictive Paradigm." *Marburg Journal of Religion* 11, no. 1 (June 2006): 1–16.

Presutti, Carolyn. "Former Egyptian Police Officer Directs Protesters from Afar." *Voice of America*, February 9, 2011.

Przeworski, Adam. *Democracy and the Market*. Cambridge: Cambridge University Press, 1991.

———. "Democratization Revisited." *Items* (Social Science Research Council) 51, no. 1 (1997): 6–11.

Przeworski, Adam, and Fernando Limongi. "Modernization: Theories and Facts." *World Politics* 49, no. 2 (1997): 155–183.

Przeworski, Adam, and Henry Teune. *The Logic of Comparative Social Inquiry*. New York: Wiley-Interscience, 1970.

Puddington, Arch. "Discarding Democracy: A Return to the Iron Fist." In *Freedom in the World 2015*. Washington, DC: Freedom House, 2015. https://freedom house.org/sites/default/files/01152015_FIW_2015_final.pdf.

Ragin, Charles C. *The Comparative Method: Moving Beyond Qualitative and Quantitative Strategies*. Berkeley: University of California Press, 1987.

Ragin, Charles C., and Howard S. Becker, eds. *What Is a Case? Exploring the Foundations of Social Inquiry*. Cambridge: Cambridge University Press, 1992.

Rector, Robert, and Rachel Sheffield. "Air Conditioning, Cable TV, and an Xbox: What Is Poverty in the United States Today?" Heritage Foundation Backgrounder no. 2575 on Poverty and Inequality. 2011. http://www.heritage.org/research/reports/2011/07/what-is-poverty.

Reno, William. "Market, War, and the Reconfiguration of Political Authority in Sierra Leone." *Canadian Journal of African Studies* 29, no. 2 (1995): 203–221.

Rhodes, R. A. W. "The Institutional Approach." In *Theory and Methods in Political Science*, edited by David Marsh and Gerry Stoker, 42–57. Basingstoke: Palgrave Macmillan, 1995.

Richards, Paul. "Out of the Wilderness? Escaping Robert Kaplan's Dystopia." *Anthropology Today* 15, no. 6 (1999): 16–18.

Rizzo, Jennifer. "China Spending Big Money to Avoid Arab Spring Fever." November 21, 2011. http://security.blogs.cnn.com.

Roberts, J. Timmons, and Amy Hite. "Editors' Introduction." In *From Modernization to Globalization: Perspectives on Development and Social Change*, edited by J. Timmons Roberts and Amy Hite, 1–24. London: Blackwell, 2000.

Robertson, Ann E. *Terrorism and Global Security*. New York: Facts On File/Infobase, 2007.

Robinson, William I. "Globalization and the Sociology of Immanuel Wallerstein: A Critical Appraisal." *International Sociology* (2011): 1–23.

Rochon, Thomas R., and Dan A. Mazmanian. "Social Movements and the Policy Process." *Annals of the American Academy of Political and Social Science* 528 (1993): 75–87.

Rosenau, James N. "Distant Proximities: The Dynamics and Dialectics of Globalization." In *International Political Economy: Understanding Global Disorder*, edited by Björn Hettne, 46–64. London: Zed, 1995.

Rosenau, James N., and Mary Durfee. *Thinking Theory Thoroughly: Coherent Approaches to an Incoherent World*. 2nd ed. Boulder: Westview, 2000.

Rosenthal, Franz. "On Suicide in Islam." *Journal of the American Oriental Society* 66 (1946): 239–259.

Ross, Mark Howard. "Culture and Identity in Comparative Political Analysis." In *Comparative Politics: Rationality, Culture, and Structure*, edited by Mark Irving Lichbach and Alan S. Zuckerman, 42–80. Cambridge: Cambridge University Press, 1997.

Rostow, W. W. *The Stages of Economic Growth: A Non-Communist Manifesto.* Cambridge: Cambridge University Press, 1960.

Rothkopf, David. "In Praise of Cultural Imperialism." *Foreign Policy,* no. 107 (Summer 1997): 38–53.

Rudolph, Christopher. "Constructing an Atrocities Regime: The Politics of War Crime Tribunals." *International Organizations* 55, no. 3 (Summer 2001): 655–691.

Rueschemeyer, Dietrich. "Different Methods—Contradictory Results? Research on Development and Democracy." *International Journal of Comparative Sociology* 32, nos. 1–2 (1991): 9–38.

Rueschemeyer, Dietrich, Evelyne Huber Stephens, and John D. Stephens. *Capitalist Development and Democracy.* Chicago: University of Chicago Press, 1992.

———. "The Impact of Economic Development on Democracy." *Journal of Economic Perspectives* 7 (1993): 71–85.

"Rushing by Road, Rail, and Air." *The Economist,* February 14, 2008.

Ryan, Jasmine. "The Tragic Life of a Street Vendor." *Al Jazeera,* January 20, 2011.

Sachs, Jeffrey D. "Poverty and Environmental Stress Fuel Darfur Crisis." *Nature* 449, no. 7158 (6 September 2007): 24.

Sarel, Michael. *Growth in East Asia: What We Can and What We Cannot Infer.* International Monetary Fund, September 1996. http://www.imf.org/external/pubs/ft/issues1.

Sarte, Jean-Paul. "Genocide." *New Left Review,* no. 48 (March–April 1968): 13–25.

Sartori, Giovanni. "Compare Why and How." In *Comparing Nations: Concepts, Strategies, Substance,* edited by Mattei Dogan and Ali Kazancigil, 14–34. Oxford: Blackwell, 1994.

Schaefer, Richard T. "The Ku Klux Klan: Continuity and Change." *Phylon* 32, no. 2 (1971): 143–157.

Schmid, Alex P., and Albert J. Jongman. *Political Terrorism: A Research Guide to Concepts, Theories, Databases, and Literature.* Amsterdam: North Holland Publishing, 1983.

Schmid, Peter D. "Expect the Unexpected: A Religious Democracy in Iran." *Brown Journal of World Affairs* 9, no. 2 (Winter–Spring 2003): 181–196.

Scott, Alan. "Violence and the State: The Political Sociology of War." In *Blackwell Companion to Political Sociology,* edited by Kate Nash and Alan Scott, 183–194. Malden, MA: Blackwell, 2008.

Seib, Philip. "Hegemonic No More: Western Media, the Rise of Al-Jazeera, and the Influence of Diverse Voices." *International Studies Review* 7, no. 4 (2005): 601–615.

Serrano, Mónica. "The Responsibility to Protect and Its Critics: Explaining the Consensus." *Global Responsibility to Protect* 3 (2011): 1–13.

Sewell, William H., Jr. "Ideologies and Social Revolutions: Reflections on the French Case." *Journal of Modern History* 57 (1985): 57–85.

Shaw, Jane. "Public Choice Theory." In *Concise Encyclopedia of Economics,* 2nd ed. (online), edited by David R. Henderson. 2002.

Sigelman, Lee, and G. H. Gadbois. "Contemporary Comparative Politics: An Inventory and Assessment." *Comparative Political Studies* 16 (October 1983): 275–305.

Singh, Susheela, Jacqueline E. Darroch, and Lori S. Ashford. *Adding It Up: The Costs and Benefits of Investing in Sexual and Reproductive Health.* New York: Guttmacher Institute, 2014.

Sitton, Claude. "Negro Groups Split on Georgia Protest." *New York Times,* December 18, 1961.

Skocpol, Theda. *States and Social Revolutions.* Cambridge: Cambridge University Press, 1979.

Small Arms Survey. *Small Arms Survey 2007: Guns and the City.* Oxford: Oxford University Press, 2007.

Smith, Steve, and John Baylis. Introduction to *The Globalization of World Politics: An Introduction to International Relations,* edited by John Baylis and Steve Smith, 1–12. New York: Oxford University Press, 1997.

Snow, David A., and Sarah A. Soule. *A Primer on Social Movements.* New York: Norton, 2010.

Snyder, Jack. *From Voting to Violence: Democratization and Nationalist Conflict.* New York: Norton, 2000.

So, Alvin. *Social Change and Development: Modernization, Dependency, and World-System Theory.* Newbury Park, CA: Sage, 1990.

So, Alvin Y., and Stephen W. K. Chiu. *East Asia and the World Economy.* Thousand Oaks, CA: Sage, 1995.

Sørensen, Georg. *Democracy and Democratization.* Boulder: Westview, 1993.

Spirkin, Alexander. *Dialectical Materialism.* Translated by Robert Daglish. Soviet Union (no city): Progress Publishers, 1983. https://www.marxists.org/reference/archive/spirkin/works/dialectical-materialism/index.html.

Srebrnik, Henry. "'Full of Sound and Fury': Three Decades of Parliamentary Politics in Mauritius." *Journal of Southern African Studies* 28, no. 2 (2002): 277–289.

Stanton, Gregory H. "The 8 Stages of Genocide." Working paper. New Haven: Yale Program in Genocide Studies, 1998.

Statista. "Countries with the Highest Number of Deaths by Terrorism in 2013, by Percentage of Total Deaths." 2015a. http://www.statista.com/statistics/377061/countries-with-the-highest-number-of-deaths-by-terrorism.

———. "Number of Fatalities Due to Terrorist Attacks Between 2006 and 2014." 2015b. http://www.statista.com/statistics/202871/number-of-fatalities-by-terrorist-attacks-worldwide.

Staub, Ervin. "The Origins and Prevention of Genocide, Mass Killing, and Other Collective Violence." *Peace and Conflict: Journal of Peace Psychology* 5, no. 4 (1999): 303–336.

———. *The Roots of Evil: The Origins of Genocide and Other Group Violence.* Cambridge: Cambridge University Press, 1989.

Steil, Benn. *The Battle of Bretton Woods: John Maynard Keynes, Harry Dexter White, and the Making of a New World Order.* Princeton: Princeton University Press, 2013.

Stepan, Alfred. "Religion, Democracy, and the 'Twin Tolerations.'" *Journal of Democracy* 11, no. 4 (2000): 37–57.

Stoker, Gerry, and David Marsh. Introduction to *Theory and Methods in Political Science,* 2nd ed., edited by David Marsh and Gerry Stoker, 1–16. Basingstoke: Palgrave Macmillan, 2002.

Straus, Scott. "'Destroy Them to Save Us': Theories of Genocide and the Logics of Political Violence." *Terrorism and Political Violence* 24, no. 4 (2012): 544–560.

Sutherland, Neil, Christopher Land, and Steffen Böhm. "Anti-Leaders(hip) in Social Movement Organizations: The Case of Autonomous Grassroots Groups." *Organization* 21, no. 6 (2014): 759–781.

Swanson, Guy. "Frameworks for Comparative Research: Structural Anthropology and the Theory of Action." In *Comparative Methods in Sociology,* edited by Ivan Vallier, 141–202. Berkeley: University of California Press, 1971.

Swidler, Ann. "Cultural Power and Social Movements." In *Social Movements and Culture,* edited by Hank Johnston and Bert Klandermans, 25–40. Minneapolis: University of Minnesota Press, 1995.

Tan, Huileng. "Why China Steel Prices Hit Record Lows." *CNBC,* November 15, 2015.

Taras, Raymond C., and Rajat Ganguly. *Understanding Ethnic Conflict.* 4th ed. New York: Routledge, 2009.

Tarrow, Sidney. *Power in Movements: Social Movements, Collective Action, and Politics.* Cambridge: Cambridge University Press, 1994.

Tehranian, Majid. "Islamic Fundamentalism in Iran and the Discourse of Development." In *The Globalization Reader,* edited by Frank J. Lechner and John Boli, 359–370. Malden, MA: Blackwell, 2000.

Thörn, Håkan. "Solidarity Across Borders: The Transnational Anti-Apartheid Movement." *Voluntas: International Journal of Voluntary and Nonprofit Organizations* 17, no. 4 (2006): 285–301.

Tilly, Charles. *Democracy.* New York: Cambridge University Press, 2007.

———. "Globalization Threatens Labor's Rights." *International Labor and Working-Class History* 47 (1995): 1–23.

Tipps, Dean C. "Modernization Theory and the Comparative Study of Societies: Critical Perspectives." In *Comparative Modernization: A Reader,* edited by Cyril E. Black, 62–88. New York: Free Press, 1976.

Toameh, Khaled Abu. "'Democracy Is Forbidden in Islam.'" Gatestone Institute, January 11, 2013. http://www.gatestoneinstitute.org/3533/jordan-democracy-islam.

Tocqueville, Alexis de. *Democracy in America.* Translated by George Lawrence. Edited by J. P. Mayer. 2 vols. New York: Perennial Library/Harper and Row, [1835] 1988.

Torre, Pablo S. "How (and Why) Athletes Go Broke." *Sports Illustrated,* March 23, 2009.

Unger, Jonathan, and Anita Chan. "China, Corporatism, and the East Asian Model." *Australian Journal of Chinese Affairs,* no. 33 (January 1995): 29–52.

United Human Rights Council. "Genocide in Darfur." 2015. http://www.united humanrights.org/genocide/genocide-in-sudan.htm.

United Nations Department of Economic and Social Affairs (UN/DESA). *World Economic Situations and Prospects 2011.* New York, 2011.

———. *World Economic Situations and Prospects 2015.* New York, 2015.

United Nations Development Programme (UNDP). "Composite Indices: HDI and Beyond." In *Human Development Reports,* n.d. http://hdr.undp.org/en/statistics /indices.

———. *Human Development Report 2000.* New York: Oxford University Press, 2000.

———. *Human Development Report 2014.* New York: Oxford University Press, 2014. http://hdr.undp.org/sites/default/files/hdr14-report-en-1.pdf.

———. "Table 2: Human Development Index Trends, 1980–2013." In *Human Development Reports,* 2015. http://hdr.undp.org/en/content/table-2-human -development-index-trends-1980-2013.

United Nations Family Planning Agency (UNFPA). *Sex Imbalance at Birth: Current Trends, Consequences, and Policy Implications.* Bangkok: UNFPA Asia and the Pacific Regional Office, August 2012.

United Nations General Assembly. Resolution 51/210. "Measure to Eliminate International Terrorism." December 17, 2010. http://www.un.org/documents/ga/res /51/a51r210.htm.

————. Resolution 260. "Convention on the Prevention and Punishment of the Crime of Genocide." December 9, 1948. http://www.un.org/ga/search/view _doc.asp?symbol=a/res/260(III).

United Nations Office on Drugs and Crime (UNODC). "Homicide Counts and Rates, Time Series 2000–2012." *Global Study on Homicide.* N.d. https://www .unodc.org/gsh/en/data.html.

————. "International Homicide Statistics." 2006. http://www.unodc.org/documents /data-and-analysis/IHS-rates-05012009.pdf.

————. *Seventh United Nations Survey of Crime Trends and Operations of Criminal Justice Systems (1998–2000).* N.d. http://www.unodc.org/pdf/crime/seventh _survey/7sc.pdf.

US Department of State. *Foreign Relations of the United States.* Vol. VI, 1948. http://digital.library.wisc.edu/1711.dl/FRUS.FRUS1948v06.

Verba, Sidney. "Comparative Politics: Where Have We Been, Where Are We Going?" In *New Directions in Comparative Politics,* edited by Howard J. Wiarda, 31–44. Boulder: Westview, 1991.

Wade, Robert. *Governing the Market: Economic Theory and the Role of Government in East Asian Industrialization.* Princeton: Princeton University Press, 1990.

Wallerstein, Immanuel. "The Rise and Future Demise of the World-Capitalist System: Concepts for Comparative Analysis." *Comparative Studies in Society and History* 16, no. 4 (1974): 387–415.

————. "What Have the Zapatistas Accomplished?" *Commentary,* no. 244 (January 1, 2008). http://iwallerstein.com/neozapatistas-twenty-years.

Wal-Mart 2015 Annual Report. 2015. http://stock.walmart.com/files/doc_financials /2015/annual/2015-annual-report.pdf.

Ward, Hugh. "Rational Choice." In *Theory and Methods in Political Science,* 2nd ed., edited by David Marsh and Gerry Stoker, 65–89. Basingstoke: Palgrave Macmillan, 2002.

Weaver, R. Kent. "Temporary Assistance for Needy Families." In *The Oxford Handbook of U.S. Social Policy,* edited by Daniel Béland, Christopher Howard, and Kimberly Morgan. Oxford: Oxford University Press, 2014.

Weber, Max. *The Protestant Ethic and the Spirit of Capitalism.* Translated by Talcott Parsons. New York: Scribner, [1930] 1958.

Weitz, Eric. *A Century of Genocide: Utopias of Race and Nation.* Princeton: Princeton University Press, 2003.

Werth, Nicholas. "Mass Crimes Under Stalin (1930–1953)." *Online Encyclopedia of Mass Violence,* 2008. http://www.massviolence.org/Mass-crimes-under-Stalin -1930–1953.

Whittaker, David J., ed. *The Terrorism Reader.* 4th ed. London: Routledge, 2012.

Wiarda, Howard J. "Comparative Politics Past and Present." In *New Directions in Comparative Politics,* edited by Howard J. Wiarda, 3–30. Boulder: Westview, 1991.

————. *Introduction to Comparative Politics: Concepts and Processes.* 2nd ed. Fort Worth, TX: Harcourt College, 2000.

Wilkins, John S., and David Hull. "Replication and Reproduction." *Stanford Encyclopedia of Philosophy.* 2014. http://plato.stanford.edu/entries/replication/#toc.

Willets, Peter. "Transnational Actors and International Organizations in Global Politics." In *The Globalization of World Politics,* edited by John Baylis and Steve Smith, 287–310. New York: Oxford University Press, 1997.

Williamson, Vanessa, and Theda Skocpol. *The Tea Party and the Remaking of Republican Conservatism.* Oxford: Oxford University Press, 2013.

Wilson, Bruce M. *Costa Rica: Politics, Economics, and Democracy.* Boulder: Lynne Rienner, 1998.

Wilson, Charles Reagan. *The New Encyclopedia of Southern Culture.* Vol. 24. Chapel Hill: University of North Carolina Press, 2013.

Wolfsfeld, Gadi, Elad Segev, and Tamir Sheafer. "Social Media and the Arab Spring: Politics Comes First." *International Journal of Press/Politics* 18, no. 2 (2013): 115–137.

Woo, Jung-en. *Race to the Swift: State and Finance in Korean Industrialization.* New York: Columbia University Press, 1991.

Woo-Cumings, Meredith, ed. *The Developmental State.* Ithaca: Cornell University Press, 1999.

Wood, Graeme. "What ISIS Really Wants." *The Atlantic,* March 2015.

Woods, Ngaire. "The Uses of Theory in the Study of International Relations." In *Explaining International Relations Since 1945,* edited by Ngaire Woods, 9–31. Oxford: Oxford University Press, 1996.

World Bank. "GDP Growth (Annual %)." N.d. http://data.worldbank.org/indicator /NY.GDP.MKTP.KD.ZG.

———. *Global Monitoring Report 2014/2015: Ending Poverty and Sharing Prosperity.* Washington, DC: International Bank for Reconstruction and Development, 2015a.

———. "The Global Poverty Numbers Debate." N.d. http://web.worldbank.org.

———. "Lending Interest Rate (%)." 2015b. http://data.worldbank.org/indicator /FR.INR.LEND/countries?order=wbapi_data_value_2014+wbapi_data_value+ wbapi_data_value-last&sort=asc.

World Health Organization (WHO). "Suicide Rates per 100,000 by Country, Year, and Sex (Table)." 2008. http://www.who.int/mental_health/prevention/suicide _rates/en/index.html.

Worstall, Tim. "By Global Standards There Are No American Poor; All in the US Are Middle Class or Better." *Forbes,* August 27, 2014.

Wuthnow, Robert. *Meaning and Moral Order: Explanations in Cultural Analysis.* Berkeley: University of California Press, 1987.

Zahariadis, Nikolaos. *Theory, Case, and Method in Comparative Politics.* New York: Harcourt Brace College, 1997.

Zuckerman, Alan S. *Doing Political Science: An Introduction to Political Analysis.* Boulder: Westview, 1991.

Zuehlke, Eric. "In Arab Countries, Mobile Internet and Social Media Are Dominant, but Disparities in Access Remain." Population Reference Bureau, 2012. http://www.prb.org/Publications/Articles/2012/arab-region-internet-use.aspx.

Index

abortion: female feticide, 92–93
absolute poverty, 107
Acheson, Dean, 176
activism, terrorism as, 245, 252–253
administrative guidance, 149
Afghanistan: clans' roles in political
   outcomes, 94–95; poverty and family
   size, 111
AFL-CIO (American Federation of
   Labor-Congress of Industrial
   Organizations), 329
Africa. *See* sub-Saharan Africa
African Americans: civil rights
   movement, 293–295; Vietnam War as
   genocide, 236–237
agency: actors' choices in regime
   transition, 217; behind globalization,
   338–339; culture of poverty as
   expression of, 123–124; defining,
   70(fig.); development and
   democratization, 203–204; elite-
   centered democratization, 205–208;
   "flying geese" model of labor, 172;
   historical structuralism, 84;
   institutionalist argument for, 94;
   limitations of the structural approach
   to social movements, 301–302; poor
   countries' dependence on loans, 132;
   theoretical assumptions contained in,
   63, 70–71; waiting for democracy,
   204–205

agricultural policies and systems:
   corruption contributing to poverty,
   117–118; creation of social class, 83;
   disjunct between self-interest and
   collective good in poverty situations,
   110; large families and poverty,
   112–113
Ahmadinejad, Mahmoud, 207(fig.), 336
Aid to Families with Dependent Children
   (AFDC), 104
Al Jazeera, 316–317
Albany Movement, 295
al-Qaeda/al-Qaeda in Iraq (AQI), 233,
   250, 254, 265
altruism as self-interested behavior, 74
Ammar, Rachid, 315
analytical induction: case study, 49–51;
   historical reality of democratization,
   203–204; rational choice view of East
   Asian economic growth, 145
anarchy, 7, 330–331; anarchic
   international system, 79; anarchic
   violence, 330–332, 334
Anderson, Kenny, 124(fig.)
anglophone Canada, 307–310
Angola: poverty and family size, 111
animal rights movements, 289
anti-apartheid movement, 283–284,
   288
antiglobalization movement, 330, 337–
   338, 340(n1)

383

anti-intellectualism: univocal, monolithic views of Islamic culture, 87–88
Anti-Saloon League of America (ASLA), 286(fig.)
Apple Corporation, 168
Arab culture: compatibility with democracy, 86–88. *See also* Islam
Arab Spring: background, 311–312; catalyst for, 207(fig.); compromise between elites and challengers, 206; cultural perspective, 220–221; diverse outcomes, 310–312; method of agreement application, 41–42; political opportunity structure explaining, 314–316; rational choice perspective, 312–314; structuralist perspective, 314–315; suppression of media coverage, 230
area studies, 45
Armenian genocide, 247
Arusha Accords, 249(fig.)
Aryan groups, 265
Asia: emerging democracies, 189; influencing globalization, 336. *See also* China; East Asia; Japan; Korea; North Korea; South Korea; Taiwan
al-Assad, Bashar, 215
associated-dependent development, 134
associational organizations, 292–293
athletes: why professional athletes go broke, 124(fig.)
Australia: estimates of civilian firearms ownership and homicide rates, 34(fig.)
authoritarian regimes: case studies comparing multiple cases, 55–56; Catholic political theology supporting, 225–226; democratic transition by regime type, 210–216, 214(fig.); diversity in democratization patterns, 213; elite-centered democratization, 205; Equatorial Guinea, 119(fig.); modernization theory of democratization and development, 196; oppression of prodemocracy protesters, 207(fig.); power of collective mobilization to shift, 315; qualitative analysis of post-authoritarian regimes, 216; relocating labor from core to periphery, 134–135; Russia's regime change path, 228; South Korea's economic growth under,

149; US support in the Middle East, 273; working class repression, 199–202; Zapatista movement challenging Mexico's, 298
autonomy, economic growth and, 180–183
Azerbaijan: modernization theory of democratization and development, 197

Bahrain: Arab Spring outcomes, 312
Baker, Ella, 294
balance of power: class power and democratic transition, 217; democratization from below, 209–210
balance of trade, 130–133
Ban Ki-moon, 46, 47(fig.)
Bangladesh: lending interest rate, 131
Barber, Benjamin, 321–322, 322(fig.)
basic needs, defining poverty through, 105–107
Bates, Robert, 143
Beck, Ulrich, 323–326
beliefs. *See* values and beliefs
Ben Ali, Zine El Abidine, 207(fig.), 314–315
bias: defining terrorism in terms of evil, 241–243; overdetermination, 51–52
binary analysis, 43, 51–53
birth control, 112
black box as metaphor, 21–22, 24(n10)
Blumner, Robyn, 86
Botswana: modernization theory of democratization and development, 197
"bottom-up" analytical approach, 340
bottom-up democratization, 213, 215–216
Bouazizi, Tarek Mohammed, 207(fig.), 220, 311
Bowling for Columbine (documentary film), 2, 32
brainwashing, 267
Brazil: estimates of civilian firearms ownership and homicide rates, 34(fig.); poverty statistics, 108
Bretton Woods institutions, 133(fig.). *See also* International Monetary Fund; World Bank
Britain: estimates of civilian firearms ownership and homicide rates, 34(fig.); India's poverty-dependence relationship, 127–129

Buddhism: in Japanese culture, 160; Taiwan's heterodox culture, 164

bureaucratic capitalism, 149

Burkina Faso: poverty and family size, 111

Burundi: genocide, 235; poverty and family size, 111

Bush, George H. W., 252(fig.)

Bush, George W., 241

Bushido (way of the warrior), 161

cadres, 212–213

Cambodia: genocide, 234; poverty statistics, 108

Canada: estimates of civilian firearms ownership and homicide rates, 34(fig.); firearm-related homicide rates in the US and Canada, 32–36, 32(fig.); nationalist movement, 306–310

capitalism: capitalist world-system and genocide, 275–276; China's economic growth, 179; creation of the modern state, 82–84; culture explaining heterogeneity in, 92; culture of poverty as adaptation and reaction to, 123–125; debate over the causes of poverty, 104–105; dependence on the existence of the poor, 127; developing public goods and infrastructure, 116–117; divergent political outcomes, 85; East Asia's postwar industrial development, 149; globalization and the expansion of, 337; impoverishment of the Middle East, 272–275; international debt as poverty mechanism, 131–132; Max Weber's view of Protestantism and, 120(fig.); mutually constitutive relationship among culture, politics, and the economy, 120–121; postcolonial East Asia, 147; requiring a periphery to support the core, 135–136; social movement organizations, 290–291; state role in East Asia's rapid economic growth, 141, 143–144; structural analysis of, 95; structural analysis of China's economy, 183–185; theorizing about violent crime in societies, 68–69; working class struggle for democratization, 199–200. *See also* development, economic; global capitalism; globalization; industrialization; poverty

Capitalist Development and Democracy (Rueschemeyer, Stephens, and Stephens), 193, 197–199, 217

Cardoso, Fernando H., 134

Caribbean economies: international debt as mechanism of poverty, 130

case studies: analytical induction, 49–51; in comparative perspective, 20–22, 43–44; comparative value of a single case study, 44–45; comparing three or more cases, 53–55; examining East Asia's economic growth, 142–143; guidelines for conducting, 45–49

Catholic Church: democratization of authoritarian regimes, 222–227

Catholic Wave, 222, 224, 226–227

causal relationships: causal power of culture, 91–93; Confucian argument for East Asia's economic success, 158; correlation and causation, 65(fig.); culture as both, 91–92; most similar systems comparison, 35; multiple causation, 40; poverty and culture, 125

Central African Republic (CAR): underdeveloped infrastructure, 114–115

Central America: international debt as mechanism of poverty, 130

Central Asia: clans' roles in political outcomes, 94–95

Central Intelligence Agency (CIA), 273

chess exemplifying historical structures, 80–82, 81(fig.)

child mortality rates, 113

children: core-periphery relationships and poverty, 129; female infanticide and feticide, 92; genocide against, 239; perpetuation of poverty, 123–124

China, 92; annual real GDP growth rate, 180(fig.); binary comparison of an authoritarian regime, 52; communism and global capitalism, 173; comparing successful social revolutions, 39–40, 56–58; democratization potential, 228–230; developmental state, 180; economic downturn, 185–186; escape from poverty, 134; explaining economic growth, 179–186; female infanticide and feticide, 92(fig.); Japanese subjugation of, 147–148, 171; modernization theory of democratization and development, 196; oppression of prodemocracy protesters, 206, 207(fig.); as postcolonial threat to Taiwan, 152; postwar political and economic goals, 148; structuralist analysis of economic growth, 183–185; systems-level analysis failing to explain economic growth, 179; US hegemony in the capitalist world-system, 175. *See also* East Asia

Christian Identity, 265

Christianity: militant groups, 265; role of the Catholic Church in the democratization of authoritarian regimes, 222–227; terrorism and genocide, 259–260

Churchill, Winston, 194

civil liberties, 190–191

civil rights: democracy and socialism, 191–192

civil rights movement, 284, 288, 293–295

civil society: historical-structural perspective of democracy, 198–199; increasing social, political, and economic equality, 193; leading Arab Spring movements, 316

civil war resulting from Arab Spring, 310

clans: clan hegemony, 208–209; institutional role in political outcomes, 94–95

"The Clash of Civilizations," 333

class-based structures. *See* feudalism

classical dependency theory, 137(n4)

classical modernization theory, 121

classification process: legitimizing elements of legitimation and genocide, 261–262

clientelist system: Mexico, 300

climate change: Darfur case study, 46–49

Clinton, Bill: welfare reform, 104

Coalition of Justice in the Maquiladoras, 329

Cold War: core development in the periphery, 135; creating and embedding authoritarian regimes, 315; divergent political outcomes, 85

collective action and behavior: culture of poverty excluding people from, 123; as deviancy, 279; eliminating free riders, 116; genocide and terrorism as

collective political violence, 257–261; the hegemon overcoming, 174; significance of culture, 89–90; social good conflicting with individual self-interest in a context of poverty, 109; structural argument for perpetual poverty, 127. *See also* social movements

collective good: developmentally-oriented state, 155; free-riders on infrastructure and public good, 116; poor parents having large families, 112–113

collective identity: Québécois nationalism, 307–310

collective mobilization, 282

collective representations, culture as, 304

Colombia: estimates of civilian firearms ownership and homicide rates, 34(fig.)

colonialism: dependency theory, 130; explaining poverty, 137–138(n4); instilling a sense of national vulnerabilities, 151; Japanese control of Korea, Taiwan, and parts of China, 146–148, 171; poor countries' dependence on loans as perpetuation of, 132; poverty-dependence relationship, 127–129; the strong state and economic development, 147–149; US role in postwar East Asia, 148

command economies: China, 181; North Korea, 144

communal organizations, 292–293

communications: social networking during Arab Spring, 316

communist regimes: capitalist economies' collective effort to demolish, 133; divergent political outcomes, 85; external behavior of states, 7–8; Korea's postwar political vacuum, 148; shrinking world markets with the rise of, 173; US economic intervention in China, 184. *See also* China; Soviet Union

comparative context, 45

comparative genocide studies, 236

comparative method: advantages of, 20–22; analytical induction, 49–51; binary comparison, 51–53; care, caution, and constraint, 42–43; case study guidelines, 45–49; choosing strategies of comparing, 29–30; comparing firearm-related homicide rates in the US and Canada, 32–36; comparing three or more cases, 53–55; critical thinking and, 28–29; emphasizing caution, care, and constraint, 42–43; importance of applying, 27; key points in, 97–99; method of agreement, 40–42; mixed design, 56–58; most different systems design, 36–40; most similar systems design, 30–31; open-mindedness and, 28; principles of research design types, 30–43; suicide rates around the world, 38–40; use of method and theory, 22–23; within-case comparison of Russian economic development, 54(fig.)

comparative politics: defining, 3–9, 6(box), 9, 23(n3); defining politics, 9–13

comparativism: theorizing about violent crime, 67–68

competition as element in Japanese capitalism, 163–164

complex causality, 20–22

complexity: element of uncertainty, 76–77; game analogy of historical structures, 80–82; integration of culturalism and rational choice theory, 96–97; prosperity in East Asia, 186–187

conditionality of IFIs, 133, 133(fig.)

conflict: civil war resulting from Arab Spring, 310; the "clash of civilizations," 333

Confucian culture: China's potential for democratization, 230; compatibility with democracy, 87, 219; competition and fairness in postwar Japan, 162–164; cultural and economic dissimilarities in Taiwan and Japan, 164–167; East Asian capitalism and, 167; East Asian economic success, 141, 157–159; obstacles to Japan's industrialization, 159–162; Taiwan's anti-Confucian bias, 165–167

Congress of Racial Equality (CORE), 294

consolidated democracies, 189–190

constraints: economic constraints of infrastructure development, 115;

imposed by capitalism, 83–84; rational choice in a global context, 329–330; rational choice theory, 77; structural explanations of poverty, 126–127; using the comparative method, 42–43

context: global approach to cultural analysis, 305

contradictions, 80

cooperative economic behavior, 156

co-optation: by the colonial state, 147; single-party regimes, 213, 215; working class struggle for democratization, 201

core-periphery relationships: colonial and postcolonial perpetuation of poverty, 129; communism and global capitalism, 173; from the "development of underdevelopment" to "dependent development," 133–136; East Asia's technology-based industries, 168–169; "flying geese" model of labor, 171–172; hegemony and, 173–174; IFIs ensuring periphery dependence on core countries, 133(fig.); international debt as mechanism of poverty, 130–133; intersection of agency and structure in globalization, 338–339; US hegemony shaping economic policy, 176–177; world-system tri-modal structure, 170–171, 170(fig.)

corporate power, 325

correlation and causation, 21, 65(fig.)

corruption: China's economic development, 182(fig.); China's economic liberation, 181; core requirements of democracy, 191; Equatorial Guinea, 119(fig.); the patrimonial state, 331; in postcolonial countries, 151; poverty and, 117–119

Costa Rica, 24(n9)

countercultures: Confucian values and the development of, 159; Taiwan's heterodox culture, 164–165

coups d'état: Central African Republic, 114; Egypt's flirtation with democracy, 203, 314–315; South Korea, 153–155

crime: analysis through self-interest, 75; firearm-related homicide rates in the US and Canada, 32–36, 32(fig.)

critical thinking, comparing and, 28–29

cross-national comparison: culture of poverty, 122–123

cross-regional comparison: examining East Asia's economic growth, 143

cultural change, social movements fighting for, 286(fig.)

"cultural richness," 126

cultural shifts, 88

culturalism, 86–88; Arab Spring, 316–317; avoiding cross-case generalizations, 167; causal power of culture, 91–93; challenging, 94; competition and fairness in postwar Japan, 162–164; "Confucian ethic" and East Asian economic success, 157–159; contextualizing Confucianism, 159–162; cultural dissimilarities in Japanese and Taiwanese Confucianism, 164–167; democracy as ideal political system, 195; democratic transition and transformation, 218; East Asia's rapid economic growth, 141, 156–167; explanations of poverty, 119–126; genocide and terrorism, 257–261; integration with other research traditions, 96–97; modernization theory, 231(n3); mutually constitutive relationship among culture, politics, and the economy, 119–121; Oscar Lewis's cultures of poverty, 121–125; poverty of professional athletes, 124(fig.); significance of culture, 89–91; social movements, 302–310; suicide terrorism, 269–270; Taiwan's anti-Confucianism bias, 165–167; view of globalization, 334–336

culture, 71; beliefs, ideology, and leadership legitimizing violence, 262–266; Canada's nationalist movements, 306–310; compatibility with democracy, 218; core features, 89(fig.); creating a global culture, 321–322; decontextualizing, 157; defining, 88–89; elements in the legitimization of terrorism and genocide, 261–271; female infanticide and feticide, 92–93; hierarchy of cultures, 332; homogenization effect of globalization, 326–327; inside-out approach, 303; integration with other research traditions, 96–97; intracivilization differences, 333–334; legitimation of killing, 260–261; malleability of Islamic culture, 270–271; outside-in approach, 303–306; rise of suicide terrorism, 268–270; role in democratization, 218–222; role of Christian culture in democratization, 223–226; role of the Catholic Church in democratization, 222–226; self-interest independence from, 73; significance of, 89–91; traditional view of globalization and the disappearance, 332–333; Weber on the contribution of Protestantism to capitalism, 120(fig.)

culture of fear, 1–2, 33–35

culture of poverty, 121

"culture wars," power as root cause of, 90

currency exchange, 177

Dallaire, Roméo, 248, 249(fig.)

Darfur genocide, 46–49, 47(fig.), 235

death: genocide statistics, 234–235

debt, international: China's public and private debt, 185; Mexico's austerity measures, 299–300; poverty and, 130–133

decision-making environment, institutional constraints on, 77

dedazo, 95

deductive logic, 73, 75, 109, 145

definitions pertaining to comparative politics, 4–8

dehumanization process: legitimizing elements of legitimation and genocide, 261–262

democracy and democratic systems: comparing gun-related homicides across industrialized democracies, 33–36; compatibility with Arab culture and Islam, 86–88, 219, 227–228; compatibility with Catholicism, 223; core requirements, 190–191; cultural compatibility with, 218; definitional debate, 190–195; democratic nature of markets, 324–325; divergent paths and key similarities, 200–201; economic development and, 195–204, 231(n4); Egypt's flirtation with, 314; emergence in Eastern Europe, Asia, and Africa, 289; external behavior of states, 7–8; global decline, 189–190; Korea's postwar political vacuum, 148; narrow definition of, 192–193; as nonexistent ideal, 231(n2); postwar Japan, 147–149; role in Arab Spring uprisings, 221; significance of the middle class, 49–50; threatening material self-interests, 221–222; US coercion of Japanese trade, 150–151; usefulness of comparative analysis, 21

democracy without democrats, 206, 208

democratic consolidation, 189–190, 231(n1)

democratic peace thesis, 23(n4)

Democratic Republic of the Congo (DRC): lending interest rate, 131; Rwandan genocide, 235

democratization and democratic transition, 192, 231(n1); agency, development and, 203–204; authoritarian regimes' oppression of prodemocracy protesters, 206(fig.); Catholic Church under authoritarian regime, 222–226; Catholic Church's opposition to, 224; complexity of a comparative perspective, 228–231; democratic transition terminology, 231(n1); democratization from above, 205–208; democratization from below, 208–210; differing authoritarian regimes, 210–216; elite-centered, 205–208; explaining variations, 213–216; importance of agency, 204–205; importance of culture, 218–221; liberation theology, 227; modernization theory, 195–197, 231(n3); qualitative analysis of post-authoritarian regimes, 216–217; rational choice principles of democratization, 216–218; Russia's regime change path, 228; working class and, 199–202

dependence: defining, 128(fig.); from the "development of underdevelopment" to "dependent development," 133–136; importance of external factors in comparison, 9; international debt as mechanism of poverty, 130–133; poverty and, 127–130, 137–138(n4)

dependency theory, 134

dependent variables: comparing identical twins, 37(fig.); defining, 31, 31(box); defining terrorism in terms of evil, 241–242; method of agreement, 41; Skocpol's comparative research design, 57(fig.); theorizing about violent crime, 67–68

deportation: Soviet oppression of kulaks, 238

development, economic: by the colonial state, 147; culturalist view of East Asia's, 156–167; democracy and, 195–204; from the "development of underdevelopment" to "dependent development," 133–136; East Asia prioritizing national development, 149–150; historical-structural view of democratization and, 197–199; link with democracy, 231(n4); as postwar priority in East Asia, 150–151; rational choice theory view of the state role in, 155–156; South Korea's strong state, 153–154; threatening political power, 118; within-case comparison of Russia's, 54(fig.). *See also* capitalism; industrialization; poverty

development, human. *See* Human Development Index (HDI)

deviancy, mass mobilization as, 279

differentiation process: globalization as, 323–327; religious bodies and state institutions, 226

discourse: preceding Arab Spring movements, 316; role of Islamic discourse in Arab Spring, 221; social movements' competition for discursive space, 306

discursive opportunity structure, 306–307

Djotodia, Michel, 114

domestic dynamics defining comparative politics, 4

domestic politics: defining comparative politics, 6(box); democratic peace thesis, 23(n4); impact of external forces, 8–9

domestic terrorism, 253–254

dominant groups' antipathy to democracy, 197–198

Dore, Ronald, 163

Dos Santos, Theotonio, 128(fig.), 129–130
Durkheim, Emile, 304

East Asia: avoiding cultural
  generalizations, 167; "Confucian
  ethic" and East Asian economic
  success, 157–159; culturalist view of
  economic growth, 156–167; economic
  growth as reflection of US hegemony,
  174–177; gauging the "richness" of,
  140(fig.); methodological examination
  of economic growth, 142; miracle
  economies, 139; prioritizing national
  development, 149–150; rational choice
  analysis of economic growth, 143–
  156; state role in economic growth,
  155–156; strong developmental state,
  145–149; systemic interaction in the
  global capitalist system, 169–171;
  world-systems theory discounting
  domestic factors in economic growth,
  178–179. *See also* China; Confucian
  culture; Japan; Korea; South Korea;
  Taiwan
Eastern Europe: democratization from
  below, 208–210; emerging
  democracies, 189; escape from
  poverty, 134. *See also* Russia
ecological violence: Darfur, 47(fig.)
ecological/environmental movements,
  284, 289, 336
economic constraints, 77
economic forces: cultural explanations of
  poverty, 119–120; culture intersecting
  with, 90–91; female infanticide and
  feticide, 92; market failure, 117;
  modern state as capitalist creation, 82–
  84; perpetuating poverty in India, 129;
  self-interested behavior, 74. *See also*
  capitalism; poverty
economic growth: China's growth rate,
  179–180, 180(fig.); declining fertility
  rates and, 113; defining dependence in
  terms of other countries', 128(fig.);
  importance of public goods and
  infrastructure for, 114–115
economic growth (East Asia): China's
  developmental state, 139, 180–183;
  China's reversal, 185–186; "Confucian
  ethic" and East Asian economic
  success, 157–159; impact of
  corruption on China's, 182(fig.);
  methodological examination, 142–
  143; postwar growth, 140(fig.);
  rational choice theory of, 143–156;
  role of the strong, developmental state
  in, 145; South Korea under
  authoritarian administration, 149;
  South Korea's strong postcolonial
  state, 153–154; structural analysis of
  China's, 183–185; US role in Japan's,
  174–178; world-systems theory
  discounting domestic factors in East
  Asia's, 178–179
economic hinterland, Japan's, 176–177,
  188(n3)
economic policy: South Korea's
  postcolonial policies, 153
economic theory: agency and structure,
  70(fig.)
economy, 82
education: Confucian values in Japan,
  161; defining poverty, 107; East Asian
  meritocratic culture, 158–159; family
  size, poverty and, 112; history of
  Japan's developmental state, 146;
  Japan's meritocratic system, 162–163;
  self-interested behavior, 74; survival in
  the patrimonial state, 331
Egypt: role of culture in Arab Spring,
  220; social movements pre-dating
  Arab Spring, 313; structural obstacles
  to democratization, 203
Eisenhower, Dwight, 176, 184
elections: definitional debate, 190–191;
  Egypt's Sisi, 203
elites: antipathy to democracy, 197–198;
  Arab Spring outcomes, 314–315;
  colonial powers co-opting, 147;
  democratization in military
  authoritarian regimes, 211–212; elite-
  centered democratization, 205–208;
  rational choice analysis of economic
  growth in East Asia and
  industrialization, 144
employment opportunities defining
  poverty, 107
"enabling" the poor, 103
endogenous forces: India's postcolonial
  poverty, 128–129
entrepreneurship, 156–157, 290–291,
  313–314

environmental justice movement, 284
environmental/ecological movements, 284, 289, 336
epistemic authorities, 270
epistemic dependence, 267–268
equality: procedural democracy, 192–193; substantive definitions of democracy, 191–192
Equatorial Guinea: corruption, 119(fig.)
equilibrium outcomes, 77
Estonia: suicide rate, 38–39, 38(fig.)
ethnic conflict: Darfur, 46–49; Rwandan genocide, 234–235, 247–250, 249(fig.), 259–260, 266
ethnicity/race defining genocide, 237–241
ethnocentrism: cultural roots of underdevelopment, 120–121; thorough comparison obviating, 28; view of the compatibility of Arab culture with democracy, 86–88
European Union: declining democratic standards in member states, 190
evaluation through critical thinking, 28–29
evidence, comparative analysis and, 98
evil, terrorism as, 241–245, 256
exogenous shocks: changing Mexico's regime, 300; democratic transition by authoritarian regime type, 214(fig.); ending authoritarian regimes, 215–216; impact on domestic politics, 8–9; precipitating democratic transitions, 213; undermining authoritarian regimes, 215
experimental method, 21, 31, 31(box)
export-oriented industrialization, 155–156
extensive research, 48–49
extreme poverty, 107

factionalism: military authoritarian regimes, 212
Fadlallah, Sayyid Muhammad Husayn, 270
fairness as element in Japanese capitalism, 163–164
"falling domino" concept, 176, 184
falsification in case-studies, 50
family: relationship between poverty and family size, 110–113, 111(fig.)

fascism, 327
female infanticide, 92
fertility rates, 110–111, 111(fig.), 112
feticide, 92
feudalism: causes of transformation, 84; Japan's strong developmental state, 146; rational choice position of universality, 73; social classes and economic forces, 83; transformation as structural change, 80
financial crisis (2009), 105
financial-industrial dependence, 130
Finland: estimates of civilian firearms ownership and homicide rates, 34(fig.)
firepower: US strength, 250–251
fluidity of culture, 87, 219, 259
"flying geese" model of labor, 171–172
food aid: US in the Middle East, 274
foreign aid, 188(n4); US aid to South Korea, 153
foreign policy: IR versus comparative politics, 4; US hegemony shaping economic policy, 175–177
formal democracy, 192–195
formal institutions, 93–95
formal political systems, 9–10
formalism/legalism in comparative politics, 10
Foxconn, 169
France: comparing successful social revolutions, 39–40, 56–58; estimates of civilian firearms ownership and homicide rates, 34(fig.)
Franco, Francisco, 225
francophone Canada, 307–310
Frank, André Gunder, 129
Fraudel, Fernand, 27
Freedom House scores: postcommunist countries, 229(fig.); Russia, 228
free-rider problem, 115–117; Japan's postwar economic and political goals, 148–149; Japan's strong developmental state, 146; rational choice explanation for East Asia's economic growth, 144; social movements and, 291–293; voluntary participation in social movements, 287–289
fukoku ky hei ("enrich the nation, strengthen the military"), 150
future-based ideological view, 263

games, structures as, 80–82
gang culture, 69–70
Geddes, Barbara, 55, 210–211, 213, 215–216
Geertz, Clifford, 304
gender: defining genocide, 240; female infanticide and feticide, 92, 92(fig.); gendercide, 92(fig.); rational choice position of universality, 73
General Agreement on Tariffs and Trade (GATT), 177
generative sectors, China's growth in, 184
genocide: beliefs, ideology, and leadership legitimizing violence, 262–266; capitalist world-system and, 275–276; casualty figures, 234; central actors, 246–247; "clash of fundamentalisms," 272–275; consolidating power by killing the helpless, 247–250; cultural perspective, 257–261; defining, 237–241; ideology, 264(fig.); importance of individual choice, 275–276; integrative approach, 277–278; leadership element, 266–268; legitimation elements, 260–262; as rational expression of self-interest, 245–246; relevance of a comparative politics approach, 235–236; strategic reasoning, 255–257; structural perspective, 271–277; UN peacekeeping in Rwanda, 249(fig.); Vietnam War as, 236
Germany: estimates of civilian firearms ownership and homicide rates, 34(fig.)
Germany (Nazi): Catholic Church's agreement with, 224; Holocaust, 234–236, 263; rationalizing Holocaust participation, 266; reliance on mass mobilization, 280(fig.)
global approach to culture, 303–306
global capitalism: China as loss to, 184; China's economic growth, 179–180; counterculture defining Taiwan's capitalism, 164–167; IFIs integrating periphery countries into, 132–133; the importance of hegemony, 173–174; postwar rise of communism, 173; the rise of East Asia, 168–179; systemic interaction, 169–171; US hegemony, 174–177

globalism, 323–325
globality, 323–324
globalization: antiglobalization movement, 330, 337–338, 340(n1); cultural perspective, 334–336; heterogeneity and, 327; homogenization effect, 321–323; implications in comparative politics, 326–328; importance of external factors in comparison, 9; intersection of agency and structure, 338–339; intracivilization differences, 333–334; McWorld phenomenon, 322(fig.); multiple dimensions of, 323–326; as political belief system, 325–326; rational choice perspective, 329–332; structural perspective, 336–340; traditional view of culture and, 332–333
goals of social movements, 286(fig.)
gold exchange system, 175
government: defining, 5; formal political systems, 9–10; process-oriented definition of politics, 11. *See also* state
Great Depression, 175
Green Movement (Iran), 206
gross domestic product (GDP): China's economic growth rate, 139, 180(fig.); corporate revenues, 12, 13(box); East Asia's postwar economic growth, 140(fig.); fertility rates, per capita GDP and, 111(fig.)
gross national product (GNP): Japan's postwar economic growth, 140(fig.); postcolonial South Korea, 153
Guatemala: genocide, 266; suicide rate, 38–39, 38(fig.)
guerrillas: Mexico's Zapatista movement, 298
gulags, 238
Gulf War (1991), 254
gun homicides, 1–2
gun rights: cultural legitimation of killing, 260–261; estimates of civilian firearms ownership and homicide rates in selected countries, 34(fig.); firearm-related homicide rates in the US and Canada, 32–36, 32(fig.)
Guyana: suicide rate, 38–39, 38(fig.)

Haiti: suicide rate, 38–39, 38(fig.)
Hamday, Faida, 311

"hard structuralists," 85–86
harder definition of genocide, 239–240
hard-liners, 50–51, 205–206, 209
Haykel, Bernard, 259
health defining poverty, 107
hegemony: China's socialist economy within the capitalist world-system, 183–184; democratization of single-party regimes, 216; East Asian economic growth, 173–174
heterogeneity: culture explaining heterogeneity in capitalism, 92; heterogeneous effects of specific historical experiences, 85
Hezbollah, 251, 255, 265, 269
hierarchical relationships: "Confucian ethic" and East Asian economic success, 158; hierarchic systems, 7; hierarchy of cultures, 332
historical context: connection with structural relationship, 84; East Asia's strong developmental states, 145–146; examining East Asia's economic growth, 143
historical particularity: culture of poverty, 125–126
"historical reality" of Quebec nationalism, 308
historical structuralism, 79, 99(n3); agency versus structure, 84; capitalist development and democracy, 197–199; economically determined categories, 82–83; importance of history in analysis, 84–85; tensions and contradictions of globalization, 339; types of dependence, 129–130
Holocaust, 234–236, 247, 263, 266
homicides: firearm-related homicide rates in the US and Canada, 32–36, 32(fig.)
homogenization process: globalization as, 323–327; structural processes, 85
homosexuals: Holocaust casualties, 234
Hon Precision Industry, 169
Hong Kong, 92(fig.), 140(fig.)
Hu Yaobang, 207(fig.)
Human Development Index (HDI), 107; East Asia's postwar economic growth, 140(fig.)
human rights: democracy and Catholic values, 224–225

Hungary: declining democratic standards, 190
Huntington, Samuel, 137(n2), 218, 333
Hussein, Saddam, 75–76, 212
Hutu population, 234–235, 247–250
hybrid research traditions: institutionalism, 93–96

identity: cultural perspective on globalization, 335–336; culture as collective identity, 90; defining nations and nation-states, 5; globalization and the "clash of civilizations," 333; intracivilization differences, 333; role in social movements, 280–281; shared identity explaining Arab Spring, 316–317; social construction of collective identity, 306; suicide terrorism, 269
ideology: defining, 264(fig.); as element in terrorism and genocide, 267; globalism as ideology of world market rule, 324–325; initiating collective political violence, 262–263; Mexico's Zapatista movement, 298; rational choice analysis of economic growth in East Asia and industrialization, 144; US economic intervention in China, 184
incentives, economic: breaking the cycle of poverty, 113; Japan's postwar economic goals, 149; rational choice explanation for East Asia's economic growth, 144–145
income defining poverty, 107–108
income inequality, China's, 185
independent variables: debate over causal power of culture, 91; defining, 31, 31(box); Skocpol's comparative research design, 57(fig.); theorizing about violent crime, 67–68
India, 92; female infanticide and feticide, 92(fig.); poverty-dependence relationship, 127–129
Indigenous Movement of First Peoples Worldwide, 285
indigenous people: Mexico's Zapatista movement, 297–301; Native Americans, 5, 236
indirect method of difference, 30
individual freedom: democracy and socialism, 191–192

individuals: collective mobilization, 282; as free-riders, 115–117; interpersonal environment shaping group behavior, 69; Marxist view of social class divisions, 82–83; rational choice analysis, 72–75; rationality and social movements, 285, 287; responsibility for poverty, 103–104; role in genocide and terrorism, 275–276; significance of culture, 89–90; social good conflicting with individual self-interest in a context of poverty, 109; structural argument for perpetual poverty, 127; as structural unit of analysis, 86. *See also* agency

Indonesia: poverty statistics, 108

industrial economy, 82–84

industrialization: case study, 45; colonial development policy, 147; dependence resulting from, 130; divergent political and economic outcomes, 85; KMT in Taiwan, 152; rational choice analysis of economic growth in East Asia, 144; state-directed development, 147; Western expansion as threat to Japan, 150–151; Westernization of Japanese society and culture, 160–161. *See also* capitalism; development, economic; economic growth

inequality: China's increasing inequality, 185; democracy as struggle for power, 198; radical view of poverty, 104–105

infant industry, 149

infanticide: female infanticide and feticide, 92

informal institutions, 95

infrastructure: China's history of investment in, 182(fig.); history of Japan's developmental state, 146; importance for economic growth, 114–115; nonexcludable element, 115–116; South Korea's postcolonial reforms, 153–154

inside-out approach to cultural analysis, 303

institutional constraints, 77

institutionalism, 71–72, 93–96

institutions: cultural view of, 96; culture of poverty excluding the poor from, 122–123; formal political systems, 9–10; internal workings of states, 7; required minimal guarantees for democratic institutions, 193–194; shaping social movements, 305; state imposition of colonial policies, 147. *See also* state

integrated regional economy, 169

integrative analysis: Québécois nationalism, 309; to social movements, 281

intensive research, 48–49

intent: of genocide, 239–241; importance to social movements, 282

interest rates: lending interest rates in selected countries, 131–132, 132(fig.); South Korea's postcolonial financial policies, 153

international financial institutions (IFIs), 132–133, 133(fig.)

international law defining genocide, 237

International Monetary Fund (IMF): antiglobalization movement, 330, 338; history and criticism of, 133(fig.); integrating periphery countries into global capitalism, 132–133; US hegemony, 175

international relations (IR), 4, 7–8

Internet access: underdeveloped infrastructure, 114

interpersonal environment, 69

interpretation, theoretical assumptions inherent to, 63–64

intersecting systems and forces: culture, 90; integration of culturalism and rational choice theory, 97

intersubjectivity of definitions, 5, 88

investment: relocating labor from core to periphery, 134–135

Iran: manipulation of identity, 335–336; modernization theory of democratization and development, 197; oppression of prodemocracy protesters, 207(fig.); US support in the Middle East, 273

Iraq: al-Qaeda attacks, 254; compatibility of Arab culture with democracy, 86; terrorism casualties, 234

ISIS/ISIL, 239, 250, 258–260, 266, 284

Islam and Islamic culture: "clash of fundamentalisms," 272; compatibility with democracy, 219, 227–228; intracivilization differences, 333; ISIS as representative of, 258–260; malleability of Islamic culture, 270–271; risks of terrorism in Islamic countries, 233–234; role in Arab Springs uprisings, 221; univocal, monolithic views of Islamic culture, 87; view of suicide, 269–270

Islamic fundamentalist regimes, 7–8

Islamist groups: ideology and terrorism, 265; suicide terrorism, 268–270

Islamization of Iran, 335–336

Israel: defense force, 251

issue entrepreneurs, 290–291, 313–314

Italy: estimates of civilian firearms ownership and homicide rates, 34(fig.)

Japan: China's generative sectors, 184; compatibility of Confucianism with democracy, 219; Confucianism as obstacle to development, 159–162; cultural contribution to economic growth, 156; cultural dissimilarities in Japanese and Taiwanese Confucianism, 164–167; economic growth as reflection of US hegemony, 174; economic hinterland, 176–177, 188(n3); economic policy, 188(n1); escape from poverty, 134; "flying geese" and regional economic integration, 171–172; history of the strong developmental state, 145–146; integrated regional economy, 169–171; large-scale firms, 165; methodological examination of East Asia's economic growth, 142–143; political role of informal institutions, 95; postwar economic growth, 140(fig.); postwar political and economic goals, 148–149; rational choice and the East Asian economy, 145; reparations to South Korea, 153; spontaneous massacre of Koreans in, 240; structuralists' pessimistic view of autonomous economic growth, 168–169; subjugation of Korea, Taiwan and parts of China, 147–148, 171; suicide rate, 38–39, 38(fig.); US hegemony in the capitalist world-system, 175–176; Vietnam as threat to the world-system, 176–177; Western expansion threatening, 150–151

Jews, 234–236, 263

John Paul II, 224

John XXIII, 224

Johnson, Paul, 241–243

Jordan, 219

judiciary: formal political systems, 9–10

Kaname, Akamatsu, 171

keiretsu (horizontally linked companies), 179

Kennan, George, 176

Khmer Rouge, 234

killings as rational act, 245–246

King, Martin Luther Jr., 293–294

Korea: "flying geese" model of labor, 171–172; Japanese subjugation of, 147–148, 171; postcolonial national vulnerability, 151–152. *See also* North Korea; South Korea

Korean War, 177

Ku Klux Klan as social movement, 285

Kulaks, 238

Kuomintang (KMT), 148, 151–152, 165

Kurland, Daniel J., 29

Kuwait: suicide rate, 38–39, 38(fig.)

labor: China's generative sectors, 184; colonial development policy, 147; "Confucian ethic" and East Asian economic success, 158; division of, 7–8; "flying geese" model, 171–172; internationalization of unions, 329–330; Japan's late industrialization, 160–162; Japan's lifetime employment policy, 163–164; Japan's meritocratic educational system, 162–163; large families and poverty, 112–113; world-systems theory of markets, 170–171. *See also* working class

labor migration: relocating labor from core to periphery, 134–135; South Korea's postliberation economic reform, 153

landlord class, 83

late industrialization, 160–161

Latin America: escape from poverty, 134; liberation theology, 227

leadership: effect on Arab Spring outcomes, 313; initiating collective political violence, 262–266; role in genocide and terrorism, 266–268

Lebanon: suicide terrorism, 251, 252(fig.), 269
legitimacy, political: democracy undermining authoritarian regimes, 222; South Korea's Park, 154
level of analysis, theoretical assumptions contained in, 63–64
Lewis, Oscar, 121–126
LG Corporation, 168
LGBT movement, 284, 286(fig.)
Li Peng, 207(fig.)
liberation theology, 227, 298
Libya: Arab Spring outcomes, 312; modernization theory of democratization and development, 197
lifetime employment: Japan, 163–164
Limongi, Fernando, 195, 231(n4)
linguistic identity: "pan-Canadian" project, 307–310
Lipset, Seymour, 195
Lithuania: suicide rate, 38–39, 38(fig.)
living conditions: Soviet oppression of kulaks, 238
The Logic of Collective Action (Olson), 288
The Logic of Comparative Social Inquiry (Przeworski and Teune), 30–31

macro-level factors, 69; genocide and terrorism, 277–278; structural view of genocide, 276–277
Malawi: poverty and family size, 111
Mali: poverty and family size, 111
manufacturing: China's overcapacity, 185–186; Coalition of Justice in the Maquiladoras, 329; textiles, 172(fig.)
Mao Zedong, 148, 175, 180
map, theory as, 66–67
maquiladoras, 329
marginalization, political, 287–289
market failure, 117
Marshall Plan, 175
Marx, Karl, 82
Marxism: development of structures, 95–96; globalization as an elemental process, 337; Mexico's Zapatista movement, 298
mass mobilization: democratization from below, 205, 208–210; social movements and, 280(fig.); success and failure of, 2. *See also* social movements

McAdam, Doug: defining social movements, 282
McFaul, Michael, 204–205, 209
McGinnis, Michael, 95
McVeigh, Timothy, 265
McWorld concept, 322, 322(fig.)
media: Al Jazeera, 316–317; social networking during Arab Spring, 316; suppression by authoritarian regimes, 230
Meiji Restoration (Japan), 146, 160–161
meritocracy: East Asian economic culture, 158–159; Japanese culture and society, 162–163
meso-level factors, 69
method of agreement (MoA), 30, 40–42; Arab Spring outcomes, 311; comparing popular uprisings, 41–42; examining East Asia's economic growth, 142; mixed design, 56–58
method of difference, 30
metropolis-satellite relationships, 129
Mexico: culture of poverty, 121; estimates of civilian firearms ownership and homicide rates, 34(fig.); improving working conditions, 329; modernization theory of democratization and development, 197; political role of informal institutions, 95; state co-optation of subordinate classes, 201; Zapatista movement, 297–301
micro-level factors, 69. *See also* individual
middle class: class alliances and democratization, 201–202; "development" in the periphery and the emergence of, 134–135; significance in democratic formation, 49–50
Middle East and North Africa (MENA): comparison of regime changes, 230; oppression of prodemocracy protesters, 207(fig.). *See also* Arab Spring
migrant labor: relocating labor from core to periphery, 134–135; South Korea's postliberation economic reform, 153
militarization of the Rwandan genocide, 248

military authoritarian regimes, 211–213, 214(fig.)

military culture, 69–70

military intervention and military capability: imposition of colonialism, 147; Japan's postwar development, 177; predicting a nation's external behavior, 7–8; terrorism as strategic action, 242; Tunisian and Egyptian military refusing to intervene, 315; US coercion of Japanese trade, 150; US deemphasizing South Korea, 154–155; US protecting Taiwan from China, 152; US strengths, 250–251

minimum wage, 106

miracle economies, East Asia's, 139, 246

mixed research design, 43, 56–58, 204

moderates' role in democratization, 205–206

modernization and modernization theory, 121; capitalist world-system and genocide, 275–276; culture and structure, 231(n3); culture of poverty, 122, 125–126; democratization as final stage of, 195; economic development and democratization, 195–197; as evolutionary process, 137(n2); India's postcolonial poverty, 128–129; industrialization and dependence, 130

monolithic view of culture, 87

Montgomery bus boycott, 293–294

Montgomery Improvement Association (MIA), 293–294

Moore, Michael, 1–2, 32–33

Morocco: Arab Spring outcomes, 312

Morris, Aldon, 293–295

Morsi, Mohammed, 203, 314

Mossadeq, Mohammed, 273

most different systems (MDS) design: basic logic, 40; case studies comparing multiple cases, 55–56; historical reality of democratization, 204; levels of observed behavior, 59(n2); limitations of, 40; mechanism of, 30, 36–40; method of agreement and, 41–42; mixed design, 56–58; suicide rates around the world, 39–40

most similar systems (MSS) design: Arab Spring outcomes, 311; binary comparison of an authoritarian regime, 52–53; case studies comparing

multiple cases, 55–56; comparing identical twins, 37(fig.); East Asia's economic growth, 142; historical reality of democratization, 204; limitations of, 34–36, 41; mechanism and practice, 32–36; method of agreement and, 41–42; mixed design, 56–58

Mothers of East Los Angeles (MELA), 285

Mousavi, Mir-Hossein, 207(fig.)

Mozambique: poverty and family size, 111

Mubarak, Hosni, 203, 314–315

multiculturalism: "pan-Canadian" project, 307–308

Multidimensional Poverty Index (MPI), 107–108; Central African Republic, 115; China, 139; Equatorial Guinea, 119(fig.)

multinational corporations: antiglobalization movement, 338

multiparty systems: definitional debate, 190–191; welfare reform in the 1980s and 1990s, 104

multiple causation, 40

mutually constitutive relationships, 119–120

Nakhle, Rami, 313

naming social movements, 306–307

nation: defining, 5. *See also* state

National Association for the Advancement of Colored People (NAACP), 294

national security. *See* security

national states: defining, 5

nationalism: Canada's nationalist movements, 306–310; cultural legitimation of killing, 260–261

nation-building, 1

nation-state: defining, 5; as unit of analysis, 7. *See also* state

Native Americans, 5, 236

Nehru, Jawaharlal, 128

neoliberal economic reforms, 324; the state as the cause of poverty, 117; undermining peace efforts, 330–332

neorealism, 7, 99(n2)

networks, 78–80

"new dependence," 130

new social movements, 280–281, 289, 289(fig.), 295
Niger: poverty and family size, 111
normative statement of democracy, 194–195
norms and traditions, 7
North American Free Trade Agreement (NAFTA), 300–301
North Korea: globalization and the disappearance of culture, 332; similar structures producing different outcomes, 85; strong state and weak economy, 144; threat to South Korea, 154
nuclear capability: legitimizing violence, 261; North Korea, 154

Obiang, Teodoro Nguema Mbasogo, 119(fig.)
objectivity, 62, 66–67
oil industry, 119(fig.), 272–275
old institutionalism, 93
Olson, Mancur, 288
one-directional view of culture, 87
open-mindedness, 28–29
operational definition of democracy, 193–194
Organization of Petroleum Exporting Countries (OPEC), 272–275
outside-in approach to cultural analysis, 303–306
overcapacity,: China's, 185–186
overdetermination, 51–52

pacts, democratization through, 208
Pahlavi, Mohammed Reza Shah, 273
Palestine Liberation Organization (PLO), 252(fig.)
"pan-Canadian" project, 307–308
Park Chung Hee, 153–155
patriarchal traditions: univocal, monolithic views of Islamic culture, 87–88
patrimonial state, 330–332
Paul VI, 224
peasant class, 83
People Power movement, 226
per capita comparisons, 33
per capita GDP, 111(fig.), 115, 139
per capita GNP, 153
per capita income, 140(fig.)

Perry, Matthew C., 150
Personal Responsibility and Work Opportunity Act (PRWORA), 104
personalist authoritarian regimes, 212–214, 214(fig.), 216
petty bourgeoisie, 201–202
Philippines: estimates of civilian firearms ownership and homicide rates, 34(fig.); People Power movement, 226–227; poverty and family size, 111
Philpott, Daniel, 222, 225–226
Poland, 209
polemical tool, concept of terrorism as, 243
policymaking: breaking the cycle of poverty, 113; genocide as last resort, 247–250
political elites. *See* elites
political empowerment defining poverty, 107
political forces: cultural explanations of poverty, 119–120; culture intersecting with, 90–91; structural realism, 79
political instability: importance of public goods and infrastructure, 114
political opportunity structure, 282, 296–297, 299–301, 314–316
political outsiders, importance to social movements, 283
political process model, 282
political theology, 224
politics: defining, 9–13
polyarchy, 231(n2)
popular uprisings, 41–42, 215–216
positivism, relevance of theory to, 62
postcommunist countries: democratization from below, 208–210; emerging democracies, 189; Freedom House scores, 229(fig.); paths of regime change, 228
post-Marxism, 296
postpositivism: mutual constitution of theory and reality, 62
poverty: breaking the cycle, 113–114; China's multidimensionally poor population, 139; corruption and, 117–119; corruption keeping Equatorial Guinea poor, 119(fig.); cultural explanations, 119–126; culturalism and modernization theory, 125–126; defining, 105–108; dependence and,

127–130; from the "development of underdevelopment" to "dependent development," 133–136; disjunct between self-interest and collective good in poverty situations, 110–113; domain of comparative politics, 1; fertility rates, per capita GDP and, 111(fig.); the free-rider problem, 115–117; importance of public goods and infrastructure for economic growth, 114–115; international debt and, 130–133; Oscar Lewis's cultures of poverty, 121–125; rational choice perspective, 108–119; the state as the cause of, 117; the state's role in rational choice view, 113–114; structural explanations, 126–136; theoretical process explaining the causes of, 63; theory of responsibility, 103–104; usefulness of comparative analysis, 21; welfare reform in the 1980s and 1990s, 104; Western impoverishment of the Middle East, 272–275; why professional athletes go broke, 124(fig.). *See also* economic growth; prosperity; underdevelopment
power: balance of class power in the struggle for democratization, 202; challenging elites, 206; consolidating power by killing the helpless, 247–250; of culture, 90; democracy as struggle for, 198; development as threat to political power, 118; postcolonial struggle in South Korea, 152–155; theoretical assumptions contained in, 63; understanding agency, globalization, and, 338–339; of values and beliefs, 220; working class struggle for democratization, 200
power, distribution of: social processes defining politics, 10–11
predatory state: China's state-level corruption, 181
preferences in self-interest, 74–75
"presentist" explanations of democracy, 202
presidential systems, 7–8
"primitive" cultures, 121, 129
procedural democracy, 192–195
process-oriented definition of politics, 10–11

Prohibition (US), 286(fig.)
prosperity: declining fertility rates, 112–113; measuring East Asia's, 140(fig.). *See also* economic growth; industrialization; poverty
protest: China's oppression of prodemocracy protesters, 206; Eastern European democratization from below, 208; Mexico's Zapatista movement, 298; terrorism as, 252–253. *See also* social movements
The Protestant Ethic and the Spirit of Capitalism (Weber), 303
Protestantism: contribution to capitalism, 120(fig.), 158
Prussia, 223
Przeworski, Adam, 30–31, 37–38, 59(n2), 195, 204, 231(n4)
public choice: agency and structure, 70(fig.); state as the cause of poverty, 117
public good: culture as, 90–91; effect of globalization, 321–323; history of Japan's developmental state, 146; importance for economic growth, 114–115; nonexcludable element, 116; social good conflicting with individual self-interest in a context of poverty, 109–110
Puerto Rico: cultures of poverty, 121
purchasing power parity (PPP), 106, 140(fig.)
Puritanism, 303
Putin, Vladimir, 53

Qaddafi, Muammar, 310
Qatar, 317
qualitative analysis, 58
quality of democracy, 191–192
quantitative analysis, 21–22, 59(n3)
Québécois nationalism, 307–310
Quran: role of Islamic discourse in Arab Spring, 221

race/ethnicity, 73
racism: US and Islamic countries, 86–88
radicalism: capitalism as the root cause of poverty, 104–105; postwar East Asia, 148; role in democratization, 205–206
Rafsanjani, Ali Akbar Hashemi, 207(fig.)

rational choice institutionalism, 95, 137(n1)

rational choice theory: agency and structure, 70(fig.); Arab Spring, 312–313; causal power of culture, 91–93; China's economic growth, 179; China's strong developmental state, 181, 183; in a comparative politics context, 77–78; defining terrorism, 242; democratization from below, 208–210; democratization in differing authoritarian regimes, 210–216; East Asia prioritizing national development, 149–150; East Asia's economic growth, 143–156; East Asia's strong, effective postcolonial states, 151–152; East Asia's strong developmental states, 145–146; elite-centered democratization, 205–208; explaining genocide and terrorism, 245–257; explaining the patrimonial state, 331–332; failing to explain Arab Spring, 220–221; the free-rider problem and poverty, 115–117; the free-rider problem in social movements, 287–289; global context, 329–332; importance of constraints, 77; India's postcolonial poverty, 128–129; institutionalism, 95; integration with other research traditions, 96–97; Japan's postwar political environment and economic goals, 150–151; key questions for analysis, 79(fig.); mass participation in social movements, 291–293; postwar strong state and development policy, 147–149; poverty and corruption, 117; public goods and infrastructure, 114–115; relationship between poverty and family size, 110–113; resource mobilization theory in social movements, 290–291; the rise in global terrorism, 254–255; Rwandan genocide, 247–250; self-interest in East Asia's economic growth, 143–145; self-interested individual, 72–75; social good conflicting with individual self-interest, 109–110; social movements, 285–295; South Korea's economic development, 154; state intervention and economic development, 155–156; state role in the poverty cycle, 113–114, 117; strategic interaction, 76; strategic reasoning in genocide and terrorism, 255–257; structural analysis of democratic transition, 216–218; structural explanations of poverty, 126–127; suicide terrorism, 268–269; terrorism as a last resort, 250–255; "thick" variant, 78, 117, 137(n1); understanding and explanation, 321; welfare reform in the 1980s and 1990s, 104; world systems theory and, 135

rationality: clan behavior, 94; neorealistic scholars embracing, 99(n2); terrorist behavior, 255; theorizing about violent crime in societies, 68; uncertainty and bad outcomes, 75

Reagan, Ronald: state role in economic struggles, 113–114

realism, 7–8

reality: importance of understanding theory, 61–62; reality as simplification and clarification mechanism, 62–64; research traditions, different views of, 96; as simplification and clarification mechanism, 62–64; theory as simplification, 66

regime types: clan hegemony, 94–95. *See also* authoritarian regimes; communist regimes; democracy

regional economic integration: East Asia, 171–172

regional economies, 169–171; East Asia's economic growth, 178–179; US hegemony shaping economic policy, 176–177

relationships: social classes and economic forces, 82–83; structural theory, 78

relative autonomy, 52–53

relative deprivation, 287

relative poverty, 106–107

religion: arguments against the "Confucian values" culture, 159; civil rights movement, 293–294; compatibility of democracy with Islam, 219; cultural similarities among religions, 227–228; liberation theology, 227; role of the Catholic Church in democratization, 222–226; Weber's study of religious calling, 303 religious fundamentalism and zealotry: "clash of fundamentalisms," 274–275; cultural context of politics, 90; genocide and terrorism, 272–275; globalism fostering, 335; globalization fostering, 339; ISIS as representative of Islam, 258–260; manipulation of identity, 335–336; role of ideology in terrorism, 265; terrorists acts, 233–234; univocal, monolithic views of Islamic culture, 87–88; US and Islamic countries, 87–88

rentier states: modernization theory of democratization and development, 196

rent-seeking activity, 181

repeated game, 292–293

reproduction of structures, 80

research design: comparative analysis and, 30; examining East Asia's economic growth, 143; institutionalism, 93–96. *See also* culturalism; rational choice theory; structuralism

resistance: antiglobalization movement as, 340(n1); Mexico's Zapatista movement, 298; terrorism as, 252–253. *See also* protest; social movements

resource mobilization theory, 290–291, 295; Arab Spring, 312–314; civil rights movement, 293–295; explaining Arab Spring, 315–316

resources and resource allocation: creating public goods and infrastructure, 115; culture as a societal resource, 332; defining poverty, 105–106; dominant group's antipathy to democracy, 197–198; export-oriented industrialization, 155–156; free-riders, 115–117; importance of the state in, 144; international debt as mechanism of poverty, 130–133; political opportunity approach to social movements, 296–297; scarcity as economic constraint, 77

Responsibility to Protect (R2P) principle, 248–249

risk management: relative poverty and extreme poverty, 110

rivalries: challenging authoritarian regimes, 216

The Roots of Evil: The Origins of Genocide and Other Group Violence (Staub), 246

Rueschemeyer, Dietrich, 197–199, 203–204, 208, 217

Russia: binary comparison of an authoritarian regime, 52–53; comparing successful social revolutions, 39–40, 56–58; declining democratic standards, 190; democratic-authoritarian hybrid regime, 209; domestic terrorism, 253–254; path of regime change, 228; within-case comparison of economic development, 54(fig.). *See also* Soviet Union

Rwandan genocide, 234–235, 247–250, 249(fig.), 259–260, 266

Rwandan Patriotic Front, 250

Salafic Jihadi movement, 219

Salinas, Carlos, 300

Samsung Corporation, 168

samurai culture, 161

San Andrés accords, 298

sanitation defining poverty, 107

satellite states, 208

Saudi Arabia, 254, 310, 315

scale of genocide, 239–241

Scandinavian countries, 30–31

scapegoating, 247

scarcity of resources: economic constraints, 77

scattering agriculture plots, 110

Second Vatican Council (Vatican II), 224–225

security: East Asia prioritizing national development, 149–150; incentive structure for combating poverty, 113; poverty and family size, 112–113; underdeveloped infrastructure and an insecure domestic environment, 114; US as existential threat to China, 181, 183

selection bias, 51–52

self-immolation, 207(fig.), 220, 311

self-interest: causal power of culture, 91; China's state-controlled enterprises, 183; class alliances and democratization, 201–202; democracy threatening, 221–222; exploring, 109;

female infanticide and feticide, 93; individuals as self-interested actors, 72–75; participation in social movements, 295; the patrimonial state undermining, 331; perpetuation of poverty, 123–125; poor parents having large families, 112–113; social good conflicting with individual self-interest in a context of poverty, 109–110; social movement organizations, 290–291; US role in postwar East Asia, 148. *See also* rational choice theory

self-organization of subordinate classes, 200

semiperiphery, 136, 170(fig.). *See also* core-periphery relationships

September 11, 2001, 233

sex ratio at birth, 92(fig.)

Shanghai index, 185

shared identity explaining Arab Spring, 316–317

sharia, 233

Shehadeh, Abed, 219

Shinto in Japanese culture, 160

shogunate, 150

Sierra Leone: overgeneralizing causes and processes, 334; undermining the patrimonial state, 331

Singapore, 92(fig.); modernization theory of democratization and development, 196; postwar economic growth, 140(fig.)

single-country case studies, 24(n8)

single-party authoritarian regimes: challenges to, 215–216; China's potential for democratization, 230; democratic transition, 212–213, 214(fig.). *see also* China; North Korea

el-Sisi, Abdel Fattah, 203

Skocpol, Theda, 39–40, 56–58, 84

slum cultures, 121–125

small-to-medium-size enterprises: Taiwan's economy, 165–167

So, Alvin, 137(n3)

social causation, multifaceted nature of, 20–21

social class: civil society increasing social, political, and economic equality, 193; class power and democratic transition, 217; cross-class alliances and democratization, 201–

202; culture of poverty excluding the poor from social institutions, 122–123; historical structural analysis, 82; participants in social movements, 279–280; working class repression in authoritarian regimes, 199–202. *See also* feudalism

social construction of collective identity, 306

social forces, culture intersecting with, 90–91

social media, 41–42, 312–314

social movement organizations (SMOs), 290–291, 293–295, 312–314

social movements: anti-apartheid movement as, 283–284; Canada's nationalist movements, 306–310; case-study method, 44; challenging elites for democratization, 205–208; civil rights movement, 293–295; cultural factors, 302–310; culture of poverty excluding people from, 123; defining and characterizing, 281–285; free-rider problem, 287–289; global approach to cultural analysis, 304–305; importance of agency in democratization, 204–205; inside-out approach to cultural analysis, 303; limitations of the structural approach, 301–302; mass mobilization and, 280(fig.), 291–293; measuring success and failure, 286(fig.); Mexico's Zapatista movement, 297–301; political opportunity approach, 296–297; rationality and, 285–295; resource mobilization theory, 290–291; resulting from social tensions and contradictions, 80; shifts in perception of, 279–281; structural accounts, 295–302; theoretical explanations for the rise of, 280–281; working class struggle for democratization, 201. *See also* Arab Spring

social networks: effect on Arab Spring outcomes, 312–314; mass participation in social movements, 291–293; networking during Arab Spring, 316

social order: India's postcolonial poverty, 128

social processes defining politics, 10–11

social revolutions, 1; comparing successful social revolutions, 39–40, 56–58; factors in the emergence and development of, 84

social variables defining poverty, 107

socialism: substantive definitions of democracy, 191–192

socially constructed interests, 199

socioeconomic status: defining genocide, 238–241; environmental justice movement, 284; mass participation in social movements, 291–292

"soft" structuralism, 86, 296–297

softer definition of genocide, 239–240

soft-liners, 50, 205–206, 209

Somalia: poverty and family size, 111

South Africa: anti-apartheid movement, 283–284, 288

South Korea, 92(fig.); colonialism and economic growth, 151; compatibility of Confucianism with democracy, 219; declining fertility rates with increasing prosperity, 112–113; escape from poverty, 134; integrated regional economy, 169–171; large-scale firms, 165; methodological examination of East Asia's economic growth, 142–143; one-directional view of Confucian culture, 87; postcolonial corruption, 151; postcolonial struggle for power, 152–155; postwar economic growth, 140(fig.); postwar economic policy, 149; similar structures producing different outcomes, 85; structuralists' pessimistic view of autonomous economic growth, 168–169; technology-based industries, 168–169; US foreign aid, 188(n4); US "invitation to develop," 177–178

South Sudan: poverty and family size, 111

Southern Christian Leadership Conference (SCLC), 294–295

sovereign nations: defining, 5

sovereignty: China-Taiwan relationship, 152; compatibility of democracy with Islam, 219

Soviet Union: communism and global capitalism, 173; democratization from below, 208–210; exogenous shocks to the one-party regime, 215–216; filling Korea's postwar political vacuum, 148; oppression of Kulaks, 238. *See also* Russia

Spain: Catholic political theology, 225–226

Sports Illustrated magazine, 124(fig.)

Stalinism: divergent political outcomes, 85

standard of living defining poverty, 106

state: China's economic development and government corruption, 182(fig.); East Asia's postwar strong developmental state, 145, 147–149, 180–183; East Asia's rapid economic growth, 141, 143–144; eliminating free-riders, 116; factors in the emergence and development of social revolutions, 84; global expansion of capitalism, 338–339; globalization undermining the patrimonial state, 330–332; modern state as capitalist creation, 82–84; poverty and, 113–114; South Korea's strong postcolonial state, 153–154; as structural unit of analysis, 86; structuralist view of China's economic growth, 185. *See also* colonialism

state-directed economic development, 147

States and Social Revolutions (Skocpol), 39

statistical analysis, 21, 24(n10), 59(n3)

Staub, Ervin, 246

steel production, 184

Stephens, Evelyne Huber, 197–199, 203–204, 208, 217

Stephens, John D., 197–199, 203–204, 208, 217

stock market, volatility of China's, 185

strategic calculation, 75

strategic environment: impact of globalization on, 329–330; South Korea's coup, 154–155; terrorism as strategic action, 241–242, 256; US as existential threat to China, 181, 183

strategic interaction, 76

strategies for comparison, 20

"structural reductionist" approach to social movements, 280–281

structuralism, 78–82; agency, development, and democratization,

203–204; Arab Spring outcomes, 314–315; capitalism and subcultures of poverty, 125; capitalist development and democracy, 197–199; causal power of culture, 91–92; China's economic growth, 179, 183–186; "clash of fundamentalisms," 274–275; defining terrorism, 242; from the "development of underdevelopment" to "dependent development," 133–136; East Asia's autonomous economic growth, 168–169; the effects of globalization, 336–340; explaining poverty, 126–136; failing to explain Arab Spring, 220–221; genocide and terrorism, 271–277; history, the economy, and Marx, 82–84; the importance of hegemony, 173–174; key questions for analysis, 85(fig.); modernization theory, 195–197, 231(n3); political opportunity approach to social movements, 296–297; poverty and dependency, 127–130; rational choice analysis of democratic transition, 216–218; rational choice in the framework of, 95–96; role of international debt in poverty, 130–133; scope of, 85–86; social movements, 295–302; systemic interaction in the global capitalist system, 169–171; understanding and explanation, 321; US role in postwar East Asia, 148. *See also* historical structuralism

structure, 70(fig.), 71; of the global economy, 9; historical structuralism, 84; intersection of agency and structure in globalization, 338–339; systems and, 80; theoretical assumptions contained in, 63, 70–71

Student Nonviolent Coordination Committee (SNCC), 294–295

subculture, culture of poverty as, 122–123

subjectivity: positivism and postpositivism, 62

sub-Saharan Africa: anarchy and violence, 330–332; emerging democracies, 189; genocide statistics, 234–235

substantive definitions of democracy, 191–192

suffrage: defining democracy, 191

suicide rates around the world: most different systems comparison, 38–40

suicide terrorism, 251, 255, 268–270

Suriname: modernization theory of democratization and development, 197

survival techniques: large families and poverty, 112–113

Sweden: estimates of civilian firearms ownership and homicide rates, 34(fig.)

Switzerland: estimates of civilian firearms ownership and homicide rates, 34(fig.)

Syria: Arab Spring outcomes, 310; challenging the personalist regime, 215

systems, structural analysis and, 79–80, 83, 86

Taiwan, 92(fig.); compatibility of Confucianism with democracy, 219; counterculture defining Taiwan's capitalism, 164–167; cultural contribution to economic growth, 156–157; escape from poverty, 134; "flying geese" model of labor, 171–172; integrated regional economy, 169–171; Japanese subjugation of, 147–148, 171; methodological examination of East Asia's economic growth, 142–143; postcolonial national vulnerability, 151–152; postcolonial political and economic success, 151–152; postwar economic growth, 140(fig.); postwar political and economic goals, 148–149; structuralists' pessimistic view of autonomous economic growth, 168–169; technology-based industries, 168–169; US "invitation to develop," 177–178

Taiwan Semiconductor Manufacturing, 169

Tajikistan: suicide rate, 38–39, 38(fig.)

Taoism, 156–157, 164

Tarancón, Vicente Enrique y, 225

technological-industrial dependence, 130

technology-intensive industries, 172(fig.); South Korea and Taiwan, 168; South Korea benefiting from the Vietnam War, 177–178

Temporary Assistance for Needy Families (TANF), 104

terrorism: beliefs, ideology, and leadership, 262–266; central actors, 246–247; "clash of fundamentalisms," 272–275; cultural legitimation of killing, 260–261; cultural perspective, 257–261; defining, 241–245; elements of legitimation, 261–262; globalization and the "clash of civilizations," 333; ideology, 264(fig.); importance of individual choice, 275–276; integrative approach, 277–278; ISIS and Islam, 258–260; ISIS targeting ethnic groups, 239; as last resort, 250–255; leadership element, 266–268; as rational expression of self-interest, 245–246; relevance of a comparative politics approach, 235–236; rise in global attacks, 254–255; strategic reasoning, 255–257; structural perspective, 271–277; suicide terrorism, 268–270; Western targets, 233

Teune, Henry, 30–31, 37–38, 59(n2)

textiles manufacturing, 172(fig.)

theology, political, 224

theory, 71; correlation and causation, 65(fig.); defining, 66–67; the differences between good and bad theorizing, 64–67; legs of comparative analysis, 98; relevance of, 61–62; a sampling of theories, 72(fig.); as simplification and clarification mechanism, 62–64; theoretical synthesis, 142; theory and practice, 22–23; violent crime in societies, 67–71

"thick" variant of rational choice, 78, 117, 137(n1)

Thörn, Håkan, 282

Tiananmen Square, 206, 207(fig.)

"top-down" analytical approach, 340

top-down democratization, 213, 215

Toward a Political Economy of Development: A Rational Choice Perspective (Bates), 143

trade relations: international debt as mechanism of poverty, 130–133; US beneficence to Japan, 177; US coercion of Japan, 150

transitional leaders in East European democratization, 209

transnational action: successful social revolutions, 84

transnational corporations: creating a global culture, 321–322; East Asia's technology-based industries, 168–169

transportation. *See* infrastructure

Truman, Harry, 152

Tunisia: Arab Spring outcomes, 314–315; civil society leading Arab Spring movements, 316; democratization success, 207(fig.); onset of Arab Spring, 311; role of culture in Arab Spring, 220; social movements pre-dating Arab Spring, 313

Tutsi population, 234–235, 247–250, 259–260

twins, differences between, 37(fig.)

two-party systems, 31

Uganda: poverty and family size, 111

uncertainty, 76–77

underdevelopment: core-periphery relationships and poverty, 129; cultural roots, 120–121; modernization theory of democratization and development, 196. *See also* poverty

understanding, 321

unequal treaties, 150

unions, 329–330. *See also* labor

United Arab Emirates (UAE): Arab Spring outcomes, 310

United Kingdom: lending interest rate, 131

United Nations (UN): peacekeeping in Rwanda, 248–249, 249(fig.)

United Nations Convention on the Prevention and Punishment of the Crime of Genocide, 237–239

United Nations Development Programme (UNDP): Central African Republic poverty statistics, 115; HDI and MPI, 107–108

United States: civil rights movement, 284, 293–295; corruption in Equatorial Guinea, 119(fig.); defining comparative politics, 4–6, 23–24(n6), 23(n2); determining poverty level, 106; economic intervention in China, 183–184; estimates of civilian firearms ownership and homicide rates, 34(fig.); as existential threat to China, 181, 183; filling Korea's postwar political vacuum, 148; firearm-related homicide rates in the US and Canada, 32–36, 32(fig.); as global hegemony, 174–177; impoverishment of the Middle East, 272–275; Prohibition, 286(fig.); relative poverty, 109–110; Rwandan genocide, 248–249; shifts in perception of social movements, 279–281; socioeconomic status and mass participation in social movements, 291–292; suicide attacks in Lebanon, 252(fig.); terrorism as obsession, 233; use of quantitative and qualitative methods, 59(n3); welfare reform in the 1980s and 1990s, 104

units of analysis, 43–44, 86

univocal view of culture, 87

upstream industries, China's history of investment in, 182(fig.)

utility calculations, 269

values and beliefs: belief in democracy, 221–222; "Confucian ethic" and East Asian economic success, 157; contributing to the perpetuation of poverty, 123–125; defining culture, 88; global approach to cultural analysis, 304; individual- and collective-level power, 220; role of Christian culture in democratization, 223; slum cultures distinguishing poor from nonpoor individuals, 122

Vatican II, 224–225

Venezuela: modernization theory of democratization and development, 197

victim blaming for poverty, 104, 123

Vietnam War: cultural legitimation of killing, 260–261; East Asia's economic growth, 154–155; economic threat of communism, 176–177; as genocide, 236–237; Japan profiting from, 177; South Korea's development resulting from, 177–178

violence: of democratic transitions, 197; distinguishing terrorism from other forms of, 243–244; power of culture, 90; rationality, uncertainty, and bad choices, 76–77; violent crime as an exercise in theories, 67–71. *See also* terrorism

violent substate activism, 245

virtuous behavior: rationalist view of poverty and corruption, 118–119

vulnerability, national, 150

wa (harmony), 156

Wal-Mart, 12, 13(box), 325

wealth-producing activities, 123–124, 124(fig.)

weapons. *See* gun rights

Weber, Max, 5, 120, 120(fig.), 303

welfare reform, 104

Western countries: postcommunist regimes, 215–216; terrorists targeting, 233; Western expansion as threat to Japan, 150

Western values: Confucian ethic and, 158; defining globalism in terms of, 336; democracy and socialism, 191–192; globalization and the "clash of civilizations," 333; impoverishment of the Middle East, 272–275; Japan's Meiji leaders embracing, 160–161; old institutionalism, 93–94; religious fundamentalism in the Middle East, 90; shifts in perception of social movements, 279–281; source of globalization, 327; terrorists targeting, 233, 253–255

"whole" arguments, theory facilitating development of, 66

within-case comparisons, 53; East Asia's economic growth, 178–179; examining East Asia's economic growth, 142–143; South Korea's postcolonial struggle for power, 152–155

Wood, Graeme, 259

working class: class power and democratic transition, 217; struggle for democracy, 199–202. *See also* labor

working poor, 106

World Bank: antiglobalization movement, 330, 338; defining poverty, 106–108; globalization as an elemental process, 337; history and criticism of, 133(fig.); US hegemony, 175

World Development Report, 337

World Summit Outcome Document, 249

World War II: cultural legitimation of killing, 260–261; Holocaust, 234–236, 247, 263, 266; postcolonial East Asia, 147

world-systems theory: colonialism and dependency theory, 138(n4); development by invitation, 177–178; discounting domestic factors in East Asia's economic growth, 178–179; economic growth in the periphery, 135; "flying geese" model of labor, 171–172; regional and national interactions, 169–170; tri-modal structure of the capitalist world-system, 170(fig.); units of analysis, 86; US hegemony and East Asian economic growth, 174–177. *See also* global capitalism

Yemen: estimates of civilian firearms ownership and homicide rates, 34(fig.)

Zahariadis, Nikolaos, 7–8
Zambia: poverty and family size, 111
Zapatista movement, 297–302
Zhao Ziyang, 207(fig.)

About the Book

This systematic, user friendly, and refreshingly unusual introduction to comparative politics has not only been updated and refined in the
third edition, but also fully revised to reflect the impact of major new developments in world politics.

Designed to teach students how to think comparatively and theoretically about the world they live in, the book is organized around a set of critical questions—why are poor countries poor? why is East Asia relatively
prosperous? what makes a democracy? how can we explain terrorism and
genocide? what leads people to mobilize around a cause?—each the topic
of a full chapter. These issue chapters are based on the solid methodological
and theoretical foundation laid out in the first part of the book, and the entire text is enhanced with case studies and graphics.

Timothy C. Lim is professor of political science at California State University, Los Angeles.